Composite Index

to

Volumes 14-17

(Revolutionary War Rolls)

of the

New Hampshire State Papers

Dr. Frank C. Mevers

Compiler

HERITAGE BOOKS
2024

HERITAGE BOOKS

AN IMPRINT OF HERITAGE BOOKS, INC.

Books, CDs, and more—Worldwide

For our listing of thousands of titles see our website
at
www.HeritageBooks.com

A Facsimile Reprint
Published 2024 by
HERITAGE BOOKS, INC.
Publishing Division
5810 Ruatan Street
Berwyn Heights, MD 20740

International Standard Book Number
Paperbound: 978-1-55613-824-9

INTRODUCTION

What follows is intended to be an exact transcription of the indexes that appear in volumes XIV-XVII of the *New Hampshire State Papers*. There has been no attempt to validate or elucidate individual entries.

The purpose of this compilation is twofold: first, it hopes to expedite the search for information from these four volumes: and, second, it will serve as a model by which a compiled index of the entire 40-volume set of the *State Papers* might be made. The compiler hopes to see such a compilation accomplished eventually. There are flaws in this one that can later be avoided. One, quickly obvious, is that the subject and name indexes should be composed as one.

In the view that an entry followed only by a string of numbers is frustrating, the device of a contents listing is included behind the indexes. Entry numbers can be correlated with the contents listing of each volume in the hope of quickly ascertaining whether the particular entry number might be useful to the researcher. This is a device here being tried.

This project was begun on October 13, 1982 and worked on nearly every day, in spare time, until its completion on February 11, 1984. Final typing of the manuscript was begun on July 10, 1983.

Inspiration for the project came from a belief in the resource value of the *New Hampshire State Papers* and immediately from a shared enthusiasm for the much larger project with Andrew S. Taylor. I believe that a suggestion for such a project was made years ago by Leon W. "Andy" Anderson and has over time been thought of, and wished for, by many others. A very special thanks goes to my wife, Kathy, and children, John and Lauren, for indulging these thousands of hours at the typewriter.

Certainly the *State Papers* series deserves a compiled index just as it deserves to be carried onward in further volumes.

Frank C. Mevers
Concord, New Hampshire

TABLE OF CONTENTS

PERSONAL NAME INDEX

NEW HAMPSHIRE'S REVOLUTIONARY WAR ROLLS

A

Abbot, Abiel XV,529
    Abraham XV,751
    Amos XV,405
    Bancroft XV,592
    Benjamin XV, 87, 510; XVII,3
    Beriah, XV, 608, 729; XVI,
       210, 239, 277, 501
    Chandler XV,515
    David XVI,785
    Ebenezer XV,612, 731
    Elias XV,129, 285, 698; XVI,
       105, 147, 530
    Ephraim XV,185, 515
    Ezra XV,129, 185, 515
    George XV,210, 212, 595, 720;
       XVI,204, 272, 516, 803-4
    Isaac XV,129
    Jacob XVI,114, 145, 157, 880-
       82
    James XV,592
    Jeremiah XV,175, 268, 271,
       274-75, 419, 514; XVI,88,
       93, 255, 501, 604, 882
    Jesse XV,185, 234
    Joel XVI,694
    John XV,129, 177, 185, 634,
       649, 732, 735; XVI,102,
       212, 279, 498, 503, 512,
       617, 726; XVII,45, 91
    Joseph XVI,145
    Joshua XV,283, 290, 405,
       407, 515; XVI,68, 79, 99

Abbot, Josiah XV,118, 138, 696,
    698
    Moses XV, 405
    Nathaniel XV,513
    Peter XVI,84, 95, 125, 190,
       209, 510; XVII,436
    Philip XV,406; XVI,529
    Reuben XV,406; XVI,915;
       XVII, 91
    Samuel XV,468, 480
    Solomon XV,595, 720;
       XVI,214, 234, 803
    Stephen XV,185, 612, 711;
       XVI,218, 239, 267, 934
    Timothy XV,695; XVI,85, 100,
       106, 194, 235, 882
    William XV,379, 419, 529,
       592, 595, 720; XVI,679;
       XVII,14, 82
    William Jr. XV,529; XVI, 881,
       883
Abbott, Aaron XIV,550
    Abiel XIV,417-18, 478, 609,
       613, 622, 632, 640; XV,
       68
    Abraham XIV,34
    Amos XIV,60, 529
    Amos Jr. XIV,454, 546
    Benjamin XIV,32, 63, 181,
       186
    Beriah XIV,304-5, 465-66,
       566, 653; XVI, 31, 34, 59,
       187, 611

2

Abbott, Chandler XIV,273
  Charles XIV,280
  Ebenezer XIV,574, 639; XVI,
    15, 26
  Elias XIV,273, 276, 289; XV,
    514
  Ezra XIV,182, 273, 276, 280;
    XVI,296, 529
  George XIV,623; XV,440; XVI,
    229, 804-5
  Gilbert XIV,8
  Jacob XIV,303, XVII,385
  James XIV,547
  Jeremiah XIV,60, 182, 273,
    277, 289, 299, 359; XV,
    267; XVI,609
  Joab XIV,246
  Job XIV,424
  John XIV,182, 227, 257-58,
    312; XVI,21, 23, 191, 225;
    XVII,655, 749
  Joseph XV,74, 472, 490
  Joshua XIV,60, 62, 102, 153,
    156, 158, 182, 208, 249,
    266,303-6, 465-66, 477;
    XV,267, 269, 272; XVI,528
  Moses XIV,304-5, 465-66
  Nathan XIV,96, 204, 301,
    303, 312
  Nathaniel C. XIV,60, 182, 299;
    XVI,529, 609
  Peter XIV,1, 380, 489, 585,
    647, 649; XV,728; XVI,13,
    40, 256, 259, 295
  Philip XIV,274, 289
  Reuben XIV,60, 182
  Samuel XIV,100, 206, 346;
    XV,81
  Solomon XIV,624; XV, 440
  Stephen XIV,60, 182, 468,
    613, 672; XVI,198
  Thomas XIV,237
  Timothy XVI,271, 522
  Uriah XIV,52, 184
  Walter XVII,513
  William XIV,167, 170, 244,
    246, 546, 624, 667; XVII,

Abbott, William (Cont.) 80, 118,
    120
  William Jr. XIV,244, 667
Abeel, James XVII,397
Abel, Phinehas XVII,104
Abercrombie, James XIV,8
Abner, Thomas XVII,153
Aboire, Pretle XVII,305
Abraham, David XIV,325, 463,
    470, 578, 592; XV,716;
    XVI, 201, 218, 270, 499,
    553, 934
Acen, John Jr. XVII,116
Acley, Samuel XVII,308
Acre, Lewis XIV,84
Adal, John XIV,263
Adams, Aaron XIV,261, 468, 578,
    594; XV, 31, 145, 717; XVI,
    202, 221, 270, 502, 597,
    935; XVII,249
  Andrew XVI,776
  Asa XIV,90, 201; XV,99; XVI,
    840
  Benjamin XIV,421; XVI,135,
    764
  Dr. Caleb G. XIV,49, 121;
    XVII,13
  Charles XVII,525
  Daniel XIV,104, 436, 524; XV,
    218; XVI,158; XVII,101
  Daniel J. XVII,16, 184
  David XIV,95, 97, 204, 325,
    463, 468, 613; XV, 20, 434,
    711, 741; XVI,198, 225,
    267, 507, 662, 914; XVII,
    124
  David Jr. XIV,204
  David 2d XIV,205
  Doctor XIV,245
  Dudley XIV,369, 483, 502,
    511, 518; XV,468, 480,
    496, XVI, 110
  Dudley G. XIV,375, 498
  Ebenezer XIV,369, 374, 482,
    498, 502, 511, 518
  Eli XIV,420; XV,100, 221;
    XVI,839-40

Adams, Eliphalet XVI,150
  Elisha XIV,596; XV,713; XVI,
    255, 502, 597
  Ephraim XIV,334, 421;
    XV,355, 536; XVI,536, 842;
    XVII, 102
  Ephraim Jr. XIV,34
  Henry XV,77-78, 346
  Isaac XIV,43, 99, 436, 524,
    631; XV,456, 643, 711;
    XVI, 198, 267, 504, 635
  Jacob XIV,244, 439, 527, 667;
    XVI,88, 96; XVII,383
  John XIV,10, 100, 200, 207,
    296; XV,134, 162, 171,
    233, 394, 428, 699;
    XVI,215, 235, 267, 270,
    301, 514, 763, 840, 899,
    910; XVII, 440, 442, 449
  Jonas XIV,333, 575, 593; XV,
    438, 716; XVI,201, 235,
    511, 725
  Jonathan XVI,263, 662-63,
    718; XVII,426
  Joseph XIV,6, 369, 374, 482,
    498, 502, 511, 518;
    XVI,110
  Joshua XVI,158
  Josiah XV,416; XVI,374, 765,
    767
  Levi XIV,91, 201, 575, 592;
    XV,716; XVI,201
  Luther XVI,247, 254
  Moses XVI,630
  Mr. XVII,389
  Oliver XV,17, 77, 138; XVI,
    150
  Peter XV,481, 501; XVI,106
  Philip XVI,83, 96
  Phinehas XIV,90, 201; XV,93,
    355; XVI,235, 275, 514,
    763
  Richard XIV,96, 203-4, 238;
    XV,754; XVII,124
  Robert XIV,73, 178; XV,394,
    428
  Rufus XV,668, 680, 690

Adams, Samuel XIV,554, 625;
  XV,20, 541, 718; XVI,5,
  110, 180, 182, 203, 233,
  237, 268, 271, 349, 517,
  525, 536, 929, 935;
  XVII,29, 268,440
  Sarah XVI,322, 333, 335, 337,
    349
  Silas XIV,418
  Stephen XIV,90, 98, 201, 205,
    333; XV,93; XVI, 236, 274,
    514, 576, 764
  Stephen Jr. XV,533
  Thomas XIV,420, 436, 524,
    583, 653; XV,99; XVI,34,
    59, 535
  William XIV,9, 107, 122, 187,
    307, 348; XV,201, 209,
    464, 466, 477, 505, 654,
    671-72, 676, 743; XVI, 51,
    53, 719, 926; XVII,464
  Winborn XIV,107, 120, 122,
    154, 187, 250, 553, 615;
    XV,137, 421, 718; XVI,4,
    322, 349, 525, 710; XVII,
    267
Addington, Secretary XVII,690
Adkens, David XIV,464
  Samuel XIV,324, 463
Agaton, Samuel XV,703
Ahern, Timothy XIV,210, 214,
  217, 219-20
Aiken, Andrew XIV,42, 60, 182,
  304, 306, 465; XV,167,
  XVI,620
  Benjamin XIV,583, 600, XVI,
    47
  James XIV,60, 182, 249, 300,
    304, 306, 328, 465, 583,
    600; XV,362, 556-58, 714;
    XVI,112-14
  James Jr. XIV,583
  John XIV,299, 362; XV,176,
    299, 557; XVI,65, 76, 97,
    106, 717-18, 876
  John Jr. XVI,314
  N. XVI,405

4

Aiken, Nenian XV,122, 552-53
    Phinehas XVI,141, 161
    Robert XV,750
    Samuel XIV,304, 306, 465-66,
        583, 600; XV,715; XVI,200
    Samuel Jr. XIV,466
    Thomas XV,122
    William XV,394
    William Jr. XVI,900
Ailsworth, John XV,492, 602;
    XVI, 310
Ainger, John XIV,332
Ainsworth, Amariah XIV,324,
        463; XV,371
    Edward XV,27; XVII,105
Ajaton, Samuel XVI,175
Akely, Francis XV,701, 704; XVI,
        175, 522, 877
Akerman, Benjamin XIV,484,
        499, 512, 518; XV,749;
        XVII, 325
    Francis XVII,296
    Henry XVII,619
    John XIV,227, 485, 499, 512,
        518
    Josiah XVI,110, 165
    Mark XIV,343
    Nahum XIV,484; XVII,325
    Noah XIV,484, 500, 512, 518
    Peter XIV,192, 648-49; XV,
        596, 728; XVI,13, 109, 209,
        327, 329, 331, 341, 343,
        345, 350
    Simeon XIV,484, 499, 510,
        512, 519; XVI,925;
        XVII,454
Akers, Joseph XV,243, 245, 247;
        XVI,116; XVII,28
    Joseph Jr. XV,243, 245-46
    Samuel XVI,156
    William XV,6
Albright, Frederick XVII,296
Alcock, Robert XV,122
Alcott, Benjamin XV,63
Alden, James XVI,608; XVII,104,
        249
    John XVI,605, 607-8

Alden, Thomas XIV,334
Aldrich, Abner XV,55; XVI,811
    Abraham XVII,110
    Benjamin XVII,94
    Caleb XIV,84, 199, 427, 646;
        XV,6, 49, 651, 732, 735;
        XVI,20, 22, 191, 212, 225,
        279, 522, 877, 879, 887
    Captain XVII,384
    Ebenezer XIV,84, 199-200,
        264
    George XIV,84, 86; XV, 700,
        702, 704, 718; XVI,46, 167,
        174, 179, 203, 302, 312,
        426, 878
    Joel XIV,264
    Luke XIV,264
    Nathan XV, 17; XVI,506
    Nathaniel XVI, 236
    Philip XV, 54
    Solomon XV,745; XVII,97
    William XIV,265; XV,745
Aldridge, Captain XVII,380-81
    Joseph XVII,301
Alexander, Aaron XIV,525; XVI,
        311
    Captain XV,457
    Elijah XVI,922
    Hugh XIV,73, 178, 348
    Jabez XV,183-84
    James XIV,425; XV,116, 175,
        511
    John XIV,426, 577; XV,426;
        XVI,927
    Medad XVI,927
    Philip XIV, 264, 437; XV,
        146
    Randal XVI,247, 254, 564
    Reuben XVI,887-88; XVII,96
    Richard XIV,99, 205, 334;
        XVI,80, 92
    Robert XIV,16
    Samuel XVI,579
    Seth XIV,355; XV,54
    Thomas XIV,612
    William XV,394, 428, 698;
        XVI,720

Alfrod, John XVII,297
Allard,--XV,455
  David XV,298; XVI,68, 79, 92
  Ezekiel XV,451
  James XIV,641; XV,423, 735;
    XVI,17, 184, 211, 228, 241,
    278, 507, 673, 803
  Joel XIV,322, 365
  Joseph XIV,361
  Noah XIV,623; XV,595, 720;
    XVI,204, 231, 272, 516,
    803-4
  Shadrach XIV,296
Allcock, Joseph XVII,139
Alld, Benjamin XIV,417; XV,616,
    753; XVI,247, 254
  David XIV,242; XV,79, 346;
    XVI,635
  Isaac XV,616, 711
  Isaac C. XIV,573
  John XIV,58, 183; XV,207,
    614
  John Jr. XIV,631
  William XIV,267; XV,435
  William Jr. XIV,573; XV,616
Allen, Aaron XV,11
  Abel XV,66
  Abijah XIV,100, 206, 639;
    XV,346
  Abner XIV,233; XVII,264
  Amasa XV,750
  Benjamin XV,145
  Charles XVII,527
  Colonel XVII,167, 189
  Daniel XIV,18; XV,168;
    XVII,705
  David XVI,178-79, 267; XVII,
    440
  Ebenezer XIV,230; XVI,202,
    223, 271, 523, 818; XVII,
    28
  Elijah XVI,122, 164
  Ira XV,139
  Isaac XIV,10; XVII,295
  Isaac Jr. XIV,10
  Jacob XIV,18
  James XVI,282
Allen, Jeremiah XIV,10
  John XIV,233, 242, 266, 361,
    468, 476, 612; XV,298,
    455, 469, 481, 506, 612,
    711; XVI,118, 198, 511,
    723, 725, 920-21, 935;
    XVII, 444
  Jonathan XIV,370, 377, 492,
    503, 515; XV,326
  Joseph XIV,229, 233, 322,
    406-7; XVI,129, 162, 623,
    628
  Joshua XIV,407
  Josiah XIV,42, 211, 215, 217,
    220, 370, 377, 387, 492,
    494, 503, 507, 515-16,
    519; XVI,287, 507, 551;
    XVII,27
  Moses XV,144; XVII,249
  Nathan XV,31
  Reuben XVI,920
  Samuel XIV,279, 288, 324,
    463, 468, 470, 478, 596;
    XV,435, 713; XVI,199, 221,
    225, 241, 268; XVII,693,
    724, 755
  Samuel G. XV,711; XVI,198,
    267, 502, 606-7
  Thomas XVII,719
  William XVI,98, 815
Alley, Daniel XIV,125, 560, 620;
    XV,442, 619-20, 724; XVI,
    206, 523, 817-18; XVII,10
  Ephraim XIV,17, 125, 188;
    XIV,312; XV,628, 641;
    XVI,731; XVII,10
  Otis XVI,237, 243, 523, 818,
    820
Alline, Joshua XIV,245
Allinwood, Joseph XIV, 359
Allison, James XVII,207
  Joseph XVI,237
  Samuel XVI,633
  Samuel Jr. XVI,898, 903
Allman, John XIV,253, 413; XV,
    487, 489, 495
Almsberry, Joseph XVI,153

Almsbury, Ezra XV,3
  Israel XV,6
Amadon, Ephraim XV,52, 223
Amazeen, John XVII,606, 616,
  667, 672
Ambler, John XIV,13; XVII,716-
  17, 721
Ambrose, Benjamin XV,185
  Jonathan XV,185
  Nathaniel XIV,296, 424; XV,
  134, 392-93; XVI,750
  Samuel XV,381
Ames, Amos XIV,268, 271, 291;
  XV,733; XVI,45, 48, 265,
  304-5; XVII,307
  Benjamin XV,747
  Daniel XIV,530
  Daniel Jr. XIV,455
  David XIV,32, 346, 572, 590,
  690; XV,18, 101, 510, 613,
  743; XVI,51, 53; XVII,61,
  464
  Francis XIV,571, 605; XV,
  651, 716
  Jacob XVI,159
  Jeremiah XV,624; XVI,689-90
  Jonathan XIV,32; XV,88
  Joseph XV,631, 650; XVI,853
  Mr. XVII,57
  Phinehas XVI,403, 678
  Samuel XIV,261, 469; XV,174,
  405, 528
  Simeon XIV,100, 206
  Simon XIV,207
  Solomon XV,175
  Stephen XV,124, 150, 160;
  XVI,236, 274, 503, 669,
  687-88; XVII,57
  Thaddeus XV,18, 138, 377
Amesbury, Israel XVII,94
Amey, Abraham XIV,225
  Heman XIV,52, 185, 587, 660
  William XIV,463, 473; XV,589
Amlan, Baptist XVII,304
Ammons, William XIV,9
Amonds, John XIV,81
Amsden, Joel XV,751

Amsden, Thomas XIV,84, 199,
  264; XVI,531
Amy, George XV,390, 569;
  XVI,124
  Heman XV,727; XVI,10, 43,
  183, 209
  William XVII,65, 113
Anasthege, Vincent XV,597
Anastie, Vincent XIV,662
Anderson, Allen XV,201, 553,
  583; XVI,235, 274, 511,
  724
  Andrew XIV,115, 141, 192,
  250, 298
  Archibald XVII,208
  Enoch XVII,205
  James XIV,16, 73; XVI,911
  James Jr. XVI,911
  John XIV,73, 178, 347; XV,
  199, 376, 631, 635, 637,
  639; XVI, 102, 287, 589-
  90, 609, 907,
  John Jr. XIV,348
  Joseph XV,628, 645; XVI,
  507,667
  Lieutenant XVII,155
  Matthew XIV, 73, 178, 347
  Michael XVII,296
  Robert XV,465, 467, 478, 505
  Samuel XV,395, 429
  Thomas XVI,262, XVII,427
  William XIV,410, 425; XVI,
  167
Andre, Samuel XIV,169
Andrews, Abner XIV,348; XVI,
  235, 272, 511, 724
  Ammi XVI,50, 186, 210, 214,
  217, 219-21, 568, 660;
  XV,729; XVI,28, 287, 504
  Ammi Jr. XIV,50
  Asa XVI,235, 511, 724
  Daniel XV,634, 644; XVI, 26,
  663
  Dennis XVI,44
  Frye XV,609
  Isaac XIV, 50, 185, 261, 302;
  XV, 409; XVI, 565, 685-86;

Andrews, Isaac (Cont.) XVII, 257
   James XV, 621
   Jeremiah XIV,35, 90, 201,
      334; XV,95 364; XVI,854
   Joel XV,31, 446, 716; XVI,
      201; XVII,457
   John XIV,5; XVI,287, 519, 930
   Joseph XIV,308-9, 668
   Nathaniel XIV,607-8; XV, 604,
      714; XVII,110
   Peter XVI,930-31
   Solomon XV,127, 165, 546,
      582; XVII,259
   Stephen XV,631, 638, 732;
      XVI,26, 40, 190, 212, 228,
      279, 508, 685; XVII,438
   Thomas XVI,156
   William XV,630, 643, 646;
      XVI,854-55, 857
Andros, Amasa XVI,607
   Levi XVI,307
Andross, Abraham XIV,476
   Edmund XVII,532, 540
   James XVII,303
   Joel XIV,594
   John XVII,253
   Levi XVII,114 253
   Solomon XVII,431
Angier, John XV,108, 541
   Silas XV,20, 96, 364
Angleson, Polis XVII,608
Annable, William XV,591
Annas, Solomon XIV,25
Anne, Queen XIV,4
Annis, Charles XV, 740
   Ezra XIV,333
   Jacob XVI,860
   James XV,348
   Michael XVI,234, 264
   Samuel XIV,55, 175, 184
   Solomon XVII,431
Anthony, Jacob XIV,5
   John XVII,307
Antill, Colonel XVII,155
   Edward XVI,265
Antoine, Garoutte XV,451
Apiere, Jean B. XVII,299

Applebee, Isaac XVI,763
   Joseph XIV,243, 259,408; XV,
      243, 245, 247, 465, 468,
      480, 506; XVI,118; XVII,38
   Thomas XIV,403, 414; XV,
      243, 245, 247, 571;
      XVI,118
   William XVI,196
Appleton, Captain XVII,509
   Francis XV,220, 355, 533
   Isaac XIV,34, 421
   Samuel XVII,298
Ap Owen, Richard XVII,646
Applin, John XV,204
   Thomas XVI,852
   Timothy B. XVI,81, 95
Arbuckle, John XVI, 417
   William XV,85, 207; XVI,911
Archer, Benjamin XV,3, 62, 741;
   XVI,531
Archibald, James XV,567
   John XIV,300, 485, 500, 512,
      518, 560; XV,722; XVI,60,
      63, 71, 94, 205, 273, 502,
      586; XVII,86
   Thomas XIV,411; XVII, 219
Ardell, William XVII,666, 674,
   675
Ardewe, Samuel XIV,169
Arendine, Jeremiah XIV,12
Arlin, Samuel XV,300-1, 305,
   308, 628, 640, 725; XVI,
   500, 570-72
Arman, John XVI,268
Armes, Edward XIV,314, 338,
   565, 662; XV,268-69, 272,
   451, 730; XVI, 31, 34, 187,
   210, 277
Armon, John XVII,116
Armour, John XV,359
Armstrong, G. XVII,207
   Robert XVII,303, 704, 743,
      754, 758
   T. F. XVII,160-62, 168, 172-
      73, 176-77, 181
Arnold, Benedict XIV,209-10,
   214, 477; XVI,104; XVII,58-

8

Arnold, Benedict (Cont.) 59, 136,
  357, 461
  Edward XIV,92, 94, 202, 213,
  221
  James XIV,338, 343, 465
  Jonathan XVII,248
  R. XVII,281
  Robert XIV,561, 620; XV,443
  Thomas XIV, 230, 351, 450,
  535; XV, 256, 258-59, 262
Arskin, John XVI,528
Artland, James XV,730
Arvine, William XV,519
Arwin, Henry XVI,900
  William XVI,296
Arwine, David XIV,159, 163;
  XV,383
Asborn, John XVII,250
Ash, John XIV,469, 568, 603;
  XV,610, 712; XVI,198, 224,
  241, 268, 499, 563-64,
  827, 918; XVII,91, 453
  Phinehas XIV,341; XV,323,
  342, 748; XVI,770
  Samuel XIV,586, 628; XV,323,
  342, 627
  Thomas XVI,898; XVII,660
  William XVII,453
Ashley, Daniel XIV,426, 429;
  XVI,137, 235, 270, 522,
  867, 887
  Martin XV,23, 147, 367, 372;
  XVI,867
  Oliver XIV,297; XV,26, 37,
  370, 372; XVI,530, 532,
  541, 607; XVII,103
  Samuel XIV,256, 297, 355,
  357, 558; XV, 1, 26, 37, 46,
  47, 50-51, 54, 57, 61, 65,
  140-41, 205, 225, 367,
  372, 433, 447, 504, 655;
  XVI, 541, 605, 608, 853,
  887; XVII,15, 52, 94, 99,
  103
  Surgeon XV,37
Ashmead, Jacob XIV,284, 290

Ashton, Edward XVI,931
  Thomas B. XIV,117, 128, 289,
  615; XV,719; XVI, 103,
  192, 235, 242, 505, 644-45
Askey, William XV,205
Askin, Christopher XIV,355;
  XV,55
Askins, John XIV,437, 525
Aspinwall, Eleazer XVII,72, 87
  Zalmon XV,17, 156; XVII,143
Asten, Abijah XIV,348
  Reuben XIV,642
Astin, Nathan XV,359
Atherton, Jonathan XVI,809
  Solomon XV,54
Atkins, David XV,27
  John XV,10
  Patience XVII,679
  Samuel XV,10; XVI,313
Atkinson, Benjamin XIV,432; XV,
  128, 172, 187
  Captain XVII,342
  George XVI,292, 533
  John XVII,656
  Dr. Joseph XIV,21; XVII, 511,
  513
  Samuel XIV,60, 62, 182; XV,
  406; XVII,91, 93
  Stephen XIV,581, 641; XV,
  423, 488, 599, 730, 734;
  XVI,17, 194, 211, 220, 239,
  278, 512, 750-51
  Theodore XIV,17, 20; XVII,
  664, 666-69, 676, 683,
  685, 691-92, 710, 713-14,
  735
Atridge, George XVI,536
Atwell, John XIV,32, 303, 312
  John Jr. XIV,301
Atwill, John XV,510
  Richard XV,541
Atwood, Benjamin XIV,587, 656;
  XV,731; XVI,35, 38, 195,
  212
  Caleb XIV,328-29; XV,350-52;
  XVI,871

Atwood, David XIV,225
  James XIV,224
  John XIV,404; XV,328, 330,
    343, 754; XVI, 530; XVII,
    32
  Jonathan XVI,871, 922
  Joseph XV,125, 150, 160; XVI,
    928
  Joshua XIV,52, 185, 354;
    XVI,141, 161, 298
  Moses XIV,381, 489, 501, 514;
    XV,396; XVI,124
Auberts, Ettinne XIV,662; XV,
  451
Aubree, Frederick XIV,272
Auld, James XVI,286, 498
Austin, Abiel XIV,52, 185
  Benjamin XVII,139
  John XIV,225, 566, 653; XV,
    175, 608, 729; XVI,30, 33,
    59
  Matthew XIV,1
  Reuben XIV,231; XV,477, 732;
    XVI,19, 40, 189-90, 212,
    774, 843, 845
  Thomas XV,209
Averet, Samuel XIV,421
Averill, Daniel XVII,436
  David XV,217; XVI,167, 259
  Ebenezer XIV,244, 667; XVII,
    307
  Elijah XIV,101, 207, 416, 572,
    597; XV,611, 713; XVI,199,
    259; XVII,436
  George XV,731; XVI,35, 38,
    212
  John XIV,324
  Moses XV,74, 210, 664, 670,
    682; XVI,749; XVII,339
Averitt, George XVI,35, 38
Averson, George XIV,585, 628
Avery, Daniel XIV,259; XVI,143
  David XIV,90, 201; XVI,536
  Elijah XIV,206
  Elisha XIV,671
  Jeremiah XIV,571; XV,697;
    XVI,260-61; XVII,432

Avery, John XIV,362, 365, 463;
    XV, 195, 267, 269-71;
    XVI,122, 164, 260
  Jonathan XIV,437, 524
  Joseph XIV,571; XVI,103,
    194, 213, 220, 279, 513-
    14, 778
  Joshua XV,544, 654
  Moses XVI,67, 75, 96
  Samuel XVI,67, 75, 96
  Thomas XIV,1; XVII,511, 513,
    655
  Timothy XIV,35, 90
Ayer, Joseph XVII,424
  Francis XVI,900, 907
Ayers, Christopher XVII,105
  Daniel XVI,796
  Edward XIV,227, 257; XV,693;
    XVII,622, 655, 680, 691
  James XVI,911
  John XIV,246, 653; XV,415;
    XVI,34, 59, 723, 796
  John Jr. XV,324
  Jonathan XVII,139
  Joseph XVI,68, 78, 99, 193,
    750; XVII, 32
  Levi XIV,118, 120, 150, 196;
    XVII,360
  Mark XIV,234; XVII,655-56
  Mr. XVII,262
  Nathaniel XVII,668, 686
  Phinehas XVI,263, 612; XVII,
    430
  Samuel XIV,73, 579, 631; XV,
    206, 453, 456, 550
  Stephen XIV,259
  Thomas XIV,14, 119, 151,
    196; XVI,110, 165, 260-61;
    XVII,432, 496
  William XIV,243, XV,549
Aymond, Jean XVII,309
    B
Babb, John XIV,228; XV,723
  Joseph XIV,333
  Moses XIV,228, 362
  Nathaniel XIV,239
  Philip XVI,930

Babb, Richard XIV,446, 540
Thomas XV,300, 302, 305,
309; XVI,128, 162, 647;
XVII,450
William XIV,234, 236, 242,
550; XV,430; XVI,286, 499
Babbitt, Isaac XV,41
Babcock, Adam XVII,353
Amos XV,23; XVI,865
Benjamin XVI,869
Babe, Joseph XV,101
Bachelder, David XV,698
Isaiah XVII,14
Jeremiah XV,319; XVI,703-5
Jethro XVII,25
John XIV,189; XV,300-1; XVI,
705, 897
Josiah XVI,237, 244
Mark XIV,385; XVI,676
Nathaniel XIV,3, 128; XV,250,
252, 341, 623, 728; XVI,
727, 897
Phinehas XVI,676
Reuben XIV,358
Samuel XV,319; XVII,740
Simon XIV,122
Thomas XIV,3
William XIV,585; XVI,285
Bachellor, Archelaus XV,209;
XVI, 332, 334, 354
Isaiah XIV,167, 170
James XV,522; XVI,28, 188,
210
John XV,523; XVI,591, 616
Jonathan XV,169
Joseph XV,118; XVI,273
Nathan XVII,50
Nathaniel XV,132, 254, 318,
335, 337; XVI,44, 79, 127,
162, 200, 709; XVII,349
Samuel XIV,551; XV, 523;
XVI,672
Simon XV,255
Uzziel XV,211
William XV,607, XVI,155, 202,
234, 264, 501
Zachariah XV,522

See also Batchelder
Bachelor, Benjamin XVII,642
Josiah XVI,28, 506
Nathaniel XVI,27, 68
Stephen XVII,642
William XVI,147
Bachiler, Nathaniel XVII,528, 643
Bacon, Butts XVII,759
John XVII,67
Nathaniel XIV,264; XVI,460
Oliver XIV,36, 571, 634; XV,
441, 626, 724; XVI,206,
229, 240, 274, 301, 518,
814; XVII, 441-42, 468
Retire XV, 750
Badcock, Solomon XV,108
Badger, Abigail XVI,338, 355
Enoch XVI,285, 501, 935
Ezra XIV,63, 181, 186, 429;
XVI,926; XVII,3, 91
James XVI,465
Joseph XIV,256, 296, 321,
361, 364, 433, 455, 478,
557, 580; XV, 140, 447,
450, 498-99, 598-601, 631-
32, 643, 650, 655, 668,
690; XVI,58, 104, 166, 410,
422, 657, 828
Joseph Jr. XIV,361, 364; XV,
393; XVI,660
Nathaniel XIV,432; XV,745
Robert XV,554
Stephen XV,561
William XIV,136, 191; XVI,
333, 335-56; XVII,5
Bagley, Alando XVI,140
Barnard, XV,694; XVI,156
David XVI,256, 500
Elijah XIV,225
Enoch XVI,130, 163
Jacob XIV,327
John XV,169, 748; XVI,155
Jonathan XV,402
Joshua XIV,532
Luther XV,48
Orlando XVI,140, 161
Samuel XV,402

Bagley, Thomas XVI,140,161
  Winthrop XVI,586
Bail, Thomas XV,598
Bailey, Aaron XV,279-80
  Amos XVI,112
  Andrew XIV,87, 200, 312; XV,
    739; XVI,26, 145
  Asa XIV,286-87
  Benjamin XIV,204, 336, 697
  Cyrus XIV,282, 286; XVI,541
  Daniel XIV,329; XV,88, 510;
    XVI,143
  Dudley XV,200; XVI,125
  Eliphalet XIV,203-4
  Frye XIV,287
  General XV,410
  Jacob Jr. XVI,306
  James XV,279; XVII,368
  Jesse XIV,324, 464; XVII, 249
  Joel XIV,33, 247, 325, 464;
    XVI,26
  Job XIV,33, 87, 200
  John XIV,304
  John Jr. XIV,304
  Joseph XIV,33
  Joshua XIV,261; XVI,265, 484
  Luther XVII,94
  Moses XIV,50
  Richard XIV,33
  Solomon XV,383
  Thomas XVII,205
  Thomas C. XV,328, 343
  Timothy XIV,160-61, 163,
    286; XVI,137, 307
  Ward XIV,463; XVII,65, 78-79,
    113
  William XIV,207, 548, 568;
    XV, 494, 610, 727; XVI, 11,
    316
  William Jr. XVI,883
  See also Bayley
Baker, Amos XVI,235, 270, 514,
    764
  Benjamin XIV,58,63, 181,
    183, 186; XVI,733; XVII,3
  Captain XVI,937-38
  Cato XV,723; XVI,206

Baker, Charles XIV,433; XV,573;
    XVII,260
  Colonel XIV,365; XV,653
  Ebenezer XVII,27
  Ephraim XIV,336; XV, 419;
    XVII,62
  Joel XVI,236, 270, 514, 764
  John XV,431, 741
  Joseph XV,693
  Moses XIV,242, 339; XV, 402-
    3; XVI,586, 588, 861;
    XVII,69
  Nathaniel XIV,459, 539; XV,
    24, 111; XVII,104
  Nicholas XVI,930
  Osman XV,32
  Otis XIV,321, 323, 331, 371,
    386, 562, 619, 621, 625,
    637; XVI, 398; XVII,140
  Samuel XIV,242, 563, 651;
    XV,416, 729-30; XVI, 28
  Thomas XIV,70, 179, 433;
    XVI, 283, 287, 511, 701,
    712
  William XVI,586; XVII,306
Balch, Benjamin XIV,14; XV,62
  Caleb XIV,86, 199, 200; XVI,
    167, 254, 878
  Cyrus XVI,167, 254, 878
  Hart XIV,96, 203-4, 576, 629;
    XV,98; XVI,237, 271, 505
  John XV,62; XVI,21, 191, 212;
    XVII,98
  John Jr. XIV,644
  Nathaniel XV,191
  Timothy XV,580; XVI,739
Balcom, Elijah XVI,296
Baldwin, Asa XV,358
  Colonel XV,432
  Daniel XV,51, 225; XVI, 152
  Ebenezer XVI,538
  Elijah XV,591; XVI,310
  Ephraim XV,51, 53
  Isaac XIV,42, 50, 51, 153, 156
  Jabez XV,40, 155; XVI, 310;
    XVII,143, 252
  Jacob XVI,247, 254

Baldwin, John XIV,578, 592;
  XV,439, 603, 717; XVII,153
  Joseph XV,566
  Loammi XV,748
  Nahum XIV,301-2, 316, 335,
    337, 481; XV,123; XVI,
    143, 251, 323, 557-58;
    XVII, 62, 214
  Nahum Jr. XVI,247, 498, 562
  Reuben XVII,428
  Thomas XV,38, 45; XVI,587
Ball, Abner XV,218, 746
  Ebenezer XIV,32, 390, 486,
    506, 512; XV,743
  Eleazer XV,87
  John XIV,346, 573; XV,96,
    614; XVI,26
  John Jr. XIV,640
  Jonathan XIV,421; XV,41
  Nathaniel XIV,32
  Peter XV,325; XVII,648, 749
  Samuel XVII,22, 34
  Thomas XV,448
  William XIV,206; XV,87
Ballard, Ebenezer XV,533
  Eleazer XVI,100
  Jeremiah XV,412, 640
  Nathan XIV,242, 244, 303;
    XV, 74-76, 196, 209;
    XVI,688
  Nathaniel XV,529, 531
  Uriah XIV,574, 639; XV,617,
    731; XVI,15, 25, 186, 211,
    278, 522
  Uriah Jr. XVI,883
  William H. XV,746, 754
Ballou, James XV,669, 680; XVI,
    810; XVII,255
  Seth XV,54
Bamford, Charles XIV,122, 189
  Charles Jr. XIV,107
  John XVI,256, 505
Bancroft, Caleb XV,220
  Captain XVI,372
  James XV,108, 541
Bane, Alexander XIV,237, 550
  Daniel XIV,550; XV,430

Bane, Nehemiah XIV,236
Banfield, Charles XVII,749
  Hugh XVII,655
  Joseph XVII,30
  Samuel XV,431; XVI,902;
    XVII, 22, 33, 37, 749-50
Banfill, George XV,586
  Joseph XIV,257
  Samuel XIV,259, 664
Banks, Daniel XV,12
  Jeremiah XIV,238
  Joseph XIV,237; XVII,293
  Zebulon XIV,238
Barbarick, Ellis XV,18
Barbe, Antoine XV,461
Barber, Anthony XVI,28
  Benjamin XIV,399
  Daniel XIV,128; XV,410
  Daniel Jr. XIV,116, 189
  Jethro XVI,147, 236, 243, 271
    510, 642
  John XIV,321
  Josiah XIV,353
  Mr. XVII,181
  Robert XV,165, 416, 630, 637;
    XVI,102, 720, 724
  Thomas XVII,261
  Zebulon XIV,232, 242, 352;
    XV,283, 287, 289
Bare, Isaac XV,494
Barefoote, Walter XVII,558, 563,
    568, 584, 586, 612 616,
    618
Barger, Stephen XVII,32
Barker, Abner XIV,162, 262, 293-
    95
  Anthony XV,729
  Benjamin XIV,229, 369, 371,
    379, 414-15; XV,228, 566;
    XVI,109, 249; XVII,6, 53
  Daniel XIV,400, 439, 527; XV,
    74, 358, 748; XVI, 143,
    235, 271, 504, 749, 882;
    XVII,57
  Ebenezer XIV,229, 402, 414;
    XV,437, 567
  Isaac XIV,52, 185

Barker, James XV,177
Jerry XIV,1
John XIV,92, 94, 202, 213,
221, 363, 365, 576; XV,49,
442; XVI,506, 654
Josiah XIV,629; XV,456;
XVII,57
Nathan XVI,845
Philip XIV,485, 500, 512;
XVII,87
Phinehas XIV,87, 200
Richard XV,229, 567
Samuel XIV,232, 641; XV,422,
423, 456, 597; XVI,17, 127,
162, 194, 211, 257, 285,
514, 520, 677
Theodore XVI,82, 100, 106,
195
Thomas XV,615; XVI,933
William XIV,244, 301; XV,90;
XVI,752
Barkhart, Jacob XIV,585
Barkley, Robert XIV,168, 288;
XVI,175, 508
Barkner, Joseph XVII,308
Barlow, Abner XIV,463, 473;
XV,700, 703, 726; XVI,171-
72 175, 208, 302, 521,
782; XVII,66, 113
John XVI,269, 517; XVII,306
Joseph XV,425; XVII 78
Nathan XIV,463; XV,425, 705;
XVI,166, 168-69; XVII,66,
113
Barnard, Charles XIV,112, 146,
195
John XVI,314
Moses XIV,387, 476, 494;
XVI,448, 526, 548, 618;
XVII,284
Seco XIV, 381, 490, 501,
514
William XIV,308; XV,549
Barnes, Amos XIV,60, 182, 304-
5, 611; XVI,632
Bill XVI,608-9
Caster XV,454

Barnes, Caesar XIV,469, 573,
603; XVI,198, 222, 268,
513, 746
Eleazer XV,616
Elisha XV,546; XVII,257
James XIV,281, 288, 657; XV,
459,731,735; XVI, 35, 38,
191, 212, 225, 278, 517,
798, 800-2; XVII,221
Jeremiah XVI,81
John XIV,239; XVII,23, 39
Dr. Joseph XIV,435
Joseph Jr. XIV,439
Moses XVII,116
Nathaniel XIV,28
Reuben XIV,346
Submit XVI,801-2
Thomas XIV,258; XVII, 669
William XV,66
Barnet, Captain XVII,167-68
Ebenezer XV,628
Hugh XVII,296
James XV,567
Jonathan XV,740
Samuel XV,362
Barnett, Benjamin XIV,607-8;
XV,425, 714
Charles XIV,34
John XIV, 29; XV,111, 176;
XVII,116
Robert XIV,73, 178; XV,710
William XIV,55, 184
Barney, Constant XV,56; XVI,809
David XIV,427; XV,54, 745
Jaffrey XV,204
Jaffrey A. XV,54
William XV, 745; XVI, 167
Barns, Caesar XV,712
Daniel XV,750
James XV,605
Joseph XV,90
Reuben XV,346
Barnum, James XIV,358
Barr, James XIV,34
John XV,199, 201; XVII, 301
Samuel XV,115
Barrass, David XV,102

Barrass, Ebenezer XV,3
  Jeremiah XV,204
  Nathan XV,745
Barrel, William XV,25
Barrett,-- XVI,741
  Benjamin XV,81, 530;
    XVI,169, 170, 200
  Elijah XV,50
  Hugh XVI,296
  Isaac XIV,101, 206; XV,221,
    360; XVI, 839-40
  John XIV,104; XVI,169-70;
    XVII, 458
  Jonathan XIV,84, 199, 427
  Joseph XIV,478; XV,81-84,
    211; XVI,741
  Moses XIV,247, 437, 525
  Nathaniel XIV,102, 207; XVI,
    235, 271, 512
  Reuben XIV,419; XV,82
  Robert XVI,197, 303, 321,
    326, 328, 332, 341, 343,
    345, 351
  Samuel XVII,141
Barron, Benjamin XVI,145
  John XVI,155
  Jonathan XV,153-54, 592;
    XVI,238, 247, 267, 306,
    513; XVII,81, 83
  Joseph XIV,527; XVI,85, 95
  Lieutenant XVII,223
  Moses XIV,244; XV,379, 592,
    654, 682; XVI,313
  Samuel XIV,58, 183; XV,207,
    715; XVI,200
  Timothy XV,279-80, 584-85,
    592-93; XVI, 307, 539
  Timothy W. XVII,39
  William XIV,335, 338, 358,
    465, 690; XVI, 143, 145-
    46, 746; XVII,62, 414
Barrowcliff, Samuel XIV,51, 156-
  57
Barrows, David XV,360
  James XVI,237
  Nathan XIV,642

Barrows, Nathaniel XV,740
  Prentice XVI,137
Barrus, Jeremiah XV,745
  John XV,55
  Michael XV,54
  Nathan XVI,809
  Oliver XV,56
Barry, Benjamin XIV,682; XVI,
  241
  Ebenezer XV,437
  James XIV,653
  John XVI,912
  Robert XVII,293
  William XVI,912
Barter, Caleb XIV,472
  Henry XIV,563, 627; XV,443,
    720; XVI,204, 233, 272,
    506, 649; XVII,27
  John XIV,25, 260, 484, 499,
    512, 518, 564, 635; XV,
    724; XVI,206, 233, 240-41,
    274, 335, 514, 767;
    XVII,46, 85
  Mark XIV,238
  Peletiah XIV,260, 484, 499,
    512, 518; XVII,46, 86
  Peter XIV,257, 382, 490, 623;
    XV,440, 595, 720; XVI,204,
    272, 516, 803; XVII,30, 383
Bartlemy, Gil XVI,28
  Joseph G. XIV,662; XV, 597,
    729
Bartlett, Abiel XV,267, 270, 273
  Benjamin XV,25; XVII,105
  Christopher XIV,70, 179
  Colonel XVI,89
  Daniel XV,398, 742; XVI,124
  Ebenezer XVI,113
  Elias XIV,625
  Gideon XV,128; XVI,592-93
  Jeremiah XV,322, 342
  Jeremy XIV,226
  John XIV,485, 500, 512, 518,
    614; XV,602, 629, 648,
    711; XVI,102, 649; XVII,
    26, 86, 656

Bartlett, John H. XVII,44
   Joseph XIV,451, 532; XV, 284,
     291, 562; XVI, 150, 827;
     XVII,2
   Josiah XIV,37, 256, 340, 453,
     475, 536, 557, 585; XV,1,
     190, 276, 328, 341, 343-
     45, 354, 366, 385, 580,
     706; XVI,62, 111, 123, 126,
     129, 132, 283, 317, 371,
     386, 642, 707; XVII,15,
     123, 217, 339, 389, 399
   Josiah H. XIV,232, 247;
     XVII,25, 140
   Matthias XV,562; XVI,770;
     XVII,2
   Moses XV1,527, 532, 796
   Nathan XIV,226
   Nathaniel XIV,116, 129, 189,
     422, 614; XV, 157, 398,
     602, 711; XVI, 168-69,
     198; XVII, 143
   Nicholas XV,323, 342
   Pelatiah XIV,225
   Philip XIV,231
   Richard XIV,112, 146, 195;
     XVI,551, 579, 785-86
   Samuel XIV,34
   Stephen XIV,358, 476; XV,
     415
   Thomas XIV,242, 330, 352,
     354, 399, 401, 435, 571;
     XV,267-68, 286, 300-1,
     303, 314-17, 381; XVI,104,
     108-34, 162-65, 215, 349,
     359, 430, 491, 639, 768,
     777-78, 781
Bartley, Robert XV,701-2, 704,
   726; XVI,46, 208, 303 679
Barton, Abraham XIV,336
   Colonel XVII,162-68, 176,
     178, 180-83, 189
   Josiah XIV,43
   Stephen XVI,906
   William XIV,454, 530
Basford, Aaron XVI,285, 875;
   XVII,438

Basford, Benjamin XIV,64, 181,
   186, 319-20; XVI,926;
   XVII,3
   Ebenezer XIV,589
   Jacob XIV,1, 14; XVI,156
   James XIV,2, 273, 289; XV,
     754; XVII,719
   Jonathan XIV,172, 174, 177
   Joseph XIV,273, 276, 289; XV,
     43, 157; XVII,143
   Moses XVI,285, 501
Bascom, Elias XVI,770
Bass, Joseph XIV,339; XVI,106-
   7; XVII,139, 359, 362, 371-
   72, 377, 417
Bassett, Samuel XIV,427; XV, 3,
   741
Bastard, Walter XVII,644
Bastrick, Samuel XVI,906
Batchelder, Benjamin XIV,224,
   380, 413, 489; XV,525
   Daniel XV,419
   David XIV,116, 128, 189, 584,
     630; XV,444, 627, 725;
     XVI,169-70
   Ephraim XIV,451, 532
   Henry XIV,118, 137, 158, 191,
     255
   Henry Jr. XIV,413
   Isaiah XIV,423
   James XIV,565, 570, 651
   Jeremiah XV,331, 339; XVI,
     863
   Jethro XV,194, 512
   John XIV,12, 117, 128, 232,
     253, 328, 353, 450, 535;
     XV,267, 269, 273, 305,
     309, 663, 670, 684, 688
   Jonathan XIV,12, 353; XV,
     267-68, 270-71, 754
   Joseph XIV,109, 131, 190;
     XV,138, 488, 498
   Joshua XV,729
   Josiah XIV,70, 179, 353, 450,
     534, 570, 651; XV,562;
     XVI, 617
   Js. XV,729

Batchelder, Mark XIV,661;
  XVI,11; XVII, 433
  Nathan XIV,70, 179, 253; XV,
    127, 130
  Nathaniel XIV,68, 87, 117,
    180, 189, 200, 451, 532,
    570, 600, 615; XV,180,
    249, 331, 333, 629, 641,
    714; XVII, 625
  Nathaniel Jr. XVI,616, 707
  Phinehas XV,180; XVII,433
  Richard XV,180
  Samuel XIV,11, 229, 253,
    450, 535; XV,339, 656,
    666, 674
  Samuel Jr. XIV,253
  Simon XIV,109, 187, 330,
    332; XV,249-51
  Stephen XIV,231, 570, 641;
    XV,423, 730; XVI,18
  Dr. Stephen XVI,411
  Theophilus XIV,24
  Thomas XIV,110, 131, 190;
    XV, 179, 321, 340
  Timothy XVI,131, 163
  William XIV,567, 611; XV,
    717; XVII,424
  Zachariah XV,412
Bates, Captain XVII,327
  Joseph XIV,34; XVI,535-36
  Nathaniel XIV,577, 597; XV,
    713
  Samuel XIV,578, 614; XV,434,
    711; XVI,198, 605; XVII,
    468
  Thomas XIV,603; XV,451, 711
Batson, John XVII,622, 668
  Nathaniel XVI,906
Batt, Sampson XVI,264
Battas, Sampson XVII,431
Batten, John XVII,302
Batter, Richard XIV,459
Baxter, Benjamin XV,29
  Elihu XIV,274, 291
  Elisha XIV,289
  John XV,153
  Simon XIV,325, XVI,531, 554

Baxter, Stephen XVII,468
  Thomas XIV,607-8; XV,436,
    604, 714; XVII,111, 468
Bayard, James XVI,929
Bayles, John XV,122, 188
  Joseph XVI,246, 516
Bayley,-- XV,699
  Aaron XVI,924, 928; XVII,89
  Abijah XV,152, 154; XVII, 253
  Abraham XV,216
  Amos XV,210
  Andrew XIV,301, 303,573
    640; XVI,510, 613
  Asa XIV,546
  Benjamin XIV,96; XVII,63
  Charles XVI,928
  Cyrus XIV,287
  Daniel XV,380, 664, 670, 682;
    XVI,690; XVII,339
  Daniel Jr. XIV,418
  David XVI,125
  Dudley XIV,77, 81, 198
  Ebenezer XIV,242
  Eliphalet XIV,96
  Enoch XIV,211, 215, 218-20
  Frye XVII,281-82
  George XV,166
  Jacob XV,278-79, 429, 584-
    85; XVI,169, 171, 923,
    928-29; XVII,72, 135-36,
    150, 223, 240, 243, 248,
    265, 275-76, 282-83, 313-
    14, 317-18, 321, 330, 344,
    347, 355, 357-58, 363, 376
  James XV,279, 281, 399, 586;
    XVI,679; XVII,91
  Jesse XV,147
  Joel XIV,573, 640; XV,613
  John XIV,306, 465; XVI,921;
    XVII,17-18
  John M. XIV,225, 405; XV,390
  Joseph XV,400; XVI,253
  Joshua XIV,453, 467; XV,162,
    182-84, 234-36, 548-49;
    XVI,540, 694, 696
  Miles XV,189
  Moses XIV,185; XV,380

Bayley, Orasmus XV,589
Phinehas XV,183
Richard XIV,247; XVI,377,
799-800
Samuel XV,44; XVI,871-72;
XVII,67
Solomon XV,120, 183
Sylvanus XIV,427
Timothy XIV,287; XV,589;
XVII,114
Ward XV,589
William XV,209
Winthrop XV,475
See also Bailey
Beach, Azariah XV,277; XVI,314
Beache, Richard XVII,405
Beal, Abigail XVI,333, 356
Benjamin XVI,167, 814
Captain XVII,312
James XIV,131, 190, 563,
627; XV,441, 720
Joseph XIV,484, 512, 518;
XVII,86
Joseph Jr. XIV,664
Josiah XVII,27
Obadiah XV,753
Thomas XIV,112, 146, 195,
660; XV,727; XVI,9, 40, 42,
189, 208
Zachariah XIV,118-19, 149,
197, 555, 647, 649; XV,
449, 457-58, 595-97, 600-
1, 726; XVI,6, 26, 333, 355,
528; XVII,269
See also Beel, Beals,
Beels
Beale, Josiah XIV,236
Beals, Aaron XV,21
Benjamin XV,217, 348
Bealy, William XIV,659
Bean, Benjamin XIV,171, 174,
176-77, 253, 261; XV,134,
172, 179, 323, 342, 406,
754
Cornelius XIV,63, 186, 316,
319; XVII,3
Curtis XIV,398; XV,564

Bean, Daniel XIV,11; XV,439;
XVI, 178-79
David XIV,433
Ebenezer XIV,66, 181, 232,
317, 320, 454, 530, 546,
563-64, 616; XV,406, 440,
719; XVI,531
Edward XIV,14, 299; XV,564;
XVI,282
George XIV,66, 181
Jabez XV,623
James XVI,125
Jeremiah XIV,14, 113, 146,
195, 341; XVI,589
John XIV,3, 12, 55, 63, 116,
128, 181, 184, 186, 189,
210, 218, 220, 231, 316,
318, 465, 565, 651; XV,
171, 512, 728; XVI,27, 105,
188, 210, 323, 330, 337,
340, 356; XVII,3
John Jr. XIV,12, 65, 186;
XVII,4
Jonathan XIV,580, 659; XV,
448, 599, 727; XVI,10, 43,
183, 209
Joseph XIV,134, 191, 391,
404, 487, 508, 512; XV, 526;
XVII,6, 44
Josiah XIV,297, 299, 387,
494, 508,516, 565, 651;
XV,162, 171, 729; XVI,28
Moody XV,133, 392
Nathaniel XVI,285, 510
Phinehas XV,514, 658-59,
668, 676; XVI,590
Richard XVI,39
Samuel XIV,12, 305, 404
Samuel Jr. XIV,12
Simeon XIV,297
William XV,400
Beane, John XV,431
Bearce, Andrew XIV,562, 637;
XV, 618, 724
Beard, John XIV,160-61;
XVI,235,242, 516, 803, 805
Robert XVII,298

18

Beard, Samuel XIV,60, 182, 304-5
    Simon XVI,113
    Simon Jr. XVI,921
    Thomas XVII,525
    William XIV,181, 186; XV,163, 188, 429; XVII,3
Beasom, John XV,118, 138
    Nicholas XV,554
Beattee, Thomas XIV,317
Beaver, Charles XVII,204
Beavins, Benjamin XV,612; XVI, 748
    Edward XVI,140, 161
Beatty, Francis XVI,541
Beck, Amos XIV,227, 257, 472
    Henry XVII,501
    John XV,577
    John Jr. XIV,239; XVII,23, 39
    Jonathan XV,325
    Samuel XV,256, 259-60, 263
Beckford, Thomas XIV,28
Beckman, John XIV,350
Beckwith, Andrew XIV,297
    Bethuel XV,30, 35, 368
    Ira XVII,383
    Jabez XIV,298; XV,9
    Martin XIV,325, 464; XV,147
    Niles XV,741
    Silvanus XV,29
Beckworth, Bethuel XVI,137, 713, 714
    Ira XVI,80, 93
    Jabez XVI,714
Bedel, Benjamin XV,177
    Daniel XV,279, 281; XVI, 924, 932
    Jacob XIV,285, 287
    John XIV,167, 170; XV,589; XVII,14, 89, 331
    Joshua XIV,173, 286-87; XV, 592; XVI,541
    Moody XV,593; XVII,253
    Richard XIV,160-61, 163, 282, 286-87
    Robert XIV,163

Bedel, Thomas XIV,317, 320; XV,185, 405
    Timothy XIV,159-62, 171, 209, 261-62, 284, 287, 295, 481, 695; XV,426, 584-85, 594; XVI,280, 306, 308-11, 459, 539, 573, 908, 921, 927; XVII,16-17, 21, 52, 57-60, 76, 114-15, 118, 128-35, 150-51, 210-13, 217-18, 222-24, 228, 232-34, 237, 239, 241, 243, 248, 250-52, 265, 275-76, 281-83, 289-90, 310-17, 321, 328-31, 343-44, 347-50, 355, 358, 363, 365, 368, 379-84, 463, 469
Beder, William XVII,306
Beebe, Peter XIV,625, 646; XV, 66, 226, 651, 732; XVI,20, 22, 191, 507, 653, 663
    Peter Jr. XVI,633
    Sebe XV,383; XVI,307; XVII, 114, 253
Beecher, Will XVII,495
Beede, Aaron XVI,416
    Bezaleel XIV,404; XV,322, 342; XVII,32
    Daniel XVI,831-32
    Daniel Jr. XIV,297
    John XVII,25
    Joshua XVI,122, 164
    Josiah XVI, 509, 709
    Phinehas XV, 748; XVI,115
    Rezia XVI,103, 202, 219, 270; XVII,359
    Thomas XVI, 657
Beel, James XIV,111
Beels, Benjamin XIV,99, 205
Belanche, Juill XVII,304
    Noel XVII,304
Belaney, Charles XVI,234
Belding, David XV,63; XVI,488
    Elisha XIV,84, 199; XV,6, 50, 224; XVII,97
    Lieutenant XV,447

Belding, Moses XIV,84, 199, 355;
   XV, 733; XVI,8; XVII,269
Bele, Joseph XV,431
Belhan, John XV,44
Belknap, Ezekiel XIV,404, 476;
   XV,388; XVI,529, 532
Nathaniel XV,664-65, 671,
   682; XVI,629
William XV,592; XVI,928;
   XVII,80, 82
Bell, Andrew XV,379; XVI,314;
   XVII,118, 120
Benjamin XIV,20, 27, 387,
   494, 507, 516; XVI,906,
   916
Elizabeth XVI,333, 341, 356
Frederick M. XIV,114, 140,
   142, 554, 623, 625-26; XV,
   440, 447, 449, 457, 595-
   98, 601, 719; XVI,5, 333,
   356; XVII,267
Henry XIV,369, 374, 482, 498
James XIV,111, 328; XVI,307,
   314; XVII,114
John XIV,343, 349; XV,111,
   122, 175; XVI,263, 315,
   725; XVII,118-19
Jonathan XIV,44, 184;
   XV,116, 557; XVII,258
Joshua XIV,358, 653; XV,729;
   XVI, 30, 33, 59, 331, 341,
   344-45, 357
Meshech XIV,380, 383, 480,
   489; XVI,317-18, 916; XVII,
   451, 459
Meshech Jr. XVI,234, 264
Samuel XVI,314; XVII,91,
   118-19
Shadrach XVII,644, 669
Thomas XIV,20, 27; XVI,234,
   906, 916; XVII,307
William XIV,270, 289, 298,
   563, 627; XV,441, 721;
   XVI, 204, 315, 358;
   XVII,47, 148
William M. XIV,115, 140, 192,
   554, 619; XV,718; XVI,4, 5,

Bell, William (Cont.) 51, 182,
   203, 271, 300, 438; XVII,
   137, 268, 441
Bellamy, John XIV,237; XVII,87
Belling, John XIV,485
   Samuel XIV,485
Bellomont (Richard, Earl of)
   XVII,680-81, 688
Bellows, Benjamin XIV,256, 461,
   577; XV, 1, 9, 13, 23, 34-
   37, 87, 90, 147-48, 367-72,
   433, 501, 629-30, 642-43,
   652, 655, 662, 669, 671;
   XVI,58, 104, 166, 249, 552,
   739, 867, 921; XVII,235,
   248, 462
Benjamin Jr. XIV,297-98, 422,
   442, 462, 478, 558; XVI,
   865; XVII,103, 106-7
John XIV,262, 264, 266, 293-
   94; XV, 23, 37; XVI, 382,
   528, 532, 866; XVII,41, 52,
   103
Peter XV,32; XVII,104
Theodore XVI,137, 866
Bemain, George XIV,51, 156-57,
   267, 336, 690; XV,608;
   XVI,685; XVII,62
Beman, Joseph XIV,264
Bemins, Edward Jr. XV,138
Bemis, David XVI,159
Henry XIV,334; XV, 541, 741
James XV,102, 109, 360;
   XVII,428
John XVI,523
Benedict, Caleb XVII,48
   Samuel XV,379
Benham, Nathan XV,30
Benjamin, Judah XV,145; XVII,
   118, 120, 249
Bennett, Andrew XVI,121, 164
Arthur XIV,134; XV,571;
   XVII,6
Benjamin XVI,333
Caleb XIV,23; XVII,205
Ebenezer XV,640; XVI,570-71
Ephraim XVII,306

20

Bennett, Henry XVII,737
  Jeremiah XV,748
  John XVI,122, 164, 287, 555,
    765, 840; XVII,57
  Jonathan XVI,839
  Joseph XVII,27
  Moses XIV,236; XV,100;
    XVII,94
  Nicholas XVII,655
  Samuel XIV,287; XVII,46
  Spencer XIV,227
  William XIV,149, 197, 352,
    388, 495, 507, 516;
    XVI,648, 928
  Winthrop XIV,255; XVII,39
Benney, Stephen XIV,516
Bennick, Ebenezer XIV,408
  Samuel XIV,13
Benson, Henry XIV,13
  Isaac XVI,809; XVII,97
  James XIV,664
  John XIV,227
  Joseph XIV,257
  Perry XVII,203
Bent, William XIV,571, 630
Bentley, William XIV,289
Benton, Abijah XIV,265
  Elijah XV,741
  Stephen XV,39, 375
  William XVII,6
Bergin, John XIV,115, 140, 193,
    371, 384, 496, 505;
    XVII,261
Berkley, James XVII,308
Berrien, John XVII,389
Berrings, Edward Jr. XV,118
Berry,-- XV, 699
  Benjamin XIV,68, 180, 469,
    570, 617; XV,723; XVI,
    128, 162, 199, 225, 274,
    647
  Benjamin B. XV,634, 649,
    712; XVI,268, 501, 505,
    604
  Ebenezer XIV,583, 600; XV,
    715; XVI,200

Berry, Edmund XVII,294
  Eliphalet XVI,913
  Ephraim XIV,18, 127, 188,
    321, 361; XVII,12
  Francis XVI,111; XVII,360
  George XIV,227-28, 257, 344;
    XVII,30
  Isaiah XVII,360
  James XIV,234, 433, 566; XV,
    609; XVI,34, 59; XVII,11
  Jeremiah XIV,118, 137, 158,
    XIV,192, 224; XVII,26
  Jeremiah Jr. XIV,248
  John XIV,15, 24, 169, 228,
    410, 583; XV,715;
    XVII,511, 527
  John B. XV,192
  Jonathan XIV,15, 600
  Joseph XIV,15, 234, 456, 531;
    XVII,667, 679
  Joshua XIV,15; XV,327
  Josiah XIV,343, 550
  Levi XV,256, 259-60, 263
  Nathan XVI,300; XVII,454
  Nathaniel XIV,118, 137, 158,
    192, 228, 248, 362; XV,
    298; XVII,26
  Samuel XIV,228, 248; XV,192,
    699; XVII,26
  Simon XV,694; XVI,171-72,
    175
  Stephen XIV,127, 188, 371,
    384, 496, 505; XVII,12
  Thomas XIV,15, 115, 141,
    193,228; XVII,360
  Thomas Jr. XVI,668; XVII,360
  Timothy XIV,224
  William XIV,28, 233; XVII,29
Beson, Nicholas XIV,425
Bethel, Stephen XIV,166, 170,
    288, 318-19; XVII,14
Bettis, Robert XIV,52, 185
Bettison, Naboth XIV,355, 644;
    XV, 732, 735; XVI,20, 22,
    191, 212, 225, 279, 510,
    701; XVII,467

Bettle, Joseph XIV,550
Betton, James XIV,219; XV,677,
    683, 686; XVI,453, 654,
    889-91; XVII,256, 431,
    433, 435
    John XIV,276, 360; XVI,527;
    XVII,211
    Richard XIV,538
Beverly, James XIV,212, 215,
    218, 220, 249, 570, 602;
    XV,712; XVI,779
Bevins, Benjamin XIV,100, 206,
    248, 572, 612; XV,711
    Edward XIV,87, 201; XV,350,
    554
Bewell, Simon XVI,138
Bezell, Robert XV,752
Bicker, David XV,295
Bickford, Aaron XIV,18, 623; XV,
    619, 720; XVI,204, 229,
    272, 503, 624
    Abner XIV,570, 617; XV,723
    Abraham XV,444
    Andrew XIV,68, 180, 408;
    XVI,236, 242, 274, 505,
    644-45
    Benjamin XIV,25, 235
    Daniel XIV,228, 456, 531,
    581, 619; XV,283, 288,
    449, 600; XVI,256, 510;
    XVII,140
    Dennis XIV,627; XV,443, 457,
    721; XVI,207, 231, 273,
    510, 527, 703-4
    Eleazer XIV,433; XVII,717
    Eli XIV,108, 122, 187, 408;
    XVI,710
    Eliakim XIV,22, 369, 375,
    483, 498; XVI,64, 74, 93
    Ephraim XIV,236, 406;
    XV,311
    George XIV,25
    Henry XIV,239; XVI,907
    Ichabod XIV,18
    Isaac XV,299
    James XIV,630; XV,597, 724
    Jethro XIV,2

Bickford, Joanna XVII,671
    John XIV,12, 211, 216, 226,
    228, 234, 330, 398, 456,
    474-75, 531; XV, 249, 251-
    52, 254, 299; XVI,68, 76,
    97, 130, 163, 256, 513,
    526, 776; XVII,29, 525,
    648, 668-69, 671, 717
    Jonathan XIV,25, 341, 363
    Jonathan Jr. XIV,12
    Joseph XIV,108, 122, 187,
    235, 250-51, 354, 467,
    548, 653, 664; XV,692;
    XVI, 214, 637; XVII,717
    Joshua XVI,317-18
    Micajah XIV,233
    Moses XIV,25
    Richard XVI,904
    Samuel XIV,369, 375, 482,
    498; XV,300, 302, 305,
    309, 311, 471, 506; XVI,68,
    79, 90
    Temperance XVII,671
    Thomas XIV,3, 12, 14, 236,
    315, 467, 475, 548; XVI,
    899; XVII, 623, 645, 658,
    671
    Winthrop XVII,22, 34
Biddle, John XVII,303
Bigelow, Benjamin XV,745; XVII,
    139, 247
    Solomon XIV,442, 544; XV,32
    Timothy XVI,406
Bigford, Joseph XIV,301, 314,
    567; XV,608, 729
Bigsby, Asa XIV,628; XV,721
    John XVI,27, 44
    Jonathan XIV,265
Bigsford, Joseph XVI,30, 33, 59
Bill, David XIV,428; XV,3
    Ebenezer XV,67; XVII,95
Billings, Christopher XIV,577,
    593; XV,439
    Daniel XIV,240
    Ebenezer XV,741, 752; XVI,
    167, 878
    Isaac XIV,264

Billings, James XVII,42
   John XV,597, 701; XVI,46,
     171, 173, 177, 303
   Nathan XIV,265
   Samuel XIV,500, 512, 518;
     XVII,87
Bingham, Abner XIV,469, 578,
     596; XV, 713; XVI,221,
     268, 512, 714
   Alvin XVI,312
   Elisha XV,155; XVII,144
   Gustavus XIV,356; XVI,23
   Ithamar XVII,263
   James XVII,105
   Mr. XVII, 343
   Nathan XV, 35, 147
   Nathaniel XV,58; XVI,602
   Reuben XV,10; XVII,105
   Ripley XIV,265, 578, 596; XV,
     435, 713
   Silas XIV,298; XVII,103
   Theodorus XV,224
Binnet, Winthrop XVII,24, 31
Birts, Rob Ben XV,604
Bishop, Bethuel XV,204, 746
   Daniel XIV,167, 170, 286-87;
     XV,61, 204; XVII,14, 98
   Enoch XIV,319
   Enos XIV,167, 288, 318, 567,
     596; XV,425, 435, 607,
     713; XVII,14
   Jean XIV,271, 282, 287, 290,
     427, 470, 596
   John XV,425, 713; XVI, 199,
     224, 239
   Josiah XV,592
   Nathaniel XVI,35
   Robert XV,541; XVI,152
   Samuel XIV,92, 202-3; XV,218
   Samuel Jr. XIV,102
   Thomas XV,669, 680; XVI,81,
     93; XVII,255
   Timothy XV,63; XVII,97
Bixby, Asa XIV,459, 539, 587;
     XV,696, 698
   Daniel XVI,137
   David XIV,105

Bixby, Edward XIV,58, 183; XV,
   207
   Jacob XVI,884
   John XV,127, 721, 634, 644;
     XVI,619
   Jonathan XIV,106; XV, 369
   Lewis XVI,884
   Thomas XV,123, 654,745
   William XV,206
Black, Caesar XIV,600; XVI,829
   Edmund XVII,427
   George XV,443
   John XV,309; XVII,296
   Jonathan XVI,235, 267, 511,
     724
   Nicholas XV,308
   Richard XIV,381, 490, 519
   Sherburne XV,308
   William XVII,300
Blackey, Mark XIV,581; XV,448,
   599
Blackman, Benajah XIV,281, 285
   Benjamin XIV,287
   Hut XIV,7
   John XIV,289, 291
Blackstone, William XVII,754
Blagden, James XVII,620
Blair, Elisha XV,733
   Hugh XVI,913
   James XVI,236, 274, 511, 725
   John XV,221, 427, 538, 739;
     XVI,47, 54, 101, 213, 279,
     303, 517, 794
   William XV,101, 221, 356, 754
   William Jr. XV,125
Blaisdell, Abijah XIV,108, 122,
     187, 251; XVI,637
   Abner XIV,227; XV,578
   Daniel XIV,391, 487, 509, 513
   Ebenezer XIV,567, 660;
     XV,456, 608, 727; XVI, 10,
     44
   Ezra XIV,316, 319; XV,180
   Henry XIV,226, 404
   Isaac XIV,457, 539; XV,169,
     464, 466-67, 478, 504;
     XVI, 65, 76, 96, 105-6,

Blaisdell, Isaac (Cont.) 601;
XVII,378
Jacob XIV,112, 146, 195, 342;
XV,250-51, 253
Jedediah XIV,238
John XIV,227, 257, 381, 413,
490, 501, 514, 585, 623,
641; XV,423, 456, 720,
730, 734; XVI,17, 69, 79,
94, 131, 163, 194, 204,
211, 220, 234, 264, 278,
508, 675; XVII,30
John Jr. XVI,133
Moses XVI,901
Nathaniel XIV,300, 457, 538
Parrot XV,472, 490
Peter XVI,87, 94, 106; XVII,
383
Philip XIV,226, 562, 585 636;
XV, 653, 656, 666, 678,
724; XVI, 207, 230, 275,
510, 642, 703; XVII, 32
Roger XV,632, 636; XVI,286,
499, 557
Samuel XIV,226, 405
Sargent XVII,427
Thomas XIV,226, 381, 489,
585, 623; XV,720
William XIV,229
Blake, Aaron XVI,897
Ariel XV,61
Asahel XV,61; XVI,768
Benjamin XIV,331; XVI,920
Christopher XVI,255, 508
Daniel XVII,512
David XVI,299
Ebenezer XIV,25, 253, 361,
365; XV, 392
Elijah XIV,56, 184; XV,400;
XVI,152, 298
Elisha XIV,228; XV,297; XVI,
127, 162
Enoch XV,320, 339, 695
Francis XIV,363-64
Henry XIV,50, 185; XV,320;
XV,339, 408

Blake, Hezekiah XV,400, 742;
XVII, 32
Isaac XVI,88, 90
Israel XIV,12
James XIV,463; XV,705; XVI,
288-92; XVII,65, 78, 113,
293, 440-42
Jeremiah XIV,230
Jethro XIV,230, 252; XV,412
John XIV,1, 11, 301, 326,
464; XV,167, 249-50, 255-
56, 258, 273, 300-1, 305,
475, 489, 572; XVI,116,
152
Jonathan XIV,55, 184, 252,
341; XV,543; XVI,568
Joseph XV,62
Joshua XIV,652; XV,456, 728;
XVI,27
Josiah XIV,110, 131, 190,
300, 387, 494; XV, 256,
258, 260, 263
Levi XIV,110, 131, 190, 413;
XV,256, 258, 260, 263, 522
Moses XIV,113, 146, 195, 350,
627; XV,457, 720; XVI,128,
162, 204, 703-4
Nathan XIV,22, 25, 299, 369,
377, 492, 503, 515; XV,61;
XVI,115
Nathan Jr. XVI,702
Nicholas XV,300-1, 304, 308
Obadiah XV,3
Obadiah Jr. XIV,428
Oliver S. XIV, 112, 146, 195,
340
Paul XIV,70, 179, 232, 312,
450-51, 532, 534; XV,482,
495, 523
Philemon XIV,12; XV,412;
XVI,490
Phinehas XV,494
Richard XIV,501, 514
Robert XIV,116, 128, 289; XV,
565
Samuel XIV,1

Blake, Sherburne XV,300-1, 304,
  308; XVI,775
  Theophilus XIV,454, 530, 546
  Thomas XIV,422, 553, 607;
    XV, 710; XVI,3, 51, 180,
    182, 197, 248, 267, 306,
    563; XVII,266
  Timothy XIV,3, 12, 23, 55,
    184; XVII,211
  William XIV,23, 451, 532,
    651; XV,729; XVI,28, 563
Blanchard, Abel XVI,131, 163
  Augustus XIV,242; XV,412;
    XVI,556, 563
  Benjamin XIV, 244; XVI,595,
    883, 903
  Colonel XVI,919
  Daniel XV,225; XVI,882
  David XIV,143, 194; XV,179,
    698; XVI,85, 100, 106, 195,
    310; XVII,9
  Edward XIV,261
  Eleazer XIV,96, 203-4
  George XIV,244; XVI,884
  Isaac XV,150
  Jacob XIV,417, 474, 639; XV,
    617, 731; XVI,15, 25, 186,
    211, 748-49
  James XIV,418, 555, 638;
    XVI,6, 40, 44, 182, 208,
    259; XVII,269, 436, 440,
    449, 458
  Joel XV,167, 269, 273
  John XIV,52, 249-50; XV,
    555, 622, 634, 644; XVI,
    27, 44, 286, 501, 631, 633
  Jonathan XVI,595
  Joseph XIV,19, 346, 436, 457,
    465-66; XV, 472, 490;
    XVI,105, 148, 158, 263,
    392, 445, 612, 921-22;
    XVII,430
  Joshua XV,529; XVI,883
  Josiah XV,189
  Js, XV,726
  Lieutenant XVII,326
  Mr. XVII,339

Blanchard, Nathaniel XIV,355
  Pelatiah XVI,924
  Peter XIV,454, 529, 546; XV,
    129, 185; XVI,264; XVII,
    304, 431
  Reuben XVI,105, 148, 247,
    253, 501, 611
  Simeon XV,100
  Simon XV,215
  Stephen XIV,96, 203-4; XV,74
  Stephen Jr. XIV,96, 204;
    XVI,749
  Thomas XIV,337, 570;
    XVI,203
  Thomas 3d XVII,63
  William XVI,909
Blancher, John XIV,185
  Joseph XIV,524
  Richard XIV,3
  Thomas XIV,9
Bland, John XVII,641
Blandon, William XVII,307
Blaney, John XVII,303
Blasol, John XVI,131
Blathwait, William XVII,544-46,
  564, 585
Blazo, Paul XVI,288, 507
  Thomas XVI,288, 507; XVII,
    360
Bliss, Abner XIV,427; XV,66
  Azariah XV,41, 156
  Azariah Jr. XVII,143
  Constant XIV,160-61, 163;
    XV,383, XVII,250
  Daniel XV,17; XVII,67, 109
  Ebenezer XIV,423; XV,374
  Isaiah XVII,143
  Josiah XV,156
  Levi XV,66; XVII,99
  Pelatiah XV,379, 586
  Stephen XV,43; XVII,111
Blith, John XVII,655
  Moses XVII,7
  William XVII,24
  See also Bly
Blodgett, Archippus XIV,463;
  XVI,288-92; XVII,65, 78

Blodgett, Asahel XIV,435
  Azel XIV,527
  Caleb XIV,635; XV,442, 624,
    719; XVI,5, 182, 203, 229,
    271; XVII,440-42
  Captain XIV,579
  David XVI,739
  Ebenezer XIV,280, 288;
    XVI,797
  Elijah XIV,173, 176-77, 288;
    XV,589; XVI,289-92
  Jacob XIV,97, 101, 203-4,
    206-7, 247, 267; XV,81,
    197, 209
  James XV,150, 160
  Jeremiah XVI,909
  Jonathan XIV,334; XV,150,
    160, 217, 536; XVI,534
  Joseph XV,206
  Joshua XIV,279, 572, 602;
    XV,612, 712; XVI,198
  Josiah XIV,463; XV,425, 700,
    725; XVI,46, 170, 172, 175,
    208, 302, 517, 521, 782;
    XVII,66, 78, 113
  Phinehas XV,698
  Samuel XIV,554, 634-35; XV,
    441, 448, 460, 595-98,
    605, 607; XVI, 5, 664; XVII,
    267
  Thomas XIV,463; XV,425,
    700, 703, 726; XVI,46, 175,
    302; XVII,65, 78, 113
Blois, Walter XIV,662; XV,16,
  602
Blood, Amos XVI,296, 539
  Asa XVI,237, 512, 741
  Captain XVII,135
  Daniel XIV,33, 346, 418, 572,
    590, 609; XV,613, 714
  Ebenezer XIV,43, 101, 206;
    XV, 553; XVI, 893
  Ephraim XIV,32, 43; XV,632,
    635, 733, 744; XV, 53, 269,
    306, 504, 634-36
  Francis XIV,33, 35; XV,88,
    743; XVI,465, 792-94, 835,

Blood, Francis (Cont.) 855, 859-
    60; XVII, 135, 415
  Jonas XIV,33
  Joseph XIV,43, 101, 206; XVI,
    144
  Josiah XIV,346; XV,88
  Lemuel XVI,84, 96, 106
  Nathan XIV,32, 43; XV,743
  Nathaniel XV,510; XVI,85, 90,
    106
  Nathaniel Jr. XV,510
  Reuben XIV,631; XV,88, 614;
    XVI,85, 90, 106
  Simeon XIV,631; XV,209, 614;
    XVI,689
  Simon XVI,167
  Solomon XIV,441, 527;
    XVI,669
  Thomas XIV,574, 639;
    XV,612, 731; XVI,15, 25,
    186, 211, 740
  Timothy XIV,418; XV,510
  Zaccheus XV,740; XVI,839
Bloy, John XIV,10
Bloyce, Zadoc XV,386
Blue, Jonathan XIV,353; XV,249,
    251-53; XVI,260-61;
    XVII,432
  Samuel XV,249, 251-53
Blunt, Arthur XIV,339
  Cornelius XV,43, 155; XVI,
    310; XVII,144
  Jeremiah A. XV,132, 513
  John XIV,248; XVII,26
  Samuel XV,452
  William XIV,239; XV,578;
    XVII,139
Bly, John XIV,1
  Moses XIV,134, 191
Boanloy, Cornelius XVII,294
Boardman, Benjamin XIV,242;
    XVI, 648
  John XVII,293
  Sherman, XV,369
Bodge, Benjamin XV,311; XVII,
    717
  Samuel XIV,233

Bodwell, John XVII,122
Boffee, John XIV,359; XV,118,
    138, 742
Bohonon, Ananias XVI,236, 271,
    521, 827
    Andrew XIV,429; XV,162, 164
    Dennis XVII,308
    Jacob XV,165
    Stephen XIV,430, 548;
        XV,663, 670, 685, 688;
        XVI,285, 286, 875;
        XVII,438
Boilant, Amiable XVII,304, 347
Bokell, Robert XVII,39
Bolds, James XIV,471
Bollay, Anabel XVII,308
Bolton, William XV,229
Boltwood, Ebenezer XIV,6
Bomford, Robert XIV,226
Bond, Asa XIV,355; XV,55, 203
    David XV,226
    Gilbert XIV,77, 81, 198;
        XVI,670
    John XV,559; XVI,121, 164;
        XVII,27
    Samuel XIV,66, 180
    Stephen XIV,325, 464; XV,3,
        66; XVI,153; XVII,96
Bonner, John XVI,238, 275, 509
Bonney, Jacob XIV,593; XV, 717;
    XVII,460
Boody, John XV,298
    Joseph XV,298
    Robert XIV,296; XVI,555, 755,
        757-58
Booker, Jotham XIV,259-550
Boone, John XVII,293
Booth, Epaphrus XV,368
    Freegrace XIV,324
    James XVII,623
    William XV,164
Boothe, Epaphrus XV,35
    Joshua XV,30, 147
Borden, Nathaniel XIV,288
    Simpson XIV,310
Borland, John XV,536
Born, Ben XIV,238

Born, Thomas XIV,7
Bornheeter, John XIV,223
Borno, Nehemiah XVII,302
Borrows, Jonathan XIV,583
Boston, Anthony XV,754;
    XVI,928
    Elijah XIV,238
    Tone XIV,145, 194
Bostwick, John XVII,297
Boswell, John XVII,430
Bosworth, Jeremiah XV,204
    Jonathan XV,54
Botts, Thomas XIV,565
Bouder, Isaac XIV,238
Bouffard, Nicholas XVII,47, 85
Boughton, Nathan XVII,295
Bounds, Richard XIV,1
Bourette, Louis XVII,305
Bourn, Mary A. XVII,278
    Patrick XVII,278
Boutell, Asa XV,715
    John XV,521
    Reuben XV,214
Boutelle, Aaron XVII,62
Boutwell, Amos XIV,267
    Asa XIV,600
    James XVI,728
    Joseph XIV,102, 207
    Reuben XIV,417; XVI,557
    Thomas XIV,102, 207
Bovier, Captain XVII,277
Bowden, William XVII,501
Bowen, Andrew XVI,11, 316
    Enoch XV,586; XVI,171-72,
        175
    Jabez XV,629, 641; XVII,349
    Jeremiah XV, 586, 743;
        XVI,296
    Jeremiah Jr. XV,743
    John XV,514; XVI,43, 184,
        908, 910
    William XVII,300
Bowers, Benjamin XV,85-86,
    196, 206
    Ephraim XVI,143, 636;
        XVII,436
    Henry XV,209

Bowers, Isaac XIV,417; XVI,259
James XV,610
Jarathmeel XV,632, 636; XVI,
44, 690-91
Jeremiah XVI,41
Jonathan XIV,251
Oliver XV,88
William XVI,921
Bowes, James XIV,569
Bowker, Edmund XV,6
Bowler, Michael XIV,287
Thomas XIV,260, 484;
XVII,47, 85,284
Bowles, Charles XIV,600;
XV,153-54, 715; XVI,200,
499, 563
James XIV,585, 611; XV,717;
XVI, 202, 219, 229, 509,
580, 708-9, 723
Samuel XV,578; XVI,803-4;
XVII,139
Thomas XVII,298
Bowley, James XVI,509, 568
John XIV,182, 548; XV,128,
487, 490-91
Bowman, Abiatha XV,131, 546;
XVII,257
Captain XVI,406
Jonas XV,162, 182, 546-47;
XVI,148, 680-81; XVII,257-
58
Zadoc XV,183; XVI,148
Boyce, James XIV,369, 375, 483,
498, 502, 518, 520;
XV,729; XVI,210; XVII,29
Boyd, David XV,362, 567
John XVI,914
Joseph XVII,247
Mary XVI,665-66
Nathaniel XIV,57, 59, 183
Samuel XIV,267, 631; XV,556,
614, 711; XVI,198, 223,
267, 320, 323, 325, 328,
331, 338, 340, 343-44,
347, 360-61, 500, 527,
664, 666, 689, 692, 755;
XVII,256, 463

Boyd, William XIV,74, 178;
XV,622, 663, 669, 676,
689; XVI, 565, 733
Boyer, P. Jr. XVI,238, 283, 285;
XVI,288, 297
Boyes, Captain XVII,259
James XIV,502, 511, 560,
579, 620; XV,454, 715,
722, 740; XVI,205, 235,
273, 511, 725
James Jr. XIV,347-48, 579,
604; XV,453, 455
John XIV,579, 654; XVI,30,
33, 59, 187
Robert XIV, 73, 178; XVI,723
Samuel XIV,17
Thomas XVI,574
William XV,552-53, 583; XVII,
259, 426
Boyle, Charles XVI,920
Boyles, Edward XVII,293
Boynton, Amos XIV,34, 92, 202,
213, 221, 576, 632;
XV,723; XVI,206, 653
Andrew XIV,265; XV,146, 473,
501; XVII,249
Benjamin XIV,33, 418;
XVI,377
Benoni XVI,840
David XV,173
Edmund XIV,65, 186, 211,
217, 219-20; XVII,4
Elias XIV,33; XV,510, 744
Isaac XIV,573, 590, 609; XV,
613, 714; XVI,200
Jacob XIV,43; XV,744
Job XV,109
Joel XIV,418
John XIV,649; XV,65, 96, 226,
614, 702; XVI,171-72, 174,
377
John 3d XIV,573, 590, 609
Joseph XIV,134, 182, 191,
555; XV,6, 726; XVI,7, 182,
208; XVII,6, 269, 440-42
Joshua XIV,31, 65, 186, 320;
XV,87, 743; XVII,4

Boynton, Lieutenant XVI,498
    Richard XV,72, 392; XVI,44
    Samuel XIV,402, 415;
        XVII,30
    Snow XIV,577, 662; XVI,814
    Solomon XV,63
    Sullivan XV,104
    William XV,132, 698
Bracewell, William XVII,691-92
Brackett, Anthony XVII,511,
    513, 527
    Ebenezer XV,695, 698
    Ephraim XVII,306
    Ichabod XVI,766
    Isaac XIV,169
    James XV,545, 559; XVI,710
    Jonathan XVI,188
    Joshua XIV,403, 415; XVII,
        125-26, 633, 664
    Thomas XIV,369, 377, 492,
        503; XVI,525
Bracon, George XVII,525
Bradbury, Daniel XVI,237, 273,
    519, 825
    Daniel E. XVI,936
    Jabez XIV,14
    Jacob XIV,55, 184
    John XVI,908
    Sanders XIV,574, 600;
        XV,437, 614, 714
Bradeen, Mr. XVII,134
    Samuel XVI,854
Bradford,-- XV,136
    Andrew XV,698; XVI,143,
        286, 498; XVII,431
    Benjamin XV,188
    Colonel XV,432
    Enos XV,520
    John XIV,242, 244, 478; XV,
        72, 196, 213, 215, 509,
        566
    Joseph XIV,87
    Lieutenant XVII,274
    Robert XIV,225; XV,390
    Samuel XIV,51, 185, 554,
        589, 632; XV,582, 718;
        XVI,5; XVII,276

Bradford, Thomas XV,622, 663,
    669, 689; XVI,872
    Timothy XV,582
    William XIV,52, 102, 184,
        207, 266, 477, 553, 595;
        XV, 122, 163, 188, 552,
        568, 710; XVI,3, 528;
        XVII,124, 216, 266, 463
Bradley, Abraham XVI,915
    Benjamin XV,698; XVI,105,
        147
    Daniel XVI,243
    David XVI,178-79
    Edward XVII,300
    Jeremiah XIV,18
    John XIV,242
    Jonathan XIV,61, 182, 304-5;
        XV,69
    Joseph XVI,125
    Keyes XVI,105, 148, 238,
        270, 306, 501, 611
    Moses XIV,136, 191; XVII,7
    Philbrick XIV,454, 529, 546;
        XV,186, 514
    Timothy XV,129
Bradshaw, John XIV,657;
        XVI,39
    Patrick XIV,304
    Richard XVII,491
    Samuel XIV,236
Bradstreet, Simon XVII,511
Bragdon, Arthur XIV,1
    James XIV,584, 630; XVI,589
    Josiah XIV,238
    Thomas XIV,236
Bragg, Benjamin XV,36, 371;
        XVII, 105
    Ebenezer XV,3, 226
    Nathaniel XIV,10
    Nicholas XV,226
    Robert XIV,413, 641; XV,423,
        457, 730; XVI,18, 190,
        211, 278, 834
    Samuel XVI,623
Brainard, Asaph XIV,464
    Barzillai XV,125
    Chiliab XV,149, 160, 662,

Brainard, Chiliab (Cont.) 668,
682; XVI,585
Church XVI,138
Daniel XIV,166, 170;
XVI,800; XVII,14
Daniel Jr. XVI,820-21
Ebenezer XVI,113
Israel XV,125, 381
Simon XV,35
Uriah XV,35, 368; XVII,105
Braman, David XIV,92, 202-3
Brannon, Richard XVII,297
Branscomb, Arthur XV,571
Charles XVI,237, 244, 268,
319, 507, 673-74
Elizabeth XVI,673
Brasbe, William XIV,229
Brasbee, John XVI,207, 275,
514, 760
Brasher, Abraham XVII,397-99
Brassbridge, John XIV,630; XV,
259-60, 263, 597, 724;
XVI, 233
William XIV,269, 375, 483,
498, 502, 511, 518
Brasbury, John XIV,381, 489
Brattlebank, Samuel XV,550
Bray, William XIV,237
Braynard, Asaph XIV,324
Brazeel, John XIV,25
Brecknel, Nathaniel XV,377
Bredeen, Elnathan XIV,594
Samuel XIV,35, 89, 201
Breed, Allen XIV,34, 333; XV,92,
219, 533; XVI,95, 106
Allen Jr. XIV,333; XV,219;
XVI,83
Charles XVI,502
John XIV,90, 201; XVI,159
Dr. Nathaniel XIV,49, 80;
XVI,285, 517, 751-53,
841, 870
Thomas K. XV,109, 217; XVI,
159
Brenton, Andrew XV,25
Brereton, Edward XVII,694, 698
Bretton, Ebenezer XV,8

Bretton, Job XV,6
Richard XVII,694, 698
Brewer,-- XV,136
Ebenezer XIV,423; XV,16, 40,
156, 376; XVII,143
James XIV,100-1; XV,102;
XVI, 738
Jonathan XV,432, 750
Peter XIV,572; XV,611, 712
Brewster, David XIV,550;
XV,201, 430; XVII,27
Ebenezer XVI,387; XVII,458
James XIV,299; XV,566
John XIV,367, 371, 384, 386,
496, 504, 510, 516-17,
519-20; XVI,526; XVII,527
Paul XV,297
Samuel XV,575
William XVII,139
Brian, John XIV,3; XVII,693
Robert XVII,667-68, 693
Briant, Charles XIV,579, 648,
650; XVI,13
David XIV,604; XVI,221, 875
Edmund XV,355, 357
Elisha XVII,645
John XIV,524, 579; XV,348;
XVI,299, 536
Robert XVII,656
Walter, XV,570
William XVI,175, 179
Briar, Robert XVII,46, 86
William XVII,87
Briard, Charles XIV,648
Robert XIV,512
William XIV,500, 512, 518;
XV,431
Brick, Arnold XIV,15; XVII,667-
68
Bride, Jabez XV,604
Bridge, Ebenezer XVI,373
Jabez XIV,632
Bridger, John XVII,677, 743
Bridges, Daniel XV,631, 650,
731, 735; XVI,16, 102,
186, 211, 221, 278, 892;
XVII,439

Bridges, Ebenezer XV 750
    John XVI,884
Bridgman, Abel XV,157; XVII,
    144
    Elisha XV,42
    Isaac XV,43; XVI,528; XVII,
        67, 109
    John XV,39, 41; XVII,109
Bridle, John XIV,308
Brier, John XV,171
    Moses XV,692
    Robert XIV,260, 484, 518;
        XV,692
    Samuel XVI,281
    William XIV,485
    See also Briar
Briggs, Daniel XVI,25
    Elkanah XVI,932
    Moses XV,47
    Nathaniel XIV,644; XV,732;
        XVI,21, 23
Brigham, Abner XV,14
    Alpheus XIV,420; XVI,536-37
    Asa XV,109, 196, 198, 360;
        XVII,428
    Asaph XVI,286, 509
    Isaac XV,18; XVII,109
    Jonathan XV,43
    Leonard XIV,334
    Levi XVI,655
    Lyman XVI,159
    Moses XVII,458
    Samuel XV,377
    Stephen XIV,92, 202-3
Bright, John XIV,560
Brightman, John XIV,10
Brimmer, Martin XVII,352
Brintnall, George XIV,662; XVI,
    38
Brissille, Joseph XVII,305
Britain, Job XIV,84, 190
    William XIV,427, 466
Britt, Seth XV,205; XVII,97
Britton, Asa XVI,254
    Captain XVII,94
    David XV,48
    Ebenezer XV,49; XVI,361,

Britton, Ebenezer (Cont.) 363,
    530, 532; XVII,94
    James XVII,300
    Job XV,48
    Joel XVII,94
    Samuel XIV,646; XV,651,
        732, 735; XVI,21-22, 189,
        212, 228, 279, 522, 877,
        879, 887
    Seth XVII,94
    William XV,49, 224, 610
Brock, Thomas XVII,114
Brocklebank, Asa XIV,36
    Daniel XV,166
    Samuel XIV,173-74, 176-77;
        XVI,161
Brockway, Asa XV,221
    Ephraim XV,221; XVI,160,
        839
    Jonathan XV,106-7
    Martin XV,471, 502
    William XVII,95
Broderick, J. XIV,42
    Joseph XIV,70
    William XV,743
Brone, John XVII,667, 669
Brookfield, Samuel XVI,140
Brookline, Godfrey XVII,611
    Hannah XVII,611
    Mary XVII,609
Brooks, Abraham XV,20;
        XVI,82, 92
    Asahel XV,27; XVI,608
    Barnabas XV,27
    Benjamin XV,27
    Benjamin Jr. XVI,608
    David XIV,50, 185, 577, 662;
        XVI,814
    Edward XVII,308
    Eleazer XV,483, 494
    Elijah XVI,178-79
    Ezekiel XVI,285
    Job XV,84
    John XIV,573, 590, 609;
        XV,92, 355, 533, 613; XVI,
        51, 53; XVII,100, 102,
        296, 464

Brooks, Jonathan XIV,34
    Joseph XIV,480; XV,748;
    XVI, 536
    Josiah XIV,484, 499, 512,
        XIV,518, 623; XVII,86
    Samuel XIV,210, 435; XVI,
        569, 616, 643, 648, 670,
        672, 694, 706, 710, 776,
        821; XVII,12, 17, 18, 43,
        80
    Simon XVI,553-54; XVII,103
    Thomas XVI,307
    William XIV,21; XV,510; XVI,
        51, 53, 259
    William Jr. XVII,464
    Willis XVII,436
    Zaccheus XV,630, 646; XVI,
        102, 517, 792, 794
Brotten, James XIV,500, 512
    Joseph XIV,227, 257, 472
    Mark XIV,259, 343
    Noah XIV,258
    Samuel XIV,664
    William XIV,260, 369, 375,
        483, 498, 502, 511
Broughton, James XIV,485,
        518; XVII,87, 205
    Mark XIV,118-19, 149, 196
    Samuel XIV,114, 119, 150,
        197
    William XIV,518; XVII,46,
        153
Brown,-- XV,699
    A. XVI,792
    Aaron XIV,357; XV,147, 525
    Abel XIV,33; XV,744; XVI,
        838
    Abijah XV,107
    Abraham XIV,72, 400, 451,
        532, 539; XV,285, 291,
        475, 494, 564; XVI,115,
        134, 285, 501, 527;
        XVII,105
    Abraham Jr. XV,147
    Abram XVI,936
    Adam XIV,455, 529; XV,392

Brown, Alexander XIV,73, 102,
        178, 208, 267; XVI,526;
        XVII, 465
    Amos XIV,627; XV,457, 487,
        489; XVI,127, 162
    Andrew XIV,12; XV,240, 245,
        261
    Anna XVI,558, 621
    Asa XVI,159
    Batchelder XV,411; XVI,127,
        162
    Benjamin XIV,22, 388, 398,
        413, 469, 494, 507, 516,
        XIV,606; XV,134, 283,
        290, 319, 339, 565, 634,
        649, 712; XVI,102, 199,
        268, 501, 604, 837;
        XVII,399, 666
    Bryant XIV,422; XV,15, 138;
        XVII,118, 120
    Caleb XIV,392, 488, 509,
        513; XV,256, 258, 260,
        262, 320, 340, 523, 526;
        XVI,65, 75, 94, 106, 901;
        XVII,205
    Captain XV,699
    Charles XIV,251; XV,573;
        XVII,260
    Clark XV,81
    Daniel XIV,96, 204, 303; XV,
        171, 225; XVI,322-23,
        330, 334, 337, 339, 361-
        62
    David XIV,441, 463, 527; XV,
        30, 35, 300, 302, 306,
        309, 371; XVI,113; XVII,66
    E. XVI,920
    Ebenezer XIV,34
    Edmund XV,586
    Edward XIV,617; XV,618,
        723, 744; XVI,206, 526,
        621
    Eleazer XV,63
    Eliada XVI,150
    Elias XV,662, 669, 680;
        XVI,552, 838

32

Brown, Elijah XIV,351, 617;
    XV,457, 723; XVI,838
Eliphalet XV,87-88, 134, 173,
    209; XVI,237, 515, 698
Elisha XV,591, 733; XVI,45,
    48, 265, 302, 305, 310,
    834
Enoch XIV,253
Ensley XIV,70, 179; XV,183
Ephraim XIV,23, 35; XV,219;
    XVII,100
Isaac XIV,96, 204; XV,663,
    670, 684, 688; XVI,156,
    591
Jabez XVI,671
Jacob XIV,11; XVII,640
James XIV,95, 97, 173, 203,
    231, 353, 605; XV,134,
    550, 628, 632, 635, 645,
    705, 716; XVI,150, 201,
    289-92, 507, 521, 667-68,
    697, 888; XVII,113
Jeremiah XIV,350; XV,256,
    259-60, 264, 300, 302,
    305, 309, 321, 340;
    XVI,111
Jesse XV,224; XVI,41, 44
Job XIV,34, 224, 253, 402,
    414, 551; XV,324, 695,
    698
Joel XVII,67
John XIV,1, 12, 50, 101, 186,
    206, 213, 221, 230, 280,
    288, 301, 313, 358, 397,
    421, 467, 548; XV,191,
    267, 269, 272, 470, 483,
    497, 502, 527, 592, 621,
    634, 644, 711; XVI,26, 65,
    76, 97, 105-6, 307, 580,
    663, 860-61, 897, 903,
    907; XVII,114, 300, 528,
    667, 739
Jonathan XIV,110, 131, 263,
    274-75, 289, 550; XV,30,
    35, 430, 487, 489, 564
Joseph XIV,11, 224, 226,
    232, 252, 325, 361, 405-6,

Brown, Joseph (Cont.) 442, 544,
    589; XV,29, 169, 321,
    669, 676; XVI,152, 262,
    689, 700-1, 705, 922;
    XVII, 32, 105, 255,. 426
Joshua XIV,1, 11, 229, 231;
    XV,243, 245, 247, 256,
    260, 263, 693; XVI,901;
    XVII,740
Josiah XIV,21, 34, 66, 89,
    91, 181, 330, 370, 378,
    446, 492, 540; XV,1, 20-
    22, 92-94, 149, 160, 249,
    251-52, 254, 483, 494,
    654, 747, XVI,255, 505,
    764, 910, 928; XVII,29,
    49, 100, 102
Josiah Jr. XV,125, 381
Levi XIV,232, XV,412, 523
Mary XVII,739
Michael XV,746
Moses XIV,114, 140, 193,
    259, 422, 614; XV,396,
    602, 711; XVII,36
Mr. XVII,509
Nathan XIV,230, 252, 299,
    367, 387, 389, 480, 494,
    506, 510, 516, 519;
    XV,28, 412, 564-65;
    XVI,156, 210, 525;
    XVII,284
Nathaniel XIV,325, 404, 564,
    581, 654; XV,449, 600,
    729, 734; XVI, 30, 33, 59,
    187, 219, 277, 520, 644-
    45, 832
Nehemiah XV,6, 225; XVI,362
Nicholas XIV,68, 180, 234;
    XVI,330, 332; XV, 528;
    XVI,130, 163
Oliver XVI,35
Paul XIV,399; XV,243, 245,
    247
Peter XIV,35, 90, 201; XV,
    542; XVI,82, 100, 106,
    194, 931
Richard XIV,118, 137, 139,

Brown, Richard (Cont.) 158,
553, 578, 593, 615; XV,
719; XVI,4, 675, 822; XVII,
145, 268
Samuel XIV,6, 11, 13, 76, 81,
198; XV,201, 346-47; XVI,
286, 515-16; XVII,307
Scipio XIV,381, 490, 585,
600; XV,437, 715
Sewell XV,402, 526, 748;
XVI, 938
Silas XIV,166, 170, 657; XV,
459, 605, 730; XVI, 35,
38; XVII,14
Simeon XVI,298
Simon XV,411
Stephen XV,412
Theodore XIV,253
Thomas XIV,34, 117, 128;
XV, 21, 92, 355, 375;
XVI,85, 95, 121, 159, 164,
616; XVII,91
Timothy XIV,253, 391, 487;
XV,113; XVI,152
True XV,267, 269, 271; XVII,
435
Trueworthy XV,270
William XIV,20, 87, 116, 129,
189, 200, 245, 266, 358,
470, 572, 596; XV,169,
350, 352, 612, 713;
XVI,199, 224, 238, 241,
246, 268, 498, 508, 558-
62, 681, 687, 917;
XVII,301
Wright XIV,428
Zaccheus XIV,118, 137, 158,
192, 351; XV,319, 339;
XVI, 127, 162
Zadoc XIV,423; XV,41
Brownell, George XVII,747-48
Browning, Nathaniel XVI,931
Brownson, Elijah XIV,423
Gideon XVI,308-9
Bruce, David XV,658
James XVII,536
Josiah XIV,247

Bruce, Simeon XV,664-65, 671,
682; XVI,812-13
Bruer, Peter XIV,613
Bryan, Charles XVI,722
James XVI,933
Robert XVII,667-68, 693
Bryant, Andrew XIV,224
Charles XIV,653; XV,728;
XVI,34, 59
David XV,715; XVI,201, 269,
527, 532, 795, 873; XVII,
438
Edmund XV,92, 357
Edward XIV,34
James XV,192; XVI,122, 164
Jeremiah XV,571
John XIV,436; XV,427, 536;
XVI,47, 55, 257, 303, 515,
578
Joseph 3d XIV,413
Matthew XIV,300, 387, 494;
XVI,526; XVII,284
Robert XIV,15, 296, 432;
XV,163, 171; XVII,215
Thomas XVI,110, 165
Walter Jr. XIV,400
William XVI,178
Bryar, Elisha XVII,679, 693
Bryent, Charles XV,452, 454
Jeremy XV,416
Walter XVI,767
Walter Jr. XV,416; XVI,766
Bryer, Peter XIV,564, 600; XV,
437, 714
Buchanan, Andrew XV,514
Annanias XV,514
Stephen XVI,147
Buchart, Jacob XIV,654
Buck, Benjamin XVI,308-9
Ebenezer XVI,234, 264
Isaac XVI,138
John XV,251
Buckland, Eli XIV,238
Buckley, Lawrence,XV,32
Richard XVII,633, 667, 679,
681, 691
Buckman, John XVI,138, 314

Bucknal, John XVII,116
Bucknam, Edwards XV,705;
    XVI, 289-91; XVII,78
Bucknell, Nathan XV,42
Budlow, William XV,315-16,
    318, 333, 338
Buel, Aaron XV,35
    Abraham XVI,169, 586
    Allan XVI,770
    Daniel XV,12, 147, 472, 501;
    XVII,105
    Jerry XVII,57
    Joseph XV,12, 35
Buell, Abraham XIV,324, 464;
    XV, 30, 35, 705-9
Buffard, Nicholas XIV,260, 484,
    500, 512, 518
Buffee, Thomas XIV, 87
Buffington, Preston XVI,236,
    518, 815
Bufford, Nicholas XVII,47, 85
Bugbee, Amasa XVI,314
    Nathaniel XIV,607-8; XV,436,
    603, 714; XVI,200
    Silvester XV,591
    Timothy XV,153
Bugby, Amasa XV,379
Bulkeley, Peter XVII,524, 532
Bullard, Asa XVI,630; XVII,428
    Benjamin XV,750
    Ebenezer XIV,90, 201; XV,92;
    XVI,83, 96, 106
    Eleazer XVI,85, 106, 286,
    512
    Ezra XVI,193
    John XVI,235, 272, 514
    Joseph XV,83
    Peter XV,211; XVI,83, 96,
    106, 235, 270, 514, 763
    Simeon XIV,332; XVI,630
    Uriah XVI,235
    Uriah Jr. XVI,882
Bullock, Hezekiah XV,42
    Jeremiah XV,54
    Nathan XV,205
    Simeon XV,17, 138, 157
    Simon XVII,110, 144

Bumford, Charles XV,619, 723
    Ishmael XIV,25
Bundy, Asa XVII,468
    Asahel XV,25
    Elias XV,25
    Isaac XV,23, 369
Bunker, Benajah XIV,258, 344
    Daniel XIV,18
    Enoch XIV,235; XV,311
    James XVII,513, 645, 658
    James G. XIV,234
    Jonathan XVI,287, 499
    Joseph XV,625, 628, 640,
    720; XVI,102, 204, 233,
    241, 272, 504, 638-39
    Zaccheus XIV,406
Buntin, Andrew XIV,476
    John XVI,926; XVII,3
    Josiah XV,713
Bunton, Andrew XIV,242, 426
    John XIV,63, 181, 186
Burbank, Aaron XIV,387, 494,
    507, 516, 519; XV,528
    Abner XIV,398
    Caleb XV,183
    David XIV,60, 113, 146, 182,
    195; XV,185
    Ebenezer XIV,246
    Gershom XV,381, 385
    Hale XVI,125
    Jacob XV,106; XVI,869
    John XIV,238, 259; XV,182;
    XVI,915; XVII,22, 33, 38
    Jonathan XIV,418; XV,517;
    XVI,171-72, 175, 208,
    240, 519; XVII,443
    Josiah XV,701, 703, 725;
    XVI, 46, 170, 172, 175,
    208, 240, 303, 500, 577
    Moses XIV,60, 182, 430; XV,
    409, 514; XVI,928
    Nathaniel XIV,60, 182; XV,
    187; XVI,238, 245, 273,
    519, 576, 928
    Samuel XIV,237, 259
    Wells XIV,274, 276; XV,185,
    515

Burbank, William XV,406
Burbe, Nathaniel XVII,67
Burbeck, Edward XV,707,.752
    Henry XVII,290
Burbee, Peter XIV,576, 634
    Peter Jr. XIV,576, 634
Burby, Peter XV,724
    Peter Jr. XV,724
Burch, James XVI,313
    Burchill, John XVII,300
Burdean, Nathaniel XVI,525
Burdeen, Nathaniel XIV,281
Burdet, George XVII,498
Burge, Ephraim XV,89; XVI,377
Burgen, John XV,575
Burgess, Jonathan XIV,297
Burget, Charles XV,729; XVI,28,
    29
Burgoyne, John XV,22, 139;
    XVII, 147
Burke, James XVI,235, 511, 725
    John XVII,307
    Jonathan XVI,285, 522, 866
Joseph XIV,578, 592; XV,716;
    XVI,201, 218, 270, 934
    Mr. XVII,154, 192
    Robert XIV,73, 178
Burkhart, Jacob XV,460, 606,
    730; XVI,32, 187, 210,
    277, 709
Burkins, William XIV,493
Burl, Samuel XIV,104
Burleigh, Benjamin XIV,362
    Edward XV,300-1; XVII,30
    Gordon XIV,370, 378, 492,
        504, 515; XV,474, 494
    Jonathan XIV,400
    Joseph XIV,116, 128, 399,
        642; XV, 474, 494; XVI,65
    Josiah XV,288, 571
    Miss XVI,766
    Samuel XIV,451, 532;
        XV,571; XVI,122, 164
    Stephen XIV,322, 661
    Thomas XV,172
    Wheeler XIV,370, 379, 493,
        503, 515

Burleigh, William XIV,323, 659;
    XVI, 63, 71
    William Jr. XVI,61
Burley, Benjamin XIV,99, 156-
    57, 365
    Edward XIV,229, 344;
        XV,325
    Jacob XV,284, 288
    John XVII,25
    Joseph XIV,189; XV,456;
        XVI, 75, 95, 106
    Josiah XIV,232; XV,284, 288;
        XVII,24
    Nicholas XVI,153
    Samuel XIV,232
    Stephen XIV,365; XVI,11,
        547, 829
    Stevens XV,448, 599
    William XIV,365, 580;
        XV,448, 599, 727; XVI,10,
        43,.98, 106, 183, 193,
        209; XVII, 26, 719
Burnam, Abraham XVI,633
    Benjamin XV,742
    Edward XV,618
    Enoch XV,619
    George XV,619
    Israel XV,664, 670
    Jabez XV,555
    John XVII,719
    Joseph XVI,624
    Josiah XVI,710
    Nathan XV,554
    Offin XVI,531
    Paul XV,284, 291
    Robert XVII,513, 719
    William XV,622, 634; XVI,26,
        729
Burnap, John XVII,67
    Samuel XV,95, 364
Burnham, Aaron XIV,427
    Andrew XV,483, 494
    Asa XIV,359
    Barachias XVI,147
    Benjamin XV,312, 628, 640,
        706; XVI,102, 674
    David XIV,244; XV,74, 214

Burnham, Ebenezer XIV,233
  Edward XIV,624; XV,440,
    720; XVI,640; XVII,315,
    466
  Elizabeth XVI,620
  Enoch XIV,371, 384, 496,
    505, 516-17, 562, 636;
    XV,445, 724; XVI,207
  George XIV,125, 188, 473,
    624; XV,624, 719; XVI,5,
    203, 849; XVII,11
  Gideon XIV,427; XV,48
  Israel XV,74, 214, 682; XVI,
    881; XVII,339
  Jabez XV,351, 353
  James XIV,140, 192, 250,
    473; XV,350, 352; XVI,86,
    99, 118; XVII,719
  James Jr. XIV,114
  Jeremiah XIV,12; XVII,645,
    658, 682, 693, 719
  Jonathan XIV,102, 207, 223,
    241-42; XV,74, 214, 256-
    58, 706
  Joseph XIV,547, 623;
    XV,440, 720; XVI,204,
    227, 272, 503, 526
  Joshua XIV,102, 208, 234;
    XVII,24
  Josiah XIV,108, 232, 286-87,
    307, 330
  Nathaniel XV,188
  Paul XV,284, 291; XVI,119
  Pike XIV,408; XVI,119
  Robert XIV,13
  Samuel XIV,235, 268, 272,
    289, 291, 330
  Stephen XV,189
  William XV,644; XVI,106
Burne, Martin XVI,235, 511,
    724
Burniston, Charles XVII,743
Burns, Amos XIV,465
  George XV,70
  Harry XVII,298
  James XIV,65, 181, 186; XVI,
    141, 161, 926
Burns, John XIV,64, 186, 210,
    337, 690, 699; XV,553;
    XVI,141, 161, 247, 254,
    926, 929; XVII,4, 64
  John Jr. XVII,4
  Patrick XVII,300
  Philip XIV,110, 131, 190,
    351, 642; XV,423, 456,
    730; XVI,18
  Robert XIV,424; XV,174;
    XVII,301
  Thomas XVI,563
  William XV,69, 556
Burnside, James XVI,288-89,
    219; XVII,113
  Thomas XVI,290; XVII,78,
    113
Burpee, Nathan XV,475, 494,
    748; XVI,588
  Nathaniel XV,402
Burr, Nathan XVII,295
Burrell, George XVI,931
Burrill, John XVII,715, 725
  Simon XV,501
Burroughs, Daniel XV,13, 367
  Edward XIV,18
  Elijah XIV,265; XV,29, 147
  Joel XIV,325; XV,29, 368
  John XIV,464; XV,28, 146
  Jonathan XV,715
  Timothy XIV,464; XV,29, 368
  William XIV,458, 537, 539
Burrows, Charles XVI,112, 235,
    273, 511, 724
  Edward XVII,435, 461
  James XVI,244, 273, 803,
    805
  Jeremiah XVI,95
  Jonathan XIV,600; XV,436
  Josiah XIV,247
  Nathaniel XV,199; XVI,23
  William XV,200
Burry, Elijah XV,443
Burt, Amasa XV,203
  Benjamin R. XVI,587
  Enos XIV,264
  Jonathan XVII,103

Burt, Joseph XV,48; XVI,362, 426, 876-79; XVII,94
  Robert XV,714; XVI,200
  Simeon XVI,536
Burton, Abraham XIV,244, 690; XVI,882; XVII,63
  David XIV,696
  John XVI,36
  Jonathan XIV,244, 335, 338, 465, 667, 690; XV,529, 531; XVI,530, 532, 540, 882-83; XVII,62
  Joseph XV,435
  Joshua XVI,199
  Josiah XIV,92, 202-3, 470, 595; XVI,223
  William XIV,639; XV,617, 731; XVI,15, 25, 885
Burts, Robert XIV,607-8
Burwash, Nathaniel XV,164; XVI, 88, 92
Busey, John XIV,3, 13
Bush, Jacob XVI,932
  Timothy XIV,423
Bushby, Robert XIV,631
Bushel, John XIV,6
Bushley, Robert XV,456
Bushnell, G. XVII,452
Buskirk, Colonel XVII,176, 178, 180, 189
Buss, Rev. John XVII,736
  John XIV,108, 122, 188, 251, 635; XV,618, 724; XVI,206, 229, 241, 274, 504, 638-39
  John Jr. XVII,719
  Silas XV,529
  Stephen XV,419
Bussell, Andrew XIV,623
  Daniel XVI,363
  David XIV,453, 532; XV,329-30, 343; XVI,824
  Elijah XIV,561; XVI,747
  Isaac XVI,913
  Jacob XIV,18
  James XVI,913
  John XIV,18; XV,160

Bussell, Joseph XIV,122
  Noah XIV,586, 600
Bussiel, Samuel XIV,226
Buswell, Daniel XVI,341
  David XV,667, 673, 691
  Elijah XIV,125
  James XIV,532
  John XIV,36, 70, 179; XV, 267-68, 270; XVI,141, 161, 264, 728
  Nicholas XVI,140
  Noah XIV,77, 81, 198; XV,715; XVI,200
  Paul XIV,141
  Richard XV,267, 269-70
  Samuel XIV,410
Butcher, John XVII,300
Butland, Samuel XIV,238
Butler, Alpheus XV,713; XVI,199, 268
  Andrew XIV,92, 202-3
  Asaph XIV,578; XVI,313, 502, 605-6; XVII,224
  Benjamin XIV,225, 231, 570; XV,712; XVI,198, 768, 780-81
  Benjamin Jr. XVI,260
  David XV,358; XVI,783-84
  Edmund XIV,255; XVII,23, 31, 39
  Elijah XVI,195
  Enoch XVI,260-61; XVII,432
  Ezra XVI,80, 98
  Gideon XV,517, 744; XVI,783
  Henry XIV,121; XV,527-28; XVI,130, 132-33, 163, 781
  Henry J. Jr. XVI,785
  Ichabod XIV,369, 376, 483, 498, 502, 511, 518
  Jacob XV,358
  James XIV,371, 384, 496, 505, 516-17
  John XIV,264, 368, 375, 483, 498, 502, 511, 518, 573, 600; XV,437, 615, 715
  Levi XIV,644; XV,732;

Butler, Levi (Cont.) XVI,21, 24
  Nathan XV,358; XVI,112
  Thaddeus XV,358
  Tobias XIV,359; XVII,426
  William XIV,369, 375, 482,
    498, 502, 511, 518
  Zephaniah XIV,397, 602;
    XVI, 780
Butman, Thomas XIV,226
Butterfield, Abraham XIV,244
  Asaph XIV,598-99
  Charles XIV,336, 690; XV,77;
    XVII,63
  Henry XV,110, 465, 467,
    479, 503
  Isaac XIV,262, 293-94, 477;
    XV,116, 351, 353, 583;
    XVI, 286, 459, 461, 523,
    530-32; XVII,60
  James XIV,183, 574; XV,47,
    426, 614; XVI,311-12;
    XVII,94
  Jonas XV,700, 702, 704, 718;
    XVI,46, 174, 203, 302,
    362; XVII,95
  John XIV,459, 537; XV,556;
    XVII,258
  Jonathan XIV,418; XVI,308-9
  Joseph XVI,884
  Major XIV,477
  Oliver XV,189, 622, 663, 669,
    682, 689; XVI,655
  Peter XIV,55, 184; XV,556;
    XVII,258
  Robert XIV,358; XVI,141, 161
  Samuel XIV,359; XVI,141,
    161, 200
  Simeon XIV,95, 204, 600; XV,
    437, 615, 715; XVI,247,
    253, 504, 515, 636; XVII,
    124
  Simon XIV,573; XVI,286
  Stephen XVI,885
  Thomas XV,77; XVI,308-9
  Timothy XIV,264; XV,48,
    465, 467, 479, 503
Butterfield, William XIV, 96,
    204-5, 336, 690; XVII,
    63
  Zachariah XIV,299, 314; XV,
    125, 149, 160
Butters, James XVI,525
Buttin, Jaques XVII,305
Buttress, Joseph XV,100
Butts, Thomas XVII,301
Buxton, John XIV,100, 206; XV,
    419, 529
Buzel, Solomon XV,250
Buzell, Aaron XVI,283
  Elijah XV,722
  John XV,698
  Jonathan XV,722; XVI,205,
    273
  Joseph XVI,282
  Nicholas XVI,161
Buzwell, Solomon XV,255
Buzzell, Andrew XIV,236;
    XV,720
  Benjamin XIV,228
  Daniel XV,747; XVI,327, 331,
    341, 344-45
  Elijah XIV,118, 620; XVI,287,
    521, 817; XVII,10
  Henry XIV,372, 384, 496,
    517, 520; XVII,434
  Isaac XIV,238
  James XIV,235
  John XIV,228; XV,125, 515;
    XVI,169-70
  Jonathan XIV,238, 323, 365,
    621
  Joseph XIV,109
  Paul XIV,115
  Richard XV,273, 515
  Robert E. XIV,187
  Samuel XIV,228; XV,525
  Solomon XV,249, 251
Byam, Benjamin XIV,35; XV,96,
    219; XVI,542
Byars, Peter XVII,298
Byng, Garret XVII,28
Byrn, Garrit XIV,233

C

Cabuii, Bartlemy XVI,28, 890; XVII,439
Cabuy, Bartlemy XIV,662; XV,451, 729
Cady, Curtis XIV,423, 607-8; XV, 436, 602, 714
  Elias XV,45; XVII,109
  Elijah XV,38
  Isaac XVI,287, 554
  Nicholas XV,39, 155; XVII,143
  Palmer XVII,204, 303
  Stephen XV,14; XVII,88
Cadwell, John XV,698
Cagville, Jacob XIV,662
Cain, John XIV,238
  Peter XVI,930
Calcord, Isaac XV,435
Calcot, David XVII,26
  Edward XVII,7
  Joseph XVII,26
  Josiah XVII,26
Calcott, Isaac XV,713
  Samuel XIV,578
Calder, William XVII,295
Calderwood, John XIV,579
Caldwell, Alexander XV,70, 555
  James XIV,266, 477; XV,69, 550, 740; XVI,527, 754; XVII,463
  John XIV,46, 48, 266, 346, 469, 611; XV,70, 517, 550, 635, 639, 712; XVI,102, 135, 199, 218, 268, 500, 589-90, 725, 874, 934; XVII,60
  Joseph XIV,411; XV,201
  Paul XV,740
  Samuel XIV,58, 183, 346, 459, 537; XV, 350, 352, 539, 550, 552, 622, 634, 644, 653, 717, 740; XVI,32, 34, 187, 202, 210, 277, 753-54, 872, 873, 898; XVII,18-19, 60, 259
  Samuel Jr. XVI,872

Caldwell, Thomas XIV,346; XV,350-54; XVII,19, 60
  William XIV,424; XVI,159
Calef, Daniel XIV,149
  John XIV,224; XVI,139; XVII, 43
  John Jr. XVII,43
  Joseph XIV,195
  William XV,514
Calfe, Daniel XIV,119, 196
  John XIV,286-87, 367, 380, 404-5, 480, 487, 500, 510, 514, 519, 579; XV,559, 581; XVI,108, 120, 123, 126, 132, 136, 139, 149, 151, 154, 290, 610, 670, 682; XVII,284, 385
  Jonathan XVI,125
  Joseph XIV,16, 147
  Joseph Jr. XIV,113; XV,560
  Oliver XVII,27, 57
  William XIV,261; XV,165
Calker, John XIV,635
Calkins, James XV,586
  John XIV,104, 578; XV,39, 626, 724
  Samuel XV,587
  Solomon XIV,263
Call, Asa XVII,252
  James XV,145, 473, 501; XVII,249
  Nathaniel XVI,285, 499
  Philip XVI,903, 915
  Silas XIV,61, 182; XV,128, 406
  Stephen XIV,318; XVI,915
Callaghan, Daniel XV,623, 629, 641; XVI,566; XVII,349
Callahan, Dennis XVII,297
  John XIV,58, 183, 304-5
  William XIV,26
Calld, Isaac XIV,613
Calle, Isaac XIV,417
Callender, John XIV,156
Calley, Edward XVI,102, 720
  Eliphalet XIV,399; XV,284, 291

Calley, John XIV,564, 616;
 XV,440, 719
 Jonathan XIV,399
 Josiah XIV,308, 532, 564,
  616; XV,719; XVI,203
 Mr. XVII,273
 Nathaniel M. XVII,266
 Thomas XIV,231, 345;
  XV,134, 171; XVII,27
 William XV,325
Callis, Christopher XV,721
Cambridge, William XIV,255,
  260; XVI,925; XVII,39, 46
Came, Arthur XIV,238
Cameron, Thomas XVII,308
Cammare, Piere XVII,305
Cammell, John XIV,240
Cammet, Jesse XVI,206
 Peter XVI,286, 500
 Samuel XIV,226, 585, 611;
  XVI,202
 Silas XVI,938
 Thomas XIV,585, 611; XVI,
  202, 510
Cammett, Jonathan XV,526
 Samuel XV,717
 Silas XV,402, 748
 Thomas XV,717
Camock, Thomas XVII,483, 490
Camond, Abel XVII,501
Camp, Amos XVI,204
 Benjamin XV,567
Campbell, Andrew XVII,308
 Annanias XIV,340; XV,560
 Archibald XIV,354, 448, 536;
  XIV,618-19; XV,596, 689,
  723; XVII,42
 Cornelius XIV,3
 Daniel XV,437; XVI,63, 113,
  287, 519, 555-56, 560
 David XIV,261; XV,228; XVI,
  73, 91, 246, 253, 891;
  XVII,439
 Duncan XIV,600, 635;
  XV,626; XVII,651
 Henry XIV,411
 Hugh XIV,59; XV,351, 353

Campbell, James XIV,87, 201,
  324, 411, 579, 602, 605;
  XV,87, 438, 453-54, 630,
  637, 712, 715, 722;
  XVI,102, 198, 201, 255,
  320, 326, 328, 332, 341,
  343, 345, 365, 510, 720,
  722, 724, 916-17;
  XVII,205
 Jesse XIV,568, 632; XV,609,
  723
 John XIV,33, 74, 178, 308,
  315, 348; XV,131, 200,
  209, 359, 472, 483, 490-
  91, 744-45; XVI,141, 161,
  263, 719, 891; XVII,22,
  32-33, 427
 Lieutenant XVII,155
 Patrick XIV,307
 Robert XIV,34, 266, 477; XV,
  546, 747; XVI,84, 527,
  754; XVII,257, 259, 306,
  463
 Samuel XIV,101, 206;
  XV,200, 517; XVI,103,
  263, 515, 687, 891;
  XVII,427
 Thomas XIV,74; XV,744
 William XIV,87, 200, 262;
  XV,123, 350, 352, 698;
  XVI, 516, 720, 898
Campredon, Joseph XV,628,
  645; XVI,507, 668
Canaan, William XV,44
Canada, James XVI,909
 Pearse XVI,931
 Robert XVII,91
Canfield, Samuel XIV,298;
  XV,25, 37, 369, 372;
  XVII,103
Canne, Joseph XVII,525
Canney, Benjamin XVI,627
 Daniel XIV,18
 Moses XVII,28
 Richard XIV,3
 Samuel XVII,648
 Thomas XIV,3, 14, 18;

Canney, Thomas (Cont.)
 XVII,525
Canning, Thomas XVII,502
Cannon, Thomas D. XIV,559
 William D. XV,722; XVI,205,
  273
 See also DeCannon
Canock, John XV, 610
Cant, John XIV,600
Canwell, Joshua XVII,46
Capee, George XIV,164, 288;
 XVI, 679
Capron, Oliver XV,54, 56, 745;
 XVI,809-10; XVII,97
 Otis XIV,645; XVI,23, 809
 Thaddeus XVI,153
 Thomas XIV,159, 161, 163,
  288, 584, 631; XV,451,
  711; XVI,588; XVII,16, 299
Carbuy, Barth J. XV,729
Card, Edward XIV,382, 490
 Joseph XIV,237
 Samuel XIV,382, 490, 623;
  XV, 719; XVI,204, 233-34,
  272
 Samuel Jr. XV,596; XVI,515
Carew, Michael XIV,340
Carey, Arthur XIV,525
 George XIV,10, 25
 Peter XIV,304, 306, 466
 William XIV,298
Carkin, Isaac XIV,88, 200; XV,
  622, 634, 644, 730;
  XVI,17, 26, 194, 211, 220,
  278, 511, 729; XVII,359,
  443
 John XIV,359; XV,118, 138;
  XVI,921
Carleton, Benjamin XIV,36, 420
 David XIV,43, 88, 225
 Dean XV,33
 Ebenezer XIV,101, 206-7,
  303, 417, 574, 639;
  XV,617
 Edward XIV,273, 289
 George XIV,36, 43, 99

Carleton, Sir Guy XIV,435; XVII,
 131, 151, 229, 274
 James XIV,6
 Jeremiah XV,138; XVI,729
 Jesse XIV,34, 90, 201
 John XIV,405; XVII,339
 Jonathan XIV,475; XVII,32
 Nathaniel XIV,34, 90, 201
 Osgood XVI,350
 Samuel XV,748
 William XIV,36; XVII, 101
Carlisle, Daniel XIV,84, 199,
 263, 291, 293; XVII,41,
 350
 John XIV,237, 258; XVII,302
 Joseph XIV,1
 William XIV,550; XV,430
Carlton, Benjamin XV,539, 742
 Dean XVI,138
 Ebenezer XV,731; XVI,15, 25,
  45, 211, 278, 301, 522,
  883
 Edward XVI,529
 Enoch XVI,286, 498
 Ezra XVI,237, 272, 515, 698
 Henry XV,355, 533; XVI,83,
  96, 106
 Jeremiah XV,118
 John XV,520, 664, 670, 682;
  XVI,556
 Joseph XVI,265, 304
 Kimball, XV,196, 223, 225;
  XVI,394
 Nathaniel XV,93
 Samuel XVI,194
 Theodore XVI,648
 Thomas XV,748
 William XV,539
Carney, Thomas XIV,292
 Timothy XIV,259; XV,752;
  XVII,37
Carpenter, Benjamin XV,66;
  XVI, 81, 92, 106
 Benjamin Jr. XV,66
 Daniel XVI,153
 Dr. XVI,538

Carpenter, Ebenezer XIV,100,
206-7, 325, 463; XV,62
George XVII,22, 33, 37
Greenwood, XV,633, 643,
647; XVI,23, 44, 236, 273,
523, 851-52
Jesse XIV,394; XV,379;
XVII,88
Jonathan XV,3, 67; XVI,298;
XVII,96
Nathan XIV,356; XVI,80, 92;
XVII,383
Nathaniel XV,701, 704; XVI,
175
Nicholas XIV,230; XVI,119
Samuel XV,55, 745
Uriah XIV,644; XV,732;
XVI,20, 22
William XIV,355, 437, 525;
XV,205
Carr, Alexander XV,359
Benjamin XV,732; XVI,40,
190, 212
Daniel XIV,641; XV,423, 730;
XVI,18
Elias XIV,585, 659; XV,727;
XVI,11, 316, 708
Jacob XIV,173, 175-76
James XIV,125, 127, 184,
211, 215, 218, 220, 554,
559-60, 620, 622; XV,443,
449, 455-56, 595-97, 600-
1, 718; XVI,4, 5, 51, 182,
203, 248, 271, 300-1, 527,
909; XVII, 216, 267, 440,
457
Jean XVII,299
John XVII,24
Jonathan XIV,61, 604
Joseph XV,179
Moses XIV,245; XV,573; XVI,
863; XVII,29
Moses Jr. XVII,260
Nathan XIV,359; XV,554, 740
Page XVI,169-70
Paul XIV,230
Reuben XV,256

Carr, Richard XVII,730
Robert XVII,253
Rowland XIV,230, 253, 351;
XV,258, 260, 262
Samuel XIV,3; XV, 115, 133,
173, 175, 556
Sanders XV,242, 244, 246,
562; XVII,25
Thomas XV,200, 229, 471,
490, 557; XVI,87, 99;
XVII,258
William XIV,358
See also Karr
Carrigain, Philip XVII,149
Carroll, James XIV,464;
XVII,298
John XIV,308
Michael XVII,297
Carson, James XIV,223
John XV,123, 350, 352
Robert XIV,115, 142, 193,
250, 581, 635; XV,449,
601, 724; XVI,207, 274,
515, 757-58
Simon XV,123
Carswell, Joseph XIV,321
Carter, Abraham XIV,380, 489;
XIV,501, 514
Andrew XIV,25; XV,586; XVII,
91
Benjamin XV,578
Bishop XIV,579
Daniel XIV,454, 530, 546;
XV, 186, 488, 490-91,
663, 670, 684, 688; XVI,
577
David XIV,316, 319
Ebenezer XV,735
Edward XIV,572, 609;
XV,613, 714; XVI,200, 691
Edward Jr. XIV,590
Ephraim XIV,112, 146, 195;
XVI,594
Ester XVI,691-92
Ezekiel XIV,261
Henry XIV,644; XV,732; XVI,
20, 22, 191, 212, 519, 809

Carter, Hubart XIV,63, 181,
    186; XV, 610, 710
  Hubbard XIV,273, 276, 289,
    568, 602; XV,624; XVI,3,
    180, 182, 197, 267; XVII,
    3, 438, 452
  Jacob XIV,60, 182, 430, 586,
    629; XV,405
  Jeremiah XVI,88, 94, 264,
    577; XVII,430
  John XIV,259, 429; XV,267,
    269, 272, 515; XVI,103,
    908, 910; XVII,38
  Jonas XIV,362, 365, 455,
    531
  Levi XIV,25, 359; XVI,167
  Lieutenant XVI,301
  Nathan XVI,264, 578
  Nathaniel XV,698; XVII,430
  Richard XIV,15
  Robert XIV,664
  Samuel XIV,25; XV,180
  Stephen XIV,92
  Thomas XV,510, 628, 640,
    656; XVI,102, 622, 816
  Timothy XVI,679
  William XVII,36
  Winthrop XIV,261; XVI,147
Cartwright, Colonel XVII,509,
    514, 519
Carty, John XVI,724
Cary, Arthur XV,473, 503, 669;
    XVI,848; XVII,255
  Barnabas XVI,159
  Christopher XVII,250
  Daniel XVI,65, 75, 99, 103,
    106, 194, 512, 750
  Samuel XV,11
  William XV,367, 372; XVI,712
Case, John XIV,244
  Samuel XIV,70
  Theophilus XIV,68
  Zenas XV,153-54; XVII,118,
    120
Casey, John XIV,68; XV,140-41,
    660; XVI,440, 647; XVII,
    300

Casey, Peter XVII,304
Cason, Robert XV,618
Cass, Amos XIV,12; XVI,895,
    897
  Benjamin XIV,129, 189, 242,
    299, 327; XV,285, 291,
    525; XVI,590
  Daniel XIV,70, 179, 584, 659;
    XV,727; XVI,9, 42, 183,
    208
  John XIV,528
  Jonathan XIV,30, 112, 146,
    195, 261, 661; XV,421,
    562, 726, 748; XVI,6, 51,
    182, 193, 195-96, 208,
    248, 301, 350, 368, 645;
    XVII, 269, 359, 364, 368,
    465
  Joseph XIV,274, 289; XV,167
  Lieutenant XVI,105
  Luke XVII,97
  Moses XIV,299, 327, 584,
    659; XV,727; XVI,10, 43
    131, 163, 184, 209, 323,
    330, 338, 340, 365-68
  Nason XIV,277, 289; XV,381;
    XVI,683
  Nason Jr. XV,124
  Nathan XIV,274
  Theophilus XIV,180, 570,
    601; XV,434, 712;
    XVI,198, 222, 268, 505,
    647
  Thomas XIV,469
Castle, Gilbert XV,446
Caswell, Eliphalet XVI,203, 219,
    501, 611
  Gilbert XIV,104, 106, 213,
    221, 578; XV,653, 717;
    XVI, 202, 218, 270, 502,
    517, 597, 768-69, 934
  John XVII,86
  Joseph XV,295, 300-1
  Mark XVII,86
  Nathan XIV,285, 287, 463,
  Caswell, Nathan XIV,473; XV,
    589, 705; XVII,65, 78, 113

44

Casewell, Nathan Jr. XVI,289-91
　　Ozias XV,589
Cate, Andrew XV,665, 684
　　Benjamin XV,423-24, 609,
　　　730; XVI,17, 211
　　Daniel XIV,259
　　Elisha XIV,143, 193-94;
　　　XVII,8
　　Elise XVII,360
　　Enoch XIV,117, 129, 189,
　　　432; XV,300-1, 304, 308;
　　　XVI,616
　　Henry XIV,227
　　Henry F. XIV,257-58; XVII,45
　　James XIV,394; XV,42;
　　　XVII,88
　　James Jr. XIV,432
　　John XIV,228, 344; XV,325;
　　　XVI,110, 165, 369, 572;
　　　XVII,693, 705
　　John Neal XVI,604
　　Jonathan XVI,121, 164
　　Joseph XIV,551; XV,324;
　　　XVII,360
　　Joseph Jr. XVII,360
　　Neal XV,660-61, 668, 685;
　　　XVI,255, 501
　　Samuel XIV,179, 402, 414;
　　　XV,300-1, 305, 309
　　Samuel Jr. XIV,239
　　Samuel W. XIV,257, 344; XV,
　　　326; XVI,260-61; XVII,30,
　　　432
　　Simeon XVII,360
　　William XIV,15, 228
　　William Jr. XIV,402, 414;
　　　XVI,569-70
Cater, Andrew XIV,370, 378,
　　　493, 503, 515
　　Benjamin XIV,566, 607-8
　　Edward XIV,13, 228; XV,619
　　Stephen XIV,231, 401, 414
Caterling, Gideon XVI,232
Cates, Elisha XV,134
　　Simeon XV,134, 173
Cauley, John XIV,116

Cavanaugh, Charles XVI,246,
　　252, 287, 511
　　James XVI,37, 103, 196, 213,
　　　241, 279, 510
Cavender, James XVI,232, 725
Caverly, Charles XV,749
　　John XIV,260, 343; XV,749;
　　　XVI,61, 64, 71, 95; XVII,46
　　Nicholas XIV,485, 500, 512;
　　　XVII,86
Cavernough, Charles XV,188
Cawdle, William XVI,930
Cayce, Peter XVII,304
Center, Abraham XIV,13, 561,
　　620
Chace, Abraham XIV,585-86,
　　657
　　Benjamin XIV,585, 660
　　Caleb XV,341
　　Daniel XV,342
　　Enoch XV,421
　　Jacob XV,168
　　Jonathan XVI,96
　　Joshua XIV,636
　　Joseph XV,606
　　Moses XVI,91-92
　　Nehemiah XVI,24
　　Robert XVI,242
　　Samuel XIV,290-91; XVI,509
　　Stephen XIV,250
　　See also Chase
Chadbourne, Benjamin XV,578;
　　　XVII,139
　　Japhet XV,326
　　Jonathan XV, 578
　　Mark XIV,239; XVII,33, 39
　　Dr. Thomas XIV,246
Chadwick,-- XIV,555
　　Edmund XV,726; XVI,367,
　　　527; XVII,91, 269
　　Edward XIV,61, 182; XVI,6
　　Job XVI,80; XVII,384
　　John XIV,185, 301, 313, 467,
　　　548, 567, 611; XV,608;
　　　XVI,202
　　Jonathan XV,717

Chadwick, Joseph XV,120, 409,
752
William XIV,238, 362, 550;
XV,430
Chaffee, Clifford XIV,51, 185,
325, 464
Nathan XVII,67
Chaford, David XV,610
Chaiser, Isaac XVI,913
Challis, Christopher XIV,585,
628; XVI,204
Enos XIV,471, 585, 611; XV,
717; XVI,202, 224, 508,
615
Thomas XIV,340, 586, 627;
XV, 400, 624, 719; XVI,5,
203
William XVII,424
Chalmers, Hambleton XV,295
Chamberlain, Aaron XIV,34; XV,
355
Abiel XV,387
Abner XIV,269, 272, 289
Amasa XVII,118-19
Asa XVI,259; XVII,436
Asher XV,586
Benjamin XIV,104, 270, 289,
295; XV,375, 746
Calvin XIV,645; XV,7, 732;
XVI,20, 22, 191
Charles XVII,118-19
Daniel XIV,280
David XIV,268, 270, 289
Eben XIV,279, 295
Ebenezer XIV,84, 199, 264,
287; XV,48
Elias XIV,269, 272, 290
Ephraim XIV,280, 288, 297;
XV,172
Francis XIV,117, 129
Henry XIV,84, 199, 264;
XV,49
Ichabod XV,243, 245, 247
Increase XV,7
Jacob XIV,304-5, 465;
XV,195; XVI,554-55

Chamberlain, James XIV,125,
188, 407; XVI, 237, 271,
505; XVII,10
Jason XIV,188; XV,575; XVII,
11, 261
John XIV,427; XV,6, 753;
XVI,748
Jonathan XV,118, 138, 350,
352
Jonathan Jr. XV,118, 138
Moses XIV,96, 204; XV,584-
85, 592; XVI,307; XVII,114
Nathaniel XIV,288
Richard XVII,116, 542-51,
558, 563-64, 567-68, 572,
575, 608, 615
Richard Jr. XVI,314
Samuel XIV,143, 194, 243,
483, 459, 527, 539, 551;
XV,387; XVII,8
Silas XIV,99, 204
Thomas XIV,234, 624;
XV,619, 725; XVI,207, 817
Wilder XV,744
William XIV,194, 304-5, 465;
XV,179, 654; XVI,912
Chambers, Benjamin XVII,160-
65, 174, 178, 198
John XVII,293
Chamlet, William XIV,7
Champaigne, Charles XVII,299
Champernowne Francis
XVII,502, 508, 511-12,
514, 519-20, 578, 599
Champlin, Peter XIV,5
Champney, Nathan XV,533
Richard XV,578; XVII,56
Chandler, Abiel XIV,36, 46, 48,
60, 62, 304-5; XVI,172,
176, 240, 269, 521, 828
Abner XVI,538; XVII,253
Abraham XV,134
Aretas XIV,269, 272, 290
Benjamin XIV,239, 255; XVII,
23, 31, 39
Captain XIV,696; XVII,150

46

Chandler, Daniel XIV,167, 169,
274, 289, 291, 586, 654;
XV,732; XVI, 31, 34, 59,
187; XVII,319
David XV,41, 375, 520; XVII,
109
Ebenezer XIV,143, 194, 244;
XVI, 529; XVI,87, 99;
XVII,7
Hill XV,384; XVI,157; XVII,
253
Isaac XV,129, 654, 656, 666,
673; XVI,675, 694; XVII,50
James XIV,34, 333-34
Jeremiah XVI,263, 612; XVII,
430
Joel XVI,554
John XIV,664; XV,300-1,
306, 310, 431, 515;
XVI,247, 251, 499
Jonathan XV,383-85;
XVI,924
Joseph XIV,143, 193-94,
225, 243, 269, 271, 290-
91, 304, 330-32, 350;
XV,284, 291, 328, 343,
564, 701, 703; XVI,46,
175, 302, 563, 749-50;
XVII,9
Josiah XIV,312; XV,663, 670,
685, 688; XVI,85, 91, 106,
264, 610; XVII,431
Moses XIV,96, 203, 205, 269,
272, 290; XV,392;
XVI,287, 503
Nathaniel XV,300-1, 305,
308, 578; XVI,108, 130,
163
Peter XIV,62, 158, 304-5,
639; XV, 731, 752; XVI,15,
25, 186, 211
Philander XVII,253
Primus XIV,267
Robert XIV,239, 255; XVII,23,
31, 39
Samuel XV,29
Sanborn XVI,918

Chandler, Thomas XIV,63, 118-
19, 149, 181, 186, 197,
664; XV,513; XVI,918;
XVII,3
William XV,41, 375
Zachariah XV,362
Zebulon XV,369
Chandonnet, Francis XIV,553,
613; XVI,3; XVII,266
Chaney, John XV,115
William XV,26, 371, 629,
642-43
Chapin, David XVII,632
Hiram XVII,97
Justus XIV,427
Sewell XIV,272, 290; XV,377
Chaplain, Micah XIV,77, 81, 198
Samuel XIV,420
Chaplin, Moses XV,20, 348
Samuel XV,20, 98, 349
William XV,377
Chapman, Benjamin XIV,542;
XV, 15; XVI,310
Benjamin Jr. XIV,444
Edmund XIV,390, 486, 512
Edward XIV,508, 513;
XVII,24
Elisha XIV,116, 129, 189;
XV, 482, 494
James XIV,8, 414; XV,320,
340
Job XIV,11; XVII,360, 464
John XVI,67, 78, 99
Jonah XIV,441, 463, 527;
XV, 706-9, 736; XVI,585-
86
Jonas XVII,251
Jonathan XVI,320, 322-23,
326, 330, 334, 337, 339,
343-44, 368-70, 489
Joseph XIV,134, 191, 391,
487, 508, 512; XVI,150,
667; XVII, 5, 74
Josiah XVII,66
Levi XIV,136, 191, 309; XV,
285, 287-88; XVI,69, 79,
92, 286, 520; XVII,6

Chapman, Micah XVI,507
 Michael XVI,286
 Nathaniel XVI,52-53; XVII,
  460, 464
 Samuel XIV,229; XVI,844;
  XVII,28, 740
 Shadrach XVI,60, 62, 70, 94
 Smith XIV,248; XV,285, 287;
  XVII,26
 Solomon XIV,469, 602;
  XV,609, 712; XVI,198,
  222, 241, 268, 501, 611
 Stephen XIV,92, 202, 264
Charbona, Augustine XVII,305
Chartie, Antoine XVII,309
 John M. XVII,309
Chartier, Joseph XVII,299
 Peter XVII,304
Chase, Abel XIV,161
 Abiel XIV,160
 Abner XV,186, 548
 Abraham XIV,225; XV,629,
  641; XVI,38, 102, 795;
  XVII,349
 Abram XV,623
 Amos XIV,298; XV,11;
  XVII,103
 Benjamin XV,727; XVI,9, 42,
  183, 208, 708; XVII,153
 Bradstreet XV,693; XVI,214,
  234
 Caleb XIV,452, 532; XV,322,
  341; XVII,424
 Captain XVI,301
 Carr XIV,423
 Charles XV,640
 Daniel XIV,394, 404; XV,155,
  157-58, 323, 342; XVII,88,
  143
 Dudley XIV,402, 555, 652;
  XV, 42; XVII,227
 Dudley L. XIV,134, 191, 415;
  XV,726; XVI,7, 51, 208,
  525, 538; XVII,6, 269
 Ebenezer XVI,145
 Edward XIV,134, 191, 402,
  414; XVII,6

Chase, Enoch XIV,115, 140,
  192, 554, 631; XV,719;
  XVI,4, 182, 203, 231, 271,
  526, 932; XVII,26, 267,
  319
 Ephraim XVII,6, 60
 Ephraim C. XIV,346
 Ezekiel XIV,92, 202-3
 Francis Jr. XVI,770; XVII,2
 Isaac XIV,430; XVI,867-68;
  XVI,920; XVII,293
 Jacob XIV,212, 217, 219-20
 John XIV,341, 394; XV,15,
  69, 129, 138, 301, 304,
  308, 376, 660-61, 668,
  698; XVI,282, 284, 287,
  499, 604; XVII,80, 82
 John Jr. XVI,284
 Jonah XVI,188
 Jonathan XIV,112, 146, 195,
  256, 395, 444-45, 556,
  559, 580, 641; XV,1, 14,
  19, 38, 45, 138, 373-87,
  408, 422-23, 433, 448,
  492, 548, 599, 602, 604,
  651, 655, 730; XVI, 17, 58,
  65, 75, 104, 106, 166,
  249, 294, 922; XVII, 27,
  108, 111-12, 143-44, 149-
  50, 236, 290, 298, 363,
  367, 369, 419
 Joseph XIV,313, 567, 656;
  XV, 346, 445, 609, 731;
  XVI, 36, 38, 130, 163,
  195, 212, 285, 520, 586
 Joshua XIV,87, 201, 340,
  346, 562, 565; XV,725;
  XVII,60, 88
 Josiah XIV,48, 143, 194, 369,
  375, 398, 482, 498, 502,
  511, 518, 651; XV,161,
  163, 597, 729; XVI,28,
  286, 520; XVII,8
 Dr. Josiah XVI,400, 424, 458,
  472
 Lieutenant XVI,181, 620
 Micajah XIV,346; XV,517;

Chase, Micajah (Cont.) XVII,160
  Moses XIV,398, 614; XV,38,
    45, 267-69, 271, 369, 537,
    660, 711; XVI,82, 87, 106,
    198, 203, 224, 528, 538,
    617-18; XVII,111
  Moses Jr. XV,602
  Nathaniel XIV,354, 427, 587;
    XV,725, 748; XVI,36, 38,
    152, 207, 275, 519, 825
  Nehemiah XIV,118, 137, 158,
    350, 645
  Parker XVI,130, 163;
    XVII,434
  Pratt XIV,64, 181, 186, 566,
    654; XV,607; XVI,31, 34,
    59, 926; XVII,3
  Robert XVI,236, 274, 503,
    617
  Salmon XV,15, 40
  Samuel XIV,269, 271, 478;
    XV, 90, 373, 386, 543,
    548; XVI,246, 251, 285,
    511, 715, 734, 771;
    XVII,108, 111
  Samuel Jr. XV,42; XVI,246,
    252, 511; XVII,111
  Samuel 3d XV,14
  Seth XV,39, 374
  Simeon XV,39, 90, 376; XVII,
    109
  Solomon XV,14, 138, 142,
    376; XVI,538; XVII,108,
    111, 144
  Dr. Solomon XVI,386, 466,
    472
  Stephen XIV,74, 97, 178,
    204, 398; XV,69, 517
  Stevens XVI,921
  Thomas XV,377
  William XIV,231, 242, 402,
    415
Chaterad, Joseph XV,729;
    XVI,28
Chating, Francis XVII,299
Chatterton, Joseph XVI,549

Chautere, Joseph XIV,662
Chellis, Enos XV,742
Chelsea, William XIV,371, 379,
    493, 504, 515; XV,284
Cheney, Benjamin XVI,112
  Elias XIV,632; XV,444, 723
  Eliphalet XV,742
  Jesse XIV,92, 202-3
  Jonathan XV,200, 465, 467,
    478, 505
  Nathaniel XIV,225; XV,200,
    398
  Richard XIV,225
  William XVI,739
Chenoweth, Richard XVII,207
Chensey, Elias XVI,206
Cherry, Samuel XIV,210, 214,
    217, 219-20, 347, 465,
    554, 579, 622; XV,718;
    XVI,5, 51, 180, 182, 203,
    233, 248, 271; XVII,267,
    440, 444
Chesley, Aaron XIV,235
  Alpheus XIV,235, 242, 476
  Andrew XIV,226, 397
  Corydon XV,723; XVI,206,
    273; XVII,435
  Daniel XIV,225
  Ebenezer XIV,108, 122, 125,
    187-88, 226, 624; XV,
    445, 619, 725; XVI,638;
    XVII,10
  Ichabod XVII, 719
  Isaac XIV,226
  James XIV,312; XV,435;
    XVI,905
  John XIV,13, 226, 330; XVII,
    719
  Jonathan XIV,13, 396-97,
    408; XV,570; XVI,640-41;
    XVII,719
  Joseph XVII,719
  Nathaniel XVI,196
  Nicholas XIV,409
  Philip XIV,225; XVII,512,
    719, 734

Chesley, Reuben XIV,373, 386, 497
Samuel XIV,235, 369, 375; XV, 312; XVII,719
Samuel Jr. XVII,719
Sawyer XIV,226, 397; XV,572
Timothy XVI,641
William XV,288
Chestnut, Robert XVII,296
William XIV,223
Chetman, Solomon XIV,566
Chick, John XIV,259; XVII,36
Child, Cyril XIV,607-8; XV,424, 714; XVI,314
Francis XVII,669
Jonathan XIV,160, 608; XV,154, 366, 385, 705; XVI,456, 924; XVII,14, 289, 331-34, 350, 355-56, 358, 365-66, 376, 381, 385
One XIV,590
Richard XVI,920
Stephen XV,15, 374
William XIV,344; XVI,314, 528; XVII,22, 667, 692
Chiswell, Wentworth XV,417
Chittenden, Thomas XVII,227, 234, 243
Choat, Ammi XVI,169-70, 255, 506
Jacob XV,548
Jonathan XIV,297
Chownes, Joseph XVII,620-21
Christie, Peter XIV,74, 178
William XV,350, 352
Christo, Indian XVI,906, 916
Christopher, George XIV,657; XV, 732; XVI,37, 195, 212, 232, 259, 278; XVII,436
Christy, George XVII,19
James XV,394, 428
Jesse XVII,19
Peter XV,394, 428; XVI,898
Thomas XVI,898, 903
Chubb, William XIV,9
Chubbet, John XIV,3

Chubbuck, Simeon XV,621, 663, 670, 682, 689; XVI,573-74
Church, Benjamin XVI,624
Ebenezer XVI,661-62; XVII,96
Iddo XIV,613; XV,732, 741; XVI,20, 22
Jabez XIV,423; XV,124, 149, 160; XVI,247, 254
James XIV,1; XV,12
Jared XV,705-6, 708-9; XVI, 586
Job XIV,310
John XIV,265, 408, 610; XV,116, 176; XVII,525
Joshua XV,717; XVI,202
Nathaniel XIV,114, 409; XV, 469, 481, 506; XVI,323, 327, 329-30, 338, 340, 344-45, 370-72; XVII,22, 33
Simeon XV,26, 367
Simon XV,741
Thomas XIV,613; XV,711, 741
Churchill, John XVII,757
Thomas XVII,424
Churchwood, Arthur XIV,90, 201
Cilley, Benjamin XVII,32
Colonel XVI,280
Cutting XIV,231, 589; XV,433; XVII,140
Daniel XIV,650
James XIV,509
John XVII,32, 440
Jonathan XIV,509, 570, 603; XV,174, 624, 727; XVI,8, 41, 181-82, 208
Joseph XIV,37, 49, 107, 121, 253, 471, 552, 591, 611; XV, 136, 276, 421, 424-25, 432, 434, 446, 456-57, 653, 710, 755; XVI,2, 51, 56, 182, 197, 387, 423, 477, 527; XVII, 25-26, 28,

Cilley, Joseph (Cont.) 33, 44,
    127, 239, 266, 278, 341,
    372
  Joseph Jr. XVII,13
  Samuel XV,113
  Thomas XIV,24; XV,457
Claggett, Horatio XVII,207
Claghorn, James XVII,669
Clantard, Joseph XV,597
Clapham, Charles XV,573;
    XVI,624; XVII,261
  George XVII,307
Clapp, Daniel XIV,553, 607; XV,
    710; XVI,3, 180, 182, 197,
    529; XVII,75, 266
  Preserved XV,367
  Supply XVI,805; XVII,123,
    139, 375, 446
Claridge, James XIV,239, 259,
    664
  Stephen XV,692; XVI,214
  William XIV,240, 259, 664;
    XV, 431, 693; XVI,214;
    XVII,22, 33, 37
Clark, Abraham XIV,1; XVII,25
  Adam XV,42
  Amiel XIV,234
  Amos XIV,225
  Andrew XV,25
  Archibald XV,464, 466, 477,
    505, 671, 677; XVI,60, 62,
    70, 99, 103, 112, 190,
    213, 228, 235, 279, 511,
    516, 719, 721, 725, 803
  Benjamin XIV,25, 337, 464;
    XV, 27, 34, 325; XVI,137;
    XVII, 64
  Bunker XIV,470, 576, 593;
    XV, 439, 716; XVI,202,
    218, 270, 517, 752, 764,
    934; XVII,468
  Caleb XIV,563, 615; XV,719
  Cephas XV,226; XVII,98
  Charles XVI,820-21; XVII,14
  Daniel XIV,406, 648-49; XV,
    457, 595, 728; XVI,13,
    138, 261; XVII,249

Clark, David XIV,66, 181;
    XV,199; XVI, 285, 506
  Ebenezer XIV,442, 581, 659;
    XV, 448, 599, 727; XVI,11,
    316
  Edward XV,153-54, 733;
    XVI,45, 48, 264, 302, 305,
    307, 679; XVII,91, 253,
    511
  Eleazer XIV,13, 544; XV,27
  Elijah XVI,237, 275, 509, 692
  Elisha XVII,25
  Ephraim XIV,266; XV,122;
    XVI, 531
  George XIV,334
  Greenleaf XIV,242
  Guy XV,380; XVII,118-19
  Hanson XIV,237, 403, 414
  Henry XV,526
  Hezekiah XIV,324, 464, 578,
    579; XV,713; XVI,199,
    223, 240, 268, 522, 866
  Isaac XIV,34, 325, 464;
    XV,92; XVI,122, 164;
    XVII,102, 629
  Jacob XIV,66, 181, 235, 240,
    404
  James XIV,267, 359; XV,487,
    498, 567, 668, 676, 690;
    XVI,862
  Jesse XV,634, 649, 720; XVI,
    102, 204, 230, 272, 513,
    778
  John XIV,14, 118-19, 151,
    211, 215, 218, 220, 227,
    231, 257-58, 291, 343,
    345, 381, 391, 456, 468,
    470, 472, 489, 501, 537,
    578; XV,150, 153-54, 194,
    277, 475, 494, 643, 649,
    698, 711, 716, 753; XVI,
    63, 72, 91, 112, 198, 201,
    218, 224, 241, 260-61,
    267, 270, 307, 313, 513,
    605, 671, 682, 720, 778,
    780-81, 928, 934; XVII,80,
    82, 116, 253, 757

51

Clark, John Jr. XVI,515, 682;
     XVII, 274
   Jonathan XIV,2, 68, 180,
     188, 279, 288, 296, 463;
     XV,160; XVI,113, 307,
     656; XVII,66, 80-81
   Jonathan D. XIV,308
   Joseph XIV,191, 251, 260,
     344; XV,27-28, 143, 152,
     154, 371; XVI,119, 157,
     285, 498, 606, 845;
     XVII,6, 47, 91, 249, 253,
     435, 465
   Josiah XIV,227, 236, 257,
     353, 445, 470, 543;
     XV,157, 377, 634, 649,
     667, 678, 715; XVI,200,
     210, 224, 241, 269, 513,
     656, 778, 780-81; XVII,
     143
   Josiah Jr. XIV,352
   Mary XVI,781
   Matthew XIV,28, 30
   Michael XIV,280, 288
   Moses XIV,190, 302, 314;
     XVI, 648, 844, 933
   Nathaniel XIV,113, 147, 587;
     XV,440, 630, 642-43, 719,
     724; XVI,207, 229, 274,
     522, 865-66
   Nathaniel S. XIV,616
   Nicholas XV,133, 171
   Page XV,439
   Paul XVI,300
   Peter XV,118, 138, 162, 188-
     90, 230, 233, 235, 350,
     352, 354, 429; XVII,207
   Richard XV,377
   Robert XIV,390, 393; XV,564;
     XVI,115, 117, 525;
     XVII,24, 629, 667
   Samuel XV,632, 636, 700,
     703, 725; XVI,26, 44, 170,
     172, 175, 556-57, 911,
     914-15; XVII,33, 42
   Samuel H. XIV,108, 122,
     188, 226, 258

Clark, Sawtelle XV,171
   Simeon XV,3
   Solomon XIV,234, 259;
     XV,297; XVI,913; XVII,37
   Stephen XIV,242, 253, 550;
     XV, 410, 699; XVI,67, 74,
     98; XVII,24-25, 44
   T. XVII,159, 161, 188
   Taylor XIV,231, XV,597;
     XVII,27
   Thomas XIV,468, 607-8;
     XV,436, 603, 714; XVII,25,
     88, 153, 465
   Timothy XV,358
   Valentine XIV,25
   Ward XIV,657; XV,731;
     XVI,36, 38, 195, 212
   Widow XVI,933
   William XIV,226; XVI,261,
     755, 781; XVII,104
   Winthrop XIV,289
Clarke, Benjamin XIV,324
   Charles XIV,166, 170
   Daniel XV,145; XVII,432
   David XV,380
   Ebenezer XV,589
   Edward XVII,114
   Henry XIV,550; XV,430
   Hezekiah XIV,104
   Isaac XV,355
   Jacob XVII,22-23
   John XIV,196, 289, 391, 487,
     514; XV,380, 584-85, 589,
     698; XVII,114, 433, 537
   John Jr. XV,589
   Jonathan XV,589; XVII,114
   Joseph XIV,134; XV,11
   Josiah XV,18
   Moses XIV, 110, 131
   Nathan XVII, 622
   Nathaniel XIV,196
   Robert XIV,486
   Samuel XVII,22
   Solomon XVII,22, 34
   Stephen XV,430
   Thomas XIV,102, 207;
     XV,754

52

Clarke, Timothy XIV,104
Clarkson, Andrew XIV,20; XVI,
  918-19
Clary, Daniel XIV,34; XV,21
  John XV,355
Clash, Samuel XVI,46, 302
Clay, Daniel XVI,285, 501
  George XVII,296
  James Jr. XIV,264
  John XIV,249, 257, 539; XV,
    169, 748; XVI,931
  Richard XIV,10; XVII,641,
    646
  Samuel XIV,550; XV,475,
    494; XVI,66, 77, 97, 904
  Timothy XV,658-59, 668,
    679; XVI,156, 252
  Walter XV,526; XVI,155
  William XVII,717
Clayes, Abigail XVI,323-24, 333,
    338, 340, 372
  Elijah XIV,92, 202, 554, 632-
    33; XV,444-45, 457, 610,
    718; XVI,5, 51, 180, 324,
    333, 372; XVII,267
Clear, Philip XIV,259; XVII, 37
Cleaveland, Solomon XIV,285,
    287
Clemens, Simon XVI,41, 44
Clement, Aaron XIV,237
  Abraham XVII,686
  Benajah XVI,568
  David XIV,66, 181
  Ezra XIV,329
  Henry XIV,302, 314
  Isaac XIV,392, 488, 509, 513;
    XVI,87, 506, 694; XVII,452
  James XIV,18; XVI,634
  Jeremiah XVII,261
  Jesse XIV,174; XV,113
  Job XIV,3, 14, 18; XVII,525,
    543, 555, 568, 605, 620
  John XIV,225; XV,658-667;
    XVI, 257, 519, 823, 926
  John Jr. XVI,824
Clement, Dr. John XV,231
  Jonathan XV,405

Clement, Merrill XVI,87, 94
  Moody XVI,696; XVII,430
  Nathaniel XIV,64, 182, 186;
    XVI,926; XVII,3
  Peter XVI,567-68
  Reuben XVII,306
  Richard XIV,587, 628;
    XV,172
  Simeon XV,568; XVII,349,
    424
  Timothy XIV,51, 185, 243,
    301, 302, 267, 390, 392,
    480, 486, 488, 508, 510,
    512, 514
  Thomas XIV,385, 496, 505,
    517, 520
  William XIV,315, 429, 467,
    548; XV,404-5
Clements, Benajah XV,543
  Henry XV,554
  Isaac XV,663, 670, 685, 688;
    XVI,91, 106, 224, 238,
    271
  James XV,350, 352
  Jeremiah XV,576
  Jesse XV,551
  John XV,549, 674, 691
  Merrill XV,698
  Moody XVI,264
  Moses XV,549
  Prince XVI,237, 244, 272,
    504, 624, 628
  Richard XV,720; XVI,204
  Simeon XV,629, 641; XVI,
    566
  Simon XV,623
  William XV,161, 163
Clemons, David XIV,223
  Thomas XIV,372
Clendinin, Robert XVI,898
Cleveland, Aquila XV,701, 704
  Eliphalet XVI,541
  Elisha XV,153-54, 279-80,
    589; XVI,83, 97, 295, 313,
    541; XVII,80, 82, 116
  Solomon XV,589; XVI,156,
    928

Clifford, Abraham XIV,23, 29,
    224, 641; XV,442, 596,
    626, 724; XVI,822
  Anthony XV,168
  Captain XV,696
  David XIV,559, 660; XV,727;
    XVI,10, 43, 184, 209
  David Jr. XIV,580; XV,448,
    598
  Dudley XIV,70, 179, 330
  Ebenezer XIV,109, 121, 133;
    XIV,190
  Isaac XIV,405, 441, 527;
    XVII, 32
  Israel XIV,12, 68, 180; XV,
    167
  Ithiel XIV,331
  Jacob XIV,198, 328; XV,377,
    402; XVI,897; XVII,109,
    643, 644, 738
  John XIV,1, 2, 76, 81, 198,
    410, 423; XV,683;
    XVI,232, 897, 901;
    XVII,528, 738
  John Jr. XV,662, 668;
    XVII,528
  Jonathan XV,150
  Joseph XIV,232; XV,402,
    412, 522, 524; XVI,938;
    XVII,738
  Richard XV,300, 302, 305,
    309
  Samuel XIV,11, 110, 131,
    190; XV,128, 412; XVI,68,
    77, 99, 115
  Stephen XIV,226
  Tristram XV,300, 302, 305,
    309
  William XIV,585, 623;
    XV,720; XVI,204, 227,
    272, 510, 642, 709
  Zachariah XIV,387, 494, 507,
    516; XV,125, 150, 160
Clinton, James XVII,310, 317,
    320
Clogston, John XVI,665
Clogstone, Paul XIV,43, 95, 204

Clop, John XVII,304
Closson, John XIV,267, 271
  Nathan XV,741
  Nehemiah XV,571
Cloud, Joseph XVII,301
Clough, Aaron XV,668, 685,
    690; XVI,658
  Abner XIV,392, 487, 509,
    513; XV,300-1
  Amos XIV,25
  Benjamin XIV,413; XV,746;
    XVI, 838-39
  Caesar XIV,628; XV,456,
    494, 721
  Caleb XV,571
  Cornelius XIV,405; XVII,32
  Daniel XVI,68, 79, 85, 91, 99,
    219, 270, 695, 875;
    XVII,438
  David XIV,172, 174, 176-77,
    362, 365, 425, 551;
    XV,180; XVI,64, 73, 95,
    694
  Ebenezer XIV,12
  Ezekiel XVI,915
  Gilman XV,304, 308;
    XVI,169-70; XVII,81, 83
  Hezekiah XVI,229
  Humphrey XIV,16; XV,658,
    667, 674, 691, 743;
    XVI,830
  Isaac XIV,225; XV,328, 343;
    XVI,909
  Jeremiah XIV,107, 143, 145,
    154, 193-94; XVI,591,
    595, 899-900, 907-8, 915;
    XVII,8
  John XIV,108, 187, 323, 560,
    580, 652; XV,447, 546,
    598, 631, 638, 722, 728;
    XVI,27, 188, 205, 210,
    273, 335-36, 508, 680-81;
    XVII,257
  Jonathan XV,400, 742;
    XVI,922
  Joseph XIV,64, 143, 181,
    193-94; XVI,180, 628,

54

Clough, Joseph (Cont.) 640,
   698; XVI,837-38, 926;
   XVII,4, 7-8
Levi XVI,148
Moses XIV,25, 261; XV,514;
   XVII,91
Nathan XIV,173-77, 380,
   398, 489, 501, 514;
   XV,321, 340, 387;
   XVI,257, 520
Nathaniel XIV,240
Nehemiah XVI,592-93, 595
Obadiah XIV,143, 194; XVII,9
Oliver XV,631, 638; XVI,41,
   44, 680
Phinehas XIV,453, 532;
Reuben XIV,112, 146, 195;
   XV, 322, 341
Richard XV,402
Samuel XIV,108, 123
Simon XV,194
Theophilus XIV,550; XV,430,
   526
Thomas XIV,219, 399;
   XVI,915; XVII,24
Timothy XIV,107, 242, 565,
   660; XVI,871
William XIV,350; XV,328,
   330, 343, 569
Winthrop XIV,143, 173-77,
   194, 291; XVII,9
Zaccheus XIV,107, 242, 565,
   660; XV,283, 290, 545,
   747; XVI,10, 43, 209, 277,
   517, 657, 711; XVII,43
Zachariah XV,727; XVI,188
Cloun, Timothy XVI,933
Cloutman, Edward XIV,3, 14
Eliphalet XIV,114, 140, 193
Thomas XIV,25
Clows, John XVI,303
Cloyd, Joseph XVI,543
Cluer, Joseph XV,350
Clutterbuck, Mr. XVII,520
Clyde, William XIV,74, 178
Coats, Benjamin XIV,263;
   XVI,313

Cobb, Ebenezer XIV,35; XV,95
Isaac XV,465, 479, 503
Samuel XIV,427; XV,6
Seth XIV,35; XV,110
Simeon XIV,356; XV,47, 224
Stephen XIV,35
Cobbett, Thomas XVII,625, 643,
   646
Cobbey, James XVI,341, 343,
   345, 373
Nathaniel XIV,232
Cobleigh, Daniel XV,51; XVII,
   95
Eleazer XIV,92, 202-3
John XVII,629
Jonathan XV,225
Oliver XV,51, 53; XVI,602
Coburn, Amasa XIV,356
Amos XIV,555
Andrew XIV,638
Benjamin XV,510
Benoni XV,740
Daniel XV,57
Ebenezer XIV,282
Ezekiel XVII,95
George XV,74, 419
James Jr. XIV,590
Merrill XIV,185, 588; XV,
   358
Nathan XIV,419
Rowlins,XV,716
Thomas XIV,309, 466
Cochran, Charles XIV,223
Doctor XVII,395
Elijah XIV,64, 186, 425; XV,
   189, 429; XVII,4
Isaac XV,358
James XIV,205, 266, 359,
   476, 572, 606, 613;
   XV,611, 711; XVI,241,
   498, 560, 562, 789-790
John XIV,28-30, 360, 411,
   417; XV,359, 552, 556;
   XVI,198, 267, 419, 666,
   753, 755; XVII,1, 55, 224,
   259
John C. XIV,30

Cochran, Jonathan XIV,29, 246,
    416, 439, 527, 572, 613;
    XV,611, 711
  Joseph XIV,360
  Major XVII,317, 320
  Robert XIV,102, 207, 266,
    307, 572; XV,611;
    XVI,287, 516
  Samuel XV,90; XVII,306
  Sarah XVII,224
  William XV,740; XVI,787-88,
    839
Cockle, John XIV,573; XV,615;
    XVI,504, 635
Cod, Richard XIV,1
Codman, Dr. Henry XVI,135
Coffin, Abner XIV,321; XV,740;
    XVI,285, 523, 820
  Benjamin XV,125
  Eliphalet XIV,134, 191, 251
  Enoch XIV,301; XV,406; XVI,
    643-44
  George XV,460, 605-6
  James XIV,99
  Jemima XVII,747
  Michael XV,701, 703;
    XVI,170, 172, 175
  Nathaniel XIV,113, 147, 195,
    250; XVI,648
  Nicholas XVI,242, 273, 502
  Peter XIV,243, 253, 304-5,
    367, 435, 466, 476; XVI,
    284; XVII,27, 513, 604-5,
    621, 623, 631, 633, 638,
    640, 647, 675, 683, 691
  Peter Jr. XVI,648
  Primus XIV,615; XV,719;
    XVI, 63, 71, 93, 106, 203
  Richard XIV,86
  Tristram XIV,12
Cogan, Patrick XIV,552, 591;
    XV, 710; XVI,2; XVII,267
  Stephen XVI,640
Coger, Enoch XVII,307
Cogswell, Amos XV,749
  Nathaniel P. XV,749
  Sibbel XVI,538

Cogswell, Thomas XV,748
  William XV,568; XVI,568
Coit, James B. XVII,470
Coke, John XVI,241
Colbath, Benjamin XIV,637; XV,
    618, 653, 725; XVI,640
  Dependence XIV,623;
    XV,618, 725; XVI,207,
    233, 241, 275, 504, 639
  Downing XIV,259, 623;
    XV,441, 618, 720; XVI,64,
    74, 93, 204; XVII,38, 290,
    327, 434
  George XV,431
  Hunking XVI,818
  John XIV,108, 122, 187; XVI,
    638
  Sarah XVI,640; XVII,327
  Winthrop XVI,121, 164
Colborne, Thomas XV,745
Colbroth, George XIV,664
Colburn, Amos XIV,101, 206,
    655; XV,726; XVI,7;
    XVII,269
  Andrew XIV,555; XV,421,
    726; XVI,6, 324, 333, 373;
    XVII, 210, 269
  Asa XIV,394; XV,156;
    XVII,89, 143
  Benjamin XV,87
  Charles XV,621, 663, 669,
    682, 689; XVI,872
  Daniel XV,6
  Ebenezer XIV,287
  Edward XV,228, 637;
    XVI,784
  Elias XV,95
  Isaac XV,698
  Jacob XV,17, 40, 156;
    XVI,178-79; XVII,89, 143
  James XIV,33, 573, 609;
    XV,613
  John XIV,607-8; XV,603,
    714; XVI,200; XVII,67
  Jonathan XVI,915
  Lieutenant XVI,60
  Merrill XIV,52

Colburn, Nathan XIV,33, 247, 264
Phebe XVI,324, 333, 340, 373
Robert XIV,274, 278, 289; XV, 39, 375
Rollins XIV,575, 592
Stephen XIV,445, 543; XV,40
Thomas XIV,33, 44, 88, 304-5, 459, 574, 604; XV,614, 715; XVI,201
Colby, Abner XIV,315, 467, 548
Abraham XIV,246
Archelaus XVI,786
Barzillai XIV,404
Benajah XIV,327-28
Benjamin XIV,226; XV,401, 561; XVII,32
Daniel XIV,225; XVI,236, 267, 502, 594-95
David XIV,301, 586, 627; XV, 120, 183, 721, 746, 748; XVI,167, 204, 226, 270, 514, 770-71
Ebenezer XIV,227, 315, 467, 548; XV,322, 329-30, 341, 343
Edmund XVI,267, 502, 594-95
Edward XV,637; XVI,236; XVII, 502, 522, 528, 607
Eli XIV,302-3, 312; XV,150, 160
Elias XIV,19
Elliot XVI,264
Enoch XIV,328; XV,169, 526
Ephraim XIV,61, 182, 304-5, 465
Ezekiel XVII,253
Hezekiah XIV,304-5, 465-66; XV,176; XVI,285, 510, 706
Humphrey XIV,143, 195; XVII,9
Ichabod XVI,156
Isaac XIV,112, 146; XV,199, 464, 466, 477, 505, 671, 673; XVI,719, 721

Colby, Israel XIV,195
Jacob S. XV,116
James XIV,564, 651; XVI,321, 326, 332
Jethro XV,465, 467, 478, 505
John XIV,19, 224, 410, 424, 584, 628; XV,720, 748; XVI, 85, 91, 106, 125, 587; XVII, 426
John S. XIV,359
Joseph XIV,167, 169, 246, 274, 425; XV,113, 175, 550, 621, 663, 669, 682, 689; XVI,872
Kimball XVI,786
Levi XIV,112, 148, 195, 452, 532; XV,183
Morse XV,608
Moses XIV,413, 567, 611; XV, 717; XVI,202, 264, 286, 509, 696; XVII,430
Nathaniel XIV,400; XVI,113
Nicholas XIV,225
Orlando XIV,19; XVI,914
Rowell, XV,165
Salem XVI,58, 103, 202, 219, 501, 611
Samuel XIV,359; XV,470, 490; XVI,31, 187, 210, 270, 277
Simeon XIV,429; XV,273
Simon XV,267, 269-70, 273
Stephen XIV,316; XVI,238, 267, 868; XVII,438
Theophilus XIV,332, 350, 617; XV,457, 719, 747; XVI,203, 226, 271, 520, 838
Thomas XIV,350; XVI,125, 257, 514
Thomas Jr. XVI,125
William XIV,348, 559, 561, 579, 621; XV,455, 725; XVI, 208, 511, 725
Zebediah XIV,463, 571, 579, 604
Zebulon XV,453-54, 715;

Colby, Zebulon (Cont.) XVII, 65,
113
Colcord, David XIV,232
Eliphalet XV,243, 245-46
Isaac XIV,597; XV,435
Job XV,284, 288
John XIV,134, 191, 554, 617;
XV,283, 290; XVI,4; XVII,
5, 268
Jonathan XVI,766
Joseph XIV,232; XV,284,
288
Josiah XIV,232
Samuel XVII,57, 642
Thomas XIV,495, 508, 516;
XV, 475, 494; XVI,155
Colcot, David XVII,26
Edward XVII,7
Joseph XVII,26
Josiah XVII,26
Cole, Abraham XVII,528, 623
Adam XIV,342, 349
Ambrose XIV,188; XV,722;
XVI,205
Benjamin XVI,153
Ebenezer XIV,237; XVII,97
Eli XIV,664
Eliphalet XV,228; XVI, 238,
267, 516, 784
Gale XIV,105; XV,602;
XVI,178-179
John XIV,43, 84, 102, 199,
259; XV,47, 49, 520; XVI,
153; XVII,37, 94
Jonathan XV,49, 223; XVII,
94
Nathan XIV,244; XV,72, 213
Noah XIV,664; XV,431
Robert XIV,372, 385, 506,
517
Samuel XIV,648, 650;
XV,279-280, 592, 595
Solomon XIV,53, 185, 587,
628; XV,443, 720;
XVI,124, 204, 331, 341,
374

Cole, Tobias XV,295, 468, 481,
507; XVI,119, 237, 245,
272, 521, 836
William XIV,259, 664;
XV,431; XVII,36
Colefax, Robert XVII,23, 31, 39
Coleman, Eleazer XVI,905
James XIV,234, 371, 384,
496, 505, 516-17
John XIV,10; XVII,694-95,
698
Plato XVI,61, 63, 72, 94, 106
William Jr. XVII,695
Colfax, Robert XIV,255
Colgrove, Jeremiah XIV,5
Colket, Thomas XIV,388
Coll, Samuel XIV,8
Collar, Nathaniel XV,225
Colley, Edward XVI,720, 724
Collier, G. XVII,343
Colliers, Nathaniel XIV,7
Collins, Benjamin XIV,172, 174,
176-77, 611; XV, 718;
XVI,632;
Charles XIV,224; XV,322,
342
Daniel XIV,101, 206-7;
XV,177, 560, 742
Ebenezer XIV,171, 174, 176-
77, 328, 576, 611;
XV,608, 717
Enoch XV,321, 340
Ephraim XIV,279, 288
Ichabod XIV,279, 288; XVI,
314; XVII,116
James XVII,293
John XIV,108, 122, 187, 265,
307, 369, 375, 482, 498,
502, 511, 518, 623;
XV,441, 618, 720;
XVI,638; XVII,297
Jonathan XIV,112, 147, 196;
XV,560
Levi XIV,279, 288
Richard XIV,159, 161, 163
Robert XV,400-1; XVI,285,

Collins, Robert (Cont.) 875, 935;
    XVII,438
  Samuel XVI,67, 78, 100
  Solomon XIV,74
  Stephens XVII,293
  Thomas XVI,42, 54
  William XIV,226
  William Jr. XIV,340
Collor, Nathaniel XVI,153
Colombon, Glaude XIV,662; XV,
    451, 453, 455, 729;
    XVI,28, 728
Colomy, John XVI,282, 756
  Richard XIV,322, 365, 581,
    624; XV,441, 449, 601,
    720; XVI,758
Colony, Richard XVI,204
Colster, Reuben XIV,632
Colston, Richard XIV,227, 257
Colter, Job XIV,543
Colton, Caleb XIV,274-75, 278,
    289; XV,156
  Job XV,17, 138
  Lemuel XV,376; XVI,178-79
  Stephen XV,156
  Thomas XVII,32
  William XVI,17
Combner, John XVII,295
Combs, John XVII,63
  Medad XVII,63
Comel, Ebenezer XIV,141, 192
Comfort, John XIV,10
  Samuel XVII,633, 679
Comings, Abraham XV,734
  Benjamin XIV,394
  Ebenezer XVI,28
Commings, Benjamin XVII,143
Comstock, Azariah XIV,645;
    XVI, 22, 809
  Azariah Jr. XIV,356
  Josiah XIV,646; XV,732;
    XVI,21
  Moses XIV,356; XVI,927
Conant, Abel XV,510, 744
  Amos XV,27; XVI,606, 608
  Ebenezer XVI,608

Conant, Jonathan XIV,104, 422,
    607-8; XV,603, 714;
    XVI,200
  Joshua XV,201
  Josiah XV,510
  Roger XV,6
  Rufus XV,379
  Rev. William XVI,315
Condon, Solomon XIV,259
Cone, Jonathan XV,124, 381
Coney, Arthur XIV,437
Conn, Daniel XV,457
  Thomas XIV,85
Conneck, James XV,745
  William XIV,572, 590
Connell, Timothy XVII,721
  William XIV,609
Connelly, Hugh XVII,297
Conner, Eliphalet XV,587
  John T. XV,608, 717
  Joseph XV,619
Connerly, William XIV,194
Connet, William XIV,419
Connick, Abraham XVII,719
  John XV,209
  Robert XVI,259; XVII,436
  William XV,613, 714; XVI,84,
    90, 106, 200
Connor, B. XVII,57
  Benjamin XIV,400; XVII,27,
    43
  Edward XVII,302
  Eliphalet XIV,70, 179, 302,
    359; XV,267, 269-70, 272,
    696, 698; XVI,255, 501,
    604
  Henry XVI,143
  Jeremiah XIV,12, 68, 180,
    249, 410; XVI,918; XVII,
    57
  John XIV,588; XVII,57
  John T. XIV,172, 174, 176-
    77, 567, 611; XVI,202,
    694
  Joseph XIV,61, 182, 430, 618
  Levi XIV,24

Connor, Moses XIV,50, 185,
315; XVII, 760
Philip XV,392
Samuel XIV,24, 242, 339,
403, 414, 630; XV,415,
456; XVII, 19-20, 57, 69
Simeon XVII,91
Timothy XIV,3, 13; XVII,719
Tristram XVI,5, 514
See also Conner
Conra, John XV,614
Samuel XV,614
Conroy, John XIV,631
John Jr. XVI,689
Samuel XIV,33; XV,745
Stephen XIV,631; XV,88; XVI,
84, 90, 106
Conton, Thomas XIV,419
Converse, Robert XV,102, 218
Samuel D. XV,58, 224
Conway, Thomas XVII,197-98,
213, 217-18
Cook, Abraham XVI,913
Andrew XVI,538
Barnabas XIV,10
Charles XV,152, 154, 727,
734; XVI,10, 43, 103, 183,
196, 208
Daniel XIV,127, 188, 234,
322, 624; XV,619, 725;
XVI,45, 103, 192, 207-8,
213, 225, 230, 241, 301,
523, 817-18; XVII,11, 29
Daniel Jr. XIV,322; XVI,818
David XVI,279
Ebenezer XIV,322, 562, 636;
XV,134, 172, 226, 618,
724, 741; XVI,207, 230,
275, 503, 624
James XIV,427; XV,55, 204
John XIV,10, 360, 396-97,
588, 623; XV,618, 632,
636, 720; XVI,204, 230,
272, 516, 526, 608, 624,
789-91, 932
Joshua XVI,314
Josiah XV,28

Cook, Lot XVI,122, 164
Matthias XVI,932
Michael XVI,930
Nicholas XVI,809
Oliver XIV,324, 464; XV,9,
144, 371, 426; XVI,312,
606; XVII,249
Paul XIV,618; XV,443, 618,
634, 649, 723; XVI,102,
206, 231, 274, 503, 617,
624-25; XVII,435
Peter XIV,13; XV,628, 640;
XVI,816; XVII,435
Richard XV,629, 648, 731,
735; XVI,37-38, 196, 212,
232, 241, 278, 506, 649,
818
Samuel XIV,236, 317, 320
Seth XVI,932
Sylvanus XV,3; XVI,153, 811
Thomas XIV,7, 223, 372,
385, 496, 505, 517, 562,
636; XV,149, 160, 444,
618, 724; XVI,207, 230,
275, 503, 624
Uriah XVI,153
William XIV,469, 573, 613;
XV, 435, 616, 712;
XVI,198, 222, 513, 746
Zack XIV,330
Zuriel XVI,81, 95
Cooke, Elisha XVII,724
John XVII,486
Nicholas XV,238, 462
Cookery, Joseph XIV,9
Cool, Tobias XV,507
Cooledge, Silas XIV,50, 186,
302-3, 312, 572, 589, 633
Coolen, Thomas XVI,929
Cooley, Edward XV,630
John XIV,279, 288, 362, 365;
XV,173
Jonathan XV,565
Coolidge, Silas XV,611, 723
See also Cooledge
Coombs, Francis XV,628, 645,
732; XVI,40, 190, 192,

Coombs, Francis (Cont.) 212,
    232, 237, 271, 279, 520,
    523, 844-46
  James XV,518
  John XIV,336, 573, 613, 642;
    XV,456, 616, 711, 732,
    735, 744; XVI,19, 41, 194,
    198, 213, 279, 286, 520,
    845
  Medad XIV,95, 204-5, 337,
    700
  Samuel XIV,10
  William XV,85
Cooper, Aaron XVII,97
  Daniel XIV,236
  Elijah XIV,84, 199
  George XIV,583, 653;
    XV,729, 734 XVI, 30, 33,
    59, 187, 189, 210, 219,
    277, 501, 600; XVII,132
  Jacob XIV,248
  Joel XV,16, 156; XVII,110,
    143
  John XIV,471, 586, 662;
    XV,16, 138, 718, 742;
    XVI,202, 219, 270, 517,
    796; XVII,89
  Jonathan XV,667, 691;
    XVI,285, 517, 797
  Joseph XV,427, 733; XVI,47,
    101, 195, 213, 303
  Mary XVI,796
  Moses XVI,285, 517, 797
  Nathaniel XV,11, 368,
  Parker XIV,112, 146, 195
  Philip XIV,497, 648-49; XV,
    595, 728; XVI,12, 192,
    209, 803
  Sherman XV,43, 156;
    XVI,178-179; XVII,143
  Thomas XVII,628
  William XIV,242, 380, 383,
    489; XVII,2, 20
Copeland, Gideon XVI,13
  Jacob XIV,436, 524; XVI,441;
    XVI,840
  Samuel XV,106-7, 369, 537

Copp, Aaron XIV,587, 656;
    XV,731, 743
  David XIV,19, 108, 122, 187,
    232, 234, 243, 251, 253,
    258, 343, 617; XV,443,
    618, 722
  Ebenezer XIV,77, 81, 198
  Joseph XIV,586-87, 656; XV,
    328, 731, 749; XVII,424
  Josiah XV,343, 486, 499-500
  Moses XIV,587, 628; XV,721
  Samuel XIV,321, 465
  William XIV,546
Copps, Aaron XVI,35, 38, 320-
    21, 323, 326, 328, 330,
    335, 337, 339, 343, 345,
    375, 914
  David XVI,206, 231, 273,
    504, 639-40, 863, 914;
    XVII,28, 45
  Ebenezer XVI, 914-15
  John XVI,918
  Joseph XVI,37-38, 212
  Joshua XVI,409
  Moses XVI,156
Corbet, Abraham XVII,511-14
Corbett, Josiah XV,120, 183,
    408, 515; XVI,247, 254
Corbit, Josiah XIV,186
Corey, Ephraim XV,745
  Hezekiah XIV,33; XV,92
  Isaac XV,40, 155; XVII,144
  Morris XVII,301
  Nathaniel XVI,310
  Simeon XIV,394; XVII,88
  Timothy XV,15
Corliss, Daniel XIV,349
  Elihu XIV,64, 186; XV,43;
    XVII, 3, 143
  Elisha XIV,181; XV,155
  Emerson XIV,53, 185;
    XV,228, 391
  James XV,390
  Jeremiah XVI,870
  Joseph XIV,348
  Samuel XIV,433
  Timothy XVI,872

Corliss, William XV,586
Cornell, Colonel XV,238
  Ebenezer XV,747
  General XV,239
Cornwall, Robert XVI,85, 100,
  106, 195
Corse, John XVII,205
Corser, Asa XV,185
  David XV,186
  Elijah XIV,182
  Esau XIV,61
  Jonathan XV,186
  Nathan XV,128, 187
  Samuel XIV,60, 182
  Simeon XVI,147
  William XIV,61; XV,187,
    754
Corson, Aaron XIV,25; XVII,29
  Ebenezer XIV,245; XV,295;
    XVI,627
  Joshua XIV,244; XVII,29
  Samuel XIV,2; XVI,898-99,
    913
  Timothy XIV,245, 369, 374,
    482, 502, 511, 518;
    XVII,29
Cortling, Michael XVII,295
Cosden, Jesse XVII,203
Cossin, Thomas XIV,15
Cossit, Ambrose XVI,609
Coste, Joseph XIV,662;
    XV,451, 453, 455, 729;
    XVI,724
Coster, Bishop XIV,604;
    XV,453-454, 715;
    XVI,112, 201, 722
  Joseph XV,729; XVI,28
Coston, Ebenezer XIV,424; XV,
    56; XVI, 285, 506, 733;
    XVII,258, 427
Cote, Samuel XVI,13
Cotter, Enos XVI,167
  Jonathan XIV,12
  William XVI,194
Cottle, William XIV,314
Cotton, Benjamin XIV,66, 180,
    469, 580, 602; XV,447,

Cotton, Benjamin (Cont.) 598,
    610, 712; XVI,198, 222,
    268, 499, 580, 659
  Caleb XV,40; XVII,144
  Job XIV,445
  John XV,487, 489; XVI,257,
    506; XVII, 27, 479-84,
    487, 494
  Joseph Jr. XIV,239
  Luther XV,27, 680
  Lydia XVI,660
  Samuel XIV,227, 257, 472,
    552, 591; XVI,2;
    XVII,266
  Seaborn XVII,528, 608
  Solomon XVII,648, 693, 749
  Stephen XVII,144
  Thomas XIV,404, 535
  Thomas Jr. XIV,450
  William XIV,13, 280, 288,
    642; XV,458, 465, 730,
    735; XVI,514, 774-75;
    XVII, 139, 511, 513,
    633, 693, 727
Couch, Benjamin XIV,77,
    81, 198
  James XVII,674
  John XIV,122
Coughlan, Richard XIV,199
Courser, Asa XIV,182
  Samuel XIV,429
  Thomas XIV,316, 319
  William XIV,182, 316, 319
  See also Corser
Courson, Ebenezer XIV,234
  Joshua XIV,234
Coussens, Enoch XIV,238
Coval, Peter XIV,326
Covel, Joseph XVI,167, 793
Coventry, Secretary XVII,520
Coverley, Nathaniel XVI,281
  Philip XV,575
Cowan, Isaac XIV,87, 200
  Thomas XV,85, 518
  William XIV,336, 631;
    XV,85, 207, 614, 744;
    XVI,135, 247, 251, 498

Cowden, Heber XVI,81, 95
Cowdry, John XIV,573, 613;
    XV, 434, 616, 711;
    XVI,198, 513, 746, 934
Cowell, Ichabod XVII,29
    Thomas XVII,611
    William XVII,62
Cowle, Silas XVII,307
Cowles, Amos XVI,607
    Timothy XVI,607
Cowsins, Josiah XIV,6
Cox, D. Powell XVII,205
    Edward XIV,348
    James XVII,298
    John XIV,177, 348, 576
    Thomas XIV,171, 174, 176-
    77
    William XIV,9
Coy, Daniel XVI,308-9
Craber, Francis XVI,509, 695
Crafford, Jonathan XVII,65
Craft, James XV,749
Craggin, Benjamin XV,219;
    XVI, 855; XVII,100, 135
    Francis XV,95, 364;
    XVII,100
    James XVI,930-31
    John XIV,35; XV,364;
    XVII,102
    John Jr. XV,95; XVI,854,
    857; XVI,860; XVII, 135
Cragin, Benjamin XIV,35;
    XV,196
Craig, Alexander XIV,441,
    463; XVI,820-21
    Andrew XVI,898, 903
    Captain XVI,902
    James XIV,566; XVI,31, 33,
    41, 59, 190
    John XIV,566; XVI,31, 33,
    59, 187
    Robert XIV,579; XVI,723,
    725, 898
Craige, Alexander XIV,348;
    XVII, 66
    Andrew XIV,280, 288
    David XIV,280, 288

Craige, James XIV,654; XV,606,
    609, 732; XVI,213
    John XIV,304-5, 465-66,
    654; XV,606, 609, 729;
    XVI,210
    John Jr. XVI,859
    Robert XIV,635; XV,454,
    724; XVI,206, 229, 274,
    510
Cram, Asa XIV,43, 96, 204
    Benjamin XIV,12; XV,189,
    475, 494
    Captain XV,695
    Daniel XIV,89, 459, 539;
    XV, 118, 138, 350, 352,
    554; XVI,140, 161
    Dudley XV,699; XVI,61, 63,
    71, 92, 106
    Ebenezer XIV,244; XV,211;
    XVI, 885
    Elijah XIV,23
    Ephraim XVI,531
    Ezekiel XV,113
    Humphrey XIV,639; XV,731;
    XVI, 15, 25, 186, 211,
    883, 885
    Jacob XVI,728
    John XIV,261; XV,300, 302,
    304, 308; XVI,885
    John Jr. XIV,417
    Jonathan XIV,65, 180;
    XV,411, 419; XVI,676,
    882; XVII,643
    Jonathan Jr. XVI,259
    Joseph XIV,244, 417, 503;
    XV, 300, 301, 306-7,
    309, 413; XVI,649, 651
    Reuben XIV,354; XV,300,
    302, 306, 309
    Samuel XIV,370, 378, 492,
    503; XIV,515; XV,563;
    XVI,155, 806
    Samuel P. XV,283, 290
    Smith XVI,68, 79, 97
    Thomas XIV,425
    Tristram XV,267, 269-71
    Wadley, XIV,454, 529, 546

Cram, Zebulon XV,211, 529;
   XVI,145, 885
Crane, Abiah XV,3
   Abiel XIV,427
   Colonel XV,707, 753;
      XVII,290
   Francis XVI,81
   John XVI,45, 597
   Jonathan XVII,436
   Obadiah XV,65
   Samuel XVI,82, 92, 106
   Zebulon XIV,265, XV,12,
      367
Cranfield, Edward XVII,502,
      563, 564, 567-86, 588-
      602, 612
Crapp, John XVII,295
Crary, John XV,383
Crater, Francis XV,631, 638
Craw, Jonathan XV,376
Crawford, Alexander XIV,223
   John XIV,566, 654; XV,606,
      609, 729; XVI,31, 59
   John Jr. XIV,566
   Jonathan XIV,167, 170,
      441, 463, 527; XV,160;
      XVI,928; XVII,14, 65
   Robert XIV,163, 226, 304-
      5, 465-66, 601; XV,460,
      605, 712
   Thomas XIV,166, 170;
      XV,149, 160; XVI,914;
      XVII,14
   William XIV,16; XV,52
Creighton, James XIV,352,
      562-563, 637; XV,444,
      724
   John XVII,294
   Stephen XVII,57
   Thomas XIV,110, 131, 190,
      350, 628; XV,441, 457,
      721; XVI, 116, 648
Cressey, Aaron XVI,153
   Andrew XIV,459, 539; XV,
      350, 352
   Barnabas XVI,916

Cressey, Benjamin XV,631,
      638; XVI,44, 102, 237,
      268, 509, 695-96
   Daniel XIV,51, 185, 567,
      611; XV,608, 717;
      XVI,202
   Henry XV,52
   Jonathan XIV,427; XV, 669,
      680; XVI,602; XVII,255
   Jonathan Jr. XV,52
   Michael XV,53, 59-60, 651;
      XVI,602-3; XVII,264
   Richard XIV,46, 75, 179
Crimball, Abraham XIV,551
   Robert XIV,370, 415, 493,
      551
Crison, Nathaniel XVI,23
   Thomas XV,63
Crisson, Nathan XIV,646
Cristie, William XV,350, 352
Critchett, Benjamin XIV,569,
      592; XV,438, 609, 717;
      XVI, 103, 202, 223,
      271, 518, 849
   Elias XIV,362, 624; XV,619,
      720; XVI,67, 78, 93, 204,
      711; XVII,24, 719
   Elias Jr. XVII,719
   James XIV,372, 385, 496,
      505, 517
   John XIV,618; XV,443, 618,
      723; XVI,66, 77, 93,
      155, 206, 627-28
   Richard XIV,388, 494, 507,
      516, 519
   Thomas XV,171
Crocker, Gershom XV,4
   Dr. John XVII,465
Crockett, Benjamin XIV,12,
      246, 296; XV,325
   Joshua, XVI,742
   Solomon XIV,233; XVII,24
   Thomas XIV,3; XVII,522
Croge, John XVII,301
Crombie, Hugh XIV,61, 182,
      299

64

Crombie, James XIV,35, 420,
   422, 554, 634; XV,725;
   XVI,5, 321, 330, 335,
   338, 376; XVII, 267
  Jonathan XIV,414
Cromey, John XIV,17
Crommell, Benjamin XIV,3, 14
  Ebenezer XIV,369, 483
  Samuel XV,468
Crommet, Ebenezer XIV,617;
   XV, 618, 723; XVI,206,
   273, 504
  Eliphalet XIV,621
  James XIV,21, 623; XV,725;
   XVI,207
  John XVII,719
  Moses XIV,308
  Philip XIV,21, 564, 623,
   626; XV,701, 726;
   XVI,175
  Samuel XV,480, 507
  Thomas XV,311-13
Cromwell, Ebenezer XIV,376,
   502, 511, 518
  Eliphalet XIV,560; XV,619,
   722
  Jacob XVII,367
  Joseph XVII,175
  Richard XVII,507
  Silvanus XIV,230, 314;
   XVII,28
Crook, Andrew XV,277;
   XVII,253
  Charles XIV,159, 161, 163;
   XVII,253
  Samuel XV,383; XVII,253
  Thomas XIV,159, 161, 163;
   XVII,253
Crosbie, Anthony XIV,11
  Jonathan XIV,226, 402,
   641; XVI,744
  Joseph XVI,744
  Josiah XVI,392
Crosby, Alpheus XV,664, 670,
   682; XVI,83, 193, 556;
   XVII, 339
  Daniel XIV,342

Crosby, Ezekiel XVI,98
  John XIV,551
  Jonathan XV,423, 597, 730;
   XVI,18, 281
  Joseph XVI,282
  Josiah XIV,38, 78, 102-3,
   155, 207-8; XV,68, 72,
   520-21; XVI,749
  Paul XVI,259; XVII,436
  Stephen XIV,102, 207;
   XV,72, 214, 520, 662,
   668, 682; XVI,83, 94,
   550
  Thomas XIV,317, 320, 365
  William XIV,244; XV,72,
   214
Crosden, William XVI,519, 825
Cross, Abiel XIV,411; XVII,32
  Benjamin XIV,227, 257,
   648-49; XV,595, 728;
   XVI,12, 60, 63, 71, 95,
   192, 209, 803; XVII,
   383
  Daniel XIV,353, 657;
   XV,150, 284, 287, 460,
   606, 732; XVI,37, 40,
   115, 190, 213, 228,
   279, 288, 505, 519, 820
  Daniel E. XIV,167, 274
  David XIV,104; XV,33;
   XVI,264
  Ephraim XIV,567, 611;
   XV,608, 718; XVI,203
  John XIV,104, 594; XV,9,
   130, 143, 179, 446,
   716; XVI, 143, 201,
   221, 241, 270, 502,
   597; XVII,91, 249, 502,
   622, 643, 648, 669,
   682, 694
  Joseph XV,69, 206
  Moses XIV,316, 319;
   XVI,63, 73, 97
  Nathan XV,664, 670, 682;
   XVI, 259, 715, 921;
   XVII,339, 436
  Nathaniel XVII,57

Cross, Peter XV,517, 519;
    XVI,237, 243, 519, 825
    Ralph XIV,431; XVI,578
    Ralph Jr. XIV,429
    Shubael XIV,269-70, 289,
      291; XV,277
    Thomas XVI,87, 90, 203,
      224, 259; XVII,436
    Timothy XV,10, 368;
      XVI,80, 91
    William XIV,227, 257
Crossfield, John XVI,34
    Timothy XIV,645-46;
      XV,732, 752; XVI,20,
      22, 191
Crosson, Asa XV,633, 648;
    XVI, 38, 185, 188, 213,
    228, 279, 519, 810;
    XVII,449
    Benjamin XVI,38
Croston, William XIV,54, 156-
    57
Crowder, John XVII,644
Crown, John XIV,391, 487
    William XIV,307, 322;
      XV,701, 703, 725;
      XVI,46, 175, 303
Crummet, Ebenezer XVI,639
    James XV,618; XVII,367
    Moses XVI,637
    Philip XV,703; XVI,46,
      302, 913
    See also Crommet
Cruson, Nathan XVII,98
    Thomas XVII,98
Cruther, Stephen XIV,477
Cseaina, Francis XVII,306
Cumings, Benjamin XV,744
    Peter XV,734
    Philip XV,744
Cummings, Abraham XIV,659;
    XV, 597, 727, 734;
    XVI,10, 316
    Andrew XIV,143, 194;
      XVI,749; XVII,9
    Benjamin XIV,33, 529;
      XV,15, 155; XVII,88

Cummings, David XV,70, 346
    Ebenezer XIV,573, 651;
      XV,613, 729; XVI,85,
      100, 106, 194
    Eleazer XIV,34, 242
    Elisha XIV,317, 320, 365
    Enoch XIV,92, 202-3, 355;
      XV, 63
    Ephraim XV,63, 204
    Isaac XIV,65, 182, 186;
      XVII,4
    John XIV,32; XV,743;
      XVI,921
    John Jr. XVI,921
    Jonathan XIV,417
    Joseph XV,63
    Jotham XIV,166, 168, 170;
      XVI, 800
    Larned XIV,391, 487, 508,
      513
    Nathaniel XIV,203
    Nehemiah XIV,92, 202;
      XV,63; XVI,487
    Reuben XIV,336, 696;
      XV,744; XVII,62
    Richard XVII,527
    Samuel XIV,355; XV,744
    Silas XV,521
    Simeon XV,85
    William XIV,438, 527, 545;
      XV, 89, 346, 517;
      XVI,693
Cunningham, Alexander XVI,
    141, 161
    Andrew XIV,179
    Archibald XV,200
    Daniel XIV,421
    David XIV,463; XV,705-6,
      708-9; XVI,586; XVII,66
    James XV,538
    John XIV,336; XV,729;
      XVI,28, 188, 210;
      XVII,63
    R. XV,712
    Robert XIV,51, 185, 572,
      603; XV,435, 612, 712,
      753; XVI, 85, 100, 106,

Cunningham, Robert (Cont.)
195, 199, 236, 268, 511,
716, 911
Robert Jr. XIV,572, 603;
XV, 612
Samuel XV,101, 197, 219,
538, 540; XVI,792, 794
Cunnit, Caleb XIV,7
Curey, Thomas XVI,264, 595
Curnell, Ebenezer XIV,115
Currier, Abner XV,35
Abraham XVI,237, 268, 509,
696
Benjamin XIV,454, 546;
XV,525
Daniel XV,267, 270-71
David XIV,76, 81, 198,
262; XV,169, 602
Dudley XIV,225, 405;
XV,390
Ebenezer XIV,391, 487,
509, 531; XVI,285, 501,
531; XVII,24
Edward XV,465, 467, 478,
505; XVI,66, 77, 97,
286, 517
Ephraim XIV,19
Ezra XV,322-23, 331, 335,
337, 341, 592
Gideon XIV,327
Henry XV,183
Isaac XV,284, 287
James XVI,178-79
John XIV,52, 184; XV,746;
XVI, 914
Jonathan XIV,16, 61, 66,
181-182, 304-5, 429,
614; XV, 267-69, 271,
602, 714, 754; XVI,300
Joseph XIV,261; XV,549
Moses XV,15, 39, 249-51,
254
Peter XV,155; XVII,144
Reuben XIV,169; XV,180;
XVI,148
Richard XV,321, 340

Currier, Samuel XIV,87, 201,
424; XV, 116, 120, 267,
269, 272
Sargent XIV,430, 455, 530,
580, 660; XV,447, 598,
727; XVI,11, 43, 209
Theophilus XV,748
Thomas XIV,342, 348, 362,
365, 580, 587, 624,
628; XV,441, 447, 598,
720; XVI,204, 233, 272,
506, 659
Timothy XIV,225, 341
William XV,268, 270, 273
Curry, John XIV,143, 193-94;
XVII,8
Thomas XV,179, 512;
XVII,430
Curtice, Ebenezer XVI,498
Isaac XIV,477, 545; XV,72,
214, 698
Jacob XIV,207, 545; XV,72
Lemuel XIV,260, 477;
XV,215
Stephen XIV,266; XV,213
Curtis, Daniel XVI,125
Ebenezer XVI,247, 251, 498
Isaac XVI,84
John XVI,22, 81, 886
Jonathan XV,18, 375
Joshua XV,375
Lemuel XVI,325
Nathaniel XV,434, 602
Noah XVI,810-11
Samuel XVI,310
Stephen XVI,94
Thomas XV,3; XVI,152
Timothy XV,717; XVI,712
Curtiss, Abel XVII,153
Amariah XIV,427
Captain XVII,377, 380
Isaac XIV,439, 527
Isaac P. XIV,266
Israel XVII,76
Jacob XIV,102, 439, 527;
XV, 213

Curtiss, James XVI,288-92;
    XVII,78-79
    John XIV,645; XVII,96, 468
    Joseph XV,41
    Nathaniel XIV,578, 596
    Samuel XV,74
    Timothy XIV,160-61, 163,
        288, 464, 578, 592;
        XVII,16
    William XIV,173, 176-77,
        463; XVII,65, 293
Curwin, Captain XVII,509
Cushing, Daniel XIV,114, 141,
    193, 406; XV,295, 574;
    XVI, 627; XVII,261
    Dr. John XVI,359
    Jonathan XVI,907
    Mr. XVII,245
    Thomas XIV,406; XV,295;
        XVI, 627-28; XVII,124
    William XIV,353; XV,284,
        287, 748; XVI,67, 76,
        98, 288, 503, 650;
        XVII,424-25
Cushman, Ambrose XIV,544
    Eleazer XV,591; XVI,310
    Solomon XV,426, 584-85,
        591-92; XVI,307, 310-11
Cutler, Benjamin XV,15
    Betty XVI,582
    Hodges XVI,150; XVII,144
    James XVII,101
    Knights XVI,178-79
    Moses XVI,236
    Nathan XV,533
    Niles XVII,144
    Richard XIV,52
    Solomon XV,98; XVII,100,
        102
    Thomas XVI,84
    Toby XVI,236, 273, 518,
        815
    William XIV,274-75, 278,
        289, 565, 635; XV, 373,
        442, 724; XVI,206, 229,
        274, 499, 582

Cutt, John XIV,372, 384, 496,
    505, 516-17; XVII,512,
    527, 537, 539, 547, 549,
    551, 556, 646, 693
    John Jr. XVII,527
    Richard XVII,512
    S. XIV,315
    Samuel XVII,667, 669
Cutter, Dr. Ammi Ruhamah
    XVII, 139, 326
    Benjamin XIV,90, 201, 420;
        XV, 536; XVI,854
    Doctor XIV,45
    Hodges XV,156
    James XIV,36; XVI,536
    John XIV,421; XV,93
    Jonas XV,437; XVI,536
    Jonathan XIV,34
    Joseph XVI,536
    Knight XV,138, 155
    Moses XVI,159, 270, 509,
        699
    Nathan XV,21; XVI,535
    Niles XV,16
    Richard XIV,185; XV,346,
        483
    Samuel XVI,923
    Seth XIV,42; XV,206
    Thomas XVI,100
Cutting, Daniel XVI,738
    Jonas XIV,55, 604; XV,715;
        XVI,575
    Joseph XIV,476
    Moses XIV,6
    Thomas XIV,183
Cutts, Samuel XVI,925-26
Cuyler, Cornelius XVII,234
    Jacob XVII,234
Cypher, John XIV,43, 58
            D
Daby, Thomas XV,57
Dady, Timothy XVII,307
Dagee, David XVII,14
Daggett, Asa XV,668, 680;
    XVI, 876; XVII,255
    Nathaniel XV,7

Daggett, Simeon XIV,356;
XV,47, 224
Dailey, Daniel XIV,259, 344
Darby XIV,257-58, 344;
XVII,30
Daily, London XV,631, 650,
721; XVI,102, 205, 226,
239, 273, 505, 658-59
Dakin, Amos XIV,528; XV,346;
XVI,740-41
Amos Jr. XV,81
Joshua XVI,932
Justus XV,69, 206
Dale, John XIV,244, 417;
XV,419; XVI,885
Timothy XVI,882, 885;
XVII,436
Timothy Jr. XVI,259
Dalling, Samuel XVII,55
Thomas XVII,139
Dalton, Caleb XIV,42, 57;
XVI, 914
Isaac XVI,88, 90
John XIV,23
Michael XIV,248, 402, 415;
XVII,26
Moses XV,564
Samuel XIV,23, 604;
XV,716; XVI,201, 900;
XVII,528, 543, 547,
555, 608
Samuel Jr. XVII,528
Timothy XIV,11, 23, 118,
137, 192, 255, 351;
XVII,740
Tristram XVII,124
Dam, Abner XVI,907
Benjamin XIV,227, 257,
259, 472, 664; XVII,30,
433
Daniel XVI,898
Ebenezer XV,593
Edward XIV,664; XV,431
Ezra XVII,433
Hatevil XIV,259, 664;
XV,431

Dam, John XIV,24, 27, 235;
XV,256; XVII,22, 34, 501,
525
John Jr. XIV,12
Jonathan XIV,664; XV,431
Joseph XVI,93, 106
Joseph P. XVI,72
Levi XIV,231
Morris XIV,12
Moses XVII,737
Nathan XIV,664; XV,431
Samuel XIV,236; XVII,24
Thomas XIV,550
Volentine XVII,360
William XVII,648, 655-56
Dame, Benjamin XIV,118-19,
149, 197; XV,577, 583;
XVI,261; XVII,37
Ebenezer XVII,81-82
Edward XV,692
George XVII,139
Jabez XV,575; XVI,815,
817, 820; XVII,261
Jacob XV,715; XVI,269
John XV,259-60, 263; XVI,
118; XVII,527
Jonathan XV,298
Joseph P. XV,666, 678;
XVI, 61, 63, 72, 759
Samuel XIV,402, 408, 415;
XV, 572; XVII,29
Theodore XIV,280, 288,
291; XV,380
Theophilus XV,693, 695,
736; XVII,137
Thomas XV,430
Timothy XV,577, 583;
XVI,760
Valentine XV,325
Dameris, Samuel XIV,25
Daming, Samuel XIV,21
Damon, Barjonah XV,591
David XV,595
Martin XVII,249
Dana, William XV,14, 373,
378; XVII,111

Dancos, Joseph XVII,299
Dane, Daniel XVI,755
Danford, David XV,537
  Edward XIV,276; XVI,247,
    251, 499
  Elkanah XIV,144, 194;
    XV,186; XVII,9
  Ezekiel XIV,320, 365
  Henry XVI,243, 659
  Jedediah XVII,92
  Jonathan XV,173
  Joshua XIV,180, 276, 289,
    469, 701; XV,610, 700,
    702-3, 712, 725;
    XVI,46, 170, 172, 174,
    198, 208, 224, 240-41,
    268, 302, 499, 576-77
  Moses XIV,272, 290;
    XV,129; XVI,907; XVII,9
  Samuel XIV,276, 289, 605;
    XV, 607, 716; XVI,201,
    269
  Simeon XIV,186; XV,186
  Solomon XV,207
  Thomas XIV,269, 271, 290
  Thomas Jr. XV,173
  William XV,185; XVII,91
  Zebadiah XVI,928
Danforth, Abel XIV,96, 204
  David XV,106, 369
  Edward XIV,274; XVI,499
  Eleazer XIV,221
  Elkanah XIV,211, 217-20
  Ezekiel XIV,317
  Henry XVI,237, 243, 506
  Jacob XIV,33, 573; XV,614,
    750; XVI,84, 90
  Jedediah XIV,317, 319
  Jonathan XIV,95, 204;
    XV,133
  Joshua XIV,66, 273, 569;
    XVI, 500, 530, 563
  Moses XVI,234, 512, 726
  Samuel XIV,273
  Simeon XIV,63, 181;
    XV,129; XVI,926; XVII,3
  Solomon XV,85

Daniel, Eliphalet XVII,22,
  33, 35-36, 135
  John XVII,717
  Joseph XVII,719
  Joseph Jr. XVII,717
  Reuben XVII,36
  Samuel XV,249
  Thomas XVII,527, 543, 555,
    563, 568, 592
Daniels, Bartholomew XVI,83,
  96, 106
  David XIV,372, 384, 496,
    505, 517, 520
  Eliphalet XIV,240, 259,
    480, 663; XV,431, 433,
    594; XVI, 67, 78, 93;
    XVII,42, 75
  Ephraim XIV,372, 384, 497,
    506, 517
  Jacob XIV,238, 373, 386,
    497, 506, 517; XVI,525,
    904
  John XIV,646; XV,62;
    XVI,24, 131, 163
  John M. XVI,839
  Jonathan XIV,372, 385,
    497, 506, 517; XVI,904
  Joseph XIV,238, 373, 386,
    497, 506, 517; XV,747
  Nathaniel XIV,233, 341,
    659; XV,620, 727;
    XVI,9, 42; XVII,24
  Pelatiah XV,311
  Reuben XVII,31
  Samuel XIV,117, 129, 289,
    353, 451, 532, 616;
    XV,251-53, 719; XVI,
    203, 252, 505, 527, 790
  Solomon XV,249, 251-52,
    254; XVI,67, 78, 98
Danielson, Charles XV,747
  James XIV,114, 140, 193,
    234, 250, 321; XV,297,
    469, 481, 506; XVI,287,
    500
  Levi XIV,228; XVI,256, 500
Dapuh, Francis XVII,306

Darbee, Jonathan XV,383, 385
Darby,-- XV,584
  David XIV,84, 199
  Jonathan XVI,538, 924
  Lieutenant XVI,307
  Nathaniel XV,277; XVI,307;
    XVII,114
  Simeon XV,154; XVII,118-19
  See also Derby
Darling, Abraham XIV,341
  Benjamin B. XIV,430;
    XVI,696
  Eliakim XV,217
  John XIV,224, 340, 450;
    XV,55; XVII,32
  Moses XIV,50, 185, 301,
    390, 393, 486, 508,
    512; XV,548, 699
  Timothy XIV,96, 204;
    XV,548
  William XIV,64, 182, 186,
    430; XV,42
Darrah, Arthur XIV,411;
    XV,744
  James XVII,298
  Robert XIV,247
  William XIV,171, 174, 177,
    346, 468, 574; XV,614,
    711, 744; XVI,198, 224,
    716, 890; XVII,439
Darrock, Nego XV,602
Darrow, James XV,90
Dart, Jesse XV,3, 67
  Josiah XV,4, 67
  Justice XV,65
  Justus XIV,326, 463
  Roger XV,65, 741
  Thomas XV,65, 741; XVI,663
  Thomas Jr. XV,66
  Thomas 3d XV,66
Darte, Nathaniel XVII,97
  Roger XVII,96
Dascomb, James XV,211;
    XVI,882
Dassance, Jesse XV,741
Dastum, Nathaniel XIV,445

Daulton, John XIV,25
  Michael XIV,224
Davenport, Charles XV,632,
    636; XVI,556-57
  John XVII,24, 31, 39
  Mr. XVII,342
Daverson, John XVI,535
  Thomas XIV,259; XVII,37
  William XIV,252
Davey, Aaron XV,7
David, Job XIV,1
Davidson, Captain XIV,2
  Charles XV,664-65, 671,
    680; XVI,792
  Daniel XIV,351; XV,747
  David XIV,347
  George XVI,918
  James XV,358
  Jesse XV,228
  John XV,57
  Nathaniel XV,483, 497
  Thomas XV,21; XVI,159, 792
Davies, Ephraim XIV,618;
    XV,609
  Isaac XV,607
  John XIV,446, 617; XV,609,
    658
  Robert XV,589
  Samuel XV,587
  Samuel Jr. XV,587
Davis, Aaron XIV,235
  Abel XV,664, 671, 685,
    733; XVI,48, 143, 259,
    264, 297, 304-5, 313,
    745; XVII,116, 339, 436
  Abel Jr. XV,733; XVI,48,
    264, 304-5, 314;
    XVII,116
  Abner XIV,225, 397
  Amos XV,51, 486, 499-500
  Amos Jr. XIV,160-61, 164
  Andrew XV,99, 537; XVI,167
  Aquilla XIV,568, 654;
    XV,610, 729; XVI,31,
    34, 59, 187, 210
  Asa XIV,346-47; XV,69,

Davis, Asa (Cont.) 346; XVI,
696-97; XVII,60-61
Benjamin XIV,1, 36, 98,
102, 205, 208, 225;
XV,18, 138, 374; XVI,
264, 528, 557, 559,
562, 728, 909; XVII,67,
430
Bezaleel XV,41; XVII,109
Briant XIV,18
Captain XVII, 710
Clement XIV,233; XVII,25
Daniel XIV,2, 15, 258,
344, 485; XV,674;
XVII,87, 253, 717
David XIV,99, 170, 205,
408, 447, 540; XV,267,
269-71, 311, 597, 656,
665-66, 673, 685;
XVI,638; XVII,14, 657,
719
Dudley XIV,108, 408;
XV,298
Ebenezer XV,204; XVII,100
Edmond XVII,139
Edmund XIV,58, 183, 254,
404; XVI,633, 678
Edward XVII,306
Elijah XIV,34, 90, 201,
321; XV,21, 92; XVI,96
Elisha XVI,68, 79
Enoch XIV,255, 344;
XVII,39
Ephraim XIV,227, 257, 316,
319, 569; XV,723;
XVI,206, 726
Ezekiel XIV,84, 199, 572,
596; XV,612, 713
Ezra XV,48
Flint XVI,362
Francis XIV,315, 467, 548;
XV,165, 549; XVI,124
Gideon XV,85, 207
Henry XIV,99, 205; XVI,150
Ichabod XVII,57
Isaac XIV,61, 182, 304-5,
454, 465-66, 530, 546,

Davis, Isaac (Cont.) 567, 585,
659; XV,629, 642-43,
719, 727; XVI,9, 42, 203,
226, 272, 522, 576, 708,
865-66; XVII,95
Jabez XIV,234, 408
Jacob XIV,85, 199, 571;
XV, 249-51, 255, 699;
XVI,850; XVII,434
James XIV,3, 11-13, 15,
24, 363; XV,312, 754;
XVII,624, 642, 645,
654, 658,.693, 710, 719
James Jr. XIV,239;
XVII,716
Jeremiah XVI,283
Jesse XV,16; XVI,300
John XIV,12-13, 43, 61,
182, 233, 236, 258,
314, 316, 321, 340,
344, 540, 569, 601;
XV,312, 322, 341, 431,
443, 542, 560, 569, 619,
667, 679, 691, 712, 723;
XVI,64, 73, 94, 250, 256,
507, 670, 726, 897;
XVII,525, 717, 719
John Jr. XV,217
Jonas XV,51; XVII,95
Jonathan XIV,34, 113, 147,
196, 225, 235, 571; XV,
52, 93, 533, 699;
XVI,141, 155, 161,
262; XVII,95, 426
Joseph XIV,211, 215, 217,
219, 220, 249, 572,
597; XV,612, 713; XVI,
141, 161, 236, 243, 273,
501, 600; XVII,719, 728
Joshua XIV,346; XV,82;
XVII, 61, 719
Josiah XIV,34, 405;
XV,100, 343, 743, 754
Malachi XV,175
Matthew XV,471, 502
Micah XIV,25, 107, 188,
233, 250, 323, 361;

Davis, Micah (Cont.) XVII,24
    Michael XIV,122
    Morris XIV,12
    Morris Jr. XIV,14
    Moses XIV,134, 191, 570,
        624; XV,441, 564, 720;
        XVI,147, 204, 229, 272,
        513, 778, 781; XVII,7
    Moses XVII,717
    Nathan XIV,60, 182;
        XV,185, 515, 603, 714;
        XVI,200, 269; XVII,226,
        236
    Nathaniel XIV,607; XV,564
    Nehemiah XIV,226
    Nicholas XIV,280, 288
    Philip XV,749
    Phinehas XV,560
    Robert XIV,281, 285, 287
    Samuel XIV,15, 60, 118-19,
        150, 182, 196, 302, 316-
        18, 432, 563, 588, 626,
        648-49; XV,6, 51, 267,
        269, 271, 322, 342, 515,
        595, 623, 628-29, 640-41,
        718, 720, 728, 734, 754;
        XVI,12, 26, 60, 63, 71,
        90, 102, 111, 192, 202,
        204, 209, 219, 241, 270,
        283, 297, 507, 603, 664,
        671, 784; XVII, 349, 383,
        717
    Simon XIV,39, 98, 205;
        XV,98
    Stephen XIV,34, 314
    Theodore XIV,256
    Thomas XIV,14, 108, 123,
        187, 573, 613; XV,153,
        616, 711; XVI,198, 259,
        922; XVII, 253, 302,
        436, 625, 628-30, 717
    Thomas Jr. XV,154
    Timothy XIV,13, 123, 188,
        297; XVI,118, 555, 638;
        XVII, 692, 717
    Timothy Jr. XVII,729-30
    Webster XV,560

Davis, Wells XIV,64, 181, 186;
        XVII,4
    William XIV,8; XV,217;
        XVII, 431
    Winthrop XVI,287, 512
    Zachariah XV,346; XVI,740
    Zebulon XIV,232, 400;
        XV,175, 576; XVII,261
Davison, Benjamin XVII,306
Dawes, Abraham XVII,494-95
Dawling, Lawrence XVII,303
Daws, John XIV,85
Dawson, John XVI,307;
        XVII,114
Day, Abner XV,746
    Amos XV,63
    Benjamin XV,293, 541;
        XVI,850
    Daniel XIV,646; XV,446; XVI,
        23, 81, 95, 106, 193
    Ebenezer XV,4
    Enos XVI,152
    Isaac XIV,358
    John XV,41, 62
    Joseph XIV,227, 257-58,
        355, 549; XV,61;
        XVII,45
    Miss XVI,930
    Noah XV,216
    Othniel XV,55, 745
    Samuel XIV,302
    Solomon XIV,682
    Stephen XV,741
    William XIV,356; XV,750
Dayton, Colonel XVII,167, 181
Dealen, Daniel XIV,408
Dealing, Daniel XV,298
Dealons, William XVII,302
Dean, Benjamin W. XV,195
    Edward XVI,238, 509, 692
    Eliphalet XVI,116
    Hiram XV,744
    James XV,102, 740
    John XV,216; XVII,100
    Jonathan XVI,536
    Lemuel XIV,607-8; XV,714;
        XVI,200

Dean, Samuel XIV,223
  Thomas XVI,902; XVII,205
  William XV,541
Deane, James XV,218
  Lemuel XV,602
Deaner, Thomas XVII,302
Dearborn, Abner XV,730;
    XVI,18
  Abraham XVI,111
  Abraham Jr. XVI,844
  Asa XIV,328; XV,525
  Asel XVI,282
  Captain XVII,52
  Daniel XIV,403, 415
  Ebenezer XIV,11; XV,168;
    XVII, 740
  Edward XIV,114, 140, 192,
    298, 617; XV,300-1,
    305, 309, 618, 723
  Godfrey XVII,528
  Henry XIV,11, 68-69, 153,
    179, 210, 214, 216-18,
    220-21, 249, 474, 555,
    638; XV,421, 461, 494,
    562, 726; XVI,6, 11-12,
    51, 103, 182, 192, 193,
    196, 208, 248, 301,
    347, 367, 416, 454,
    525, 777, 780, 893;
    XVII,145, 210, 225,
    239, 269, 359, 446, 453
  James XIV,231, 236, 448,
    535; XV,256, 259-60,
    264
  Jeremiah XIV,232
  John XIV,11, 118, 137,
    144, 158, 192-94, 252,
    316, 319; XV,402, 411,
    422, 578; XVI, 127,
    162, 262, 774; XVII,9,
    432, 740-41
  John Jr. XV,422, 455
  John 3d XV,456
  Jonathan XIV,11, 410
  Joseph XIV,118, 137, 158,
    191, 242, 255, 317,
    327-28; XV, 525-26;

Dearborn, Joseph (Cont.) XVI,
    61-62, 72, 98, 106, 127,
    162, 193; XVII,360, 740
  Josiah XIV,253, 411, 450,
    534; XV,522; XVII,424
  Levi XIV,253, 415, 551;
    XV, 412, 578; XVI,775-
    76
  Dr. Levi XV,318, 331, 333,
    335, 337, 339, 509;
    XVI,448
  Levi Jr. XIV,403
  Michael XV,125
  Nathan XIV,144; XVI,705
  Nathaniel XIV,66, 181,
    194, 330; XV,180, 249-
    51, 255, 571; XVII,9
  Peter XVI,796
  Samuel XIV,11, 66, 118,
    137, 158, 191, 228-29,
    255, 551, 581; XV,169,
    423, 449, 456, 482-84,
    497, 600, 730; XVI, 17,
    531, 656, 774; XVII,
    360, 642, 667-68, 713,
    740
  Samuel Jr. XVII,740
  Samuel C. XIV,403
  Sherburne XIV,66, 181, 330;
    XVI,169; XVII,49
  Shubael XIV,143, 193-94,
    316, 319; XVII,9
  Simeon XIV,233; XV,191;
    XVI, 862-63
  Simeon Jr. XIV,564
  Simon XIV,68, 116, 128,
    242, 391, 399, 487,
    513; XV,410, 564, 728,
    734; XVI,27, 116;
    XVII,24
  Simon Jr. XIV,117, 129
  Stephen XV,162, 167, 170,
    235, 237
  Thomas XIV,11; XV,167,
    476, 748; XVI,587;
    XVII,619, 642, 644-46
Dearing, Ebenezer XIV,239,

Dearing, Ebenezer (Cont.) 255,
  260, 267, 368, 484, 511,
  518; XVI,234, 264, 283,
  378, 527, 619; XVII,23,
  31, 38, 46-47, 49-50, 85-
  87, 284, 383, 421, 466
  Elliot XIV,255, 484, 500,
    512; XVII,31, 39, 85
  Joseph XIV,237
  Mr. XIV,45
  William XIV,240, 484, 499,
    512; XVII,85
De Borre, General XVII,154,
  156, 161-72, 178-91
DeCannon, William XVI,205,
  273, 510, 517, 725, 794
Deck, Jacob XVII,302
Dedois, Joseph XIV,662;
  XV,597
Dego, Peter XIV,308
Degroaf, John XVI,932
  John Jr. XVI,932
Delancy, Thomas XIV,624
Delano, Abishi XV,25
  Gideon XV,29, 368
  Nathan XIV,265
Delanoe, Phillip XVII,669
Delap, James XV,635
Delelance, Delevarne XV,65
Delil, John XVII,304
DeLong, Arca XVI,933
Demary, Ezekiel XIV,98, 205,
  559, 561, 576; XV,722;
    XVI, 205, 273, 518,
    814-15
  John XIV,98, 205; XV,97-
    98, 348, 539
  John Jr. XIV,36; XVI,236,
    518, 815
Demeritt, Daniel XV,312
  Ebenezer XV,312
  Eleazer XIV,13
  Eli XVII,721
  Eli Jr. XVII,719, 721
  Elijah XIV,25
  Ezekiel XIV,621

Demeritt, John XIV,108, 119,
  123, 188, 371, 384, 496,
  505, 516-17, 617; XV,722
  Joseph XV,571-72
  Robert XV,469, 481
  Samuel XIV,107, 123, 187,
    251, 406, 446; XVI,904
Demery, Ezekiel XVII,428
  Thomas XVI,83, 96, 106
Deming, Alpheus XVI,150
  Gamaliel XIV,104
  John XVI,55
  Israel XVII,306
  Martin XIV,104; XV,146,
    473, 501
Demmick, Timothy XVII,96
Denbow, Cornelius XIV,362;
  XVII, 24
  Elijah XIV,233
Denmark, Patrick XVII,513
Dennett, Alexander XIV,13;
  XVII,655
  Ephraim XIV,255; XVII,31,
    39
  John XIV,118, 149, 197,
    255, 484, 499, 512,
    555, 648-49; XV,726;
    XVI,7, 11, 37, 51, 180,
    182, 195-96, 208, 232,
    248, 350, 395, 480,
    528; XVII,38, 85, 269,
    441
  John Jr. XVII,31
  Joseph XIV,13, 287;
    XVII,737
  Lieutenant XVI,105
  Moses XV,325
  Robert XV,507
  Samuel XIV,540
  Thomas XVI,60, 62, 70, 94
  William XIV,119
Dennie, Albert XVI,571
Denning, William XVII,336,
  344
Dennis, Amos XIV,308
Dennison, Hugh XIV,223

Dennison, John XV,25;
    XVII,104
    Jonathan XV,25
    Jedediah XV,11, 147
    Major XVII,509
    Samuel XVI,931
Densmore, Abraham XIV,90
    Doctor XVI,466
    Elijah XIV,242; XVI,282,
        284; XVII,24
    Peter XVII,717
    Salathiel XVII,717
    See also Dinsmoor,
        Dinsmore
    Thomas XVI,860
Derburne, John XIV,641-42
    Samuel XIV,641
    Simon XIV,651
Derby, Elias XIV,40-41
    Simeon XV,153
Derry, James XIV,283, 287
    John XVII,682
Dessane, Martin XV,472, 503
D'Estaing, Count XVII,290,
    351
Detrap, Gasparell XV,461
Deuel, Jonathan XVI,932
    Robert XVI,932
    Silas XVI,932
    Timothy XVI,932
Deverin, Robert XIV,310
Deverno, Lewis XV,461
Devincaux, Lewis XV,729
Devine, Thomas XVII,118-19,
    250
Devins, Lewis XVI,28
Dewey, Aaron XV,50
    Ebenezer XV,67
    Martin XV,17, 138
    Simon XV,14
    Timothy XIV,265; XV,741,
        752
    William XV,374; XVII,109
Diamond, Ezekiel XIV,16, 61,
    182; XV,129, 405
    Isaac XV,406

Diamond, Israel XIV,226;
    XV,401, 742
    John XIV,564, 628; XV,451
Diamond, John XV,721; XVI,87,
    91, 106, 204, 651
    Reuben XV,186
Dibble, Alexander XIV,105;
    XVI, 137
Dibell, Alexander XV,13, 147
Dickerson, Ashbel XVI,313
    Gilbert XVI,933
    Joel XV,696
    Joseph XV,61
    Dr. Nathaniel XVI,424
Dickey, Adam XV,201; XVI,263,
    725, 911; XVII,426
    Benjamin XV,713
    Captain XVII,176, 180-81
    David XIV,579, 604;
        XV,438, 453-54, 716;
        XVI,201, 723
    Elias XIV,346; XV,744
    James XIV,33, 346, 425,
        469, 573; XV,87, 616,
        712, 740; XVI,198, 222,
        268, 513, 746; XVII,61
    Jesse XVI,236, 273, 507,
        665
    John XIV,425
    Joseph XIV,267
    Matthew XIV,411; XV,199,
        201; XVI,112
    Nathaniel XIV,469; XV,632,
        635-36, 712; XVI,199,
        222, 268, 513, 745-46
    Samuel XIV,74; XVI,898
    William XIV,74, 178, 347-
        48, 561, 579, 604, 629;
        XV,455, 566, 715, 722;
        XVI,201, 263, 721, 726,
        920; XVII,427
Dickinson, General XVII,238
    Joseph XVI,487
    Nathaniel XVII,98
Dickson, James XVII,301
    John XIV,428

Dickinson, Stephen XIV,664
Dike, Adam XVI,313
  Benjamin XIV,87, 200, 266,
    572, 595; XV,611;
    XVII,463
  Calvin XVI,313
  Stephen XV,622, 663, 669,
    677, 689; XVI,754
Dimock, Abner XV,65
Dimond, Jack XVII,364
Dinsmoor, John XVII,258
  Samuel XVI,246, 251, 564
  William XVI,889
  See also Densmore, Din-
    smore
Dinsmore, Abraham XV,96, 471,
    502, 752
  Abraham Jr. XIV,35
  Elijah XIV,361; XVI,282,
    284
  John XV,359, 556, 567
  Robert XIV,347; XV,169,
    358, 362
  Samuel XIV,327, 348
  Zebediah XIV,35; XV,364
Disco, John XV,442, 724
Dix, Joseph XIV,439, 527; XV,
    80; XVI,143, 259, 636;
    XVII,436
  Timothy XIV,261
Dixon, Stephen XV,431
  William XVI,917
Doaney, Andrew XVII,293
Dobbin, John XIV,210, 214,
    217, 218, 220
Dobbins, Alexander XVII,300
Dockham, Bemain XIV,415
  Benjamin XIV,15, 21, 24,
    119, 149, 197, 403,
    415; XV,456, 725; XVI,
    58, 103, 202, 207, 219,
    227, 270, 275, 507, 611,
    644-45, 673; XVII,757
  Benjamin Jr. XIV,403
  Enoch XIV,330, 564, 576,
    617, 630; XVI,103, 206,
    274, 505, 645

Dockham, James XV,697;
    XVI,68, 79, 97, 207, 227,
    275, 506, 649
  John XIV,15
  Jonathan XIV,330; XV,699
  Samuel XIV,682
  Thomas XIV,455, 530;
    XV,133, 475, 498;
    XVII,9
Dockum, Enoch XV,723
Dodge, Andrew XV,746
  Benjamin XIV,233, 244,
    562, 581, 637; XV,350,
    352, 449, 600, 631,
    638, 724, 753; XVI,27,
    44, 207, 230, 275,
    685, 753, 862; XVII,438
  Brewer XIV,264
  David XVI,256, 272, 511,
    607
  Elijah XV,55; XVI,888
  Elisha XV,552
  Elisha Jr. XVII,259
  Gideon XV,622, 663, 670,
    682, 689; XVI,141, 161,
    754
  Gideon Jr. XVI,141, 161
  Jacob XV,189, 429
  John XIV,160-61, 164, 547,
    632; XV,279-80, 592,
    667, 678, 723; XVI,206,
    542, 644, 653; XVII,468
  John 2d XVII,468
  Joseph XIV,524; XV,99,
    103, 360, 537, 740;
    XVI,158, 442, 839-40
  Joseph Jr. XIV,436
  Lemuel XIV,562
  Malachi XV,753
  Nathan XVI,81; XVII,383
  Nathaniel XVI,128, 162
  Nathaniel B. XV,55
  Nehemiah XV,189
  Nicholas XVI,236, 267,
    504, 634
  Noah XV,350, 352; XVI,755
  Samuel XV,396, 428;

Dodge, Samuel (Cont.) XVI,555, 556
  Shadrach XV,7, 633, 648; XVI, 23, 877
  Simon XVI,86, 100
  Solomon XV,350, 352; XVI,82, 92, 106
  Thomas XIV,592; XV,716; XVI, 201; XVII,468
  William XIV,426, 645; XV,54, 746; XVI,23, 886
  Zadoc XIV,104, 576, 578, 632; XV,723; XVI,206, 653; XVII, 468
  Zebulon XV,632, 636; XVI,740
Dodridge, Jacob XVII,300
Doe, Bradstreet XV,416
  Daniel XIV,251, 581
  David XIV,126, 188, 635; XV, 442, 449, 601, 724; XVI,206, 229, 274, 515, 756, 758, 818; XVII,11
  James XV,243-45, 247-48; XVI,757
  John XIV,571; XV,441, 698; XVI,122, 164, 282; XVII,137, 719
  Jonathan XIV,581, 624; XV, 441, 449, 601, 619, 719; XVI,758
  Joshua XV,311
  Josiah XVI,757
  Nicholas XV,571
  Reuben XIV,400; XVII,435
  Sampson XIV,13; XVII,719
  Simeon XV,191
  William XIV,72; XV,259, 262, 267, 270
  Zebulon XIV,134, 191, 307, 353; XVII,6
Doen, David XVII,669
  Thomas XVII,669
Dolbear, Stephen XV,596
Dolbeer, Nicholas XIV,253
  Stephen XIV,118, 137, 158, 191

Dolce, Thomas XVII,669
Dole, Benjamin XIV,99, 205, 334; XV,348; XVI,237, 270, 509, 534, 699
  Captain XVI,383
  John XIV,99, 213, 221, 334, 576, 613; XV,711; XVI,198, 237, 273, 509, 534, 699
  Parker XV,568; XVI,568
  Stephen XIV,225, 405; XV,398
Dolf, Matthew XV,226
Dollar, Daniel XIV,112
  Joseph XV,748
  Noah XIV,70, 179
  Richard XIV,515
Dolloff, Daniel XIV,147, 196; XV,242, 244, 246
  John XIV,246, 559; XV,721; XVI,204, 272, 512, 742; XVII,27
  John Jr. XIV,246
  Joseph XIV,370, 378, 493, 659; XV,457, 727; XVI,11, 62, 71, 94, 316, 838
  Josiah XIV,246
  Noah XIV,312
  Phineas XV,243-46, 248
  Richard XIV,370, 378, 493, 503; XVII, 27, 57, 732, 738
  Samuel XIV,12
  Thomas XIV,312, 584-85, 660; XV,727; XVI,10, 43, 184, 209, 285, 501, 708; XVII,57
  William XIV,246
Dolten, Samuel XIV,583
Donald, Stephen XIV,411
Donaldson, James XVI,717
  John XVI,452
  Mary XVI,340, 452
  Thomas XVII,293
Donally, Christopher XIV,631
  Thomas XIV,304, 466

Dongan, Colonel XVI,189, 598
Donnell, Reuben XIV,600
  Samuel XIV,237
  Donovan, Richard XVII,204
  Doolittle, Captain XVI,544
  Ephraim XV,745-46
  John XVI,362, 879
Door, Jonathan XIV,369, 375,
  483, 498, 502, 511, 518
  Philemon XIV,14
  Richard XIV,372, 385, 497
  William XIV,602
  See also Dore, Dorr
Dore, Benaiah XVI,119
  John XIV,368, 375, 483,
  498, 502, 511, 518,
  572; XV,612; XVI,913
  Jonathan XVI,118
  Richard XVII,656
Dorrety, Charles XIV,282,
  287, 470, 577, 596
Dorman, John XIV,468, 611;
  XV, 718; XVI,202, 221,
  241, 270, 504, 633
Dorothy, Charles XVI,502, 597
Doroughty, Mr. XVII,347
Dorr, William XV,752
Doss, Martin XVI,932
Dosson, Jesse XV,4
  Martin XV,4
Doty, Elias XVI,933
Doud, James XVI,219, 240,
  270, 875
Dougherty, Charles XV,713;
  XVI, 199, 223, 268, 502
  Edward XVII,301
  John XIV,223
  Michael XVII,204
Doughty, Hugh XVII,303
  William XVI,933
Douglass, Alexander XIV,99,
  156-157; XV,751
  Generall XV,239
  John XIV,470, 585, 605;
  XV,716
  Thomas XV,741
Douse, John XIV,11

Douse, Ozem XVI,912
Dove, Daniel XIV,9
Dow, Amos XVI,823
  Benjamin XIV,11, 232, 469,
  564, 571, 602; XV,116,
  256, 258, 260, 264,
  393, 712; XVI, 65, 74,
  106, 198, 222, 239,
Dow, Benjamin XVI,767-68, 776
  Daniel XV,486, 499-500,
  564, 658, 667, 691;
  XVI,124, 708; XVII,528
  David XVII,740
  Ebenezer XIV,23, 116, 128,
  189, 399; XV,284
  Ela XV,400; XVI,831
  Eli XIV,227
  Elijah XVI,196
  Enoch XIV,312; XV,640,
  706; XVI,102, 674
  Evan XV,510, 744
  Gideon XIV,23
  Henry XIV,11; XVII,32,
  528, 623, 627, 631-32,
  638, 646, 648, 659,
  683, 687, 689, 740
  Henry Jr. XVII,659
  Isaac XIV,225; XV,488,
  499, 500; XVII,32
  Jabez XIV,618; XV,443,
  457, 723, 747; XVI,206;
  XVII,740, 741
  James XIV,408; XVI,530
  Jeremiah XIV,25, 249, 252,
  587; XV,331, 390-91;
  XVI,768, 776
  John XIV,253, 432, 580;
  XV,180, 447, 598, 667,
  698, 712, 720; XVI,64,
  105, 656
  Jonathan XIV,249; XVI,106,
  875
  Joseph XIV,110, 131, 190;
  XV, 256, 259, 261-62,
  265-66, 306, 309, 695,
  698; XVI,672, 673;
  XVII,632

Dow, Joshua XIV,408; XV,398; XVII, 612
Josiah XV,512; XVI,673; XVII, 25
Lemuel XV,41
Moses XVI,508, 586, 680; XVII,416
Nathaniel XIV,362, 364, 580, 660; XV,447, 598; XVI,64, 74, 106
Noah XIV,297; XV,393
Oliver XIV,261; XV,120-21, 548; XVII,430
Peter Jr. XIV,19
Percy XIV,225
Phinehas XIV,342, 348
Reuben XIV,32, 39, 41, 43; XV, 510, 743; XVI,321, 323, 326, 328, 331, 334, 337, 339, 343
Reuben XVI,345, 377, 431, 495, 687, 690
Richard XIV,253, 347, 587; XVI,914
Richard Jr. XIV,342
Samuel XV,398; XVI,632, 659
Simon XIV,11; XVI,767; XVII, 676, 713
Solomon XVI,178-79
Stephen XIV,418; XV,88; XVI,377
Thomas XIV,405, 586; XV,499, 500, 743; XVI,38, 530
Widow XVI,933
Winthrop XIV,399; XV,565; XVII,25
Zebulon XIV,399; XV,410; XVII, 25
Dowboard, Abraham XVI,933
Dowd, James XIV,471, 578; XV, 653, 718; XVII,438
Dowe, Asa XIV,225
Benjamin XV,523; XVI,74, 98, 268, 513
Daniel XV,673

Dowe, Ebenezer XV,290
Jeremiah XIV,68, 180, 225
John XVI,148
Jonathan XIV,68, 180; XVI,74, 98, 118
Joseph XV,523
Lemuel XV,375
Nathaniel XVI,74, 98
Richard XIV,225
Stephen XV,89; XVI,144
Thomas XIV,657; XV,485
Dowell, Henry XVII,522
Dower, William Jr. XIV,422
Dowley, William XVI,929
Dowling, Lawrence XVII,303
Downer, Dr. Abraham XVI,400
Josiah XV,375
William XV,18, 375
Zaccheus XV,15, 138, 374; XVII, 109
Downes, Thomas XVII,525
Downey, Edward XVII,296
Downing,-- XVI,102
Bartholomew XVI,761
Captain XVI,900
Colonel XIV,23
Daniel XIV,5; XV,529, 632, 635, 730, 735; XVI,17, 194, 211; XVI,220, 298, 522, 880-81
George XIV,562, 637; XV,619, 643, 725; XVI,207, 230, 240, 275, 523, 817, 818
John XVI,904; XVII,648, 737
Jonathan XIV,114, 141, 193, 562, 620, 637; XV,619, 719; XVI,203, 226, 271, 523, 817, 818
Joseph XIV,18
Richard XVI,761
Samuel XVI,192, 213, 232, 279, 504; XVII,438
Simon XVI,286, 514
Thomas XVI,502
Timothy XIV,687

Downs, Aaron XIV,236
  Gershom XIV,125, 188;
    XVII,10
  James XIV,369, 376, 401,
    414; XVI,623
  John XIV,104
  Noah XIV,631; XV,451, 723;
    XVI, 206, 227, 274,
    504, 620, 635
  Paul XIV,314
  Robert XIV,226, 635;
    XV,724; XVI,902
  Samuel XIV,257; XVI,620;
    XVII, 28, 30
  Thomas XIV,13, 236
  Timothy XIV,347
  William XIV,236, 563; XVI,
    514, 767
  Zephaniah XVI,198, 223,
    267, 506, 649
Dowsett, Dennis XVI,931
  Peter XVI,931
Doyen, Daniel XVI,141, 162,
    286, 501
  Jacob XIV,604, 606;
    XVI,83, 240, 516, 789
  Jacob Jr. XVI,790
Doyle, Henry XVII,301
  John XIV,223
  William XIV,413
Drake, Abraham XIV,66, 181;
    XV, 267, 269, 272, 276,
    318-45, 433, 475, 494,
    639-40; XVI, 833;
    XVII,528
  Ephraim XIV,117, 129, 189;
    XV, 172; XVI,749
  Francis XVII,511, 513
  George XVII,511
  James XIV,400
  John XIV,350, 362, 365;
    XV, 522; XVII,66
  Jonathan XV,320, 340
  Nathaniel XIV,11, 22;
    XVII, 511, 513
  Robert XIV,252

Drake, Samuel XIV,230, 450;
    XV,411
  Simon XIV,118, 137, 158,
    192, 352
  Thomas XIV,143, 194;
    XVII,8
  Weare XVI,642
Draper, Jacob XIV,463;
    XVI,796; XVII,65
Dresser, Jeremiah XVI,914
  Jonathan XIV,167, 274,
    288; XV,106
  Asa XV,165
  Ebenezer XV,15
  Stephen XIV,169
Drew, Andrew XV,469, 481,
    507; XVI,627
  Benjamin XVI,192
  Benoni XVI,87, 90, 103,
    232, 279, 502, 594
  Clement Jr. XVI,904
  Daniel XIV,232, 433
  Elijah XVI,628
  Enoch XV,628
  Francis XIV,259, 480, 624;
    XV, 618, 720; XVI,204,
    624; XVII,42
  Henry XVI,200
  John XIV,234, 242, 321,
    323, 338, 365, 465,
    476, 554, 617, 619,
    624; XV,573, 651, 718;
    XVI,5, 526, 626, 905;
    XVII,260, 267, 270-71,
    757
  Capt. John XV,443, 448-49,
    457, 595-601, 618
  Jonathan XIV,228
  Joseph XVI,904, 929;
    XVII,420
  Samuel XIV,167, 170; XVII,
    14
  Silas XV,575; XVI,570
  Theophilus XIV,236, 373,
    386, 497, 507, 517
  Thomas XV,671, 677; XVI,

Drew, Thomas (Cont.) 721;
  XVII,717
  Thomas Jr. XIV,13
  William XIV,13
  Zebulon XIV,107, 122
Drinkwater, John XVI,308-9
Drisco, Cornelius XIV,13;
  XVII; XVII,719
  John XIV,3, 107, 122, 187,
    635; XV,442, 618, 724;
    XVI, 638, 640
Drought, Richard XIV,469; XV,
    634, 649, 712; XVI,102,
    199, 222, 268, 505,
    646-47
  Robert XIV,500, 512
Drown, Benjamin XVI,108
  Joseph XIV,446, 540
  Moses XIV,234, 321
  Peter XVI,371, 756
  Samuel XIV,353
  Solomon XVI,285, 523, 820
Drowne, John XV,493
  Peter XV,416, 468-69, 480-
    81, 493
  Samuel XV,577; XVII,139
  Thomas XV,469, 481, 496
Drowt, Robert XVII,87
Druce, John XV,16, 377
Drummer, Henry XIV,265
Drury, Captain XV,750
  Daniel XIV,35
  David XV,664-65, 671;
    XVI,855; XVII,428
  Ebenezer XIV,35, 575, 639;
    XV, 731; XVI,15, 25,
    186, 211, 857-59
  Gershom XIV,35; XV,95-96,
    364-365, 534, 654, 682;
    XVI,542; XVII,100,
    135, 214
  John XIV,575, 639; XV,731;
    XVI,15, 25, 857-58
  Manoah XV,24
  Moses XV,108
  Needham XV,220
  Thomas XV,751

Drury, William XIV,35; XV,95,
    364
  Zedekiah XIV,35; XV,364
  Zedekiah Jr. XIV,35
Dublin, John XIV,5
Dublisse, Joseph XVII,305
Duca, Joseph XVII,299
Ducale, Theodore XVII,305
Duce, Cato XIV,133, 190;
    XVI,648
Ducet, Philemon XIV,468, 575
    612; XV,711; XVII,444
Ducit, Philamon XVI,198, 856,
    858, 860
  Philip XVI,521
Ducker, Thomas XVII,111
Duclan, Alleais XVII,305
Ducros, Francois XVII,299
Duda, Asa XIV,235, 322
  Eliphalet XIV,233, 242
  Joseph XIV,13; XVII,719
  Lemuel XIV,235; XV,618,
    725; XVI,230, 239, 275,
    504, 639
  Moses XVI,18, 185
  Obadiah XV,448, 599;
    XVI,30, 33, 59
  Samuel XVI,207
Dudee, Lemuel XIV,637
  Obadiah XIV,654
Dudey, Obadiah XIV,581-82
Dudley, Billy XVII,526, 652,
    676, 693
  Daniel XV,147, 194;
    XVI,64, 74, 98, 106
  Daniel Jr. XV,35
  Davidson XV,748
  Elias XVI,137
  Eliphalet XIV,117, 129
  Ephraim XIV,312, 659;
    XV,457, 727; XVI,10,
    43, 66, 71, 98, 184,
    209, 237, 245, 277,
    506, 649, 838
  Gilman XIV,410
  Jeremiah XIV,340
  Jeremiah Jr. XV,746

Dudley, John XIV,327-28;
    XV,12, 135, 178, 241,
    371, 660; XVI,361, 376,
    394, 418, 473, 551, 588-
    89, 656, 806, 808, 920;
    XVII,57, 105, 217, 230,
    264, 288, 323, 455
  John Jr. XVI,905
  Jonathan XIV,12, 112, 247,
    195, 304; XV,283, 288
  Jonathan S. XIV,134, 191,
    400, 563, 627; XV,442,
    720; XVI, 204, 272,
    514, 767; XVII,6
  Joseph XIV,227, 257, 377,
    492, 564, 651; XV,729;
    XVI,28; XVII,689-90,
    701-4, 711
  Nathaniel XV,562; XVI,806
  Samuel XIV,12, 311, 313,
    335; XV,243, 245-46,
    475, 494; XVI,581, 583;
    XVII,53, 526
  Rev. Samuel XVII,608
  Stephen XIV,66, 181, 362,
    365; XVI,64, 75, 98,
    106
  Theophilus XVII,526, 617,
    710
  Trueworthy XIV,563, 588,
    616, 659; XV,457, 557,
    719; XVI; XVI,10, 43,
    65, 72, 97, 184, 209,
    650, 838; XVII,424-25
  Trueworthy Jr. XV,727
  Winthrop XIV,242; XVII,57
Dufan, Jean XVII,299
Duff, Henry XVII,205
Duffee, Cornelius XVII,301
  James XVII,300
Duffey, Daniel XVII,308
  Matthew XVII,155
Duford, David XV,109
Dufronce, Joseph XVII,299
Dugen, John XVII,301
Dukin, Thomas XIV,607
Dully, William XVII,302

Duman, David XV,595
DuMaulin, Frederick XVII,305
Dunbar, James XVII,674
  John XIV,423
Duncan, Captain XVI,305;
    XVII, 345
  Colonel XVII,167
  David XIV,387, 494, 647,
    649; XV,728, 734;
    XVI,12, 209, 320, 326,
    332, 341, 343, 345,
    378, 803-4
  David XIV,74, 178, 424
  George XVI,911
  James XV,583; XVII,295,
    301
  John XIV,324, 463; XV,115,
    362-63, 369, 583;
    XVI,403, 437, 528, 540,
    549, 564, 893; XVII,19
  Robert XVI,679
  Thomas XV,603, 714
  William XVI,911
Duncklee, Hezekiah XIV,425;
    XV, 189
Duncomb, Anthony XVII,694
Dunfee, James XV,144
Dunham, Gershom XVII,67
Dunlap, Adam XV,394, 428, 566
  Hugh XIV,420; XVI,536
  James XIV,560; XV,635,
    639, 721; XVI,204, 272,
    518, 807-8
  Robert XIV,394; XVII,89
  Samuel XIV,411; XV,175
  Thomas XV,519
Dunley, John XVI,930
Dunn, Benjamin XV,221;
    XVI,839
  James XVI,930
  Nicholas XIV,2
Dunnel, Reuben XV,437, 715
Dunsey, Cornelius XIV,263
Dunsler, Henry XV,81
Dunstar, Thomas XVII,502
Dunster, Isaiah XVI,85, 100
  Josiah XVI,106

Dunton, Zachariah XIV,579
Dupire, Jean B. XVII,299
Duplaines, Auris XVII,299
Durant, Jonathan XIV,51, 185
  Joseph XV,226
  Joshua XVI,152
  Levi XIV,93, 202-3, 437,
    525; XV,63, 293;
    XVI,850; XVII,98
Durbin, Edward XV,443
Durgan, Eliphalet XV,311
Durgen, Francis XV,431
  Gershom XV,177
  Joseph XV,129
  Silas XV,309
  Winthrop XV,195
Durgin, Benjamin XIV,25, 647,
    649; XV,619, 728; XVI,13
  Daniel XIV,408
  David XIV,235
  Ebenezer XV,249-51, 253
  Eliphalet XIV,108, 123,
    188
  Ephraim XIV,231
  Francis XV,698; XVI,766
  Henry XIV,322; XV,619,
    653, 725; XVI,207, 230,
    275, 504, 639, 641
  Jacob XIV,232
  James XIV,235; XVII,644,
    719
  John XIV,580, 659; XV,448,
    599, 727; XVI,10, 43,
    184, 209
  Joseph XIV,233, 398;
    XV,666; XVI,818, 898
  Josiah XIV,126, 288;
    XV,312, 656, 673;
    XVI,711; XVII,10, 24
  Josiah Jr. XIV,233
  Levi XVI,64, 74, 93
  Philip XIV,119, 150, 196
  Richard XV,256, 259-60,
    263
  Silas XV,300, 302, 305,
    309

Durgin, Thomas XIV,235, 446,
  540, 608, 664
  Trueworthy D. XIV,107,
    123, 188, 235; XV,312,
    571
  William XVII,657, 719
  Winthrop XIV,363-64;
    XVI,121; XVI,164
Durgy, Andrew XIV,9
Durham, Caesar XIV,21
Durkee, Adam XV,19, 138
  David XIV,422
  John XV,41; XVI,178-79
  Nathan XV,377
  Thomas XV,38, 45; XVII,236
  Timothy XV,18, 138
Durell, Lemuel XVII,281
  William XIV,176
  See also Durel
Dustin, David XVI,167, 172,
  175, 521, 828
  Ebenezer XV,328, 464, 477,
    504; XVI,87, 91, 106
  Eliphalet XV,552; XVII,259
  Gardner XVII,65
  Gordon XVII,253
  James XV,183
  John XVI,141; XVII,463
  Moody XIV,553, 613;
    XV,710; XVI,2, 180,
    182, 197, 223, 229,
    267; XVII,266, 440, 442
  Moses XIV,554, 629;
    XV,718, 748; XVI,5,
    112, 182, 203, 271,
    588; XVII,216, 267, 466
  Nathaniel XIV,543
  Paul XIV,329, 459, 467,
    539
  Peter XVII,91
  Phinehas XIV,263
  Samuel XV,464, 466, 478,
    504; XVI,88, 95
  Dr. Samuel XVI,914
  Stephen XIV,599, 611; XV,
    328, 718; XVII,224, 438

84

Dustin, Thomas XV,27; XVI,608
  Timothy XVI,605, 607
  Zaccheus XIV,314, 467,
    560, 621; XV,455, 722;
    XVI,723
Duston, Caleb XVI,823
  Ebenezer XV,343, 466;
    XVI,106, 823
  Gardner XIV,463
  John XVI,161
  Dr. John XIV,172, 176-77
  Josiah XVI,195
  Nathaniel XV,39
  Obadiah XIV,53, 185
  Paul XV,177
  Stephen XIV,471; XV,343
  Timothy XIV,158, 342, 347
Dutch, Jeremiah XVI,237, 244;
    XVI,273, 511, 712
  John XIV,309, 390, 486;
    XV,747
  Samuel XIV,353
Dutcher, Dirck XVI,932
Dutton, Abel XIV,436, 524; XV,
    221, 535; XVI,159, 839
  Asa XIV,425
  Ezra XIV,88, 200, 425;
    XV,188
  Jacob XIV,87, 200; XV,188,
    482, 497; XVI,140, 161
  John XIV,101, 206, 345,
    561, 572, 621; XV,529,
    612, 722; XVI,685-86;
    XVII,61
  Jonas XIV,421
  Jonathan XIV,247, 302
  Josiah XVI,908
  Nathan XIV,419
  Roger XIV,102, 207, 266,
    439, 527; XV,72, 213,
    467, 479
  Stephen XV,48; XVII,94
  Thomas XV,536
  William XV,99; XVI,840
Duty, Mark XVI,167, 285, 503,
    734

Duty, Moses XIV,159, 161, 163,
    272, 290, 547, 607-8;
    XV,423-24, 733; XVI, 213,
    228, 279, 508, 679;
    XVII,330
  Philip XIV,3; XVII,717
  Philip Jr. XVII,717
  William XIV,52, 185;
    XVI,825; XVII,719
Duvall, Isaac XVII,207
Dwickee, Heman XV,375
  John XV,375
Dwinell, Amos XVI,151
Dwinnel, Jonathan XV,227
  Thomas XV,62
Dwire, John XV,712
Dwyer, John XIV,68, 180, 259,
    570, 602
Dyer, E. F. XVII,208
  Edward XVI,296
  Eliphalet XVII,124
  Joseph XVII,308
  Samuel XIV,21, 273, 276,
    289, 291; XV,284, 288
  William XV,387
Dyke, Benjamin XVI,528
  Calvin XVII,252
  Eden XVII,252
Dyle, John XV,47

E

Eager, Dr. George XIV,262, 294-
    295; XV,426, 584-85; XVI,
    306, 528
  Luke XIV,183
  Samuel XIV,178
Ealy,-- XV,699
  Paul XV,465, 504
Eames, David XVII,110
  Jeremiah XIV,463, 473;
    XVI, 289, 292, 782;
    XVII,65, 78, 113, 416
  Jeremiah Jr. XVI, 113
  Jonathan XIV,267
  Thaddeus XVII,110
Earle, Caleb XIV,105
Earl, John XVII,28

Early, John XIV,223
Easterbrooks, Abel XV,20, 108
    Abraham XV,369
    Jonathan XV,93
    Nehemiah XV,15, 138, 374
    Samuel XV,38, 45, 155,
        157-58
Eastham, Edward XVI,527
    William XV,608
Eastman, Aaron XVI,86, 99,
        106
    Abner XIV,571; XV,698
    Abiatha XIV,246
    Abigail XVI,704-5
    Amos XIV,33, 438
    Benjamin XIV,232; XV,742;
        XVI,147, 530
    Caleb XV,744; XVI,296
    Collins XIV,51; XVI,694
    Daniel XVII,430
    David XVI,263, 612
    Ebenezer XIV,36, 66-67,
        144, 193-94, 587, 628;
        XV,720; XVI,204, 264,
        659-60, 709, 910;
        XVII,9
    Edmund XIV,463; XVI,296;
        XVII, 65
    Edward XIV,352, 429, 627;
        XV, 457, 514, 720;
        XVI,204, 226, 240, 272,
        510, 614, 703-4;
        XVII,27
    Enoch XIV,51, 185, 315;
        XV, 120, 182, 548
    Ezekiel XIV,273, 276, 289;
        XV,285
    Henry XVI,148, 238, 246,
        268, 296, 508, 681
    Ichabod XIV,346, 418
    Isaac XIV,224
    Jacob XIV,470, 581, 606,
        654; XV,449, 599, 631,
        637, 716, 729; XVI,30, 33,
        59, 102, 189, 201, 210,
        269, 501, 609, 611

Eastman, James XIV,574, 626;
        XV,24, 589, 615, 719;
        XVI,204; XVII,80, 82, 104,
        114
    Jeremiah XIV,316, 318;
        XV,187; XVI,490, 776
    John XIV,340, 471, 567,
        611; XV,129, 525, 560,
        608, 631, 638, 718;
        XVI,102, 124, 126, 509,
        695; XVII,443
    John Jr. XVI,270
    Jonathan XIV,33, 104, 315,
        467, 548, 578; XV,25,
        34, 182, 279-80, 405;
        XVI,308, 439; XVII,80,
        82, 114
    Jonathan Jr. XIV,105, 596
    Joseph XIV,567, 611;
        XV,129, 405, 608, 717;
        XVI,910, 915, 938
    Joshua XIV,453, 532
    Josiah XVI,237, 271, 512,
        726
    Mary XVI,694
    Moses XIV,25, 50, 186,
        242; XV,113, 405, 550;
        XVI,664
    Nathaniel XIV,167, 274;
        XV,129
    Nathaniel Jr. XIV,299;
        XVI,609
    Nehemiah XIV,586, 600;
        XV,437
    Nicholas XV,70
    Noah XIV,246
    Obadiah XIV,405; XV,279,
        281, 568; XVI,308, 541;
        XVII,114
    Pearson XIV,566; XV,607
    Peaslee XV,663, 670, 684,
        688; XVI,86, 92, 106,
        247, 253, 286, 501,
        504, 610-11
    Peter XV,425; XVI,308;
        XVII, 80, 82, 114

Eastman, Philip XV,146;
XVII,103
Richard XV,129
Samuel XIV,64, 181, 186,
329, 598; XV,146, 183,
550, 715; XVI,131, 133,
163, 264, 696, 926;
XVII,4, 430, 711, 731
Simeon XVI,124, 296
Stephen XIV,454, 529, 546;
XV,742
Stilson XV,405
Stinson XV,129
Thomas XIV,51, 185, 329,
567; XIV,611; XV,323,
342, 439, 550-51, 608,
718; XVI,202
Thomas Jr. XV,323
Timothy XIV,316, 319
William XIV,323, 365, 456,
566, 653; XV,608, 729;
XVI, 30, 33, 59, 105,
187, 210, 263, 541,
725, 853, 914; XVII,92,
426
Zachariah XIV,579; XV,452,
740
Easton, William XVII,294
Eastwick, Pheasant XVII,513,
633, 646
Easty, Aaron XIV,36
Eaton, Abigail XVI,740
Abijah XV,530, 632, 636;
XVI, 26, 44, 259;
XVII,436
Alexander XV,475, 494;
XVI,66, 77, 97
Amos XV,256, 258, 260, 262
Asaph XIV,252
Benjamin XIV,144, 193-94,
350, 587, 656; XV,169,
321, 340, 475, 494;
XVI,37-38, 66, 76, 97,
124, 128, 162, 914;
XVII,9, 425
Collins XIV,656; XV,731;
XVI, 36, 38

Eaton, Daniel XVI,246, 251, 509
David XIV,413; XV,41, 99,
321, 340, 348, 373; XVI,
913
Ebenezer XIV,315, 467,
548; XV, 182; XVI,286,
500
Elisha XIV,351; XV,747
Enoch XV,116, 174; XVI,69,
79, 90
Ephraim XIV,242, 252;
XVII,295
Henry XIV,268, 271
Ithamar XV,408, 550-51;
XVI, 873, 875
Jabez XIV,229; XV,524
Jacob XIV,144, 193-94;
XV,133
James XV,189, 323, 342,
483, 497, 749
Jeremiah M. XIV,238
Jesse XV,402, 748
John XIV,11, 459, 537,
556; XV,90, 726; XVI,7,
66, 77, 97, 237, 270,
509, 696; XVII,269, 536
Jonathan XIV,9, 629; XV,
456, 730, 735; XVI,17,
194, 211, 220, 236, 243,
274, 278, 498, 507, 567,
834
Joseph XIV,404; XV,323,
341; XVI,65, 75, 98,
281, 744
Joseph T. XIV,382, 491,
501, 514
Joshua XIV,658
Levi XIV,229, 252, 350;
XV, 319, 339
Obadiah XV,408
Paul XIV,456, 539
Reuben XVI,128, 162; XVII,
433
Samuel XIV,23, 225, 268,
271, 290, 524; XV,176,
328, 343, 586; XVI,246,
252, 313; XVII,116, 433,

Eaton, Samuel (Cont.) 438
  Sylvanus XIV,413; XV,747
  Timothy XIV,252; XV,321,
    340
  Tristram XIV,252
  William XIV,203, 229;
    XV,488, 489
Eayers, John XIV,579; XV,454
  Joseph XVI,51, 53;
    XVII,457, 464
  Samuel XV,454; XVI,198,
    201, 722
  Thomas XIV,8
  William XIV,412
Eccleston, John XVII,208
Eddy, Abiel XV,47; XVI,878-
    79; XVII,95
  James XIV,428, 644;
    XV,732, 741; XVI,20,
    22, 191, 212, 225, 279,
    522, 877, 879
  Thomas XIV,423
Edes, Captain XVII,130
  James XVII,296
  Jonathan XIV,280, 288;
    XV,633, 647; XVI,37,
    191, 669; XVII, 364
Edgerley, Benjamin XVI,569
  James XIV,368, 375, 483,
    498, 502, 511, 518,
    567, 611, 648-49;
    XV,608, 619, 717, 728;
    XVI,12, 192, 202, 209,
    640
  John XVI,281, 744;
    XVII,717
  Jonathan XV,392
  Joseph XIV,2; XV, 433;
    XVII,717
  Joshua XIV,125, 188, 560,
    581, 620; XV,449, 600,
    722; XVII,11
  Josiah XIV,117, 128, 399
  Richard XV,468, 480, 507
  Thomas XIV,235; XVII,525,
    640, 658, 716

Edgerley, Zebulon XIV,116, 128,
    189, 476; XV,581
Edgerly, Samuel XVII,717
Edmonds, Jonathan XVII,30
Edmunds, Jonathan XIV,239,
    257-258, 344; XV,267,
    269, 273; XVI,317-19
Edmundson, Richard XVII,294
Edson, Caleb XIV,210, 214,
    217, 219-21
  Ebenezer XVI,607
  Jonas XV,48
Edwards, Daniel XIV,238
  E. XVII,203
  Ebenezer XVI,835
  John XIV,126, 188, 248,
    251, 560, 620; XV,619,
    626, 724; XVI,207, 236,
    243, 506, 527, 649;
    XVII,11
  Jonathan XV,495
  Malachi XIV,5
  William XIV,309
Egan, Luke XIV,58
Ela, David XIV,371, 379, 493,
    504, 515
Elbridge, Mr. XVII,491
Eldridge, Joseph XIV,238
Elger, Waitsill XIV,355;
    XV,205
Elkins, Abel XV,166
  Chase XVII,25
  Henry XIV,107, 117-18,
    120, 137, 139, 158,
    191, 229, 242, 252-53,
    341; XV,400, 748;
    XVI,672, 915
  John XV,242, 244, 246,
    474; XVI,920
  Jonathan XVII,92, 253,
    642, 644
  Jonathan Jr. XVII,253
  Joseph XIV,585, 611
  Josiah XIV,286-87, 291,
    546; XV,279-80;
    XVI,308; XVII,114

Elkins, Mr. XVII,366
  Moses XV,165, 411;
    XVII,643
  Obadiah XIV,25
  Peter XV,322, 342
  Samuel XIV,14, 369, 377,
    492, 503, 515; XV,300-
    1, 305, 308
  Thomas XIV,11
Ellerson, John XIV,623;
    XV,440, 627
Elley, David XIV,579
Ellinwood, Benjamin XV,188-89
  James XV,521
  Jedediah XV,214
  Joseph XIV,88; XV,350, 352
  Ralph XIV,244, 631;
    XV,711; XVI,198, 267
  Samuel XIV,247
Elliot, Amos XV,72, 213, 698
  Benjamin XV,186
  Bernard XV,323, 342
  David XV,93, 211
  Edmund XV,149, 151, 158
  Edward XV,149
  Ephraim XVI,156
  Francis XVII,24
  Jacob XV,168, 464-66, 477,
    654, 658-59, 668, 678;
    XVI, 166, 168, 379
  Jedediah XVI,287, 512
  John XV,170, 425, 464,
    466, 477, 504, 619,
    658, 667-78, 691, 712,
    714; XVI,144, 576, 771;
    XVII,4, 30
  Jonathan XVI,791
  Oliver XV,211, 346
  Samuel XV,211,746;
    XVII,23, 39, 61
  Robert XVII,527, 584, 599,
    622, 628-29, 638, 641,
    646, 652, 660, 672,
    683, 685, 701, 703
  Thomas XV,405
  William XV,743; XVI,4,
    909; XVII,268

Elliott, Amos XIV,244
  Andrew XIV,409
  Barnabas XV,26, 143, 145,
    158
  Barnard XIV,404
  Benjamin XIV,431
  David XIV,90, 201
  Ezekiel XIV,423; XV,584-
    85; XVI,307
  Jacob XIV,43; XVI,168-69
  John XIV,61, 90, 182, 186,
    227, 235, 257-58, 589,
    602, 607-8; XV,748
  Jonathan XIV,313, 359,
    588; XV,748
  Oliver XIV, 346
  Samuel XIV,239, 346
  Thomas XIV,224
  Timothy XV,748
  William XIV,553, 615
Ellis, B. XVI,605
  Barnabas XVI,607;
    XVII,104, 249
  Benjamin XIV,355, 555,
    644; XV,66, 633, 643,
    648, 726, 741; XVI,8,
    21, 23, 44, 51, 180-82,
    191, 208, 225, 248,
    506, 702, 810-11;
    XVII,269, 440, 443, 468
  Caleb XIV,428; XV,741
  Colonel XVI,104, 249, 293-
    94
  Edward XV, 655, 666,
    676;XVI, 67, 77, 96,
    623, 627-28
  Ephraim XIV,233
  Gideon XV,62
  Henry XIV,356
  John XV,4, 54, 57, 203-4,
    633, 647, 733, 745;
    XVI,40, 190, 522, 813,
    886-87; XVII,97
  Jonathan XIV,406; XV,297;
    XVI, 286, 523, 820
  Joseph XIV,125, 188;
    XV,66, 192; XVII,10

Ellis, Joshua XIV,43, 93, 202-3, 326
  Lawrence XIV,485, 500, 512; XVII,86
  Major XV,447, 633, 643, 668
  Robert XVI,192, 213, 232, 279, 523, 748, 817-18
  Simeon XV,4
  Thomas XVI,286, 523, 820
  Timothy XV,2, 61, 196, 198, 647-48; XVI,58, 166, 527, 531, 700, 876; XVII,97, 255
  William XIV,5, 555, 644; XV, 726; XVI,8, 20, 25, 50, 208, 411; XVII,269
Ellishanes, John XVI,220
Ellison, John XIV,381, 489; XV, 596, 627; XVI,515
  Joseph XVI,269, 512, 726
  Thomas XIV,108
Ellsworth, Aaron XV,173; XVII, 28, 57
  John XV,483
  Oliver XV,27; XVI,608
  Peleg XVII,307
  Samuel XVII,57
Elmore, Daniel XV,11
  Elijah XIV,85, 199
Eltinge, Solomon XVI,933
Elwyn, Joseph XVII,644
Ely, David XV,454
  Paul XV,478
  Samuel XIV,82
Emerson, Amos XIV,76, 81, 83, 553, 600-1; XV,710; XVI,2, 51, 197, 477, 530, 599; XVII,266
  Asa XV,16, 138
  Benjamin XV,195
  Benjamin H. XIV,418
  Caleb XV,396
  Captain XV,436, 602; XVI,180
  Charles XIV,58, 183, 304-5, 465; XVI,733, 914

Emerson, Daniel XV,87, 89, 510, 654, 682, 686
  Daniel Jr. XIV,346; XVI,378, 438-39, 496
  David XIV,316, 319; XV,109; XVI,683
  Edward XVI,287
  Edward W. XVI,196, 516, 805; XVII,434
  Eleazer XIV,55, 184, 656; XV, 731; XVI, 35, 38
  Enoch XV,42, 155; XVII,110,
  George XIV,58, 183; XVI,285, 504
  J. XV,713
  John XIV,331, 363; XVI,65, 75, 98
  Jonathan XIV,53, 97, 185, 204, 296, 553, 601; XV,710; XVI, 3, 321, 323, 330, 334, 337, 339, 379, 569; XVII,266
  Jordan XV,350, 353
  Joseph XVI,914
  Mr. XVII,326
  Moses XIV,45, 248, 251, 447, 540; XV,113, 120, 169, 183, 312, 696; XVII,29, 279, 284
  Nathaniel XIV,335; XV,161-62, 509; XVI,587, 590, 840
  Oliver XV,90, 206, 483; XVI, 85, 100, 106
  Peter XV,464, 466, 478, 504, 654, 672, 688
  Ralph XIV,346, 572, 609; XV, 613, 714; XVI,200, 529, 688
  Richard XVI,36
  Samuel XV,382, 664, 671, 682; XVI,381, 683, 690, 797, 799-802; XVII,17, 339
  Seth XV,85, 207
  Smith XIV,233, 408; XVI, 710

Emerson, Solomon XVI,730
  Thomas XIV,346
  Timothy XV,571; XVI,118,
    120, 641
  William XIV,236; XV,177-78
Emery, Amos XIV,424; XVII,102
  Anthony XIV,24, 246, 253;
    XVII,502
  Benjamin XIV,242, 299,
    429, 431; XVI,609
  Caleb XIV,237, 425;
    XVI,915
  Daniel XV,99, 348, 536;
    XVI, 238, 245, 267,
    498, 534-36, 567, 699
  Daniel Jr. XIV,420; XV,99
  David XVII,36
  Eliphalet XIV,134, 191;
    XVII,7
  J. XVI,923
  James XIV,664; XV,431;
    XVI,119
  Jane XIV,503
  Jesse XV,698
  Joel XIV,56, 184
  John XIV,36; XV,20, 536
  Joseph XIV,588; XVI,785
  Josiah XIV,432; XVI,547
  Moses XIV,225; XV,399;
    XVI,125
  Noah XIV,70, 179, 311,
    498, 510, 521, 588,
    604; XV,5, 19, 64, 67-
    68, 73, 76, 86, 96,
    103, 110, 117, 119,
    121, 132, 142, 148,
    151, 158, 161, 163,
    166, 170, 173, 177,
    181, 184, 187, 195,
    197-98, 205, 218, 227,
    244, 255, 265, 274,
    281, 282, 285, 313,
    347, 359, 378, 380,
    384, 387, 391, 407,
    410, 461, 495, 709,
    416; XVI,158, 742, 787-
    88, 843 XVII,22, 83,

Emery, Noah (Cont.) 93, 102,
    113, 145, 225, 374-75
  Noah Jr. XV,462; XVI, 145,
    376, 394, 396, 400,
    403, 932
  Rama XV,628, 640; XVI,102,
    622, 627
  Richardson XIV,421; XV,739
  Thomas XIV,15, 98, 205,
    334; XV,396
  William XIV,261; XV,162,
    164; XVI,158, 254
  Zachariah XIV,35;
    XVII,101, 135
Emmons, Benjamin XV,149, 151,
    158, 160
  John XIV,77, 198, 501
  Joseph XIV,329
  Noah XV,223; XVI,153
Emms, Richard XVII,51
Endicott, John XVII,490, 518
English, Ensign XVI,314
  James XV,383, 385; XVI,924
  Jonathan XVI,113
  Thomas XIV,178, 359
  William XIV,658; XV,732;
    XVI, 39, 190, 212, 228,
    498, 567
Ennis, Richard XVII,308
Enos, General XVI,543, 545
  Roger XIV,209
Epes, Francis XV,350, 353,
    554
Epeson, Samuel XVI,886-87
Epperson, Samuel XV,633, 647
Erinson, David XIV,586
Erskine, Jacob XVII,619
  John XVII,203
Ervine, John XVI,722
Erving, Henry XVI,375, 915
  John XIV,579, 653; XV,431,
    452, 454; XVI,59, 253
  Morris XVI,915
Erwin, David XIV,161
  Henry XVI,907
  John XVI,247, 516
Esinau, Ichabod XVII,60

Estabrook, Abel XIV,93, 202-3, 420
  Deacon XVII,149
  Joseph XIV,262, 288, 292; XVII,48
  Samuel XVII,144
Estaing, Charles Hector, Count de XVII,290, 351
Etheridge, Stephen G. XIV,362, 365
Eustace, J. O. XVII,160-61, 168, 179-80, 182
Evans, Benjamin XV,749, 752
  Daniel XIV,22, 227, 257-58; XVII,340
  Edward XIV,61, 182, 280, 288, 468, 567, 590, 607-8; XV, 161, 163, 459, 607; XV,631, 637, 714; XVI,200, 224, 241, 269, 321, 323, 326, 330, 338, 340, 343-44, 609, 798, 800-1
  Eldad XIV,264; XVII,96
  Elizabeth XVI,800, 802
  Elzy XV,223
  Ephraim XIV,114, 140, 142
  Eri XV,602
  George XIV,70, 179; XV,175; XVI,551
  Ira XIV,85, 199, 264, 470, 593; XV,717
  Rev. Israel XV,726; XVI,208; XVII,459
  James XVI,898
  John XIV,269, 272, 290, 302-3; XV,7, 181, 406, 698, 744; XVI,313, 452; XVII,116, 525
  Jonathan XV,747
  Joseph 3d XVI,904
  Joshua XIV,264
  Lemuel XV,249, 251-53
  Moses XIV,274
  Peter XVI,93
  Robert XIV,233, 409; XVII,623

Evans, Samuel XIV,236
  Stephen XIV,256, 321, 361, 366, 406, 409, 446, 461, 478, 556; XV,276, 286-317, 433, 507, 581, 618, 620, 628, 640-41, 655, 666; XVI,58, 104, 196, 526, 528, 623, 625, 816, 850, 899; XVII,213, 270
  Tappan XVI,868
  Thomas XV,575
  Wiggins XIV,550; XVI,168-69
  William XIV,125, 188, 235, 307; XV,297, 747; XVI,103, 207; XVII,359
Eveleth, William XIV,114, 141, 193, 298
Everdon, John XIV,477; XV,214, 520
Everett, Edward XIV,279, 287, 292, 295
  George XIV,279, 288, 586, 657; XV,460, 606; XVI,195; XVII, 221
  John XIV,35; XV,220; XVII,649, 651
  Nicholas XIV,259; XVII,37
  Thomas XV,748
Evers, Morris XVI,900
Everton, John XIV,267
Eviston, George XV,199
Ewers, Rufus XIV,400
Ewing, David XVII,294
  James XVII,208
Ewins, James XIV,347
  John XVI,720
  Peter XIV,324, 464; XVI,80
Extill, Benjamin XV,48
Eyers, Christopher XV,144
  John XV,452
  Samuel XIV,348, 605; XV,711, 716
  Stephen XV,350, 352
Eyre, Eleazer XVII,479-84, 487-488

Eyre, Thomas XVII,479-84, 487, 492, 496

F

Fabes, John XVII,625
Fabins, Elizabeth XVII,634
Fabyan, John XVII,737
Facy, Eliphalet XVII,137
  Joseph XIV,555; XV,726; XVI,8; XVII,269
Fahey, William XIV,274, 277, 289
Fairbanks, Aaron XVI,840
  Jonas XIV,437
  Levi XIV,437, 525
  Zenas XIV,525; XV,58
Fairfield, Elijah XIV,585, 611; XV,717; XVI,202
  Ensign XVI,315
  Jeremiah XIV,579, 653; XV,452, 454, 729, 739; XVI, 31, 33, 59, 65, 73, 100, 187, 210, 235, 277, 511, 723-24; XVII, 319
  John XV,152; XVI,314; XVII,645
  Joseph XVI,46
  Samuel XIV,394; XV,15; XVII,88
  Walter XVI,315
Fairman, Benjamin XVII,296
Fairweather, William XIV,13
Falker, Michael XIV,235
Fall, Aaron XVI,234
  Betty XVI,863
  George XIV,233, 559, 561, 581, 621; XV,449, 600, 619, 722; XVI,205, 273, 836, 862, 863; XVII,29, 438
  Joshua XVI,103, 202, 223, 271
Fannell, John XVI,931
Fannin, Phinehas XIV,329
Farley, Benjamin XIV,33, 381, 490, 501, 514
  Benjamin Jr. XIV,346

Farley, Caleb XIV,392, 488, 509, 513; XV,510; XVI,377, 689
  Ebenezer XIV,33, 438
  Jonathan XIV,307
  Kendall XV,751
  Joseph XV,88-89
  Samuel XV,125, 149, 160
  Solomon XIV,309, 576
  William XIV,576, 644; XV,732; XVI,20, 22, 191, 212, 840
Farmer, David XIV,56, 184; XVI, 733
  James XIV,53, 185, 588
  Minot XIV,32; XV,743
  Samuel XVII,207
  Simeon XV,748
  William XIV,264
Farms, David XV,176
Farnham, Ebenezer XIV,265, 653
  Jacob XV,698
  John XIV,267; XV,638; XVI,202, 219
  John S. XV,718; XVI,695
  Joseph XV,74, 76
  Samuel XIV,268, 271
  Timothy XV,163, 182, 548; XVI, 268, 696
Farnsworth, David XIV,32; XV,743
  Edmund XV,664, 671, 684; XVI, 741; XVII,339
  James XIV,297; XV,31, 37; XVI, 920; XVII,148
  Joseph XV,32, 367
  Moses XIV,575, 593; XV,438, 716; XVI,201
  Oliver XV,11, 144
  Paul XVI,159
  Samuel XV,535
  Silas XIV,85
  Thomas XIV,34; XV,355; XVII, 100
Farnum, Asa XIV,102, 207
  Daniel XV,129, 405

Farnum, Ebenezer XIV,566;
  XV,23, 129; XVI,31, 34,
  59, 187
 Ephraim XVI,931
 John XIV,100, 198, 206-7,
  471, 477; XV,405, 631;
  XVI,611
 John S. XVI,270, 509
 Joseph XIV,244, 319;
  XV,197, 213
 Joseph Jr. XIV,317
 Nathaniel XVII,10
 Roger XV,24
 Stephen XIV,416; XV,520
 Theodore XV,185
 Timothy XVI,237, 509
Farr, Aaron XIV,437, 525;
  XVII, 95
 Charles XV,7, 223
 Daniel XV,6, 223
 Ebenezer XV,51
 Ephraim XIV,93, 202-3;
  XV,7
 Isaac XIV,427
 Jacob XV,7
 Jacob Jr. XV,225
 Jonathan XIV,93, 202-3,
  427; XV,224
 Jonathan Jr. XV,51
 Jonathan 3d XIV,428
 Joshua XIV,93, 202-3
 Nathaniel XIV,34, 101,
  206-7; XV,21
 Samuel XVII,95
 Samuel B. XIV,247
 Thomas XV,7; XVI,35;
  XVII,95
 William XV,223, 355
Farrar, Isaac XV,133, 173
 Jeduthan XIV,300, 399;
  XVI,657
 John XIV,310; XVI,236,
  272, 506, 654-55
 Joseph XIV,267; XV,21, 79,
  108, 360, 470
 Stephen XVI,762
 Rev. Stephen XIV,34

Farrar, Timothy XIV,34; XV,79,
  82, 84, 105, 470, 754;
  XVI,762; XVII,102
Farren, Phinehas XIV,174
Farrill, John XIV,353
Farrington, John XIV,25
 Phinehas XIV,336; XV,211;
  XVII,62
 Samuel XV,408
 William XIV,52, 185
Farris, William XIV,34
Farrow, William XV,542
Farwell, Absalom XV,217
 Eleazer XVI,921
 Elisha XV,367
 Isaac XIV,34, 104, 106,
  553, 592; XV,21, 438,
  595-97, 602, 710;
  XVI,2, 51, 182, 197,
  218, 267, 385, 712,
  934; XVII,153, 266,
  440, 460
 J. XVI,248
 John XV,108
 Jonathan XIV,427; XV,57;
  XVI, 246, 253, 296,
  314, 515; XVII,116, 253,
  265
 Joseph XIV,43, 105
 Josiah XV,31, 367
 Levi XIV,646; XVI,23
 Noah XVI,296
 Richard XV,217
 Timothy XIV,34
 William XIV,84, 199
Fassett, Joseph XIV,93-94,
  202, 213, 221; XV,630,
  643, 646, 725; XVI,102,
  506, 653-54
Favor, Thomas XIV,404
Favour, -- XV,699
 Cutting XV,124, 126, 381,
  385; XVI,681
 Samuel XVII,425
Faxon, Christopher XIV,239
 Hunking XIV,227, 257, 387,
  494, 507, 516

Fay, Daniel XV,209
    Joseph XIV,265, 578, 644;
        XV, 732; XVI,20, 22,
        191, 212, 333, 382
    Joseph Jr. XIV,644
    Josiah XV,751
    Lucy XVI,333, 341, 382
    Nathan XVI,553
    Nathaniel XVII,103
Fears, Humphrey XV,206
Felch, Benjamin XIV,329
    Daniel XIV,454, 530, 546,
        568, 759; XV,610, 727;
        XVI,10, 43, 184, 209,
        901
    Jabez XIV,252, 390, 486,
        508, 512-13; XV,524
    Nicholas XIV,229, 253,
        390, 487, 508, 512-13;
        XV,174
Felker, Joseph XIV,362;
    XV,747
    Michael XVI,196
Felix, Philip XIV,55, 184
Fellows, Benjamin XV,167,
        754; XVI,287, 510
    Daniel XV,699
    David XV,408; XVII,198,
        306
    Ebenezer XVI,922
    Hezekiah XIV,62, 158;
        XV,752
    Isaac XIV,24, 232
    Jeremiah XV,522
    John XV,150, 160; XVI,236,
        273, 521, 827
    Jonathan XIV,110, 131,
        190; XVI,255, 508
    Joseph XIV,273, 277, 289;
        XV, 165, 486, 499-500;
        XVI,65, 74, 98, 107,
        147, 264, 530; XVII,30,
        730
    Josiah XIV,441, 527;
        XV,382; XVI,928
    Moses XIV,211, 215, 218-
        20, 548, 568, 659;

Fellows, Moses (Cont.) XV,610,
        727; XVI,9, 42, 183, 208,
        264; XVII,430
    Nathan XIV,267, 271;
        XVII,114
    Nathaniel XIV,226, 290;
        XVI, 308
    Samuel XV,379, 561;
        XVI,308; XVII,32, 92,
        114
    William XIV,13; XV,199;
        XVII, 712
Felt, Aaron XVI,859
    Jonathan XV,360
    Joseph XIV,90, 201; XV,93,
        470, 502
    Peter XV,364
    Samuel XV,107, 534
Felton, John XV,102, 360
Fenix, John XIV,237
    Joshua XIV,485; XVII,86
Fenner, Joshua XIV,518
Fenton, Francis XIV,159, 161,
        163; XVI,538; XVII,118,
        120
Fergerson, Eleazer XVI, 116
Ferguson, Archibald XIV,240,
        259; XVII,22, 33, 37
    Eleazer XIV,299, 352, 629;
        XV, 456, 748
    Henry XIV,242
    James XIV,411; XV,566;
        XVI,63, 72, 90, 106
    John XIV,74, 178, 411;
        XV,200; XVI,401
    Joseph XVII, 294
    William XV, 632, 650; XVI,
        13, 44, 102, 236, 275,
        520, 832
Ferid, Alexander XVII,304
Fern, Philip XV,556, 558
Fernald, Amos XIV,109, 124,
        187; XVI,710
    Benjamin XIV,259; XVII,36
    Ebenezer XIV,240
    Edward XIV,259; XVII,36
    Joel XIV,240

Fernald, John XIV,119, 259, 664; XV, 431, 692; XVI,234; XVII,37
Joseph XIV,259, 480, 664; XV, 431; XVII,36
Mark XVII,420
Noah XIV,664; XV,431
Robert XIV,259, 480, 664; XVII,24, 31, 36
Samuel XVII,511
Simeon XVI,925
Theodore XIV,260
Thomas XIV,299
Tobias XV,749
William XIV,259, 344, 664; XV, 431; XVI,705
See also Furnald
Ferren, Ebenezer XV,174
Jonathan XV,455; XVI,38, 633, 724
Moses XIV,586, 627; XV,720, 742; XVI,204, 233, 241, 272, 514, 526, 771
Philip XV,115, 556, 558; XVII, 258
Ferson, James XIV,254
Robert XV,189
Fessenden, William XIV,46
Fever, John XVI,928
Timothy XV,562
Field, Andrew XIV,68, 180
Elihu XIV,355
Gains XVI,167, 298, 849, 878
Henry XIV,416, 478
Israel XV,55
John XIV,336; XVII,62, 436
Moses XV,67, 197, 226
Moses D. XVII,97
Robert XVI,237, 518, 815
Thomas XVII,98
Waitsill XIV,93, 202-3; XV,3, 205
Zachariah XIV,355
Fielding, Ebenezer XV,144; XVI, 313, 606; XVII,249

Fields, John XVI,259
Robert XVI,273
Fife, Silas XVI,738
Fifield, Abraham XIV,60, 182; XV,164
Benjamin XIV,273, 276, 289; XV,406; XVI,909, 915; XVII, 612, 659, 687
David XVII,57
Ebenezer XIV,226; XVII,32
Edward XIV,112, 146, 430, 585, 616; XV,165, 440, 719; XVI, 902
John XIV,112, 147, 195, 279, 288, 342, 546; XV,165
Jonathan XIV,25, 71, 179, 266, 548; XV,127, 165, 249-51, 254, 267-69, 272, 470, 490, 515; XVI,147, 236, 521, 528, 827, 897
Joseph XIV,25, 159, 161, 164, 286-87, 430, 546; XV,165, 424, 514, 700-3, 725; XVI, 170-71, 174, 208, 302, 508, 679; XVII,16
Mark XV,327; XVI,110
Moses XV,621, 663, 669, 682, 689; XVI,872
Nathaniel XIV,302, 390, 480, 486; XVII,19
Samuel XV,194; XVI,173
Sherburne XVI,147
Stephen XIV,565, 660; XV,727, 743; XVI,11, 316, 581
Weare XIV,195
William XIV,61, 182; XVII,528
Winthrop XV,698; XVI,147
Filbert, Antoine XVII,299
Finch, Simeon XIV,87, 200
Finlay, Joseph XV,394-95, 428-29; XVI,436

Finney, Robert XVI,88, 95, 236, 508, 685
Finniston, Winthrop XVII,307
Fish, David XIV,513
   John XIV,100, 206-7
   Jonathan XV,695
   Nathan XIV,573, 576, 629; XV, 613, 731; XVI,15, 26
   Nathaniel XIV,639
   Simeon XV,81, 632, 636; XVI,23, 44, 740
Fisher, Anne XVII,323
   Edmund XIV,264
   Ichabod XVI,922
   Janvrin XVI,357
   John XVII,322-23, 325
   Nathan XV,188
   Nathaniel XVI,931
   Samuel XIV,411; XVI,911
   Thomas XIV,22
   Timothy XV,39; XVII,109
   William XV,99
Fishley, George XIV,642; XV,457, 494, 733; XVI,19, 41, 192, 213, 232, 279, 774
Fisk, Aaron XV,224
   Amos XVI,539
   Cato XIV,564; XV,451, 725; XVI,207, 227, 275, 505, 644-645
   David XIV,301, 391, 487, 509, 513
   Ebenezer XV,207
   Eleazer XVI,113, 635
   Eleazer Jr. XV,664, 671; XVII, 339
   Ephraim XIV,304, 306, 465; XV, 186; XVI,105, 148
   Ephraim Jr. XV,129, 186
   James XIV,33; XV,743-44
   Jonathan XIV,25
   Dr. Joseph XVI,479
   Josiah XIV,33, 346; XV,87, 510, 743
   Lieutenant XVII,312
   Mashon XIV,6

Fisk, Nathan XVI,84, 91
   Simeon XV,211
   Solomon XIV,566; XV,608; XVI, 31, 33, 59
Fiske, Cato XIV,630
   David XIV,244
   Eleazer XV,677
   Solomon XIV,653; XV,729
   William P. XVI,59; 926
Fitch, Abigail XVII,747
   Caleb XVI,286, 510, 702
   Jedediah XVII,747
   Paul XV,97
   Samuel XIV,394; XV,39, 156; XVII,88, 143
   Thaddeus XIV,102, 207; XV,97, 103, 197-98, 539
   Zebediah XIV,394; XV,39
   Zebulon XVII,88
Fitts, Abraham XV,402; XVI, 588, 590, 936
   Isaac XIV,317, 319
   J. H. XVI,936
   Nathan XV,402; XVI,599-600
   Richard XIV,112, 147, 196, 453, 532
Fitzgerald, John XVII,37
   Joseph XVII,47
   Joseph M. XIV,260; XV,749
   Michael XIV,570, 616; XV,637, 722; XVI,521, 784, 849
   Thomas XIV,283, 287
Fitzgibbons, William XVII,297
Flagg, Asa XVI,93
   Asa Jr. XVI,81
   Elijah XIV,34
   Isaac XIV,100, 206-7, 346; XV,530
   James XIV,581, 659; XV,449, 600, 727; XVI,9, 42
   Jonas XV,510; XVI,144
   Josiah XV,402; XVI,262, 479; XVII,432
   Dr. Samuel XV,388, 557
   William XIV,356
Flahane, Thomas XVII,296

Flanders, Abner XIV,430;
    XV,185; XVI,295
  Captain XV,657, 696
  Christopher XIV,34
  Daniel XV,321, 340, 408, 698
  David XIV,60, 182, 280, 288,
    341; XV, 187, 329, 343
  Enos XV,408
  Ezekiel XV,187, 194, 486,
    499-500, 658, 667, 673,
    691, 742; XVI,125, 255,
    287, 508, 516, 708, 918
  Isaac XIV,226
  Jacob XIV,184, 471, 566,
    611, 617; XV,457, 663,
    670, 684, 688, 718, 722,
    747-48; XVI, 202, 270,
    610, 838, 874; XVII,438
  James XVI,869
  Jesse XV,128, 186; XVI,908
  John XIV,184, 211, 215, 217,
    220, 611; XV,187, 515,
    717; XVI,140, 161, 202,
    576, 871, 874
  Jonathan XIV,181; XVI,657
  Joseph XIV,317, 320;
    XV,187; XV,195, 515
  Josiah XV,267, 269-70, 273,
    663, 670, 685, 688; XVI,
    105, 148, 610
  Levi XIV,350
  Micah XIV,63, 181, 186;
    XVII,3
  Micajah XV,515
  Michael XV,406
  Moses XVI,246, 251, 509,
    838
  Nathaniel XIV,226
  Parker XV,640
  Philip XIV,16, 261, 316, 318,
    568, 601; XV,610, 712;
    XVI, 222, 268, 521, 827,
    914-15
  Seth XVI,148
  Stephen XIV,55, 184, 341,
    585, 657; XV, 328, 330,
    343, 485, 499-500, 742;

Flanders, Stephen (Cont.)
    XVI,38
  Thomas XIV,67, 181, 432;
    XVI, 140, 161
  William XIV,287
Fleming, James XVII,332
  Mary XVII,332
Flennon, Simon XVII,301
Fletcher, Charles XVI,884
  E. XVI,694
  Ebenezer XIV,555, 574, 622;
    XV,52, 443, 722; XVI,205
  Francis XIV,34; XV,97, 103,
    355; XVII,100
  Gideon XVI,236, 270, 503
  Henry XVII,101
  John XIV,336, 700; XV,24,
    741; XVII,62, 527
  John Jr. XV,77, 79
  Jonathan XV,26, 147;
    XVI,159; XVII,249
  Joshua XV,381; XVII,91
  Josiah XV,93, 100; XVII,92
  Levi XIV,441, 527; XV,160;
    XVI,113
  Levi Jr. XVI,113
  Nicholas XVII,653
  Oliver XVI,884
  Peter XIV,34, 436, 524;
    XV,93, 220, 533; XVII,100,
    102
  Philip XIV,358
  Phinehas XVI,236, 267, 513,
    772
  Robert XIV,35, 420, 422; XV,
    79, 96, 518, 533, 535, 654
  Samuel XV,12, 147, 741;
    XVII, 42, 47, 249
  Simeon XV,118, 350;
    XVI,140, 161, 729; XVII,
    426
  Simeon Jr. XV,138
  Simon XV,353
  Thomas XIV,34
  Timothy XVI,553-54
Fleury, Major XVII,200
Fling, Anthony XIV,322

Fling, John XVI,109, 165
Patrick XIV,211, 215-20,
348, 649, 653; XV,728;
XVI,12, 192, 209, 247,
251, 500, 575
Flint, Amos XIV,103, 207
Jacob XIV,302, 313, 467, 548
Dr. Thomas XVI,366
Flood, Aaron XVI,235
Amos XIV,105, 265, 568,
653; XV,610, 729; XVI,30,
33, 59, 187, 210
Benjamin XIV,442, 542;
XV,369, 372
Daniel XIV,261, 611; XV,408;
XVI,874
Humphrey XIV,230, 252,
351, 450, 535; XV,256,
258, 260, 262; XVI,65, 75,
94, 106
James XIV,404; XV,102, 108;
XVI,190, 738; XVII,32, 296
Jonathan XIV,110, 132, 190,
312, 563, 651; XV,728,
734; XVI,27, 188, 210,
231, 277, 505, 648-51,
922
Joseph XIV,173, 176-77,
611; XVI,246, 252, 874;
XVII,438
Moses XIV,172, 175-77, 329;
XVI,247, 253; XVII,438
Richard XIV,61, 182, 454,
564; XV,185; XVI,68, 79,
97, 236, 243, 501, 600
Stephen XIV,16
Flossington, Valentine XVII,252
Flower, Benjamin XVI,51, 53
Flowers, Benjamin XVII,457,
460
Elisha XIV,291
Floyd, James XIV,642; XV, 597,
730, 735; XVI,17, 211,
228, 278, 507, 520, 668,
845-46; XVII,220
Richard XIV,529
Flyard, Morey XVII,301

Fogg, Abner XV,732
Caleb XV,284, 291, 565
Chase XIV,312; XV,474, 494;
XVII,25
Daniel XIV,132, 190
David XIV,116, 128, 189,
352, 451, 532; XV,242,
244, 247, 412
Dearborn XIV,229
James XIV,110, 131, 190,
413, 551; XVII,642, 741
Jeremiah XIV,49, 121;
XV,320, 340, 461, 718;
XVI,4, 51, 115, 182, 203,
230, 271, 286, 875, 935;
XVII,13, 268, 280-81,
438, 440, 443-44
Jerry XIV,553, 615
John XVI,932
Jonathan XIV,118, 137, 158,
192, 212, 214, 217-18,
220, 255; XV,300-1, 305,
308; XVI,905
Joseph XIV,49, 110-11, 121,
154, 413; XV,240-41
Josiah XV,559; XVI,806-7
Phinehas XV,565
Samuel XIV,370, 378, 387,
492, 494, 507, 516, 519;
XV,169, 474, 494; XVII,25
Seth XIV,352; XVI,643, 645
Simeon XV,300, 302, 304
Simon XV,308
Stephen XV,168, 475, 496;
XVI,116; XVII,25
William XIV,244
Follansbee, Moses XVII,426
Nathan XVII,424
Thomas XVII,511
Follensby, John XIV,424
Moses XIV,212, 215-20
William XV,483, 497
Follet, Benjamin XIV,356, 443,
543; XV,204, 277, 380
Gibbs XIV,543
Giles XIV,443; XV,277, 380
Ichabod XIV,13

99

Follet, John XIV,225, 397
  Robert XIV,237
  Samuel XIV,93, 202-3
  William XV, 360
Follett, Benjamin XVII,48
  Giles XVII,48
  Ichabod XVII,717
  John XVII,98, 501
  William XVII,513, 611
Follinsby, James XVI,84, 90,
    106
  Nathan XVI,78, 100
  Nathaniel XVI,67
  See also Follensby
Follinton, Jonathan XIV,584
  Joseph XIV,584
Folsom, Abraham XIV,12; XVI,
    742
  Asa XV,416, 571
  Benjamin XIV,71, 179, 353,
    476, 564, 616; XV,478;
    XVI,616
  Colonel XV,450
  David XVI,853
  Ebenezer XVII,640, 643
  Edward XIV,232
  Ephraim XVII,526
  General XV,489, 496, 623,
    655
  Israel XIV,11, 13
  Jacob XIV,353
  James XVII,27
  Jeremiah XIV,12, 341;
    XV,256, 258, 260, 263,
    657, 667, 674; XVI,64, 74,
    94, 641
  John XIV,66, 148, 180, 195,
    232, 235, 259, 321, 364,
    451, 532, 563, 617;
    XV,171, 284, 287, 544-45,
    723; XVII, 22, 34, 36, 512,
    526, 625, 643, 693
  John Jr. XIV,322
  Jonathan XIV,144, 194, 232,
    248, 563, 618, 639;
    XV,571, 723; XVI,11, 206,
    231, 273, 316, 514, 660,

Folsom, Jonathan (Cont.) 766;
    XVII,26-27
  Josiah XIV,142, 193, 298;
    XV, 574; XVI,624, 932-33;
    XVII, 29, 261
  Levi XV,416
  Moses XIV,312
  Nathaniel XIV,37, 41, 44-45,
    48-49, 120, 338, 398, 475;
    XV,14, 577, 690; XVI,165,
    299, 406, 420, 463, 651-
    52, 803-4, 923; XVII,15,
    50, 53, 79-80, 123, 139,
    247, 255, 335, 349, 387,
    693
  Nicholas XV,173
  Peter XVII,526
  Samuel XV,651; XVI,242,
    245, 257, 505, 582, 648,
    717; XVII,15, 526, 624
  Theophilus XVI,316-17
  Thomas XV,418, 565; XVI,
    648; XVI,650; XVII,25
  Tristram XIV,398; XV,300,
    302, 305, 309
  Trueworthy XVII,57
  Widow XVI,933
Foot, Challis XVI,869
  Isaac XIV,25, XV,664, 670,
    683; XVI,84, 92, 106, 141,
    161, 697; XVII,339
  Thomas XVI,125
Footman, Benjamin XVII,717
  John XIV,13, 235; XVII,717,
    719
  Joseph XVII,717
  Thomas XIV,120, 124, 151,
    187, 197, 251; XVI,623;
    XVII,513-514, 636, 638,
    670, 717
Ford, Benjamin XVII,191, 204
  Charles XIV,223
  Daniel XV,27, 143; XVI,541;
    XVII,249
  Hezekiah XV,153-54;
    XVII,208, 253
  James XIV,247, 478; XV,69,

Ford, James (Cont.) 71, 196,
206-8; XVI,249, 322, 331,
334, 382
Job XV,153
Joseph XV,154; XVII,253
Miles XIV,362
Noah XV,277; XVI,539
Paul XV,153-54; XVII,134
Richard XVII,536
Robert XIV,237
Seth XV,279-80; XVII,253
Foreman, John XV,592
Foret, Samuel XIV,447
Forgerson, Ebenezer XIV,495
Eleazer XIV,388
Forgison, William XVI,13, 44,
242
Forrest, John XV,387
Major XVII,160
Robert XIV,144, 193-94, 304,
306, 569, 605; XV,609,
716; XVI,201, 269, 512,
726
William XIV,144, 193-94,
211, 215, 218, 220, 316,
319, 454, 529, 546;
XV,181, 487, 490-91;
XVI,87, 94
William 3d XVII,9
Forsaith, David XIV,554, 634
Jonathan XIV,583, 635
Josiah XIV,456, 537
Robert XV,381, 385
Forst, Benjamin XIV,244
Samuel XIV,637
Forster, Asa XVI,148
Captain XVII,462
Daniel XVI,148
David XVI,595
George XIV,477
William XVI,148
Forsyth, David XV,719; XVI,5;
XVII,268
Jonathan XV,724
Fosbury, John XVI,930
Fosgate, Ebenezer XIV,203-4,
267, 573, 596; XV, 615,

Fosgate, Ebenezer (Cont.) 713;
XVI,199, 223, 241, 268,
504, 635
Fosgood, Ebenezer XIV,470
Foskett, Robert S. XV,723
Foss, Abner XVI,106
Benjamin XIV,229, 253, 351,
540, 551; XV,320, 340;
XVI, 61, 63, 71, 98, 107,
193, 251, 520
Daniel XIV,372, 385, 497,
506, 517; XV,297
Ebenezer XV,387; XVI,87, 90
George XIV,235, 248, 408;
XV, 298; XVII,26
George Jr. XIV,409
Henry XIV,20, 27, 382, 490;
XV,749; XVII,55
Isaac XVI,129, 162
Isaiah XV,299
Jacob XV,249-51, 254
Jeremiah XIV,135, 191, 228,
400; XVII,6
Job XIV,381, 490, 501, 514;
XV,243, 245, 487, 496;
XVI, 61-62, 72, 98, 107,
193, 261; XVII,432
Job Jr. XVI,822
John XIV,127, 188, 224, 229,
232, 248, 316, 319, 402,
415, 473, 564, 627, 671;
XV, 324, 441, 627, 720;
XVI,103, 185, 213, 228,
272, 279, 507, 514, 668,
767; XVII,26, 434
Jonathan XIV,231, 397
Joseph XV,247
Joshua XVI,372
Joshua Jr. XVI,571
Mark XIV,235; XVII,26
Moses XIV,228, 423; XVI,
860
Nathan XIV,114, 141, 193,
447, 540
Nathaniel XIV,141, 193, 235,
400; XV,242, 244, 246,
248, 298, 527; XVI,261,

Foss, Nathaniel (Cont.) 822,
   912; XVII,432
Nathaniel Jr. XIV,114
Richard XIV,565, 660;
   XV,727; XVI,10, 43
Robert XV,129
Samuel XIV,15, 228, 245,
   540, 562; XV,619, 725
Stephen XIV,228
Thomas XIV,135, 191, 231,
   309, 564, 624; XV,441,
   512, 720
Timothy XIV,273, 289
Wallace XVI,912
William XIV,15, 448, 536
Zachariah XVI,906
Fosse, Martin XVII,305
Foster, Abiel XIV,194, 317; XVI,
   592, 594, 727
Anthony XIV,607-8
Asa XV,515; XVI,148
Asa Jr. XIV,359
Asaph XVI,910
Caleb XIV,588; XVI,790
Daniel XIV,34, 575, 622, 646;
   XV,47, 95, 220, 722, 732;
   XVI,20, 22, 148, 205, 212,
   887
David XIV,425; XV,4; XVI,595
Enoch XVI,159
Ephraim XIV,34, 169, 333,
   575, 592; XV,163, 179,
   716; XVI, 580, 920-21
Frederick XV,698; XVI,147
Isaac XV,75, 211; XVII,388
Jacob XV,95
James XIV,348, 401, 414;
   XV, 220; XVI,235, 272,
   506, 654-655
Jedediah XVI,124
Jeremiah XIV,76, 81, 198,
   452, 532; XVI,286, 498
Jerry XVII,427
Joel XIV,272, 289
John XIV,53, 185, 259; XVI,
   144, 678; XVII,37, 226

Foster, Jonathan XIV,100, 144,
   194, 206, 316, 318, 454,
   529; XIV,546, 573;
   XV,127, 164, 179, 468,
   480, 512, 612, 698, 731;
   XVI,15, 25, 186, 211;
   XVII,9
Joseph XIV,62, 156-57;
   XV,751; XVI,81
Joshua XIV,35, 334; XV,534
Luke XIV,259, 343; XVII,22-
   23, 38
Mr. XVII,361, 384
Nathan XV,698; XVI,144,
   237, 270, 512, 741
Nehemiah XV,63
Samuel XIV,34, 575, 622;
   XV, 412, 443, 722
Simeon XV,624, 632, 636;
   XVI, 23, 44, 691
Thomas XV,133
William XV,698; XVI,148
Fosto, Antona XV,714
Fothergill, Moses XIV,237
Foward, John XV,693
Fowle, James XIV,105
Jeremiah XV,714; XVI,200
Oliver XVI,920
Fowler, Abner XIV,566, 660; XV,
   587, 607, 727; XVI,9, 42,
   183, 208, 594; XVII,81, 83
Ebenezer XV,747
Jacob XIV,413; XV,457
Jacob Jr. XV,587
John XIV,297; XV,134;
   XVI,903
Josiah XV,400
Mary XVI,594
Moses XVI,933
Philip XIV,299, 313, 408,
   452, 532, 571, 586, 616,
   618; XV, 311, 719, 723,
   743; XVI,203, 206, 226,
   239, 272, 274, 519, 766,
   831
Robert XIV,413

Fowler, Samuel XIV,253, 273,
288, 295; XVI,525; XVII,47
Simon XVI,169-70
Thomas XVI,128, 162
Fox, Benjamin XIV,15, 233, 370,
378, 492, 503, 515;
XVI,529; XVII,25
Daniel XVII,80, 82
Edward XIV,21, 135, 191,
226; XV,300-1, 304, 308,
417, 528
Eliphalet XV,25
Israel XIV,226
Joel XIV,657; XV,459, 605,
731; XVI,37-38
John XV,41, 194, 375, 693,
698; XVI,156, 286, 505
Dr. Jonathan XV,624;
XVI,689-690, 692
Joseph XV,451-52
Nathaniel XIV,66, 181
Robert C. XIV,239
Silas XIV, 317, 320, 657; XV,
459, 605, 731, 735;
XVI,36, 38, 190, 212, 228,
278, 502, 585-86, 680
Sinkler XV,169
Timothy XIV,34; XV,93
Uriah XV,149, 160, 633, 647;
XVI,585
Winthrop XV,633, 647, 721;
XVI, 205, 233, 241, 272,
517, 586, 798
Foxlesory, Henry XVII,293
Foy, Benjamin XIV,447
Daniel XIV,451
James XIV,273, 277, 289
John XIV,238, 446, 540
Thomas XIV,381, 489, 501,
514
Timothy XIV,277
Foye, John XV,575; XVII,26
Francis, -- XV,136
Colonel XV,432
Joseph XVI,313
Levi XVI,507
Richard XV,518

Francis, Thomas XVII,22, 34
Frankford, William XV,718; XVI,
852
Franklin, Ichabod XV,55, 204;
XVII,96
James XIV,355
Nathan XIV,427; XV,6;
XVI,877
Stephen XV,471, 503;
XVII,96
Frasier, General XV,421
John XV,256
John G. XIV,671
William XIV,71, 179, 302,
588, 604; XV,438, 716
Frazier, Dennis XVII,297
John XVII,51
Samuel XVII,302
Freeland, Richard XVII,293
Freeman, Captain XVII,216-17
Constant XVII,469
Daniel XIV,356
Edmund XV,14, 38, 45, 373,
378; XVII,111
Ezra XIV,645; XVI,24
Frederick XIV,576, 655; XV,
729; XVI,31, 33, 59, 737
James XVII,469
John XIV,160-61, 164
Jonathan XV,38, 44-45; XVII,
108, 111
Josiah XVII,307
Moody XIV,160-61, 163;
XV,39; XVII,109
Peter XVI,510
Rufus XVI,159
Russell XV,18, 41, 138
Sampson XVI,920
Samuel XVII,18
Sylvanus XV,374
Titus XIV,274-75, 289, 292
William XIV,10
Freese, Gordon XIV,391, 487,
509, 513
Zachariah XIV,299, 312
Freeze, Andrew XV,660;
XVI,617-618

Freeze, Gordon XV,249-51, 254, 565; XVI,115
Jacob XVII,25
Joseph XIV,118, 137, 158, 192; XV,522
French, Abel XVII,2
Abraham XIV,226; XVI,706-7, 709
Amos XV,267-69, 273, 565; XVI, 115
Andrew XIV,229; XV,325
Arthur XVII,303
Benjamin XVI,67, 78, 99, 193, 915
Daniel XIV,229; XV,183, 544; XVI,131, 163, 261, 286, 516, 805; XVII,432
David XIV,392, 427, 487, 509, 513
Ebenezer XIV,110, 132, 190
Elijah XIV,370, 378
Elisha XIV,229, 370, 378, 492; XV,544
Enoch XIV,117, 129, 189; XVI, 616
Ephraim XIV,336; XV,10; XVII, 62
Ezekiel XIV,116, 129, 189, 332; XIV,350
Ezra XIV,224; XV,400; XVII,32
Gould XIV,330
Haynes XIV,281, 286-87, 473; XV,700, 703, 725; XVI,171, 175, 314, 315, 782; XVII,117
Hezekiah XV,42
Isaac XIV,419
Jabez XIV,117, 129, 189, 392, 487, 509, 513
James XV,128, 186, 217, 680; XVI,921
James Jr. XV,664-65, 671; XVI, 698
John XIV,12, 113, 147, 173, 176-77, 195, 288; XV,107, 217, 285, 291, 537, 564,

French, John (Cont.) 589, 664, 671, 696; XVI, 167, 751; XVII,78, 113, 675
Jonathan XIV,234; XV,209, 510, 665, 680; XVI,257, 520, 751; XVII,32
Jonathan 4th XV,561
Joseph XIV,247, 391-92, 487, 508, 512; XV,79-80, 197, 206, 249-51, 254, 256, 482, 494; XVI,82, 92, 106, 256, 507, 530
Joshua XIV,146, 195
Joshua Jr. XIV,112
Levi XIV,24; XV,696, 699
Matthias XIV,210, 215, 218-20
Moses XIV,300
Nathaniel XIV,116, 129, 189; XV,285, 291, 400-1
Nehemiah XIV,247; XV,88
Obadiah XIV,413
Offen XVI,287, 516
Richard XV,421
Samuel XIV,226, 340, 574, 626; XV,70, 441, 615, 720; XVI, 237, 265, 274, 509, 696, 915; XVII,32, 465
Silas XV,4, 698, 741; XVII,98
Thomas XIV,296, 452, 532; XV, 328, 343, 754; XVI, 922
William XIV,23, 33, 229, 223; XV,524, 545, 740; XVI, 705; XVII,433
William Jr. XIV,219
Winthrop XIV,299, 312, 565, 651; XV,729; XVI,28
Friend, Charles XVII,302
John XIV,114, 141, 193, 407
Frink, Dr. Calvin XIV,46, 48, 311; XV,293; XVI,389, 411, 487-88, 852
Thomas XV,46; XVI,434
Frison, Peter XVII,304

Frohock, Thomas XIV,210, 214,
217, 219-20; XV,133
Frost, Elkiah XV,717
George XIV,149, 622;
XV,652; XVI,203, 408,
441, 528
George P. XIV,119, 196, 554;
XV,718; XVI,5, 51, 182,
271, 301; XVII, 268, 449
John XIV,237, 314; XVII,511
Joseph XIV,578, 610;
XV,439; XVII,429
Joshua XV,225
Mark XIV,236
Mr. XVII, 517
Nathaniel XIV,624; XV,441,
620, 725; XVI,207, 233,
241, 275, 511, 710
Nicholas XV,192
Simon XIV,237
Thomas XIV,9
Wentworth XV,192
Winthrop XIV,233; XVII,24
Frye, Captain XV,437-38, 453-
55, 597, 606-8
Colonel XIV,42, 44
David XIV,359
Ebenezer XIV,70, 552, 604-6;
XV,710; XVI,2, 51, 182,
197, 248, 267, 301, 610-
11; XVII, 216, 266, 274,
361, 445
Isaac XIV,38, 48, 78, 80, 155,
555, 639-40; XV,458-59,
726; XVI,7, 15, 17, 50,
182, 194, 208, 220, 875;
XVII, 145, 269, 291 440,
442-43
James XV,746
Richard XVI,920
Fryer, Nathaniel XVII,512, 527,
584, 599, 621, 631, 638-
39, 641, 644, 654, 670,
674, 683, 692
Fugard, Samuel XIV,358, 468,
604
Fullam, Elisha XV,24

Fuller, Amasa XV,144, 662, 669,
689; XVI,313; XVII,249,
252
Amos XIV,303, 575, 639;
XV,731; XVI,15, 26, 857-
58
Andrew XV,558; XVI,728
Asa XIV,233; XVII,28
Benjamin XIV,224; XV,42,
169; XVII,110
Benoni XVII,740
Chase XVI,928
Daniel XIV,422, 468, 607-8;
XV,436, 714; XVI,159
David XV,603; XVI,153; XVII,
236
Enoch XIV,244
Ezra XIV,90, 573, 639;
XV,613, 731; XVI,15, 26
Francis XIV,334
Hezekiah XIV,443, 542, 547;
XV,589; XVII,73
James XV,41; XVII,109
Jesse XV,204
John XIV,1, 112, 147, 195;
XV,400, 732; XVII,528
Jonathan XIV,263, 265, 644;
XVI,20, 22
Joseph XV,211
Joshua XV,65, 227, 741;
XVII, 97
Josiah XIV,408
Lemuel XV,43, 156, 375;
XVII, 143
Levi XIV,578, 644; XV,732;
XVI, 20, 22
Peter XIV,265
Samuel XIV,356; XV,67, 149,
160, 226; XVI,247, 253,
286, 519
Silas XIV,100, 206
Theodore XV,666, 685;
XVI,843
Thomas XIV,11, 112, 147,
195, 341, 470, 586, 600,
606; XV, 715; XVI,200,
269, 516, 831

Fuller, William XVII,528, 628
Fullerton, David XIV,189
  James XV,192; XVI,65, 76,
    99, 105-6
  John XIV,364; XVI,807
  Jonathan XIV,580; XV,447,
    598
Fullington, David XIV,116, 129
  Ezekiel XV,562
  Francis XV,279, 281, 592
  James XIV,370, 378, 492
  John XIV,362
  Jonathan XIV,630; XV,725
  Joseph XIV,630; XV, 725
Fullonton, John XVII,57
  Jonathan XV,444
  Joseph XV,444
Fulmer, George XVII,301
Fulton, John XIV,171, 175-77
  Robert Jr. XVII,149
Fund, Nicholas XVII,304
Funde, Alexander XVII,307
Furber, Benjamin XIV,234
  Eli XIV,233; XVII,25
  Jethro XV1,760
  Joshua XV,249-51, 253, 571;
    XVI,776
  Levi XV,324; XVII,29
  Mary XVI,429
  Moses XIV,234
  N. XIV,257-58, 550
  Nathaniel XV,430
  Richard XIV,233; XV,298,
    576; XVI,429; XVII,28
  Thomas XIV,115, 141, 193;
    XV, 575
  William XV,324, 331, 578,
    583; XVII,502, 525, 620,
    625, 632, 668, 693
  William Jr. XVII,525
Furbish, Benjamin XIV,497, 517
  Samuel XIV,406
Furbush, Benjamin XIV,372,
    385, 506
Furgerson, Eleazer XVI,116
Furgit, Ebenezer XIV,96
Furguson, Joseph XVII,294

Furnace, John XV,573
Furnald, Charles XV,249, 251-
    53
  Edmund XIV,227, 257
  Edward XVII,42
  John XVI,214; XVII,139
  Joshua XIV,237
  Renald XVII,31, 39, 86
  Rendall XIV,255, 485
  Robert XIV,255; XV,326;
    XVII,39
  Theodore XIV 484, 499, 512,
    518; XVII,46, 85
  Thomas XV,249-51, 255
  William XIV,583, 651;
    XV,579, 729; XVI,28, 109,
    165, 188, 210
  See also Fernald
Furness, John XIV,237, 242;
    XVII,260
  Robert XVII,139
  William XIV,362
Fycount, Francis XVII,302
Fyence, Joseph XIV,358
          G
Gaffet, James XVI,267
  John XVI,103, 510, 720, 725
Gage, Aaron XV,85
  Abner XIV,42, 53, 185, 588;
    XVI,322-23, 327, 329-30,
    334, 337, 339, 343, 345,
    383
  Amos XV,345, 359, 566
  Andrew XIV,53, 185, 587,
    660; XV,727; XVI,9, 42
  Asa XV,25
  Benjamin XV,359, 698;
    XVI,720
  Captain XVI,914
  Daniel XIV,348; XV,359, 567,
    718; XVI,102, 202, 223,
    246, 253, 271, 516, 784
  David XIV,53, 185; XV,228
  Isaac XV,358, 740
  James XIV,478
  Job XIV,247
  John XIV,126; XV,286, 294,

Gage, John (Cont.) 296, 315,
  317, 329, 343, 574;
  XVI,357, 526, 622-23,
  913-14; XVII,11, 32, 261
John Jr. XVI, 627
John 3d XIV,188
Jonathan XIV,52, 185, 476
Joseph XIV,430; XVI,933
Joshua XIV,58, 183, 254
Josiah XV,358; XVI,783-84
Phinehas XV,207
Pierce XIV,611
Solomon XV,187
Gaile, Asa XV,57
Gains, George XIV,233, 367,
  376, 383, 389, 393, 415,
  520; XV, 282, 428, 578-
  79, 675; XVI, 111, 129,
  142, 317-18, 451, 804-5;
  XVII,36, 38, 289, 350,
  362-63
Samuel XIV,423
Thomas XIV,8
Gale, Amos XVI,706-7
Asa XIV,93, 202-3
Bartholomew XIV,451, 532;
  XVII, 57
Colonel XVI,58, 104
Daniel XIV,144, 193; XV,171,
  243, 245, 247; XVI,13;
  XVII,9-10
Jacob XIV,405, 475, 478; XV,
  318, 331, 333, 341, 420,
  559-69, 623, 629, 641,
  655, 658, 667, 691;
  XVI,566, 795, 823;
  XVII,43-44, 349
John XV,165; XVI,169
John C. XVI,170, 281, 564
Joseph XIV,399; XVII,25
Nathan XIV,578, 644; XVI,21,
  24
William XIV,484, 499, 512,
  518, 648-49; XV,595, 728;
  XVI,12, 192, 209, 803;
  XVII,85, 288-289
See Also Gaile

Gallop, Asa XV,42; XVII,89
Benjamin XV,16
Thomas XV,40, 155;
  XVII,108, 111
Thomas Jr. XVII,144
William XVII,422
Galloway, Charles XVII,295
Robert XVII,303
Gallup, Asa XIV,394
Gallutin, Samuel XVI,307
Galusha, Jacob XVI,308-9
Samuel XIV,268, 272, 290;
  XVII, 114
Gambier, Admiral XVII,324
Gamble, Archibald XV,622, 663,
  669, 677; XVI,732-34
Gambling, Benjamin XVII,710,
  750, 762
Gammel, Hugh XV,592
William XV,546, 582
Gammell, William XVII,259
Gammet, John XV,168
Gammon, Thomas XIV,227,
  257-58, 344, 472; XV,324
Gamsby, John XV,705
Gandra, Gabriel XVII,305.
Louis XVII,305
Gansey, John XVI,167, 878
Ganzier, John XIV,645
Gardner, Christopher XIV,119,
  150, 196, 448, 535;
  XVII,486
David XV,578
Ebenezer XIV,424; XVII,747
Gardner, Ezekiel XIV,445, 543;
  XV,377
Henry XVII,479-84, 487-88,
  494, 506
John XIV,239, 255, 283, 287,
  425; XV,417, 435, 577;
  XVI, 108-9, 143, 165;
  XVII,23, 46, 715
John Jr. XIV,260; XVII,31,
  38, 139
Josiah XV,754
Nathaniel XVI,197, 267
Thomas XIV,127, 188, 251,

Gardner, Thomas (Cont.) 618;
    XV,444, 618, 722; XVII,12
  William XV,577; XVII,139,
    146-47, 274
Garey, Daniel XV,430
  James XV,430
  Moses XV,30
  Samuel XV,430
  See also Gary
Garfield, Nathaniel XV,508, 580,
    582; XVI,135, 150
Garland, Amos XV,523;
    XVII,424
  Dodivah XIV,476; XV,750;
    XVI, 904
  Ebenezer Jr. XIV,361;
    XVI,913
  Gideon XV,469, 481, 506
  Jacob XIV,11, 144, 593; XV,
    166; XVII,8
  James XIV,68, 180; XV,300,
    302, 306, 309
  Jeremiah XIV,354
  John XIV,11, 25, 252, 413,
    534, 642, 654; XV,423,
    448, 455, 468, 481, 507,
    523, 527, 599, 619, 725,
    729; XVI,18, 31, 33, 59,
    207, 370, 627, 913;
    XVII,740
  Jonathan XV,522, 524, 750
  Joseph XIV,253; XV,134,
    527; XVI,918
  Moses XIV,430; XV,515
  Nathaniel XIV,230
  Peter XVII,501
  Richard XV,655, 666, 685;
    XVI, 67, 77, 96, 623, 627-
    28
  Robert XVII,692
  Simeon XIV,22
  Simon XVI,912
  Thomas XIV,114, 141, 192
Garling, Gideon XIV,408
  John XIV,406-7, 580, 637
  Thomas XIV,406

Garnet, Amos XV,740
  Robert XVII,296
Garnsey, David XVI,81
  John XV,745; XVI,167, 809,
    878
  Samuel XVI,81
Garonte, Antoine XIV,662;
    XV,728
Garoutte, Antoine XVI,210
Garrelty, Richard XVII,297
Garrett, Anthony XVI,27, 189
  Samuel XVI,931
Garrison, William XVI,235, 242,
    501, 600
Garvin, Eliphalet XV,175, 513
  Ephraim XIV,171, 174, 176-
    77, 359; XVI,66, 78, 91
  James XV,573; XVII,260
Gary, Daniel XIV,549
  James XIV,549
  Moses XIV,325
  Samuel XIV,549
  See also Garey
Gasemore, Thomas XVII,46
Gaskell, Jonathan XVI,412
Gassaway, John XVII,208
Gassett, John XIV,606; XV,465,
    467, 478, 504, 698
Gatchell, Increase XVII,749
Gates, Daniel XIV,264, 291
  Elias XIV,394; XV,15, 138,
    373; XVII,88
  Elisha XV,171
  Ezra XIV,280, 288; XV,733;
    XVI,45, 48, 264, 302, 305,
    313, 332, 341, 385, 679,
    783; XVII,116, 253
  Ezra Jr. XIV,280, 288
  George XIV,604
  Horatio XV,219, 276, 278-79,
    367; XVII,72, 94, 100,
    106, 108, 136, 147, 150-
    51, 210, 218, 232, 239,
    241, 243, 265, 281, 290,
    311-12, 328-29, 382, 393,
    405-6

Gates, Isaac XIV,51, 186
  Jacob XIV,167, 170, 280,
    288; XVII,14
  James XV,376
  Nathan XV,374
  Stephen XIV,280, 288;
    XVII,253
  Thomas XV,39; XVII,108, 111
Gauding, Samuel XIV,634
Gault, Adam XVI,910
  George XV,716; XVI,141, 161
  John XV,587, 632, 636;
    XVI,34, 44, 85, 236, 268,
    500, 575, 746
  Matthew XIV,173-77; XV,174
  Patrick XVI,911
  Samuel XIV,171, 174-77;
    XV,587
  Samuel Jr. XV,587
  William XV,128; XVI,169-70,
    787, 911
Gaustie, Mauterin XV,461
Gawen, William XIV,240
Gay, Isaac XIV,658; XVI,39
  James XV,116
  Robert XVI,917
  Thomas XV,499-500
  Zebulon XIV,268, 270, 290
Gearfield, Nathaniel XV,508,
  580, 582
Geary, Oliver XV,7
Gee, Luman XV,147; XVII,249
  Solomon XVII,104
Geer, Charles XIV,598; XVI,80,
  91; XVII,384
  Ebenezer XV,32
  Matthew XIV,578; XVI,201
  Shubael XVI,598
  Walter XIV,598
Gefford, Joseph XVII,508
Geoghegan, John XVII,204
George, Austin XIV,55, 184,
  657; XV,731; XVI,36, 38,
  195, 212, 284
  Benjamin XIV,58, 183, 602;
  XV, 712; XVI,199, 733,
  735

George, Charles XV,113
  Daniel XV,637
  David XIV,212, 214, 217,
    219-220, 348, 561, 579,
    621; XV, 187, 455, 722;
    XVI,205, 723
  Fanny XVI,724
  Gideon XV,322, 342
  Gideon Jr. XV,322, 342
  Henry XIV,253, 350
  Isaac XIV,602; XV,434, 712;
    XVI,199, 735
  James XIV,13, 258
  John XV,698; XVI,86, 91,
    107, 297
  Jonathan XIV,348, 560, 579,
    620; XV,455, 722, 740;
    XVI, 724
  Joseph XV,557; XVI,733;
    XVII,256
  Josiah XIV,642; XV,422, 456,
    730; XVI,19; XVII,291, 354
  Michael XIV,347, 560, 563
    579, 620; XV,455, 722;
    XVI, 103, 205, 222, 241,
    273, 506, 649, 724-25
  Moses XVI,237, 273, 498,
    564
  Moses S. XIV,632; XV,444;
    XVI, 206, 335-36;
    XVII,467
  Samuel XIV,350; XV,747;
    XVI, 141, 161, 256, 297,
    507
  Thomas XIV,397, 570, 602,
    611; XV,712, 717;
    XVI,198, 202, 632, 777,
    779-81
Gerould, Reuben XVII,108
Gerrald, James XIV,316, 319
  Monsieur XVII,343
Gerrish, Alexander XIV,237,
  369, 377
  Benjamin XIV,239; XVII,28
  Captain XIV,13, 15, 26; XVII,
    710
  Colonel XVII,15

Gerrish, Enoch XIV,316-18,
   465; XV,128, 405, 514
Henry XV,127, 130-31, 404-
   8; XVI,576-77; XVII,10, 50
Jacob XV,751
James XIV,322; XV,295;
   XVI,627
John XVII,525, 621, 629,
   648, 655-56, 665, 676,
   683
Joseph XIV,118-19, 149,
   196, 260; XV,515; XVII,46
Paul XIV,322; XVI,128, 162,
   628, 904
Richard XVII,678
Samuel XIV,236, 298, 429;
   XVI, 592-94, 904
Thomas XIV,236, 372, 384,
   496, 505, 517; XV,699
Timothy XIV,255, 260, 368,
   375, 483, 498; XV, 468,
   480, 507, 517, 656, 666,
   674; XVI,639; XVII,31, 39,
   46
William XIV,485, 500, 512;
   XVII,87
William Jr. XIV, 518
Gerry, Mr. XVII, 352, 389, 391
Getchell, David XV, 15; XVII,
   111
Egburton XV, 350, 352
Jesse XVI, 632; XVII, 427
Zebulon XIV,341; XV, 115,
   742
Ghiselin, John XVII,204
Gibbon, Fitch XVI,81, 93
Gibbons, Ambrose XVII,534
Gibbs,-- XVII,6, 406
Abraham XIV,264; XV,7
Asa XIV,436, 524, 575, 622;
   XV,443, 722
Benjamin XIV,34; XV,533
Caleb XVI,45
David XIV,264, 607-8;
   XV,436, 714; XVI,200
Elisha XV,100; XVI,840

Gibbs, Isaac XIV,264, 607-8;
   XV,714; XVI,200
James XIV,55, 184
Joseph XIV,276
Joshua XIV,264, 607-8;
   XV,714; XVI,200
Robert XIV,336; XVII,63
Thomas XIV,264; XVI,460
William XIV,20; XV,632, 635;
   XVI,504, 634-35
Gibson, Abel XVII,257
Archibald XIV,95, 204-5
Barnabas XV,358
Daniel XV,546, 582; XVII,
   259
David XVI,153
Ebenezer XIV,33
Enoch XIV,144, 193-94;
   XV,134; XVII,9
James XIV,29, 51, 58, 96,
   144, 171, 175-77, 193-94,
   204, 296, 430, 653;
   XV,165, 206, 358, 472,
   490-91, 671, 676, 730;
   XVI,31, 34, 59, 719, 783-
   84, 903
James Jr. XVI,783; XVII,9
Jedediah XIV,194
Jeremiah XIV,144, 193;
   XVII,9
John XIV,463, 473; XV,630,
   646, 671, 677; XVI,82,
   100, 102, 167, 719, 783-
   84, 812, 814, 878, 898-99;
   XVII,66, 113
Mr. XVII,493
Samuel XIV,417; XV,85
William XV,346; XVI,921
Giddens, Simeon XIV,298
Giddinge, Eliphalet XV,416;
   XVII, 140, 213, 220, 224,
   226, 236
John XVI,537
Giddinge, Lydia XV,451
Nathaniel XV,416
Zebulon XV,451

Giddings, Eliphalet XIV,601, 604, 615-20, 627, 629, 633, 659, 662
Gidney, Colonel XVII,661
Joshua XVI,932
Gigo, Francis XVII,304
Gilbert, Abel XV,225
Ebenezer XVI,152
Elias XV,370
Enos XV,633, 648; XVI,41, 44, 877
John XVI,68, 79, 100, 250, 256, 507
Larraford XV,214
Lenaford XIV,267, 477
M. XVII,299
Samuel XV,745
Seth XIV,357
Thomas XV,384; XVI,315
Gilbertson, Edward XVII,307
Gilbor, Amiable XVII,304
Gilbus, James XVII,294
Gilchrist, Alexander XV,556
Charles XIV,265
Robert XV,115
Gilcreast, Alexander XVII,258
Gilder, Reuben XVII,205
Gile, Abraham XIV,309; XVI,314; XVII,116
Asa XIV,226
Benjamin XVI,125, 255, 517, 713, 769-70
Captain XVII,390, 404
Ephraim XIV,341; XVI,914
Ezekiel XIV,242; XV,398-99, 485, 488, 499-500; XVI,566, 795
Jacob XVI,37, 44, 103, 191, 213, 225, 279, 875; XVII,438
James XVI,246, 252; XVII,438
John XIV,225, 476
Jonathan XIV,19; XV,128, 387
Joseph XIV,16; XVI,914
Moses XIV,19; XVI,914

Gile, Nathan XIV,452; XV,398
Nathaniel XIV,532
Giles, Benjamin XIV,478; XVII,22, 126
Daniel XIV,316, 318
Ezekiel XIV,225, 340
Jacob XVI,664
John XIV,231; XV,249, 252, 254; XVI,779-81; XVII,712, 722-23
Joseph XIV,273, 289
Mark XIV,13, 25
Nicholas XVII,27
Richard XV,745
Solomon XV,249, 251-52, 254, 698; XVI,66, 76, 95, 776; XVII,434
Thomas XIV,103, 208
Gilkie, Sampel XV,43
Gill, Joseph XVII,328
Silas XIV,90, 201, 575, 593; XV,438, 716; XVI,323, 331, 338, 340, 385
William XIV,231, 330, 350
Gillen, John Jr. XVII,526
Gillespy, John XVII,303
Richard XV,630, 637
Gillett, Jonathan XVII,153
Simon XIV,268, 272, 290; XVII, 118-19, 250
Gillispee, Richard XVI,102, 720, 724
Gilman, Andrew XIV,232, 243; XV, 416; XVII,28
Anthony XIV,471, 610; XV,718; XVI,202, 219, 270, 517, 795
Antipas XVI,525, 659
Benjamin XIV,116, 129, 189; XV,191
Bradbury XVI,273
Bradstreet XIV,232
Caleb XIV,580, 661; XV,172, 448, 599, 748; XVI,11, 547, 829
Captain XVI,221; XVII,608
Carter XIV,3, 314, 563, 585,

Gilman, Carter (Cont.) 618, 661;
    XV,444, 723; XVI, 11, 206,
    231, 274, 505, 649, 651,
    708
  Colonel XVI,58, 104, 180,
    901
  Constantine XIV,464; XV,23,
    370
  Daniel XIV,226, 341;
    XV,514, 746; XVII,526
  David XIV,299, 301-2, 435,
    461, 479, 481, 522, 554,
    619; XV, 719; XVI,5;
    XVII,48, 50, 75, 140, 268,
    285
  Doctor XVI,933
  Dudley XIV,112, 117, 129,
    147, 189, 195, 250, 390,
    486, 508, 512; XV,194,
    482, 495; XVII,29
  Edward XVII,526
  Edward Jr. XV,194
  Eliphalet XVII,27
  Ezekiel XIV,71, 179, 580,
    627; XV,447, 598, 720;
    XVI,149, 204, 226, 272,
    506, 649, 659, 928
  Israel XIV,37-38, 48, 78, 80,
    685
  J. XVI,549
  James XIV,103, 207 232,
    458, 537; XV,213
  Jeremiah XIV,552, 591;
    XV,162, 191, 193, 235,
    710, 742; XVI, 2, 197,
    221, 541; XVII,127, 225,
    266, 705
  Jeremy XVI,527
  John XIV,15, 116, 128, 189,
    233, 581; XV, 243, 245,
    247, 449, 600, 729, 748;
    XVI,28; XVII, 27, 29, 526,
    543, 555, 563, 568, 584,
    601, 665, 693
  John Jr. XIV,233, 309, 651
  John M. XIV,25, 144, 194,
    221, 304, 465; XVII,9

Gilman, John Taylor XIV,389,
    446, 459, 531; XV,22,
    154, 157, 198, 208, 212,
    215, 246-47, 251-252,
    258, 269-70, 278, 281,
    327, 330, 341, 384, 688;
    XVI,322, 380, 396, 400
  Jonathan XIV,43, 68, 180,
    354, 362, 365; XVI,747
  Joseph XIV,162, 216, 407,
    461, 662; XV,630, 642,
    643 etc. as examiner of
    rolls; XVI,13, 117, 120,
    136, 146, 149, 154, 160,
    202, 238, 271, 288, 292,
    297, 299, 360, 364, 373,
    458, 522, 547, 552, 829,
    866; XVII,102, 111, 113,
    226, 274, 289, 314, 322,
    357, 361-63, 368, 375,
    396, 458
  Joseph S. XV,242, 244
  Joshua XIV,12, 324, 464;
    XV,11, 147; XVI,321, 331,
    334, 386, 659
  Joshua Jr. XVI,659
  Josiah XVI,166, 318; XVII,90;
    XVII,444, 449
  Josiah Jr. XV,2, 5, 8, 13, etc,
    as examiner of rolls;
    XVI,103, 108, 111, 114,
    117, 123, 126, 129, 139,
    142, 151, 283, 285, 290,
    297, 299, 322, 360, 381,
    395, 490, 550-892;
    XVII,99, 107, 112, 258,
    315
  Major XVI,901-2
  Michael XV,22
  Morris XIV,12
  Moses XIV,210, 214, 217,
    220, 455, 530
  Mr. XVII,18
  Nathaniel XIV,247, 555, 649;
    XV,726, 748; XVI,7, 121,
    164, 766; XVII,25, 269
  Nicholas XIV,12, 15, 119,

Gilman, Nicholas (Cont.) 218,
    256, 275, 299, 369, 389,
    410, 434, 478, 531, 555-
    56, 638; XV,2, 141, 193,
    202, 208, 212, 215, 218,
    229, 283, 286, 303, 314,
    330-31, 416, 629, 648,
    655, 657, 667, 688, 726;
    XVI,6, 22, 121, 164, 182,
    186, 208, 264, 281, 292,
    304, 317, 384, 426, 581,
    628, 839; XVII,126, 269-
    70, 288
    Noah XIV,227, 257; XV,324
    Peter XIV,160-61, 164, 302,
        459, 539; XV,194, 592-93;
        XVI,281; XVII,88
    Samuel XIV,23-24, 107, 134,
        136, 154, 191, 232, 250,
        286-87; 353; XV,249-50,
        416, 592; XVI,316-17,
        902; XVII, 5, 7, 13, 114,
        215
    Samuel Jr. XIV,432; XVI,410;
        XVII,20, 57
    Samuel F. XV,456
    Samuel T. XIV,629
    Simeon XIV,196; XV,444
    Simon XIV,112, 147, 150,
        195, 312, 353, 451, 532,
        618; XV, 599, 722;
        XVI,206, 297, 648
    Smith XV,246
    Stephen XIV,105; XV,30,
        371; XVII,80, 83
    Sumersbee XVI,659
    Theophilus XVI,933
    Thomas XIV,261
    Trueworthy XV,657; XVI,
        650-51
    William XV,132, 392, 475,
        498, 742
    Zebulon XIV,399; XV,283,
        287, 289, 315, 317, 513;
        XVI,296
Gilmant, Francis XVII,304

Gilmore, James XIV,74, 178,
    242, 335, 338, 348, 605,
    699; XV, 566-67, 638,
    715; XVI, 201 888, 890;
    XVII,62
    John XIV,411; XV,99, 116,
        176; XVI,534
    Jonathan XV,394, 428
    Robert XIV,334; XV,162, 174,
        217; XVI,536; XVII,41
    Roger XV,98, 103; XVI;700
    Samuel XVI,307
    Thomas XIV,578, 593;
        XV,596, 716
    Whitefield XIV,358
Gilner, Henry XVII,307
Gilson, David XV,79, 518; XVI,
    84, 91
    Joel XV,100, 360; XVI,840
    John XIV,100, 206-7
    Solomon XVI,287, 516, 805
    Timothy XV,656
    William XVII,124
Gisgory, John XVII,298
Gist, John XVII,207
Gladding, James XIV,183, 254
Gladin, William XVII,295
Glasier, David XIV,85, 199-200
    Joseph XIV,6
Glass, David XIV,234
    James XVI,131, 163
Glazier, David XV,225
    John XVI,922
Glazon, Joseph XIV,6
Gleason, Eliab XV,9, 31, 367
    James XV,47
    Joab XVII,97
    Job XV,226
    Timothy XIV,226, 300, 312;
        XV, 654, 666, 672, 678;
        XVI,117, 570-72
    Windsor XV,143
Glen, Captain XVII,739
Glidden, Andrew XV,36
    Charles XIV,143, 194
    Daniel XIV,312

Glidden, David XVI,155
Gideon XIV,68, 180, 249,
617; XV,619, 627, 723
James XIV,58
John XIV,13, 111, 131, 190,
296-97, 362, 365; XV,172,
319, 339
Peter XV,297
Simeon XIV,298
William XV,733; XVI,45, 48,
264, 302, 305
Glinds, Israel XIV,269
Nathaniel XIV,65
Glines, Benjamin XVI,87, 90,
107
Eli XVI,297
Elizabeth XVI,592-95
Israel XIV,252, 271, 290,
429; XV,129, 186
James XIV,261
John XIV,144, 194, 269, 271,
290; XV,392; XVI,749;
XVII,9
Nathaniel XIV,181, 186, 304,
316, 319, 566, 605-6; XV,
617, 716; XVI,201, 271,
502, 592-93, 926; XVII,4
Richard XV,179
Robert XVI,65, 75, 100
William XIV,144, 194;
XV,128, 387; XVI,236,
267, 502, 594-595;
XVII,717
Gliten, Charles XVII,526
Glover, David XIV,88, 201
Henry XIV,42, 58, 183, 267;
XV,188, 483, 497; XVI,753
John XIV,108, 123, 187, 233
Robert XIV,87, 201; XV,517
Goatham, Edward XIV,562, 637
Samuel XIV,637
Goddard, John XVII,513, 535,
604
Samuel XVI,930
William XV,55
Godding, Samuel XV,724;
XVI,206, 813

Godfree, Isaac XV,695
James XV,249-51
John XIV,302-3, 545
Jonathan 3d XV,456
Godfrey, Edward XVII,478, 504,
506, 508-9
Ezekiel XV,564; XVI,657
Humphrey XVII,528
James XV,255
John XIV,151, 197, 303, 312,
527, 573, 639; XV,613,
731; XVI,15, 25, 186, 211,
236, 275, 509, 692;
XVII,528, 643
Jonathan XIV,230, 252, 351,
621; XV,412, 722;
XVI,205, 273
Oliver XVII,506, 508
Tristram XV,656, 666, 673;
XVI, 127, 162, 672
William XIV,430; XVII,740
Goffe, Captain XVI,902
John XIV,16-17, 24, 26, 58,
183; XV,111, 362, 557;
XVI, 908-9, 913, 921;
XVII,461
Joseph XV,435
Thomas XVI,102
William XIV,605; XV,715
Gofoney, John XIV,119
Goggin, Hugh XVI,285, 504, 935
Going, John XV,259, 431
See also Gowen
Goings, William XIV,338
Golding, Windsor XV,671, 674;
XVI,63, 73, 91, 719, 721
Goldsmith, John XV,171
John Jr. XV,172
Josiah XV,25; XVI,865
Goodale, Asa XV,714
Enos XIV,35; XV,95, 364
Ezekiel XIV,35, 242, 476,
555, 640; XVI,8, 525;
XVII,134, 269
Jonathan XVI,314
Titus XVI,314
Goodall, Asa XIV,607-8

Goodell, Asa XV,424
Gooden, Robert XVII,298
Goodenough, Adino XIV,655;
    XV, 727; XVI,9, 42, 59,
    513, 737
    Benjamin XIV,334; XV,102
    Calvin XIV,655; XV,730;
        XVI,31, 34, 59, 513, 737-
        38
    Daniel XIV,420
    David XV,704
    Ebenezer XVI,236, 274, 513
    Jonathan XV,541
    Levi XVI,286, 510, 702
Goodenow, Adino XIV,101, 206-
    7, 576
    Calvin XIV,576
    Edmund XIV,427
    Israel XVII,95
    Nahum XIV,84, 199; XV,6, 47
    Timothy XV,7
Goodhue, George XV,589
    James M. XVII,294
    John XV,695
    Josiah XVI,169-70
    Lieutenant XVI,902
    Nathaniel XVI,781
    Phinehas XIV,53, 184
    Stephen XIV,418; XV,511
    William S. XIV,129
Gooding, James XIV,564
    Samuel XIV,576
    Theophilus XIV,459
Goodman, James XIV,7
    Richard XIV,87, 200, 301,
        572, 639; XV,611, 731;
        XVI,15, 25
    William XVII,297
Goodrich, Benjamin XV,300
    Eleazer XV,19
    Ezekiel XV,754
Goodridge, Allen XV,75, 213,
    520
    Thomas XIV,336; XVII,63
Goodspeed, Nathaniel XVII,108
Goodwin, Amariah XVI,119
    Amos XIV,236

Goodwin, Benjamin XIV,403,
    414; XV,302, 304, 308;
    XVI,647
    Caleb XIV,238
    Daniel XIV,225, 236, 403,
    414
    Edward XV,27; XVI,541;
    XVII, 105
    Ezekiel XIV,302, 314, 469,
    548; XV,549
    Henry XV, 539
    James XIV,135, 191, 236,
        243, 265, 321, 361;
        XVI,288; XVII,6
    John XIV,242
    Jonathan XIV,380, 489, 501,
    514
    Matthew XVI,83, 90, 107
    Noah XIV,473; XV,749
    Paul XIV,345
    Richard XIV,430; XV,408;
        XVI, 899
    Samuel XIV,224, 227, 234,
        257, 343, 472; XV,323,
        342; XVI, 539
    Simeon XV,385; XVI,539;
        XVII, 150
    Solomon XIV,16
    Theophilus XIV,224, 380,
        389, 501, 514, 538-39
    Thomas XIV,236
    William XIV,237
    Willoughby XIV,125, 188,
        473; XVII,12
Gookin, Daniel XIV,351, 562,
        636; XV,424, 456, 624,
        719; XVI, 5, 180, 182,
        203, 248, 271, 514, 528,
        774-75; XVII,441
Gordon, Alexander XIV,12
    Amos XV,182
    Caleb XV,746
    Daniel XIV,242, 399, 451-52,
        532; XV,562; XVI,115, 117
    Daniel Jr. XVI,807
    David XIV,242; XV,390, 483,
    495

Gordon, Dudley XVI,116
  Eliphalet XIV,457, 538, 584,
    630; XV,725; XVI,207,
    227, 239, 275, 519, 808
  Enoch XV,172
  Ithiel XIV,584; XV,445, 725;
    XVI,207, 807
  Ithiel Jr. XIV,630
  James XIV,116, 129, 189,
    309, 369, 377, 402, 492,
    503, 515, 564, 647;
    XV,283, 287, 629, 648,
    723; XVI,31, 33, 39, 206,
    227, 241, 274, 286, 500,
    517, 644, 657; XVII,27,
    57, 428
  John XIV,64, 182, 186, 612;
    XVI,926; XVII,3, 640
  Jonathan XV,328, 330, 344
  Joseph XIV,67, 304, 465,
    563, 585, 627; XV,482,
    495, 720; XVI,204, 226,
    241, 272, 509, 649, 709
  Josiah XIV,71, 179, 299; XV,
    169, 256, 258, 283, 288,
    696, 698, 748; XVI,85,
    100, 107, 115, 195, 589,
    650; XVII, 424-25
  Peter XVII,297
  Phinehas XIV,225
  Thomas XIV,14, 300, 397;
    XV, 514, 562; XVI,155,
    582, 807, 928; XVII,27
  Timothy XIV,71, 179
  William XIV,67, 181, 563,
    618-619, 627; XV,359,
    442, 566, 596, 720;
    XVI,204, 226, 240, 246,
    253, 272, 505, 516, 649
  William Jr. XV,566
  Zebulon XV,667, 679; XVI,
    581
Goreley, Benjamin XIV,7
Gorges, Edward XVII,489
  Ferdinando XVII,475-79,
    484-96, 500, 503, 506,
    516, 529, 533, 538, 540

Gorges, John XVII,691
  Robert XVII,500
Gorham, S. XV,266
  Stephen XVII,460
Gorman, Joseph XIV,231
Goss, B. XIV,514
  David XVI,234
  Eben H. XV,515
  Ephraim XVI,286, 498
  James XIV,76, 81, 198;
    XVI,690
  Jean XVII,609
  John XIV,32, 229, 369, 377,
    478, 492, 503, 515, 528;
    XV, 196, 209, 211-12,
    325, 743; XVI,377, 562;
    XVII,214
  John A. XVI,236, 269
  Jonathan XIV,118, 137, 158,
    192, 255; XV,256, 259-60,
    263; XVII,220
  Joseph XV,695, 698
  Mary XIV,317
  Nathaniel XV,27; XVI,609
  Peter XIV,102, 207; XVI,286,
    498
  Philip XV,55
  Philip Jr. XIV,427
  Richard XIV,380, 489, 501,
    647, 649; XV,596, 728;
    XVI,12
  Robert XIV,15
  Samuel XIV,503, 515
  William XIV,76, 82
Gotha, Matthew XV,729
Gotham, Edward XV,595, 724;
    XVI, 207, 229, 274, 516,
    803-5
  Henry XVI,256, 500
  Matthew XVI,28
  Samuel XV,596, 653, 725;
    XVI, 516, 803
Gotton, Henry XV,754
Goudy, Samuel XIV,382, 490,
    501, 514, 519
  Thomas XIV,244
  William XIV,381, 489, 501,

Goudy, William (Cont.) 514,
    519, 648-49; XVI,13
Goulay, John XVII,304
Gould, Abijah XV,96
    Amos XIV,243
    Christopher XIV,118, 138,
        158, 191, 255; XV,182
    Daniel XIV,302; XV,554, 664-
        665, 671, 673; XVI,235,
        269, 506, 653
    Daniel Jr. XVI,654-55
    Elias XIV,430
    Elijah XIV,574, 636; XV,440,
        615, 719; XVI,204
    George XV,741
    Gideon XIV,430
    Jacob XV,98, 348; XVII,100,
        102
    Jacob Jr. XV,631, 646; XVI,
        699, 812
    James XIV,162, 170, 422,
        553, 590, 607; XV,605,
        710; XVI, 3, 320-25, 330,
        334, 337, 339, 343-44,
        387, 525, 527; XVII,14,
        266
    Jeremiah XIV,114, 141, 193;
        XV,192
    Jeremy XIV,331
    John XVI,83, 96, 107, 298;
        XVII,428
    John Jr. XVII,428
    Jonathan XVI,144
    Moses XIV,597; XV,435, 713
    Nehemiah XIV,597; XV,713
    Noah XV,229
    Oliver XV,98
    Robert XV,164
    Samuel XIV,16
    Silas XV,207
    Simeon XIV,34, 524, 590,
        607-8; XV,355, 436, 459,
        571, 502, 533, 605, 714;
        XVI,200; XVII, 91
    Simon XV,424
    Stephen XIV,247, 439, 527;
        XV, 217; XVI,86, 99

Gould, Thomas XIV,224
    William XIV,382, 391, 487,
        490, 501, 508, 513-14;
        XV, 747
Gove, Abraham XVI,620
    Ebenezer XIV,350; XVI,835
    Edward XV,523; XVII,584,
        587, 589, 591, 594-97
    Eleazer XIV,23, 111, 132,
        190, 229, 642; XV,422,
        457
    Elijah XV,113
    Jeremiah XIV,23
    John XVII,675, 693, 710
    Jonathan XIV,11; XVI,491,
        755; XVII,149
    Dr. Jonathan XVI,359
    Joseph XIV,13
    Levi XV,412
    Moses XV,747
    Nathan XV,457; XVI,872
    Winthrop XVI,834
Gowdy,-- XV,596
    See also Goudy
Gowell, Benjamin XIV,236
Gowen, John XV,260, 263;
    XVI,898
    William XIV,255, 260, 312;
        XVII,22, 31, 33, 39, 46
Goy, James XV,174
Goyer, Bartholomew XV,109,
        630, 643, 646; XVI, 102,
        237, 274, 505, 629
Grace, Benjamin W. XVI,238,
        268, 509, 629
    Charles XIV,260; XVII,46
    John XIV,118-19, 150, 197
    Joseph XIV,63, 182; XVII,3
    Manuel XIV,33, 101, 206
Graffort, John XVI,198
Grafton, Caleb XIV,13
Graham, Alexander XIV,347
    George XV,557; XVI,147;
        XVII, 256
    Hugh XIV,347; XV,663, 670,
        674, 688; XVI,684
    John XIV,42, 333; XV,566,

Graham, John 582, 739; XVII, 259
  Jonathan XVI,101
  Joshua XVI,86, 92
  Josiah XVI,107
  Nathaniel XIV,469, 603; XV, 712; XVI,199, 225, 268, 504, 686
  William XIV,577; XV,739
Grandy, Besaleel XIV,264
  Clement XIV,20, 27
  John XVI,23
  Robert XV,50
Granes, William XVII,28
Grannis, Edward XV,145; XVI,313; XVII,249
  Timothy XVI,608
Grant, Asa XVI,922
  Benjamin XIV,231, 257, 267-68, 289, 295-96; XV,267, 269-70, 273; XVI,315, 924; XVII,30
  Charles XV,295
  Christopher XVI,922
  Daniel XIV,473, 622; XV,619, 719, 750
  David XIV,259
  Duncan XIV,470, 586, 600, 606; XV,715, 742; XVI,200, 507, 671, 930
  Edward XIV,230, 559, 561, 621; XV,443, 619, 722; XVI,205, 239, 273, 520, 836
  Elias XIV,237
  Elijah XIV,236
  John XIV,236, 248; XV,325; XVII,360
  Joseph XIV,603; XV,597, 712; XVI,199, 237, 244, 267, 503, 617, 846; XVII,296
  Joshua XIV,127, 188, 230, 258, 343, 473; XVII,12, 45
  Nathaniel XVI,668; XVII,360
  Nelson XIV,388, 495, 507, 516, 519

Grant, Noah XIV,268, 271; XVI,314
  Paul H. XIV,116, 129, 189, 330
  Peter XIV,126, 288, 382, 490; XV,152; XVI,314-15; XVII,11
  Peter Jr. XIV,380, 489
  Reuben XVI,314
  Samuel XIV,126, 188, 236, 323, 559, 621; XV,619, 722; XVI, 205, 273, 521, 836; XVII,12
  Silas XIV,237
  Thomas XVI,109, 165
  William XIV,561, 621; XV,443, 619, 722; XVI,205
Grapes, Philip XIV,167, 288;XV, 589; XVI,928; XVII,81, 83
Graves, Aaron XV,24; XVI,137
  Abner XVII,97
  Darius XV,24, 370
  Elijah XV,293; XVII,98
  Elijah Jr. XVI,850
  Elinda XVII,105
  Israel XIV,312; XVI,124; XVII, 30
  Jacob XV,421
  John XV,23; XVI,930
  Joshua XV,63; XVII,98
  Josiah XVI,116
  Mr. XVII,710
  Nathaniel XVII,57
  Reuben XV,58; XVII,95
Gray, Aaron XV,62; XVII,98
  Billy XIV,281, 285, 287
  Ebenezer XVI,105, 148
  Ellis XVII,245
  Francis XVII,513
  George XIV,228, 447, 540; XVII, 511
  Hannah XIV,472
  Hugh XV,741, 753
  James XIV,13, 49, 178, 225, 556, 659, 661; XV,447-49, 457-58, 597-600, 610, 726, 753; XVI,6, 42, 316,

118

Gray, James (Cont.) 526;
    XVII,269
  John XV,18, 538; XVI,237,
    244, 274, 504, 624, 628,
    917; XVII,717
  Jonathan XIV,43, 96, 204
  Joseph XIV,235, 249, 265,
    574, 639; XV,617, 731,
    741; XVI, 15, 25, 186,
    211, 235, 278, 522, 882
  Kalso XVI,792
  Moses XIV,464; XV,747
  Reuben XV,230
  Samuel XIV,225, 235, 242,
    361, 397, 408; XV,572;
    XVI,781
  Solomon XVI,237, 244, 500,
    572
  Thomas XVI,109, 165
  Timothy XIV,244; XV,75
  William XIV,115, 141, 192,
    321, 361, 624; XV,619,
    719, 741
  See also Grey
Grear, James XVII,427
  John XIV,662; XV,451, 453,
    455, 728; XVI,27, 724
  Matthew XIV,470, 594;
    XVI,218, 270, 499, 549,
    934
  See also Greer
Greele, Enoch XIV,113
  John XV,211, 529
  Jonathan XIV,691
  Joseph XIV,527
  Matthew XIV,548, 659;
    XV,610
  Nathaniel XV,75
  Reuben XIV,548, 659;
    XV,610
Greeley, Aaron XVI,483
  Benjamin XIV,247
  Daniel XVI,286
  David XVI,87, 90, 875; XVII,
    438
  Edward XIV,404; XV,421
  Enoch XIV,147, 195

Greeley, Ezekiel XVI,908
  John XIV,103, 207; XVI,85,
    100, 107, 236, 271, 516,
    784
  Jonathan XIV,103, 207, 336;
    XVI,883; XVII,62
  Joseph XIV,97, 204-5, 438;
    XV, 69, 346
  Josiah XIV,43
  Matthew XIV,568; XV,727;
    XVI, 10, 43, 184, 209,
    264; XVII,430
  Nathaniel XIV,103, 208;
    XV,419
  Noah XIV,388, 495, 507, 516,
    519; XVI,66, 73, 95;
    XVII,57
  Philip XV,408
  Reuben XIV,568; XV,727;
    XVI,11, 316
  Samuel XV,323, 342, 420-21
  Thomas XIV,13; XVII,654
  See also Greele
Green, Benjamin XIV,12
  Benajah XIV,422
  Bossett XVI,58
  Boswell XVI,103, 611
  Bradbury XIV,350, 561, 606,
    620; XV,319, 339, 443,
    457; XVI,103, 184, 189,
    205, 519, 834, 934;
    XVII,254
  Caleb XIV,264
  Captain XIV,11, 15
  David XIV,244; XV,213
  Eaton XIV,230
  Eben XVI,280
  Ebenezer XIV,162-66, 267-
    68, 270, 274, 289, 291,
    295-96; XVI,568; XVII,48,
    357-58, 461
  Edward XVII,253
  Elijah XV,113
  Enoch XIV,109, 122, 187
  Dr. Ezra XIV,48, 80; XVI,431;
    XVII,4
  Henry XVII,623, 629, 631,

Green, Henry (Cont.) 638, 669,
    683
  Isaac XVII,676, 753
  James XIV,484; XVII,86
  John XIV,11; XV,116, 633,
    643, 648; XVI,125, 700-1
  Jonathan XIV,354, 584, 628;
    XV, 320, 339, 748;
    XVI,205
  Joseph XIV,642; XV,204,
    597, 733, 740; XVI,19, 41,
    194, 213, 220, 279, 520,
    668, 845; XVII,235-36
  Richard XIV,642; XV,458,
    735; XVI,19, 185, 211,
    228, 278, 514, 773-75,
    822
  Robert XIV,642; XV,456; XVI,
    103, 514, 774-75
  Rowland XVII,693
  Thomas XIV,42; XV,740;
    XVI,82, 92, 107, 322, 327,
    329, 331, 335, 342, 345,
    388
  W. XVI,470
  William XIV,227, 257-58,
    472; XVI,296
  See also Greene
Greenaway, Abraham XV,724
Greene, Bradley XV,722
  General XVII,382, 407, 412
  Jonathan XV,721
  Richard XV,730
  William XV,246, 261
Greenfield, Charles XIV,304-5,
    465-66; XV,186, 714; XVI,
    202
  Paul XIV,23
  Thomas XIV,16
Greenleaf, Captain XVI,902
  David XIV,160-61, 164, 286-
    87; XVI,307; XVII,114
  Nathan XIV,450, 534, 642;
    XV, 422, 734; XVI,17, 190,
    211, 228, 278, 519, 834
  Nathaniel XV,730
  Samuel XIV,229, 252

Greenleaf, Stephen XVII,749-50
  William XVI,286, 501
Greenough, Epes XVII,139
  William XIV,166, 170;
    XVI,928; XVII,14
Greenway, Abraham XVI,124,
    256, 510, 642
  Abram XIV,585, 616
Greenwood, Joseph XVI,628,
    630, 752
  Joshua XV,21, 109, 536
  Noses XV,109
  William XIV,334; XV,217
Greer, James XV,621, 634, 644;
    XVI, 27, 44, 574
  Matthew XV,716
  See also Grear
Gregg, Adam XV,101, 538
  Alexander XV,350, 352, 359;
    XVI,753
  Colonel XV,630
  David XIV,74; XV,197, 228,
    567
  Ebenezer XV,567
  Ephraim XV,201, 567
  George XIV,279, 288;
    XVI,314; XVII,116
  Hugh XIV,99, 205, 334;
    XV,164
  Isaac XV,589; XVII,124
  Jacob XV,739
  James XIV,17, 183; XVI,263,
    725, 911
  John XIV,58, 183, 425;
    XV,189, 458; XVI,753,
    911-12
  Jonathan XIV,348
  Joseph XIV,242; XV,566-67;
    XVI, 719
  Leslie XIV,425
  Reuben XV,189, 429, 552;
    XVII, 259
  Samuel XV,394, 428
  William XIV,396-97, 453,
    532, 579, 588; XV,196,
    198, 637; XVI,58, 104,
    166, 719, 898; XVII,426

Gregory, Captain XVII,76, 324
  David XIV,358
  John XVII,324-25
  William XIV,387, 494, 507,
    516; XVI,237, 244, 269,
    518, 822
Grenier, Augustine XVII,305
Gressell, John XV,18
Grey, Corporal XIV,2
  Hugh XIV,248
  James XIV,46
  John XIV,227, 257
Gridley, Richard XIV,39; XV,751
  Samuel XV,752
Griffin, Abraham XIV,93, 202,
    356
  Anne XVII,270
  Benjamin XIV,231; XVI,922;
    XVII,80, 83
  Daniel XVI,915
  David XV,29
  Dominicus XIV,231, 570,
    651; XV,728; XVI,27;
    XVII,80, 83
  Dudley XIV,99, 205
  Ebenezer XV,743
  Israel XIV,327; XV,563;
    XVI,807
  James XIV,353
  Jeremiah, XV, 643, 719;
    XVI,203, 226, 271, 512,
    600, 742, 901
  John XIV,77, 81, 107, 122,
    198, 256, 260, 484, 499,
    512, 518; XV,323, 341;
    XVI, 124, 235, 250, 255,
    500, 507, 625-26, 925;
    XVII,39, 47, 85, 270
  Jonathan XIV,348; XVI,85,
    107, 195, 236, 242, 268,
    271, 503, 575, 617
  Joseph XIV,571, 651;
    XV,729; XVI,28, 188, 210;
    XVII,80, 83
  Nathaniel XV,167, 465, 467,
    479, 505; XVII,642-44
  Nicholas XVI,235

Griffin, Obadiah XIV,589
  Richard XIV,227, 452, 532,
    585, 657; XV,459, 606,
    731; XVI, 37-38, 709
  Samuel XIV,35, 90, 201, 334;
    XV,498, 743; XVI,752
  Theophilus XIV,77, 81, 198;
    XV,111, 176; XVI,901
  Thomas XIV,317, 320;
    XV,199
  Timothy XVI,100
  William XIV,623; XV,627
Griffith, David XVII,35
  George XVII,479-84, 487-88,
    494
  John XIV,29; XVII,49-50, 757
  Samuel XVII,207
  William XIV,381, 489, 501,
    514; XV,441, 596; XVI,931
Griggs, John XIV,265, 644; XVI,
    661-62
Grill, John XVII,644
Grimes, Alexander XVII,298
  Francis XV,122, 189
  Charles XV,63
  James XIV,425; XV,63, 122,
    553
  John XIV,417
  Jonathan XV,427; XVI,47,
    55, 303
  Moses XIV,346; XV,745
  Nathaniel XVI,504, 620, 685
  Samuel XVI,898
  Samuel Jr. XVI,896
  William XIV,247; XV,61;
    XVII,97
Grindall, John XVII,761
Grindle, Daniel XIV,325, 464;
    XV,143
Griswold, Ebenezer XVII,306
  Gilbert XV,370, 629, 642-43,
    723; XVI, 206, 233, 274,
    522, 865-66
  Isaac XIV,325, 463; XV,62,
    741
  Jeremiah XV,156; XVII,143
  Joseph XV,11

Griswold, Josiah XV,11
  Oliver XVII,111
  Stephen XVII,95
Gross, David XVI,64, 73, 94
  William XIV,22, 198; XVI,599
Grout, Amasa XV,9, 31
  Benjamin XIV,270
  Elijah XIV,323, 326; XV,121;
    XVII,147
  John XIV,471; XV,716
  Jonathan XV,367
  Solomon XV,33
Grover, Amasa XV,12
  Amaziah XV, 29, 368
  Joseph XV,329
  Joseph Jr. XV,343
  Samuel XIV,238
  Simon XIV,238
  Stephen XIV,307
Groves, John XVI,103, 223, 271,
    520, 845
  William XVI,178-79
Grow, Isaac XIV,563, 627;
    XV,720, 748
  James XVI,28
  John XVI,202
  William XIV,237
Grush, Thomas XVII,467
Grushe, John XIV,261; XVI,579
  Thomas XIV,600; XV,715;
Grusha, John XV,512
Guernsey, Amos XIV,356
  David XVI,93
  John XVI,23
  John Jr. XIV,356
  Oliver XIV,356
  Samuel XVI,93
Guild, Daniel XV,61
Guile, Ezekiel XVII,32
  Joshua XV,182
Guille, Jean Jacque Jr. XV,450
Guinn, William XIV,4
Guire, Daniel XIV,568
Gunby, John XVII,206
Gunn, Daniel XV,63; XVI,153
  Samuel XIV,645; XVI,141,
    161

Gunn, Wyatt XIV,356
Gunnison, Christopher XIV,239
  Elihu XVII,667
  Elisha XIV,119, 149, 197
  Henry XIV,29
  John XIV,239; XV,324, 749;
    XVII,22, 33, 37
  John Jr. XIV,259
  Josiah XIV,549; XV,430
  Pelatiah XIV,258, 549
  Samuel XIV,298, 325, 463;
    XV, 10, 30; XVI,847
  William XIV,29, 118-19, 150,
    196; XVI,61, 64, 71, 94
Guppy, James XV,294; XVI,901,
    912-13
  James Jr. XVI,627
  Joshua XIV,233; XVI,747
Guptail, Moses XIV,237; XVII,28
  Nathaniel XIV,236
  Stephen XIV,237
  William XIV,230
Gustin, Elisha XIV,105, 325,
    464
  John XIV,562; XV,11
  Joshua XIV,265
  Josiah XIV,265
  Thomas XIV,464; XV,12
  Thomas Jr. XIV,324
Guthrie, John XVII,445
Gutridge, Benjamin XV,226
  Jedediah XIV,406
Gutterson, Josiah XV,229
  Samuel XV,529; XVI,748-49
Guy, Edwin XVII,479-84
  Thomas XV,398, 486
Gyles, John XVII,712, 722-23,
    746
                H
Hackaday, William XVII,22, 33,
    37
Hackens, Peter XV,637
Hackett, Allen XIV,269, 271,
    290
  Barnabas XIV,577, 596
  Charles XVI,30, 34, 187, 299,
    522, 853-54

122

Hackett, Daniel XIV,425
Ebenezer XIV,424; XVI,634
Ephraim XIV,432
Ezra XV,172
George XVI,87, 90
Hezekiah XV,173
James XIV,223, 255-56;
XV,416, 577; XVI,537;
XVII, 30-31, 46-47
Jeremiah XIV,261; XV,127
Josiah XVII,95
Judah XIV,370, 378, 492,
503, 515
Moses XIV,459, 537; XV,116,
267-68, 270, 272
William XVII,526
Hadd, John XIV,604
Hadley, Abel XV,622, 663, 670,
683, 689; XVI,140, 161,
631
Abijah XVI,167
Amos XV,116
Daniel XV,175
Enos XIV,418
Ephraim XIV,51, 185, 424
Ezekiel XIV,454, 529, 546;
XV, 182
George XV,351, 353; XVII,19
Jacob XIV,55, 184
James XVI,914
Jonathan XV,588
Joseph XIV,159, 161, 164,
283, 287, 546, 595;
XV,424, 435, 713;
XVI,679; XVII,16
Noses XV,70
Obadiah XV,176; XVI,141,
161
Peter XVII,428
Samuel XV,586
Stephen XIV,346; XV,206;
XVII, 60
Hadlock, Hezekiah XV,122
Nathaniel XIV,26
Hadon, James XVII,294
Haes, Henry XIV,418
Hagar, Amos XVII,110

Hagerman, Francis XVII,306
Hagerty, Barnabas XIV,289, 292
Haggart, Robert XIV,605
Haggett, Benjamin XIV,359
Haggs, Jacob XVII,298
Hailstock, Michael XVII,299
Haines, Abner XVI,668
Elisha XV,698; XVI,131, 163;
XVII,433
Jacob XIV,252; XV,544;
XVII,360
Jeremiah XV,300, 302, 305,
309
Joseph XV,191; XVI, 360
Joshua XIV, 252; XVI, 668
Joshua Jr. XVII, 360
Josiah XV, 476, 489, 663,
670; XV,678, 688; XVI,
297, 563
Matthias XIV,327; XVII,527,
612, 619, 693
Nathan XV,256, 259, 263
Nathaniel XV,665
Noah XVII,432
Reuben XVII,621
Richard XVII,8
Robert XVII,622
Samuel XIV,316; XVII,9, 501,
527
Samuel Jr. XVII,527
Simeon XIV,391, 487, 508,
512, 563-64, 616; XV,719;
XVI,119
Simon XIV,550; XV,430
Stephen XIV,316; XV,130
Thomas XIV,604; XV,609,
715; XVI,237, 269, 320,
326, 328, 331, 340, 343,
345, 391, 512, 726, 864;
XVII,713
Walter XIV,566, 605; XV,607
William XIV,564, 615;
XV,440, 719
Hainson, Nathan XV,685
Hakins, Peter XVI,720, 724
Hale, Aaron XIV,304-5, 466,
567, 635; XV,607, 626,

Hale, Aaron (Cont.) 724; XVI,
  274, 500, 577; XVII,418
Abigail XVI,333, 342, 390
Abraham XIV,336; XVII,63
Benjamin XV,399
Captain XIV,250
Cato XVI,238, 245, 267, 498,
  567
David XIV,99, 205, 333;
  XV,98, 511, 749
Edward XVI,261
Eliphalet XV,657; XVI,850-51
Enoch XIV,256, 332, 335,
  420-421, 437-38, 460,
  478, 558, 575; XV,1, 20,
  22, 92, 97, 106, 108, 216,
  218, 502, 532-42, 630-31,
  643, 646, 655, 664-65,
  671; XVI, 58, 104, 166,
  294, 376, 813-14, 835;
  XVII,100, 102
Ephraim XIV,644
George S. XVII,47, 129
Henry XV,346, 742; XVI,143
Israel XVI,235, 268, 511,
  729, 935
James XVII,293
Job XVI,158
John XIV,50-51, 185, 304,
  306, 438, 527, 552, 591;
  XV,408-9, 511, 698, 710;
  XVI,2, 197, 536; XVII,30,
  267
Dr. John XVI,377, 381, 529
Jonathan XVI,52, 924
Joseph XV,346, 640;
  XVI,237, 275, 501, 531,
  611, 914-15
Joshua XVI,158
Major XIV,156
Moses XV,20, 66; XVI,531
Moses Jr. XV,217
Nathan XIV,35, 37-38, 48,
  78, 80, 552-53, 615;
  XV,136, 276, 421, 425,
  432-33, 440, 445, 456-57,
  718, 755; XVI, 4, 86, 333,

Hale, Nathan (Cont.) 390;
  XVII,137, 267
Nathaniel XVI,91
Richard XVI,746
Robert XIV,77, 82, 198
Samuel XV,426, 584-85;
  XVI,306
Silas XVII,29
Stephen XV,690
Thomas XIV,135, 191, 587,
  627, 657; XV,345, 732;
  XVI,36, 38, 909; XVII,7, 67
William XIV,572, 590, 609;
  XV, 436, 613, 714;
  XVI,200, 529
Haley, Ebenezer XVI,234
James XIV,258, 550
Joshua XIV,279, 590; XV,430
Nathaniel XVI,902
Richard XV,38
Samuel XIV,129, 189, 399;
  XV, 249, 251, 253, 565
Thomas XIV,239, 344;
  XVI,234
Halfpenny, John XV,739
Halicom, John XVII,646
Hall, Aaron XIV,465
Abiel XV,129, 186
Abijah XIV,394; XV,15;
  XVI,298, 614; XVII,88
Abraham XV,12, 24, 146;
  XVII, 105
Amos XV,11; XVI,138
Ananias XV,741
Avery XVI,861-62, 864
Benajah XIV,167, 170, 546;
  XVI,679; XVII,14
Benjamin XIV,52, 115, 141,
  185, 192, 235, 265, 308,
  321, 328, XIV,651;
  XV,328, 331, 343, 619,
  729, 741; XVI,28
Caleb XV,525, 749
Christopher XIV,10; XV,386,
  681
Colonel XVII,160
Daniel XIV,90, 201

Hall, David XIV,52, 185, 464,
    573; XV,170, 369, 612,
    728; XVI, 12, 15, 25, 209
David Jr. XVII,205
Ebenezer XIV,269, 271, 290-
    91, 322; XV,298, 469,
    481, 506; XVI,284, 910
Edward XV,16, 43, 138, 156;
    XVI,150, 822, 902;
    XVII,89, 143, 432
Edward Jr. XIV,394
Elijah XIV,225; XV,592, 656,
    666, 679; XVI,287, 500,
    570, 572
Eliphalet XV, 667, 681; XVII,
    255
Elisha XV,11, 370
Emerson XV,16
Enoch XIV,285, 287;
    XVII,434
Ephraim XIV,119, 150, 197;
    XV, 596
Ezekiel XV,42
George XVI,910
Henry XIV,346, 423; XV,149,
    151, 158, 530; XVII,61
Isaac XIV,361; XV,721
Jacob XV,14, 138, 374, 592,
    726; XVI,208
Jacob Jr. XVI,6
James XIV,18, 53, 185, 233,
    326, 394, 464, 570, 651;
    XV,346, 620, 633, 647,
    729, 732; XVI,28, 40, 189,
    212, 279, 522, 886-87;
    XVII,89
James Jr. XV,729; XVI,28
Jesse XV,62
John XIV,7, 243, 260, 571,
    605, 623; XV,370, 716;
    XVI,169, 201, 269, 640,
    645, 734, 823, 897;
    XVII,27, 47, 502, 525, 625
John Jr. XVII,525
Jonathan XIV,423; XV,24
Jonathan Jr. XIV,442, 544

Hall, Joseph XIV,118, 138, 158,
    192, XIV,228, 248, 261,
    305; XV, 568, 628, 693,
    725; XVI, 102, 178-79,
    207, 228, 230, 275, 500,
    570-71, 779, 782; XVII,26,
    108
Josiah XV,168, 699
Jude XIV,85, 199, 572, 632;
    XV, 444, 457, 612, 723;
    XVI,206, 227, 274, 498,
    510, 512, 703
Kingsley XVII,526, 612, 625,
    643, 663, 666
Laban XIV,662; XV,17, 138,
    386, 602; XVI, 310
Moody XV,39
Moses XIV,61, 182, 299, 304,
    306, 465; XV, 16, 138;
    XVI, 609; XVII,109
Nathan XV,84; XVII, 384
Nathan Jr.XIV,346; XVII, 61,
Nathaniel XIV, 226, 330; XV,
    15, 138, 373, 378; XVII
    458
Nicholas XIV, 566, 587, 657;
    XV, 607, 633, 647, 731,
    735; XVI,37, 39, 102, 196,
    212, 232, 278, 517, 795,
    798
Obadiah XIV,328
Obededom XV,526
Peirce XVII,255
Pelatiah XV, 370
Pierce XV, 4, 668, 681; XVI,
    153, 885
Ralph XV, 298, 575; XVII,
    526
Ralph Jr. XIV,235
Reuben XIV,299, 583, 600;
    XV, 437, 714; XVI, 200
Richard XVII,411; XV, 566
Rowland XV, 24; XVII, 105
Samuel XIV,18, 82, 115, 141,
    192, 198, 234, 428; XV,
    227, 250; XVI, 861-63;

Hall, Samuel (cont.) XVII, 139, 526
Samuel B. XV, 16
Samuel R. XV,156; XVII, 143
Stacy XVII,22, 33
Stephen,XIV, 61, 182, 304-5, 465; XV, 267-69, 271, 668, 681; XVI, 287, 500, 569; XVII, 434
Thomas XV,635-36,721; XVI, 205, 226, 273, 513, 778, 780-81
Thomas Jr. XIV,394; XV, 39
Timothy XIV,88, 304, 465; XV,406
William XVI,285, 501, 823, 929
Ziba XIV,428, 644; XV,732; XVI, 21, 24, 152
Ham, Benjamin XIV,236, 447, 540; XVI,60, 62, 70, 94; XVII,22
Benson XIV,261; XV,300, 302, 305, 309
Daniel XIV,228; XV,620
David XV,574; XVII,261
Dodavah XVI,625-26
Ephraim XIV,233; XV,574, 619, 719; XVI,109, 165, 204, 530, 620; XVII, 139, 261
George XIV,409; XV,242, 245, 247, 469, 481, 722; XVI,110, 165
George Jr. XV,326
Ichabod XVII,435
Israel XV,575; XVII,261
John XIV,18, 114, 140, 193, 234, 298, 307, 623; XV,620, 628, 645, 720, 730, 735; XVI,17, 64, 73, 99, 110, 165, 189, 204, 211, 230-31, 241, 272, 278, 503, 514, 624, 756-57, 759; XVII,525
Jonathan XVI,904

Ham, Joseph XV,243, 245, 247; XVII, 22
Moses XV,573; XVII,261
Samuel XIV,18, 323; XV,577; XVI,166
Thomas XVI,527
William XIV,447, 540; XVI,109, 165, 260-61; XVII,139, 432, 527
Hamack, Thomas XIV,18, 620; XV, 619
Haman, Ezekiel XV,695
Hamblet, Asa XVI,84, 90, 107
Benjamin XV,698; XVI,720
David XVI,113
Hezekiah XIV,359; XV,350, 353
Phinehas XV,229, 698
Reuben XIV,588, 626
Samuel XVI,259, 882; XVII,436
William XIV,267; XVI,169, 247, 254, 287, 506
Hambleton, Abial XIV,237
Jonathan 3d XIV,237
Paul XIV,237
Richard XIV,237
Samuel XIV,370, 379, 493, 504, 515, 579, 647, 649
Hamilton, A. XVII,200
Edward XVI,285, 501
J. Lenox XVII,489
James XV,318
John XVI,236, 273, 518, 815
Joseph XV,18
Samuel XV,454; XVI,13
Hamlet, Reuben XV,720
Hammedleton, David XVII,513
Hammet, Moses XIV,234, 407
Thomas XV,725
Hammock, Ebenezer XIV,29, 142, 193
John XIV,3, 14
Richard XIV,3
Thomas XIV,30; XV,443, 619; XVI,907

Hammon, Philip XIV,4
  Thomas XV,435
Hammond, Abel XV,55; XVI,927
  Abiel XVII,96
  Benjamin XIV,428
  David XV,623, 629, 641, 730;
    XVI,32, 34, 187, 210, 220,
    277, 519, 824-25;
    XVII,349
  Isaac XV,63; XVI,469, 487-
    88, 852
  Joseph XIV,36, 426, 428-29,
    437-38, 478; XV, 46, 446-
    47 XVII,99
  Joseph Jr. XIV,92, 202-3,
    428
  Josiah XIV,258
  Oner XVII,204
  Simpson XIV,356
  Thomas XVI,489
  W. XV,467, 469
Hammons, Thomas XIV,603
Hamock, Thomas XVII,525
Hamon, Elijah XVII,153
Hanagin, Joseph XVII,293
Hancock, Henry XVI,924
  Jacob XIV,19; XVI,914
  John XIV,309, 481; XVII,68,
    75, 159
  Joseph XV,129, 180
  Robert XVII,673
  Thomas XIV,560
Hand, Aaron XIV,280, 288
  Amos XV,348
  Edward XVII,350
  Ira XIV,160-61, 164; XV, 593;
    XVI,155, 928
  J. XVII,452
  Landfar XVI,156
  Oliver XIV,173, 177, 288;
    XVI, 307; XVII,114
  Willard XIV,286-87
Handey, Jacob XVII,424
Handsome, John XIV,333, 634;
    XVI 814
Handy, Bradbury XIV,110
  Cyrus XIV,185

Handy, Jonathan XIV,110
Haniford, Thomas XVII,6
Hanley, Henry XVI,286, 498
  John M. XVI,238, 509, 692
Hannaford, John XIV,36
  Peter XV,179
  Thomas XIV,191
Hannah, John XVII,300
Hanscom, Reuben XIV,664
  Thomas XIV,331, 361, 623
  Uriah XIV,236, 446, 540
Hanscomb, Reuben XV,431
  Thomas XV,619-20, 720
Hanson, A. XVI,239
  Aaron XIV,242
  Abraham XV,572, 574;
    XVII,261
  Anthony XIV,114, 140, 192,
    406, 559, 561, 621;
    XV,443, 618, 722;
    XVI,205, 273, 503, 527,
    624
  Benjamin XIV,245; XV,619
  Benjamin Jr. XVI,904
  Charles XIV,583, 600;
    XV,715; XVI,68, 79, 92
  Daniel XIV,230
  David XVI,68, 92
  Ebenezer XIV,369, 374, 482,
    498, 502, 511
  Enoch XV,699; XVI,128, 162,
    628
  Ephraim XVI,914; XVII,711
  George XVI,904
  Hannah XVI,624
  Isaac XV,628, 641; XVI,731;
    XVII,435
  Jacob XVI,818-19, 903
  James XIV,13
  John XIV,126, 188, 298, 576;
    XV,724; XVI,235, 503,
    760; XVII,11
  John B. XIV,298; XVI,231,
    521; XVI,622-24; XVII,385
  Joseph XVI,904, 914
  Joseph Jr. XVI,905, 914
  Joshua XV,295; XVI,627

Hanson, Lieutenant XIV,26
  Nathan XV,192, 668, 690;
    XVI, 747
  Nathaniel XV,676
  Robin XVI,503, 624
  Sergeant XIV,2
  Solomon XV,311
  Thomas XVII,513
Harall, Jo XVII,527
Harbard, Jonathan XV,698
Harben, James XVII,513
Harbor, John XVI,189-90, 231
Harbour, John N. XV,732; XVI,
    522, 886-87
  Michael XVII,309
  Nehemiah XVI,40, 213, 279
Harbower, John XV,633, 647
Hard, Oliver XV,593
  Robert XVI,118
Hardie, Nicholas XV,283
  Silas XV,441
  Theophilus XV,748
  Thomas XIV,554
Hardman, John XVII,208
Hardnay, John XIV,289
  Joseph XIV,289
Hardwick, William XIV,265, 336;
    XVII,62
Hardy, Aaron XIV,33
  Asa XVI,246, 253, 516
  Bradbury XIV,111
  Charles XV,358, 566;
    XVI,113
  Cyrus XIV,53, 588, 626;
    XV,720
  Daniel XV,70, XVI,143
  Edmund XV,228
  Henry XVI,144
  Isaac XV,70, 518
  Isaiah XVI,520, 840-41
  Jacob XIV,53, 156-57;
    XV,228, 623, 629, 641;
    XVI,27, 44, 547, 824;
    XVII,349
  James XIV,53, 173, 177, 184,
    288, 588, 607-8, 626;
    XV,424, 714, 720; XVI,44

Hardy, Jedediah XIV,53, 185,
    347
  Jerry XIV,371
  Jesse XIV,53, 185
  John XIV,342, 349
  Jonathan XV,69
  Joseph XV,695
  Josiah XVI,238
  Lemuel XV,88; XVI, 144;
  Nathaniel XIV,116, 129, 189,
    418, 574, 600; XV, 614,
    715
  Nehemiah XIV,423
  Nicholas XV,290
  Noah XIV,301, 303, 312; XV,
    87, 511; XVI,159
  Perry XIV,379, 418, 493, 504,
    515; XV,693
  Phinehas XIV,88, 200, 301,
    303, 312
  Robert XIV,433; XVI,861-62;
    XVII,29
  Samuel XIV,398
  Silas XV,695
  Simeon XIV,60; XV,637, 722;
    XVI,102, 205, 241, 273,
    516, 784-85
  Theophilus XV,575
  Thomas XIV,52, 54, 88, 200,
    577, 588, 625-26, 662;
    XV, 210, 718; XVI,5, 158,
    688; XVII,216, 267
  William XIV,348; XV, 358;
    XVI, 287, 516
Harford, John XIV,245
  Nicholas XIV,3, 14
  Paul XIV,230, 245, 497
  Samuel XIV,21
  Solomon XIV,373, 386, 497,
    506, 517
Harkness, John XIV,89, 91; XV,
    100
  Robert XIV,34; XV,355
Harman, Stephen XIV,321, 338,
    642
Harmon, Benjamin XVII,85
  John XVII,86

Harmon, Nahum XVII,85
  Noah XVII,86
  Simeon XVII,85
  Stephen XV,423; XVI,194,
    220, 514, 760
Harper, Captain XIV,338
  Daniel XVI,236, 270, 509,
    699
  John XIV,98-99, 192, 578,
    593; XV,438, 717; XVI,537
  Samuel XIV,105-6, 221, 298,
    544, 578, 563; XV,33, 37,
    172, 438, 717
  Samuel Jr. XIV,442, 593
  Thomas XIV,578, 592;
    XV,439, 717
  William XIV,71, 179, 311-13,
    365, 476
Harriman, Ebenezer XIV,261
  Edmond XVI,914-15
  Jacob XVI,155
  Joab XV,754
  John XV,743
  Joseph XIV,341
  Joshua XVI,63, 94
  Leonard XIV,19, 167, 246,
    274
  Levi XIV,454, 529, 546;
    XV,131; XVII,257
  Matthew XVII,756
  Matthew Jr. XVII,756
  Moses XIV,172, 176-77
  Nathaniel XVI,914
  Page XIV,593; XVI,201
  Peter XIV,452, 532; XVI,125
  Philip XIV,174
  Samuel XIV,16; XVI, 914
  Stephen XV,183; XVI,211,
    694, 696
  William XIV,77, 82; XVI,670
  See also Herriman
Harrington, Francis XIV,5
  Hezekiah XIV,4
  Jeremiah XIV,246
  John XIV,203, 487, 545, 647,
    650; XV, 109, 596, 728,
    734; XVI,12, 209, 232,

Harrington, John (Cont.) 241,
    277, 516, 803
  Jonah XIV,420
  Jonathan XV,102
  Joshua XIV,93, 202-3;
    XV,109, 541; XVI,73
  Samuel XIV,259, 480;
    XVII,36
  Timothy XIV,336, 604;
    XV,453-54, 715; XVI,485,
    721; XVII,63
Harris, Abraham XIV,15
  Azel XV,55
  Benjamin XV,156, 471, 502;
    XVI, 82, 99; XVII,143
  David XV,197-98, 227, 741
  Ebenezer XVI,144
  George XVI,587
  Henry XIV,572, 597; XV,612,
    713; XVI,199
  Jacob XVI,113
  James XVI,63, 73, 91
  Job XV,124
  Jonathan XIV,95, 204; XV,77
  Joseph XIV,53, 185, 587,
    628; XV,721
  Joshua XV,19
  Robert XVII,204
  Samuel XIV,337; XV,214;
    XVI, 316-17; XVII,64
  Solomon XIV,578, 598;
    XV,713; XVI,199, 223,
    268, 313, 502, 605-6
  Stephen XV,109; XVI,167,
    878
  Thomas XIV,14, 337; XV,77,
    207, 518; XVII,63
  William XIV,95, 204; XV,77,
    79, 518; XVII,124
  William Jr. XIV,95, 204-5
Harrison, Colonel XVII,158
  Samuel XIV,4
  William XIV,550
Harriton, John XV,26
Harrod, Archibald XVI,144
  James XV,90
Harrop, Martha XV,613

Harrow, Thomas XV,125
Harsey, Peter XIV,353
    Samuel XIV,147, 195, 309
Hart, Aaron XV,677, 679;
    XVI,765
    Arthur XIV,58
    Constantine XV,32
    Daniel XV,577; XVII,139
    Edward XVII,139
    George XV,577
    John XIV,326; XV,10, 145,
        326, 579
    Josiah XV,31, 143
    Mary XIV,27
    Samuel XIV,227, 257-58,
        472; XVII,711
    Simeon XIV,543; XVI,137
    William XIV,245, 343, 372,
        385, 496; XVII,142
    William Jr. XIV,239, 255;
        XVII, 23, 31, 39
Hartley, William XVII, 307
Hartman, George XVII,296
Hartshorn, Aaron XIV,433
    Edward XVI,259; XVII,436
    James XIV,244, 267; XV,40,
        375; XVI,560-61
    John XIV,244, 417; XV,698
    Jonathan XIV,439, 527;
        XV,211, 529
Hartwell, Captain XVI,545
    Jonathan XV,369; XVII,103
    Joseph XVI,603
    Josiah XVI,654-55
    William XV,12, 662, 669,
        680; XVI,866; XVII,105
Harvell, James XVI,797
    Joseph XIV,171, 174, 176-77
Harvey, Alexander XVII,223
    Archibald XIV,269, 285, 290
    Archibald Jr. XIV,287
    Barnet XIV,61, 182, 249,
        304, 465
    Bernard XIV,305
    Calvin XVI,241
    Ebenezer XVI,603
    Edmund XIV,265

Harvey, Enoch XIV,424; XV,176;
    XVI,733
    James XV,249, 252, 254,
        527; XVI,103, 184, 213,
        228, 241, 279, 513, 645,
        778; XVII,288
    John XIV,16, 69, 180, 571,
        660; XV,249, 252-53, 624,
        727; XVI,8-9, 14, 42, 182,
        208, 301, 480, 914;
        XVII,440, 468
    Kimber XIV,645-46; XV,446-
        47, 732; XVI,20, 22, 191,
        212
    Lemuel XIV,59, 183
    Levi XV,300-1, 304, 308
    Moses XV,750
    Peter XIV,12
    Samuel XVI,110, 165
    Theophilus XVI,914
    Thomas XIV,471; XV,46, 631,
        638, 718; XVI,103, 192,
        202, 213, 219, 232, 241,
        270, 279, 516, 779, 786-
        87, 790, 803, 849; XVII,96
    Timothy XIV,265
    William XV,427; XVI,47, 55,
        303, 920
Harwood, Archibald XVI,259,
    636; XVII,436
    James XIV,97, 203-4, 267,
        573, 600; XV,207, 437,
        615, 622, 634, 644;
        XVI,27, 44, 656
    John XVI,921; XVII,124
Haseltine, Timothy XVII,81, 116
    David XIV,639; XV,587, 731;
        XVI,25, 211, 883-84
    Jeremiah XIV,77, 82, 198,
        313, 586
    John XIV,242, 463, 546;
        XV,698
    John Jr. XVI,696
    Jonathan XV,448, 598;
        XVI,199, 225
    Joseph XIV,359
    Maxi XVI,539

Haseltine, Nathan XVI,884
  Nathan Jr. XVI,884
  Nathaniel XIV,206, 244, 335;
    XVI,885
  Solomon XVI,191, 213, 225,
    279, 523, 852
  Thomas XV,733
  Timothy XV,592; XVI,313
  William XIV,574; XV,590;
    XVI, 322, 331, 334, 393
Haselton, Benjamin XV,525
  David XVI,186
  John XV,436, 714; XVI,200
  Jonathan XV,712; XVI,268
  Joseph XVI,198
  Moses XV,403
  Nathaniel XVII,62, 428
  Richard XV,224
  Samuel XV,402
  Solomon XV,633, 643, 647
  Timothy XVII,83
  William XV,224
  See also Haseltine
Hasham, Benjamin XVI,92
Haskell, Abijah XIV,576, 634;
    XV,724; XVI,813; XVII,101
  David XVI,285, 502
  Henry XV,753
  Jason XV,744
  Job XIV,455, 534; XV,256,
    259, 262, 528, 747
  Lurel XV,42
  William XV,259-60, 263
Hasket, Ebenezer XV,177
Haskins, Samuel XIV,26
  William XVII,610-11
Haslet, William XVII,301
Hassell, Abel XV,207
  Jason XV,517
Hastings, Amos XV,405
  Andrew XV,58
  Asa XV,126
  Benjamin XV,751
  James XIV,566, 657; XV,329-
    30, 731; XVI,36, 38
  James Jr. XV,343
  Jedediah XVII,424

Hastings, John XIV,16; XV,199;
    XVI,931
  Jonas XIV,55, 184
  Joseph XIV,238, 315, 467,
    548; XV,390, 548
  Josiah XIV,92, 202-3, 427;
    XV, 51, 53, 197, 223;
    XVI,531
  Moses XVI,124
  Oliver XV,10, 143
  Robert XIV,566, 583, 657;
    XV, 607, 731; XVI,36, 38,
    286, 507
  Sylvanus XIV,105, 594;
    XV,446, 717
  Thaddeus XIV,436, 524;
    XV,541
  William XV,483, 494;
    XVI,320, 323, 325, 328,
    330, 334, 337, 339, 343-
    44, 391
  William Jr. XVI,322
Hastons, Benjamin XIV,525
Hatch, Adrian XIV,422
  Amos XIV,238
  Asa XIV,423; XV,12, 29, 147;
    XVI,81, 93; XVII,249
  Benjamin XV,19, 43
  Elisha XIV,238
  Isaac XV,656, 666, 681; XVI,
    816
  John XV,4, 55, 204; XVII,96
  Joseph XIV,166, 170, 268,
    270, 423; XV,379; XVII,14
  Josiah XV,27, 145; XVI,312;
    XVII,249
  Mason XVI,138
  Nathan XIV,290, 325, 464;
    XV, 147
  Reuben XVI,554
  Thomas XVI,83, 97, 928
Hathorne, Benjamin XVI,158
  Collin XV,217
  Ebenezer XVI,534
Haven, Daniel XVI,311-12
  John XIV,550-51
  Samuel XVI,356, 452

Hawes, David XV,535
  Nathan XV,116, 175, 557
Hawkes, John XVI,930, 932
Hawkins, Benjamin XIV,361
  John H. XVII,307
  Lieutenant XVI,180
  Nathaniel XIV,3
  Peter XV,630
  William XIV,205, 235, 408,
    555, 640; XVII,269
  William A. XIV,95, 204, 574;
    XV,617, 726; XVI,40, 208
Hawkley, James XIV,471, 577;
    XV, 439; XVI,218, 517,
    934
Hawley, Ezekiel XVII,118-19
  James XV,716; XVI,308-9
Hawse, Nathan XVII,258
Hay, Thomas XV,85
  Thomas Jr. XV,85
Haydon, Samuel XIV,650
Haye, Robert XVII,528
Hayes, Aaron XIV,228, 236; XV,
    252; XVI,119, 236, 243,
    270, 511, 512, 781
  Amos XIV,234, 245, 372,
    385, 497, 506, 517;
    XV,298
  Arthur XVII,645
  Benjamin XV,574; XVI,571-
    72; XVII,261
  Daniel XIV,19
  Daniel R. XVI,178-79
  David XV,18, 43; XVII,67,
    109
  Ebenezer XIV,447, 540
  Enoch XIV,447, 540; XV,297,
    576; XVII,261
  George XIV,322; XV,298,
    576; XVII,261
  Hezekiah XV,575
  Ichabod XVI,623, 905
  James XVI,569; XVII,297
  John Jr. XVI,904
  Joshua XVI,128, 162
  Michael XVI,930

Hayes, Nathaniel XIV,245, 575,
    593; XV,716; XVI,201
  Paul XV,575
  Richard XIV,363
  Samuel XIV,228, 470; XV,41;
    XVI,569
  Solomon XIV,451, 532;
    XV,249, 251-52, 254
  Thomas XVI,127, 162
  William XIV,144, 193-94; XV,
    57; XVI,287, 513, 772
  William Jr. XVII,8
Hayman, John XVII,300
Haynes, Elisha XV,695; XVI,262
  James XVII,57
  Joseph XV,584-85, 592; XVI,
    307; XVII,114
  Joseph Jr. XV,593
  Lewis XVII,360
  Nathan XIV,228; XV,260
  Nathaniel XIV,228
  Noah XVI,261
  Robert XVII,644
  Samuel XIV,15, 143, 194,
    319
  Simeon XIV,236
  Stephen XIV,319
  Thomas XIV,569; XV,438
  Walter XV,438
Hayward, Benjamin XIV,270,
    543
  Captain XVII,150, 223
  David XV,741
  James XVI,534
  John XVI,519, 825
  Joseph XV,741
  Joshua XIV,442-44, 462,
    542, 544, 547; XV,281,
    379-80; XVI,539, 924;
    XVII,80, 131-132
  Nathan XV,741
  Peter XVI,849
  Samuel XIV,34
  Thomas XIV,626
  Urijah XVI,179
  William XV,37, 142

Haywood, Benjamin XVII,105
    Eleazer XV,10; XVII,104, 468
    Joseph XIV,464
    Joshua XVI,259; XVII,82, 436
    Samuel XIV,588; XV,100
    Samuel S. XV,720; XVI,204
    William XV,23, 37, 145;
        XVI,920
Hazard, David XIV,464
    James XIV,411; XV,402, 464,
        466, 477, 504
    James C. XV,749
    Jason XVI,286, 500
    Mr. XVII,396, 404
Hazeltine, Barnes XIV,167, 169,
    275
    Benjamin XIV,410; XV,169
    Daniel XIV,225
    David XVI,15, 25
    Jeremiah XVI,670
    John XIV,161, 164, 288, 546;
        XV,459, 605; XVI,679;
        XVII, 65
    Jonas XIV,53
    Jonathan XIV,185, 305, 342
    Nathaniel XIV,101, 207
    Peter XIV, 410
    Samuel XIV,410; XV,381
    Timothy XV,380
    See also Haselton,
        Haseltine
Hazelton, Daniel XV,568
    Jeremiah XIV,602; XV,712
    John XIV,590, 607-8;
        XVI,155
    Jonathan XIV,304, 603
    Joseph XV,712
    Nathaniel XV,213
    Solomon XVI,23, 851
    Thomas XV,7; XVI,48, 265,
        302, 305
    Timothy XV,153-54
    See also Haselton
Hazen, Benjamin XIV,436;
    XV,61, 203
    Colonel XVI,539, 597, 679
    Edward XV,63

Hazen, General XVI,265
    John XVII,351
    Joshua XVII,67
    Moses XV,707, 733; XVI,45,
        48, 217, 304-5; XVII,156,
        162, 167, 169, 178, 187,
        191, 193-194, 197, 203,
        210, 212, 218, 240-41,
        243, 48, 282, 292-309,
        316, 329-33, 343-47, 350,
        355-58, 363-69, 376, 379-
        81, 384
    Nancy XVII,351
    Solomon XV,591
Hazzen, Captain XIV,26
Head, Arthur XVII,644
    Daniel XVI,169-70
    Isaac XVI,287, 515
    James XIV,359, 588; XV,161-
        62; XVI,287, 506, 900
    John XIV,74, 178, 470, 579,
        606; XV,453-54, 715;
        XVI,201, 269, 510, 723,
        725
    Moses XIV,269-70, 289;
        XVII,9
    Moses Jr. XIV,269, 272, 290
    Nathaniel XIV,242, 424;
        XV,512-513; XVI,787-89;
        XVII,430
    Richard XV,512
    Samuel XIV,278
    Timothy XVI,287, 506
Heald, Amos XV,98
    Daniel XV,534
    Ephraim XIV,35
    Joseph XIV,35; XV,95, 221
    Oliver XIV,35; XV,96;
        XVI,854, 856; XVII,102,
        135
    Peter XIV,35
    Thomas XIV,33-34; XV,95,
        97, 103-4, 665; XVI, 762;
        XVII; 100, 102
Healey, Nathaniel XIV,11; XVI,
    933
    Nehemiah XIV,427

Healey, Paul XV,467, 694;
  XVI,125
  Samuel XIV,1, 76, 116, 198;
  XV,203
  Thomas XVI,214
Heard, Benjamin XIV,321
  Captain XV,449, 600
  Dame XVI,621, 629
  David XIV,244
  George XIV,234, 406, 625;
  XV, 445, 506, 619
  Jacob XIV,245
  James XVI,898
  Jethro XIV,125, 127; XVI,5;
  XVII,10, 267
  John XIV,244; XVI,899; XVII,
  502, 525
  Joseph XVII,435
  Josiah XIV,245
  Meshech XIV,234, 322
  Nathaniel XVII,648, 653,
  655-656
  Reuben XIV,234
  Robert XIV,372, 385;
  XVI,627-628; XVII,435
  Samuel XIV,18, 236, 245
  Tristram XIV,15, 236, 321,
  361; XVII,693, 711
  William XIV,236
Hearl, James XIV,237, 246
  Robert XIV,246
Hearle, William XVII,511
Hearsee, Peter XIV,611
Heath,-- XV,699
  Abiel XVII,424
  Amos XIV,211, 214, 217,
  219-220, 547; XVII,254
  Asa XIV,328-29, 404, 663;
  XVI, 85, 91, 107, 874;
  XVII,384
  Bart XIV,19
  Bartholomew XVI,125
  Benjamin XIV,167, 246, 274,
  288, 317, 319; XV,733;
  XVI, 45, 48, 265, 302,
  304-5, 502; XVII,307
  Caleb XVI,914, 922

Heath, Daniel XV,329, 343, 488,
  499-500, 742; XVI,88, 97
  David XIV,586, 611
  Dearborn XIV,410, 457, 538;
  XV, 464, 466, 477, 505,
  693
  Enoch XIV,135, 191, 341,
  586, 657; XV,485, 499-
  500, 742; XVI,38, 124;
  XVII,7
  Enoch Jr. XVI,38
  Ephraim XIV,548, 568, 659;
  XV, 610, 727; XVI,9, 42
  Isaac XIV,225, 340
  Jacob XV,129, 398
  James XV,587, 658, 667,
  679, 691; XVI,255, 307,
  510, 642, 670, 914;
  XVII,114
  Jared XVII,32
  Jesse XIV,224, 404, 546,
  586, 600; XV,396, 586,
  715; XVI, 200, 313, 530;
  XVII,32, 116
  John XVI,922
  Jonathan XIV,135, 143, 191,
  193, 586, 657; XV, 512-
  13; XVI,38-39; XVII,7-8
  Joshua XIV,52, 185, 246;
  XVII,427
  Josiah XIV,16; XVI,914
  Moses XV,568; XVI,85, 90,
  237, 243, 270, 504, 519,
  634, 825, 913
  Nathaniel XVI,922
  Reuben XIV,76-77, 82, 198;
  XVI,928
  Richard XIV,77, 82, 341, 586,
  656; XV,731; XVI,36, 38,
  670, 918
  Robert XIV,211, 215, 218-20
  Samuel XIV,16, 77, 83, 198,
  341; XV, 329-30, 343-44,
  485, 499-500, 587, 749,
  754; XVI, 37, 103, 125,
  196, 212, 232, 278, 517,
  567, 670, 795; XVII,92,

Heath, Samuel (Cont.) 296
  Samuel Jr. XV,329-30
  Sargent XV,183, 546;
    XVII,257
  Solomon XVI,579-80
  Sterling XIV,279, 288, 587,
    657; XV,460, 606, 731,
    735; XVI,36, 38, 212, 278,
    515, 565, 567, 682;
    XVII,221, 756
  Stephen XV,742
  Timothy XIV,225, 453, 532
  William XIV,19, 315, 467,
    548, 566, 650, 653; XV,
    183, 425, 609, 623, 629,
    641, 728-29; XVI,13, 31,
    33, 59, 187; XVI,190, 209-
    10, 228, 277, 507, 671;
    XVII,349
  General W. XVII,382, 421
  Zebadiah XIV,76, 83, 198,
    586-587, 656; XVI, 915
  Zebedee XV,731; XVI,36, 38
Heaton,-- XV,4
  Charles XVII,295
  James XIV,355; XV,61, 197,
    203; XVI,487
  Jonathan XIV,325, 464;
    XV,61; XVI,673
  Luther XV,61; XVI,152
  Nathan XIV,355
  Samuel XIV,436
  William XIV,92, 202
Heden, Robert XVII,513
Hedges, Dr. Silas XVII,286, 339,
    342
Heffrin, Dennis XVI,46, 171-72,
    175, 208, 303, 523, 852
Heffron, Dennis XIV,264;
    XV,446, 701, 703, 725
  Michael XIV,264
Heirs, Christopher XV,10
Hemenway, Phinehas XV,633,
    643, 648
Hemingway, Jason XIV,420
  Philip XVI,44
  Phinehas XVI,13, 603

Hemmingway, Joseph XV,109
Hemphill, James XVI,112, 256,
    519
  Nathaniel XIV,348; XV,638
  Robert XVI,286
Hendee, Joshua XV,14, 155,
    157-158; XVII,144, 153
  Mr. XVII,508
Henderson, Andrew XVI,298
  John XVI,82, 96, 106
  Joseph XIV,231, 403, 414,
    575, 612; XV,327, 711;
    XVI,517, 794
  Samuel XVII,29
  Stephen XIV,372, 385, 496,
    505, 517
  Thomas XIV,99, 205
  Zoath XIV,114, 140, 193,
    298, 624; XV,441, 618,
    720; XVI, 204, 233, 241,
    272, 503, 624
Hendrick, Daniel XV, 19
  James XV, 621, 634, 644;
    XVI, 34, 44, 663
Henry, Joseph XIV,425; XV,518
  Dr. Robert R. XV,719; XVI,4,
    203, 271; XVII,440, 450
  Samuel XIV,244; XVI,83, 100
  William XV,57
Herbert, James XV,267-69, 272,
    515
  Richard XV,127, 130, 163,
    185
  Samuel XIV,302
Hermon, Asa XV,565
  Levi XV,546
  Stephen XV,597, 730;
    XVI,18, 278, 514
Hern, James XV,631, 650; XVI,
    102, 274, 506, 658-59
Heron, Captain XVII,155, 165,
    175, 178
  James XVII,298
Herrick, Amos XVI,259;
    XVII,437
  Daniel XV,189
  Edmund XV,189, 429

Herrick, Joseph XIV,100, 206;
    XV,81, 350, 353; XVI,728
  Samuel XV,543
  Shadrach XV,81, 211, 530
Herriman, Esop XV,398
  Moses XV,399
  Page XV,717
  Peter XV,399
  William XV,752
Herrin, John XIV,269, 271, 290
Herring, John XVI,920
  Thomas XVI,928
Herrington, John XIV,391
  Timothy XIV,579
Harrod, James XV,714
  John XV,473, 518
Herron, Captain XVI,305
  James XVI,928
Hersey, Ichabod XIV,424
  James XVI,829
  Jonathan XIV,233
  Josiah XIV,233; XVII,29
  Peter XV,718; XVI,632, 905
  William XIV,232; XVII,29
Hervey, Ebenezer XVI,603
  Enoch XVI,733
Herwood, John XV,77
Heustis, Daniel XIV,268, 270,
    289; XVI,527
Hewes, Benjamin XIV,93, 202-3;
    XV,63
  Joseph XIV,443, 543;
    XV,153; XVI,314
  Nathaniel XV,383; XVI,315
  Nathaniel Jr. XVI,314
  Samuel XIV,210, 216, 218,
    220, 607; XV,424, 714;
    XVI,200; XVII,32
  William XVI,81
Hewey, Henry XVI,921
  James XVI,921
Hewit, William XIV,471, 575
Hewitt, George XVII,340
  William XV,653, 717;
    XVI,202, 218, 270, 514,
    764, 934

Heywood, Benjamin XVI,138
  Eleazer XIV,597
  John XVI,237, 274
  William XV,145, 158;
    XVI,286, 498
Hibbard, Rev. Augustine
    XIV,262, 295, 573, 615;
    XV,23, 37, 142, 230;
    XVII,279
  Augustus XIV,294
  Daniel XIV,265
  Eliphalet XIV,283, 287
  James XV,375
  Jedediah XV, 39, 373
  Moses XV,41
  Sarah K. XVII,47
  Thomas XIV,162, 262, 284,
    290, 292, 295, 465;
    XV,379, 385, 426, 584-85;
    XVI,306
Hickcox, Benjamin XIV,422,
    556, 658; XV,605; XVI,7
Hickety, Barrabus XV,713
Hickey, Daniel XV,464, 466, 505
Hickox, Benjamin XVII,269
Hicks, Amos XIV,356
  Asa XIV,356
  Barnard XIV,427
  Benjamin XIV,233; XV,441,
    627; XVII,24
  Eliphalet XV,204
  John XV,192
  Samuel XIV,235; XV,203
  Simeon XV,205
Hickson, Ebenezer XIV,332
Hidden, Jeremiah XV,187;
    XVII,91
Hide, Levi XV,17, 138, 375
Higbee, Charles XVI,313
  Levi XVI,313
Higby, Charles XIV,105, 324,
    464; XV,27, 371
  Levi XVII,249
  Stephen XVII,105
  See also Higbee, Higsbyy
Higgins, Daniel XVI, 243

Higgins, Joseph XV,52
    Joseph Jr. XV,52
Higginson, Stephen XVII,244
Hight, James XIV,227, 257-58,
    472, 550; XV,430;
    XVII,139
    Joseph XV,310
Higsby, Levi XV,27, 144, 371
Hilands, Michael XVII,301
Hildrich, Samuel XIV,51
    Simeon XIV,333
Hildrick, Levi XVI,908
    Martin XV,669, 680
    Simeon XV,100
Hildrith, David XVI,247, 251,
    498
    Ephraim XV,356; XVI,237,
        268, 509, 696; XVII,428
    Isaac XV,52
    Jesse XV,58
    John XV,90
    Jonathan XVI,602
    Jonathan Jr. XV,224
    Levi XIV,76, 82, 198; XV,548;
        XVI,670, 921
    Martin XVI,602; XVII,255
    Reuben XV,58
    Simeon XIV,34, 101, 206
    Simon XV,219
    Stephen XV,92, 356
    William XV,6; XVI,601
Hilger, Henry XVII,301
Hill, Alpheus XIV,263
    Benjamin XIV,330, 332;
        XVI,103
    Benoni XVI,202, 224, 241,
        271, 502, 597
    Captain XIV,12, 15
    Charles XIV,273, 276, 288,
        294-295; XV,426; XVI,284,
        312, 527
    Colonel XVI,766
    Daniel XIV,237, 259; XV,12
    David XIV,119, 150, 196,
        309, 327, 584, 600; XV,
        715, 748; XVI,192
    Dudley XV,249-51, 254

Hill, Ebenezer XIV,264, 613;
    XV,191, 744; XVI,66, 77,
    96, 469
    Edward XIV,233
    Eleazer XV,41, 375; XVI,528
    Elijah XV,346
    Elisha XVII,139
    Henry XIV,235, 446, 540; XV,
        298; XVI,235, 242, 274,
        502, 905, 921
    Isaac XVII,43
    James XIV,232; XV,416;
        XVII, 139
    John XIV,234-35, 598;
        XV,575-576, 633, 643,
        648, 669, 681, 720;
        XVI,257, 514, 700-1;
        XVII,27, 525, 664
    John B. XVI,69, 80
    Jonathan XIV,563, 627;
        XV,443, 721; XVI,205,
        239, 272, 505, 526, 649,
        659
    Joseph XIV,10, 15, 613;
        XV,544
    Moses XV,408
    Mr. XVII,604
    Nathan XVI,106
    Nathaniel XIV,93, 202-3,
        235, 264; XVI,908;
        XVII,693, 719
    Nicholas D. XIV,330
    Oliver XIV,418
    Reuben XVI,607
    Richard XIV,233
    Robert XIV,235; XV,249;
        XVI,51
    Robert H. XVI,502
    Samuel XIV,33, 227, 233,
        257-258, 346, 572, 590,
        609; XV, 436, 613, 714,
        743; XVI,200; XVII,139,
        667, 692, 719
    Simeon XIV,204
    Stephen XV,85
    Thomas XIV,186, 570;
        XV,312, 408, 663

Hill, Volentine XVII,719
William XIV,18, 26, 233, 624;
XV,191, 441, 619, 720;
XVI, 167, 204, 230, 292,
511, 572-73, 710;
XVII,717
See also Hills
Hiller, Joseph XVII,742-43
Hillery, John XIV,459, 538, 654;
XV,729; XVI,31, 33, 59,
187, 210; XVII,319
Hillhouse, David XVII,459
Hilliard, Benjamin XVI,102, 674
Jonathan XVI,65, 75, 106,
282
Luther XVI,150; XVII,118,
120
Robert XIV,2
Samuel XV,155; XVI,313;
XVII, 143
Sergeant XVI,897
Hilliard, Simeon XVI,604
Timothy XVII,623, 676
Zebulon XIV,109, 131
Hills, David XIV,328
Ebenezer XV,434, 616, 711;
XVI,198, 487
Ebenezer Jr. XIV,573
Elijah XV,70
Jacob XIV,410
James XVI,921
John XIV,76, 81, 198;
XV,402
Joseph XIV,573; XV,434,
616, 711; XVI,198
Joseph Jr. XIV,328
Levi XIV,341
Moses XIV,328; XV,120, 548
Moses Jr. XV,120
Nathan XVI,850
Nathaniel XV,293; XVI,152,
927
Parker XIV,43, 76, 82
Philip XV,70
Samuel XV,168; XVI,389, 851
Simeon XIV,96

Hills, Stephen XIV,103; XV,403,
751
Thomas XIV,51; XV,70, 670,
685, 688; XVI,694
Reuben XIV,82, 198
William XV,70; XVI,849, 927
Hillsgrove, John XIV,35, 225,
468, 575, 612; XV, 434,
711, 740; XVI,221, 521,
854, 856, 858-60
Hilton, Charles XV,285, 291;
XVI,530
Colonel XVII,702
Daniel XV,242, 244, 246;
XVI, 765; XVII,612
Dudley XIV,232; XV,242,
245-46; XVII,26
Edward XV,416, 571-72;
XVI,764; XVII,484, 490,
512, 514
Ichabod XVI,765-66
John XIV,119, 151, 196, 250,
563, 628; XV,443, 721;
XVI, 204, 233, 272, 506,
648-49; XVII,7, 513
John P. XIV,212, 216, 218,
220, 570; XV,716; XVI,282
Jonathan XIV,233; XV,249,
251-252, 255
Joseph XIV,555, 652;
XV,726; XVI,7, 321, 330,
334, 337, 395, 526;
XVII,269
Levi XV,246
Nathan XVI,843
Nathaniel XV,666, 684;
XVI,111, 844
Pike XIV,651
Richard XVII,693
Samuel XVI,921
William XIV,269, 272, 290,
581; XV,242, 245-46, 449,
600, 724; XVI,207, 229,
274, 520, 832
Winthrop XVII,629, 739
Hilyard, Benjamin XIV,351; XV,

Hilyard, Benjamin (Cont.) 320,
    339, 523, 628, 640, 706
  John XIV,432
  Samuel XIV,542
  Simeon XV,523
  Zebulon XIV,109, 131;
    XV,522
  See also Hilliard
Hinckes, John XVII,631, 637,
    665, 679, 683, 703
  Samuel XVII,723
Hinckley, Christopher XIV,273,
    276, 289
Hinckson, John XIV,15, 172,
    175-177, 268, 289, 299
Hindman, Benjamin XVII,295
Hinds, Barzillai XIV,115, 141,
    193, 250
  Jacob XIV,38, 78, 84, 86,
    155, 199
  Jacob Jr. XIV,85, 199
  John XVI,153
Hinkley, Mr. XVII,585
  Seth XVI,141, 161
Hinksman, Robert XVII,667-68
Hinkson, Samuel XV,186;
    XVII,92
Hitchcock, Captain XIV,25
  Ichabod XVI,608
  Lyman XVII,204
Hix, Benjamin XIV,624; XV,619
  David XV,54
  Eliphalet XV,54
  Joseph XIV,22; XVII,717
  Samuel XV,54
  Simeon XV,54
Hoag, Eben XVI,68, 73, 505,
    644
  Ebenezer XV,565; XVI,235,
    242, 270, 645
  Elijah XIV,23
  Hussey XIV,111, 132, 190,
    641; XV,456, 730; XVI,18,
    194, 211
  Nathan XVI,933
  See also Hoeg

Hoar, Benjamin XIV,34
  Jotham XV,100, 220
Hoat, Israel XIV,543
Hobart, Amos XV,224
  David XIV,256, 440-41, 558;
    XV,140, 142-43, 146, 149,
    151-52, 155, 158-60, 231,
    385, 459-60, 605-6, 655;
    XVI,386, 798; XVII,13
  Eliphalet XV,724
  Francis XV,560; XVI,125
  Gershom XV,150, 160
  Hezekiah XV,97
  Isaac XIV,43; XV,744;
    XVI,238, 273, 509, 692
  Jacob XV,632, 636; XVI,236,
    273, 509, 689-92
  James XIV,118, 138, 158,
    192, 350, 458, 538;
    XV,358, 381, 523, 573;
    XVI,800; XVII,109
  John XV,88, 147; XVI,88
  John Jr. XV,664, 671;
    XVI,690; XVII,339
  Jonas XIV,590, 607-8;
    XV,459, 605, 714; XVI,200
  Jonathan XIV,527, 545
  Jonathan Jr. XVI,690
  Joseph XIV,280, 288, 657;
    XV, 459, 605, 731, 735;
    XVI, 36, 39, 190, 212,
    228, 278, 517, 798
  Joshua XV,88-89, 209, 212,
    510
  Oliver XV,58
  Richard XV,560
  Samuel XIV,24, 37, 49-50,
    77, 80, 109, 111, 687;
    XV,657, 688, 706;
    XVI,116; XVII,8, 11, 34,
    53, 279
  Solomon XIV,590; XV,88,
    125, 150, 160, 511;
    XVI,51, 53; XVII,464
  William XIV,423; XVI,286,
    288, 502

Hobbs, Benjamin XVII,740
  Caleb XIV,404
  David XIV,413; XV,522
  Jacob XIV,99, 404; XVI,657
  James XVII,260
  James Jr. XIV,361
  John XIV, 3; XVII,619
  Joseph XIV,411; XV,201;
    XVI, 286, 515
  Josiah XVI,128, 162
  Morris XVI,774-75; XVII,528,
    659, 667-68, 704, 740
  Nathaniel XIV,229
  Samuel XIV,192, 351
  Sheldon XIV,237
  Simon XIV,23
  Solomon XIV,609
Hobby, Sir Charles XIV,6; XVII,
  724
  William XIV,6
Hobson, John XIV,423
Hockley, James XIV,593;
    XVI,201, 218, 270, 794
  See also Hawkley
Hodgart, Robert XIV,579;
    XV,715; XVI,201, 484, 722
Hodgdon, Aaron XIV,664
  Abel XV,683
  Amos XVI,66, 77, 96
  Benjamin XIV,236, 323;
    XV,325
  Caleb XIV,235, 253, 367-68,
    374, 376, 498; XVI,525,
    622-624; XVII,261, 284
  Charles XIV,641; XV,423,
    730; XVI,18, 194, 211
  Daniel XIV,298, 549
  David XIV,114, 141, 193,
    406, 562, 636; XV,618,
    725
  Hanson XIV,369, 375, 482,
    498; XVI,628
  Isaac XIV,236
  Israel XIV,18
  James XIV,664
  John XIV,18, 280, 288, 546;
    XV,424, 700, 702-3, 726;

Hodgdon, John (Cont.) XVI,46,
    170, 172, 174, 208, 240,
    302, 508, 679
  John Jr. XIV,287
  Jonathan XIV,141, 192
  Jonathan Jr. XIV,115
  Joseph XIV,120, 149, 197,
    231, 233; XV,660-61, 668,
    681; XVI,237, 777; XVII,29
  Major XVII,121
  Moses XIV,235, 446, 540-41
  Phinehas XIV,228, 616;
    XV,440, 719; XVI,203, 257,
    507; XVII, 360
  Richard XIV,369, 375, 482,
    498, 502, 511, 518, 550
  Samuel XIV,236, 485, 500,
    512, 647; XV,728, 734;
    XVI,12,
Hodgdon, Samuel XVI,192, 209,
    232, 277, 516, 803;
    XVII,86
  Stephen XIV,236, 314;
    XVI,131, 163
  Stephen Jr. XIV,236
  Thomas XIV,242; XV,579
  William XIV,406; XV,751
Hodge, Alexander XIV,443, 542;
    XV,592; XVII,73, 81, 83
  Asa XVII,67, 252
  David XIV,280, 288
  John XV,696, 698
  Robert XV,554
  Samuel XIV,280, 288, 441,
    527; XVI,904, 928;
    XVII,251
  William XV,483, 497, 698;
    XVI,85
Hodgent, Robert XV,453
Hodgkins, Francis XIV,476
  Henry XV,146
  William XIV,34, 567, 611;
    XV, 533, 608, 718
Hodgman, Abel XV,664, 671;
    XVI, 741; XVII,339
  Job XV,211
  John XIV,419

Hodgman, Joseph XIV,100, 206, 208; XV, 211, 530; XVI, 270, 512, 741
  Joseph Jr. XV,82
  Josiah XV,517
  Nathan XV,211, 530
  Oliver XIV,346; XVII,61
  Zaccheus XIV,100, 206-7; XV,81
Hodgskin, Aaron XV,23; XVI,549
  Francis XVI,807-8
  Jonas XVI,137
  William XVI,202
Hodgskins, Henry XV,24
  William XV,92
Hodsden, Alexander XIV,14
  Jonathan XIV,12
  Joseph XIV,14
Hodsdon, Aaron XV,431
  Charles XV,597
  Daniel XV,430
  Phinehas XV,597
  Richard XV,430
  Samuel XV,595
Hody, John XVII,527
Hogg, Abner XIV,359, 653; XVI, 30, 33, 40, 59, 189, 212
  Alexander XIV,547; XV,380; XVI,620, 917
  Ebenezer XIV,670; XV,742; XVI,98
  George XIV,59, 183, 611; XV, 725; XVI,103, 632; XVII,212
  Hussey XV,423
  James XIV,58; XVI,140, 161
  John XIV,219, 254; XV,122; XVI,141, 161, 630, 633
  Mr. XVII,454-55, 713
  Robert XIV,254; XVI,630
  Simpson XV,221
  William XIV,329, 579, 616; XV, 122, 189, 215, 454, 719; XVI,91, 107, 724
Hogskins, William XVII,92
Hoisington, Isaac XVI,312
  Major XVII,130

Hoisington, Ucline XVI,313
  Vespasian XVI,313
Hoit, Aaron XVI,932
  Abner XIV,194; XV,180; XVI, 287, 502, 914
  Benjamin XIV,224, 299, 312, 371, 563, 650; XV,113, 728; XVI,12, 192, 771
  Daniel XV,250, 253; XVII,213
  David XV,564
  Ebenezer XV,742
  Elisha XVI,45, 301
  Enoch XIV,567, 611; XV,439, 608, 718; XVI,202, 633
  Ensign XVI,60
  Ephraim XV,670, 684, 688; XVI,247, 253, 501, 867
  Israel XIV,12, 14, 445
  Jabesh XV,525
  Jabez XVI,601
  Jacob XV,409
  Jedediah XV,186
  Jeremiah XV, 515
  John XIV,274, 278, 291, 294; XV,164, 291; XVI,131, 163
  Jonathan XV,747; XVI,932
  Jonathan Jr. XIV,338
  Joseph XV,300-1, 306; XVI,577; XVII,111
  Joseph B. XVI,87, 236, 243, 264, 270, 932
  Levi XIV,312; XV,564, 716; XVI, 201 269, 517
  Lieutenant XVI,180
  Micah XIV,554; XVI,5, 770; XVII,268
Hoit, Michael XIV,629; XV,719
  Moses XVII,32
  N. XVI,854
  Nathan XIV,42, 71, 555, 655; XV,726, 735; XVI,7, 29, 102, 182, 208, 212, 225, 279, 521, 526, 751, 827-28; XVII, 269, 453
  Nathaniel XV,732; XVI,21, 23, 191
  Nicholas XVI,130, 163

Hoit, Peaslee XIV,340
  Philip XVI,914
  Reuben XIV,548, 568;
    XV,323, 342, 727; XVI,10,
    209
  Richard XIV, 532; XV,323,
    342
  Samuel XIV,410, 600;
    XV,175, 548, 715;
    XVI,200, 224, 241, 269,
    501, 600, 770; XVII,2
  Simeon XV,742
  Stephen XIV,50-51, 231, 315,
    330, 467; XV,408
  Thomas XIV,71, 566; XV,115,
    150, 160, 163, 174, 607,
    658, 667, 679, 729;
    XVI,31, 33, 59, 167, 771,
    878
  William XIV,14, 385, 563,
    650; XV,728; XVI,13
  Zebadiah XIV,224
  See also Hoyt
Holaboat, John XV,671
Holbert, John XV,465
Holbrook, Abijah XIV,239
  Adam XVII,98
  Aden XV,226
  Amos XIV,263
  Benjamin XIV,227, 257, 259,
    262; XVII,30, 37
  David XVI,178-79
  John XV,256, 258, 260, 263,
    705; XVI,290, 292
  Joseph XIV,239
  Peter XV,54
  Robert XIV,239; XVI,110, 165
Holcomb, Matthew XIV,292,
    567, 601; XV,435, 607,
    712; XVI, 500, 525
Holden, Adonijah XIV,159, 161,
    164, 288
  Ephraim XV,539
  Febeus XIV,114, 140, 192
  James XIV,694; XVI,885
  John XIV,64, 181, 186, 566;
    XV,607; XVII,4

Holden, Nathaniel XIV,324;
  XV,31
  Phebeus XIV,298; XV,294;
  XVI, 627
  Richard XV,10; XVI,167, 311,
    878
  Samuel XIV,25
  Timothy XV,32, 143
  William XV,32, 369, 426;
    XVI, 311
  Zachariah XV,90, 176, 557;
    XVII,256
Holdridge, Jehiel XIV,265; XV,
    67, 226, 741, 752;
    XVI,531
Holland, Daniel XVI,906
  Jeremiah XV,632, 636
  Mark XVI,116
  Nathaniel XIV,580, 659; XV,
    448, 598, 727; XVI,11,
    316
  Robert XIV,211, 215, 218-20,
    283, 287, 584, 600;
    XV,715; XVI,269, 514, 766
  Stephen XVI,717; XVII, 139,
    447
  Thomas XVII,667
Hollicome, John XVII,701
Holliday, Noah XV,593; XVII,92
Hollis, Benjamin XVII,527
Holloway, Curtis XIV,7
Hollowell, John XV,677; XVI,889
Holman, Ezekiel XIV,370, 379,
    493
  Jeremiah XIV,70, 179, 584,
    604; XV,715; XVI,529
  Joseph XVI,237, 244, 269
Holmes, Benjamin XV,182
  James XIV,21
  Jeremiah XVII,360
  John XV,459, 731; XVI,36,
    38, 237, 244, 274, 499,
    572, 585
  John Jr. XV,605
  Jonathan XIV,74, 178, 411;
    XV, 394, 428
  Jonathan P. XIV,355

Holmes, Joseph XIV,235, 406;
    XV,203
  Joshua XIV,227; XVI,572
  Lazarus XIV,118, 120, 151,
    196, 258, 343; XV,325
  Lemuel XVI,167, 531, 547,
    849
  Nathaniel XIV,421; XV,394,
    429
  Oliver XV,350, 352, 354; XVI,
    655
  Philip XV,741
  Robert XIV,239, 485, 500,
    512; XVII,87
  Samuel XIV,423; XVI,586
  Stetson XV,205, 746; XVI,887
  Thomas XIV,211, 215, 218-
    20, 579, 653; XV,452,
    454, 730; XVI,31, 34, 59,
    187, 210, 723
  William XIV,29; XV,555; XVI,
    141, 161
  William Jr. XV,176
Holowboat, John XVI,719
Holt, Abiel XIV,439, 527; XV,
    364; XVII,214
  Amos XIV,244, 574; XV,419,
    529, 617, 731; XVI,15, 25,
    186, 211, 883
  Amos Jr. XIV,639; XVI,885
  Asa XIV,592; XV,716; XVII,67
  Barachias XV, 75, 419
  Daniel XV,214, 520, 664,
    670, 682; XVI,145, 235,
    271, 522, 881-82;
    XVII,339
  Enoch XV,698; XVI,883
  Fifield XIV,244
  Frye XIV,588; XV,175
  Humphrey XIV,411
  Jabez XIV,102, 207, 266;
    XVI, 140, 161, 531;
    XVII,468
  Jeremiah XIV,101, 206, 303;
    XV,419; XVI,883
  Joel XVI,235, 271, 522, 882
  Nathan XIV,179; XV,631

Holt, Nehemiah XIV,574, 639;
    XV,617, 731; XVI,15, 25,
    186, 211, 883
  Obadiah XIV,266, 477;
    XV,75, 214, 698; XVI,84,
    94
  Oliver XVI,729, 884; XVII,427
  Reuben XVI,43
  Samuel XV,95
  Simeon XIV,101, 206, 417;
    XV,75
  Solomon XVI,883
  Thomas XV,217
  Valentine XVI,145
  William XV,118, 138, 189
Holton, Darius XV,11
  Dr. XVII,389, 405
  Edward XV,4
  Jonathan XIV,427; XV,47,
    197, 223; XVI,321, 331,
    334, 396
  Nehemiah XV,55
Homans, John XVI,417, 509
  Joseph XVI,709
Homer, Joseph XVII,655
Honaway, Jack XVI,29
Honeway, Jock XV,729
Honey, Calvin XIV,470; XV,632,
    636, 651, 714; XVI,200,
    224, 269, 498, 556-57,
    562
  John XIV,699
  Joseph XIV,573, 632;
    XV,615-16, 723; XVII,124
  Peter XIV,95, 204, 337, 418,
    470, 600, 606; XV,207,
    347, 715; XVI,200, 269,
    504, 635; XVII,63
  Peter Jr. XIV,573; XV,615
Honeyford, Thomas XIV,135
Honorej, Jaques XIV,662
Honwell, Israel XVII,762
Hood, Aaron XVI,515, 698
Hook, Abraham XIV,227
  Daniel XIV,229, 253
  Dyer XV,300, 302
  Humphrey XIV,226; XV,560

Hook, Israel XV,400
Moses XV,400
Hooker, John XIV,239; XVII,24,
31, 39
Rev. Mr. XVII,105
Hooper, Daniel XIV,236
James XIV,283, 287; XV,435
Levi XIV,297; XV,23, 37; XVI,
528, 532; XVII,103
Thomas XV,189, 230, 429;
XVI, 901
Hope, John XVII,296
Hopkins, Allen XIV,74, 178, 348
Benjamin XVI,558
Benjamin Jr. XVI,559
James XIV,457-58, 537;
XV,429; XVI,112
John XIV,74, 178
Johnes XVII,302
Lieutenant XVII,132
Mr. XVII,126
Richard XIV,302, 391, 487,
509, 513
Robert XIV,425
Solomon XIV,307
Stephen XVII,124
William XIV,9, 273, 277, 289;
XV,394; XVI,85, 100
Hopkinson, Caleb XV,589
David XV,589; XVI,314; XVII,
89, 116
John XV,590; XVI,650
Jonathan XIV,563, 627;
XV,443, 589, 721;
XVI,205, 314, 649-50;
XVII,80, 82, 116
Jonathan Jr. XV,589
Moses XVII,27
Noyes XVII,17
Horn, Andrew XIV,473; XV,295,
574; XVII,10, 260
Andrew Jr. XVII,10
Benjamin XIV,230, 322;
XV,295
Bernard XV,322
Caleb XIV,126, 188, 230; XV,
574; XVII,10, 29, 260

Horn, Daniel XIV,114, 141, 193,
560, 624; XV,440, 618,
719; XVI, 203, 239, 271,
503, 526, 624, 818, 905;
XVII,137
Ebenezer XIV,115, 126, 141,
188, 193, 298, 446, 540;
XV, 295, 468, 480, 506
Ebenezer Jr. XVII,10
Elisha XIV,238
George XIV,363
Hurd XV,294; XVI,627
Ichabod XIV,559; XV,469,
481, 506, 628, 640, 651,
719; XVI,203, 271, 523,
816, 818
Isaac XIV,244; XVI,904
Jacob XV,468, 480, 507; XVI,
627; XVII,300
James XIV,114, 140, 192,
238, 298; XVII,29
Jonathan XIV,114, 140, 192,
298; XV,295; XVII,29
Nathan XV,294, 205
Thomas XV,294; XVI,627;
XVII, 644
William XIV,476
Horne, Andrew XIV,125, 188
Benjamin XIV,365
James XIV,250
John XIV,13
William XIV,13
Horner, James XV,587
Thomas XVI,297
Horney, John XIV,25
Horseman, Joseph XVII,205
Horslee, James XVII,669
Horsom, David XIV,236; XVI,79
Hoskins, Nicholas XIV,8
Hosley, Samuel XIV,33; XV,744
Hosmer, Aaron XV,592;
XVI,313; XVII,116
Nathaniel XV,84, 530
Reuben XIV,101, 206, 574,
639; XV,419, 529, 617,
731; XVI, 15, 25, 186,
211, 220, 278, 512, 741

144

Howard, Eleazer XV,446
  Enoch XIV,53, 185, 236
  Isaiah XV,379; XVI,314
  John XIV,53, 156-57;
    XV,327; XVI,63, 73, 243
  Joseph XIV,325; XV,379;
    XVI, 144, 314
  Joshua XV,279, 385
  Nathan XIV,427; XV,4, 66,
    226; XVI,921
  Peter XV,67
  Roswell XIV,607-8; XV,424,
    714
  Samuel XIV,35; XV,20, 364;
    XVI, 859-60; XVII,135
  Solomon XIV,136, 191; XVII,7
  Sylvanus XV,66
  Thomas XV,42-43, 157;
    XVII,144
  Urijah XVI,178
Howe, Aaron XV,473, 490
  Antipas XVI,23, 44, 810
  Baxter XV,751
  Barzillai XIV,103, 552, 604
  Benjamin XV,203
  Bezaleel XIV,207; XV,710;
    XVI, 3, 51, 180, 182, 197,
    267; XVII,266, 418, 440,
    442
  Caleb XV,47
  Daniel XV,48
  David XV,182, 548; XVI,87,
    91, 103, 203, 224, 271,
    509
  Elijah XVI,208, 503
  General XVII,127
  Isaac XVII,100
  Israel XIV,97, 204-5, 303;
    XVI, 235, 269, 522
  James XIV,367, 543;
    XVII,214
  Joel XIV,103, 207
  Jonathan XIV,662; XV,472,
    490, 602; XVI,87, 91
  Joseph XIV,262; XV,726;
    XVI, 46, 208
  Josiah XIV,491, 648

Howe, Dr. Mark XVI,108, 208,
  445, 447
  Moses XV,50
  Moses M. XVI,287, 510, 702
  Nehemiah XV,47
  Peter XIV,51; XV,182
  Richard XIV,628; XV,721;
    XVI, 327, 329, 332, 341,
    345
  Samuel XV,44, 182, 473;
    XVI,87, 100
  Selah XV,733; XVI,522, 827
  Simeon XV,293
  Thomas XIV,618; XVI,128,
    206, 526
  Uriah XV,63, 205
  William XIV,40-41, 44;
    XVI,931
  See also How
Howell, Joseph Jr. XVI,304-5
Howlett, Davis XIV,326, 463;
  XV, 3, 5, 61, 64; XVI,701
Hoyt, Abner XVI,502
  Benjamin XIV,25, 384, 387,
    494, 496, 505, 516-17,
    647; XVII, 39
  Eben XV,43
  Enoch XVII,430
  Ephraim XV,663; XVI,501,
    611
  Israel XV,43
  Jacob XVI,915
  Jared XVII,25
  John XV,284; XVI,133
  Joseph XV,698; XVI,90, 148;
    XVII,430
  Joseph B. XVI,243, 510, 703,
    706
  Levi XIV,468; XVI,221, 657
  Micah XVII,2
  Nathan XV,650
  Nicholas S. XVI,257, 517
  Peaslee XIV,224
  Reuben XIV,659; XV, 610
  Richard XIV,341, 453
  Samuel XIV,23, 583
  Stephen XIV,465, 467, 548;

146

Hoyt, Stephen (Cont.) XVI, 694, 696
  Thomas XIV,179, 654; XV,691
  William XIV,494, 507, 516, 647; XVII,27
  See also Hoit
Hubart, John XIV,404
Hubbard, Benjamin XV, 402
  Captain XV,750
  David XV,741
  Elisha XIV,89, 201
  Ephraim XVI,531-32, 602; XVII,95
  Jacob XVI,23, 44
  James XIV,236
  John XV,683; XVI, 90, 107, 399, 598-99
  Jonas XV,436
  Jonathan XIV,438; XVI,921
  Joseph XV,9; XVI, 190, 606
  Lemuel XIV,297, 326, 463, 465
  Nathan XVI,814
  Richard XIV,226, XVI,707
  Roswell XV,31
Hubert, Paul XVII,304
  Pierce XVII,309
Huckins, Israel XIV, 373, 386, 497, 506
  James XVI,287
  John XIV,235; XVI, 164, 906-7
  Jonathan XIV,225; XV,300-1
  Robert XVII,719
  Stephen XIV,362, 364; XVI, 121, 164
  Thomas XIV,233
Hudson, Benjamin XIV,578, 597; XV,713; XVII,104
  Brooks XVI,152
  Samuel XV,629, 642-43; XVI,44, 865
  Thomas XV,417
Huff, Daniel XIV,238
  Israel XIV,239
  Lemuel XV,15

Huggins, David XIV,394; XV,42; XVII,88
  John XIV,233
  Jonathan XV,376
  Nathaniel XVII,705
  Robert XVII,501, 710, 719
  Samuel XVII,360
Hugh, Jeremiah XIV,6
Hughes, Clement XVII,630, 739, 758
  James XVII,298
  John XV,199, 201; XVII,294
  Jonathan XV,197, 322
  Major XVII,306
  Richard XIV,639; XV,612, 731; XVI,15, 25, 186, 211
  William XVI,95
  See also Huse, Hughs
Hughs, John XIV, 412
  Richard XIV,88, 200, 572
  Robert XIV,9
  Solomon XIV,13
Huit, William XV,356
Hull, Benjamin XVII,513
  Israel XIV,257-58, 587, 628; XVII,30
  John XIV,227,XV,618; XVI,204; XVII,226
  Joseph XIV,225, 246, 304, 465-466, 648, 650; XV,595, 728; XVI,12, 192, 209, 804
  Josiah XV,24
  Nathaniel XIV,656; XV,459, 605, 731; XVI,36, 38
  Samuel XIV,657; XV,459, 605, 731
  Walter XVII,729
Humble, John XV,693; XVI,103, 198, 222, 267, 516, 803-5
Humphrey, Amherst XVI,153
  James XV,200
  John XIV,348; XVI,902-3
  Willard XV,205
  William XIV,355, 423; XV,46; XV,125; XVI, 153, 887
Hungerford, Oliver XVII,88

Huniston, Daniel XVII,308
Hunking, Captain XVII,710
John XVII,513, 527
Mark XVII,511-12, 566, 626, 713, 715
William XVII,749
Hunkings, John XIV,149, 196
Hunkins, John XIV,118, 120, 225; XV,587
Richard XV,723; XVI,206
Robert XV,584-86; XVI,307
Hunnuile, Roger XIV,448
Hunt,-- XV,599
Abel XV,300-1, 304, 308
Asahel XVI,80, 91, 598
Bartholomew XVII,501
Caleb XIV,577, 634; XV,442, 626, 724; XVI,246, 251, 400, 562; XVII,468
Daniel XV,592; XVI,314; XVII, 116
David XIV,300, 388, 470, 495, 505, 516, 565, 586, 600, 606; XV,249-53, 714; XVI, 200, 269, 517, 657, 831
Enoch XIV,586, 656; XV,731; XVI,36, 38, 195, 212
Ephraim XVI,296
Gideon XIV,345; XVI,93, 106; XVII,37, 42
Henry XV,742; XVI,159, 247, 251, 498, 562
Humphrey XIV,662; XVI,10, 121, 164, 287, 547, 829
Jacob XIV,391, 487, 509, 513; XVI,130, 163
James XIV,646; XVI,887
Jonathan XV,120, 183
Joseph XV,593
Leroy XVII,8
Levi XIV,144, 193-94
Moses XIV,340, 380, 489, 501, 514, 519, 564; XV,701-3, 726, 742; XVI,46, 170, 172, 174, 302, 505, 644

Hunt, Nathan XIV,404; XV,658, 667, 674, 691; XVI,830; XVII,425
Nathaniel XVI,908
Philip XIV,144, 193-94
Philip Jr. XVII,8
Samuel XV,23, 37, 367, 372; XVI,315, 596-98, 701, 866; XVII,103, 137, 443
Stephen XVI,933
Thomas XIV,10, 283, 287, 597; XV,446, 718; XVI,202, 223, 271, 518, 597, 809; XVII,446
Willard XIV,420, 629
William XIV,238; XV,329, 343; XVI,635, 637
Dr. William XVI,636
Zachariah XVI,200, 241, 519, 563
Zaccheus XIV,569, 586, 600, 606; XV,610, 714; XVI,269, 499, 831
Zebulon XIV,285, 287, 546; XV, 593; XVI,314; XVII,116
Hunter, David XIV,332
Ebenezer XIV,8
John XIV,43, 59, 183, 249; XV, 395, 428; XVI,929
Lieutenant XIV,699
Robert XV,754; XVII,27
Theophilus XVII,369
Thomas XIV,1
Huntington, John XIV,425; XV,177-178
Joshua XVI,85, 92, 107
Sampson XVI,232, 248
Timothy XIV,413
William XV,323, 342, 742; XVI, 543
Huntley, Aaron XV,26
Andrew XV,26, 30, 147; XVI, 138; XVII,105
Elisha XV,26; XVI,80, 93
Isaiah XV,26
Nathan XIV,325, 464; XV,26,

148

Huntley, Nathan (Cont.) 741
  Rufus XV,25
  Russell XV,11
  Samuel XIV,265
Huntoon, Aaron XV,322, 342
  Benjamin XIV,316, 318;
    XV,164, 514; XVI,826
  Caleb XIV,25, 113, 147, 196;
    XV, 143
  Charles XV,12, 30, 34, 144;
    XVI,137
  Hilton XIV,325, 464
  John XIV,325, 464; XV,12;
    XVI, 709
  Jonathan XIV,60, 182;
    XV,754
  Joseph XIV,25, 194, 556,
    661; XV,458, 733; XVI,6,
    234; 320-21, 323, 326,
    330, 334, 337, 339, 343,
    345, 397, 713; XVII,269
  Josiah XIV,113; XV,30
  Moses XIV,112, 147, 195,
    404
  Nathaniel XIV,24, 26, 298;
    XVII,103
  Philbrick XIV,195; XV,30,
    371
  Philip XIV,104; XV,30
  Reuben XIV,585, 660;
    XVI,234, 708
  Sampson XVI,232
  Samuel XV,12, 56, 528, 746;
    XVI,163
  Samuel Jr. XVI,131
  Thomas P. XIV,112, 147, 404
Huntress, Christopher XIV,246,
    618; XV,618, 723; XVI,627
  George XIV,14; XVII,612
  Gideon XVI,61, 63, 72
  James XIV,246
  John XIV,18
  Jonathan XIV,118-19, 149,
    196, 227, 344, 635;
    XV,325, 596, 724
  Joshua XVII,22, 34
  Joshua L. XIV,256; XVII,39

Huntress, Noah XV,325
  Pearson XIV,580, 619;
    XV,448, 598, 721;
    XVI,207, 273; XVII,140
  Seth XIV,664; XV,431
  Solomon XIV,316, 319
Hunwill, Robert XIV,535
Hurd, Christopher XVI,930
  George XV,725
  Jacob XV,379
  John XVII,52, 69, 72, 79, 84,
    93
  Jonathan XVI,119
  Justus XV,67; XVI,663
  Nathan XV,35
  Robert XV,295; XVI,118
  Samuel XIV,298; XV,11, 30,
    371; XVI,531-32; XVII,105
  Shubael XV,65; XVI,714;
    XVII, 96
  Stephen XV,36, 147; XVI,80,
    99, 193
  Uziel XIV,324, 464; XVI,531
  Zadoc XIV,645; XVI,24, 546
Hurey, Job XIV,3
Hurlbert, Richard XIV,261
Hurlburt, John XV,467, 478,
    505, 529
  Josiah XV,81
Hurlbut, Abel XVI,308-9
  Asahel XVI,308-9
  Daniel XVI,308-9
Hurst, John XVII,692
Huse, Arthur XVII,621, 667
  Carr XV,381; XVI,420, 681-
    82, 684
  James XIV,134, 191, 341;
    XV, 699; XVI,68, 79, 100,
    250, 255, 507; XVII,7
  Jonathan XIV,112, 147, 195;
    XV,341
  Joseph XIV,425, 432
  Robert XIV,369, 498
  Samuel XIV,225, 341;
    XV,486, 499-500
  Serjeant XV,564
  Thomas XIV,58, 183, 254,

Huse, Thomas (Cont.) 359
    William XV,483, 495
    See also Hewes, Hughes,
        Hughs
Hussey, Christopher XVII, 528,
    543, 555, 608
    Job XIV,14
    John XVII,620, 641
    Richard Jr. XVI,904
    Robert XIV,375, 483, 502,
        511, 518
    Samuel XIV,112
Huston, John XVI,911
    Samuel XV,138; XVI,921
Hutchins, Asa XIV,93, 202-3;
    XV, 203, XVII,97
    Benjamin XIV,432
    Captain XV,439, 607-8;
        XVII,223
    Daniel XVI,165
    Edman XIV,664
    Edmund XV,431
    Ephraim XIV,77, 81, 198
    George XIV,225
    Gordon XIV,63, 65, 153, 156,
        181-82, 186, 416, 431;
        XVI, 926; XVII,3-4, 21
    Hezekiah XIV,38, 76, 78, 81,
        83, 155, 198; XV, 396-97,
        569; XVI,599, 670; XVII,36
    Isaac XIV,93, 202-3; XVII,96
    Israel XIV,517
    James XIV,408, 611;
        XVI,512; XIV,408, 611;
        XVI,512, 729, 872, 874;
        XVII,26
    Jeremiah XIV,233
    John XIV,25, 82, 118-19,
        149, 197-98; XV,128, 186,
        693; XVI,121, 145, 214
    Jonathan XV,306, 310
    Joseph XIV,448, 534, 664;
        XV, 279, 281, 431;
        XVI,539
    Josiah XV,552; XVII,259
    Levi XIV,63, 181, 186; XVI,
        726, 926; XVII,3

Hutchins, Lieutenant XVI,180
    Moses XIV,239, 468, 593; XV,
        596, 716; XVI,201, 221,
        241, 270
    Nathaniel XIV,210, 214, 217,
        219-21, 475, 553, 610-11;
        XV,710; XVI,2, 182, 197,
        611, 769; XVII,212, 266,
        443, 655
    Phinehas XV,110
    Samuel XIV,35, 90, 239, 255,
        260, 484; XV,439;
        XVI,528; XVII,23, 31, 38,
        46, 85, 289, 434
    Simon XIV,597; XV,713
    Solomon XIV,664; XV,431
    Theophilus XIV,25
    Thomas XIV,664; XV,431
    William XIV,85, 199, 553,
        610; XV,47, 710, 742;
        XVI,3, 50, 769, 872;
        XVII,94, 266
Hutchinson, Alexander XIV,59,
    156-57, XV,751
    Asa XV,518, 664, 671, 683;
        XVI,745; XVII,339
    Azariah XVI,44
    Benjamin XIV,244
    Captain XV,610
    Dudley XIV,69, 180, 569; XV,
        609
    E. XV,712
    Ebenezer XV,72
    Elisha XIV,69, 180, 432, 603;
        XV,194; XVI,199, 222,
        506, 659
    George XVI,885
    Israel XV,622, 634, 644; XVI,
        26, 729
    James XIV,43, 87, 103, 200,
        575, 639; XVI,16, 26, 85,
        XVI,99, 857-858; XVII,427
    John XIV,101, 206, 607-8;
        XV, 118, 138, 436, 603,
        714; XVII,236
    John Jr. XV,731
    Levi XIV,433, 603; XV,712;

Hutchinson, Levi (Cont.)
 XVI,199, 268
 Nathan XV,74
 Nehemiah XIV,88, 201;
  XV,118, 138, 188, 230
 Samuel XIV,87, 200; XV,189,
  554; XVI,885
 Solomon XIV,59, 183, 254,
  439, 527, 545; XV,85, 207
 Thomas XIV,99, 205, 576,
  634; XV,442, 724;
  XVI,206, 814
 Timothy XIV,55, 184, 579,
  604; XV,453-54, 716;
  XVI,723
 William XVI,921
Huttele, Aaron XVII,308
Hyde, Levi XV,138; XVII,252

I

Ide, Israel XIV,428
Indian, James XV,619
 Lewis XIV,265
Ingalls, Amos XV,21, 217; XVI,
 144
 Benjamin XV,54, 204
 Benjamin P. XV,698; XVI,147
 Caleb XV,97, 218
 Captain XVI,902
 Ebenezer XIV,98, 205;
  XV,217; XVI,535-36, 928
 Edmond XVI,809-10
 Edmund XV,3,5
 Henry XV,54, 56, 196, 203,
  754
 Israel XIV,82, 198, 337, 387,
  494, 507, 516, 519, 586,
  600; XV, 77, 79, 436,
  518, 715; XVI,200; XVII,63
 Jonathan XIV,420; XV,20,
  125, 150, 160
 Joseph XV,204
 Moses XV,568; XVI,568
 Nathaniel XIV,36; XV,97;
  XVI, 297
 Simeon XIV,36, 98, 205
 Timothy XV,658-59, 668, 679
Ingalls, William XVI,37, 278

Ingersoll, Colonel XIV,25-26
Ingerson, Richard XIV,549; XV,
 692; XVI,214
 William XIV,259; XVII,37
Ingham, Joseph XIV,238
Ingleherst, Christopher XV,724
Inglish, William XV,732; XVI,39
Ingliss, Thomas XIV,73
Ingraham, Junia XIV,422;
 XV,379
 Morris XIV,13
Iraf, George XVII,513
Ireland, Asa XIV,110-11
 Benjamin XIV,9
 George XVII,204
Irving, Caleb XIV,247
Isaki, August XVII,304
Isamen, Peter XVII,304
Isham, Benjamin XVI,80
Ives, Elizabeth XVI,608
 Jesse XVII,104
 Joseph XV,28; XVI,605-6

J

Jack, John XVI,64, 71, 93
Jackman, George XVI,576-78;
 XVII,418
 Humphrey XV,515
 John XIV,317, 319; XV,187
 Moses XIV,341; XV,328, 330,
  343, 486, 499-500
 Richard XVI,255, 522, 903
 Samuel XIV,304, 306, 466
 Simeon XV,406
 William XV,128, 187, 488,
  490-491, 663, 670, 684,
  688; XVI,88, 94, 577
Jackson, -- XV,695
 Asa XVI,82, 92, 106, 237,
  269, 523
 Benjamin XIV,21, 233, 432;
  XV, 527
 Caleb XVI,819
 Clement XIV,570, 649;
  XV,595, 728; XVI,13
 Clement Jr. XIV,255, 260,
  484, 647; XVII,31, 39, 46,
  86

Jackson, Daniel XIV,272, 385,
   496, 505, 517, 617; XV,
   444, 722; XVII, 29
Daniel Jr. XIV,239; XVII,23,
   39
Doctor XVI,925
Eleazer XIV,444, 543; XV,654
Ephraim XVII,648, 749
George XVII,39
George Jr. XIV,255, 260;
   XVII, 23, 31, 46
Dr. Hall XIV,239, 367;
   XV,428; XVII,4, 23, 35, 38,
   280
Henry XV,137, 427, 432,
   753; XVI,47, 54-55, 101,
   217, 266; XVII,354, 415,
   466
James XVII,719, 721
John XIV,344; XV,577;
   XVI,930; XVII,139, 513,
   527, 749
Dr. John XVI,413
Joseph XIV,68, 180, 408; XV,
   305, 309, 528; XVI,730
Mr. XVII,646, 710, 757
Nathaniel XIV,13
Richard XVII,527
Samuel XIV,233; XVII,24,
   655
Simeon XIV,430
Stephen XV,172
Thomas XV,284, 287
William XIV,192; XVII,92,
   719
Jacobs, Andrew XV,194
Daniels XVI,150
David XV,195
Elias XIV,238
George XVII,204
John XIV,238; XV,518, 744;
   XVI,143
John J. XVII,204
Jaffrey, George XVII,615-16,
   625, 643, 661, 664, 691-
   92, 701, 730, 746
Jaiques, Jean XIV,585

Jalbert, Francis XVI,271
Jallen, Simon XIV,10
James, Benjamin XVII,642
Caleb XV,284, 288
David XV,320, 340
Francis XVI,776
Henry XVI,931
Jabez XIV,362, 365; XV,411,
   523
James XIV,236
John XIV,664; XVII,22, 33,
   207
Jonathan XIV,362, 365
Joshua XVI,672
Kinsley XIV,239
Kinsley H. XIV,353
Samuel XIV,4, 110, 132, 190
Thomas XVII,307
William XVII,22, 33
Jameson, Alexander XV,351,
   353, 362; XVI,140, 161
Daniel XV,555; XVI,632;
   XVII, 427
Hugh XIV,605; XV,453, 455,
   740; XVI,247, 253, 500,
   575, 724, 726
John XIV,53, 185, 359;
   XV,165, 228
Patrick XVII,512
Thomas XIV,611; XVI,632;
   XVII, 212
Jandes, Barnabas XIV,2
Jannison, John XIV,297
Janvrin, Ebenezer XIV,345, 664;
   XV,431; XVII,22, 33, 47
Mendum XIV,240, 259;
   XVII,36, 42, 135
Jaques, Louis XVII,305
Jaquith, Benjamin XVI,535-36
Ebenezer XIV,33; XV,88
Jarvis, Leonard XVII,381
Robert XIV,660; XV,727; XVI,
   43
Jeffers, John XIV,532; XVII,32
John Jr. XIV,452
Jenkins, Benjamin XV,431, 587
Ebenezer XIV,5

Jenkins, Joseph XVII,710, 717
  Lyonell XVII,575, 591, 598,
    600
  Mark XVII,360
  Nathaniel XIV,108, 123, 188,
    362; XVI,710
  Peter XIV,74, 178, 348, 579,
    604; XV,453-54, 715; XVI,
    201, 721
  Richard XIV,227, 257-58,
    472, 549; XV,430; XVII,45
  Rowland XVII,679
  Stephen XVII,42, 716
  William XVII,360
  William Jr. XVII,360
Jenks, Cornelius XIV,263
  Jeremiah XV,371
  Zachariah XV,277
Jenne, Ebenezer XV,14, 374,
  602
  Ephraim XV,40
  Silas XV,18
Jenness, Benjamin XIV,571; XV,
  663, 670, 684, 688;
  XVI,88, 786
  David XIV,52, 184
  Francis XVI,821
  Francis Jr. XIV,402, 414
  Job XIV,585, 647, 450;
    XV,596, 728; XVI,13
  John XIV,224, 343, 360; XV,
    527, 634, 649, 712;
    XVI,199, 505, 646-47
  John S. XVII,475
  Jonathan XIV,118, 138, 158,
    192, 627
  Joseph XIV,370, 378, 414,
    492, 503, 515
  Joshua XIV,641; XV,456
  Nathaniel XV,256, 259-60,
    263
  Noah XVI,111
  Peter XIV,224
  Richard XIV,224; XV,527;
    XVI, 548
  Samuel XIV,588; XVI,351
  Samuel Jr. XIV,224

Jenney, Ebenezer XVII,89
Jennings, Abel XVII,114
  Benjamin XVI,93, 247, 253,
    499
  Ebenezer XIV,662
  Ephraim XIV,607-8; XV,436,
    604, 714; XVII,468
  Hezekiah XVII,642, 741
  John XIV,469; XVI,102, 221,
    268
  Jonathan XIV,586; XV,441,
    627, 721
  Joseph XV,750
  Mark XVII,29
  Michael XVI,307
  Stephen XIV,607-8; XV,604,
    714; XVI,200; XVII,468
Jennison, John XV,23, 37; XVI,
  528, 532; XVII,103, 445
Jenville, Alexir XVII,304
Jepson, John XIV,563
Jerould, Reuben XV,38, 45, 373,
  378, 386
Jewell, Bradbury XVI,854
  Daniel XIV,415; XV,544; XVI,
    109-11, 165, 803, 844-45,
    847
  David XIV,308, 401, 586-87,
    650; XV,731; XVI,36, 39,
    212, 286, 520; XVII,221
  Enos XIV,583, 586, 627;
    XV,457, 627, 749;
    XVI,103, 205, 501;
    XVI,520, 600, 838
  Henry XIV,413
  Jacob XVI,921
  James XIV,267; XV,80, 347,
    518, 615; XVII,63
  John XV,172, 634, 649, 721;
    XVI,205, 226, 241, 273,
    503, 617
  Joseph XIV,381, 490, 623;
    XV, 457, 719, 747;
    XVI,204, 233, 241, 272,
    520, 838
  Nathaniel XIV,8
  Timothy XIV,300, 456;

Jewell, Timothy (Cont.) XVI,68,
    79, 97
Jewett, Abel XIV,333; XV,630,
    643, 646
    David XIV,400; XV,571; XVII,
        27
    Ebenezer XV,88
    Edward XIV,36; XV,97; XVII,
        121
    Enoch XVII,124
    Enos XV,721
    Ezekiel XIV,35
    Jacob XV,698
    Jacob Jr. XV,624
    Jacob 3d XV,511
    James XIV,337
    Jedediah XIV,172, 174-77;
        XVII, 145, 280, 291, 417-
        18, 445, 448, 459
    Jonathan XV,88, 217, 476
    Joseph XIV,580, 661; XV,
        215, 448, 599, 727
    Moses XIV,452, 532
    Nathaniel XV,534
    Noah XIV,229, 419; XV,324,
        544; XVII,27
    Paul XVII,57
    Samuel XIV,33; XV,89, 285,
        287, 744
    Stephen Jr. XIV,419
Jilson, James XVI,809
Job, John XIV,348, 560, 620;
    XV, 722; XVI,205, 288,
    890; XVII, 439
Joel, Esar XIV,10
Johannes, Pierre XVII,309
Johns, Peter XIV,283, 287
Johnson, Abraham XIV,57, 183;
    XV,658, 667, 691; XVI,65,
    73, 106, 707-8
    Abram,XVI,90
    Adam XV,394, 429, 554; XVI,
        298
    Amos XV,228
Johnson, Andrew XIV,223, 363;
    XV, 625, 628, 640, 720;
    XVI,204, 230, 272, 504,

Johnson, Andrew (Cont.) 572,
    638-39
    Asahel XIV,324, 464
    Asael XIV,645
    Benjamin XIV,9, 109, 123,
        187, 308, 321; XV,179;
        XVI,173, 240, 274, 521,
        828
    Calvin XIV,59, 183, 304, 306
    Captain XIV,475; XVII,130,
        132
    Charles XIV,93, 202-3;
        XV,142
    Colonel XVII,338
    Daniel XV,48; XVI,255, 505
    David, XIV,25, 265, 442, 544,
        578, 596, 610; XV,443,
        713; XVI,199, 223, 268,
        296, 399, 522, 878-79;
        XVII,360
    Davis XIV,258
    Dennis XIV,343
    Ebenezer XVI,884, 914-15
    Edmond XIV,12
    Edward XIV,33; XVII,521
    Ezra XIV,417
    Gideon XIV,233; XV,191;
        XVII,29
    Isaac XIV,63, 105, 181, 186,
        265; XV,12; XVI,926
    Isaiah XIV,286, 657
    Ithamar XV,746
    James XIV,22, 25, 54, 235,
        252, 316, 318, 321, 465-
        66, 548; XV,128, 166,
        406, 514, 663, 670, 684,
        688; XVI,826; XVII, 511-
        12, 535, 642, 692
    Jesse XVII,339
    Job XV,143
    John XIV,15-16, 88, 108,
        201, 225, 235, 242, 398,
        405, 455, 529, 575; XV,
        249-51, 255, 544; XVI,
        900, 907, 914; XVII,128,
        131, 511, 527, 655, 691-
        692, 740

Johnson, John M. XIV,392, 487,
    509, 513
  Jonathan XIV,167, 275, 304-
    5, 405, 465; XVII,32
  Joseph XIV,25; XV,69, 206,
    486, 499-500, 517;
    XVI,66, 75, 97, 125, 137,
    235, 242, 274, 505, 644-
    45; XVII,92
  Joshua XIV,253; XV,666,
    685; XVI,843
  Josiah XIV,265; XVI,39
  Jotham XVII,360
  Michael XVI,156, 522,
    866
  Moses XIV,61, 182, 317, 319;
    XV,109, 536
  Mr. XVII,342
  Nathan XVI,668
  Nathaniel XIV,252; XVI,686
  Noah XIV,404; XVI,125
  Oliver XIV,85, 199; XV,370
  Peter XIV,43, 64, 181, 186,
    224; XVI,335, 926; XVII,
    667-68
  Philip XIV,149, 197, 312; XV,
    422, 544, 597, 730, 735;
    XVI,17, 61, 63, 72, 99,
    194, 211, 220, 239, 278,
    286, 507, 668
  Philip Jr. XIV,120, 338, 641
  Samuel XIV,33, 82, 198, 370,
    379, 381, 397, 438, 489,
    493, 501, 514, 527, 545,
    592; XV,439, 593, 597,
    698; XVI, 66, 77, 96, 403,
    491-92, 670, 775-76;
    XVII,643
  Silas XV,358
  Simeon XV,746
  Simon XIV,247; XV,391, 527;
    XVII,26
  Sylvanus XV,31
  Thomas XIV,228, 235, 322,
    578, 596; XV,713; XVI,69,
    79, 268; XVII,18, 283, 360
  Timothy XIV,358; XV,186

Johnson, William XIV,18, 210,
    216-17, 220, 474-75, 579;
    XV, 452, 623, 629, 641,
    730, 740; XVI,31, 34, 59,
    671, 722, 783; XVII,341,
    349
  Willis XVII,95
  Zebediah XIV,332
Johnston, Charles XIV,395, 547
  Elisha XIV,9
  Isaac XVII,3
  John XIV,622
  Michael XVII,254
  Nathaniel XIV,9
  Peter XVII,3
  Samuel XIV,501, 504, 515;
    XVII, 295
  William XIV,10, 653
Johnstone, Abraham XV,322,
    341, 673
  Charles XV,142, 158;
    XVI,249, 293, 539, 679,
    815, 924; XVII,69, 73, 81,
    93, 344; XVII,385, 416,
    423
  Joseph XVI,645
  Michael XVI,293, 295, 680
  Robert XV,153
  William XV,454
Joice, Thomas XV,753
Joiner, Francis XV,713
  John XV,716
Jones, Abraham XVII,749
  Asa XIV,297; XV,26, 34, 37;
    XVI,605, 607
  Benjamin XIV,2, 233, 362;
    XV, 294; XVI,728;
    XVII,249
  Caleb XV,213
  Captain XVII,287
  Corporal XIV,2
  E. XVI,605
  Ebenezer XIV,18, 233; XVI,
    907
  Edward XVI,286, 891; XVII,
    439
  Ephraim XIV,574, 626;

Jones, Ephraim (Cont.) XV,615, 720; XVI,204
Evan XV,568
Ezra XVI,608
Francis XVII,511, 512, 648, 667, 669
Hannah XVII,609
James XIV,244; XV,15, 138; XVI,237, 244, 274, 516, 803, 805; XVII,109, 513, 527
Jenkins XVII,525
Jesse XIV,458, 538; XV,201
Joel XVI,88, 95
John XIV,13, 606, 648; XV,42, 595, 727; XVI,9, 42, 183, 208, 277, 516, 803-5, 920; XVII,307, 511, 513, 667
John Paul XVI,430; XVII,145, 454
Joseph XIV,398; XVII,2, 307, 710, 719, 734
Joshua XIV,257
Josiah XV,747
Lazarus XIV,238
Lloyd XIV,566, 654; XV,607, 730; XVI,31, 34, 59
Moses XIV,51, 185; XV,183
Mr. XVII,132
Nathan XIV,404
Pearson XVII,315
Robert XIV,586; XVI,295; XVII, 526
Samuel XIV,227, 257-58, 263; XIV, 472-73, 550; XV, 430, 619, 749; XVI,60, 62, 70, 99, 106; XVII,108, 207
Stephen XVII,525, 607, 645, 658, 719, 734
Thomas XIV,227, 238, 257-58, 265; XV,28; XVII,45
Timothy XIV,244, 319
William XIV,244, 697; XV, 127, 469, 481, 490; XVI, 287, 508; XVII,300, 501, 513

Jordan, Dominicus XIV,3
Ebenezer XIV,92
Eleazer XIV,202-3, 264; XV,7; XVI,287, 460, 519
Jedidiah XVII,667
Jeremiah XVII,667
John XIV,57, 183, 425, 468; XV,711, 749, 753; XVI,753, 906
Joseph XIV,180
Nathaniel XIV,383, 491
Samuel XVII,746
Jose, Richard XVII,626, 643, 665-66, 672
Joslin, James XV,546
Taylor XVI,285, 504
Joslyn, Henry XVII,483, 508, 510, 514-19, 532, 535
James XVII,257
Jourdan, Thomas XVII,508
Joy, Ebenezer XVI,150
Ephraim XV,40, 155; XVII,144, 655
Joyner, Francis XIV,265, 578, 596
John XIV,265, 578, 592
William XV,741
Judd, Amos XVI,608
Judkins, Benjamin XIV,69, 180
Eben XV,721
Ebenezer XIV,628; XV,173, 627, 748
Ebenezer Jr. XIV,565
Jacob XVI,257, 517
Job XIV,181, 281, 288
Joel XIV,112, 148, 195, 370, 377, 492, 503, 515, 586, 600; XV,715
John Jr. XVII,32
Jonathan XIV,71, 179, 312, 567; XIV,603, 611; XV,300, 302, 305, 309, 435, 449, 600, 608, 712, 718; XVI,202
Joseph XIV,172, 174, 176-77, 300, 312, 398; XVI,694

Judkins, Philip XIV,176, 578, 596;,XV, 713; XVI,103
  Samuel XIV,565, 567, 651, 653; XV,323, 341, 609, 727-28, 734; XVI,9, 27, 30, 33, 42, 59, 183, 188, 190, 194, 208, 210, 220, 233, 241, 277, 499, 509, 582, 695, 732; XVII,467

K

Kade, Noah XIV,176
Kane, Barnabas XIV,424
  Francis XIV,658
Karr, Benjamin XIV,57, 184, 654; XVI, 30, 34, 59
  George XVII,340
  Jacob XIV,177; XVI,630
  James XIV,55, 184; XVI,898; XVII,10
  Jesse XIV,55, 184; XVI,666
  Jonathan XIV,182, 304, 306, 465, 583
  Samuel XIV,56; XVI,140, 161; XVII,258
  Thomas XIV,56, 184; XVI,106
  William XIV,459, 537
  See also Carr
Karswell, John XIV,484; XVII,86
  Joshua XIV,260
  Mark XVII,86
Kaughow, Andrew XVI,246, 253, 504
Kavanah, Charles XVI,506
Kay, John XIV,212, 215, 217, 220
Kearns, James XVII,301
  William XVII,306
Keas, Samuel XVII,527, 625, 665, 713
Keath, Jeremiah XVI,635
Keconomah, Josiah XIV,10
Keef, James XV,623, 629, 641; XVI,566
  Michael XVI,246, 251
Keene, William XIV,421
Keep, Daniel XVII,298
  Doneal XVII,301

Keep, James XVII,349
  Leonard XV,2, 48, 370
  Michael XV,740
Keezer, David XVI,40, 44, 102, 680
  George XVI,108
  Reuben XVI,287
Keith, Jeremiah XV,79, 615
Kellet, Geoffrey XVII,674
Kelley, Colonel XVI,293-94
  Daniel XVI,920
  David XIV,113, 128, 146, 195, 233, 322
  Dudley XVI,255, 499, 582
  Edward XV,635, 639; XVI,102; XVII,29
  Ensign XIV,26
  Ephraim XIV,42, 53
  Holdridge XIV,3
  James XIV,323, 563, 635; XV, 724; XVI,62, 71, 93, 234, 931
  John XVI,67, 78, 95, 823; XVII,432
  Jonathan XIV,116, 129, 189, 312, 471, 564, 593; XV,717; XVI,201, 218, 270, 505, 644-645, 772, 934
  Joshua XIV,246; XVI,284
  Josiah XIV,451
  Micajah XV,668, 673, 690; XVI, 658
  Moses XIV,329, 358, 360, 652; XV,115 117, 543-58, 621, 634, 644-45, 663, 669, 689, 696; XVI,58, 104, 166, 663, 665; XVII,258
  Mr. XVII,18
  Nathaniel XV,623, 629, 641, 681; XVI,44, 282, 547, 758-759, 824; XVII,349
  Nehemiah XV,329-30, 343, 569
  Nemijah XIV,404
  Philip XVI,920

Kelley, Richard XIV,349; XVII,32
  Richard Jr. XIV,342
  Samuel XIV,71, 179, 242,
    359, 452, 532; XV,133,
    176, 654, 668, 680, 690;
    XVI,457, 622, 758-59
  Seymour XIV,104
  Timothy XVII,294
  William XIV,391, 406, 487,
    508, 512; XV,249, 254,
    294, 483, 494, 667, 678;
    XVII,435
  Zachariah XVI,65, 106
Kellogg, Captain XV,750
Kelsey, Absalom XV,33, 35;
    XVII, 104
  Giles XIV,578, 593; XV,717;
    XVII,467
  Hugh XVI,282
  Jesse XIV,324
  Jonathan XVI,287, 513
  Moses XIV,71, 179, 570, 580;
    XV,448, 599, 728; XVI,27,
    188, 210, 282
  Seymour XV,30, 147;
    XVII,105
  Zaccheus XV,723
  Zachariah XVI,75, 93, 206,
    529
Kelso, Jonathan XV,200
Kemp, Amos XIV,588, 626;
    XV,441, 720
  Benjamin XV,698; XVI,113,
    720
  Elijah XVI,88, 95
  John XV,382; XVI,928
  Nathaniel XV,79
  Reuben XIV,42, 56, 184, 267
  Thomas XIV,33, 419; XV,210,
    733, 744; XVI, 51, 53;
    XVII, 214, 457, 460
  William XIV,55, 184, 602;
    XV, 712, 740; XVI,839
Kempfield, Ebenezer XIV,463
Kempton, Rufus XVI,150
  Samuel XIV,93, 202;
    XVI,236, 272, 523, 852

Kempton, Stephen XV,54
Kenan, William XVII,291
Kendall, Daniel XVI,690, 716,
    909
  Ebenezer XVI,669
  Eber XVII,57
  Edward XIV,280, 288, 566,
    587, 657; XV,606, 609,
    732; XVI, 35, 38, 795
  Jabez XV,530
  Jacob XV,90, 698
  James XVII,308
  John XV,109
  Joseph XIV,301
  Nathan XIV,247
  Reuben XV,7
  Samuel XV,108, 360; XVI,654
  Samuel Jr. XVII,10
  William XIV,34, 577, 662;
    XV, 92
Kendrick, Benjamin XVI,556
  Daniel XIV,478; XV,138, 374,
    511, 670, 683; XVI,687;
    XVII,339
  Daniel Jr. XV,664
  Samuel XV,38, 373
Keneson, John XV,252; XVI,779
Keneston, Joseph XVI,582
  Lewis XVI,96
Kenfield, Benjamin XV,134
Keniston, Alexander XIV,15;
    XVII,655
  Benjamin XIV,354
  Christopher XIV,15;
    XVII,610, 612
  James XIV,67, 181, 191, 381,
    490-91; XV,260; XVII,49
  Job XVI,517
  John XIV,15
  Joseph XVI,499
  Lewis XIV,123, 187, 400
  Nathaniel XIV,354
  Thomas XIV,385
  Winthrop XIV,211, 214, 217,
    220
Kenistone, Andrew XV,698
  Jonathan XVII,25

Kenistone, Valentine XV,300, 302, 305, 309
Kennard, Edward XIV,664
  Mr. XVII,646
  Moses XVI,917
  Nathaniel XIV,259; XVII,38
Kennecomb, Arthur XIV,245
Kennedy, David XVII,298
  John XIV,159, 161, 164, 172, 176-77, 288; XV,104, 427; XVI,47, 101, 303
  Matthew XIV,358
  Patrick XV,587; XVI,157
  Robert XIV,159, 161, 280, 288; XV,586; XVI,910
Kennerston, James XV,597
Kennerstone, Isaac XVII,434
Kenneson, James XV,719; XVI,203
  Job XVI,204
  John XIV,271, 414
  Joseph XIV,22
  Valentine XV,309
Kenneston, Benjamin XIV,289, 291
  David XV,640; XVI,34, 97, 102
  James XVI,233
  Job XV,618
  Josiah XV,656
  Nicholas XVI,97
Kennestone, David XV,483, 490-91; XVI,210
  James XIV,536, 563, 615
  Job XIV,623
  Joseph E. XVI,282
  Josiah XV,673
  Winthrop XV,733
Kenney, Amos XIV,346, 369, 375, 482, 498, 502, 511, 518, 574, 600, 623; XV, 614, 619, 715, 720; XVI, 921; XVII,60
  Archelaus XIV,103, 208, 336; XVII,63
  Benjamin XV,295
  Daniel XV,374, 529, 535

Kenney, David XV,211; XVI,145
  John XIV,623; XV,619; 720; XVI, 204, 229, 286, 292, 508, 520, 836
  Jonathan XIV,421; XV,534
  Joseph XV,19, 138, 374
  Moses XIV,420; XVI,840
  Samuel XIV,574; XV,615
  William XVI,931
Kennison, Andrew XVI,130, 163
  Benjamin XIV,25
  David XV,284; XVI,78, 277, 504
  Henry XIV,370, 492
  James XIV,135, 402, 414; XVI, 271
  Job XV,720; XVI,239, 272, 503
  John XIV,176, 402; XV,597; XVI,846
  Jonathan XIV,403
  Joseph XIV,126, 188, 371, 379, 493, 503, 515; XVI,115; XVII,10
  Josiah XVI,711
  Lewis XVI,78
  Nicholas XVI,78
  Samuel XIV, 370, 379, 493, 504, 515
  Thomas XIV, 505, 517
Kenniston, David XV, 180, 288, 730; XVI, 32, 34, 67
  Ebenezer XVI, 287, 522
  Henry XIV, 378
  James XIV,448
  Job XIV,565
  John XV,251, 295
  Jonathan XIV,415
  Joseph XVI,255, 286
  Joseph E. XIV,312
  Josiah XIV,408; XV,311
  Lewis XVI,67
  Nicholas XVI,67
  Thomas XIV,520; XVI,241
  Winthrop XVI,45, 48, 264, 304-5
Kennistone, David XV,129, 628;

Kennistone, David (Cont.)
    XVI,514
    James XV,264; XVI,767
    John XV,254
    Joseph XVI,517
    Josiah XV,666
    Solomon XV,194
    Waldron XV,192
Kennyon, Christopher XV,587
Kent, Benjamin XVI,907
    Ebenezer XVI,64, 74, 93;
        XVII, 434
    Isaac XV,29
    Jacob XIV,283, 287, 291,
        443, 543, 547; XVI,307;
        XVII,73, 114
    Job XV,396; XVI,124
    John XIV,13, 470, 584, 606;
        XV,591, 714; XVI,200,
        269, 500, 590; XVII,717
    Joseph XV,469, 481, 506,
        699; XVI,67, 74, 93;
        XVII,383, 716
    Josiah XIV,16
    Peter XIV,82, 198
    Robert XIV,235; XVII,717
    Thomas XVI,213
Kentfield, Ebenezer XVII,65
    George XIV,166, 169, 274,
        288, 317, 320, 441, 527,
        545; XV, 124, 149, 160
    Josiah XVI,920
    Samuel XIV,287
    Shem XVI,237, 513
Keries, Morris XVI,907
Ketchum, Jonas XV,18, 157
    Jonathan XVII,144
    Nathaniel XVI,178-79
    Zophar XV,41
Kettell, Andrew XVII,418
Keyes, Abner XIV,33, 247, 301,
        390, 486, 508, 512;
        XV,698; XVII,437
    Amos XV,368
    Andrew XV,693
    Christopher XIV,268, 271,
        290

Keyes, Daniel XV,48, 225;
        XVII,94
    Ebenezer XIV,441, 527
    Edward XIV,104; XV,662,
        669, 681; XVI,549;
        XVII,106
    Elias XIV,8; XV,470, 502
    Ephraim XVI,85, 100, 106,
        194, 259
    Ezekiel XIV,280, 288;
        XV,149, 160
    Frederick XIV,442, 544;
        XV,33
    Israel XV,20
    Joseph XVI,157; XVII,118-19
    Leonard XVII,94
    Peter XV,705-6, 708-9;
        XVI,88, 90, 586
    Samuel XVI,876
    Silas XV,74, 211, 530;
        XVI,883
    Stephen XIV,280, 288, 657;
        XV, 381, 459, 606; XVI,37,
        41, 190, 236, 243, 275,
        501, 600, 928
    William XIV,298; XV,33, 37;
        XVII,103
Keyser, Reuben XVI,513, 772
Kezar, David XV,631, 638
    Edmund XV,127
    Reuben XV,165
Kiason, Daniel XV,57
Kibby, Nathaniel XVI,28
Kid, Benjamin XV,419
Kidd, Charles XVII,205
Kidder, Daniel XIV,469, 572,
        603; XV,612, 712;
        XVI,198, 222, 239, 268
    Elijah XV,556; XVII,258
    James XVII,414
    John XV,125, 150, 554, 662,
        668, 677, 696, 698;
        XVI,88, 681-82, 938
    Jonas XV,554, 696; XVI,140,
        142, 161-62, 729-30
    Joseph XIV,35, 420; XV, 364,
        534

Kidder, Noah XIV,172, 175-77
  Reuben XIV,34; XV,556;
    XVI,235, 268, 507, 665;
    XVII,258
  Samuel XV,28, 37, 367, 372;
    XVII,105
  Stephen XV,144; XVI,313;
    XVII, 249
  Thomas XIV,221
  Wilder XIV,90, 221; XVI,854
Kiding, Christopher XVII,608
  Kief, Daniel XIV,258
  Jeremiah XV,207
Kielle, James XIV,323
  John XIV,298; XVI,526, 625,
    628
  William XVI,627
Kier, David XV,631
Kilburn,-- XV,43
  Ebenezer XIV,326; XV,46, 65,
    67; XVII,95
  Eliphaz XIV,464
  Joel XV,66
  John XIV,463; XV,23, 369,
    372
  Josiah XV,374
Killam, Benjamin XIV,35
Killerist, Hugh XVI,917
Killey, David XVII,24, 308
  William XV,250-51, 656; XVI,
    703; XVII,424-25
Killicut, Charity XIV,348; XV,79,
    207, 754
  Reuben XIV,266; XV,80
  Thomas XIV,337, 700;
    XVII,63
Kimball, Aaron XV,348;
    XVI,264, 789; XVII,431
  Abel XV,664-65, 671, 683;
    XVI, 695, 812-13
  Abraham XIV,43, 64, 182,
    186, 211, 216, 218, 220,
    283, 287, 474; XV, 183,
    231, 435; XVI, 322, 332,
    334, 400
  Amos XV,169; XVI,155
  Asa XVI,130, 163

Kimball, Benjamin XIV,134,
    239, 432, 552, 591; XV,
    331, 358, 710; XVI, 2,
    333, 401, 530, 719;
    XVII,5, 7, 145, 267, 270,
    280, 348
  Caleb XV,125
  Charles XIV,192
  Daniel XV,14; XVI,131, 133,
    135, 150, 163, 286, 509;
    XVII,108
  David XIV,244; XV,120, 408,
    548; XVII,431
  Dudley XV,396; XVII,57
  Ebenezer XIV,261, 430;
    XV,512, 569; XVII,32
  Edward XV,698; XVI,720
  Eli XIV,244; XV,213
  Eliphalet XV,38, 707; XVI,45;
    XVI,301, 597
  Haines XVI,45, 301
  Hansel XV,707; XVI,597
  Henry XIV,584; XV,74, 451-
    52; XVI,145, 588
  John XIV,53, 185, 296, 455,
    529, 564, 588, 626, 628;
    XV, 75, 284, 288, 392,
    451, 720-721, 742;
    XVI,789; XVII,431
  Jonathan XV,323, 342
  Joseph XIV,329, 428; XV,17,
    568; XVII,109
  Joshua XIV,328; XV,564
  L. XVI,180
  Mellen XVI,263, 612;
    XVII,430
  Moses XIV,50, 77, 82, 185,
    212, 216, 218, 221, 230;
    XV,285, 408
  Nathaniel XIV,404, 430;
    XV,194, 388, 742
  Obadiah XIV,566, 653;
    XV,608, 729; XVI,30, 33,
    59
  Oliver XIV,52, 185
  Peter XIV,261, 429; XV,127,
    130, 162, 185, 187, 233,

Kimball, Peter (Cont.) 235-236,
  283, 288; XVI,215, 577-
  578
Philip XIV,16
Phinehas XIV,51, 185;
  XV,368
Porter XIV,242, 397; XV,283,
  290, 292-93, 315, 317
Reuben XIV,50, 186, 261;
  XV, 405, 548
Richard XIV,405; XV,390-91
Robert XIV,402, 503, 515
Samuel XIV,224, 341, 359
Sarah XVI,333, 340, 401
Sargent XVI,65, 75, 99, 282
Thomas XIV,631; XV,451,
  711; XVI,198, 267, 508,
  561, 686
Timothy XV,633, 647;
  XVI,102, 207, 232, 275,
  519, 820
William XIV,244, 442, 544;
  XV, 211, 707; XVI,169-70,
  238, 245, 268, 512, 597,
  750-51; XVII,131
Wills XV,483, 492, 602
Ziba XIV,53, 185, 411, 588
Kiming, Moses XIV,2
Kimmen, Benjamin XIV,67, 181
Kincaid, David XVII,655, 719
  John XIV,53, 185, 458, 539;
  XV,228; XVII,92
Kinelty, John XVII,293
  Patrick XVII,293
Kineson, Andrew XIV,571
  Elizabeth XVI,657
  James XVI,845
  Thomas XIV,496
Kineston, David XVI,219
King, Benjamin XIV,91, 201; XV,
  753; XVII,298
  Eleazer XVI,938
  Ezra XIV,645; XVI,21, 23,
  809
  Frederick XIV,29
  George XIV,29; XV,141; XVI,
  361, 376, 394, 473; XVII,

King, George (Cont.) 19, 22-23,
  123
George Jr. XIV,255, 260;
  XVII, 39, 46, 125
Issachar XIV,424
James XVI,246, 252;
  XVII,301, 438
James P. XVII,139
John XIV,119, 151, 196, 309;
  XV, 630, 633, 637, 643,
  647; XVI,720, 724, 848
Richard XIV,237
Robert XVII,302
Samuel XIV,15; XV,753; XVI,
  603; XVII,655, 667, 669
Silas XV,29
Thomas XIV,246
William XIV,645; XV,446;
  XVI, 21, 23, 83, 100
William Jr. XIV,645; XVI,21,
  23, 809
Kingman, John XVI,570
  William XIV,228
Kingsbury, Absalom XV,29, 369
  Daniel XV,61, 64; XVI,701
  Ebenezer XIV,105, 303;
  XV,29, 752; XVII,249
  Elisha XVI,35
  Ephraim XVI,167, 553
  E. W. XIV,102, 208
  Jeduthan XV,17
  Jonathan XIV,607-8; XV,603
  Joseph XIV,274-75, 278,
  289; XV,603
  Nathaniel XV,62
  Obadiah XV,630, 642-43,
  723; XVI,233, 499, 553,
  865
  Sanford XVI,467
Kingsley, Alpheus XV,713; XVI,
  199, 268, 606; XVII,224
  John XVII,118, 120
  Jonathan XIV,427; XV,4, 204
Kiniston, James XVII,6
Kinkard, John XIV,538
Kinnekum, Alpheus XIV,578,
  598-599

Kinnekum, John XIV,652
Kinneston, David XVI,187
    Job XVI,657
Kinney, Israel XIV,33; XV,744
    Samuel XIV,34; XV,745
Kinnison, John XV,249
    Josiah XVI,710
Kinniston, Winthrop XVII,307
Kinsman, Aaron XIV,66-67, 153,
    180-81, 429, 431; XV,404;
    XVI,105, 611
    Ephraim XIV,429
    Nathan XIV,273, 289
Kinston, Ephraim XIV,238
Kirkland, Gideon XIV,650;
    XV,629, 642-43, 728;
    XVI,192, 209, 277, 502,
    606, 608
    Robert XVI,929
Kirkwood, Alexander XIV,240,
    259, 334; XVII,22, 33, 37,
    42
    Arthur XIV,35
    Robert XVII,205
Kitson, Richard XIV,239; XVII,
    23, 39
Kittredge, Solomon XIV,103,
    208, 266, 477; XV,214
Kittridge, Asa XVI,286, 891;
    XVII,439
    Benjamin XVI,296
    Dr. Benjamin XVI,383
    David XVI,287
    Doctor XVI,386, 466, 482
    John XVI,384
    Dr. John XVI,525
    Joshua XVI,86, 99
    Solomon XVI,525
    Dr. Thomas XV,231; XVI,444
    Zephanaiah XIV,244, 302-3,
    212
Klanckerfus, Asa XVI,102
    Esaias XV,631, 637; XVI,609
Knap, Abiel XIV,427, 645;
    XV,503, 745; XVI,24, 809
    Cyprenius XVI,81
    Phinehas XVI,95

Kneeland, Joseph XIV,93, 202-3
Knight, Abiel XV,742
    Abraham XIV,226, 480;
    XV,656,
Knight, Abraham XV,666, 679;
    XVI,66, 75, 287, 516, 570-
    572, 779, 805
    Abram XVI,95
    Amariah XV,27
    Amos XIV,420
    Baptist XV,635, 639; XVI,102
    Benjamin XIV,135, 191, 587,
    656; XV,732; XVI,35, 38,
    195, 212; XVII,7
    Caleb XIV,452, 532, 587,
    656; XV,731; XVI,36, 39
    Daniel XIV,259; XVII,37
    Ephraim XV,284, 288
    Francis XIV,66; XV,751
    Gideon XIV,136, 191, 251;
    XVII,6
    James XV,541
    Jo XVI,902
    John XV,93, 220, 249, 251-
    52, 254, 483, 506, 534,
    628, 640, 735; XVI,287,
    513, 530, 570-71;
    XVII,679
    John Jr. XVI,565
    Joseph XIV,1, 225
    Lucius XIV,287
    Moses XIV,452, 532, 587,
    656; XV,731; XVI,36, 39,
    195, 212
    Samuel XV,399
    Thomas XIV,259; XVII,37
    William XIV,119, 149, 196,
    255, 321, 330; XV,295;
    XVI,627, 804, 818, 926;
    XVII,39, 139
Knock, Jedediah XV,715
    John XVII,29, 674
    Jonathan XIV,583; XV,715;
    XVI, 200
Knocks, Jedediah XIV,583
    Timothy XIV,301
Knolleys, Hansard XVII,502

Knott, Jesse XV,713
Knowland, John XV,557
Knowles, Amos XIV,1, 76, 82,
    198, 253, 456, 539;
    XV,169, 526
  David XV,249-51, 255
  Deacon XIV,338, 366
  Ester XVI,822
  Ezekiel XIV,229, 253, 328,
    351; XV,256, 258-59, 262;
    XVI,111, 260-61;
    XVII,432, 740
  Hansard XVII,502
  Isaac XV,660-61, 668, 674,
    748; XVI,588, 646
  James XIV,361, 363-64;
    XV,317; XVI,893
  Jeremiah XVII,140
  John XIV,117, 129, 189, 327,
    447, 540, 589; XV, 169,
    474, 494; XVI,65, 76, 97,
    105-6; XVII,528, 740
  Jonathan XIV,230; XV,319,
    339
  Joseph XIV,589; XV,525;
    XVI, 912
  Joseph Jr. XIV,327
  Nathan XVI,46
  Nathaniel XIV,304, 566, 581,
    656; XV,449, 461, 600,
    609, 701, 703; XVI,171-
    72, 176, 302, 520, 832
  Samuel XIV,224, 248, 380,
    489, 501, 514, 602, 647,
    649; XV,728; XVI,12, 912
  Simeon XIV,255; XV,728;
    XVI, 277; XVII,740
  Simon XIV,118, 138, 158,
    192, 469, 565, 571, 647,
    650; XV, 712, 734; XVI,12,
    189, 198, 209, 222, 232,
    241, 268, 513, 518, 657,
    76, 821-22; XVII,659
Knowlton, Asa XIV,247, 588,
    635; XV,626, 724
  David XIV,261

Knowlton, Ebenezer XV,249,
    251-52, 254
  Henry XVII,92
  John XIV,420; XV,216, 536
  Jonathan XIV,23, 39-40
  Thomas XIV,247, 309, 579
Knox, David XVI,551
  George XIV,445, 543, 607;
    XV, 603, 714; XVI,200,
    269, 898; XVII,226
  Henry XVI,345-46; XVII,159,
    161, 188
  James XIV,360; XV,174
  John XIV,360
  Samuel XIV,604; XV,715
  Timothy XIV,459, 538;
    XVI,510, 910, 920-21
  William XIV,246, 359;
    XVI,551
Kury, John XVII,301
Kyle, Ephraim XIV,185; XV,228
Kynaston, Aaron XIV,232
  David XV,625; XVI,638-39
  James XV,257
Kynaston, John XIV,226
  Josiah XIV,233
  Lewis XIV,109
  Thomas XIV,372
          L
Labaree, Peter XIV,464; XVI,597
  Peter Jr. XIV,324
Lacosta, Jacob XVII,114
Lacroix, Michael XVII,305
Lacy, William XVII,295
Ladd, Asa XVI,293, 295, 680
  Benjamin XV,300, 302, 748
  Daniel XIV,3, 25, 342, 349;
    XV, 391; XVI,616-17, 812
  David XIV,167, 170, 286-87,
    546; XV,424, 701, 703,
    725; XVI,46, 171-72, 176,
    208, 240, 302, 508, 679;
    XVII, 14, 253
  Eliphalet XVI,537, 648
  Ephraim XV,358
  Ezekiel XIV,547; XV,584-85;

Ladd, Ezekiel (Cont.) XVI,307,
539; XVII,253
Ezekiel Jr. XVII,253
James XIV,159, 161, 164;
XV, 152, 154, 426, 584-
85; XVI, 293, 295, 307,
313, 539, 580; XVII,91,
116, 223, 253, 330, 355
Jeremiah XVI,88
John XIV,455, 529; XV,125,
152, 154, 749; XVI,539,
924
Jonathan XIV,424; XVI,293,
295, 680; XVII,92, 254
Joseph XVI,293, 295, 680;
XVII,254
Josiah XIV,455, 530; XV,172
Nathaniel XV,285, 287
Samuel XIV,297; XV,163,
194, 279-80; XVI,539, 924
Simeon XVI,931-32
Timothy XVI,112, 380, 824,
889
Trueworthy XIV,425
Lafayette, Marquis de XVI,57;
XVII,199, 213, 218, 222-
23, 227, 229, 264, 281,
391
LaFramboise, Nicholas XVII,304
Laighton, George XV,583
Gideon XIV,228
Hatevil XIV,187
James XIV,187
Joel XV,259, 262
John XIV,234; XVII,655
Thomas XIV,18; XVII,502
Tobias XIV,187, 374, 498
Valentine XVI,103, 227, 639
See also Leighton
Laiken, Lemuel XV, 188
Laister, Matthias XVI,932
Lajunesse, Jean Jacque Gilli
XIV,662; XVI,615
Lake, Daniel XIV,36, 98, 205;
XV,98, 348; XVII,102
Daniel Jr. XIV,36

Lake, Enos XIV,36, 98, 205;
XV,98, 348
Henry XV,97, 217, 348, 539;
XVII,101
John XIV,576
Jonathan XIV,577, 662;
XV,348; XVI,83, 96, 107,
236, 273, 518, 814-15
Reuben XIV,415
Samuel XVII,57
Lakeman, Nathaniel XIV,359
Lakerman, Amos XVI,147
Lakin, Robert XVI,159
Simeon XV,214
William XIV,632; XV,444,
723; XVI,103, 201, 269,
321, 323, 331, 335-36,
338, 340, 347, 402, 508,
678
Lamb, Colonel XVI,217
James XIV,56, 184, 567, 604;
XV,608, 716; XVI,201
John XV,451-52
Josiah XVII,95
Samuel XIV,314, 338
Lambert, Paul XIV,330, 389,
495, 647, 650; XV,728;
XVI,13
Richard XVI,931
Lamkin, Joshua XVI,288-92
Lammy, Michael XV,612;
XVI,498, 568
Lamont, Samuel XVI,321, 326,
341, 343-44, 403
Lamos, Nathaniel XVII,717
Lamphere, Luke XVII,252
Lamphrey, Daniel XVII,528
Lamprey, Benjamin XVI,287,
506, 643
Daniel XIV,11, 118, 138, 158;
XIV,191
Levi XIV,118, 138, 158, 192,
255, 581, 641; XV,423,
449, 456, 600, 730;
XVI,17
Samuel XIV,351

165

Lamprey, Simon XV,522
Lamshier, Joshua XV,425
Lamson, Benjamin XVI,387
  Constable XVI,649
  Ensign XIV,26
  Jeremiah XIV,103, 266;
    XV,751
  Dr. John XVII,20
  Jonathan XIV,337; XV,72,
    214; XVII,64
  Joseph XVI,40, 44, 107, 635
  Joseph Jr. XV,632, 636
  Samuel XV,748
Lancaster, Ebenezer XV,569,
    658, 667, 674, 691;
    XVI,125, 824
  Jacob XVI,307
  John XIV,225, 342, 349;
    XV,391
  Jonathan XV,428
  Joseph XVI,922
  Joshua XV,394, 465, 467,
    479, 505; XVI,112
  Moses XIV,325
  Samuel XV,747; XVII,667,
    669
Landee, John XV,722
Lander, John XVI,206, 240,
    273, 516, 529, 789
Landers, John XIV,618; XV,722
Landphire, Luke XVI,313
Lane, Daniel XV,562; XVI,807
  Elkanah XVII,97
  Ezekiel XV,162, 167
  Isaac XIV,589
  Jacob XIV,299, 589; XV,464,
    466, 477, 505, 749
  James XIV,253; XV,412, 487,
    489
  Jesse XIV,298; XV,36
  John XIV,190, 198, 300, 324,
    424, 463, 583, 635;
    XV,30, 35, 162, 167, 237,
    414, 525, 724; XVI,127,
    162, 206, 590, 829
  John Jr. XIV,76
  John 3d XIV,76, 82, 198

Lane, Jonathan XIV,442, 544;
    XV,696, 699; XVI,128, 162
  Joseph XIV,589
  Josiah XV,412
  Nathan XIV,327
  Noah XV,411
  Peter XIV,7
  Primus XVI,285, 510
  Samuel XIV,299, 646;
    XVI,23; XVII,98, 526
  Simon XIV,118, 138, 158
  Thomas XV,147, 596
  William XIV,11; XVI,672;
    XVII, 642-44, 680
Lang, Benjamin XIV,247;
    XVII,26
  Daniel XVII,336
  George XV,422, 544
  Gilbert XV,192
  Henry XIV,239; XVI,60, 62,
    70, 94
  John XIV,20; XVII,669
  Josiah XIV,403, 415;
    XVII,360
  Lowell XIV,110, 131, 190; XV,
    523
  Richard XIV,227, 257-58,
    472
  Richard W. XIV,344
  Robert XVII,680
  Samuel XIV,443, 542, 547;
    XV, 325, 379; XVII,73
  Stephen XIV,119, 150, 196;
    XV, 300, 302, 306, 309
  Thomas XIV,224
  William XIV,298, 578, 606,
    610; XV,326, 439, 717;
    XVI,239, 270, 847
Langde, Francis XVII,304
Langdell, Thomas XIV,359
Langdon, H. S. XVI,449
  John XIV,31, 403; XV,139,
    416-418, 577-79, 655;
    XVI,371, 375, 380, 397,
    414, 449, 533, 806, 925;
    XVII,124, 126, 136, 154,
    286, 351, 389, 447

Langdon, Livermore XV,351,
    353; XVI,753
    Richard XIV,13; XVII,139
    William XIV,119
    Woodbury XVI,405; XVII,352
Langley, Benjamin XV,300-1,
    306, 310; XVI,131, 163
    David XIV,235, 259, 664; XV,
    431; XVII,22, 34, 36
    Elihu XVI,64, 71, 95
    Elisha XVI,60
    James XVII,716
    Jonathan XIV,226
    Joseph XIV,226; XV,300-1,
    306, 310
    Winthrop XIV,226; XVI,130,
    163
Langmaid, Harvey XIV,501
    Henry XIV,383, 491, 514,
    519, 545, 648, 650;
    XV,596, 628; XVI,12, 192,
    209; XVII,226, 622, 644,
    669, 757;
    John XV,300-1, 304, 308
    Joseph XVI,906, 916;
    XVII,757
    Margaret XVII,629
    Samuel XV,300-1, 305, 308
    Stephen XVII,435
Langtop, Henry XVII,525
Lannon, Michael XV,435
Lapish, Dorothy XVI,573
    John XIV,167, 170, 287, 318-
    19, 470, 596; XV,425,
    435, 596, 713; XVI,199,
    223, 268, 573
Lapool, Henry XVII,308
Larey, John XIV,574
    Stephen XIV,501, 514
Larkin, Patrick XV,362
    Thomas XVII,302
Larnard, Abijah XVI,314
    David XVI,314
    James XVI,170-71, 176, 208
    Silvanus XV,589
Larned, Abel XIV,463
    Abijah XIV,463

Larned, David XIV,463
    Ezekiel XIV,36, 98
Larney, Michael XIV,572, 603
Larrabee, Benjamin XIV,263;
    XVII, 153
    John XIV,578, 610; XV,718;
    XVI,103, 218, 270, 308-9,
    502, 597, 934
    Peter XV,367
    Samuel XIV,263, 578, 592;
    XV, 716
    Samuel Jr. XIV,263
    Stephen XV,741
    Thomas XIV,13
    William XIV,263
Larrey, Jacob XV,326
Larry, Jonathan XIV,362, 365
Larvey, Peter XIV,279
Lary, Daniel XV,482, 495, 748
    Jacob XVII,22, 33
    James XV,701, 703, 726;
    XVI, 46, 172, 240, 302, 521,
    828
    John XIV,144, 194; XV,134,
    392, 434, 614; XVII,8, 300
    Stephen XIV,647, 650;
    XV,728; XVI,13
    Thomas XIV,12
    William XVI,196
    See also Larry
Lasell, John XV,373, 378
Late, Francois XVII,299
Latham, Arthur XV,55, 203
    Henry XVII,502
    Joseph XIV,355
    Richard XVII,502
Lathly, James XV,724
Lathrop, Mr. XVII,585
    Samuel XV,42, 377
    Sluman XIV,422; XV,17
Latten, William XIV,471, 578,
    593; XV,717
Lattin, William XVI,202, 218,
    270, 512, 597, 712-13
Lauder, John XIV,360
Laughlin, James XIV,223
Laurens, Henry XVII,152

Laurens, John XVII,200
Laurent, Joseph XVII,304
Lauson, Louis XVII,299
Lavers, George XVII,527
    Jacob XVII,655
Lavigne, Jaques XVII,305
La Voise, Francis XVII,304
Law, Andrew XIV,35; XVI,236,
    270, 521, 835, 860;
    XVII,291
    Richard XVII,124
Lawler, David XIV,215, 218-20;
    XVI,715
    John XVII,47
Lawrence, Abraham XIV,644;
    XV, 732; XVI,20, 22, 191,
    212, 279, 322-23, 331,
    340, 403, 522, 886-87
    Abram XV,750
    Asa XV,511
    Colonel XVII,167, 189
    Cornelius XVI,933
    David XVI,933; XVII,526, 623
    Enoch XV,82, 84
    Enos XV,530
    Gordon XV,133
    Jacob XVI,933
    John XIV,438, 527; XVII,274
    Joseph XIV,12, 265, 553,
        595; XV,710; XVI,3;
        XVII,266
    Martin XV,744
    Nicholas XVI,144
    Oliver XV,475; XVI,687-88
    Oliver Jr. XIV,346
    Samuel XIV,71, 312, 451,
        532
    Seth XV,471, 503
    Silas XVI,144
    Stephen XIV,292; XV,81, 530
    William XIV,645; XVI,23,
        886, 927
Lawrey, Stephen XIV,382, 490,
    519; XV,596
Layn, John XIV,476
Layton, Thomas XVII,502
    See also Laighton

Leach, Alexander XV,260
    Benjamin XIV,565, 628;
        XV,258, 260, 263, 725;
        XVI,207, 230, 241, 275,
        499, 582; XVII,22, 33
    Billy XV,172
    Ebenezer XVII,307
    James XIV,2
    John XIV,484, 500, 512, 518;
        XVII,86, 667
    Joseph XIV,109, 131, 190,
        413
    Josiah Jr. XV,224
    Samuel XV,277
    Thomas XVI,273
    Thomas G. XVI,235, 242, 502
    William XIV,327-28; XV,694,
        754
Leader, Richard XVII,502-4,
    535-536
Lealand, Isaac XIV,99, 205, 576,
    634; XV,724; XVI,813
Lear, Alexander XV,256, 259,
    263
    George XIV,298; XV,30
    John XIV,248, 381, 490, 501,
        514; XV,326
    Joseph XV,9; XVI,847
    Nathaniel XIV,248, 381, 489,
        501, 514; XVII,26
    Samuel XIV,248, 490;
        XVI,61, 63, 66, 72, 77, 93,
        98, 107, 193, 512
    Tobias XVII,139, 527
    William XIV,239, 485, 500,
        512, 647, 650; XV,595,
        728; XVI, 13; XVII,86
Learmon, John XVII,205
Learned, Abel XVII,66
    Abijah XVII,65, 116
    Colonel XV,137
    David XVII,66, 78, 116
    Ezekiel XIV,205; XV,98, 539
Learney, John XIV,417
Leary, Cornelius XVII,526
    John XIV,603, 626; XV,712
    Samuel XIV,118

Leash, Richard XV,591
Leathers, Abednego XIV,231
  Abel XIV,226, 353; XVI,69,
    79
  Benjamin XIV,446, 540;
    XVI,64, 74, 93, 118
  Ebenezer XIV,226, 274, 276,
    289, 308
  Edward XIV,187, 362, 617;
    XV, 619, 722; XVI,118;
    XVII,719
  Enoch XVI,118, 287, 516,
    805
  Ezekiel XIV,22
  John XIV,109, 123, 187; XVI,
    710
  Jonathan XIV,616; XV,719
  Joseph XIV,226
  Levi XV,249, 251-52, 254,
    483, 506, 628, 640;
    XVI,570-71; XVII,434
  Nicholas XIV,451, 532, 570,
    616; XV,440, 719;
    XVI,203, 271, 513, 778,
    780; XVII,434
  Robert XIV,108, 123, 187
  Thomas XV,311; XVI,905
  Vowell XIV,225; XVI,491,
    780-782
  William XVII,435, 644, 719
Leathley, James XVI, 877
Leaver, William XV,440, 620,
  719; XVI,203
Leavins, Peter XIV,265
Leavitt, XV,699
  Abraham XV,496
  Amos XIV,584; XV,725
  Amos D. XIV,630; XVI,708
  Andrew XIV,103, 207
  Aretas XIV,642; XV,422, 455,
    696, 699; XVI,18
  Benjamin XIV, 345, 448,
    536; XV, 524, 748; XVI,
    110, 676, 775, 833;
    XVII, 273, 279, 321,
    350, 372-73, 377, 404,
    741-42

Leavitt, Brackett XIV,212, 216,
  474-75, 611; XVI,874
  Captain XV,458, 696;
    XVI,933; XVII,491
  Carr XV,163, 191
  Daniel XIV,446, 550; XVII,57
  Dudley XVII,57
  Edward XIV,624; XV,457,
    720; XVI,204, 227, 239,
    272, 510, 703
  James XIV,11, 450, 534, 642;
    XV,423, 455; XVI,18;
    XVII,727
  Jeremiah XV,246, 694;
    XVI,933
  John XIV,1, 14, 18, 328, 370,
    378, 402, 414, 493, 504,
    515, 651; XV,411, 544,
    597, 729; XVI,28, 61-62,
    71, 92, 107, 128, 162,
    188, 210, 285, 508, 615;
    XVII,27
  Jonathan XIV,135, 191, 230,
    252, 345, 413, 450, 534,
    564, 616; XV,256-57, 259,
    261-62, 265-66, 327, 485,
    488-89, 654, 673, 719;
    XVI,61-62, 71, 92, 106,
    423; XVII,6, 219
  Joseph XIV,103, 113, 147,
    196, 207, 281, 288, 433,
    589; XV,192, 240-41, 246;
    XVI,122, 164, 648;
    XVII,27, 57
  Joseph D. XIV,585
  Josiah XIV,231, 402, 415;
    XV, 544; XVII,27
  Levi XV,666, 685; XVI,111,
    843-44
  Lydia XVI,864
  Morris XIV,11
  Moses XIV,118, 137, 139,
    158, 192, 255, 353;
    XV,168, 319, 321, 333,
    337, 339, 475, 496, 522,
    524; XVI,115, 127, 129,
    162, 772-75, 902; XVII,57,

Leavitt, Moses (Cont.) 526, 642, 683, 740
  Nathaniel XIV,3, 43, 77, 82, 198, 555, 643; XV,422-23, 255, 726; XVI,7, 182, 186, 190, 208, 228, 670; XVII,269
  Nehemiah XIV,67, 212, 216, 474, 571, 584, 630, 651; XV,242, 245, 724, 728; XVI,27, 188, 210, 235, 242, 277, 506, 589-90, 659; XVII,693
  Peter XIV,353; XV,268, 270, 273
  Reuben XIV,230, 402, 414
  Reuben T. XV,256
  Samuel XIV,22, 135, 191, 353; XV,268, 270, 273; XVI,111, 616; XVII,620
  Samuel Jr. XVI,111; XVII,6
  Samuel 3d XVI,844-45
  Sarah XVI,661
  Sealey XIV,12
  Simon XIV,118, 137, 158, 191, 255
  Stephen XIV,116, 129, 189, 308, 370, 378, 492, 503, 515; XV,482, 495; XVII,27
  Thomas XIV,11, 229-31, 350; XV, 300, 302, 305, 309, 318, 331-335, 337, 339; XVII, 27
  William XIV,627; XV,443, 457, 721, 748; XVI,205, 226, 272, 531
Lebil, Girelaumd XVII,299
Lebourveau, Zenas XVI,254
Lebourvue, John XIV,428; XV,62
Lee, Andrew XVII,293
  Arthur XVII,412
  Colonel XV,137
  Ensign XVII,155
  General XVII,182, 239
  Nathan XV,632, 650
  Nathan Jr. XVI,750

Lee, Noah XVII,306
  Richard H. XVII,411, 413
  Samuel XIV,577, 612; XV,711
  Simon XVII,512
  William XIV,87, 200, 553, 600-601; XV,554-55, 710; XVI,3, 81, 93, 298; XVII,266
Leek, William XIV,223
Leland, Eleazer XV,14, 750
  Jacob XV,42
Leeman, Nathaniel XV,89, 698; XVI,144
  Samuel XIV,33, 88, 200, 555, 640; XV,88, 726; XVI,8; XVII, 269
Leet, Asa XVI,608
Leggins, William XVII,298
Le Grand,--- XVII,347
Legrand, John XVI,929
Legro, John XVII,28
Leigh, Joseph XIV,227, 257-58; XVII,21, 230, 237, 246, 262, 270-75, 278, 284, 313, 321, 326, 348, 361, 365, 367, 448
  Thomas XVII,139
  William XV,715
Leighton, Aaron XIV,114, 142, 193, 310, 363; XV,249, 251-253
  David XV,297, 299
  George XV,577, 654; XVI,457
  Hatevil XIV,123, 187
  Jacob XIV,361
  James XIV,108, 123; XVI,638; XVII,667
  Jedediah XV,469, 481, 506
  Joel XV,256; XVI,760-61; XVII, 29
  John XIV,361
  Joseph XIV,108; XV,325, 655, 666, 685; XVI,731
  Paul XVII,139
  Robert XV,655, 666, 685; XVI, 731
  Samuel XIV,179; XV,749

Leighton, Solomon XIV,127,
188; XVII,12
Tobias XIV,107, 122, 251,
480, 482
Valentine XV,656, 666, 685;
XVI,207, 275, 504, 639
William XV,438; XVII,44, 104
Leland, John XVI,158; XVII,428
Lemmon, Joseph XIV,248
Leonard, Ephraim XIV,85, 199-
200, 427; XV,49
John Jr. XVI,551
Solomon XV,739
Lesage, Pierre XVII,299
Lesambert, Antoine XVII,299
Leslie, Jonas XIV,419
Lesperance, Joseph XVII,305
Lester, Enoch XVI,932
Francis XVII,300
Letruman, Joseph XVII,299
Letteby, James XV,633, 648
Letton, William XVI,934
Levans, Noah XVI,176, 235,
268, 522, 877, 879
Leverett, John XVII,518, 536-37
Levi, William XIV,615
Lewey, William XIV,566;
XV,597, 715; XVI,47, 201,
269, 303, 507, 668
Lewis,--- XVII,152
Aaron XV,118, 138, 554
Asa XIV,101, 206-7; XV,75,
123, 189, 215
Benjamin XIV,14, 346; XV,
519
Eber XIV,298; XV,11
Eli XV,741
Gideon XV,27
Henry XIV,239
Isaac XVII,19
James XV,102-3, 360-61,
541-42, 630, 643, 646,
751; XVI,102, 736-37
Jo Count XVII,294, 296, 298
John XIV,18, 119, 150, 196,
325, 464; XV,26, 102,
109, 360, 541; XVII,628,

Lewis, John (Cont.) 672
Joseph XIV,574, 639; XV,38,
617, 731; XVI,16, 26, 308-
9; XVII,276, 282, 298
Samuel XV,10, 101, 104, 219
Thomas XV,698; XVI,88, 95;
XVII,324, 490
William XIV,237, 258;
XVII,22, 33
Libbee, Abraham XIV,11, 118,
137, 158, 192; XV,256,
259, 262
Benjamin XV,673
Bennet XIV,69, 180
Daniel XV,494, 635, 639,
734; XVI,188, 500, 589-90
James XIV,535; XV,635, 639,
754
Jeremiah XIV,13
Job XVI,163
Joseph XV,247; XVI,679
Josiah XIV,69, 180
Luke XVI,188
Thomas XVI,188
Libbey, Abraham XIV,115, 141,
193, 224; XVII,25
Benjamin XIV,381, 489;
XV,668, 690; XVI,257,
506, 554, 624, 898
Daniel XV,475, 728; XVI,27,
102, 188, 210, 233, 241,
277
Ephraim XVI,122, 164
George XVII,139
Isaac XIV,372, 385, 496, 505,
517; XVI,912
James XIV,415, 448, 489,
501, 514; XV,169, 286,
294, 296, 315, 317, 728,
734; XVI,27, 102, 210,
231, 277, 518, 621, 807-8;
XVII,26, 655
Jeremiah XVI,356, 804;
XVII,139
Job XVI,131, 920
John XIV,344; XVI,912
Joseph XIV,165, 288

Libbey, Luke XIV,652; XV,456, 728; XVI, 27, 62, 71, 99, 107, 188, 210; XVII,383
Nathaniel XV,693
Reuben XV,68, 690; XVI,891-92
Samuel XIV,381, 489, 501, 514; XV,243, 245
Libby, Abraham XIV,247; XV,527
Ebenezer XIV,237
James XIV,248, 381, 403, 406
Paul XIV,234
Reuben XV,674
Lickey, James XIV,603
Licot, John XVII,304
Liebert, Ph, XVII,305
Light, Ebenezer XIV,554, 563, 625; XV,748, 718; XVI,5, 50, 905; XVII,268
John XV,748
Lieutenant XVI,180
Prince XVI,63, 71, 94, 107
Liggot, James XVI,917
Lilless, Patrick XIV,240, 259; XVII,22, 33, 37
Lincoln, Benjamin XV,277, 366
General XVII,136, 393
Luther XIV,445, 543, 607; XVI, 45, 302; XVII,67, 109, 236, 289
Nehemiah XVI,85, 91, 106, 285, 500
Lind, Christopher XVII,33
Lindley, Jacob XIV,223
Lines, Charles XV,438, 716; XVI, 605
Peter XVII,295
Linkhorn, Luther XV,603
Linn, Joseph XVI,601
Linnin, John XVII,293
Linsey, David XVII,301
Linton, Joseph XVII,301
Lippitt, Charles XVII,270
Liscomb,---XVI,597

Liscomb, Samuel XIV,471, 577, 593; XV, 439, 716
Lisot, Louis XVII,299
Little, Abner XV,396
Benjamin XV,186, 388; XVI,922
Bond XV,122, 552
Caleb XV,557; XVII,258
Daniel XIV,405; XV,396; XVI, 530; XVII,756
Doctor XVI,466
Friend XIV,317, 319; XV,186
George XIV,358; XV,115, 556; XVII,258
George Jr. XV,557
Hugh XIV,25
John XIV,56, 184, 420; XV,115
Joseph XV,128, 398, 754; XVI, 88, 94, 530, 928
Lot XV,398, 568; XVI,568
Moses XIV,55; XV,396; 557, 568-569, 751; XVI,361, 667; XVII, 258
Nathaniel XV,328, 331, 343; XVI,795
Robert XIV,265
Samuel XIV,219, 404; XV,396
Samuel N. XV,398
Taylor XVI,86, 97
Thomas XV,221, 753
Tristram XV,568; XVI,568
Littlefield, Benjamin XIV,239
Daniel XIV,238
Eliab XV,430
Elial XIV,550
Jesse XIV,239
Jotham XIV,238
Nathaniel XIV,238
Noah XIV,238
Seth XIV,238
Timothy XIV,239
Littlehale, Abraham XVI,557
Abram XV,632, 636
Livermore, Daniel XIV,63, 65, 186, 555, 653, 655; XV,

Livermore, Daniel (Cont.) 425,
    448-49, 454, 458-59, 598-
    600, 606-8, 610, 726;
    XVI,7, 11, 14, 19, 29-30,
    32-33, 41, 59, 105, 182,
    187, 208, 219, 248, 753,
    926; XVII,3, 269, 319,
    440, 442-43
  Matthew XVI,917
  Samuel XVII,387, 390
Livey, John XV,441
Livingston, Robert XV,729, 734;
    XVI,30, 33, 59, 187, 210,
    219, 277, 500, 611, 753,
    755, 926; XVII,3
  William XV,553; XVI,755,
    926; XVII,3, 259
Livingstone, John XIV,74-75,
    178
  Lieutenant XIV,1
  Robert XIV,63, 181, 186,
    267, 653
  William XIV,63, 181, 186
Lloyd, James XVII,308
  John XVII,64
  Richard XVII,293
  See also Loyd
Lock, Abner XV,256, 259-60,
    263, 487, 496
  Benjamin XV,256
  David XVI,530
  Ebenezer XVI,329, 332, 344-
    45, 405
  Edward XIV,24; XV,320, 340,
    523
  Elijah XIV,224, 248; XVII,26
  Elisha XV,593; XVI,97, 295,
    313, 912; XVII,82, 116,
    254
  Elisha Jr. XVI,680; XVII,80
  Ephraim XVI,646
  Francis XIV,180; XVI,912
  Francis Jr. XIV,180
  Henry XVII,307
  James XIV,11, 116, 177; XVI,
    260-61
  Job XVII,360

Lock, John XIV,224; XV,108,
    596, 724; XVII,26, 428
  Jonathan XV,442, 527;
    XVI,67, 99, 178, 503;
    XVII,434
  Joseph XIV,11; XV,441;
    XVI,902
  Joshua XIV,224, 308, 381,
    489, 501, 514, 623;
    XV,596, 720; XVI,822
  Josiah XIV,111, 132, 190;
    XV, 256, 258-59, 262
  Moses XIV,180, 469, 570,
    602; XV,712, 747;
    XVI,198, 222, 505, 647;
    XVII,450
  Nimshi XIV,248, 402, 414;
    XVII,26
  Ozzom XIV,430, 602; XV,457,
    712
  Reuben XIV,402; XV,300-1,
    305, 309; XVI,680
  Richard XIV,118, 138, 158,
    248, 382, 490, 501, 514,
    650; XVI,12, 192, 209,
    912; XVII, 26
  Samuel XIV,469, 471, 570,
    602; XV,629, 648, 712,
    718; XVI, 199, 203, 219,
    222, 241, 505-6, 647, 649,
    675
  Simeon XV,326
  Simon XV,256, 258, 260, 263
  Timothy XV, 664-65, 671,
    677; XVI, 90, 221, 794,
    835
  Timothy B. XIV, 109, 111,
    350
  William XIV,289, 291; XVI,
    97, 295, 313, 680; XVII,
    116, 254
Locke, Elisha XV,153-54;
    XVI,83, 97, 293
  Francis XIV,69
  Francis Jr. XIV,69
  John XIV,635
  Jonathan XVI,78, 179, 286

Locke, Joshua XVI,518
  Moses XIV,69; XVI,268
  Reuben XVI,293
  Richard XIV,647; XV,728
  Samuel XVI,268, 508
  Timothy XVI,82, 268, 517
  William XV,153-54; XVI,83,
    97, 293
Logan, Andrew XVI,911
  Michael XVI,929
Lolar, David XVI,715
Lomas, James XVI,898
Lomiss, Jerome XV,371
Loney, Caesar XIV,351
Long,--- XV,136
  Benjamin XV,749
  Enoch XV,408, 684
  Enoch Jr. XV,663, 670, 688;
    XVI,694
  George XIV,450, 534, 642;
    XV, 455; XVI,18; XVII,
    622, 629
  John XIV,351
  Joseph XV,749
  Moses XIV,388, 495, 507,
    516, 519; XVI,526
  Paul XIV,351, 450, 535, 642;
    XV,423, 457; XVI,18, 774
  Pierse XIV,260, 367, 481-83,
    499, 509, 511; XV,428;
    XVI, 530; XVII,121, 283
  Solomon XVII,208
  Stephen XIV,227
  William XVI,202
Longfellow, Constable XVII,753
  Nathan XIV,309
  Samuel XIV,111, 132, 190
Looney, Michael XVII,303
Lord, Aaron XIV,381, 490
  Benjamin XIV,257
  Daniel XIV,664; XV,431, 656,
    666; XVI,833
  Eliphalet XIV,110, 132, 190;
    XV,283, 287; XVI,648
  Jeremiah XIV,236
  Joel XIV,370, 378, 493, 503,
    515

Lord, John XIV,344; XVII,693
  Joseph XIV,236; XVI,287,
    512
  Nason XIV,237, 406
  Nathan XIV,236, 307
  Nathaniel XV,138, 375
  Nicholas XIV,236-37
  Paul XV,573; XVII,260
  Richard XIV,127, 188;
    XVII,12
  Robert XVII,27
  Samuel XV,667, 676;
    XVI,116, 581
  Simon XV,431
  Stephen XIV,610; XV,718;
    XVI, 202
  Thomas XIV,370, 379, 493,
    503, 515
  William XIV,406, 432
Loring, John XIV,172, 174, 176-
    177, 346, 574; XV,614;
    XVI, 237, 271 516, 715-
    16, 784; XVII,60
Lothrop, Samuel XVII,109
Louchong, Louis XVII,304
Loud, Benjamin XIV,113, 147,
    195; XV,430; XVI,110, 165
  Daniel XIV,227, 257-58, 472
  Edmund XIV,239
  George XIV,239, 255, 260,
    484, 499, 510, 512, 518;
    XVII,23, 31, 39, 46, 85
  Mark XIV,227, 257-58, 472,
    550; XV,430
  Solomon XIV,239; XVII,23,
    31, 39
  William XIV,227, 257-58, 472
Loudon, Anthony XVII,656
  Samuel XVII,337
Lougee, Jesse XV,195
  John XV,129, 180, 512
  Jonathan XV,748
  Joseph XVII, 28
  Moses XIV,563, 627; XV,719,
    748; XVI,203, 226, 271,
    506, 649
  Nicholas XV,698

Lovees, Joseph XIV,246
Lovegrove, William XVI,930
Lovejoy, Abel XIV,463, 590, 607-
    608; XV,459, 605, 714;
    XVI, 84, 90, 200; XVII,65
    Abiel XIV,246
    Asa XIV,418, 590, 609;
        XV,613, 714; XVI,84, 90,
        106, 200
    Captain XV,698-99
    Chandler XV,406
    Christopher XIV,29
    Daniel XV,591
    Francis XIV,417; XVI,236,
        275, 498, 562
    Henry XIV,96, 204-5; XV,211,
        530; XVI,142, 145, 149
    Hezekiah XV,520-21, 695
    Jacob XIV,422
    John XV,72; XVI,157
    Jonathan XIV,36, 43, 90
    Joseph XIV,267, 477;
        XVI,237, 275, 498, 528,
        562; XVII,463
    Moses XV,419
    Obadiah XIV,70
    Peter XIV,51, 185, 325, 464
    Samuel XIV,244; XV,419
    Theodore XIV,550
    Zebulon XIV,179
Lovekin, Benjamin XVI,83, 97
    Levi XVI,237
    Philip XV,610
    Stephen XIV,583; XV,724
Loveland, Joseph XV,15
    Joshua XV,138
Lovell, Ichabod XIV,600; XV,715
    J. XVII,391-95, 403-6, 413
    Jacob XVI,100
    John XVI,47
    John Jr. XVI,921
    Michael XVI,918
    Nehemiah XVII,469
    Splan XVII,621, 655
Lovering, Benjamin XIV,98, 205;
    XVI,116, 527, 650;
    XVII,32, 425

Lovering, Dearborn XVI,282
    Ebenezer XIV,118, 138, 158,
        192, 229, 253
    Ebenezer A. XIV,413
    Jeremiah XVI,284
    John XIV,159, 161, 164, 443,
        469, 542, 547, 551; XV,
        412, 635, 639, 712; XVI,
        102, 193, 199, 224, 241,
        268, 296, 307, 500, 589-
        90; XVII,16, 73, 114, 383
    Jonathan XVII,254
    Joseph XIV,211, 215, 217,
        220; XV,283, 288, 748;
        XVI,282
    Nathaniel XV,657, 667, 673;
        XVI,64, 74, 94, 107
    Richard XVI,65, 71, 98, 256,
        510
    Samuel XV,164
    Simeon XVI,194, 211;
        XVII,435
    Simon XIV,229, 413, 432,
        641
    Simon D. XIV,253; XV,423,
        456, 730; XVI,18, 773-75
    Theophilus XIV,299, 312,
        584, 630; XV,445, 724;
        XVI,207, 227, 239, 275,
        518, 808
    Thomas XIV,229, 351; XV,
        320, 340; XVI,127, 162
Lovewell, Colonel XVI,294
    Henry XIV,97, 204-5;
        XVI,313; XVII,116
    Ichabod XIV,97, 203, 205,
        573; XV,615, 715;
        XVII,124
    John XIV,95, 204, 418;
        XV,346
    Jonathan XV,78, 80, 206;
        XVI, 313; XVII,116
    Jonathan Jr. XV,79
    Joseph XV,160
    Nehemiah XIV,97, 204;
        XV,426; XVI,313; XVII,82,
        116-17

Loverwell, Nehemiah Jr. XVII,80
   Noah XIV,439-40, 478, 631;
      XV,451; XVI,259, 547,
      588, 635
   Zaccheus XVI,314; XVII,116
Low, Simon XVII,427
   William XIV,416, 418
Lowe, David XVI,63, 72, 90, 106
   Joseph XVI,897
   William XV,72
Lowell, Barnard XVI,238, 868;
      XVII,438
   Daniel XVII,57
   David XV,249-51, 254, 369,
      565
   Ebenezer XV,664-65, 671,
      685; XVI,869-71, 897;
      XVII,457
   Isaac XVI,237, 271, 868;
      XVII, 438
   Jacob XVI,82, 100, 107, 194
   James XV,560
   John XVI,63, 73, 303
   John M. XV,615
   Joseph XIV,100, 206-7;
      XV,150, 530
   Moses XVI,465
   Peter XIV,91
   Samuel XIV,87, 200; XV,219;
      XVII,458
   Stephen XIV,171, 174, 177
   Timothy XIV,100, 206-7
   William XIV,44; XVI,237,
      271, 335, 868; XVII,438
Lowney, John XVII,298
Lowther, John XVI,480
Loyd, John XIV,337
   Nathaniel XV,19
Loynes, Michael XV,718
Lucas, Elijah XIV,657; XV,459,
      605, 731; XVI,37, 39
   James XIV,115, 140, 193,
      250; XV,191, 426, 584-85;
      XVI,306
   John XIV,233, 331, 639;
      XVI,16, 373, 406
   Thomas XIV,280, 288

Lucas, William XIV,331
Luce, David XVI,236, 243, 509,
      709
   Zimri XIV,265
Lucy, Alexander XV,301-4, 306,
      308, 528
   Thomas XVII,360
   William XIV,370, 379, 493,
      504, 515, 604; XV,437,
      609
Ludden, Michael XVI,125
Ludington, Moses XVII,14
Luenonault, Paul XVII,205
Lufkin, Levi XVI,269, 521, 827
   Philip XIV,548, 568, 665
   Stephen XIV,635
   William XVI,11, 316
Lull, Zenas XIV,265
Lund, Ephraim XV,87
   Jesse XIV,43, 88, 201;
      XV,188, 554
   Joel XIV,418; XV,347;
      XVI,635
   John XIV,95, 203-4, 335,
      696; XVII,62
   Joseph XIV,273, 276, 289
   Levi XIV,337, 698; XV,347;
      XVII,63
   Noadiah XIV,288
   Noah XV,77, 79, 207;
      XVI,143
   Stephen XIV,101, 206-7;
      XVII, 254
   Willard XVI,140, 161
   William XV,715
   William Jr. XIV,573, 600; XV,
      615
Lunt, Daniel XIV,258; XVII,139
   Ezekiel XIV,316, 318
   Henry XIV,259
   Timothy XIV,61, 182, 304,
      306, 465
Lurvey, Peter XIV,288, 291; XV,
      153-54, 383, 590;
      XVI,307; XVII,114
   William XV,425
Lush, Richard XVII,250-52

176

Luskin, William XV,727
Lutberry, Abram XVII,293
Lutterells, Francis XVII,508
Luttington, Henry XIV,288
    Moses XIV,166, 170, 288
Lutwyche, Edward Goldstone
    XIV, 418, 478
Lyford, Billy XV,283, 290
    Fifield XVI,147
    Francis XV,284, 288
    John XV,512
    Jonathan XV,483, 495, 657,
        667, 679
    Nathaniel XV, 667, 679;
        XVI,581
    Oliver XIV,179; XVII,57
    Oliver S. XIV,71, 312
    Stephen XIV,232
    Thomas XIV,143, 145, 194;
        XV, 700, 702-3, 718;
        XVI,46, 170, 172, 174,
        203, 302, 815; XVII,8
Lyman, Abel XIV,,444, 542;
    XV,38, 373, 378; XVII, 67
    Elias XV,17, 138, 377
    John XV,38, 373, 378; XVII,
        67
Lynde, Charles XIV,578, 592
    David XIV,263
    Noadi XIV,280
Lyndston, William XIV,480
Lyne, Matthew XVII,311, 320,
    330-31, 335, 358, 363,
    381
Lynn, Joseph XIV,328
Lyon, Ebenezer XV,29
    Jonathan XV,72
Lyons, Ebenezer XVI,909
    Edward XIV,302
    James XIV,55, 184
    Jonathan XIV,302
    Michael XIV,471; XVI,202,
        219, 875; XVII,438
    Samuel XVI,513
    Stephen XVII,300
    William XIV,458, 538-39;
        XVI; 237, 274, 501, 546,

Lyons, William (Cont.) 611, 686
M
Mabbet, Joseph XVI,932
    Samuel XVI,932
Maccarty, Ester XVII,749
Maccluer, James XIV,480
Macclure, Captain XV,451
Mace, Andrew XIV,340; XV,323,
        342; XVI,124; XVII,425
    Joseph XIV,118, 120, 151,
        196
    Levi XVI,110, 165
    Richard XIV,110, 132, 190,
        413
Macgregore, Duncan XIV,166,
    170
Mack, Archibald XIV,75; XV,744
    Andrew XIV,226
    Daniel XV,33, 369
    Elisha XIV,325, 464; XV, 3,
        5, 65, 67, 196, 226-27
    James XV,635, 639, 744;
        XVI,807
    Jeremiah XV,741
    John XIV,605; XV,11, 437,
        454, 716; XVI,201
    Joseph XIV,75, 178, 348,
        605; XV, 12, 28, 147, 437,
        454, 642-43, 715, 724;
        XVI,201, 207, 229, 274,
        327, 329, 332, 341, 345,
        407, 499, 553, 721;
        XVII,105
    Joseph Jr. XV,630, 642;
        XVI,553
    Joshua XIV,265, 578
    Nathan XV,29
    Robert XIV,46, 75, 178;
        XV,32
    Silas XV,26, 146; XVII,104,
        249
    Zopher XV,25
Mackay, Benjamin XVII,139
    John XIV,73, 75, 178;
        XV,753
Mackres, Samuel XIV,317, 319,
    365, 550-51

Macling, Caesar XVII,25
MacMurphy, Robert XVI,717
Macres, Benjamin XIV,2, 15
Madden, Patrick XVII,307
Maddin, George XIV,21, 25
Maddox, John XIV,9
Magett, David XVII,266
Maggart, Alexander XVI,930
Magoon, Alexander XIV,586,
    628; XV,172, 721
  Edward XIV,112, 147, 195
  Ephraim XV,180, 512
  John XIV,565; XVI,10, 777,
    829; XVII,667-68, 675
  Jonathan XIV,252, 362, 365
    Joseph XIV,317, 319;
    XV,513 Josiah XIV,494,
    507, 516; XV, 660-61;
    XVI,235, 269, 323, 325,
    328, 331, 338, 340, 343-
    44, 407, 409
  Moses XV,747
  Samuel XIV,14, 624
  Samuel Jr. XIV,563
  Thomas XV,513
  See also Megoon
Mahane, Phillip XV,711
Mahew, Peter XV,125; XVI,928
Mahony, Cane XIV,4
Mahurin, Ephraim XVI,311
Main, Isaac XV,14
  Joshua XV,138
Major, Samuel XIV,7
Malcham, Joseph XVII,29
Malcom, Joseph XIV,233,433
Malham, Matthew XIV,375
Maliete, Baptiste XVII,304
Malim, Matthew XIV,482
Mallen, Matthew XVI,515
  William XVI,10, 43, 65, 75,
    209
Mallery, Peter XIV,288, 441
Mallum, Matthew XV,440, 596,
    627
  William XIV,580, 659;
    XV,448, 598, 727

Malloon, Samuel XIV,362, 365,
    579
  Timothy XIV,299
Malony, Peter XIV,280
Maloy, John XV,629; XVI,102,
    516
  Thomas XV,595; XVI,803
Malvan, Francois XVII,305
Manahan, John XIV,211, 215,
    217, 219-20, 337; XVII,64
Manchester, Thomas XIV,286-
    87, 546
Mandel, John XV,751
Mangum, Daniel XIV,223
Manifold, John XVI,205, 226,
    272, 890; XVII,439
Manly, Commander XVII,51
Mann, Andrew XV,420-21
  Benjamin XIV,38, 44, 78,100-
    1; XIV,155-56, 206-7;
    XV,243, 245, 247, 529,
    531; XVI,467, 893
  Charles XIV,422
  Edward XIV,18
  Hezekiah XVI,811
  James XIV,299, 358, 424;
    XV, 530, 639; XVI,833
  John XVI,255, 507, 538
  Joseph XV,586; XVI,168,
    170, 787
  Nathan XIV,613; XV,711;
    XVI,254 Nathaniel
    XVI,198; XVII,468 Peter
    XIV,13; XVII,139
  Robert XIV,335, 576; XV,106;
    XVI,840; XVII,468
  William XIV,576, 613;
    XV,632, 635, 711, 733;
    XVI,53, 198, 504, 547,
    634-35
Mannifold, John XV,630, 638,
    721
  See also Manifold
Manning, Eliphalet XIV,470,
    573, 600; XV,615, 714;
    XVI,200, 224, 241, 269,

Manning, Eliphet (Cont.) 504,
    635
  John XIV,470, 573, 600;
    XV,437, 615, 714;
    XVI,200, 269, 504, 635
  Jonathan XIV,606
  Stephen XIV,394; XVII,89
  Thomas XVI,925; XVII,139
  William XVI,908
Mansfield, Daniel XIV,34
  Elijah XIV,334, 436, 524,
    575, 639; XV,731; XVI,16,
    26, 857-859
  George XVI,238, 275, 501,
    600 James XV,58
  John XIV,6; XV,630, 638;
    XVI, 241
  Levi XVII,101
  William XVII,644
Mansel, Peter XIV,7
Manson, Samuel XIV,14
  William XVII,204
Mansur, William XIV,35; XV,95
Manuel, John XIV,42, 67;
    XVI,915
  Moses XIV,429
  Peter XV,180, 754
  Samuel XIV,304-5, 465;
    XV,180, 754
Manwell, Amos XVI,140, 161
  Peter XVI,67, 78, 93
Maranack, Matthew XVII,656,
    667; XVII,669
Marble, John XVI,61, 64, 71, 99
  Joseph XIV,427; XV,55;
    XVI,927
Marbury, Joseph XVII,207
March, Benjamin XIV,484, 499,
    512; XVII,85
  Chavil XVII,301
  Christopher XVI,36, 39
  Henry XV,476, 498
  James XIV,485; XVII,87
  John XIV,81; XV,321, 340,
    569 Joseph XIV,433;
    XV,609; XVI, 201;
    XVII,215

March, Moses XV,4
  Samuel XIV,405; XVI,198,
    922
  Stephen XIV,25, 586, 657;
    XVI,39
Marchand, Bernard XVII,304
Marcy, Cato XIV,578, 596
  Griffin XVI,932
  John XIV,38, 78, 104, 106,
    155; XV,147; XVI,864;
    XVII, 105
  John Jr. XIV,105
  Samuel XIV,105; XV,11
  Stephen XV,24
Marden, Benjamin XIV,224,
    248; XVI,912; XVII,26
  David XIV,53
  David Jr. XIV,185
  Edward XV,700, 703, 726;
    XVI, 171-72, 176, 208,
    240, 714, 782
  James XIV,228, 560-61, 621;
    XV,300, 302, 305, 309,
    527, 619, 722; XVI,98,
    205, 241, 273, 369, 520,
    836; XVII,139
  John XIV,234, 239, 245, 255,
    381, 490, 501, 514, 545,
    647, 650; XV,596, 728;
    XVI,12, 192, 209; XVII,23,
    31, 38, 139, 664
  Joseph XIV,247; XVII,26
  Nathaniel XIV,247; XV,527;
    XVII,26
  Samuel XIV,248; XVII,26
  Thomas XVII,669
  William XIV,228, 402, 414,
    535, 651; XV,597, 729;
    XVI, 28, 260-61; XVII,432
Margery, Jonathan XIV,247,
    589, 633; XV,444, 723;
    XVI,206, 274, 500, 619,
    755
Mariner, Nicholas XIV,119, 151,
    196, 370, 377, 492, 503,
    515
Marion, Joseph XVII,725

Markham, Isaac XVI,80, 91
  William XV,33, 367; XVI,138
Marks, John XV,67
Marlen, John XVI,237, 244, 274
  Marnay, Louis XVII,305
Marr, Daniel XVI,917
  John XVI,922
Marre, James XVII,205
Marriner, Nicholas XV,325, 544
Marrow, Alexander XV,228
Mars, Cyrplus XIV,388
  Surples XIV,495
Marsdin, George XV,750
Marsh, Christopher XIV,587,
  656; XV,459, 605, 731;
  XVI,39, 795 Daniel
  XVI,235, 273, 511
  David XIV,96, 204; XVII,124
  Dudley XIV,628; XV,721, 748
  Elisha XV,23
  Ephraim XIV,225
  Ezra R. XV,359
  Gershom XIV,353
  Jacob XV,358; XVI,63, 72,
    90, 106, 784
  James XV,228
  John XIV,588, 626; XV,720;
    XVI, 28, 908
  Jonathan XV,206
  Joseph XIV,112, 147, 195,
    347, 568, 579, 605;
    XV,277, 453, 465, 467,
    479, 505, 715; XVI,648;
    XVII,215
  Moses XV,57, 62
  Noah XIV,312, 628; XV,443,
    721; XVI,320, 326, 329,
    332, 341, 343, 345, 409;
    XVII,7, 465
  Obadiah XIV,98, 205
  Onosepherous XV,160
  Samuel XIV,463; XV,69, 149,
    347, 517, 561; XVI,103,
    223, 267, 506, 649, 651-
    52, 697-698, 801-2;
    XVII,66

Marsh, Stephen XV,284, 288;
  XVI,450, 494, 650; XVII,
  424-25
  Zebulon XIV,69, 180
Marshall, Aaron XIV,35
  Andrew XIV,240, 259;
    XVI,905; XVII,22, 33, 36,
    75, 135
  Benjamin XIV,247; XV,228
  Benjamin Jr. XIV,247
  Caleb XIV,463; XVI, 288-91;
    XVII,66, 78
  Colonel XV,137, 432
  Daniel XV,517
  David XIV,91, 201, 458, 538
  George XIV,257, 472
  Gideon XIV,110, 131, 190
  Henry XV,698
  John XIV,247; XVII,124, 139
  John Jr. XVII,139
  Jonathan XV,21, 534
  Joseph XV,517; XVI,63, 73,
    92, 235, 515, 698
  Obadiah XIV,227, 257, 472,
    550; XV,430; XVI,110, 165
  Richard XIV,346; XVII,60
  Robert XIV,110, 132, 190,
    351; XV,256, 258, 260,
    263, 443
  Simeon XIV,150, 196, 352;
    XVI, 648
  Thomas XV,753; XVII,644
  William XIV,3
Marster, Dr. John XVI,766
Marston, Abraham XIV,229,
    413; XV,320, 340
  Asa XIV, 451, 532; XVI, 131,
    163
  Benjamin XV,132, 180
  Caleb XIV,252; XV,319, 339;
    XVII,714, 740
  Captain XVI,546
  Christopher XIV,9
  David XIV,116, 118, 129,
    138, 189, 192, 255
  David Jr. XIV,158, 351

Marston, Ephraim XIV,230;
    XVII,528, 659, 666-68,
    693
  George XVI,850
  Gilman XIV,24
  Isaac XVII,528, 740,
  James XIV,307, 312, 565,
    660; XV, 727; XVI, 10,
    43, 66, 75, 184, 209,
    287, 510, 584; XVII,
    57
  Jeremiah XIV,24-27, 118,
    129, 138, 158, 189, 192,
    255; XV, 133, 412;
    XVI,642
  John XIV,23, 118, 137, 158,
    191-92, 255, 269, 362,
    364, 443, 450, 534, 543;
    XV, 523; XVI,37, 122, 127,
    162, 164; XVII,48, 118-19,
    131, 528, 659, 676, 740
  Jonathan XIV,118, 138, 158;
    XIV,192, 641; XV,411,
    422, 456, 458, 523, 730;
    XVI,18, 774
  Joseph XIV,15; XV,658-59,
    668, 676; XVI,130, 163,
    590; XVII, 670
  Josiah XV,319, 339
  Lemuel XIV,485, 500, 518;
    XVI, 61, 64, 71, 95
  Levi XIV,118, 138, 144, 158,
    192, 194, 255, 351;
    XV,320, 339, 522, 663,
    670, 673, 688; XVI, 727
  Matthias XIV,642; XV,423,
    456; XVI,18
  Nathan XIV,150, 196, 403,
    414; XV,496; XVI,507
  Nathan Jr. XIV,120
  Nathaniel XIV,253, 403, 571,
    635; XV,422, 456, 724;
    XVI, 18, 207, 288, 501,
    604
  Nathaniel Jr. XIV,415
  Nathaniel 3d XIV,642
  Paul S. XV,128, 164

Marston, Samuel XIV,23, 118,
    138, 158, 192, 230, 253,
    255, 350, 512, 662; XV,
    411, 522, 730; XVI, 17,
    127, 162, 169-70; XVII,
    86, 334, 740
  Simeon XIV,229
  Simon XIV,338, 352, 365,
    476; XV,267-68, 270-71,
    273-75, 470-73; XVI,261,
    776; XVII, 215, 740
  Theodore XIV,71; XV,267,
    269-270, 272, 473, 506;
    XVI,260-261, 616;
    XVII,432
  Thomas XIV,3, 228, 338,
    351; XVI,128, 162;
    XVII,528, 740
  Thomas Jr. XVII,740
  William XIV,448
  Winthrop XIV,129, 189;
    XVI,584
Martaile, Joseph XIV,8
Martin, Abraham XIV,176
  Agrippa XVI,932
  Amos XVI,247, 253, 503, 735
  Asa XIV,350
  Benjamin XIV,160-61, 164;
    XV, 587; XVII,16
  Christopher XIV,303, 574,
    639; XV,617, 731, 740;
    XVI,15, 25, 186, 211
  Ebenezer XIV,16; XV,584-86;
    XVI,307
  Edward XIV,562, 636;
    XV,445, 618, 724;
    XVI,207, 275
  Eleazer XIV,645; XV,745;
    XVI, 22, 322-23, 330, 334,
    337, 339, 410, 809
  Ephraim XV,587
  Francis XVII,309
  Francois XVII,299
  Ichabod XIV,470, 604, 606;
    XV, 715; XVI,201, 269,
    507, 664, 666, 734-35
  Jacob XIV,391, 487, 508, 513

Martin, James XIV,265, 360;
    XV,267, 271, 274-75, 362,
    750; XVI, 28, 28, 88, 99,
    575; XVII,427
  Jean B. XVII,229
  Jeremiah XV,173
  Jesse XIV,304-5, 459, 466,
    539; XV,744; XVI,679
  John XIV,272, 282, 286-87,
    290-291, 579, 653; XV,
    452, 454, 701, 703, 705-6,
    708-9, 733; XVI,31, 33,
    41, 59, 112, 171- 172,
    176, 190, 213, 586, 723,
    812, 814, 862, 921;
    XVII,254, 438
  Jonathan XV,113, 587
  Joseph XV,374
  Joshua XIV,243; XVI,921
  Jubael XVII,24
  Louis XVII,299
  Moses XIV,62, 210, 217, 220,
    309
  Nathan XVI,26, 102, 867
  Nathaniel XIV,71, 179, 211,
    215, 218-20, 360; XV,111,
    267, 269, 273, 362, 622,
    631, 634, 638, 644; XVI,
    34, 44, 516, 631, 633,
    733, 786
  Reuben XIV,391, 487, 508,
    513 Richard XIV,13;
    XV,324; XVII, 527, 543,
    547, 555-56, 559-579,
    584, 594, 612, 618, 620
  Robert XIV,383, 491; XV,267,
    269-71, 698; XVI,234,
    317-19
  Samuel XIV,391, 487, 508,
    513; XV,188, 590, 696,
    698; XVI, 928; XVII,296
  Scipio XIV,338, 363
  Seth XV,14, 138, 373, 378
  Sidon XIV,233, 652; XV,620,
    729; XVI,28; XVII,24
Martin, Thomas XIV,551

Martin, Timothy XIV,59, 183,
    266, 459, 537, 573, 603;
    XV,616, 712; XVI,198, 733
  W. XVI,307
  William XIV,356; XV,430,
    593, 701, 726; XVI,46, 60,
    62, 70, 99, 106, 176, 208,
    302, 522, 877, 879, 924;
    XVII,115
Martling, Deliverance XVII,307
Marton, Arthur XVII,301
Marvel, Caleb XV,329, 343
  John XVII,6
Marvin, Giles XV,12
Mascarene, Paul XIV,4
Mason, Anne XVII,502, 504,
    517-520, 535
  Benjamin XIV,3, 14, 413,
    570, 641; XV,216, 423,
    730; XVI, 18; XVII,80, 83
  Bradstreet XIV,471; XV,268,
    270, 273, 634, 649, 718;
    XVI, 202, 219, 241, 270,
    513, 778, 780
  Edward XIV,135, 191, 606;
    XV, 597, 727; XVI,9, 27,
    42, 183, 188, 208, 277,
    520, 845; XVII,6
  Francis XIV,576, 634;
    XV,441, 724
  James XIV,581, 659; XV,448,
    599, 727, 734; XVI,10, 43,
    183, 228, 512, 750
  Jeremiah XIV,150, 635;
    XV,442, 597, 724
  Jeremy XIV,196
  John XIV,135, 191, 229, 400,
    402, 414, 569-70, 651;
    XV, 609, 729; XVI,28, 168,
    236, 243, 274, 510, 703,
    706; XVII,6, 27, 475-84,
    487, 490-496, 499-510,
    516-22, 529-40
  Jonathan XIV,232, 563, 651;
    XV, 277, 729; XVI,28, 188,
    210, 765; XVII,26

Mason, Joseph XV,217; XVI,
  920; XVII, 24, 502, 504,
  508, 514-20, 235-37
  Joseph 3d, XVII,27
  Josiah XIV,118, 138, 158,
    192; XV,412
  Lemuel XIV,562, 637;
    XV,444, 596, 724;
    XVI,207, 230, 239;
    XVI,275, 514, 760
  Lemuel B. XVI,301; XVII,440
  Moses XIV,334, 577; XV,109,
    217; XVI,630
  Nathaniel XIV,12; XV,17,
    157; XVII,144
  Nicholas XIV,369, 377, 492;
    XV,693; XVI,109, 252, 520
  Perez XV,17
  Peter XVII,719
  Robert XIV,11, 423, 445,
    543, 607; XV,18, 43, 157,
    603, 714; XVI,200, 269;
    XVII,144, 226, 236, 506,
    516-22, 529-554, 559,
    561, 563, 571-81, 591-95
  Russell XV,155; XVII,144
  Simeon XIV,564, 616;
    XV,440, 719; XVI,203
  Stephen XIV,23-24, 297; XV,
    134
  Thaddeus XIV,476
  Thomas XIV,354
  Ward XIV,231, 402, 414;
    XVII, 27
  Widow XVII,667, 669
  William XVII,298, 646
Massey, Jonathan XV,390
  Thomas XV,465
Mather, Asaph XV,25, 371
  Rev. Mr. XVII,599
Mathes, Abraham XVI,66, 77,
    282, 747; XVII,26, 717
  Benjamin XVII,717
  Daniel XVI,503
  Francis XVI,747; XVII,716-
    17, 721
  Hugh XIV,183, 299, 459

Mathes, John XIV,577; XV,653
  Joseph XIV,183, 299
  Thomas XIV,459; XV,437;
    XVI, 503, 551, 617
  Valentine XVII,466
  Volentine XVI,640-41, 904
Mathies, John XVI,223
Matthews, Abner XIV,265
  Abraham XIV,224, 248;
    XVI,288, 505
  Abram XVI,96
  Arthur XIV,265
  Benjamin XIV,12
  Daniel XV,634, 649; XVI,102,
    617
  David XVI,608
  Eben XV,716; XVI,605
  Ebenezer XIV,324, 464, 578,
    594; XV,27; XVI,201, 221,
    248, 270, 313, 502, 606
  Gideon XIV,233
  Hugh XIV,59, 183, 539;
    XVI,259; XVII,437
  Jesse Jr. XVI,607
  Joel XV,27
  John XIV,35, 468; XV,717,
    739; XVI,270, 306, 517,
    536, 794, 854; XVII,370,
    386, 392
  Joseph XIV,59, 183; XVI,169
  Robert XV,175
  Thomas XIV,65, 156-57, 470,
    538, 571, 604, 628;
    XV,267, 269, 273, 715,
    721; XVI,201, 205, 219,
    226, 269, 272, 500, 575;
    XVII,4
Mattison, Alexander XVII,301
Mattoon, Ebenezer XIV,272, 290
  Mark XIV,448, 535
Maurin, Jean XV,628, 645;
    XVI,844
Maverick, Antipas XVII,526
  Samuel XVII,510
Maxfield, David XV,587
  Hugh XV,744
  Joshua XIV,173, 175-77

Maxfield, Nathaniel XV,168;
    XVI,587
  Natt XIV,2
  Robert XV,256, 259-60, 262
  William XV,587; XVI,297
Maxwell, James XV,106-7, 536;
    XVI,159, 286, 523
  Thomas XIV,102
May, Benjamin XVI,809-10
  Zebulon XIV,348
Maydwell, Thomas XVII,489
Mayes, John XIV,682
Maynard, Caleb XIV,420; XV,96,
    364
  Jedediah XV,750
  William XVI,372
Mays, William XVII,298
McAdams, William XIV,16
McAffee, Hugh XIV,328
McAllester, William XV,537
McAllister, Andrew XIV,173-77;
    XVI,307; XVII,115, 134
  Ananias XIV,244
  Archibald XV,552; XVII,259
  Benjamin XIV,267, 274, 276,
    289; XIV,601; XV, 712;
    XVI,47, 55, 101, 303, 779
  Isaac XV,109, 216
  John XIV,267; XV,188, 429,
    552, 663, 670, 677, 689;
    XVI,573-574, 917;
    XVII,259
  Joseph XVI,141, 161
  Mary XVI,101
  Peter XIV,436
  Randall XIV,42; XV,104, 427,
    733, 739; VXI, 47, 55,
    101, 213, 303
  Reuben XIV,576; XVI,737
  Richard XIV,477
  William XVI,537
McAlpin, George XVI,285, 504
McAnnaio, Hugh XVI,931
McBean, Evan XV,425
McBride, Barnabas XIV,134,
    191, 563, 615; XV,719;
    XVII,6

McBride, Hugh XIV,29, 232, 245
  Jabez XIV,576; XV,723; XVI,
    254, 737
  John XV,541
  Thomas XVI,254
McBriton, William XIV,568, 578,
    610; XV,718
McCallester, Benjamin XV,460,
    605 McCalley, Alexander
    XIV,417
  Edward XIV,560; XVI,205,
    273, 510, 725
  Florence XIV,246, 304-5,
    465-466, 469, 566, 601;
    XV,434, 712; XVI,198,
    222, 268, 502, 611-13
  James XV,350, 352; XVI,619,
    684-85
  John XIV,261; XV,408
  L. XVI,180
  Nathaniel XIV,603; XV,710;
    XVI,3
McCallister, John XVI,917
McCan, Henry XIV,283, 287
McCann, Moses XVII,301
  Phillip XVI,930
  Thomas XV,593
McCarr, Daniel XIV,576
McCarter, Charles XIV,585
  John XV,465
McCarthy, Charles XIV,56, 184,
    654
McCartney, Thomas XVI,930-31
McCarty, Charles XV,729;
    XVI,30, 33, 59
  Daniel XV,442, 626; XVI,64,
    73
  John XV,466, 478, 505, 671,
    677; XVI,63, 72, 91, 235,
    272, 511, 721
McCauley, Alexander XVI,920
  James XIV,172, 175-77,
    183
  Nathaniel XIV,552, 604
McCay, Daniel XIV,470, 571
  Francis XVI,920
  James XIV,156,-57

McCay, John XIV,18, 178, 347;
    XV,394, 428
  Jonathan XIV,468, 571
  Paul XIV,469
  Stephen XIV,470
McCerly, John XVI,719
McClanachin, James XVI,910
McClary, Andrew XIV,37, 40,
    42, 46, 48, 180
  Daniel XVII,91
  David XIV,75; XV,196, 199
  John XIV,261, 454, 529, 546,
    570; XV,201, 289, 292,
    447-48, 506, 553, 583,
    597-99, 634, 649, 655,
    660-61, 668, 695, 707;
    XVI,58, 104, 166, 294,
    369, 604, 617, 646, 778
  Joseph XV,350, 352
  Michael XIV,68-69, 555, 651-
    52; XV, 458, 726; XVI, 7,
    368-69, 396, 458, 488,
    525, 605; XVII,269, 450
  Nathaniel XVII,268
  Thomas XIV,59, 183, 267,
    458, 538-39; XV,201, 477;
    XVII,132
  William XVII,91
McCleary, William XV,111
McClellan, Hugh XVII,297
  John XIV,328, 583, 600;
    XV,715; XVI,200
McClench, Joseph XV,213, 740
McClenen, John XVII,300
McClennan, John XVI,156
McClintock, Alexander XV,546,
    582; XVI,918; XVII,259
  John XIV,267, 597; XV,435,
    713; XVI,199
  Samuel XIV,49
  William XIV,584; XV,597
McCluer, Alexander XV,562
  Benjamin XIV,642; XV,457,
    730
  David XV,115, 175, 206, 744
  David Jr. XV,174

McCluer, James XIV,73, 178,
    367; XV, 143, 158, 748;
    XVII,106
  John XV,85, 207, 300-1, 518
  Joseph XV,123
  Robert XIV,347; XV,33
  Samuel XV,17
  Thomas XIV,210, 214, 217,
    219-220, 336; XV,85, 207,
    578; XVII,63
  William XIV,336; XV,744;
    XVII, 62-63
McClure, Alexander XVI,807
  Benjamin XVI,17, 514, 774-
    75
  John XVI,908
  Joseph XVI,246, 251, 504
  Thomas XVI,113
McClurg, Charles XVI,159
  Daniel XIV,634
  George XIV,333; XV,739; XVI,
    911
  John XIV,347
  Robert XIV,333; XV,723, 739;
    XVI,206
McCoil, Andrew XVI,169-70
McColgen, John XVII,301
McCollester, Benjamin XV,427
  John XV,621
  Reuben XV,723
McCollister, Reuben XVI,206
McCollom, John XIV,212, 214,
    217, 219-20
McColly, Edward XV,722
McComel, John XVII,301
McConnell, Jonathan XIV,159,
    161, 163
  Matthew XVII,394
  Moses XIV,70, 179; XV,590
  Samuel XIV,226, 242, 360,
    424, 426, 456-57, 537;
    XV,162, 174, 177-78, 235;
    XVI,424, 728, 791
  Thomas XIV,225; XV,152,
    154, 590; XVI,307, 924;
    XVII,115

McConnor, James XIV,32;
XV,743
McCordy, John XVI,922
McCorey, John XV,628, 640
McCorliss, James XVI,667
McCormack, Robert XV,744
McCormick, James XIV,17
John XVI,45
McCoy, Charles XIV,63, 186,
210; XV,175, 221, 415,
539; XVI, 86, 93, 926;
XVII,3
Daniel XIV,605-6; XV,716;
XVI, 201, 269, 503, 634;
XVII,298
James XIV,62; XV,751;
XVII,295 John XVI,206,
256, 269, 322, 325, 328,
330, 334, 337, 339, 343-
44, 412, 503, 505, 566,
570-71
Jonathan XIV,605; XV,716;
XVI, 102, 201, 221, 634
Paul XV,634, 649, 712;
XVI,102, 199, 222, 268,
513, 778, 780-781
Stephen XIV,606; XV,631,
637, 716; XVI,102, 201,
269, 499, 580, 634
Thomas XV,504
William XV,359, 538
McCrillis, Henry XIV,261, 454,
530, 546
James XV,133, 392
John XIV,233, 242, 451, 532;
XV,528
Robert XIV,234, 322; XVII,29
William XIV,42, 69, 354
McCrosky, Alexander XVI,929
McCuggen, Andrew XVI,28
McCurdy, Archibald XV,116,
176
John XVI,287, 511
Samuel XV,66
McCutchen, Cunningham
XVII,10
McCutchins, Cunningham

McCutchins, Cunningham
(Cont.) XIV,126, 188, 234
McCutten, Phedris XIV,360
McDaniel, Andrew XV,438
Edmond XV,753
James XV,619, 720
McDaniels, Andrew XIV,605
James XIV,624; XVI,204
John XVI,839
Randall XIV,33, 438, 527,
545
Robert XIV,234
William XVI,252, 505
McDole, Alexander XVI,141, 161
William XV,556; XVI,141, 161
William Jr. XV,556
McDonald, Edmond XV,753
George XVII,302
James XV,210; XVII,299
John XIV,391, 487, 647, 649;
XV,745; XVI,13
Neal XVI,153
Philip XVII,302
Robert XIV,409
McDorman, John XVI,39
McDougal, Alexander XVII,159,
161, 188
John XVI,920
McDowell, Alexander XVI,887;
XVII,97
William XVII,258
McDuffee, Daniel XV,297, 299,
315, 317
John XIV,37, 44, 49, 107,
121, 234, 361; XV,297,
469, 481, 507; XVI,319;
XVII,13, 213
Mansfield XV,200
Samuel XIV,285, 287; XV,175
William XIV,406, 425
McElvin, Ebenezer XV,722; XVI,
205
McFarland, Andrew XVII,328
James XIV,300, 328; XV,168
Jesse XV,587; XVI,307;
XVII,114
Joseph XIV,579, 605;

McFarland, Joseph (Cont.)
  XV,453-54, 716, 745;
  XVI,201, 722
Moses XIV,61, 182, 328;
  XV,742; XVI,353
Samuel XVII,258
McFee, Matthew XVI,907
McFerson, James XIV,183;
  XV,552; XVII,259, 427
John XIV,183; XV,694, 699
Joseph XIV,17
Paul XIV,181; XVI,926;
  XVII,4
Robert XVII,64
William XIV,425
McGaffee, Andrew XVII,269
McGaffey, Andrew XIV,43, 68,
  180, 352, 555, 652;
  XV,726; XVI,7, 103, 189,
  213, 231, 279, 320, 323,
  325, 328, 330, 338, 340,
  343-44, 415, 505, 647
Neal XIV,69, 180, 354, 570,
  651; XV,624, 727; XVI,8-9,
  27, 29, 42, 182, 208, 416,
  647, 726
Samuel XVI,113, 121, 164
McGaw, Jacob XVI,715
Titus XIV,573; XV,616
McGee, John XIV,578, 586, 597;
  XV,713
Neal XV,671, 677; XVI,719,
  721
Patrick XVII,306
William XIV,578, 586, 597;
  XV, 713
McGilvary, William XIV,59, 156-
  157; XV,427, 616, 751
McGilvery, William XVI,47, 55,
  101, 303
McGinnis, John XIV,85, 199,
  597; XV,596, 713
McGlaughlin, James XIV,167;
  XV, 288
Thomas XV,716; XVI,201,
  263, 271
McGlosphin, Owen XVII,294

McGood, Thomas XVII,298
McGoon, Alexander XVI,920
John XIV,312, 411; XVI,44
Josiah XIV,388; XVI,99; XVII,
  383
Samuel XV,720
McGovin, John XV,656, 666
McGrath, Daniel XIV,43; XV,750
James XIV,304-5, 465
McGraw, Patrick XVII,294
McGregor, Captain XVII,226
McGregore, Daniel XVI,910
David XIV,555, 579, 655; XV,
  452, 726; XVI,7, 38, 51,
  182, 189, 208, 228;
  XVII,269, 441
Duncan XIV,288; XVII,14
James XIV,157-58
Lieutenant XVI,60
London XVI,287, 507
Robert XV,115, 117, 140-41,
  543; XVI,663-64; XVII,258
McHorn, John XIV,620
McIlvain, Daniel XIV,299;
  XV,359
Ebenezer XIV,74, 178, 299,
  314, 560, 579, 620;
  XV,443, 455; XVI,205, 721
McIlvaine, James XVI,113, 247,
  253; XVII,439
William XVI,112
McIntire, Andrew XIV,391, 469,
  487, 508, 512-13, 602;
  XV, 712; XVI,198, 224,
  241, 268, 500, 755
Daniel XVI,929
James XIV,240, 258, 343,
  345; XVII,22, 37, 43,
  302
John XIV,602; XV,712;
  XVI,198
Neal XVII,139, 247
Neil XV,579
Samuel XIV,238
Timothy XIV,89, 201;
  XVI,297
Tobias XIV,550; XV,430

McIntire, William XIV,227, 257;
  XV,326; XVII,34
McIntosh, Archibald XV,210,
  745
  Ebenezer XV,279-80; XVI,539
  James XIV,32; XV,87, 743;
    XVI, 689
  John XV,753
McKeach, Thomas XIV,269, 271,
  290
McKean, Hugh XIV,266, 477;
  XVI, 526
McKeen, Daniel XV,698;
  XVI,720
  Hugh XVII,465
  James XV,739; XVI,297
  John XV,199, 632, 636;
    XVI,44, 557, 717
  Joseph XV,566
  Robert XV,567
  Samuel XVI,557
  William XV,395, 429
McKensey, James XVI,762
McKillips, Daniel XIV,289
  David XIV,19, 291
McKim, William XIV,111, 381,
  490; XV,693; XVI,214, 234
McKinsey, James XV,664-65,
  671
McKissick, John XIV,25
McKnight, David XIV,59, 183
  Doctor XVII, 388
  James XVI,909
  Robert XIV,336, 464, 635;
    XV, 441, 626, 724, 742;
    XVI,274, 503, 733-35
McKown, Joseph XVI,917
McLain, Obed XV,614, 716
McLane, Obed XIV,56, 184, 574,
  604; XVI,103, 238, 247,
  269, 507, 716
McLaughlin, Collins XVII,302
  James XIV,170; XV,557, 587;
    XVII,14, 427
  John XVI,285, 506, 910, 935
  Patrick XVII,301

McLaughlin, Thomas XIV,57,
  59, 183, 249, 254, 605;
  XV,111-12, 351, 353;
  XVI,725; XVII,426
  William XV,175, 587; XVI,296
McLean, Thomas XVII,302
McLeod, George XIV,42
McLoy, Thomas XV,439
McLurg, Samuel XV,362
McMahon, James XVI,100
  John XIV,29, 312, 338;
  XV,595; XV,722
McMarthan, James XVI,64, 73
McMaster, Alexander XIV,470,
  579, 604, 606; XV,453,
  715; XVI, 201, 239, 510,
  723, 725, 890
  Samuel XIV,88, 200
  William XIV,425; XV,351, 353
McMasters, Moses XVII,439
McMichael, John XIV,84
McMillan, Andrew XIV,246;
  XVI,613
  Archibald XIV,43, 283, 287;
    XVI, 740; XVI,320, 322,
    324, 326, 331, 334, 337,
    339, 343, 345, 417-19,
    753
  John XIV,459, 537; XV,351,
    353, 552; XVI, 323, 753
  John Jr. XVII,259
McMitchell, Patrick XVII,95,
McMullen, James XVI,141, 161;
  XVII,293, 300
McMurphy, Alexander XV,454;
  XVI, 263, 725; XVII,426
  Archibald XVI,725
  Daniel XV,124, 149, 151,
    158; XVI,112, 321, 323,
    325, 328-331, 334, 337,
    339, 343-44, 419, 499,
    917
  George XIV,73, 178, 579,
    604; XV,453-54, 716;
    XVI,201, 722
  John XIV,59, 183, 579, 605;

McMurphy, John (Cont.) XV,
453-54, 716; XVI,201,
722, 917
Patrick XV,619
Robert XIV,75, 178; XV,482,
484
Sanders XVI,236, 273
William XIV,75, 178, 266;
XVI, 928
McMurrey, William XIV,223
McMurtry, John XIV,223
McNamara, John XVII,308
McNeal, Daniel XV,189; XVII,3
James XVI,911, 922
John XV,165, 409; XVI,527,
910; XVII,301
Robert XVII,132
Thomas XV,711; XVI,198,
267
William XV,298
McNeale, John XIV, 302-3
McNee, James XVII,291
William XV,355, 538; XVI,792
McNeil, Daniel XIV,64, 115, 141,
181, 186, 193, 321, 425,
465; XV,429; XVI,926
John XIV,50, 53, 185, 312
John C. XIV,59, 183, 477
Thomas XIV,425, 612;
XV,434; XVI,221, 500, 755
McNelle, John XVI,519, 825
McNight, Robert XVII,63
McNorton, Fenley XVI,113
McPherson, James XIV,59, 183;
XV, 350, 353
John XIV,59, 183
Paul XIV,64, 186
Robert XIV,337; XV,122
William XV,122, 553
McQuaid, Jacob XV,176
McQuesten, David XIV,417
McQuig, David XIV,57, 183;
XV,90-91, 197
John XIV,417
McRian, John XIV,576
McRobert, John XV,143, 604

McRoberts, John XIV,594;
XVI,614; XVII,249
McShannon, George XIV,65
Meacham, Asa XVI,608
Jeremiah XIV,445, 543;
XV,42; XVII,67, 110
Zebah XV,31
Mead, Colonel XV,47, 65
David XVI,53
Duncan XVII,298
John XV,392, 409; XVI,149
Joseph XIV,13
Nicholas XIV,13
Stephen XVI,925; XVII,139
Thomas XIV,485, 500, 510,
512, 518-19; XVII,86
William XVII,57
Meader, Ebenezer XVI,892
John XIV,400; XVII,645, 716
Joseph XVII,657, 716-17,
720
Lemuel XIV,280, 288
March XIV,477
Mark XIV,540
Moses XIV,108, 123, 187
Nicholas XIV,476; XVII,717
Samuel XIV,114, 141, 193,
362; XVI,69, 79; XVII,434
Stephen XIV,236, 618;
XV,444, 618, 723;
XVI,206, 231, 274, 503,
624, 629
Thomas XIV,114, 140, 193,
298
Timothy XIV,234; XVI,853-54
Meale, Walter XIV,13
Means, Robert XVI,445, 562
Medbery, John XVII,669
Medole, William XV,115
Medraff, Burgess XV,384
Meele, Andrew XVII,14
Walter XVII,26
Meggs, Abner XVI,608
Doctor XVI,466
Ebenezer XVII,105
Megill, James XV,431

Megoon, Alexander XVI,205
  John XV,448, 599, 727
  Josiah XV,668, 679; XVI,66,
    75, 242, 409, 505, 644-45
  Samuel XV,743
  See also Magoon
Mehany, Thomas XIV,258
Mehorn, John XIV,561
Meken, William XIV,16
Melcher, Edward XV,320, 340
  James XV,325
  John XIV,239, 256; XVII,23,
    31, 38
  Matthew XIV,368
  Robert XV,246
  Samuel XIV,11, 230;
    XVII,667, 669
Melendy, Thomas XIV,266
Mellen, Daniel XV,108
  John XV,108, 110, 532, 622,
    663, 670, 683, 689;
    XVI,653-654, 736
  Matthew XIV,498, 623;
    XV,618
  Thomas XV,189
  William XVI,255, 257, 505
Melony, Robert XIV,632
Meloon, David XVI,288, 505
  Ebenezer XV,392
  Enoch XV,749
  Joseph XV,127
  Josiah XIV,67, 180, 312, 554,
    617; XV,725; XVI,4, 237,
    245, 271, 505, 529, 644-
    45; XVII, 268
  Mark XVII,360
  Samuel XIV,253
  Timothy XIV,312; XV,427;
    XVI, 47, 55, 101
Meloy, Daniel XIV,235; XVI,617
  John XV,623, 641, 719
  Jonathan XVI,617
Meloye, Arthur XV,259-60, 264
  Arthurmore XV,258
Melton, William XVI,232
Melvin, Abraham XIV,173-77;
  XV, 551

Melvin, David XIV,34, 91, 201;
  XV,93; XVI,144
  John XIV,34, 43, 105, 333
  Nathaniel XIV,34, 333; XV,93
Menard, Antoine XVII,304
Mendum, Mr. XVII,372
  Nathaniel XIV,2, 344;
    XVI,902; XVII,22, 33, 47
  Robert XVII,522
Mercy, Cato XV,713
Meriner, N. XVII,360
Merle, Clement XVII,301
Merlin, John XV,469, 481, 496;
  XVI,122, 164
Merriam, Abraham XVI,85, 94,
  106, 237, 275, 512, 741
  Ezra XVI,287, 515
  John XV,11, 25, 146;
    XVI,137, 866; XVII,104,
    528
  John Jr. XV,25
  Joseph XV,346
Merrick, Ezra XIV,656; XV,731
  Moses XV,477, 504
Merrifield, Joseph XV,55
Merrill, Abel XIV,332, 613; XV,
  711; XVI,198, 515, 935
  Amos XIV,180, 246
  Barnard XIV,583, 600;
    XV,715; XVI,200
  Barnet XV,437
  Benjamin XV,72, 214
  Daniel XV,511; XVI,144, 259,
    377; XVII,437
  Daniel P. XV,329, 343-44
  David XV,390, 435, 712; XVI,
    198, 735
  Dudley XIV,225, 342;
    XV,283, 290
  Enoch XIV,246
  Ezekiel XIV,340; XV,358, 562
  Rev. Gyles XVI,402
  Hallowell XIV,93, 203
  Henry XVI,167, 878
  Holava XV,57
  Isaac XIV,438, 527; XV,70;
    XVI, 698

Merrill, Jacob XV,721
James XIV,286-87, 597; XV,
    435, 446, 713; XVI,105,
    519, 806, 808-9; XVII,
    330
Jeremiah XIV,285, 287
Jesse XV,568; XVI,111
John XIV,93, 202-3, 249,
    304-5, 465, 469, 566;
    XV,153-54, 206, 380, 589,
    609, 628, 645, 712;
    XVI,198, 225, 307, 501,
    541, 611, 789, 909;
    XVII,81, 83, 95, 115
John Jr. XV,390
Joseph XVI,838-39; XVII,2
Mark XV,754
Marston XIV,144, 193
Moses XIV,70, 179; XVI,256,
    507, 908; XVII,57
Mr. XVII,377, 385
Nathaniel XIV,160-61, 164-
    65; XV,732; XVI,20, 22,
    191, 539
Nehemiah XV,475, 494, 699;
    XVI, 236, 243, 268, 499,
    935
Peasley XIV,405
Perley XIV,225
Peter Jr. XVI,890
Roger XV,664, 670, 683; XVI,
    697; XVII,339
Samuel XV,88, 210, 511;
    XVI,64, 73, 91, 909
Simeon XIV,601; XVI,51
Simon XIV,76, 82, 198, 601;
    XV, 710; XVI,3, 197, 599
Stephen XVI,282, 284
Thomas XIV,246; XVI,901
Thomas Jr. XIV,246
William XIV,87, 200, 246,
    346; XV,70; XVI,868;
    XVII,61
Merritt, Ebenezer XV,35
John XVI,102, 507, 668;
    XVII, 338
William XVI,933

Merrow, Alexander XIV,537
Benjamin XVI,913
Joshua XIV,126, 188, 554,
    631; XV,719; XVI,4, 50,
    180, 182, 203, 230, 271;
    XVII,11, 216, 220, 268,
    378, 440, 442, 449
Samuel XIV,125, 188, 406;
    XVII, 10
Merry, Benjamin XVI,907
John XIV,662
Meserve, Clement XIV,540
Henry XIV,260
Meservy, Clement XVI,904
Meskill, Lawrence XIV,233
Messe, Daniel XVI,196
Messenger, Nathaniel XIV,422;
    XVI,310
Messer, Abiel XIV,167, 169, 274
Benjamin XV,210
Daniel XV,329, 343
David XIV,342, 347; XV,390
John XV,568
Nathaniel XV,11; XVII,105
Richard XVI,823
Thomas XIV,265; XV,370
Messerve, Henry XVII,31, 39, 46
Jonathan XVI,730, 732
Joseph XVI,731
See also Meserve
Metcalf, Asa XV,58
Burgess XV,384; XVI,924
Ezra XV,227, 741
Joseph XIV,93, 202-3, 355;
    XV, 7, 57, 223
Joseph Jr. XIV,356; XV,59-
    60; XVII,264
Jotham XV,3
Luke XV,741
Michael XV,227; XVII,97
Mr. XVII,130, 224, 282
Nathan XV,57; XVII,95
Thomas XIV,356; XV,58, 223
Meuke, James XVI,102
Michel, John XIV,7
Middle, John XIV,85, 199
Middleton, Alexander XIV,28

Middleton, Reuben XIV,273, 289
  Richard XVI,68, 75, 95
  Thomas XIV,119, 151, 196
Mifflin, General Thomas XIV,523
Miguel, Joseph XVI,122, 164
Miles, Abel XV,356
  Abner XV,512
  Abraham XIV,34
  Henry XIV,355
  Josiah XV,133; XVI,903
  Michael XIV,223
  Moses XIV,432, 580, 624; XV,
    447, 598, 720; XVI,204
  William XIV,100, 346; XV,
    512; XVI,903
Miller, Bethuel XIV,442, 544;
    XV, 26, 371
  Daniel XV,279
  David XV,256, 259-60, 263,
    524; XVI, 128, 162
  Eliakim XIV, 126, 188; XVII,
    11
  Ephraim XVII, 669
  Farrar XIV,35, 91, 201, 561,
    575, 621; XV,722; XVI,
    205, 233, 273, 498, 521,
    559, 561-62, 854, 856,
    858-60
  Francis XVII,293
  Frederick XVII,300
  Heber XV,8, 49, 59-60;
    XVI,394, 426
  Henry XVII,674
  Hugh XIV,265, 291; XVI,313,
    920-21; XVII,14, 35, 116
  Jacob XV,746
  James XIV,61, 182, 266;
    XV,696, 698, 754; XVI,920
  John XIV,647, 650; XV,356,
    595, 630, 646, 728;
    XVI,14, 102, 169-70, 516-
    17, 792, 794, 803, 911,
    920; XVII, 648, 656
  Jonathan XIV,111, 132, 190,
    300, 312, 641; XV,423,
    456, 730; XVI,18, 194,
    211, 237, 244, 278, 508,

Miller, Jonathan (Cont.) 675-77
  Joseph XV,101, 538
  Lemuel XV,12, 371
  Matthew XIV,265, 291, 607-
    8; XV,425, 714; XVII,35
  Robert XIV,111, 132, 159,
    161, 164, 190, 304-5, 465,
    607-8; XV,425, 714;
    XVI,200
  Samuel XV,221, 587, 693;
    XVI, 898-99, 910
  Thomas XIV,283, 287;
    XV,189, 556; XVII,259
  William XIV,61, 182; XV,475,
    494
Millet, John XIV,468, 575,
    612; XVI,521, 856, 858,
    860; XVII, 470-71
  Morris XIV,573, 612;
    XVI,521, 856, 858, 860;
    XVII,470-71
Milliken, Alexander XIV,183
  James XIV,307, 333
  Robert XV,530
  Samuel XIV,43
  William XIV,421
Milling, John XVII,307
Millington, Solomon XV,17, 375
Millins, Charles XIV,93, 202
Millit, John XV,711
  Morris XV,711
Mills, Alexander XIV,442, 544,
    XV,24
  Benjamin XV,513
  Bradbury XV,740; XVI,778
  Daniel XV,280; XVII,114
  David XIV,410; XVI,80
  J. XVI,29, 474
  Jacob XVI,926
  James XIV,314, 467
  John XIV,59, 102, 183, 208,
    258, 266, 344, 359, 477,
    566, 570, 624; XV,116,
    196, 213, 520, 554, 607,
    722; XVI,206, 259-61,
    528, 780; XVII,211, 253,
    432, 436, 463, 536

Mills, Jonathan XV,566;
    XVI,155
  Joseph XV,122, 189, 191,
    414, 528, 624, 710; XVI,3,
    180, 182, 197, 267;
    XVII,441, 449, 453
  Levi XIV,77, 82, 198; XVI,670
  Richard XVII,139
  Samuel XIV,406; XVI,235,
    274, 522
  Thomas XVI,914
  Thomas Jr. XV,176
  William XV,525; XVII,61
Millson, Timothy XVI,303
Miltimore, Daniel XIV,73, 242;
    XV,116, 163, 188, 583;
    XVI, 720
  John XV,567
  William XVI,113
Mimell, James XIV,281
  Jeremiah XIV,281
Minchin, Richard XIV,282, 287
Miner, Nathaniel XV,19, 138
  Thomas XV,374; XVI,539;
    XVII, 69, 89
  William XIV,443, 542, 547;
    XV, 279-80; XVII,73
Minot, Benjamin XIV,199-200,
    356
  Joseph XIV,33
Mintler, James XIV,259
Mirick, Ezra XVI,36, 39
  Moses XV,464, 466
Mishorn, Daniel XVII,717
Mitchell, Benjamin XIV,421; XV,
    221
  Caleb XV,748
  Charles XIV,239, 257-58, 344
  David XIV,28
  Francis XIV,605; XV,453,
    455; XVI,724
  George XIV,287; XV,437
  Hugh XVI,138
  Isaac XIV,471, 577, 612, 629;
    XV,456, 717; XVI, 270,
    517, 739-40, 794, 934

Mitchell, James XV,101, 221,
    405, 613, 739
  John XIV,383, 287, 562, 584,
    631, 637; XV,427, 445,
    451-452, 618, 653, 723-
    24; XVI, 55, 101, 206-7,
    230, 274, 504, 557, 560-
    61, 588, 639, 641, 897,
    922; XVII,495
  John Jr. XVI,898
  John W. XIV,199
  Joseph XV,294; XVI,627
  Joshua XIV,627; XV,721
  Josiah XVII,87
  Michael XVII,298
  Philip XV,164
  Robert XIV,232, 564; XV,242,
    244; XVI,110, 165; XVII,7,
    26, 301-2
  Samuel XIV,91, 201; XV,101,
    219, 357, 427, 733;
    XVI,47, 55, 101, 213, 303,
    793; XVII, 354, 415
  Samuel Jr. XVI,898
  Thomas XV,553, 623, 629,
    641; XVI,64, 73, 671;
    XVII,349
  William XI,42, 61; XV,326,
    739; XVI,436; XVII,22, 34
Mixer, Ezekiel XIV,334
  Nathan XV,216
  Timothy XV,101; XVI,47,
    101, 303, 517, 794
Mixter, Ezekiel XV,109
  Nathan XV,109
  Timothy XV,427, 739
Moar, John XIV,19
Moisan, Michael XVII,304
Molay, John XVII,349
Molloy, Arthur XV,256
Molony, John XVII,149
Monreau, Francois XVII,299
Monroe, John XV,311
  Josiah XV,710, 739
  See also Munroe
Monson, Richard XVII,648

Montague, Samuel XIV,7
Montgomery, General XIV,171;
    XVII,76
    George XVI,235, 242, 267,
        506, 659
    Henry XVI,910
    Hugh XIV,74, 178, 425;
        XVI,898, 911
    John XVI,807, 933
    Lieutenant XVII,296, 350
    Martin XIV,42, 75, 178, 266,
        560, 579, 620; XV,455,
        722; XVI,723
    William XIV,358
Monty, Glaude XVII,304
Moody, Abner XIV,116, 129, 189
    Captain XVII,702, 725, 728,
        746
    Clement XIV,12, 69, 180;
        XVII, 25
    Daniel XIV,457, 537; XV,36,
        562; XVI,807
    Edward XIV,116, 129, 189,
        300, 399; XV,285, 291
    Elisha XV,183
    James XIV,353, 451, 532,
        563
    John XIV,297, 432, 434;
        XV,393; XVII,214
    Rev. Joshua XVII,512, 527,
        544, 556, 581, 584, 588,
        592-94, 599
    Josiah XIV,68, 180, 476
    Levi XVI,155
    Samuel XIV,400, 452, 532;
        XV, 285, 291
    Thomas XIV,236; XVI,907
Mooney, Benjamin XIV,24, 26,
        235, 312-13, 365; XVI,66,
        77, 96, 757
    Hercules XIV,20, 367, 479;
        XV, 654, 672-87, 736;
        XVI,457, 527; XVII,121,
        284, 457
    John XIV,368, 375, 498
    Obadiah XVI,593-94

Moor, Abijah XVI,311-12
    Abraham XV,517
    Archelaus XVI,458, 591, 593
    Captain XIV,33
    Daniel XIV,219, 329, 358,
        424, 459-60, 539, 557;
        XV, 122-23, 210, 300,
        302, 345, 351-64, 497,
        581; XVI,68, 872; XVII, 18,
        214, 256, 259
    Ephraim XIV,425; XV, 267,
        269, 272; XVI,579
    Ephraim Jr. XV,273
    Ezra XV,426; XVII,118-19,
        250
    George XIV,443, 543, 547;
        XV, 426, 584-85; XVI,92,
        295; XVI,307, 679; XVII,
        132
    Isaac XIV,570; XVI,163, 188
    Jacob XV,210
    James XIV,179, 304-5, 348,
        468, 577, 612; XV,115,
        267, 269, 272; XVI,223,
        518, 740
    John XIV,305, 469; XV,111,
        113, 115-16, 428, 566,
        622, 663, 669, 689; XVI,
        167, 579, 721, 733, 786
    Joseph XIV,305; XV,744
    Josiah XVI,164
    Reuben XVI,141, 161
    Robert XVI,214
    Samuel XV,749; XVI,734-35,
        903
    Sampson XV,387
    Thomas XVI,847
    Thomas Jr. XVI,842
    William XIV,178, 628;
        XV,128, 180, 429, 464,
        466, 477, 505, 696, 748;
        XVI,96, 162, 262, 595;
        XVII,426, 428, 742
    William Jr. XVII,118, 120
Moore,--- XVII,347
    Alexander XVII,301

Moore, Benjamin XV,362;
  XVII,303
  Colonel XV,113
  Daniel XIV,70, 153, 158, 179,
    256, 426, 478, 539;
    XV,122, 177-78, 190, 212,
    305, 309, 345, 453, 645,
    655; XVI,78, 98, 920
  David XIV,59, 183, 195
  Elkins XIV,566; XV,607, 721;
    XVI,148, 204, 236, 272,
    502, 594-95
  Ephraim XV,513, 754
  Ezekiel XV,697; XVI,148
  Ezra XIV,160-61, 164;
    XV,584-585; XVI,307;
    XVII,119
  Fortain XV,597
  George XIV,67, 279, 287,
    291; XV,279, 280; XVI,86,
    106, 307, 898; XVII,114
  Gideon XVI,311-12
  Goffe XIV,59, 183
  Harvey XIV, 134, 136;
    XV,324, 331; XVII, 5-6
  Henry XIV, 260, 401, 414;
    XVII, 46
  Hugh XVI, 113, 236, 268,
    890-91; XVII, 439
  Isaac XIV,71, 179, 652;
    XV,728; XVI,130, 210,
    262; XVII,432
  Jacob XVI,259; XVII,437
  James XIV,59, 70, 75, 156-
    57, 179, 420; XV,200,
    613, 711, 739, 751, 754;
    XVI,198, 238, 267, 286,
    499, 506
  James Jr. XVI,898
  John XIV,48, 57, 59, 70, 153,
    156, 167, 169, 260, 274,
    552, 605; XV,170, 175,
    394, 513, 635, 639, 677,
    710, 712; XVI,3, 199, 286,
    500, 518, 715, 720, 807-8,
    898; XVII, 46, 266

Moore, John W. XVI,236, 243,
    275, 712
  Joseph XV,128
  Joshua XIV,327
  Josiah XVI,122
  Moses XVI,286, 499
  Patrick XVII,298
  Ralph XVII,298
  Robert XIV,424; XVI,898
  Samuel XIV,18, 59, 339;
    XV,116, 169, 345, 362,
    748; XVI,564, 589, 593;
    XVII,69, 256
  Thomas XV,522; XVI,127,
    162, 458
  William XIV,75, 160-61, 164,
    312, 321, 355, 410-11,
    583; XV,175, 221, 394,
    442, 557, 698, 720;
    XVI,65, 76, 105-6, 112,
    128, 141, 161, 204, 252,
    311-12, 520, 628;
    XVII,383
  William Jr. XIV,338
Moores, Peter XIV,327
  Samuel XIV,328
  Sylvanus XIV,430
Moorland, James XIV,411
  William XIV,587, 628
Moors, Benjamin XVI,922
  Elias XVI,103
  John XVI,222, 268
Moose, John XIV,574; XV,617
More, Daniel XVI,193; XVII,654
  George XV,279
  Isaac XVI,27
  Jacob XV,735
  John XVI,918
  Martha XVII,605
  Thomas XV,695
  William XVII,526
Morehouse, John XVI,597
Moreland, William XVII,349
Morey, Captain XVII,317-18,
    321
  Ephraim XV,152, 154, 158,
    426; XVI,538; XVII,118-19

Morey, Israel XIV,161, 163, 170, 175, 256, 270, 273, 275-76, 278-295, 443-44, 558; XV, 154, 157, 278, 366, 385, 424-25, 655, 705; XVI,58, 104, 134, 249, 538, 924; XVII,15-18, 21, 47-48, 52, 73, 134, 136, 150, 321, 330, 335, 358
Israel Jr. XV,379; XVI,538; XVII,118-19, 150
James XVI,157
John XVI,538
Samuel XVI,203, 248, 271
Thomas XVI,699
William XV,165
Zenas XIV,160-61, 164
Morgan, Abraham XIV,14
Ashley XV,74, 211
Baptiste XVII,304
Benjamin XIV,231
Daniel XV,421
David XIV,118, 138, 158, 191, 565, 620; XV, 443, 596, 722; XVI,205, 233, 273, 308, 310, 499, 582-83, 821
David Jr. XVI,241
Henry XIV,547
James XVII,303
John XIV,12, 63, 186, 211, 215, 218-20, 459, 538-39, 561, 579, 621; XV, 452, 722; XVI, 203, 224, 239, 271, 504, 634, 723, 897; XVII,3, 298
Jonathan XIV,53, 185; XV,228, 631, 650; XVI,102, 199, 221, 268, 531, 779, 783, 862, 884; XVII,438
Josiah XV,351, 353; XVI,753
Nathaniel XVI,131, 133, 163, 920
Reuben XIV,451, 532
Richard XVII,526, 693
Simeon XVII,57

Morgan, William XVII,293
Morland, William XV,623, 629, 641, 720, 730; XVI,32, 34, 187, 210, 219, 277, 519, 824-25
Morley, George XVII,694, 698
Morony, William XIV,681
Morrill, Abel XIV,312, 330, 565, 617; XV,722; XVI,206, 231, 273, 285, 499, 582-83
Abner XIV,25
Abraham XV,128, 181, 512; XVII, 57
Amos XIV,68-69, 552, 601, 604; XV,460, 605, 710; XVI,2, 51, 180, 182, 197, 248, 267, 646; XVII,266, 440, 442
Benjamin XIV,247
Captain XV,434, 447-49, 457, 598-600
Charles XIV,252
David XIV,602; XV,387; XVI,238, 246, 274, 591, 681
David E. XVI,508, 920
Dudley XIV,349
Ezekiel XIV,261; XV,387, 512
Hannah XVI,582-83
Hibbard XIV,398, 571; XV,300-1, 304, 308, 571, 698; XVI,322, 332, 335, 420
Isaac XV,132, 179, 512
Jacob XIV,69, 180, 340, 563, 627; XV,300, 302, 305, 309, 457; XVI,838
James XV,267, 269, 273
John XIV,6, 116, 129, 189, 602; XV,322, 342, 421, 562, 658, 667, 679, 691, 699; XVI,236, 243, 268, 274, 498, 566-67, 657; XVII,44
Joseph XIV,231; XV,256, 264-65; XVI,257, 320-21,

Morrill, Joseph (Cont.) 323, 327,
  329, 331, 334, 339, 343,
  345, 506
  Joseph Jr. XVI,421
  Laban XIV,261; XV,162, 179
  Levi XIV,392, 487, 509, 513;
    XVI,584; XVII,57
  Marston XIV,193-94; XV,387;
    XVII,8
  Micajah XIV,351
  Nathaniel XIV,397; XVI,65,
    75, 98, 297
  Nehemiah XVI,582
  Oliver XV,283, 290, 292, 317
  Robert XIV,21, 654; XV,729;
    XVI,31, 33, 59, 286, 891;
    XVII,439
  Samuel XIV,43, 76, 82, 198;
    XIV,261; XV,515; XVI,
    148, 285, 498
  Sargent XIV,430
  Simeon XIV,553
  Simon XVII,266
  Thomas XVI,660
  William XIV,71, 179, 313;
    XVI, 582-84; XVII,43
Morris, John XIV,13; XVI,241
  Lewis XVII,127, 160-61, 178-
    81, 208
  Richard XIV,361
  Solomon XVII,698
  Timothy XIV,14
Morrison, Abraham XIV,238,
  373, 385, 497, 506, 617
  Alexander XIV,458
  David XIV,411; XV,176;
    XVI,82, 92, 106, 112, 335,
    511, 724, 840, 928
  Ebenezer XIV,239
  Halbert XIV,16
  James XIV,75, 135, 178, 191;
    XV,201, 285, 287; XVII,6
  John XIV,74, 76, 82, 178,
    198, 238, 327, 411, 550,
    580, 659; XV,101, 176,
    430, 448, 455, 474, 494,
    538, 599, 727, 739-740;

Morrison, John (Cont.) XVI,10,
  43, 82, 92, 106, 183, 208,
  840, 898, 903; XVII,640
  John Jr. XVI,898, 903
  Jonathan XIV,317, 319, 365,
    398, 406, 455, 530; XV,
    133, 173, 393; XVI,121,
    164, 241, 898; XVII,27
  Joseph XVI,898
  Moses XVI,678-79
  Robert XIV,69, 180, 224,
    412; XV,200, 285, 291;
    XVII,26
  Samuel XIV,260, 468, 484,
    499, 512, 575; XV,228,
    557, 711; XVI,198, 221,
    241, 267, 520, 840-41,
    898, 903; XVII,46, 85
  Thomas XIV,91, 201, 421;
    XV, 101, 219, 356, 394,
    429; XVI, 898, 903
  William XVI,237, 244, 273,
    520, 703, 706
Morse, Asa XV,390
  Benjamin XIV,224; XV,284,
    287; XVI,103, 189, 213,
    231, 279, 505, 649-52
  Caleb XIV,71, 179
  Daniel XIV,563, 656; XV,21,
    322, 331, 341, 536, 731;
    XVI, 37, 39, 212, 232,
    278, 505, 649, 694;
    XVII,291
  Edmund XIV,16
  Elijah XIV,90, 201; XV,92,
    356
  Enoch XIV,563, 599; XV,713;
    XVI,199, 223, 268, 505,
    649
  Ezekiel XIV,328, 465
  Ezra XV,20, 536, 741
  Gershom XIV,422; XV,591;
    XVI, 310
  Gilbert XVI,262; XVII,426
  Isaac XIV,584, 628; XV,721;
    XVI,205
  Jacob XV,634, 649, 731;

Morse, Jacob (Cont.) XVI,16, 25,
102, 186, 211, 221, 278,
503, 617; XVII,453
James XVI,130, 163, 257
Job XV,591
John XIV,333, 639; XV,108,
376; XVI,16, 82, 95, 106,
193, 516
John M. XVII,428
Jonathan XIV,334, 577, 662;
XV, 20, 217, 746; XVI,82,
95, 106, 193, 237, 271,
505
Joseph XV,164
Joshua XIV,261, 429, 431;
XV, 548
Josiah XIV,82, 198
Josiah Jr. XIV,76; XVI,599
Micah XV,217; XVI,82, 95,
106
Michael XVI,193
Moody XV,415; XVI,823-25
Moses XVII,92
Nathan XVI,750
Obadiah XIV,13; XVII,527
Parker XVI,262; XVII,426
Peter XIV,224
Philip XV,169, 526; XVI,588
Reuben XV,197, 216;
XVI,630
Samuel XIV,76, 83, 198, 411;
XV,101, 186, 471, 490-91;
XVI,588, 599, 928
Stephen XV,175, 513;
XVI,600
Theodore XVI,262; XVII,426
Thomas XV,66, 467, 479,
503, 741; XVII,96
Uriah XIV,282, 285, 287;
XV,593
William XVII,620
Morss, John XV,749
Moody XVII,43
Moses XV,748
Philip XV,748
Samuel XV,381, 748

Morton, Edward XVI,230
John XVI,204
Mr. XVII,486
Thomas XVII,486, 490, 496
Moses, Lieutenant XIV,330
Timothy XVII,719
William XVI,109, 165;
XVII,22, 33
Moshier, Hugh XVI,932
Timothy XVI,231, 507, 664
Mosman, James XIV,4
Mott, Samuel XVI,932
Moulton, Abraham XIV,11
Benjamin XVI,933; XVII,528
Cato XIV,413, 450, 529;
XV,456
Daniel XIV,237; XVI,295;
XVII, 26, 642, 740
David XIV,11, 118, 138, 158,
192, 350; XV,488-89;
XVI,130, 163
Edmund XIV,341; XV,569
Edward XIV,138, 192
Edward B. XIV,118, 158, 413
Elisha XIV,413
Ezekiel XIV,23, 25; XV,134
Henry XVII,528
Jacob XV,411
James XIV,280, 288, 566,
573, 607-8; XV,423, 425,
609; XVI, 18, 194, 211;
XVII,642-43
Jeremiah XIV,1, 110, 132,
190; XV,523
Job XIV,167, 170, 443, 543;
XV, 380, 593; XVI,924;
XVII,14, 73, 81, 83
John XIV,28, 138, 351;
XV,487; XVII,528, 619,
713
John M. XIV,118, 158, 192,
350; XV,411, 489
Jonah XVII,354
Jonathan XIV,256, 413-14,
449-450, 478, 556; XV,
276, 279-280, 319, 411-
14, 433, 457, 489, 593,

Moulton, Jonathan (Cont.) 628,
    639-40, 655-656, 666;
    XVI,58, 86, 92, 104, 106,
    285, 313, 501, 672, 703,
    750; XVII, 73, 81, 83, 116,
    644, 659, 667-68, 692
Joseph XIV,11, 546; XV,720;
    XVI, 672; XVII,434, 528
Joseph Jr. XV,730
Joses XIV,580, 624; XV,447,
    598
Josiah XIV,11, 117-18, 158,
    192, 313, 450, 534, 642;
    XV, 411, 423, 730; XVI,17,
    194, 673; XVII,15, 291,
    359
Josiah 3d XV,455-56
Michael XIV,25; XVII,26
Moses XIV,67, 181, 304-5
Nathan XIV,578, 597;
    XV,435; XVI,900
Nathan S. XIV,118, 138, 158,
    192, 413
Nathaniel XIV,71, 179, 469,
    570, 602; XV,712-13; XVI,
    198, 222, 268, 503, 617
Nehemiah XV,324
Noah XV,425, 593; XVI,293,
    205, 680, 912
Redmond XIV,230, 252;
    XV,319, 331, 339, 524
Reuben XVI,282, 299
Robert XIV,11; XVII,713
Samuel XVII,434
Simeon XIV,621; XV,456,
    722; XVI,205, 273, 673
Simon XIV,118, 137, 158
Smith XVI,751
Thomas XIV,25, 230
William XIV,11, 253, 258;
    XV, 656, 666, 674;
    XVI,103, 186, 213, 241,
    279, 507, 672-73, 900-1;
    XVII,740
Much, James XVII,108
Muchmore, Jaffrey XIV,238

Muchmore, James XIV,588,
    604; XV,715; XVI,201, 788
Mudget, Thomas XV,172
Mudgett, David XIV,69, 180,
    552, 580, 602, 604;
    XV,448, 598; XVI, 3
John XIV,66, 181, 432, 660;
    XV, 113, 727; XVI,9-10,
    42, 208, 917
John Jr. XIV,581; XV,449,
    600
Joseph XIV,433
Mugridge, William XIV,111, 132,
    190; XV,256, 258, 260,
    264; XVI,648
Mulit, Francis XVII,306
Mullen, James XIV,387, 494,
    507, 516
William XVI,184
Mulloy, Martin XVII,302
Mumford, Cato XVII,306
Munhall, George XIV,227
Munroe, Josiah XIV,553, 613;
    XV, 710, 739; XVII,266,
    440, 443-444
John XV,311
Josiah XVI,3, 51, 180, 182,
    197, 224, 267, 526
Munsel, James XV,25-26
John XV,629; XVI,713-14
Munsey, John XVII,719
Timothy XV,312
Munson, Ezra XVII,295
William XVII,308
Muny, Philip XIV,7
Murch, James XV,15, 39;
    XVI,929
Stephen XV,41, 375
Murdock, Samuel XIV,530, 546
Thomas XIV,633; XV,723;
    XVI, 206, 908
Murdough, Samuel XIV,454
Thomas XIV,568, 589;
    XV,444, 610
Murlet, John XIV,238
Murphy, James XIV,289, 292

Murphy, John XIV,230, 252,
251, 642; XV,422, 455;
XVI,18
Labach XIV,620
Patrick XIV,211, 216, 258,
474; XV,443, 722
Thomas XIV,307
William XIV,307
Murray, Beriah XV,27; XVI,605,
608; XVII,105
Daniel XIV,171, 174-77, 430
David XVII,307
James XVII,302, 434
John XIV,168-69, 275, 571;
XV, 572; XVII,235
Patrick XIV,561
Samuel XIV,248; XVII,26
Murro, John XVI,846
Musheway, Peter XVII,46
Musserway, Peter XIV,260
Musset, Joseph XVII,644
Mary XVII,605
Mussey, Benjamin XIV,419
Diamond XIV,244
Muzzey, John XV,406, 550, 698;
XVI,628
Joseph XV,630, 643, 646;
XVI, 102, 653
R. Diamond XV,521
Thomas XV,746
William XIV,433

N

Nado, Basil XVII,304
Nahor, James XV,90
Nainby, William XVII,420-21
Nanearron, John XVII,304
Nanney, Robert XVII,501
Nash, Christopher XVII,300
Littlefield XV,17; XVII,88
Samuel XV,590; XVI,314;
XVII, 71, 113, 116
Nason, David XIV,369, 374,
482, 498, 502, 511, 518;
XVI,674
Jacob XIV,257; XVII,22, 34,
37
Silas XIV,5

Nason, Willoughby XVII,655,
667
Nay, John XVII,670
Joseph XV,412
Samuel XIV,350; XV,658-59,
668, 674; XVI,155
Neal, Andrew XIV,231, 402, 415;
XV,327; XVI,842; XVII,6,
27
Clement XVI,257, 507
Ebenezer XIV,229, 413, 641;
XV, 456, 730; XVI,17, 774
Eliphalet XIV,134, 191, 408;
XVII,5
Hubartus Jr. XVI,765
James XIV,535; XV,259-60,
264
Jeremiah XIV, 312; 338,
XV,665, 684; XVI,843
John XIV,15, 107, 122, 187,
232, 353, 369, 374, 482,
498, 502, 511; XV,443,
618-20, 631, 646, 722;
XVI,261, 402, 485, 527,
626, 640, 841-42, 906,
916; XVII,432
Joseph XIV,232, 451, 514,
532; XV,284, 288
Joshua XIV,228, 382, 490;
XVII,29, 360
Robert XVI,916
Samuel XIV,15; XVI,65, 75,
99, 221, 267, 750, 860
Thomas XVI,111, 166, 257,
507
Walter XIV,118, 138, 158,
192, 232, 255, 351, 400,
551
William XIV,237, 494; XV,
693; XVI,214, 234, 317-19
Neale, Andrew XIV,423
Benjamin XIV,67, 580; XV,
448, 598, 712
Ebenezer XV,423
John XIV,617
Walter XVII,478, 484, 498,
500, 516, 522-23, 527,

Neale, Walter (Cont.) 532, 535
Nealey, David XVII,301
   Joseph XV,422, 730, 734;
     XVI, 18, 184, 211, 228,
     513, 778
   William XVI,320-21, 326,
     332, 342, 344, 423, 649
Nealy, Andrew XIV,69, 166, 170,
    180, 191, 231, 330, 332
   Benjamin XIV,211, 216, 474,
    563
   John XIV,69, 180, 476
   John Jr. XIV,400
   Joseph XIV,570, 641
   William XIV,563
Neas, Elisha XV,728; XVI,27,
    188, 210, 277
Necoth, James XVII,513
Needham, Nathaniel XIV,574,
    597; XV,617, 713
Negros--Archelaus XV,742;
    XVII,7, 8
   Cato XIV,618; XV,619
   Corridon XIV,618-19
   Dan XV,618, 653
   Daniel XIV,637
   Fortunatus XVI,845
   Fortune XIV,281, 285, 287
   George XIV,618
   Gloster XIV,618; XV,619
   Jubael XVII,24
   Oliver XIV,564
   Oxford XIV,564
   Peter XV,648; XVI,102, 709
   Primus XIV,564
   Prince XV,437, 580
   Richard XIV,618
   Robin XV,743; XVII,7, 8
   Scipio XV,742; XVII,7, 8
   Sidon XVII,24
   Zack XIV,618; XV,619
Neil, James XIV,345, 348
   Joshua XIV,501
Nelle, Benjamin XIV,304-5, 602
   Joseph XVI,211, 278, 529
   William XIV,304-5, 465, 602

Nelley, Benjamin XV,712
   William XIV,469; XV,434,
    712; XVI,199, 268, 342, 506
Nelson, Andrew XVI,286, 502
   Captain XVII,240, 243
   Charles XIV,159, 161, 163;
    XV, 584-85; XVI,307, 315;
    XVII, 16, 52, 240, 243,
    250-51
   Daniel XIV,664; XV,434
   George XIV,586, 656;
    XV,732; XVI,36, 39
   James XIV,2, 25; XV,384;
    XVI, 315
   John XIV,259, 480; XVII,37
   Joseph XIV,119, 151, 196,
    259; XV,195; XVII,37
   Mark XVI,139
   Matthew XIV,13; XVII,619,
    654, 668
   Richard XIV,119-20, 149
   Richard L. XIV,196, 258, 550
   Thomas XIV,356
Nesmith, Arthur XIV,458, 539;
    XVI,263, 725; XVII,426
   Benjamin XIV,458, 538-39
   George W. XIV,42
   James XIV,75, 178, 454, 538,
    579, 653; XV,200, 452,
    733; XVI,31, 34, 41, 59,
    190, 213, 722
   James Jr. XIV,75; XV,454;
    XVI, 716-18
   James 2d XIV,178
   John XIV,73, 178, 347, 465;
    XV, 427, 726; XVI,47, 55,
    101, 303
Nevens, Benjamin XV,210
   David XV,381, 459, 606, 633,
    647, 734; XVI,34, 39, 102,
    210, 219, 277, 550, 910;
    XVII,221
   David Jr. XVII,116
   John XV,210
   Robert XV,358, 567
   Thomas XVII,14

Nevens, William XV,743
Nevers, David XV,734
Nevins, Benjamin XIV,33
    David XIV,280, 288, 587,
        656; XV,647, 730-31;
        XVI,30, 34, 36, 187, 240,
        499, 799, 909
    David Jr. XIV,280, 288;
        XVI,314
    John XVI,921
    Joseph XIV,33; XV,88
Nevins, Phinehas XIV,43;
        XV,744
    Thomas XIV,167
    Thomas Jr. XIV,170
    William XIV,32
New, Angus O. XVII,303
Newcomb, Daniel XVI,434
Newell, Andrew XIV,56, 184,
        657; XV,732; XVI,36, 39
    Jacob XV,218
    James XIV,420
    Pearson XIV,93, 202
Newland, Jonathan XV,701,
        704, 726; XVI,176
Newman, Ebenezer XV,97, 622,
        634, 644; XVI,23, 44, 734-
        35; XVII,461
    John XVI,236, 273, 517, 752
    Thomas XIV,160-61, 164,
        286-87, 291, 468, 607-8;
        XV,425, 436
    William XIV,59, 183
Newmarch, Benjamin XIV,119,
        149, 151, 197
Newton, Benjamin XV,62
    Elnathan XV,102
    Isaac XV,11
    John XV,325; XVII,32
    Jonas XV,701, 704
    Nahum XIV,430
    Phinehas XV,41, 374
    Robert XIV,355
    Thomas XIV,391, 487, 508,
        512, 585, 648, 650;
        XV,728; XVI,3; XVII,32,
        621

Newton, Timothy XIV,578, 593;
        XV,717; XVI,202, 218,
        270, 502, 597, 599, 934
    William XV,165
Nichola, Lewis XVI,40
Nichols, Aaron XIV,244, 266,
        477; XV,75, 213
    Adam XV,116, 621, 634, 644;
        XVI,564
    Alexander XV,567; XVI,898
    Andrew XIV,264; XV,63, 203,
        633, 643, 647, 740;
        XVI,23, 44, 851, 927
    Colonel XVII,519,
    Daniel XV,116, 362
    David XIV,425
    Dudley XVII,27, 275, 284
    Francis XVI,254
    G. XVII,362
    George XV,631, 638, 706;
        XVI, 521, 826-27
    Humphrey XIV,341; XVII,32
    James XIV,113, 554, 565,
        617, 660; XV,725; XVI,4,
        581; XVII,268
    John XIV,233, 358, 627;
        XV,123, 187, 441, 457,
        533, 696, 698, 721, 748;
        XVI,205, 226, 272, 279,
        510, 527, 703; XVII,29
    Jonathan XV,204, 377; XVI,
        927
    Joseph XV,695; XVI,145,
        247, 251, 498, 655
    Lewis XVI,354
    Lieutenant XVI,180
    Moses XIV,256, 528, 557,
        572, 574; XV,68, 72, 74,
        83, 90, 140, 196-99, 203,
        206, 209, 216, 219, 223,
        226, 228, 419, 509-31,
        610-17, 632, 635-36, 650-
        51, 655, 664, 670, 695;
        XVI,58, 104, 135-61, 166,
        215, 246, 248, 369, 371,
        375, 380, 393, 440, 557,
        561, 584; XVII, 339-40,

Nichols, Moses (Cont.) 414
    Mr. XVII,509
    Nathan XVII,420
    Nicholas XVII,27, 145, 231-
        32, 237, 261-62
    Richard XVII,306, 513, 537
    Samuel XIV,298; XV,35, 37
    Thomas XVI,215
    Timothy XIV,324, 463;
        XV,30, 72, 146
    Timothy Jr. XV,521
    Trueworthy XV,284, 287
    William XV,633, 643, 647;
        XVI, 41, 44, 603
Nicholson, John XVI,269, 523
Nickelson, William XIV,157
Nickerman, John XVI,930
Nickerson, John XVI,254
    Reuben XV,173
    William XIV,54
Niles, Gains XIV,576; XV,713;
        XVI,199, 223, 268, 508,
        679
    James XIV,470
    Nathaniel XVII,254
    Zadoc XV,62
Nims, Asahel XV,741
    Eliakim XIV,326, 464;
        XV,741
Nixon, Colonel XVII,127
    James XV,623, 629, 641,
        722; XVI,519, 824-25;
        XVII,349
    John XV,742
Noble, Benjamin XIV,465
    Christopher XIV,14; XVII,642
    Lazarus XIV,13; XVII,655
    Mark XIV,239, 343; XV,326
    Moses XIV,239, 344
    Obadiah XV,385
    Sergeant XVI,818
    Stephen XIV,21, 123, 187,
        623; XV,295, 618, 625,
        715; XVI, 66, 77, 96, 204,
        229, 272, 504, 638-41
Nock, Drisco XIV,236
    Ebenezer XIV,18

Nock, Eleazer XIV,237
    James XVI,904; XVII,719
    Jedediah XIV,600; XV,437,
        596, 715
    John XIV,230, 362
    Jonathan XIV,600; XV,437,
        715
    Joseph XIV,236
    Nathaniel XIV,237
    Zachariah XIV,13
Noel, Francis XVII,304
Nokes, James XVI,257, 287,
        517, 519
    Timothy XVI,703; XVII,25
Noles, Nathaniel XV,701
Nookes, Timothy XV,457
Noraway, James XVII,656, 670,
        679
Norce, John XVII,669
Norcott, John XIV,7
Norcross, Jeremiah XIV,36;
        XV,539
    Page XIV,36
Norris, Andrew XVI,86, 93
    Benjamin XIV,71, 179, 360,
        588; XV,557, 748
    Captain XV,440, 451, 596-97
    David XIV,330, 451, 454,
        530, 532, 546; XV,127,
        179; XVI, 645
    David Jr. XIV,564
    Eliphalet XIV,116, 128, 189,
        360, 563, 615; XV,557,
        719; XVI,203, 527
    James XIV,107, 116-17, 128,
        154, 189, 554, 563-64,
        571, 615-17, 627; XV,440,
        719, 721, 726, 735;
        XVI,4, 6, 27, 51, 180, 205,
        208, 226, 272, 285, 505,
        649, 776; XVII,461
    James Jr. XIV,129
    James 3d XIV,116, 189
    James 5th XIV,564
    John XIV,2
    Jonathan XIV,14, 211, 214,
        217, 219-20, 399, 564;

Norris, Jonathan (Cont.)
  XV,283, 287, 289;
  XVI,286, 500; XVII, 57,
  267, 461, 639
  Joseph XIV,571, 605;
  XV,175, 716; XVI,201, 271
  Josiah XIV,399; XV,285, 291,
  410
  Moses XVI,169, 286, 500
  Samuel XIV,559, 563, 627;
  XV, 721, 748; XVI,205,
  239, 272, 505, 526, 649;
  XVII,449
  Theophilus XIV,370, 378,
  492, 503, 515
  Zebulon XIV,451, 532
Norton, Amos XIV,253, 317, 320
  Bonas XIV,11; XVII,633, 659
  Francis XVII,517, 522, 535
  James XVII,301
  John XIV,382, 490, 501, 514,
  545, 623; XV,596, 720;
  XVI, 227, 234, 272, 518,
  821; XVII,511
  Joseph XV,28
  Samuel XIV,233
  Samuel Jr. XVII,29
  Simeon XV,325
  Simon XIV,76, 83, 198, 299;
  XV, 754
  Thomas XVI,64, 74, 93
  William XVII,301
Norvie, Archibald XIV,272
Norwood, Francis XIV,645;
  XVI,23, 809; XVII,97
Nose, Enoch XV,435
Nosterous, Vincent O. XVI,29
Nott, Jesse XIV,105, 324, 464,
  578, 596
  Thomas XV,10
Notton, Benjamin XIV,8
Nowell, Mr. XVII,599
Nowland, Jonathan XVI,46, 176,
  303
Noyce, Aaron XV,406
  Benjamin XV,513
  Caleb XV,398

Noyce, Elijah XV,511
  George XV,377
  Humphrey XV,398
  James XV,398-99
  John XV,227
  Joseph XV,569
  Moses XV,399
  Nathan XV,513
  Nathaniel XV,398
  Oliver XV,329
  Samuel XV,399
Noyes,--- XVI,35
  Benjamin XVI,579-80
  Caleb XVI,530
  Cutting XIV,219; XV,406;
  XVI, 578
  Daniel XV,698
  Elijah XIV,346; XV,89
  Enoch XIV,346; XVI,530
  Friend XV,623, 629, 641;
  XVI, 547, 824; XVII,349
  Isaac XVI,255, 517
  James XIV,225, 405
  John XIV,265
  Moses XIV,71, 179, 454, 530,
  546; XVII,32
  Nathan XV,663, 670, 684,
  688; XVI,579
  Nathaniel XIV,225, 405
  Oliver XIV,405; XV,342; XVII,
  724
  Peter XVII,32
  Samuel XVI,788, 790;
  XVII,32
  Stephen XVI,527
  Thomas XVI,124, 568;
  XVII,714
  Timothy XIV,405
Nudd, Benjamin XV,327
  David XVI,300
  James XV,522
  John XIV,23, 229; XV,319,
  339
  Samuel XIV,119, 129, 150,
  189, 196, 228, 253;
  XVI,61-62, 72, 98, 106;
  XVII,360, 741

Nudd, Simon XVI,672
  Thomas XVI,64, 74, 98, 193;
    XVII,528
  William XV,656, 666, 685;
    XVI, 61-62, 72, 98, 675;
    XVII,360
Nurse, Benjamin XV,61, 110,
    541; XVI,745
  Ebenezer XVII,428
  Jonas XV,360
  Jonathan XV,360
  Joseph XV,109
  William XIV, 437, 524; XV,
    108, 542
Nute, Benjamin XIV, 631
  Captain XV, 699
  Daniel XIV,108, 123, 187
  Isaac XIV,236, 368, 375, 483,
    498, 502, 511, 518
  James XIV,18, 446; XVI,731;
    XVII,502
  John XIV,234, 407; XV,299;
    XVII,213
  Jotham XIV,369, 375, 482,
    498, 502, 511, 518, 562;
    XV,445, 724; XVI,207,
    230, 275, 335-336, 503,
    624
  Jotham Jr. XV,618
  Paul XIV,371, 384, 476, 496,
    520; XVI,526
  Samuel XIV,1, 3, 125, 188,
    554; XV,653; XVI,4, 818;
    XVII,10, 213, 268
  Simon XIV,2
Nutis, Daniel XIV,7
Nutt, John XV,176
  William XV,123, 351, 353;
    XVI, 246-47, 252-53, 503,
    506, 735
Nutter, Anthony XVII, 525,
    605,
  Benjamin XIV,296
  Ebenezer XV,256, 260, 263,
    469, 481, 496; XVI,110,
    261; XVII, 29, 433
  Grafton XV,192; XVII,29

Nutter, Hatevil XIV,345; XV,577;
    XVII, 29, 737
  Hatevil Jr. XV,583
  Henry XVII,139
  Jacob XIV,237, 259
  John XIV,235; XV,256, 259-
    60, 263; XVII,623
  Jonathan XIV,12; XVI,110
  Joseph S. XVII,360
  Jotham XIV,636
  Lemuel XIV,108, 123; XVI,
    119
  Mark XV,628, 645, 730, 734;
    XVI,18, 102, 194, 211,
    220, 239, 278, 514, 759-
    60
  Nathaniel XVII,360
  Samuel XIV,14
  William XV,749
Nutting, Ephraim XVI,259; XVII,
    437
  John XV,744

O
Oak, Nathaniel XIV,355
Oakes, John XIV,119, 150, 196
Oare, James XVII,512
Ober, Samuel XVI,534
Obrey, Dr. Frederick XIV,290;
    XV, 366, 429
O'Brian, Daniel XIV,259, 344
  John XIV,470, 604; XV,454;
    XVI, 722
O'Briant, John XV,453
O'Bryan, Charles XV,597
  John XV,716; XVII,302
Occum, Matthew XIV,289
O'Connor, William XVII,296
Odell, Ebenezer XIV,302, 439,
    527; XV,75, 215, 465,
    467, 478, 504; XVI,166-67
  John XV,520, 664, 670, 683;
    XVI,556; XVII,339
  Joseph XIV,246
  Thomas XIV,231
Odiorne, John XIV,402, 415,
    448, 534, 648, 650;
    XV,596, 728; XVI,12, 192,

Odiorne, John (Cont.) 209;
  XVII,26
  Jotham XVII,710
  Nathaniel XIV,242
  Robert XVI,264, 287, 512
  Samuel XIV,240, 258, 382,
    390, 484, 486, 490, 500-1,
    512, 514, 518-19, 549,
    647; XV, 430, 595, 728,
    734; XVI,12, 192, 209,
    232, 239, 277, 516;
    XVII,22, 33, 85
  Samuel Jr. XVI,803
  Thomas XV,458; XVII,280,
    341
Odlin, Dudley XVI,336, 905
  Elisha XV,475, 498
  Lieutenant XIV,26
  Mr. XVII,79
  William XVI,316-17
Ogden, M. XVII,154, 160, 162-
    63, 165, 167, 173, 181,
    189
O'Hara, James XVII,293
Okins, Benjamin XVI,47, 303
Olcott, Benjamin XV,203
  Peter XVII,376, 379-80
Oldham, Captain XVII,165
Oliver, Aaron XIV,35, 91, 201,
    334, 575, 639; XV,731;
    XVI, 16, 26, 857-58
  James XIV,7
  Russell XVI,737
  William XIV,380, 489, 623;
    XV,
  William XV,596, 693, 720;
    XVI,214, 234
Olivie, Laurens XVII,304
Olmstead, Ebenezer XVI,307;
    XVII, 115
  Israel XIV,164, 288; XV,733;
    XVI,45, 48, 314; XVII,116,
    254, 307
  Timothy XV,593; XVI,313;
    XVII, 116
Olney, Hezekiah XIV,264

O'Neil, John XIV,57, 183;
    XV,345, 363; XVI,840;
    XVII,308
  Samuel XVII,444
Onvelliers, Count de XVII,343
Orchard, Mr. XVII,585
Orcutt, Samuel XIV,258, 343
Ordway, Enoch XVI,729;
    XVII,427
  Jacob XIV,404
  John XIV,169, 173-74, 177,
    273, 276; XV,41; XVI,529
  Joseph XIV,19, 273, 276;
    XVI, 529
  Moses XVI,235, 268, 511,
    729, 935
  Samuel XVI,86, 91, 303
  William XVI,169-70, 246,
    253, 303, 504
Oriant, Joseph XIV,654
Orient, John XV,459, 605
  Joseph XV,460, 605
Orman, John XIV,271; XV,586
Ormond, John XVI,314
Orne, Azor XVII,124
O'Rourke, James XVI,931
Orr, Alexander XVI,920
  George XIV,358, 411;
    XVI,919-20
  James XIV,59, 183, 220, 439,
    469, 573, 693; XV,616,
    712; XVI,225, 268, 513,
    746
  John XIV,212, 215, 217, 347;
    XV,162, 174, 427, 616;
    XVI, 47, 198, 303, 320-25,
    328, 330, 334, 337, 339,
    343-44, 423-25
  Samuel XV,427, 616; XVI,47,
    55, 101
  William XV,427, 616; XVI,47,
    55
Osborn, Isaac XVII,153
  John VII,250
Osborne, George Jerry XIV,239;
    XVI,413

Osborne, Isaac XV,377
    Samuel XV,542
Osgood,--- XV,10; XVII,241-42
    Abner XIV,463, 473; XV,590;
        XVII,65, 78
    Benjamin XIV,246, 574;
        XV,616; XVI,701
    Consider XVI,752
    Ebenezer XIV,399; XV,285,
        290
    Elijah XV,63
    Enoch XIV,300; XV,168;
        XVII,25
    Hazen XV,514
    James XIV,166, 168-70, 246,
        273-76, 278, 288, 291-92,
        295; XVI,284, 529; XVII,17
    John XIV,88, 201, 246;
        XV,267-269, 272, 565;
        XVI,115
    Nathaniel XV,300, 302, 305,
        309
    Oliver XVI,81, 95, 106, 193
    Richard XIV,273, 276, 289
    Samuel XIV,326, 433, 464;
        XV, 61; XVI,284, 647
    Thomas XIV,578, 594; XV,27,
        717; XVI,201, 218, 270,
        502, 605-7, 934
    William XV,144, 242, 245-46,
        565; XVI,138, 535;
        XVII,105, 249
Osman, Richard XVII,302
Osmond, Henry XV,740
Ossy, Francis XVII,303
O'Sullivan, Valentine XVI,31,
    34, 59
Otis, Elijah XIV,115, 141, 192,
    362
    John XIV,228, 362, 618;
        XV,619, 722; XVI,206
    Paul XIV,618; XV,619, 723,
        747; XVI,206
    Richard XV,26
Otterson, James XV,267, 269,
    273
Ovendon, John XVII,22, 33, 37

Ovington, John XIV,664
Owen, Benjamin XV,603;
    XVII,220
    Jonathan XVI,932
    Robert XVII,301
    Silvanus XIV,160-61, 164,
        288; XVI,312; XVII,16
    Timothy XV,17
Oxford, Derrick XIV,607;
    XV,436, 714; XVI,200;
    XVII,422
            P
Pace, Thomas XV,626, 719
Packard, Gideon XV,227, 732;
    XVI, 22, 212; XVII,94
    Joseph XVI,153
    Oliver XV,633, 647; XVI,810-
        11
    Robert XV,662, 669, 680;
        XVI, 152, 866
    Madam XVII,692
    Samuel Jr. XVI,921
    Thomas XV,544; XVII,632,
        634, 638, 648, 660-61,
        667, 753
Paddleford, Philip XV,17; XVII,
    110
Page, Aaron XIV,110, 132, 190;
    XVII,12-13
    Abner XV,412
    Abraham XIV,570, 651;
        XV,729; XVI,28, 67, 78,
        188, 210
    Abram XVI,94
    Asa XV,568; XVI,568
    Benjamin XIV,229, 252, 641;
        XV, 411, 422, 456, 660,
        730; XVI, 18, 194, 211,
        260-61, 531, 616-17, 674,
        856; XVII,432
    Dr. Benjamin XVI,379, 477
    Caleb XIV,254; XV,349;
        XVI,168, 814, 921,
    Caleb Jr. XV,176
    Charles XVI,128, 162, 705;
        XVII,433
    Chase XIV,570, 651; XV,729;

Page, Chase (Cont.) XVI,28, 189, 210
    Coffin XIV,118, 139, 158, 191, 255, 351, 642; XV,457; XVI, 774
    Daniel XIV,242, 474; XV,320, 340, 527-28, 699; XVI,122, 164, 255, 501, 604, 617
    David XIV,67, 169, 180, 212, 216, 242, 246, 252, 309, 391, 487, 509, 513, 618; XV,457, 590, 722; XVI,206, 231, 239, 273, 281, 284, 299, 520, 613, 836, 838-39, 918; XVII,29, 49, 78
    David Jr. XIV,69; XVII,78
    Doctor XVII,320
    Edward XIV,485; XVII,87
    Eli XV,55, 204, 745
    Elijah XVI,235, 274, 522
    Enoch XIV,24; XV,249-51, 253, 255, 578, 746; XVI 876, 918
    Esquire XVII,71
    Francis XVII,528, 612, 644
    Jacob XVI,144
    James XVI,921
    Jeremiah XIV,246, 329, XVI,631, 634
    Jesse XIV,225; XV,328-31, 335, 337, 343, 568-69; XVI, 568
    Job XVI,125, 250, 255, 507
    John XIV,232, 463; XV,113, 192, 279-80, 475, 494, 522, 550, 696, 699; XVI,69, 74, 98, 127, 162, 256, 295, 507, 539; XVII, 65, 680
    John Jr. XV,473
    Jonas XVI,290
    Jonathan XIV,247, 432; XV,113, 399, 551
    Joseph XIV,229
    Josiah XIV,233

Page, Lemuel XIV,36, 98, 205, 421; XV,97, 343, 538
    Moses XIV,71, 83, 179, 198, 463, 564, 654; XV, 449, 590, 624, 727; XVI, 8, 30, 33, 59, 182, 208, 289, 291, 314; XVII,78, 113, 117, 441
    Peter XV,31, 37, 367, 372; XVI, 137, 139, 866-67; XVII,414
    Philip XIV,246, 304-5, 465-66; XVI,284, 299
    Phinehas XIV,111, 132, 190, 442, 542; XV,31, 300, 302, 305, 309
    Reuben XIV,36, 98, 205, 333; XV,217, 539; XVI,295, 812, 814-15
    Robert XVI,616-17
    Samuel XIV,36, 329, 459, 463, 538-39, 611; XV,425, 539; XVI,812, 874; XVII,78, 113, 642
    Serjeant XIV,333
    Simon XIV,118, 138, 158, 192, 255
    Stephen XIV,11; XV,398
    Taylor XIV,26, 229, 253
    Thomas XV, 15, 323, 333, 336-37, 342, 559
    Timothy XIV,586-87, 656; XV, 732; XVI,36, 39
    William XIV,116-17, 129, 189, 230, 569, 662; XV,609, 717; XVI,113, 202, 270, 358, 396, 630, 726
    William Jr. XIV,130, 189
Paige, Caleb XIV,420; XV,98
    Chase XIV,398
    John XIV,421; XV,498
    Jonathan XV,392
    Moses XIV,581; XV,600; XVII,66
    Samuel XVII,66
    Sargent XV,221

Paige, Silas XV,98
Paine, James XVII,644
  John XIV,229, 240, 253;
    XV,283, 288; XVI,528;
    XVII,22, 33, 153
  Noah XIV,274, 277, 289; XVI,
    178-79
  Richard XIV,229, 327
  Samuel XV,373, 378;
    XVI,178-79, 215, 528;
    XVII,72, 108, 111
  William XIV,27, 394
  See also Payne
Paling, Stephen XVII,101
Palmater, William XVII,300
Palmer,--- XVI,679
  Abraham XIV,159, 161, 163,
    443, 542; XV,277
  Amos XV,153-54; XVII,120
  Barnabas XVI,815-17
  Benjamin XIV,253, 652;
    XV,597; XVI,28, 846
  Christopher XVII,528, 676
  Daniel XIV,18
  Ebenezer XIV,588, 626;
    XV,358, 725; XVI,207
  Edward XIV,11
  Elnathan XIV,160-61, 165;
    XVII, 16
  Ensign XIV,2
  Henry XIV,286-87, 547
  Ichabod XV,278; XVII,118-19
  Isaac XVI,262
  Jacob XV,411
  Jaffrey XVII,536
  James XIV,64, 181, 186; XVI,
    110, 926; XVII,432
  Jeremiah XIV,413; XV,320,
    340
  John XIV,64, 181, 186, 282,
    287, 315, 467, 548, 605;
    XV, 165; XVI,130, 163,
    926; XVII, 4, 435
  Jonathan XIV,253, 351;
    XV,126, 150, 160; XVI,125
  Joseph XIV,390, 463, 486,
    508, 512-13; XV,256,

Palmer, Joseph (Cont.) 258,
  260, 263; XVII,66
  Moses XVI,538
  Ozias XIV,421
  Philbrook XIV,232
  Samuel XIV,126, 188;
    XV,294, 575, 589;
    XVI,627; XVII,11, 642
  Simeon XIV,353; XVI,316-17
  Simon XV,165; XVI,131, 163
  Stephen XIV,1; XV,402, 748,
    754; XVI,938
  Thomas XIV,240; XVII,4, 22,
    33, 323
  Trueworthy XIV,112, 147,
    195, 404
  William XIV,233, 253, 343,
    407, 625; XV,256, 259-60,
    263, 619, 722; XVI,205,
    817, 928; XVII,29
  Zadoc XV,496
Pallet, Nathaniel XIV,430
Pangborn, Richard XIV,289, 293
Pappon, Philip XIV,18
Parcey, Samuel XIV,647
Parcher, Elias XIV,344; XV,693;
  XVI,60, 70, 94; XVII,655
  Henry XVI,60, 70, 94
Park, Elijah XV,102, 664-65,
  683; XVI,736
  Phinehas XV,102, 541
Parker, Abiel XVI,159
  Abijah XV,24, 370; XVI,137
  Alexander XIV,171, 174, 177
  Amasa XIV,93-94, 202, 355,
    646; XV,732, 735; XVI,20,
    22, 191, 212, 225, 279,
    522-23, 852, 887
  Annan XIV,9
  Asa XV,92
  B. XIV,43
  Benjamin XIV,99, 205, 417,
    645; XV,446; XVI,23
  Benjamin W. XVI,259
  Colburn XV,500, 623, 629,
    641, 718; XVI,202, 219,
    270, 517, 795; XVII,349

Parker, Cole XV,486
  Coleman XIV,471; XV,499
  Daniel XV,19; XVI,252, 501,
    600; XVII,115
  Ebenezer XIV,417; XV,399;
    XVI, 530
  Elias XVI,62
  Esquire XVII,15
  Ezekiel XIV,445, 543;
    XV,157; XVII,131, 144
  Ezra XVI,888
  Henry XVI,62
  Isaac XIV,9; XVI,920
  Isaac Jr. XVI,920
  James XIV,265, 371, 379,
    647, 650; XV, 435, 595,
    635, 639, 728; XVI,13,
    102, 920; XVII, 308
  John XIV,171, 173-77, 603;
    XV, 519; XVI,147, 715,
    804; XVII, 125, 132
  Jonathan XIV,573, 590, 609;
    XV, 21, 220, 511, 613,
    631, 646; XVI,82, 100,
    106, 763
  Joseph XIV,33, 332, 335;
    XV,62, 532; XVI,168
  Josiah XIV,336, 698-99; XVI,
    885, 921; XVII,62
  Lemuel XV,593
  Leonard XIV,34, 333; XV,93,
    533
  Matthew Stanley XVI,892-93
  Mr. XVII,372
  N. XIV,531
  Obadiah XIV,243, 346;
    XV,347; XVI,740; XVII,61
  Paul XIV,464
  Pearl XIV,324; XV,370
  Peter XVI,13, 44
  Phinehas XV,740
  Reuben XV,54, 205; XVII,96
  Robert XIV,301, 303, 312,
    572; XV,207, 612, 713;
    XVI,199; XVII,139
  Samuel XIV,36, 98, 171, 174,
    176-77, 205, 247, 333,

Parker, Samuel (Cont.) 443,
    542; XV, 24, 153-54, 356,
    424; XVI,45, 301; XVII,73
  Solomon XIV,443, 542, 547;
    XVII,73
  Stephen XIV,34, 436; XV,93,
    100, 196, 219, 221-22;
    XVI, 238, 275, 509, 692,
    752; XVII,100
  Thomas XIV,265, 648, 650;
    XV, 25, 595; XVII,644
  Widow XVI,938
  William XIV,29-30, 75, 101,
    175, 178, 206-7, 346, 439,
    527, 553; XV, 213, 347,
    718; XVI,4, 336, 395, 407,
    451, 476; XVII,730
  Dr. William XVII,268, 271-72,
    281, 379
  William Jr. XIV,615
  Woods XVII,437
  Zachariah XIV,463; XVII,65
Parkhurst, Andrew XV,530
  George XIV,93, 202
  Jesse XV,75, 211
  John XVII,293
  Jonathan XV,17, 138, 376;
    XVI, 150, 310
  Jonathan Jr. XV,17, 376
  Nathan XV,40, 376
  Noah XV,633, 647; XVI,167,
    851
  Phinehas XV,591
  Samuel XIV,93, 202, 263
  Simeon XV,377
  William XIV,336, 698;
    XVII,62
Parkinson, Henry XIV,48, 75,
    153, 178; XVII,132
Parks, Elijah XV,671
  Joseph XIV,105-6, 213, 221
  Michael XIV,312, 565, 660;
    XV, 727; XVI,9, 42, 183,
    208, 581
  Noah XV,643
  Robert XIV,597; XVI,898
  Samuel XVI,840

Parks, Thaddeus XVI,158
  Thomas XV,626
Parlin, Stephen XIV,35; XV,95,
  364
Parmalee, Ezra XIV,298; XV,35,
  37
  John XV,25
Parr, James XIV,223
  Robert XVI,929
  William XVII,296
Parrish, Jacob XVII,306
Parrott, John XVII,139
Parry, James XV,533
  John XIV,600
  Joseph XIV,342
  Thomas XV,718; XVI,202
Parshley, George XIV,321;
  XV,619, 747
  John B. XIV,363
  Richard XV,747
  Samuel XV,297
  Thomas XIV,362; XV,619
Parsival, Jeremiah XVI,310
  Stephen XVI,310
Parsley, George XIV,618;
  XV,444, 723; XVI,206
  Thomas XIV,618; XV,723
  XVI,206
Parsons, Abraham XIV,232;
  XV,284, 288
  Captain XVII,220
  Daniel XIV,537; XV,550
  Dole XIV,400; XVI,93, 106;
  XVII,383
  Ebenezer XIV,93, 202; XV,63
  Edward XVII,13
  Eli XVII,205
  George XV,188
  Jethro XIV,14
  Job XV,564
  John XIV,228, 361, 364;
  XV,267, 699; XVI,660;
  XVII,29
  Joseph XIV,224, 242, 247-
  48, 253, 448-49, 534, 536;
  XV, 256-59, 261-62, 265-
  66, 527-528; XVI,62, 93,

Parsons, Joseph (Cont.) 106,
  261; XVII,25, 385, 432
  Josiah XIV,257-58; XV,668,
  679, 690; XVI,831; XVII,30
  Kendall XVI,699, 812
  Moses XV,138
  Nathaniel XV,699; XVII,25
  Noah XIV,51; XV,120, 182
  Richard XIV,237, 255, 260;
  XVII,39, 46
  Samuel XIV,310; XVI,143
  Stephen XIV,53; XV,359
  Thomas XIV,364; XV,118,
  138
  Timothy XV,118, 138, 351,
  353
  William XV,472; XVI,143
  See also Pearson
Partridge, Amos XV, 7, 57, 224
  Captain XVII,141, 335
  Eli XV,7
  John XVII,511, 527, 618,
  656, 693
  Levi XV,109
  Mr. XVII,390
  Nehemiah XVII,619
  Reuben XV,62; XVII,98
  William XVII,663, 680, 683,
  685, 691
Passmore, Thomas XIV,260
Patch, David XV,750
  Jonathan XIV,388, 495, 507,
  Jonathan XIV,516, 519
  Samuel XIV,388, 495, 507,
  516, 519
  Thomas XIV,33, 346
Patrick, Joseph XVI,562
  Matthew XIV,265
  Rufus XVI,287, 506, 655
  Samuel XV,108; XVI,159
Patridge, Amos XIV,356
Pattee, Asa XIV,171-77; XV,21
  Asa Jr. XIV,174, 176-77
  James P. XVI,257, 519
  Jeremiah XVI,141, 161
  John XIV,171, 175-77
  Loammi XV,658, 667, 674,

Pattee, Loammi (Cont.) 691;
    XVI,124, 257, 519, 823-24
  Seth XV,390; XVI,898
  William XIV,463; XV,343
  Zephaniah XIV,274
Patten, Benjamin XIV,574;
    XV,616
  Caleb XVII,14
  Daniel XIV,9
  David XV,169, 743, 754
  Grace XVI,689
  J. XIV,43
  James XIV,105, 635; XV,557,
    626; XVI,206, 274
  John XIV,73, 183, 424, 538;
    XV, 21, 168, 362, 693,
    743; XVI, 91
  Jonathan XIV,459; XV,122;
    XVI, 86, 106
  Matthew XIV,218-19; XV,71,
    112, XVI,383, 425, 909
  Nathaniel XIV,346, 572, 590,
    609, 631; XV,613-14, 714,
    744; XVI,84, 90, 106, 200,
    688
  Robert XV,111
  Samuel XIV,58, 183
  Sargent XIV,46
  William XVI,155, 256, 500
Patterson, Adam XIV,247;
    XV,72; XVI,286, 498
  Alexander XIV,43, 64, 181,
    186; XV,629, 647-48, 721;
    XVI, 205, 227, 273, 649,
    861, 926; XVII,3, 438
  Benjamin XVI,307; XVII,115,
    254
  Captain XVII,198
  Ephraim XV,152, 154, 158,
    585; XVI,307; XVII,223,
    253
  George XV,149, 160, 629,
    647-48, 721; XVI,205,
    272, 649, 861; XVII,438
  Ichabod XVII,254
  Isaac XIV,430; XV,183, 553,
    583; XVI,85, 91, 106, 285,

Patterson Isaac (Cont.) 498,
    538-39, 935
  James XV,111
  John XIV,75, 178; XV,72,
    197, 213, 394, 429
  Jonathan XVII,300
  Joseph XIV,430-31
  Peter XV,207
  Robert XIV,359; XV,351, 353;
    XVI,148, 753
  Robert Jr. XVII,259
  Robert 3d XVII,259
  Samuel XIV,64, 181, 186,
    299, 359; XVI,141, 161,
    926; XVII, 4
  Thomas XIV,35, 91, 201
  William XIV,57, 183; XV,189,
    429; XVI,921; XVII,298,
    301
Pattman, Thomas XVII,655-56
Patton, John XVII,205
Paul, Benjamin XVII,28
  Daniel XIV,369, 376, 483,
    498, 502, 511, 518;
    XVII,29
  James XV,146
  John XIV,231
  Joseph XIV,259; XVII,37
  Matthew XV,24; XVII,105
  Robert XIV,160-61, 165, 288;
    XVII,305
Paulin, Samuel XVII,297
Paulint, Antoine XVII,309
Payne, Elisha XVII,149
  Lemuel XIV,422
  Samuel XV,373, 378
  William XV,15; XVII,88
  See also Paine
Peabody, Aaron XVI,748
  Abigail XVI,402
  Daniel XIV,246
  David XV,517; XVI,259;
    XVII,437
  Isaac XIV,336, 698; XV,636;
    XVI,880; XVII,63
  Isaac Jr. XIV,417
  John XVI,286, 498

Peabody, Major XIV,701
  Moses XV,75; XVI,535
  Nathaniel XV,225, 508, 580;
    XVI, 365, 375-76, 389,
    427; XVI,487, 568;
    XVII,122, 235, 248, 336,
    338, 341-46, 349-52, 370,
    386-414
  Stephen XIV,38, 48, 78, 80,
    311, 464; XV,72-73, 140-
    41, 462-507, 594; XVI,89,
    114, 146, 391, 555-57,
    729; XVII, 225, 229
  Thomas XV,73, 283, 286,
    314-15, 317; XVI,286, 498
Peaca, Thomas XIV,616
Peacefull, Thomas XVI,930
Peach, John XIV,308
Peacock, James XV,50, 224
  John XIV,356; XV,52
  Samuel XV,225
Peak, Lemuel XVI,315
Peake, Israel W. XV,15
  Matthew XV,17
Peaple, Robert XVII,261
Pearcival, John XVII,301
Pearl, Benjamin XIV,235
  John XIV,363, 407
  Joseph XIV,562, 637
  Paul XIV,625
  Simeon XIV,625
Pearle, John XVI,913
  Joseph XV,445, 619, 724;
    XVI, 207, 230, 275, 523,
    818
  Paul XV,619, 724
  Phinehas XV,31
  Simeon XV,619
  Simon XV,724
Pearse, Joseph XIV,320
  Peter XVII,142
Pearson, Daniel, XIV,459
  Dole XVI,62, 71
  Isaac XV,186, 515
  Jethro XVI,905
  John XIV,345; XV,267, 270,
    273; XVII,297, 360, 705

Pearson, Joseph XIV,474, 544;
    XV,5, 13, 59, 84, 187,
    232, 282, 289, 580, 582,
    691, 751; XVI,71, 166,
    285, 333, 345, 350, 356,
    367, 539, 555; XVII, 22,
    84, 93, 113, 422
  Kendall XV,631, 646
  Morse XV,267, 270, 273
  Moses XIV,417; XV,19, 138,
    267; XVII,80, 83
  Nathan XV,554
  Nathaniel XIV,391, 487, 508,
    512
  Noah XIV,185, 250
  Richard XVII,261
  Stephen XIV,185
  Thomas XV,138
  Timothy XV,554
  William XIV,105; XV,490;
    XVI, 749
  See also Parsons
Pease, David XVI,116
  Eliphalet XV,284, 288
  John XV,283, 290; XVI,112,
    235, 273, 511, 725
  Joseph XIV,232; XV,284, 287
  Nathaniel XIV,232
  Noah XVI,578
  Samuel XIV,66, 181, 304,
    465
  Zebulon XV,243, 245-46
Peaslee, Abraham XIV,317, 319
  David XV,623, 641; XVII,349
  Jacob XIV,226
  Jonathan XIV,225
  Mr. XVII,379, 385
  Robert XIV,312, 465, 476;
    XVII, 314, 316, 329
  Samuel XVI,850
  Zaccheus XVI,265
Peasley, David XV,629; XVI,830
  Joseph XVI,909
  Robert XV,574
  Zaccheus XV,733; XVI,48
Peavey, Abel XIV,3
  Anthony XVI,122, 164

Peavey, Daniel XIV,361
  Durgin XVI,625
  Edward XIV,372, 385, 496,
    581, 648, 650; XV,449,
    601; XVI, 13, 758
  Ichabod XVI,220
  John XV,324
  Joseph XIV,230; XV,167
  Thomas XVI,625
  William XIV,446; XVI,6, 68,
    79, 92, 286, 523, 820
  William C. XIV,322, 365
  Winthrop XVI,235, 242, 274,
    504, 624, 628
Peck, Captain XVII,542
  Eba, XV,374
  Ebenezer XVII,110
  Jeremiah XVI,159
  Matthew XIV,274, 289; XV,
    138, 377
  Richard XV,25
  Simeon XVII,369
  Walter XV,156; XVII,67, 109,
    143
Pecker, Ebenezer XVII,261
  James XVII,306
Peckouth, John XIV,1
Pedrick, Joseph XVI, 236,
    498
Pegley, Benjamin XIV,463
Peirce, Abraham XV,471
  Asa XIV,631; XV,740; XVI,15,
    25, 186, 588; XVII,63
  Benjamin XIV,3; XV,47, 246,
    502; XVI,234, 264, 426,
    522, 879
  D. XIV,17
  Daniel XVI,246, 515, 899
  David XV,47, 643, 648
  Ebenezer XV,47
  Edward XIV,12
  Ephraim XIV,419; XV,636;
    XVI,41
  Ezra XVI,427
  Israel XIV,18
  Jacob XIV,205; XVI,535
  John XVI,652; XVII,142
Peirce, Joseph XIV,320, 391,
    509, 513; XVI,234, 264
  Joshua XIV,264; XVII,733,
    735, 738
  Nathaniel XIV,12
  Nehemiah XIV,573, 590, 609
  Noah XIV,227, 257
  Oliver XV,696, 698
  Robert XIV,9
  Samuel XIV,410; XVII,328
  Simon XV,643, 648
  Solomon XIV,346
  Stephen XIV,421
  Timothy XIV,264
  See also Pierce
Peirson, Samuel XV,320, 331,
    335-337, 340
  See also Pearson
Pelham, Stephen XIV,268, 270,
    290
Pemberton, James XIV,88, 200;
    XV, 206, 517, 632, 636;
    XVI,246, 253, 515, 697
  James Jr. XVI,636
Pendall, Elisha XV,66; XVI,661-
    662; XVII,96
  John XV,603; XVI,206, 229,
    274; XVII,236
Pender, Benjamin XV,618
  Jeremiah XV,311
  John XV,43
Pendergast, Edmund XV,311
  Thomas XV,635, 639
Pendexter, Samuel XVI,925
  William XIV,28
Pendlebury, James XVI,931
Pendleton, Bryan XVII,512, 527
Penhallow, John XVII,19, 139,
    220-21, 244-45, 262, 264,
    270, 273-74, 373, 448
  Samuel XIV,2-3, 386; XVI,
    378; XVII,139, 324-25,
    655, 664, 680, 683, 690,
    693, 695, 699-700, 702,
    710, 715, 728, 753
  Samuel Jr. XIV,3
Penn, Mr. XVII,156

Penner, Benjamin XV,445
Penniman, Adna XIV,556, 661;
    XV, 726; XVI,6, 51, 180-
    82, 208; XVII,269
Penny, Henry XIV,8; XVII,629,
    658, 665, 669, 679, 704
Peoples, John XVI,930
Pepperell, Andrew XVII,333
    Mary Anne XVII,333
Percell, John XVII,298
Percival, See Perseval
Perham, Asa XIV,436, 525, 575,
    622; XV, 443, 722
    John XVII,461
    William XVII,461
Perigo, David XVI,303
Perkins, Abraham XIV,243, 369,
    374, 376, 480, 482-83,
    498, 501, 509, 511, 518,
    520
    Adam XIV,562, 636; XV,618,
    724; XVI,207
    Barnabas XV,17
    Benjamin XIV,370, 379, 433,
    493, 504, 515, 564, 599;
    XV,169, 191, 562, 713;
    XVI,122, 164, 199, 807;
    XVII,435
    Daniel XIV,270; XVI,241
    David XIV,300, 399, 423; XV,
    168; XVI,585
    Ebenezer XIV,125, 188;
    XV,745; XVII,11
    Elisha XIV,36; XV,217;
    XVII,101
    Ephraim XIV,114, 141, 192,
    259; XV,294; XVI,627;
    XVII,36
    Ezra XIV,445, 543; XVII,109
    Gideon XIV,233
    Gilbert XIV,372, 385, 497
    Isaac XVI,241; XVII,629
    James XIV,11, 18, 229;
    XVII,41
    James Jr. XIV,11
    John XIV,3; XV,512; XVII,435
    John Jr. XVII,25

Perkins, Jonathan XIV,210, 214,
    217-18, 220, 350-51, 564,
    599, 628; XV,457, 710,
    721; XVI,3, 51, 121, 164,
    180, 182, 197, 223, 248,
    267, 527; XVII,266, 441,
    446
    Joseph XIV,225, 312, 405;
    XV, 191, 474, 494, 632;
    XVI, 18, 115, 295, 534,
    557; XVII, 25
    Joseph Jr. XV,636
    Joshua XIV,18
    Josiah XV,667, 679; XVI,528,
    765
    Lemuel XIV,372, 385, 497
    Moses XIV,110, 132, 190; XV,
    284, 321, 340
    Nathaniel XIV,65, 125, 182,
    186, 188, 446, 540;
    XV,294; XVII,4, 10, 214
    Pelatiah XIV,237
    Peter XV,277; XVI,314
    Reuben XIV,117, 129, 189;
    XVI, 281
    Samuel XIV,22, 228, 361;
    XVI, 918
    Solomon XIV,407
    Thomas XIV,550; XV,430;
    XVI,864
    William XIV,156, 182, 371,
    504, 515; XV,179, 751;
    XVI,115, 529; XVII,296,
    716
    William A. XIV,65, 186;
    XVII,4
Perrin, Eliphalet XV,756
    Thomas XV,753; XVII,753
Perry, Abijah XVI,884; XVII,62
    Abraham XIV,627; XV,619,
    721, 748; XVI,205, 226,
    240, 272, 504, 639, 920
    David XIV,334
    Ebenezer XIV,302, 390, 438,
    440, 480; XV,79, 108,
    196, 216, 451, 517, 519;
    XVI,885

Perry, Dr. Ebenezer XVI,885
Edward XV,728
Ephraim XVI,922
Ichabod XIV,639; XV,730;
XVI, 15, 17, 26, 194, 211,
241, 278, 522, 752
Jacob XIV,247, 579
James XV,700, 704, 740;
XVI,174
John XIV,586; XV,715;
XVI,200
Jonas XIV,103, 207, 303,
585, 631; XV,451-52, 731;
XVI,16, 26, 588, 885
Joseph XIV,349
Martin XV,324; XVI,108
Moses XIV,344; XVI,172, 174
Richard XIV,260, 484-85,
550; XV,430; XVI,214,
906, 916; XVII,47, 85
Richard Jr. XVII,86
Samuel XIV,381, 489, 586,
650; XV,728; XVI,13
Solomon XIV,264
Stephen XVI,906
Thomas XIV,471; XV,632,
635; XVI,697
William XIV,53, 185, 540;
XVI, 906, 916
Perseley, John XV,575
Perseval, Azel XV,591
Jeremial XV,591
Pervear, Joseph XIV,413
Josiah XIV,110, 133, 190
Noyes XIV,110, 132, 190
Pervue, Henry XVII,306
Petegrence, Monwell XIV,345
Peters, Abel XVI,933
Colonel XVII,241
Daniel XV,746
David XIV,7
David Jr. XIV,8
Ebenezer XIV,356
George XVI,933
Hugh XVII,508, 599
Israel XV,4, 746
James XIV,568; XV,723

Peters, James Jr. XIV,632
John XV,129, 186, 406, 731,
735; XVI,37, 39, 87, 99,
190, 212, 228, 278
Philip XIV,471, 594
Robertson XV,243, 245-46
Peterson, Andrew XVII,619,
Daniel XV,161, 163
Dr. Daniel XVI,424
John XIV,145, 194; XVI,576;
XVII,9
Jonas XVII,608
Robert XV,552
Willet XVI,827; XVII,43
Petiher, George XVII,306
Pettee, James P. XVI,257, 519
Loammi XVI,124, 257, 519,
823-824
William XVII,65
Pettegrew, William XIV,578, 598
Pettes, Joseph XIV,356
Pettibone, Jacob XVI,308, 310
Petties, James XIV,4
Pettigrew, Alexander XV,17, 138
William XV,711; XVI,198,
267, 313
Pettingill, Abbot XV,568; XVI,
825-26
Abraham XIV,69, 180
Andrew XIV,261; XV,127,
163, 185
Benjamin XIV,570, 601;
XV,515, 712, 742
Caleb XIV,167, 170; XVII,14
David XV,127, 166
Ephraim XV,300, 302, 305,
309
Jethro XIV,468, 570, 605;
XV, 716; XVI,201, 224,
269, 503, 617
John XV,717
Jonathan XIV,469, 578, 593;
XVI,202, 221, 248, 270
Joshua XIV,103, 208;
XV,215, 464, 466, 477,
504
Matthew XIV,242; XV,127,

216

Pettingill, Matthew (Cont.) 165
  Moses XV,214; XVI,297
  Nathaniel XIV,84, 199
  Samuel XIV,100; XV,75, 529
  William XIV,574, 639;
    XV,617, 731; XVI,15, 25,
    186, 211
Pettis, John XVI,239, 568
Petts, Isaac XIV,12
  Thomas XVII,14
Petty, Reuben XVI,606, 608
  William XV,329
  Zephaniah XIV,167, 169
Peverley, Benjamin XIV,240,
    343; XVII,22, 33
  Frederick XIV,259; XVII,37
  John XIV,648-49; XV,595,
    728; XVI,12, 192, 209
  Joshua XV,705-6
  Kinman XVII,139
  Thomas XIV,463, 473;
    XVII,66, 78
Phelps, Alexander XVII,118,
    120, 250
  Captain XIV,17
  Daniel XIV,548
  Davenport XV,142, 158-59,
    426; XVI,387; XVII,118-
    19, 233
  Jeremiah XIV,160-61, 163
  John XIV,267
  Joshua XVI,247, 253, 516
  Dr. Martin XVII,375
  Nathan XIV,33
  Nathaniel XVI,728
  Samuel XIV,346, 588, 593;
    XV, 277-78, 438; XVI, 247,
    253, 259, 516; XVII,261,
    437
Phenix, Joshua XIV,500, 512
Philbrick, Abner XVI,933
  Benjamin XV,568; XVI,568
  Caleb XVII,435
  Daniel XIV,138, 158, 192,
    565, 660; XV,319, 339,
    727; XVI, 209

Philbrick, David XIV,23, 118;
  XV,256, 259-260, 264;
  XVI,65, 75
  Ebenezer XVII,740
  Edmund XIV,351
  James XIV,19; XV,357; XVI,
    158, 912
  Jedidiah XVI,615
  John XIV,33
  Jonathan XIV,269, 271;
    XV,411; XVI,284;
    XVII,675, 693
  Joseph XIV,296; XVI,129,
    162
  Nathaniel XIV,189; XVI,616,
    661; XVII,434
  Page XV,696
  Richard XIV,230, 413; XV,
    523
  Samuel XIV,443, 354;
    XV,113-14, 256, 259-60,
    263, 327, 428, 527;
    XVI,870; XVII,53
  Simon XIV,118, 139, 158,
    192, 351
  Thomas XVII,675
Philbrook, Daniel XVI,10, 43,
    184, 581
  David XVI,94, 106
  Ebenezer XIV,3
  Edmund XIV,230
  George XVII,360
  Isaac XIV,2
  Jedidiah XVII,32
  John XIV,252, 551; XVII,360,
    667, 669
  Jonathan XIV,23, 290
  Joseph XVI,659
  Major XIV,363
  Nathan XIV,253
  Nathaniel XIV,117, 130
  Perkins, XIV,230
  Richard XIV,230
  Robert Tufton XVII,360
  Samuel XIV,402, 415;
    XV,747; XVII,360

Philbrook, Thomas XVII,612, 619
Phillips, Alpheus XVII,118-19, 250
   Benjamin XIV,657; XV,459, 605, 731, 735; XVI, 36, 39, 41, 190, 212, 400, 798, 800, 802; XVII,221, 235
   Israel XVII,527
   James XIV,88, 200, 334; XVII, 629, 694
   John XIV,657; XV,459, 590, 605, 731; XVI,36, 39, 41, 190, 212, 233, 278, 307, 517, 798; XVII,80, 82, 115, 502
   Nathaniel XVI, 225
   Nehemiah XV,633, 647, 732, 735; XVI,21, 23, 102, 191, 212, 241, 279, 517, 798
   Noah XVII,17
   Norton XIV,238
   Peter XV,717; XVI,201, 218, 270, 934
   Samuel XV,717
   William XIV,317, 320
Philpot, James XIV,550; XV,430
   James Jr. XIV,550; XV,430
   John XIV,125, 188; XV,286, 294, 296, 315, 317; XVII,10
   Richard XVI,904
Phinney, Colonel XV,750
Phipps, Captain XIV,13
   Justice XVII,693
   Thomas XIV,6; XVII,693, 711, 713, 730, 738
   William XVII,631
Piasett, Benjamin XIV,10
Picard, Alexandre XVII,305
Picker, Thomas XVI,119
Pickering, Boston XVI,61, 68, 72, 99
   Colonel XVII,403, 406
   Ephraim XVI,369, 760
   James XIV,248; XVII,26

Pickering, John XIV,22; XVI,481; XVII,511, 513, 527, 620, 622-23, 625; XVII,627, 629-31, 635, 643, 650-51, 658, 665, 676, 710, 727, 749
   John Jr. XVII,656
   Levi XIV,232, 248, 452, 532; XVII,26
   Thomas XIV,227, 257; XVII,737
   Timothy XVII,159
   Tumbril XVI,237, 245, 274, 507
   Winthrop XIV,314; XV,468, 480, 496; XVI,505
   Winthrop Jr. XIV,338
Pickett, James XIV,343
   John XIV,250
Pickoway, Nicholas XIV,10
Pidge, Henry XV,750
Pierce, Amos XV,48, 196, 223; XVII,94
   Asa XIV,336, 584; XV,211, 451-452, 731; XVI,211
   Benjamin XV,224; XVI,145, 153, 235, 269, 882; XVII,100
   Calvin XVI,153
   Daniel XV,48; XVI,253, 805; XVII,95, 139
   David XV,633; XVI,18, 603; XVII,94
   Ebenezer XVII,28
   Ephraim XIV,33; XV,88, 210, 632, 743; XVI,44, 691
   Israel XIV,230
   Jacob XIV,98
   James XV,525
   Joseph XIV,487
   Nehemiah XV,541, 614, 744; XVI, 320-21, 327, 329, 331, 339, 345, 426
   Nehemiah Jr. XVI,335
   Simeon XV,633
   Simon XVI,18, 44, 603
   Thomas XIV,235, 520; XV,48

218

Pierce, William XV,75, 530
  See also Peirce
Piercy, John XVII,298
Pigeon, David XIV,9
  Samuel XIV,7
Piggsley, Robert XIV,4
Pigsley, Alexander XV,604
  Benjamin XV,604; XVII,66,
  110
Pike, Benjamin XVI,676
  Dudley XIV,234; XV,298
  Henry XVI,282; XVII,29
  Isaac XVII,124
  Jacob XVI,748
  James XIV,44; XVII,28
  Jeremiah XVI,109, 165
  John XV,438
  Jonathan XVI,296
  Joseph XVII,124
  Moses XIV,160-61, 165;
    XV,279-280, 592-93;
    XVI,313, 541, 914;
    XVII,89, 116
  Nathaniel XIV,13; XVI,63, 73,
    97
  Perkins XV,242, 245-46;
    XVI,67, 78, 98
  Robert XIV,134, 191; XV,242-
    44, 246, 248; XVII,538,
    597, 602, 617
  Robert Jr. XVII,5
  Samuel XIV,9
  Simeon XIV,44
  Uriah XV,347
  William XIV,135, 191, 251;
    XV, 392
Pile, George XVII,300
Pillsbury, David XVI,66, 77, 93,
  257, 520
  Edmund XIV,398
  Ezra XVI,874
  Jacob XVI,915
  Jonathan XIV,232
  Joseph XV,169; XVII,426
  Josiah XVII,254
  Richard XVI,314; XVII,116,
    254

Pillsbury, Richard Jr. XVII,254
Pilsbury, Benjamin XV,400
  Jonathan XV,526
Pindell, John XIV,607
Pinder, Benjamin XVI,504, 639;
  XVII,717
  Jeremiah XIV,323
  John XV,596; XVI,241;
    XVII,717
  Thomas XV,257
Pingree, Ebenezer XV,25
Pingrey, Sylvanus XVI,314
Pinkerton, John XIV,457-59,
  539; XV,583
  Major XV,453
Pinkham, Abijah XIV,234
  Daniel XIV,108, 123, 187,
    235, 406; XV,628, 645,
    722; XVI, 206, 273, 507,
    667-68
  Isaac XIV,235, 618; XV,619,
    722; XVI,206, 233, 710
  John XVI,889
  Joseph XIV,21, 235; XV, 573;
    XVI,118
  Moses XIV,18, 236, 363; XVI,
    907
  Paul XIV,618; XV,619, 723
  Richard XVII,501
  Samuel XVI,119
  Thomas XIV,361; XVI,119
Pinkney, Charles C. XVII,196
Pinner, Benjamin XIV,369, 375,
  400, 498, 562, 636;
    XV,243, 245, 724;
    XVI,207, 230, 241, 275
  Jeremiah XV,571
  John XVII,644
  Thomas XIV,448, 535;
    XV,260, 264
Pinson, John XVII, 293
Piper, David XIV,660;XV, 449
  600, 727; XVI,10, 43, 184,
    209, 281
  Gideon XVI,264, 789
  Jabez XIV,525
  James XIV,346; XV,346

Piper, John XIV,362, 364, 581,
  660; XV,419, 600, 727;
  XVI,10, 43, 184, 209, 281
  Josiah XVII,27
  Mr. XVII,262-63, 272-75
  Nathan XIV,229
  Nathaniel Jr. XIV,588
  Samuel XIV,71, 179, 229,
  257, 402, 415, 424;
  XV,175, 544, 654, 684;
  XVI,196, 215; XVII,30
  Thomas XIV,159, 161, 165,
  233, 288, 580, 660;
  XV,448, 598, 727; XVI,10,
  43, 45, 103, 310, 920
Pitcher, William XVI,840
Pitio, Thomas XIV,653
Pitman, Connor XIV,372, 384,
  496, 505, 517
  Deliverance XVII,682
  Ebenezer XVI,68, 79, 96;
  XVII, 435
  Ezekiel XIV,13, 239; XVII,23,
  39
  Francis XVII,719, 721
  Isaac XIV,502
  James XVII,757
  John XIV,239; XVII,23, 39
  Joseph XIV,322, 617; XV,723
  Mark XIV,343; XVII,23, 31,
  39
  Nathaniel XIV,239; XVII, 23,
  39, 139, 682
  Nehemiah XIV,18
  Samuel XIV,14, 296
  William XIV,13; XVII,716
Pitts, Ephraim XV,525
  Thomas XIV,167, 170, 280,
  288, 566; XV,606, 609,
  729; XVI, 31, 34, 59, 103,
  187, 210, 220, 277, 501,
  611, 820
Place, Abraham XIV,18
  Amos XIV,234, 372, 385,
  497, 505, 516; XV,619
  David XIV,234, 242; XVII,465

Place, Ebenezer XIV,28-29
  George XIV,234; XV,575;
  XVII,261
  John XIV,234, 447, 540
  Joseph XIV,69, 180, 402,
  415, 448, 535; XV,324
  Joshua XIV,624; XV,619, 724
  Richard XVI,817; XVII,664
  Samuel XIV,234
Plaisted, Elisha XVI,109, 165
  Ichabod XVII,633, 676, 692
  John XVII,625, 643, 665,
  683, 693, 710, 713
  Joseph XIV,258, 343
  Samuel XV,172
  William XIV,1, 296, 343, 432;
  XV,325
Plastridge, Caleb XV,42, 376;
  XVII,88
Platt, John XIV,419
Platts, Abel XV,20, 98, 471; XVI,
  274, 814
  Abel Jr. XIV,36; XV,502; XVI,
  236, 518, 815
  Ebenezer XV,539; XVI,83, 96,
  106
  John XV,744
  Joseph XIV,36; XV,217, 539
  Joseph Jr. XV,97
  Thomas XVI,103
Plumer, Beard XVII,261
  Bitfield XIV,429; XV,187
  David XIV,579; XV,453-54
  Gershom XIV,550; XV,430
  Jabish XV,329
  John XIV,340; XV,608
  Joseph XIV,407
  Nathan XIV,579; XV,453-54
  Nathaniel XV,716
  William XVI,645
Plumley, John XV,12, 368
  Joseph XIV,442, 544; XV,28,
  368, 750
Plummer, Anna XVI,427
  Beard XV,576
  David XVI,722

Plummer, Davis XIV,604; XV,715
  Gershom XIV,230, 363; XVII,29
  Jabez XIV,225; XV,343; XVI,427
  John XVI,756, 817-18
  Joseph XIV,234
  Nathan XIV,411; XVI,201
  Nathaniel XIV,604; XVI,721, 914-15
Plunkeld, Abraham XVII,29
Poland, Josiah XV,172
Pollard, Amos XV,69
  Barnard XV,748
  Barton XIV,650; XV,562, 658, 667, 674, 691; XVI,103, 156, 192, 196, 209, 232, 277, 518, 708, 807-8
  Benjamin XIV,34
  Ebenezer XIV,346; XVII,61
  Elijah XIV,327, 628; XV,283, 290, 721; XVI,204, 233, 241, 272, 518, 808
  Ezekiel XIV,341, 564, 628; XV, 283, 290, 721, 748; XVI,204, 226, 241, 272-73, 518, 808
  Hezekiah XV,635, 639, 721; XVI, 205, 518, 807-8
  John XVI,68, 79
  John Jr. XIV,346; XVII,60
  Jonathan XIV,226, 340; XV,560
  Joseph XIV,34; XV,93, 355, 534
  Samuel XV,70, 517
  Thomas XV,69, 207
  Timothy XIV,247, 346; XVII,60
Polley, Joseph XIV,605; XV,715; XVI,201, 888-89
Polluck, Thomas XIV,109, 123, 187, 251
Pomeroy, Eleazer XVI,603
  Dr. Josiah XVI,435
  Richard XVII,621

Pomeroy, William XVII,655-56, 664
Pomfret, William XVII,502
Pomp, Peter XIV,570, 651; XV, 729; XVI,28
Pool, Henry XVII,308
  Jonathan XVII,267
  William W. XV,511
Poole, John XVI,2
  Jonathan XVI,197
  Dr. Jonathan XIV,552, 591; XV, 710; XVI,529
  William XVI,377
Poor, David XV,396
  Eliphalet XV,396
  Enoch XIV,37, 48-49, 107, 111, 120-21, 154, 187, 307, 309, 481, 552, 615; XV,138, 276, 421, 432-33, 726; XVI,4, 56-57, 105, 208, 217, 333, 335, 356, 923; XVII,13, 210, 227, 230-31, 238, 246, 262, 267, 285, 291, 354, 378
  Jeremiah XIV,225; XV,398; XVI, 530
  John XIV,338
  Jonathan XVI,402
  Martha XVI,333, 335, 338, 342
  Michael XV,635, 639; XVI,102, 589-90
  Moses XIV,42, 53
  Peter XIV,43; XV,744
  Sarah XVI, 333
Pope, Simeon XV,621, 634, 644; XVI,872, 874
  Simon XV,670, 688; XVII,431
  Thomas XV,183
  William XIV,261, 568, 589, 633; XV,163-64, 546-47, 582, 610, 723; XVI,535, 699
Popham, William XVII,303
Popkin, Captain XV,751
Popple, Charles XVII,205
Porter, Calvin XV,277; XVI,314

Porter, Chandler XV,31-34
Daniel XV,745
Ebenezer XIV,356
Eleazer XV,43, 379; XVI,314
Eleazer M. XV,156; XVI,312;
XVII,143
Elijah XV,383; XVI,314
James XV,32-34
John XV,58
Joseph XIV,655; XV,729;
XVI,32, 34, 59
Nathan XIV,351
Nathaniel XIV,542; XV,18,
375
Nathaniel Jr. XIV,445; XV,40
Dr. Nathaniel XIV,339, 555,
638
Nehemiah XIV,99, 205
Noah XIV,594; XV,32, 144,
446, 717; XVI,202, 519,
809; XVII,457, 467
Silas XVI,238, 268, 510, 597,
701, 935
Thomas XV,153; XVI,315
Thomas Jr. XVI,314
William XV,591; XVI,789
Post, Aaron XVII,118-19, 250
Eldad XV,153; XVI,924
Eldad Jr. XV,154
Jeremiah XV,152, 154, 158
Pottell, John XVII,513
Potter, Aaron XVI,255, 287
Abraham XIV,570, 652;
XV,729; XVI,28
Anthony XV,187
Barnabas XVII,306
Ebenezer XV,108, 216;
XVI,702-3
Ephraim XV,752
Jacob XIV,575; XVI,915
James XV,609
John XV,412
Joseph XIV,93, 202-3, 553,
632; XV,718; XVI,4-5, 51,
182, 203, 271; XVII,268,
440, 442
Josiah XV,14

Potter, Lieutenant XVI,301
Samuel XIV,592; XV,438,
716; XVI,201, 270, 303,
323, 330, 338, 340, 428,
515, 764
Stephen XV,482
Thomas XVII,250
Pottle, Levi XVI,237, 245, 269,
518, 822, 845
Samuel XVI,933
Potts, Thomas XV,460
Povey, Thomas XVII,508-9, 536
Powder, Tobias XVII,293
Powell, Arthur XVII,669
Benjamin XV,621, 634, 645,
732, 735; XVI,40, 102,
186, 212, 221, 279, 872,
874-75; XVII, 438
Elisha XV,426; XVI,307, 933;
XVII,114
John XIV,304, 322, 365;
XV,670, 688, 697, 717;
XVI, 506, 649; XVII,469
Moses XV,183
Oliver XVII,496
Robert XVII,526
Samuel XIV,302, 391, 487,
508; XIV,513
Thomas XIV,14, 102, 208,
266, 572, 639; XV, 611,
727, 747; XVI,9, 42, 183,
208, 259, 529; XVII,436
William XIV,3, 301, 391, 487,
509, 513, 574, 600, 663;
XV, 615, 698, 715;
XVI,200, 874; XVII,124,
639-40
Powers, Abner XIV,471, 594;
XV, 446, 717; XVI,202,
224, 241, 270, 518, 597,
809; XVII,468
Andrew XVI,312
Asahel XV,144, 631, 646;
XVI, 763, 812
Benjamin XV,9, 42
David XV,39
Elliot XIV,35; XV,96

Powers, Ezekiel XIV,427; XV,51
  Francis XIV,43; XV,210, 624,
    632, 636, 744; XVII,214
  Francis G. XVI,691
  Gideon XIV,420
  Gideon Jr. XV,534
  Grant XVI,23, 44, 145
  Isaac XIV,280, 288
  Jerusha XVI,598
  John XVI,200
  Jonah XVI,341
  Jonathan XIV,258, 343, 600;
    XV, 715, 743
  Jonathan Jr. XIV,573;
    XV,615
  Joseph XIV,105, 326, 464,
    594; XV,11, 31, 143, 446;
    XVI,519, 809; XVII,468
  Josiah XIV,85, 199, 356, 644;
    XV,732; XVI,21, 332, 428
  Lydia XVI,598
  Moses XVI,235, 522, 853
  Nahum XIV,33, 280, 288;
    XV,381, 593, 744; XVI,797
  Nathaniel XIV,471, 594;
    XV,9, 446, 717; XVI,202,
    218, 239, 270, 518, 597-
    99, 809, 934; XVII,468
  Paul XV,220, 534
  Pierce XVI,332, 341, 429
  Samson XIV,32; XV,210, 743;
    XVI, 377
  Simeon XIV,471, 578, 593;
    XV, 438, 717; XVI,218,
    270, 499, 549, 597-99,
    934; XVII,104, 468
  Simon XVI,202
  Stephen XIV,258, 302, 391,
    487, 508, 513; XVI,26,
    614; XVII, 10
  Thomas XV,717; XVI,202,
    218, 270, 597, 934
  Whitcomb XIV,34, 326, 333,
    464; XV,9, 32, 93, 145,
    219, 533
  William XIV,172, 174, 176-
    77, 441, 527; XV,150, 160

Prady, Christopher XVII,307
Pratt, Abel XVI,303
  Asa XV,217, 701, 704;
    XVI,159, 176, 522, 877
  Ebenezer XIV,91, 201
  Eleazer XV,360
  Ezra XV,745
  John XIV,356; XV,57;
    XVI,152
  Jonathan XV,733; XVI,48,
    265, 302, 305, 679, 783
  Joseph XVI,783
  Josiah XV,590, 733, XVI,48,
    265, 302, 305, 679;
    XVII,114
  Nathaniel XIV,34; XV,21,
    356; XVII,101
  Thomas XIV,33, 43, 572,
    590, 609; XV,436, 613,
    714, 743; XVI, 200, 223,
    269, 331, 340, 431, 509,
    529, 607, 692
  William XIV,607; XV,425, 714
Pray, Captain XVII,371
  Ebenezer XIV,240, 259;
    XVII,42
  Joseph XIV,250
  Joshua XIV,240, 259; XVII,36
  Peter XIV,236
  Samuel XIV,240; XVII,28
Prebble, Joseph XIV,623
  Jerediah XIV,344
Prentice, Benjamin XV,153-54
  Nathaniel Sartal XIV,297,
    416; XV,29; XVI,551
  Solomon XV,29
Prentiss, Simeon XIV,105
  Thaddeus XIV,105
Presbury, James XV,168
  Richard XVI,207, 239, 275
  William XVI,920
Presby, Joseph XIV,51, 185, 410
  Richard XIV,623; XV,725
Prescott, Benjamin XVI,534
  Captain XV,449, 601
  Colonel XVI,378
  Dominicus XIV,589

Prescott, Dudley XV,267, 269,
271, 474, 494
Ebenezer XIV,230, 413; XV,
319, 339
Edward XIV,451, 532; XV,
283, 290; XVII,27
Elisha XIV,132, 190, 231,
312-313, 351; XV,319,
339, 565
Elisha Jr. XIV,110
Elizabeth XVI,615
James XV,319, 331, 339;
XVI, 255, 508; XVI,287,
621
James Jr. XVI,676
Jeremiah XIV,261; XV,301,
304, 306, 308; XVI,116,
369, 646-647
James XIV,110, 132, 190,
450, 534
John XIV,11, 327, 399, 452,
532
Jonas XV,532
Dr. Jonas XVI,445
Jonathan XIV,11, 232, 253,
413, 565, 651;XV, 256,
258, 260, 263, 470, 506,
729; XVI,28, 131, 163,
210; XVII,80, 83, 641
Jonathan Jr. XIV,253
Joseph XIV,399; XV,283,
286, 314-17; XVII,25
Joshua XIV,11, 297
Josiah XIV,398
Marston XIV,111
Martin XIV,110
Nathan XIV,299; XVII,25
Samuel XIV,116, 130, 189;
XV, 302-3, 305, 309, 524,
565
Solomon XV,19
William XIV,33, 39, 44, 67,
181, 229, 252, 354, 413;
XV, 412, 743; XVI,97
William P. XV,169; XVI,68,
79, 285, 508, 615

Pressey, Benjamin XVI,285, 520
James XVI,88, 91, 106
Paskey XIV,314, 467, 548;
XV, 164, 698
Percy XIV,302
Presson, Benjamin XIV,463,
657; XV,731; XVI,36, 39,
195, 212
Isaac XIV,333
Moses XVI,169
Richard XIV,14; XVI,514, 766
William XIV,566, 656;
XV,609; XV,732; XVI,40,
212
Preston, Abner XIV,575, 593;
XV, 716; XVI,201; XVII,92
Benjamin XV,460, 605;
XVI,799; XVII,66
Isaac XIV,268, 271, 289; XVI,
158, 314
John XVII,655
Moses XVI,170
Samuel XV,165, 546, 582;
XVII, 259
Theophilus XV,66
William XIV,211, 215, 217,
219-220, 230; XV,609;
XVI,35, 189, 915; XVII,655
William Jr. XV,460, 605
Pribble, See Prebble
Price, Benjamin XVII,208
John XIV,7
Nathaniel XVII,114
Thomas XVII,158-60, 168,
180, 182, 184, 207-8
Prichard, Amos XV,100, 356
Jeremiah XV,710; XVI,3, 51,
180, 197, 525; XVII,266
Paul XVI,762-64; XVII,102
William XV,716
See also Pritchard
Pridham, Isaac XIV,369, 374,
482, 498, 511; XVI,234
Priest, Asa XVI,534
Joel XIV,264; XV,633, 648;
XVI, 41, 44, 311
Jonathan XVI,536

224

Priest, Quick XIV,226
    Thomas XIV,240, 256, 259;
        XVI, 325; XVII,22, 33, 37,
        39
    Thomas Jr. XVII,22, 33
    William XIV,259, 334, 344,
        436; XV,95; XVI,926;
        XVII,36
    Zadock XIV,274
Primas (Negro) XIV,564
Prime, Joshua XVI,23, 44
    Joshua J, XV,643, 648;
        XVI,810-811; XVII,468
    Josiah XIV,355; XV,293;
        XVI,850
Primer, Benjamin XIV,483
Prince, Abel XIV,244, 417;
    XV,72
    James XIV,246, 451, 532
Pringle, Thomas XV,189
    Wilson XIV,307
Pritchard, Jeremiah XIV,91,
    201; XIV,553, 592
    William XIV,575, 593
Proby, Jonathan XIV,315
Proctor, Ebenezer XIV,113, 147,
    196
    Ezekiel XIV,33; XV,743; XVI,
        238, 271, 509, 692
    Isaac XIV,334, 436, 525; XV,
        217, 536; XVI,254
    James XIV,25, 340
    Jeremiah XV,221, 740;
        XVI,839
    Joel XIV,468, 631; XV,614,
        714; XVI,200, 224, 235,
        241, 269, 509, 692
    Joseph XIV,7; XVI,274, 515,
        764
    Moses XV,89
    Nathan XV,106-7, 537
    Oliver XVI,535
    Reuben XIV,417; XV,518
    Robert XIV,283, 287
    William XV,106
Prosser, Philip XVII,293

Prouse, Thomas XV,728;
    XVI,277, 516
    Thomas Jr. XIV,648, 650;
        XV, 595; XVI,803
Prouty, John XV,31
Provinder, Benjamin XIV,6
    Jonathan XIV,6
Pry, Thomas XVII,296
Puffer, Amos XIV,265; XV,62,
    277; XVI,152
    Job XIV,436
    Simeon XIV,265
Pulling, Joseph XVII,429
Pulsifer, David XIV,104
    John XIV,105
    Joseph XV,125
Punchard, John XVI,140,.161
    Samuel XV,351, 353;
        XVI,235, 274, 511, 729
Purchase, Thomas XVII,491,
    500
Purdee, Levi XVI,608
Purington, Elias XIV,3
    Jonathan XVI,932
    Robert XVII,527
Purmont, Hannah XVII,633,
    646, 672, 679, 681
Purmort, Joseph XV,285, 287,
    748
    Mark XIV,113, 147, 195
    Richard XV,164
Purple, John XV,622, 634, 644,
    732; XVI,40, 194, 212,
    220; XVI,279, 511, 729
Purvis, George XVII,205
Putnam, Aaron XIV,459, 537;
    XV, 118, 138, 554
    Archelaus XIV,696, 698
    Archelaus Jr. XIV,336;
        XVII,63
    Benjamin XV,427, 733;
        XVI,47, 101, 213, 303,
        884
    Caleb XIV,244, 336, 694;
        XVII, 63
    Daniel XIV,265, 607-8;

Putnam, David (Cont.) XV,436,
602, 714; XVI,200, 223,
269, 431, 502; XVII,466
David XV,351, 353
Ebenezer XIV,326, 464;
XV,368
Ephraim XVI,729-30
Francis XIV,95, 203-4, 303;
XV, 25
Israel XVII,194
Jacob XV,74; XVI,883
John XV,669, 681; XVI,80,
91, 235, 268, 511, 602,
729, 935; XVII,255
Jonathan XIV,36; XV,20
Levi XV,31
Peter XVI,145, 883
Philip XIV,303, 416; XV,419-
20; XVI,447, 748, 883
Seth XIV,325, 464; XV,24,
367, 370; XVII,104
Seth Jr. XIV,326
Stephen XVI,927
Thomas XV,10, 144; XVI,80,
91
Thomas Jr. XV,33
Timothy XV,9, 31
Putney, Aaron XIV,67, 181, 289,
291; XVI,293, 680;
XVII,118, 120
Amos XVII,118
Asa XIV,185, 301; XV,131,
182; XVI,285, 332, 432,
504
Asahel XIV,51
David XVI,67, 77, 93
James XIV,67, 181; XV,120
John XIV,51, 185, 302;
XV,131, 183
Jonathan XIV,185, 315, 467,
548
Joseph XIV,51, 185, 315,
467, 548
Stephen XVI,131, 133, 163,
264, 286, 509, 696;
XVII,430

Putney, Thomas XIV,301, 314,
467, 548; XV,131
William XV,548; XVI,130,
133, 163, 234, 264
Pyncheon, Charles XVI,53

Q

Quailman, Peter XVII,296
Quanting, David XV,394
Quickett, Moses XIV,7
Quig, David XV,206
Quigley, Edward XVII,303
Quimby, Aaron XIV,532
Andrew XVI,243, 269, 862;
XVII, 438
Benjamin XIV,585, 660; XV,
573, 727, 747; XVI,41,
124, 209, 246, 615, 836;
XVII,260, 424
Caleb XV,173; XVI,75, 95
Daniel XIV,113, 147, 195;
XVII, 424
David XIV,532; XV,331, 486,
499-500, 560; XVI,75, 98,
615
Ebenezer XV,441
Eleazer XIV,584, 628;
XV,721; XVI,156, 205
Eliphalet XIV,113, 147, 195,
471, 585, 611; XV,717;
XVI, 202, 241, 270;
XVII,29
Isaac XV,183
Jacob XV,742
James XIV,71, 564, 630;
XV,445, 725; XVI,75, 94,
207
Jeremiah XIV,441, 527
John XIV,24, 63, 181, 186
Jonathan XIV,233, 252, 269,
272, 290, 561, 581, 621;
XV, 449, 600, 722;
XVI,205
Joseph XVI,871
Moses XIV,77, 83, 198;
XV,590; XVI,871
Samuel XV,746

Quimby, Sergeant XVII,3
  Timothy XIV,113, 146, 195;
    XV, 560
  William XVI,871-72
  William D. XV,742
  Zaccheus XV,727; XVI,209
  Zachariah XIV,565, 660
Quinby, Aaron XIV,171, 175-77,
    452; XV, 550-51
  Andrew XVI,236
  Benjamin XVI,11, 41, 44,
    251, 287, 508-9, 708
  Bradbury XVI,157
  Caleb XVI,68
  David XIV,340, 452; XV,322,
    341, 561; XVI,65
  Ebenezer XIV,173, 175-77
  Eliphalet XVI,219, 509, 708-9
  James XVI,68, 581
  John XIV,360; XVII,27
  Joseph XV,113, 550
  Moses XVI,670
  Samuel Jr. XIV,340
  Timothy XIV,341
  William XIV,329
  Zachariah XVI,10, 43;
    XVII,27
  Zaccheus XVI,184
Quinin, Peter XVI,102, 574-75
Quinlon, William XV,695
Quinn, John XVI,69
  Michael XVII,307
  Peter XV,621, 634, 645
Quint, John XIV,14
  Joseph XVI,110
  Thomas XIV,560, 620;
    XV,595, 722; XVI,205,
    234, 931-32
  Thomas Jr. XIV,21
  William XIV,237
Quinton, David XV,428
        R
Racine, Charles XVII,299
Racliffe, William XVII,656
Radcliffe, John XIV,14, 25
Rae, Abner XVII,307
Raino, Elias XIV,43

Raino, John XIV,572, 613; XV,
    612, 711, 740; XVI,499,
    562-63; XVII,445
Railing, John XVII,306
Ralph, Ephraim XV,511
Ramoch, Isaac XIV,248
Ramsey, David XIV,102, 208
  Hugh XIV,166
  James XIV,280, 288
  John XIV,348; XVI,246, 252,
    521; XVII,29
  Matthew XV,125
  Nathaniel XVII,160, 207
  Samuel XVI,246, 252, 504
  Thomas XIV,166, 170; XV,
    124; XVII,14
  William XV,200, 631, 637;
    XVI, 102, 609
Rand, Benjamin XV,259
  Benoni XIV,248; XV,260,
    263; XVII,26
  Daniel XIV,35, 332, 465; XV,
    348-49, 542; XVI, 815
  David XIV,108, 123, 187,
    251, 307, 341; XV,311
  Ebenezer XIV,361
  Edward XIV,11
  Ephraim XIV,119, 150, 197
  Ezekiel XIV,36, 98-99;
    XV,538, 540
  Francis XVII,527, 610
  Israel XVI,131, 163, 234, 264
  John XIV,13, 22, 224, 248,
    382, 448, 490, 501, 514,
    519, 535, 648, 650;
    XV,596, 78; XVI, 13, 912;
    XVII,26, 527, 640, 717
  Joseph XIV,224
  Joshua XIV,224, 248
  Lemuel XIV,432
  Moses XIV,244
  Nathaniel XIV,448, 535;
    XV,527
  Nehemiah XVI,446
  Reuben XV,634, 649, 731,
    735; XVI,16, 25, 102, 186,
    211, 220, 278, 503, 617

Rand, Samuel XIV,248, 448, 535; XVI, 111; XVII,26
Samuel Jr. XVII,26
Solomon XIV,36, 421; XV,349, 539
Stephen XIV,224
Thomas XV,660-61, 668, 676; XVI,111
Thomas J. XV,256
William XIV,224, 345, 353, 448, 535, 651; XV,300, 302, 305, 309; XVII,26
Randall, Aaron XIV,236
Benjamin XIV,101, 206-7, 380; XVI,168, 878, 906; XVII,26
Daniel XIV,145, 194; XV,295
Ebenezer XIV,233
Edward XV,441; XVI,241; XVII,26
Ephraim XIV,126; XVII,12
George XVII,26
Jacob XVI,165; XVII,22, 33
James XIV,68, 76, 83, 224, 514, 545, 648; XV,596; XVI,13, 97, 287, 508; XVII, 26, 622, 624-25, 638, 643
James Jr. XIV,648, 650; XVI,13
James M. XVI,64, 73
John XIV,3, 14, 21, 231, 407, 540; XV,703; XVI,102, 174, 287, 511, 707, 709, 712; XVII,24, 349
Jonathan XIV,300; XVI,64, 74, 99, 107
Joseph XV,468-69; XVI,131, 163
Mark XV,325; XVII,26
Moses XIV,317, 365
Nathaniel XVI,513, 778
Paul XIV,514
Samuel XIV,126, 188, 246
Simon XVI,904
Thomas XIV,234; XVII,24
William XIV,76, 83, 198

See also Rendell, Rendel, Rendall
Randel, Benjamin XIV,22
Daniel XIV,28
Edward XIV,224; XV,725
James XIV,570, 650
John XIV,226; XV,629
Joseph XIV,123; XV,494
Nathaniel XIV,21, 469; XV,572, 712
William XIV,21, 589
Randell, Gideon XV,249, 251-52, 254
Samuel XV,694
Randlet, James XVII,25, 640
Randolph, Barnard XVII,588
Edward XVII,520, 539, 555, 564, 566, 571-81, 584-92, 596-99, 612, 615, 618
Rankin, Andrew XIV,237, 549
Jonathan XIV,583, 600; XV,437, 715
Joseph XVI,899
Samuel XVI,898
Thomas XV,630, 637, 719; XVI, 203, 226, 271, 510, 720, 724-25
Rann, Francis XVII,511, 513, 527
John XVII,525
See also Rand
Rannis, Thomas XIV,238
Ranoc, John XIV,569
Ransom, Ebenezer XVI,66, 77, 96, 628
Samuel XVII,306
Ranson, Ebenezer XIV,314
Ranstead, John XIV,86, 199-200; XV,48, 225
Ranton, William XIV,134, 191
Ratcliffe, Mr. XVII,486
William XVII,527
Rate, Charles XVII,309
Rawlands, John XIV,110
Rawlings, Aaron XV,448, 598, 697; XVI,206

Rawlings, Daniel XV,597
    Edward XV,294
    Jeremiah XV,728; XVI,27, 71,
        210
    John XV,243, 245, 260, 263,
        626
    Joseph XV,285, 291, 520,
        597; XVI,68, 77, 760-61
    Moses XV,298, 302; XVI,648
    Moses Jr. XV,299
    Nathaniel XV,180
    Nicholas XV,324, 327, 331-
        33, 337-38
    Robert XV,723; XVI,206
    Susannah XVI,761
    Thomas XV,449, 600
    William XV,253
Rawlins, Aaron XIV,14, 117,
        119, 130, 145, 149, 196,
        564, 580, 635; XVI,207,
        229, 274, 512, 742
    Benjamin XIV,288, 641;
        XV,730; XVI,17
    Benjamin Jr. XIV,564
    Charles XVI,930, 932
    Daniel XIV,370, 378, 493,
        647; XV,728; XVI,12, 192,
        209
    Edward XIV,141, 193, 234;
        XV, 575
    Eliphalet XIV, 53, 61, 182,
        312, 641; XV,132, 730;
        XVI,18, 211, 278, 649
    George XIV,227, 257
    Ichabod XIV,234
    James XIV,2, 363; XVII,502,
        656
    Jeremiah XIV,14, 179, 300,
        652; XVI,99, 520, 846
    Jeremy XIV,71
    John XIV,71, 119, 132, 150,
        179, 190, 196, 234, 351,
        361, 380, 489, 560, 641;
        XV, 573, 575
    John XV,730; XVI, 17-18, 79,
        198, 211, 267, 278, 508,
        675-77; XVII,719

Rawlins, John 3d XVI,18
    Jonathan XIV,117, 130, 189
    Joseph XIV,14, 28, 71, 179,
        641; XV,730; XVI,18, 100,
        211, 220, 278, 514, 557
    Joshua XV,544
    Jotham XV,134
    Moses XIV,110, 133, 190,
        496, 505, 516, 563, 635
    Nathaniel XIV,532
    Nicholas XIV,231, 242
    Robert XIV,370, 377, 492;
        XVI, 274; XVII,30
    Samuel XIV,3; XV,666;
        XVI,274, 818
    Thomas XIV,581, 627;
        XV,457; XVI,510, 703,
        862-63; XVII, 438
    Simeon XIV,369, 374, 498,
        502, 511
    See also Rawlings and Rollins
Rawson, Asa XV,643
    Edward XVII,538, 604
Ray, James XV,465, 467, 478,
        504
    John XIV,424; XVI,733
    Matthew XVI,308, 310
    Peter XIV,5
    Silas XIV,646; XV,732;
        XVI,20, 22, 191, 212, 225,
        279
    William XIV,296, 361, 364;
        XV, 133; XVI,121, 164
Rayes, Simon XVI,883
Raymond, William XV,632, 635-
        36; XVI,511
Raynes, John XVII,139
Razey, Joseph XVI,81, 95
    Pelatiah XIV,646; XV,4, 205,
        732; XVI,20, 23, 191, 212,
        279, 887; XVII,468
Rea, Ebenezer XIV,336;
        XVI,558; XVII,62
    James XIV,416; XV,215
Read, Abijah XVII,62
    Benjamin XV,430
    Daniel XV,56; XVI,810

Read, Eliphaz XIV,211, 215, 217, 219-220, 503, 515, 647; XV,605
George XIV,257
Jacob XV,743
Joel XV,707; XVI,45, 48, 502
John XIV,499, 512, 525; XV, 7; XVI, 723
Matthew XVI,898
Samuel XVI,690
William XIV,418; XV,7, 57, 90
Zadoc XVI,240, 268, 500, 755
Reading, Eleazer XIV,214, 336, 698; XVII,62
Reamer, John XIV,585, 611
Reckord, John XVI,310
Reddell, James XIV,604
Redding, John XIV,239, 255; XVII, 23, 31
John Jr. XVII,39
Reddington, Asa XV,483, 632, 636
Reddinton, Thomas XV,400
Reden, John XV,4
Reder, John XV,160
Redfield, William XIV,576, 614; XV,711
William Jr. XVII,263
Redford, William XVII,625, 634, 637, 650-51, 658, 660-61
Reding, John XV,66, 227
Redington, Asa XVI,13, 44, 235, 269, 522, 880, 882
Isaac XVII,41
Thomas XVII,425
Redland, Duncan XIV,6
Redman, Benjamin XIV,314, 338
John XVII,641-43, 666, 671, 694, 740
Joseph XIV,240, 314, 338; XVII, 22, 33
Moses XIV,466
Redmond, Moses XIV,304, 306

Reed, Abijah XIV,203-4, 335; XV, 69, 518
Alpheus XIV,649; XV,597; XVI, 12, 499
Andrew XVII,328
Benjamin XIV,257-58, 550
Daniel XVI,138
Darius XVI,287
David XVII,328
Eliphaz XIV,492, 647; XV,460, 631, 637; XVI,580
George XIV,227, 258; XVII,45
Hinds XIV,85, 199
Isaac XIV,236, 312
Jacob XIV,33
James XIV,576; XV,723; XVI,320, 332, 341, 426, 433, 923; XVII,465
James Jr. XIV,632
Col. James XIV,37-45, 48, 76, 78, 80, 155, 198, 481, 552, 677, 681
James R. XVII,160, 164, 166, 187
Joel XVI,302, 305, 597
John XIV,437, 571, 605; XV,57, 223, 437, 596; XVI,106, 287; XVII,85, 622
John Jr. XIV,484
Joseph XVII,328, 638
Joshua XIV,179
Josiah XV,10
Matthew XVI,911
Micah XIV,436, 524
Moses XVI,263, 287, 504, 612; XVII,430
Nathaniel XIV,34
Robert XVII,300
Samuel XVI,259; XVII,436
Sylvanus XIV,92, 203; XV,463; XVI,654
Stephen XVI,112
William XIV,247, 298; XV,25, 37; XVI,687
Zadoc XIV,602; XV,435
Reid, Abijah XIV,95

Reid, Abraham XIV,73
George XIV,73, 75, 153, 178-79, 552, 591; XV,276, 421, 626, 718; XVI,2, 4, 51, 56, 182, 203, 227, 231, 233, 271, 280, 301, 306, 354, 374, 407, 475, 530, 888, 893; XVII, 266, 364, 440, 442, 444, 465
Isaac XIV,105
Joel XV,733; XVI,48, 265
John XIV,606; XV,716; XVI, 80, 92, 201 269; XVII,679
Joseph XIV,222
Major XVII,345
Peter XVII,296
Zadoc XIV,469; XV,712
Reese, David XIV,223
Reley, Jesse XIV,464
Remick, Daniel XIV,564
David XIV,343, 448, 535
Isaac XVII,26
Jacob XV,324
James XIV,564
John XV,573; XVI,63, 72, 91; XVII,261
Samuel XIV,664; XV,175, 431; XVI,435
Thomas XV,693; XVI,111
William XVII,36
Remington, Samuel XIV,325, 464, 594; XV,11, 143, 501, 604
Rendall, Aaron XIV,321
Benjamin XIV,248, 489
Edward XIV,248, 623; XV,595; XVI,207, 233, 241, 275; XVII, 644
Ensign XVII,664, 668
George XIV,248
Israel XVII,434
Jacob XVI,109, 165
James XIV,180, 381, 490, 501; XV,435, 728; XVI,234; XVII, 652
James Jr. XIV,382, 490; XV,728

Rendall, John XIV,446; XV,623, 641, 724; XVI,707, 709, 904
Joseph XIV,108, 187; XV,480, 493
Mark XIV,248
Moses XIV,320
Nathaniel XVI,199, 222, 268
Paul XIV,381, 490, 501
Samuel XIV,251; XVI,118; XVII, 434
See also Randall
Rent, Job XIV,404
Renton, William XIV,314
Reshworth, Edward XVII,520
Revere, Paul XIV,31
Reynolds, Alexander XVI,178-79
Daniel XV,464-66, 477, 479, 504, 654, 671-72, 676; XVI, 249, 283; XVII,211, 219, 222, 424-37, 461
Enoch XVI,710
Hezekiah XV,662, 669, 682; XVI, 98, 769
Jedediah XVII,104
Job XVII,644
John XIV,358
Joseph XV,444
Nathaniel XV,681; XVI,876
Owen XIV,14
Robert XV,377; XVI,97, 178-79
Samuel XVI,98, 166
Timothy XVII,307
Winthrop XVI,69, 79
Rhines, William XVI,236, 267
Rhodes, David XV,109
James XV,109
John XVII,205, 293
Matthew XVI,178-9
Timothy XV,227
Rhymes, Samuel XVI,110, 165
Riant, John XIV,320, 317, 587; XVI,733; XVI,36, 39, 502, 586, 795; XVII, 14
See also Ryant
Rice, Aaron XIV,105, 265; XV,13

Rice, Abel XV,700, 704; XVI,
174, 522, 608, 877
Abraham XVI,82; XVII,428
Amos XVI,605
Charles XIV,43; XV,66, 741
David XIV,8
Ebenezer XIV,443, 542, 547;
XV, 152, 154, 158;
XVI,608, 924
Elias XIV,443, 543
Elijah XV,131
Hezekiah XV,27
Isaac XVI,935
Jacob XIV,598-99; XVI,605;
XVII,224
Jacob Jr. XVI,605
Jason XV,21
Jedediah XIV,442, 542, 597;
XV, 31, 446
Joel XIV,324; XVI,605
Lemuel XV,717; XVI,270,
809; XVII,464
Nehemiah XVI,608
Peter XVI,254
Reuben XVI,608
Samuel XIV,594; XVI,202
Seth XV,439
Silas XIV,631; XV,451;
XVI,606
Rich, Amos XIV,160-61, 163,
270, 289; XV,424; XVII,16
David XIV,267, 271, 290-91;
XVI,608
John XV,279-80; XVI,156,
293, 307; XVII,115
John Jr. XVI,680
Jonathan XVII,118, 120
Josiah XVI,608
Richards, Amos XV,175, 568;
XVI, 568
Bartholomew XV,656, 666,
674; XVI,66, 74, 93, 638
Benjamin XIV,14, 19
Bradbury XVII,624, 727;
XVI,208
Bradley XIV,586-87, 657; XV,
749; XVI, 8, 35, 182, 248

Richards, Charles XIV,263
Christopher XIV,586
Daniel XVI,567-68
David XIV,56, 184; XV,115,
630, 637, 721; XVI,102,
205, 231, 273, 511, 720,
724-25
Eliphalet XV,174, 500, 557;
XVII,258
Heath XV,752
Hezekiah XV,294; XVI,627
John XIV,141, 192, 372, 385,
505, 517; XV,297;
XVI,538; XVII,253
John Jr. XIV,115
Jonathan XIV,234
Joseph XIV,12, 35, 234;
XV,297; XVI,907
Joshua XV,486
Mary XVII,612
Samuel XIV,55, 153, 156,
183, 372, 384, 496, 505,
516-17, XV,469, 481, 506,
556; XVI, 526, 666;
XVII,258
Theodore XVI,68, 79, 92
Thomas XV,383; XVII,253
Tristram XVI,119
Wentworth XIV,125
William XIV,308; XV,93, 356;
XVII,612, 621-22, 628,
654
Richardson,--- XV,699
Andrew XIV,247
Asa XIV,588; XV,566
Bradbury XIV,296; XV,161-
62; XVI,122, 164, 750;
XVII,414
Caleb XIV,112, 147, 195;
XVI, 262; XVII,426
Colonel XVI,299
Daniel XIV,626; XV,621, 634,
644, 720; XVI,23, 44, 204,
663, 686
David XVII,251
Ebenezer XV,590; XVII,330
Elab XIV,147

Richardson, Eliphalet XV,396, 487, 499
  Enoch XIV,380, 489, 501, 514; XV,396, 485, 499-500
  Eri XV,359
  Ezekiel XVI,63, 72, 90, 107
  Godfrey XIV,99, 205; XV,539
  James XIV,410; XV,168
  Jeremiah XIV,327, 363, 365; XV, 194, 485, 499-500, 698
  Jesse XVI,920-21
  Joel XV,590; XVI,296
  John XIV,225, 381, 490, 496, 501, 514; XV,569; XVI,35
  Jonas XV,359
  Jonathan XIV,172, 176-77, 288; XV,55; XVI,144
  Joseph XIV,115, 141, 193, 250, 253, 296, 624; XV,95, 364, 368, 618, 719; XVI,204, 751, 921
  Joshua XV,499-500, 534; XVII,32
  Josiah XIV,584; XV,196, 226; XVI,527, 531, 662, 700-2, 850-51
  Lemuel XVI,597, 935
  Luther XIV,160-61; XV,279, 281, 426, 584-85, 589; XVI,307, 924, 928-29; XVII,80, 82, 223, 330
  Major XV,620
  Matthew XV,556; XVII,258
  Nathaniel XIV,575, 584, 597, 627; XV,713, 721; XVI,203, 226, 272, 518, 808, 840
  Obadiah XV,150
  Paris XIV,30, 594; XV,604, 717; XVI,202, 218, 270, 326, 328, 331, 338, 340, 343, 345, 435, 499, 549, 614, 934
  Perez XV,33
  Philip Jr. XVI,783

Richardson, Phinehas XVI,650; XVII,424-25
  Richard XIV,575, 597; XV, 713, 740; XVI,199, 839-40
  Robert XIV,426
  Samuel XIV,56; XVI,237, 244, 274, 501, 600; XVII,297
  Silas XV,57
  Stephen,XIV,573, 639; XV,613, 696, 698, 730; XVI,15, 18, 26, 140, 161, 186, 211, 232, 235, 269, 278, 327, 329, 331, 341, 344-45, 438, 506, 509, 655, 692
  Thomas XV,749
  W. XVII,202
  William XIV,105, 224, 340, 453, 532, 614; XV,15, 39, 42, 57, 377, 396, 485, 488, 602, 654; XV,715; XVI, 313; XVII,109
  Zachariah XIV,438, 527, 548
  Zebediah XIV,167, 170; XV,160; XVI,796; XVII,14
Richmond, Sampson XIV,1
  Zephaniah XV,50, 503
Richey, James XV,739
Ricker, Benjamin XIV,18
  Charles XIV,372, 384, 496, 505, 516-17, 520
  Ebenezer XIV,230, 242, 446, 473, 540; XV, 573, 575; XVI,836; XVII,26
  Ebenezer Jr. XIV,447
  Enoch XIV,127, 188; XVII,11
  Ephraim XIV,18
  Ezekiel XIV,188, 473
  George XIV,372, 385, 473, 497, 505, 517; XV,749; XVI,527
  Gershom XIV,236
  James XIV,369, 374, 482, 502, 511, 518; XV,656, 666, 681; XVI,196, 234, 836

Ricker, John XIV,230, 664
 Jonas XIV,498
 Jonathan XIV,18; XVI,913
 Joseph XIV,237; XV,628,
  640, 656, 725; XVI,207,
  230, 275, 523, 816, 818
 Maturin XVI,68, 79, 92; XVII,
  754
 Moses XIV,18, 230
 Nicholas XVI,623
 Paul XVI,103 XVII,299
 Phinehas XIV,230; XVII,29
 Reuben XIV,372, 385, 496,
  505, 517; XV,294;
  XVI,526, 627, 907
 Samuel XIV,245
 Simeon XIV,236
 Stephen XIV,239
 Timothy XIV,234, 361, 625;
  XV, 619, 722; XVI,45, 205,
  301, 818
 Tobias XIV,322, 369, 375,
  482, 498, 502, 511, 518;
  XV,297, 656, 666, 679;
  XVI,816
 Wentworth XIV,188, 480;
  XVII,10
 William XVI,628
Rickery, Valentine XVII,29
Riddle, Hugh XV,176
 Isaac XVI,141, 161, 247, 251;
  XVI,141, 161, 247, 251,
  500, 575
 James XIV,569; XV,437, 610,
  716; XVI,201, 920
 John XIV,424, 571, 605; XV,
  716; XVI,201, 269
Rider, Ebenezer XV,183;
  XVI,933
 James XIV,281, 286-87, 470;
  XV, 713; XVI,575
 Stephen XV,593
Rigby, Edward XVII,506
 John XIV,5
Riggs, Gawen XIV,307
 Stephen XIV,145; XVII,9
 Thomas XV,108, 541

Rimmeck, Samuel XV,115
Rindge, Isaac XVII,142
Rine, John XVI,679
Rines, John XIV,23, 249, 356,
  547
 Nathaniel XIV,233
 Thomas XIV,22, 369, 375;
  XVII, 717
 William XIV,316, 319
 See also Rhines
Ring, Abram J. XIV, 14
 Elijah XV,527; XVI,604
 Eliphalet XVI,931
 Jonathan XV,279, 281, 379,
  402; XVI,155, 539;
  XVII,254
 Samuel XVI,661
 Seth XVII,729
Ripley, Jenuel XV,655
 Lemuel XVI,627
 Samuel XV,666, 676; XVI,623
 William XV,38, 45, 155; XVII,
  143
Rishworth, Edward XVII,520,
  523
Ritter, Daniel XIV,442, 578,
  595; XV,713
Rivington, James XVII,411
Rix, Nathaniel XV,279, 281,
  589; XVI,307; XVII,80, 82,
  331
Roach, Frederick XIV,579;
  XV,454, 740
 George XVI,929
 Morris XVII,300
 Patrick XV,174
 Thomas XIV,75
Robb, Alexander XIV,333
Robbe, Alexander XV,101, 103
 Andrew XVI,840
 David XV,104, 740; XVI,839-
  40
 John XV,104, 219; XVI,287,
  323; XVI,331, 334, 337,
  339, 439, 441, 839-40
 Samuel XV,101, 357;
  XVI,286, 840; XVII,428

Robbe, William XV,20, 221
Robbinette, Jaques XVII,305
Robbins, David XIV,36, 85, 199;
    XVI,311; XVII,95
  Eleazer XIV,85, 199; XV,224
  Isaiah XVII,429
  John XIV,267; XVII,95
  Jonas XVII,95
  Jonathan XIV,100, 206; XV,
    224; XVI,166; XVII,91
  Richard XV,102-3
  Samuel XIV,85, 199; XV,223,
    633, 648; XVI,44, 686
  Solomon XV,224, 633, 648;
    XVI,311, 877
  Thomas XIV,8
  William XIV,8
Roberson, Benjamin XV,309
  Levi XV,249
  William XV,640
Roberts, Amaziah XV,746
  Benjamin XIV,114, 141, 193;
    XVII,434
  Benjamin Jr. XIV,298
  Captain XV,690
  Cornelius XV,63; XVI,35
  Daniel XIV,19; XVI,914
  Ebenezer XVI,907
  Edmund XIV,29; XVII,139
  Elisha XV,621, 634, 644,
    730; XVI,18, 26, 186, 211,
    232, 278, 834, 873-75;
    XVII,438
  Ephraim XIV,322, 365; XVII,
    29, 756
  Francis XIV,126, 188, 473;
    XV,191; XVI,904; XVII,10
  George XIV,125, 188, 238,
    245, 473; XVI,196, 628;
    XVII,10, 29
  Griffith XVII,302
  Hatevil XIV,127, 188; XVI,
    907; XVII,11
  James XVI,491
  James Jr. XIV,230
  Jeduthan XV,701, 704;
    XVI,176, 517, 522, 877,

Roberts, Jeduthan (Cont.) 879
  Jeremiah XV,128, 749
  Joel XV,668; XVI,152, 855;
    XVII,255
  John XIV,3, 14, 230, 281,
    288, 327, 362; XV,436,
    749; XVII,29, 306, 525,
    561
  Jonathan XIV,25, 401; XV,
    457
  Joseph XIV,14, 25, 297; XV,
    195, 681; XVI,321, 331,
    341, 659-660, 757
  Joseph Jr. XIV,3; XVI,442
  Joshua XV,294, 296
  Love XIV,473; XV,749; XVI,
    620
  Love Jr. XVI,904
  Molly XVI,620
  Moses XIV,71, 179, 451, 532,
    565, 616; XV,440, 575,
    719; XVI,103, 202, 224,
    241, 271, 499, 582;
    XVII,261
  Nathan XIV,369, 375, 482,
    498, 502, 511, 518, 520;
    XVI,66, 77, 96; XVII,28
  Nathaniel XIV,3, 14
  Paul XIV,550; XV,430;
    XVI,66, 77, 96
  Perley XIV,394; XV,17; XVII,
    88
  Reuben XIV,469, 563, 611;
    XV, 718, 743; XVI,202,
    221, 270, 514, 766; XVII,7
  Samuel XIV,230, 369, 375,
    482, 498, 502, 511, 518,
    520; XVI, 60, 62, 70, 94;
    XVII,28
  Seth XV,4
  Simon XVI,66, 77, 96
  Stephen XIV, 371, 384, 496,
    505, 516-17
  Thomas XIV,23, 127;
    XVI,898; XVII,11, 502,
    513, 525
  Timothy XIV,244, 476;

Roberts, Timothy (Cont.)
   XVI,899
   William XIV,372, 385, 497,
     505, 517; XV,469, 481,
     507; XVI, 627; XVII,308
   Ziba XV,16
Robertson, Amos XVI,259;
   XVII,437
   Andrew XVI,791
   Chase XVI,281
   David XIV,353; XV,218
   Edmund XV,436
   Gilman XVII,27
   James XIV,560, 570; XV,6,
     57, 59-60; XVI,580, 787-
     88; XVII, 264
   John XIV,7, 62, 157, 219,
     221, 317, 319, 330, 567;
     XV, 310, 435, 607, 622,
     663, 689, 712; XVI, 113,
     233, 577, 742, 786;
     XVI,917; XVII,52
   Joseph XV,553
   Levi XIV,352
   Peter XV,200, 521; XVI,322-
     23, 327, 329-30, 334, 337,
     339, 345, 417-18, 443
   Richard XIV,583
   Samuel XIV,103, 234, 407
   Thomas XIV,515
   Timothy XV,3
   William XIV,93, 202; XV,628;
     XVI,579, 622; XVII,383
Robeson, Jonathan XVII,652
   Joseph XIV,184
   Thomas XIV,14
Robey, Ichabod XVII,667, 669
   Captain XVI,900
   Jonathan XVI,926; XVII,4
   Samuel XVI,901; XVII,511,
     644
   Sarah XVII,675
   Thomas XVII,528, 625, 643,
     687
   Thomas Jr. XVII,740
   See also Robie, Roby

Robie, Benjamin XV, 207;
   XVI,287
   Edward XV,403
   Ichabod XIV,410, 456, 537;
     XV, 168; XVI,86, 97
   John XVI,527, 870, 874
   Jonathan XIV,186, 467
   Nathan XVI,155
   Samuel XIV,253; XV,168,
     300, 302, 306, 309;
     XVI,253, 501, 600
   Walter XVI,588
   William XVI,528
Robins, David XV,47, 97, 370,
   539
   Eleazer XV,47, 370
   John XV,48, 225
   Jonas XV,47
   Jonathan XV,124, 142, 158
   Peter XV,80, 207
   Solomon XV,7
   Thomas XV,347
   William XV,349
   See also Robbins
Robinson, Andrew XIV,411
   Benjamin XIV,231, 458, 538-
     39, 588, 626; XV, 300,
     302, 305, 309, 720; XVII,7
   Caleb XIV,554, 627, 629;
     XV,441-442, 447, 449,
     451, 456-58, 600, 650,
     706, 718, 748; XVI, 5, 51,
     182, 203, 226, 271;
     XVI,395, 505, 525, 743,
     830, 933; XVII,216, 267,
     334, 338, 341, 441, 444,
     449, 465
   Daniel XVI,115, 905
   David XIV,135, 191, 300; XV,
     326, 630, 646; XVI,812,
     814; XVII,6, 57
   Edmund XIV,283, 287
   Eleazer XV,17, 138
   Ephraim XV,416, 640;
     XVI,349, 369, 380-81,
     402, 537, 648-651, 905;

Robinson, Ephraim (Cont.)
XVII,219-21, 261, 264,
273-75
Gideon XIV, 432; XVII,
215
Gilman XVII,57
J. XIV,42
Jack XIV,309
James XIV,110, 131, 190,
554, 563, 634; XV, 637,
722, 752; XVI,584, 609;
XVII,57
Jeremiah XIV,116, 128, 189,
308, 371, 379, 492, 503,
515, 564, 616; XV,440,
626
John XIV,128, 145, 156, 194,
210, 215-17, 220, 226,
251, 289, 370, 378, 492,
503, 515, 580, 601, 635;
XV,175, 199, 300, 302,
306, 327, 448, 598, 669,
677, 724, 740; XVI,206,
229, 237, 241, 273-74,
500, 509, 512, 611, 696,
742, 920, 933; XVII,9
John D. XIV,469
Jonathan XIV,134, 191, 400,
404, 415; XVI,843; XVII,6
Joseph XIV,56; XV,122, 173,
327, 699; XVI,140, 161,
555; XVII,445
Leonard XVI,424
Levi XIV,139, 158, 192, 226;
XV,251-53
Matthew XVII,730
Noah XIV,110, 131, 190, 554,
563, 634; XV,719; XVI,5,
51, 180, 182, 203, 648;
XVII,268
Peter XIV,43, 242, 247, 412,
588; XVI, 323, 330
Prince XIV,312; XV,285, 288
Richard XIV,71, 179, 399,
599; XV,713; XVI,199,
223, 268, 418, 529, 808
Samuel XV, 25

Robinson, Simeon XIV,143, 193-
94; XVII,8
Terence XVII,308
Thomas XIV,171, 174, 176-
77, 369, 377, 492, 503;
XVI,920; XVII, 24, 308,
673
Timothy XV,746
William XIV,173-74, 176-77;
XVI,62, 71, 99, 102, 107,
920
Winthrop XV,259, 262, 267-
68, 270, 475, 494, 657,
678; XVI,115, 837
Zebulon XIV,588
Roby, Abbott XIV,477; XV,518
Ichabod XIV,11
James XIV,247
Jonathan XIV,64, 181, 548
Philip A. XIV,95, 204, 267
Samuel XIV,417; XV,464-67,
477, 505
Samuel Jr. XV,478, 504
Silas XV,518, 744
Thomas XV,207
William XIV,95, 97, 203, 266
See also Robey, Robie
Roche, Frederick XVI,722
Rock, Edward XVII,297
Nathaniel XIV,289
Nathaniel Jr. XIV,269, 272
William XIV,8
Rockwell, Jabez XVI,137
Rockwood, Elisha XV,58
Micah XV,50
Reuben XV,4
Thomas XVII,97
Rodney, Admiral XVII,411
Rodrue, Manuel XVII,304
Roe, Abner XVI,45, 48, 265,
304-5
Anthony XIV,13
John XV,66; XVII,656
Richard XVII,525
Robert XIV,11-12
Thomas XIV,14
Thomas Jr. XIV,14

Roen, John XIV,61, 530
Rogers, Cato XIV,664
   Daniel XIV,408, 426, 585,
      611; XV,577, 718;
      XVII,756
   Daniel Jr. XIV,625
   Daniel D. XVII,341
   James XIV,234; XV,33, 143;
      XVI, 900, 907; XVII,106
   John XIV,234, 298; XV, 102,
      469, 481, 507, 628, 640,
      725, 753; XVI,207, 241,
      275, 523, 816, 818, 917
   Jonathan XIV,324, 464
   Joseph XIV,5, 181; XV,179,
      512; XVI,579
   Josiah XIV,34; XV,93, 321,
      340
   Levi XIV,101, 206-7
   Matthew XVII,303
   Nathaniel XV,383; XVI,538
   Perley XIV,269-70, 290, 547;
      XV,424, 437, 668, 681;
      XVI, 176, 208, 273, 522,
      876-77, 879; XVII,255
   Richard XIV,607-8
   Richard C. XV,409, 424, 714
   Robert XV,454; XVI,919-22
   Samuel XIV,57, 67, 156-57,
      323; XV, 751; XVI, 234,
      264, 906, 916
   Thomas XIV,16, 664; XV,201,
      431
   Timothy XIV,98, 205, 576;
      XVI, 513, 737
   William XIV,17, 261, 347,
      362, 364; XV, 33, 578,
      635, 639; XVI,102
Rokes, John XIV,105
Rolfe, Benjamin XIV,425;
   XV,129; XVI,620, 908
   Ephraim XIV,88, 200;
      XV,210, 511
   Ezra XVI,908
   James XIV,438, 527, 545;
      XVI, 235, 274, 509, 692
   Jesse XIV,430

Rollings, Aaron XV,528, 723;
   XVII,9
   Anthony XIV,517
   Benjamin XIV,566; XV,423
   Daniel XVII,27
   Edward XIV,407
   Elijah XIV,451
   Eliphalet XIV,338; XV,422,
      456
   George XIV,344
   Jeremiah XIV,312, 338
   John XIV,606; XV,256, 422-
      23, 443, 456, 656, 747;
      XVII, 383
   John 3d XV,422
   Jonathan XV,249-51
   Joseph XV,422
   Moses XIV,515; XV,300, 724
   Nathaniel XIV,451
   Samuel XIV,344; XV,656
   Williams XV,249-52
Rollins, Aaron XIV,189, 194,
      618-619; XV,724; XVI,231,
      514, 766
   Anthony N. XIV,371, 384,
      496, 505, 516
   Benjamin XIV,279; XV,608
   Daniel XIV,503, 515
   Edward XIV,115, 625;
      XVI,627, 819; XVII,261
   Elijah XIV,532
   Eliphalet XIV,185, 249, 433;
      XVI,194, 237, 244, 506
   Francis XV,660, 668, 676
   Henry XVII,29
   Ichabod XIV,195, 222, 248
   James XV,109, 630, 643,
      646; XVI,102, 629;
      XVII,654
   Jeremiah XIV,3; XVI,62, 107,
      189, 234, 286
   John XIV,228, 432, 473, 571,
      620, 641; XV,247, 595,
      666; XVI,103, 194, 237,
      244, 251, 286, 500, 505,
      516, 570, 572, 803;
      XVII,260

Rollins, Joseph XIV,18; XV,169,
  228, 632, 636; XVI,103,
  194, 760; XVII,428
Josiah Jr. XIV,400
Moses XIV,372, 384;
  XVII,435
Nathaniel XIV,433
Robert XIV,228, 503, 515,
  618-619; XV,596; XVI,231,
  514, 766
Samuel XV,678; XVI,235,
  242, 523, 816, 818-20
Simeon XIV,253, 482
Thomas XIV,67, 181, 300,
  312; XV,721; XVI,862;
  XVII,526
See also Rollings, Rawlings,
  Rawlins
Romer, Wolfgang W. XVII,691-
  92
Rone, Andrew XIV,660
John XIV,660
Rooks, Ezekiel XVI,503, 935
Root, Ephraim XIV,159, 161,
  165; XV, 383
Samuel XV,278; XVI,538
Simeon XVI,307; XVII,115,
  254
Solomon XVII,115, 250
Roque, Bryan XIV,211, 217, 220
Rose, James XIV,287; XV,425,
  436; XIV,714
Thomas XV,11, 368
Rosebrook, Eleazer XV,425, 700,
  702-3, 725; XVI,170, 172,
  174, 208; XVII,78, 113
James XV,700, 703, 726;
  XVI, 171-72, 176, 208,
  515, 782
Ross, Abraham XV,217
Abram XVI,534
James XIV,468, 607-8;
  XV,748
John XIV,317, 320, 459, 538;
  XV,362, 671, 676;
  XVI,168-69, 719, 721;
  XVII,761

Ross, Joseph XIV,573; XV,613;
  XVI,16
Josiah XIV,639
Lemuel XV,183
Moses XVI,110, 165
Sarah XVII,761
Zebulon XVI,932
Rots, Jean XIV,662; XVI,724
John XV,455
Rouncival, Joseph XVI,442;
  XVII, 235
See also Rounseval
Roundy, Asahel XIV,578, 610
Israel XV,718
Samuel XV,369
Rounseval, Joseph XV,107, 501
See also Rouncival
Rouse, William XVII,722
Row, Daniel XIV,25
Ephraim XIV,24-25
Isaiah XV,402
John XV,128, 698, 703, 747,
  749
Lazarus XIV,388, 495, 507,
  516
Robert XIV,3
William XIV,581; XV,449, 599
Rowe, Aaron XIV,229
Abner XV,733
Anthony XIV,268, 271, 290
Benjamin Jr. XV,509
Caspar XVI,933
Daniel XVI,918
Enoch XV,240-41, 256, 258,
  264
Ichabod XV,528
Jeremiah XV,283, 291
John XIV,88, 201, 269, 272,
  290, 358, 600, 617;
  XV,226, 461, 596, 715,
  723, 729, 754; XVI,29,
  171-72, 176, 200, 206,
  231, 239, 252, 273, 298,
  514, 520, 750-51, 760,
  832
John Jr. XVII,96
Joseph XV,321, 340

Rowe, Josiah XV,120, 183
  Lazarus XIV,236
  Moses XVI,68, 79, 92
  Nathan XIV,316, 318
  Paine XVI,933
  Reuben XV,172
  Robert XV,167; XVI,583, 897;
    XVII,57
  Sergeant XVI,938
  Simon XVII,27
  Thaddeus XV,409
  Webber XVI,287, 500
  William XV,730; XVI,31, 34,
    59, 187, 210; XVII,527
  Winthrop XIV,107, 109, 131,
    154, 189-90, 654; XV,523;
    XVI,542, 932; XVII,12-13
Rowell, Asa XVII,92
  Benoni XIV,16
  Captain XV,444, 447, 457,
    596-598; XVII,226
  Christopher XV,569
  Daniel XIV,228; XV,297, 299,
    747; XVI,236, 243, 273,
    505, 644
  E. XVI,938
  Eliphalet XVI,914
  Enoch XIV,327-28; XV,402,
    748
  Israel XIV,53, 185, 587, 628;
    XV,441, 720; XVI,204
  Jacob XVI,918
  James XIV,587, 628; XV,441,
    721; XVI,203
  Job XIV,135, 191; XVI,670;
    XVII,7
  John XV,176, 593; XVI,93,
    541
  Jonathan XIV,424; XVI,64,
    73, 250, 256, 507
  Josiah XVI,908, 914
  Lemuel XIV,53, 185, 587,
    660; XV,727; XVI,43, 184,
    209
  Moses XVI,287, 516
  Nathaniel XIV,25, 350
  Nehemiah XV,577; XVII,139

Rowell, Peter XIV,249
  Philip XIV,568, 654; XV,730;
    XVI,31, 34, 59
  Samuel XIV,211, 216, 307,
    347, 663; XV,200; XVI,10,
    874
  Thomas XIV,261, 300, 398;
    XV, 548
  William XIV,69, 75, 178, 180;
    XIV,554, 564, 630-31;
    XV,719; XVI,4, 51, 182,
    203, 227, 271, 644, 831;
    XVII,267
Rowen, Andrew XIV,566;
    XV,607, 727
  John XIV,182, 454, 546, 566;
    XV,607, 727; XVI,10, 209
Rowley, James XVI,207, 275
  John XIV,249
  Joseph XIV,624; XV,440,
    596, 719
  Matthew XIV,7
Rowling, John XVII,360
Rowlings, Aaron XIV,571
  Daniel XIV,650
  Francis XV,660-61
  Jeremiah XV,597
  Nathaniel XVI,847
  Nicholas XIV,414
  Robert XIV,503
  Stephen XVI,776
Royal, Philip XV,610
Royce, Abram XVI,99
  Amos XIV,578, 614; XV,711
  Elias XVI,314
  Jacob XIV,578; XVII,105
  Joel XIV,578, 614; XV,711;
    XVI,198
  John XV,32; XVI,230
  Lemuel XV,10, 143; XVI,218,
    519, 597, 692, 934
  Ruel XV,25, 37
  Samuel XV,29
  Silas XV,144, 662, 669, 683;
    XVI,83; XVII,249
Royse, Joel XIV,464
  Ruel XIV,298

Rudd, Gideon XV,604
Rugg, John XIV,264
    Levi XIV,355
Ruggles, Nathaniel XIV,422
Rumery, Simon XVI,903
Rumrill, David XV,219
    Simon XV,28, 147, 471;
    XVI,900; XVII,249
Rundlet, Charles XV,195
    Jacob XVI,842, 847
    John XVI,905
    Solomon XVI,109, 165, 260-
    61
Rundlett, Benjamin XVII,57
    Charles XVII,673
    George XIV,448, 535
    James XIV,352, 563; XV,
    440, 626, 719; XVI,203,
    316-17, 651; XVII,27
    James Jr. XIV,615
    John XVII,28
    Jonathan XV,475, 494;
    XVI,115, 285, 505
    Joshua XIV,398; XV,325
    Josiah XV,285, 291
    Noah XV,667, 676; XVI,581
    Reuben XV,699; XVI,111,
    261; XVII,432
    Solomon XVII,432
    Theophilus XV,242, 245, 247
    Thomas XIV,312
    William XV,597, 729; XVI,27,
    188, 210
Runnells, Miles XV,656, 666,
    679; XVI,711
    Nathaniel XV,669
    Robert XV,525; XVI,65, 76,
    105, 107
Runnels, Abraham XIV,372,
    385, 496, 505, 517;
    XV,192; XVI, 898
    Alexander XVI,498, 935
    Allen XVI,523
    Daniel XIV,242, 410; XV,196,
    199, 202; XVII,219
    Enoch XIV,109, 123, 187,
    233, 408; XVII,24

Runnels, Enos XIV,211, 215,
    217-20
    Hezekiah XVI,80, 193
    Isaac XIV,234, 696; XV,297,
    299
    Israel XIV,624; XV,619, 725;
    XVI,207, 227, 275, 511,
    710
    James XV,668, 684, 690;
    XVI,555
    Job XIV,233; XVII,719
    Job Jr. XVI,711
    John XIV,69; XVI,571; XVII,
    719
    Joseph XIV,321, 365, 581,
    617; XV,449, 601, 620,
    723, 747; XVI,758
    Moses XIV,233, 624; XV,619,
    720; XVI,204, 230, 272,
    511, 710-12
    Nathaniel XVII,255
    Samuel XIV,123, 187, 505,
    642; XV,451, 654, 684,
    686, 729; XVI,27, 66, 72,
    166, 168-69, 215, 638
    Solomon XIV,108, 123, 187;
    XVI, 165, 638
    Stephen XIV,369, 374, 482,
    498, 623; XV,210, 510,
    619, 725; XVI,207, 231,
    240, 275, 511, 710
    Thomas XVI,825
    See also Runnells
Rushmore, Silas XVI,933
Russ, James XIV,317, 320, 583,
    592; XV,717
    John XIV,424; XVI,732
    Jonathan XIV,33; XV,209;
    XVI,734-35
    Peter XIV,358
Russell, Andrew XIV,419; XV,
    87, 210; XVI,246, 253,
    518
    Aquila XV,741
    Benjamin XVII,428
    Calvin XVI,158
    Daniel XIV,36, 98, 205, 576,

Russell, Daniel (Cont.) 634;
  XV,442, 626, 724; XVI,
  207, 321, 323, 326, 328-
  30, 338, 340, 343, 345,
  445, 813
  David XV,745
  Edward XVI,580
  Eleazer XVII,286, 334, 450
  George XIV,605
  Isaac XVI,885
  Isaac Jr. XIV,238
  Jacob XIV,561, 621; XV,483,
    618, 722
  James XIV,23, 453; XV,744
  Jason XIV,95, 204; XV,81
  Jeduthan XV,23
  Jeremiah XIV,36, 98, 205,
    333; XV,348
  Joel XIV,36, 99, 205; XV,356
  John XIV,180, 604; XV,149,
    272, 379, 592, 715;
    XVI,285, 507; XVII,80, 82,
    628-29, 692
  Josiah XIV,394; XV,14, 375;
    XVII,88-90
  Josiah Jr. XVII,89
  Josiah 3d XIV,394; XV,16, 43
  Moors XV,593; XVII,89
  Nathaniel XIV,36
  Pomp XV,211
  Reuben XV,97, 217, 349
  Robert XV,749
  Robert E. XIV,321
  Samuel XIV,9, 36; XV,97,
    539
  Silas XVI,237, 268, 518, 849
  Thomas XIV,246, 417; XV,25;
    XVI,538
  William XIV,311, 333, 577,
    648, 650; XV,539, 595,
    728, 734; XVI,12, 192,
    209, 232, 277, 516, 803-4
Rust, Henry XVI,892
  Nathaniel XIV,325, 464
  Samuel XVI,316-17
Rutherford, Robert XIV,13

Ryan, Benjamin XIV,334
  James XIV,224, 248, 314,
    338, 369, 375, 508, 516,
    519, 623; XV,595; XVII,26,
    293
  John XIV,61; XVII,298, 302
  Michael XIV,257, 369, 375,
    483, 498, 502, 511, 518;
    XVII,30
  Samuel XIV,562, 637;
    XV,619, 653
Ryant, John XIV,166, 170, 656;
  XVI, 36, 39, 502, 586, 795
  Joseph XVI,34
  See also Riant
Rymes, Samuel XVII,621
  Thomas XIV,498
Rynes, Thomas XIV,13, 22
  William XVI,236, 267, 502,
    594-595

S

Sabe, Pierre XVII,309
Sabin, Noah Jr. XVII,458
Sackomy, Robert XIV,10
Sadler, Joseph XVII,656
Safford, Benjamin XV,100, 219
  Ebenezer XVI,152
Saint Clair, General XV,81, 83,
    136
  Jacob XV,565
Saint Houge, Joseph XVII,299
Saint Laurens, E. XVII,299
Saint Luke, Landon XVII,307
Salabray, Marston XVII,698
Salter, Alexander XIV,224; XVI,
    912; XVII,25
  John XV,578
  Michael XV,733; XVI,45, 48,
    265, 302, 305, 679, 783
  Richard Jr. XV,430
  Titus XIV,227, 257-58, 472,
    549; XV,429, 433, 594;
    XVI, 300, 319, 451, 926;
    XVII,21; XVII,30, 35, 45,
    74, 126, 135, 285, 336,
    454

Salter, Titus Jr. XIV,227, 258;
    XVII, 30
    William XVI,930
Saltistone, Mr. XVII,601
Saltmarsh, Isaac XIV,66, 180,
    246
    Thomas XV,557; XVII,258
Saltonstall, Colonel XIV,26
Saltsman, George XIV,223
Sampson, Daniel XVI,67, 73, 98
    John XIV,334, 604, 606;
    XV,716; XVI,201, 269
Sanborn, Aaron XIV,143, 145;
    XVI, 829; XVII,8
    Abner XIV,118, 137, 158,
    192; XV,411, 489
    Abner Jr. XVI,674
    Abraham XIV,109, 131, 413,
    432; XV,249, 251-53, 564;
    XVI,933; XVII,12, 32
    Abraham Jr. XIV,453
    Benjamin XIV,22, 116, 128,
    189; XV,392, 754;
    XVI,236, 243, 264, 273,
    286, 500, 513, 776, 928;
    XVII,28, 251, 431
    Bradbury XV,242, 244, 246
    Captain XVI,903
    Coffin XVII,57
    Daniel XIV,317; XV,267, 269,
    273; XVI, 457, 829; XVII,
    57
    Daniel T. XV,134, 171
    David XIV,25, 388, 494, 507,
    516; XVI,526; XVII,32
    Dudley XIV,229, 253, 350
    Ebene er XIV,118, 139, 158,
    166, 192, 255, 547; XV,
    587; XVI,542, 924; XVII,14
    Edward XIV,12, 398
    Eleazer XIV,170
    Elijah XV,249, 251-53
    Elipha XVII,57
    Enos XIV,226
    Ephraim XIV,227, 430
    James XIV,129, 189, 252,
    300, 392, 486, 509, 513;

Sanborn, James (Cont.) XV,
    319, 339, 523, 631, 650,
    732, 735; XVI,37, 102,
    127, 162, 196, 212, 232,
    278, 521, 827-28
    James Jr. XIV,116, 252
    Jeremiah XIV,111, 133, 190;
    XVI,65, 75, 96, 103;
    XVII,24
    Jethro XIV,19, 404; XV,323,
    342; XVI,615; XVII,32
    Jewett XIV,111, 133, 190,
    413; XV,258
    John XIV,160-61, 165, 261,
    450, 534, 546, 564, 603,
    616; XV, 164, 279, 281,
    411, 440, 449, 513-14,
    600, 627, 712, 719;
    XVI,203, 286, 299, 519,
    645, 727; XVII,528, 667-
    69, 740-41
    John Jr. XVII,528
    John P. XIV,67
    John S. XIV,109, 133, 190,
    232, 312, 627; XV, 442,
    457, 721
    Jonas XVII,633
    Jonathan XIV,23, 116, 128,
    189, 194; XV,323, 342,
    684
    Jonathan Jr. XV,342, 561
    Jonathan H. XV,173, 668,
    690; XVI,828
    Joseph XIV,465, 563, 565,
    611, 660; XV, 125, 439,
    718, 727; XVI,10, 43, 103,
    184, 209, 514, 581, 766;
    XVII,29
    Joseph C. XVI,614
    Josiah XIV,296, 370, 378,
    432, 434, 492, 504, 515,
    531; XV, 133, 393, 475,
    494; XVI, 281, 286, 520;
    XVII,215
    Levi XIV,230, 413; XV,256,
    259-260, 262
    Mark XIV,547; XV,593;

Sanborn, Mark (Cont.) XVI,514
Matthew XIV,231, 570;
XV,734; XVI,220
Matthew H. XVI,17
Matthew N. XIV,641; XV,422,
730; XVI,194, 211, 245,
278, 499, 582
Meshech XV,523
Moses XIV,232, 327-28, 370,
377, 492, 504, 515, 663;
XV, 285, 291; XVI,874;
XVII,24
Nathan XIV,397; XV,300-1,
303-304, 306-8, 315, 317;
XVI, 320, 328, 331, 341,
343-44, 447, 617-18
Nathaniel XIV,253; XV,285,
291; XVI,325; XVII,25
Paul XIV,561, 581, 621;
XV,449, 600, 722;
XVI,205, 257, 514
Peter XIV,12, 476; XV,323,
342; XVI,897
Phinehas XIV,25
Reuben XIV,76, 83, 198;
XV,400, 528, 587; XVI,
116, 599, 897
Richard XIV,12, 285, 287,
388, 495, 507, 516, 546;
XV,153; XVI,103, 184,
213, 228, 279, 513, 778,
897, 905; XVII,528
Sherburne XIV,111, 133,
190, 228; XV,249, 251-53;
XVI,115
Simeon XIV,210, 214, 217,
220, 454, 529, 546
Simon XIV,69, 145, 180, 194,
230, 450, 534; XV,180;
XVII,8
Stephen XIV,11
Theophilus XV,249, 251-53,
524
Timothy XIV,226; XVII,57
Tony XVII,9
William XIV,12, 118, 139,
158, 192, 255, 261;

Sanborn, William (Cont.)
XVII,528, 644
Zadoc XVII,27, 424
Sanders, Avery XVI,83, 97, 293,
295, 307, 680; XVII,115,
254
Bama XV,377
Benjamin XIV,33
Daniel XV,44
David XIV,34, 436, 572, 590;
XV,279-80, 356, 590;
XVI,225, 928
George XIV,224, 501, 514;
XV, 249-51, 255, 528
Henry XIV,405
John XIV,10, 286-87;
XV,279-80; XVII,253
Jonathan XIV,286-87;
XV,424, 700, 702-3;
XVI,46, 170, 172, 174,
302
Joseph XIV,225, 342, 348;
XVI, 734-35; XVII,461
Joshua XVI,308, 924;
XVII,115
Obed XIV,287
Obededom XIV,286; XVI,812
Oliver XVI,898
Samuel XVI,243, 510, 703,
706
Thomas XIV,577
Timothy XIV,24
Sanderson, David XIV, 419,
438, 468, 609; XV,613,
714; XVI, 200, 269, 509,
692
Enoch XIV,253
James XVI,312
John XIV,581, 616; XV,7,
719
John Jr. XIV,581; XV,448,
599
Thomas XIV,468, 612; XV,
711
William XIV,2
Sands, George XIV,223
Sanford, Samuel XVII,302

Sanger, John XV,43, 376;
    XVII,110
    Nathaniel XV,50
Sankey, Caesar XIV,540
    Carson XIV,447
Saratoga, John XVII,306
Sargeant, Benjamin XV,729
    Ebenezer XV,723
    John XV,720
    Samuel XV,731
    Valentine XV,455, 722
Sargent, Aaron XIV,211, 214,
    217, 219-20
    Abel XVI,84, 100, 246, 253,
        285, 515, 935
    Anthony XV,183
    Barnard XVI,236, 242, 270,
        503, 548, 617-18
    Benjamin XIV,567, 653;
        XV,609; XVI,31, 34, 59,
        187, 210, 789, 869;
        XVII,430
    Charles XV,742
    Daniel XIV,606; XVI,103,
        198, 267, 523, 624, 626,
        818; XVII,364
    David XIV,268, 271, 290
    Ebenezer XIV,568, 632;
        XV,113, 610; XVI,206
    Elias XIV,56; XV,464, 466,
        505
    Enoch XV,174
    Ephraim XIV,663; XVI,874
    Isaac XV,175
    Jacob XV,149; XVI,872
    James XVI,141, 161;
        XVII,427
    John XIV,16, 309, 383, 410,
        491, 624; XV,402;
        XVI,204, 229, 241, 272,
        510, 725; XVII,648, 660
    Jonathan XV,267, 269, 271
    Joseph XIV,202, 314;
        XV,199, 464, 466, 505,
        554, 742
    Joshua XV,555
    Lemuel XIV,265

Sargent, Moses XV,550;
    XVI,141, 161
    Nathan XV,409
    Paul D. XV,739
    Philip XVI,169
    Phinehas XIV,231, 341
    Richard XIV,354
    Robert XVI,131, 163
    Roger XIV,404
    Samuel XIV,173, 177, 288,
        586, 657; XVI,35, 38, 195,
        212
    Thomas XV,132
    Timothy XIV,405
    Valentine XIV,211, 215, 218-
        20, 561, 579, 621;
        XVI,205, 236, 243, 273,
        501, 600, 723
    See also Serjeant
Sarler, Thomas XVII,60
Sartell, Ephraim XV,530;
        XVI,739
    Hezekiah XV,539
    John XV,31
    Jonathan XV,538
    Jonathan Jr. XV,217
Sartwell, Captain XVII,456
    Hezekiah XV,631, 646
    Jeremiah XIV,291; XV,701,
        703
    John XIV,34; XV,100;
        XVII,104
    Jonathan XV,97; XVI,272,
        518
    Jonathan Jr. XV,218, 630,
        646
    Simeon XV,710
    Simon XIV,553, 610; XVI,2,
        180, 182, 197, 222, 267,
        769; XVII,266
Satterlee, William XVII,307
Saunders, Avery XIV,547
    David XIV,525
    George XIV,248, 381, 589;
        XV, 565
    John XIV,546; XVI,539
    Jonathan XIV,546; XV,725;

Saunders, Jonathan (Cont.) XVI,
208, 508, 679
Joshua XVI,541
Peter XVI,914-15
Samuel XVI,236, 243, 269
William XIV,265
See also Sanders
Satchwill, Jeremiah XVI,46,
174, 302, 523, 852
Satterlee, Captain XVI,304
Sautridge, John XIV,257-58
Savage, Abijah XVII,361
Benjamin XVI,111, 166
Elizabeth XVII,609
Henry XVII,511
John XIV,239, 358
Thomas XIV,343; XV,749
Sawtell, Edmund XV,93, 220
Hezekiah XVI,763, 812
John XV,745
Jonathan XVI,812, 814
Jonathan Jr. XVI,236, 815
Sawyer,--- XV,699
Abel XV,152, 154; XVII,118-
19
Benjamin XIV,159, 161, 273;
XIV,279, 288-89, 463;
XV,75, 214, 426, 584-85,
589; XVI,307, 313;
XVII,66, 78-79, 113, 116,
223
Bezaleel XV,99, 349, 664-65,
671, 681; XVI,158, 698
Canet XVII,67
Charles H. XVII,604
Colonel XVII,15
Dill XIV,463, 473; XVII,66,
78, 113
Edmund XIV,454, 529, 546;
XV, 165, 472, 487, 490,
499-500
Edward XVI,285, 498, 538
Enoch XVI,666
Enos XIV,159, 161, 165;
XV,589; XVI,313; XVII,116
Ephraim XV,6, 47, 223, 633,
648; XVI,547, 877; XVII,94

Sawyer, George XVI,116
Ichabod XIV,443, 543;
XV,278; XVI,48
James XV,227
Jeremiah XVII,435
Jesse XIV,405
John XIV,167, 170; XV,383,
568, 590, 743; XVI,314,
530, 920; XVII,14, 78,
117-19
John Jr. XV,590
Jonathan XIV,135, 191, 567,
611; XV,47, 211, 223,
608, 718; XVI,202, 538;
XVII,7
Jonathan Jr. XV,328, 330,
343
Joseph XIV,135, 191, 547;
XVI, 670; XVII,7, 92
Josiah XIV,102, 208, 398;
XV, 73, 267, 269-71, 520,
698
Jotham XIV,226; XV,486,
499-500
Manassah XV,700, 702, 704,
725; XVI,46, 174, 208,
302, 522, 877
Manassah Jr. XIV,356
Moses XVI,131, 133, 163
Nathaniel XIV,356
Nurse XIV,103, 207, 303
Phinehas XV,42
Rufus XV,99, 536
Samuel XIV,123, 187
Sylvanus XVI,297
Thomas XVI,538
William XIV,49, 121
Saxton, Charles XV,18, 40
Sayer, Abraham XIV,238
Samuel XIV,108
Sayward, Henry XIV,238
Saywood, John XIV,1
Scagell, Jacob XV,730,734
Scales, Doctor XVI,898
Isaac XV,620
James XVI,915
Joshua XIV,403

Scales, Matthew XIV, 316, 567,
    585, 659; XV,607, 727;
    XVI,316, 708
  Moses XIV,319
  Samuel XIV,234
Scammell, Alexander XIV,49,
    80, 248, 552, 555, 638,
    688; XV, 136, 276, 421-
    22, 424, 432, 446, 455-58,
    726, 755; XVI,6, 9, 12, 15,
    17, 42, 56, 59, 182, 185-
    89, 208, 248, 280, 412;
    XVII,134, 269, 354, 419
  Robert XVI,98
Scammon, Colonel XV,749
  Humphrey XIV,3
  Richard XVII,513, 526
  William XIV,231, 403, 414
Scates, Joshua XIV,414
Schoof, Jacob XVII,114
Schoop, Jacob XVI,307, 928
Schrives, Frederick XVII,301
Schuyler, Philip XVII,16, 128-
    33,141, 152, 229, 311,
    370, 386, 398
Scilley, James XIV,513
  Jonathan XIV,513
  Samuel XIV,223
Sclate, Edward XIV,27
Scobey, David XIV,358
Scofield, John XV,42, 377
Scott, Abel XVI,153
  Abraham XV,55
  Alexander XVI,840
  Benjamin XVII,204
  Charles XIV,274-75, 278,
    289; XV,43
  David XIV,43, 91; XV,427,
    733, 740; XVI,47, 54, 101,
    303, 508, 839-40
  Ebenezer XIV,427; XV,55
  George XVI,918
  Henry XIV,28-29
  Hezekiah XIV,93, 202
  James XV,99, 104, 360, 740,
    746; XVI,830-40, 842

Scott, John XV,356, 711, 739,
    753; XVI,198, 267; XVII,
    445
  John Jr. XVI,153
  Joseph XVI,159
  Nathan XV,61
  Robert XIV, 445, 543; XV,16
  Samuel XV,205; XVII,96
  Sergeant XIV,2
  Theophilus XVI,239
  Thomas XIV,469, 575, 602;
    XV, 712, 739; XVI,198,
    222, 268, 517, 520, 794,
    840-41; XVII, 293
  Waitsill, XIV,426; XV,6, 8;
    XVI,876-77
  William XIV,43, 91, 153, 201,
    333, 553, 575, 577, 612-4,
    622; XV,101, 357, 427,
    434, 456, 602, 710, 722,
    726, 739, 754; XVI,2, 47,
    51, 54-55, 90, 101, 182,
    197, 205, 221, 267, 273,
    303, 418, 514, 518, 764;
    XVII,266, 291, 350, 415,
    441, 470
Scovel, Peter XIV,464
  Thomas XIV,464
Scovill, Jeremiah XV,33
  Jesse XV,10, 147; XVII,249
  John Jr. XVII,109
  Thomas XV,35
Scranton, Stephen XIV,606;
    XVI, 103, 198, 267, 515,
    770
Scribner, Benjamin XV,165
  Daniel XV,754
  Ebenezer XVI,236, 243, 269,
    510, 642
  Edward XV,165
  Josiah XIV,316, 318
  Manoah XV,283, 290
  Nathaniel XV,172
  Noah XV,564
  Samuel XIV,316, 318, 398;
    XV, 514; XVI,564

Scribner, Stephen XIV,362, 364; XV,172

Scripture, James XIV,346; XV,529

Samuel XIV,100, 206-7; XV,530

Samuel Jr. XIV,100, 206; XV,81, 530

Scriven, William XVII,296

Scrivner, Samuel XIV,12

Scrowley, Florence XVI,930, 932

Seagell, Jacob XVI,19, 194, 211, 220, 241, 278

Sealia, Lewis XIV,283, 287

Seals, James XIV,468, 631; XVI, 198, 224, 267, 286, 504, 515, 588, 635

Searle, Elnathan XV,698
John XV,471, 502; XVII,667
Rev. Jonathan XV,81, 83; XVI, 739
Joseph XV,96, 751
William XV,164; XVI,860

Searles, Thomas XIV,346

Sears, James XVI,245

Seaver, Caleb XIV,405
Comfort XVII,153
Elijah XVII,424
John XVII,153, 656
Robert XIV,33, 243
Thomas XIV,478

Seavey, Aaron XV,326
Benjamin XVII,638
Daniel XVI,67, 78, 94, 257
Elijah XIV,228
George XIV,398
James XIV,224, 248; XVI,144; XVII,26
John XIV,247, 574; XV,615, 725; XVI,207
Jonathan XIV,119, 150, 196, 642; XV,422, 456; XVI,18; XVII,360
Joseph XIV,247, 402, 414; XV, 18, 138; XVI,130, 163; XVII, 25

Seavey, Levi XIV,228, 642; XV,422, 456; XVI,19
Mark XVII,131
Noah XIV,25
Samuel XIV,139, 192, 255, 403, 415; XV,256, 258-59, 262
Stephen XV,431, 692; XVI,214
Thomas XVII,527
William XIV,224, 247, 415; XV, 298; XVI,109, 165; XVII,25, 513, 522, 527, 666, 693, 742

Seaward, Benjamin XIV,345
George XV,249, 251-52, 254
James XIV,258, 345
John XVI,926; XVII,420
Joseph XVII,139
Thomas XVII,205
Shackford XVII,23, 31, 39, 46, 85

Secomb, Stephen XIV,546

Secombe, Stephen XVI,709

Sedocks, Isaac XIV,5
John XIV,5

Seetown, James XVI,555-56

Seils, James XV,711

Sellers, Francis XVII,297

Selley, James XIV,391, 487, 513
Jonathan XIV,391, 487, 513
Samuel XIV,424
See also Scilley

Sellingham, Henry XIV,168, 170, 654; XV,460, 605; XVI,34; XVII,14
Jacob XIV,654; XV,460, 605; XVI,34

Senter, Abel XIV,75, 178; XV,519
Abraham XV,443, 595, 725, 749; XVI,207, 803
Asa XIV, 73-74, 178, 552, 605; XV,710; XVI,3, 51, 182, 197, 222, 248, 267, 531; XVII,216, 266, 274,

Senter, Asa (Cont.) 441-42, 456
    Benjamin XIV,425
    Joseph XIV,311, 464;
        XV,238-39, 240-75, 433,
        462; XVI, 550, 798, 801,
        911; XVII,215
    Levi XVI,84, 95
    Lieutenant XIV,579; XVI,105,
        301
    Moses XV,392; XVI,122, 164,
        281, 744, 918
    Samuel XIV,75, 178
    Simeon XV,199
    Thomas XIV,247
Serjeant, Anthony XV,120
    Elias XV,478
    Elisha XV,733
    Jacob XV,160
    Joseph XV,478
    Lemuel XV,23, 37
    Roger XV,563
    Stephen P. XV,495
    Timothy XV,587
Seshings, John XV,732, 735;
        XVI, 36, 39, 196, 212,
        232, 278, 507, 664
Setchell, Jeremiah XV,446
    Jonathan XIV,238
Sever, Comfort XV,377
    Robert XV,87, 89
Severance, Abbe XV,630, 643,
        646
    Abel XIV,91, 201; XVI,855,
        857, 859
    Asa XV,664-65, 671, 683;
        XVI,159, 762
    Benjamin XV,21, 220, 534,
        754; XVI,159
    Caleb XV,206
    Daniel XIV,91, 201, 420
    Eben XV,21
    Ebenezer XIV,35, 91, 201,
        420; XV,220
    Ephraim XIV,575, 593;
        XV,716, 743; XVI,509, 709
    Jonathan XIV,135, 191;
        XV,322, 342, 561; XVII,7

Severance, Joseph XIV,261,
        574; XV,615
    Joshua XIV,97, 204; XV,519;
        XVI,261; XVII,432
    Peter XIV,69, 76, 83, 180,
        198, 249, 327, 457, 537;
        XV, 128, 165; XVI,599
    Samuel XIV,113, 147, 196
    Thomas XIV,585, 611;
        XV,718; XVI,202, 708;
        XVII,424
    William XIV,76, 83, 198; XV,
        200; XVI,156
Sewall, Jonathan Mitchell XVII,
        125
    Stephen XVII,757
    Thomas XV,752
Seward, Shackford XIV,239,
        260, 484
Sewell, Benjamin XIV,238
    Edward XVII,526
    Thomas XVI,511, 729
Shackford, John XVII,340, 655
    Jonah XVII,139
    Josiah XV,577
    Mr. XVI,925
    Samuel XV,416, 577, 583;
        XVI, 759
    Seth XIV,345; XVII,29
    Seth R. XIV,641; XV,423,
        597, 730; XVI,17
    William XVII,525
Shade, Nathan XIV,470, 606;
        XV, 716; XVI,201, 269
Shadwick, Daniel XV,225
Shafter, James XIV,264, 437,
        525; XV,55, 204; XVI,927
    Simon XV,746
Shalletoe, Michael XVII,619
Shalote, Francis XVII,621, 644,
        694
Shandonet, Francis XVII,266
Shannon,--- XV,699
    Abigail XVII,762
    Andrew XIV,201; XV,215
    George XIV,42, 186; XVII,4
    John XIV,300, 388, 494, 589,

Shannon, John (Cont.) 647,
    650; XV,465, 467, 478,
    504, 694; XVI,13, 515
  John Jr. XV,596
  Nathaniel XVII,738
  Richard Cutts XV,624;
    XVI,690
  Samuel XV,465, 467, 478,
    505; XVI,66, 77, 97
  Thomas XIV,389, 495, 508,
    516; XV,465, 467, 478,
    505
  William XIV,76, 83, 198, 299,
    387, 494, 507, 516;
    XV,526; XVI,599
Shapleigh, Major XVII,572
  Nicholas XVII,514, 537
Shapley, David XVI,151
  Henry XIV,224, 248; XVII,26
Sharp, Gilbert XVI,933
  Jonathan XIV,322, 562, 636;
    XV, 618, 725
  Thomas XVII,303
  William XVII,303
Sharper, William XV,437, 620
Sharpstone, Jacob XVI,932
Shattuck, Benjamin XV,82;
    XVI,465
  Cyrus XVI,686
  Daniel XV,50-51; XVI,531;
    XVII, 97
  Edmund XV,124; XVI,669
  Henry XV,84
  Isaac XIV,392, 488, 509, 513
  Jeremiah XV,744
  Joseph XIV,51
  Nathaniel XIV,35; XV,220
  Peter XIV,333; XV,21, 93,
    356
  William XIV,34, 67, 180, 572,
    602; XV,612, 712
Shaw, Abraham XV,256, 258,
    260, 264
  Benjamin XIV,230-31;
    XV,300, 305, 309;
    XVI,131, 163; XVII, 81, 83,
    687

Shaw, Caleb XIV,99-100, 133,
    156-57, 190, 206; XVI,687
  Caleb Jr. XIV,110, 413
  Daniel XIV,109, 122, 187,
    251; XVI,710; XVII,644
  Daniel O. XVII,667
  David XIV,413; XV,256, 258;
    XIV,413; XV,256, 258,
    260, 263, 273
  Ebenezer XV,349
  Edward XIV,11
  Follonsby XV,749
  George XIV,233, 321
  Gilbert XIV,448, 535
  Henry XVI,287
  Ichabod XIV,118, 139, 158,
    192
  Isaac XV,695, 699; XVI,128,
    162
  James XVII,301
  John XIV,390, 486, 508, 512-
    13; XV,249-51, 254;
    XVI,583, 932; XVII,27, 57,
    740
  Jonathan XVII,57
  Jonathan H. XIV,232, 350
  Joseph XIV,110, 133, 190,
    413; XV,286, 314; XVII,22,
    37
  Josiah XV,319, 339
  Levi XV,323, 342, 420-21;
    XVI, 130, 163
  Moses XIV,131, 190, 232,
    413; XV,240-41
  Moses Jr. XIV,109
  Nehemiah XVI,83, 99, 193
  Richard XVII,24
  Roger XVII,643, 667-68, 687
  Samuel XIV,230, 238, 252,
    280, 288, 549; XV,125,
    430; XVI, 131
  Simeon XIV,252
  Thomas XIV,485, 562, 637,
    647, 649, 660; XV,597,
    619, 653, 728, 734;
    XVI,12, 190, 209, 228,
    277, 498, 551, 668, 789-

Shaw, Thomas (Cont.) 790, 803-
    4, 818; XVII,85, 312
    Timothy XVI,255, 508
    William XIV,317, 320, 453,
        532, 641; XV,711
Sheafe, Henry XVI,67, 78, 93
    James XVII,142
    Mr. XVII,691
    Sampson XVI,319
    Samuel XVI,906
Shearer, James XV,553, 718;
    XVI, 202
    Nathan XVI,890-91
    Samuel XV,122, 698
Shearman, Daniel XIV,427
    David XV,746
    Richard XIV,487; XV,595,
        728, 734
Shears, Ebenezer XIV,7
Shed, Daniel XV,82, 211, 632,
        636
    Jonas XV,210
    Nathaniel XV,631, 637
Shedd, Alexander XVI,308
    Daniel XVI,18, 44, 584
    Edward XVI,611
    Nathan XVI,102, 501
    Nathaniel XVI,113, 609; XVII,
        427
    William XVI,263, 890
Shedrick, Joseph XVI,102
    Michael XVI,102
Shelburne, Major XVII,59
Sheldon, Abraham XV,95
Shelley, Abraham XVII,295
Shepard, Amos XV,9, 28, 37;
    XVI, 553
    Corporal XIV,2
    Daniel XV,165, 405, 514;
        XVI, 88, 94, 264, 578,
        914; XVII, 430
    Elisha XV,128, 631, 638;
        XVI, 264, 576; XVII,431
    George XIV,145, 193, 317,
        320, 566-67, 656; XV,606-
        7, 731, 735; XVI, 35, 38,
        195, 212, 232, 278, 500,

Shepard, George (Cont.) 577,
    594; XVII,9
    Isaac XIV,451, 532; XV,268,
        270-71; XVII,83
    Isaac Jr. XVII,80
    Israel XVII,32
    James XIV,243, 261, 316-18,
        365
    John XIV,123, 187, 331, 397,
        618; XV,607, 619, 723;
        XVI, 206, 237, 245, 273,
        520, 838
    Joseph XV,124, 126
    Joshua XV,29
    Luke XIV,387, 494, 507, 516
    Morrill XVI,237, 271, 502,
        594-595
    Nathaniel XV,29; XVII,105
    Oliver XIV,297; XV,28, 37
    Roswell XIV,325, 464
    Samuel XIV,301; XVI,687,
        903; XVII,13
    Thomas XIV,350; XV,742
Shepardson, Zephaniah XIV,264
Shepell, Rona XVII,306
Sherard, Samuel XV,696
Sherburne, Andrew XIV,248;
    XVII, 26
    Benjamin XV,359
    Colonel XVI,902
    D. XVII,139
    David XIV,239, 448, 535;
        XV,325
    Edward XVII,160, 166, 170,
        191
    General XV,239
    Henry XIV,14; XV,416, 577;
        XVI, 803-4; XVII,139, 361,
        512, 606, 695
    Jacob XV,387
    James XIV,145, 193, 304-5,
        465; XV,179; XVII,8
    Job XIV,71, 179, 330, 399,
        451, 532; XV,483, 495
    John XIV,227, 248; XV,692;
        XVI, 60, 62, 70, 98, 106,
        193, 804; XVII,26, 511,

Sherburne, John (Cont.) 513,
527, 669
John S. XV,508
Joseph XV,528; XVI,911
Love XVII,633, 646
Major XIV,477
Nathaniel XVII,139
Noah XIV,382, 490
Pomp XVI,63, 73, 93, 235,
272, 511
Pompey XVI,107, 725
Samuel XIV,13, 67, 181, 345,
403, 415; XV,249-52, 255,
580; XVI,320-21, 323,
326, 328, 330, 338, 340,
343, 345, 449; XVII,49,
139
Samuel Jr. XVI,449
Thomas XVII,23, 38
Thomas Jr. XIV,255; XVII,31
Sheriden, Bartholomew XVII,308
Sheriff,--- XVII,362
Abraham XIV,353; XV,283,
290; XVII,27
Samuel XIV,256; XVII,23, 31,
39
Sherlock, Francis XVII,599
Sherman, John XIV,257
Richard XIV,391, 647, 650;
XVI, 12, 189, 209, 277,
320, 326, 332, 341, 343,
345, 451, 516, 803-4
Sherrer, David XIV,611
Sherwick, Samuel XIV,7
Sherwin, Asa XV,20
David XV,217
John XV,539
Samuel XV,97
Sherwood, Zachariah XVII,307
Shield, Alexander XVI,314
Shields, Alexander XV,383; XVII,
115
James XVII,308
Shillaber, Joseph XIV,259
Shinner, Charles XV,595
Shipman, Abraham XV,370

Shipman, Eliphalet XV,732;
XVI,20, 23, 191, 212
Eliphaz XIV,644
Shipway, John XVII,527
Shirley, Alexander XIV,410
Daniel XIV,583, 600; XV,
715; XVI,200, 262; XVII,
427
James XIV, 406, 410; XV,
754
John XIV,410
Mr. XVII,491
Robert XVI,262; XVII,427
Thomas XV,115, 556, 754;
XVII, 258
Shoar, John XVII,656
Shoars, Ichabod XIV,239, 255,
260
William XIV,227, 257, 472
Shoff, Jacob XV,152
Shoot, Henry XIV,223
Shore, Peter Jr. XVII,139
Shorer, Ichabod XVII,24, 31, 38,
46
Shores, Peter XVI,925
Shorey, James XIV,237
Short, Benjamin XVI,218, 250,
832, 934
Daniel XV,16, 40, 138
Ebenezer Jr. XVI,153
Simeon XIV,444; XVII,89
William XVI,310
Shortridge, Benjamin XVI,333
John XIV,227, 472, 549;
XV,430
Mary XVI,333, 452
Richard XIV,118-20, 149,
151, 154, 196-97, 250;
XVI,452; XVII,527, 749
Samuel XIV,118-19, 151, 197
Shower, Nathaniel XIV,22
Shrive, Samuel XIV,239
Shroder, Thomas XIV,583, 604
Shrouder, Thomas XV,715
Shuff, Jacob XVI,924
Shurtleff, Asa XVI,83, 193

252

Shurtleff, Simeon XVI,635
Shute, John XV,728; XVI,14,
  192, 209, 277, 804
  Jonathan XIV,648, 650;
  XV,595; XVI,41, 232, 516,
  803, 805
Shutir, Lapool XVII,308
Sias, Benjamin XIV,261, 454-
  55, 529, 531, 545-46;
  XV,132, 162, 179, 181,
  235, 386, 512-13, 697-99
  Charles XIV,454, 529, 546
  Eliphalet XVI,282
  John XIV,109, 123, 187, 408;
  XV,312; XVI,710; XVII,719
  Joseph XVI,711
  Samuel XIV,211, 215, 217,
  219-220; XVII,414
  Samuel Jr. XIV,21
Sibley, Samuel XV,173; XVI,282
  William XIV,432; XVI,659
Siegert, Samuel XVII,304
Siel, James XIV,584; XV,451,
  615, 711; XVI,588
  John XVI,235
  See also Seals
Signout, Ephraim XIV,10
Sikes, Othniel XV,753
Silaway, Benjamin W. XVII,32
Silk, Humphrey XVI,113, 236,
  243, 508, 615
  Michael XIV,468, 576;
  XV,653, 711; XVI,198,
  223, 239, 267, 509, 699
Sillaway, Amos XIV,302-3, 312
  Benjamin W. XV,560
  Hezekiah XV,587
  Jacob XIV,113, 147, 195
  John XV,406
Sillery, Hugh XVII,298
Silley, Daniel XIV,494
  Jonathan XV,551, 747
  Thomas XIV,450
  See also Cilley
Silloway, Henry XVII, 667,
  669
Sills, John XV,754

Silsby, Eliphaz XV,10, 144, 368
  Eusibius XV,33; XVII,106
  Henry XVI,549
  Jonathan XV,367; XVI,436;
  XVII, 103
  Julius XV,9
  Lasell XIV,324, 464; XV,9, 33
  Samuel XV,740
Silver, Daniel XV,390
  David XVI,63, 73, 97
  Jacob XVII,424
  Obadiah XVII,426
  Samuel XIV,587, 660;
  XV,727; XV,735; XVI,11,
  40, 44, 189-90, 209, 233,
  241, 277, 519, 825
  Zebediah XVI,125
Silvester, Levi XV,587
Simmons, Nathaniel XIV,225
  Simon XVI,148
Simms, William XVI,322, 332,
  334, 470, 608
Simonds, Benjamin XVI,143
  Eli XIV,145, 193-94
  James XIV,85, 199, 593;
  XV,439; XVI,287, 519
  John XVI,809, 928; XVII,104,
  249, 457
  Jonathan XIV,140, 193
  Joseph XVI,678
  Levi XV,9; XVII,457, 468
  Samuel XIV,50
  Silas XV,31; XVII,457, 468
  Timothy XIV,61
  William XIV,289, 319; XV,29,
  127
Simons, Eli XVII,9
  James XV,370, 717; XVI,149
  John XIV,599; XV,144, 538,
  717; XVI,202, 519, 887;
  XVII,224
  Jonathan XIV,114
  Joseph XV,231; XVI,903
  Levi XV,143, 717; XVI,202
  Richard XIV,11
  Samuel XVI,914
  Silas XV,717; XVI,202

Simons, Simeon XV,182
Timothy XIV,182
William XIV,25, 273, 277,
316; XV,146,165
Simpson, Alexander XV,359,
566
Andrew XIV,226; XVI,920;
XVII, 80, 82
Benjamin XIV,237, 430;
XVII,30
David XIV,242, 414; XV,544;
XVII,360
Ebenezer XIV,238
Henry XIV,550; XV,430
James XIV,103
John XIV,42, 53, 69, 180,
185, 398; XV,470, 473,
566; XVI, 141, 162, 320,
322, 324-25, 328, 331,
334, 337, 339, 343-344,
452
Joseph XIV,426; XV,267,
269-71
Josiah XVI,66, 75, 95, 286,
520
Mr. XVII,358
Patten XIV,398; XV,527
Pelatiah XIV,237
Robert XIV,547, 607-8;
XV,154, 422, 424, 730;
XVI,18, 67, 78, 95, 194,
211, 281, 538; XVII,80, 82
Theodore XVI,906
Thomas XIV,160, 164, 555,
608, 643; XV, 154, 422-
23, 726; XVI,7, 320-21,
324, 326, 330, 335, 337,
339, 343-44, 454-457;
XVII,80, 82, 84, 269
Thomas Jr. XIV,161, 547;
XVII, 80, 82
William XIV,135, 171, 174,
176-77, 191, 288, 398,
470, 604, 606; XV, 284,
287, 634, 649, 715-16;
XVI,102, 200, 269, 513,
516, 668, 778, 783, 789;

Simpson, William (Cont.) XVII,6,
52
Sims, Joseph XIV,119
Sinclair, Bradbury XV,712
Ebenezer XV,712
George XVII,304
Jacob XIV,71
James XIV,476; XV,701, 703,
726; XVI,46, 171-72, 176,
208, 240, 302, 742;
XVII,27
John XIV,231; XVI,891;
XVII,27
Joseph XV,590, 701, 703,
712, 726; XVI,46, 171-72,
176, 208, 240, 302, 828,
928
Joseph Jr. XV,590; XVI,928
Joshua XVI,199
Noah XV,727; XVI,184, 208,
320, 458
Richard XIV,476; XVI,121,
123, 164, 185
Richard Jr. XVI,164
Samuel XV,712; XVI,199
Singleton, Lieutenant XVII,219,
228, 242, 281
Sinkler, Barnabas XIV,325, 464
Benjamin XIV,432
Bradbury XIV,361, 365, 603;
XV, 449, 600; XVII,25
Captain XVII,414
Charles XIV,3
Ebenezer XIV,56, 184, 603;
XVI, 871-72, 874
Edward XIV,67
Jacob XIV,179
James XIV,243; XVI,512;
XVII,57, 652
Jeremiah XVI,282
John XIV,331
Joseph XVI,521
Joshua XIV,361, 365, 603;
XV, 449, 600
Noah XIV,68, 180, 569, 652;
XV, 609; XVI,9, 42, 320,
325, 328, 332, 341, 343-

Sinkler, Noah (Cont.) 44, 458,
    726
  Richard XIV,296, 361, 365;
    XV, 172, 393; XVI,10, 43,
    123, 569
  Samuel XIV,14, 603; XV,449,
    600
  Sergeant XIV,2
  Thomas XV,173
  Zebulon XV,134
Sippio XIV,21, 226
Siphors, John XIV,183
  See also Cypher
Sisco, Samuel XV, 717; XVI,201;
    XVII,467
  William XV,144, 604, 717;
    XVI, 202, 218, 270, 520,
    614, 870, 934; XVII,467
Skeels, David XVI,308-9
  John XVII,254
Skerry, John XV,351, 353
Skiffe, John XIV,1
Skillin, Benjamin XIV,15
Skinner, Abel XIV,443, 542;
    XVI, 314
  Abner XV,65, 67
  Amos XIV,420; XVI,314;
    XVII,250
  Charles XIV,388, 495, 507,
    516, 647, 650; XVI,13
  Ephraim XIV,268, 270, 289;
    XV, 379; XVII,118-19
  General XVII,163, 167-68,
    174, 178
  Joseph XIV,272, 290, 292;
    XVI, 315
  Joseph Jr. XVI,314
Skipper, John XIV,1, 7
Slack, Joseph XIV,101, 206-7;
    XV, 446, 723; XVI,206,
    523, 852
Slade, James XVII,108
  John XV,29, 741
  Samuel XIV,227, 255, 257,
    472; XV,38, 324, 662,
    669, 681; XVI,552

Slapp, Edward XIV,607-8;
    XV,436; XV,603, 714
  John Jr. XIV,422
  Simon XV,40
Slaughter, Deadloff XVII,308
Sleeper, Benjamin XIV,565, 660;
    XV,727; XVI,10, 43, 184,
    209, 581; XVII,19
  Corporal XIV,2
  David XIV,279, 288
  Gideon XV,125
  Hezekiah XIV,12
  Jacob XV,564
  Jedediah XIV,230; XV,164
  John XIV,388, 495, 507, 516,
    519; XV,401; XVII,7, 32
  John Jr. XVII,32
  John B. XV,322, 342
  Jonathan XIV,113, 147, 195
  Joseph XIV,284, 287;
    XV,587, 742
  Moses XIV,227; XV,400;
    XVI,314, 525; XVII,117,
    254
  Nathan XIV,112, 147, 196
  Nehemiah XVI,615
  Peter XIV,441, 527; XVI,682
  Richard XIV,226
  Robert XV,243, 245, 247
  Samuel XIV,24
  Sanborn XVII,28
  Thomas XV,165
Sleman, John XVII,205
Sloan, James XIV,635
  John XIV,101, 206; XV,277-
    78, 626; XVI,314, 924
  Matthew XVI,314
  William XIV,563
Slocum, Hezekiah XIV,5
Sloper, Benning XIV,485, 500,
    512; XVII,86
  B. W. XIV,258
  Henry XVI,66, 76, 98;
    XVII,754
  John XIV,239, 257-58, 344,
    409; XVII,30

Sloper, Richard XVII,511, 513, 656, 660
Small, Benjamin XIV,123, 187, 251, 564, 624; XV,441, 619, 720; XVI,907
　Caesar XIV,351
　Hix XV,349
　Isaac XIV,22, 233, 408; XVI,118
　John XIV,616; XV,249, 251-53, 719; XVI,203
　Jonathan XIV,102
　Joseph XIV,25, 208
　Samuel XV,192; XVI,257, 515
　William Jr. XIV,337; XVII,64
Smalley, Benjamin XIV,287
Smallwood, William XVII,158, 160-170, 175-90
Smart, Bartholomew XVII,434
　Benjamin XIV,25, 116, 227, 257, 472, 565, 616; XV,451, 694; XVI,156, 234, 285, 505
　Caleb XIV,567, 611; XV,608, 718; XVI,202
　Dudley XIV,400; XV,243, 245, 247; XVII,29
　Elijah XIV,301, 567, 611; XV, 608, 718; XVI,202
　Jeremiah XIV,312, 564, 599; XV, 713; XVI,527
　John XIV,564; XV,243, 245-46
　Jonathan XIV,321; XV,243, 245, 247; XVI,287, 514
　Moses XIV,280, 288, 657; XV, 732; XVI,36, 39, 195, 212
　Moses Jr. XV,460, 605
　Nathaniel XVI,507
　Richard XIV,61, 182, 273, 289, 566, 657; XV,609, 732; XVI, 37, 39, 195, 212, 530; XVII, 319
　Richard Jr. XV,460, 605; XVI, 800
　Robert XV,171; XVII,435, 526
　Samuel XVI,169-70

Smart, William XIV,25, 43, 109, 123, 187; XV,243, 245, 312; XVI,28
　Winthrop XV,194; XVII,24
Smeed, Dennis XVI,521
Smiley, David XV,77, 518
　Francis XV,536
　Hugh XVI,898
　John XIV,334; XV,217
　William XIV,334; XVI,536, 698-699, 898
Smith, Aaron XIV,263, 273, 277; XV,52; XVI,320-21, 323, 325, 330, 335, 337, 339, 343-44, 459, 531
　Abijah XIV,420
　Adam XV,175
　Alexander XIV,67, 181, 304-5, 465, 469, 565, 602; XV,712; XVI,199, 222, 241, 268, 499, 529, 582
　Alexander G. XVII,57
　Amos XV,52
　Asahel XIV,342, 349
　Bartholomew XVII,501
　Benjamin XIV,35, 91, 229, 268, 271, 290, 351, 353, 417, 470, 575, 596, 600, 606, 639; XV, 11, 52, 168, 285, 291, 311, 320, 339, 425, 437, 464, 466, 478, 505, 571, 713, 715, 731, 735; XVI, 15, 26, 278-79, 194, 199-200, 211, 220, 255, 268-269, 278, 285, 505, 511, 521, 729, 750, 854, 857-60, 876
　Benjamin Y. XIV,324, 464
　Billy XIV,76, 83, 198
　Burleigh XV,526
　Caleb XIV,410; XV,562; XVI,807
　Cato XVI,285, 499
　Cheney XIV,114, 141, 193, 250, 298; XV,295; XVI,627
　Christopher XV,18, 138; XVII, 108

Smith, Colonel XVI,294
   Cortroit XVI,933
   Daniel XIV,14, 226, 229, 416,
      426, 450, 534; XV,75,
      283, 290
   David XIV,14, 231, 567, 600,
      611; XV,437, 608, 715,
      718; XVI,86, 100
   Eben XVI,236, 499
   Ebenezer XIV,246, 296, 456;
      XV, 133, 135, 389;
      XVI,243, 270, 473, 582,
      742-44, 758-59, 827-28;
      XVII,454-55
   Edward XIV,172, 175-77,
      588, 600, 604, 616, 635;
      XV,437, 457, 596, 615, 618,
      716, 724-725; XVI,201,
      528, 659
   Eli XV,10
   Elias XV,392
   Elijah XV,41, 375
   Eliphalet XIV,232, 565;
      XV,284, 287, 699;
      XVI,122, 164
   Elisha XIV,628; XV,43, 374,
      721, 748; XVI,204;
      XVII,27, 96, 713
   Enoch XV,630, 643, 646,
      723; XVI,206, 227, 274,
      523, 870
   Ephraim XIV,88, 201
   Ezekiel XVI,286, 500
   Francis XV,38, 44-45, 386;
   Francis XVII,91, 108, 111,
      236
   Gideon XIV,463; XV,15, 39,
      375; XVII,65, 78, 113
   Gideon Jr. XV,41
   Hannah XVI,796
   Henry XV,218; XVI,237, 245,
      285, 521, 523, 818, 820
   Ichabod XV, 66
   Isaac XIV,244, 280, 288, 566,
      572, 587, 597, 656; XV,
      435, 460, 605, 609, 611,
      713, 726, 732; XVI,6, 36,

Smith, Isaac (Cont.) 39, 112,
      195, 199, 208, 212, 795
   Israel XIV,113, 147, 195
   Ithiel XIV,14, 25
   Jabez XVI,842; XVII,57, 714
   Jacob XIV,296, 451, 532; XV,
      285, 291, 393; XVI,249,
      281, 293, 744, 831-32;
      XVII,639, 642
   James XIV,243; XV,101, 563,
      593, 635, 639, 742;
      XVI,102, 296, 575, 806,
      911; XVII,419, 512
   Jedediah XIV,324
   Jeremiah XIV,273, 289, 580,
      659; XV,221, 242, 244,
      246, 448, 599, 727;
      XVI,11, 41, 44, 190, 209,
      523
   Jeremy XIV,341; XVI,287
   Jesse XV,106-7, 221, 369,
      471, 502, 669, 680;
      XVI,158, 662; XVII,255
   Jethro XIV,307; XV,747
   Joel XV,24; XVII,104
   John XIV,11, 75, 178, 289,
      292, 334, 359, 380, 468,
      489, 500, 514, 567, 585,
      612, 615, 642, 659;
      XV,116, 125, 165, 189,
      196, 199, 201, 283, 288,
      351, 353, 446, 456, 553,
      571, 583, 597, 605, 625,
      656, 666, 673, 696, 698,
      711, 719, 722, 727, 729,
      744; XVI,11, 27, 87, 90,
      118, 128, 162, 189, 198,
      203, 205 210, 218, 224,
      233, 236, 241, 257, 267,
      271, 273, 277, 303, 316,
      320, 325, 328, 332, 341,
      343-44, 463, 500, 504,
      514, 519-21, 638-41, 708,
      755, 772, 809, 827, 836,
      934; XVII, 27, 54, 78, 207,
      528, 620; XVII,625, 643,
      719, 740

Smith, John Jr. XIV,597;
XVII,27
John 3d XVI,464
John W. XIV,25
Johnson XIV,612; XV,711
Jonathan XIV,3, 145, 194,
212, 215, 218-20, 254,
316, 319, 322, 365, 398,
455, 530, 611; XV,65,
133, 227, 434, 569, 658,
667-68, 674, 677, 690,
691, 717; XVI,116, 294,
298-299, 512, 552, 566,
630, 632, 739, 742, 848
Jonathan Jr. XIV,365; XV,66,
643; XVI,742-43
Joseph XIV,76, 83, 92, 108,
123, 145, 187, 194, 198,
202-203, 211, 215, 217-
18, 220, 232, 251, 396-97,
404, 432, 565, 567, 587,
656, 660; XV, 44, 58, 155,
158, 267, 269, 273, 388,
425, 437, 459, 606-7, 631,
650, 663, 670, 674, 688,
727, 731, 742; XVI, 11,
36, 39, 41, 195, 212, 232,
278, 286, 316, 501, 517,
577, 599, 605, 727, 743,
795-96, 799, 876, 890;
XVII,9, 27, 108, 144, 435,
620, 632, 642, 645-46,
657, 659, 663, 682, 693,
710, 713, 715, 760
Joshua XV,125
Josiah XV,300, 302, 305,
309; XVI, 236, 521, 827
Lemuel XIV,394; XV,155;
XVII, 89, 144
Lieutenant-Colonel XVII,160,
191
Luther XVI,235, 268, 511,
729, 935
M. XVI,439
Major XIV,11; XVII,710, 713
Mary XVI,856
Moody XVII,3

Smith, Moses XV,57, 59, 183
Moses Jr. XVI,602
Nathan XIV,312; XVI,286,
520
Nathaniel XIV,12, 16, 67,
181, 246, 355, 359, 574,
639; XV, 267, 269, 272,
613, 731; XVI, 15, 25,
186, 211, 908-9, 914
Nicholas XIV,532; XVII,435
Nicholas Jr. XIV,451
Obadiah XV,65; XVII,96
Oliver XIV,67, 180, 580, 635;
XV,169, 448, 526, 598,
724; XVI,207, 229, 274,
512, 742
Page XV,69
Pearson XIV,145, 194, 432;
XV, 392; XVII,9
Peter XIV,565, 660; XV,727;
XVI,10, 43, 184, 209, 581
Philip XVII,305
Rebecca XVI,876
Reuben XV,552; XVII,259
Richard XIV,229, 268, 271;
XV, 120, 182, 285, 288,
437, 548, 660-61, 668,
673, 698; XVI, 87, 91,
107, 264, 297, 604, 642,
696; XVII,430
Robert XIV,261, 332, 421;
XV, 127, 162, 164, 196,
198, 237, 514; XVI,718
Robinson XVI,287, 506
Russell XIV,445, 543; XV,19
Samuel XIV,22, 56, 108, 111,
119, 123, 133, 150, 172,
174-175, 177, 184, 187,
190, 196, 231, 238, 251,
312, 346, 358, 400, 430,
452, 470, 532, 567, 587,
602, 627-28, 653; XV, 65,
69, 206, 267-68, 270, 273,
442, 457, 474, 494, 522,
609, 627-28, 641, 657,
678, 700-1, 703, 712,
720-21, 729, 740, 748;

Smith, Samuel (Cont.) XVI, 30,
  33, 45-46, 59, 176, 199,
  225, 268, 301-2, 507, 510,
  664, 694, 703, 731, 750;
  XVII,61, 97, 756
 Seth XVII,295, 739
 Simeon XIV,432; XVI,65, 75,
  100; XVII,254
 Simon XIV,2
 Solomon XIV,25, 135, 191,
  312, 338; XV, 256, 259-
  60, 263; XVII,6
 Stephen XV,593; XVI,156,
  541; XVII,80, 82
 Stevens XV,242, 245-46, 475,
  489
 Theophilus XVI,932;
  XVII,139, 693
 Thomas XIV,359; XV,21, 42-
  43, 65, 356, 436, 539,
  693; XVI, 214, 929
 Timothy XIV,7; XV,173;
  XVI,246, 253, 515
 Trueworthy XV,748
 Wadleigh XIV,300; XV,747
 Willard XV,40, 386
 William XIV,237; XV,635,
  639; XVI,842, 911;
  XVII,302
 Winthrop XV,260, 263
Smyth, Jonathan XV,749
Snagg, Henry XIV,239, 255;
  XVII, 23, 31, 39
Snebly, Henry XIV,223
Snedeker, Richard XVI,932
Snell, George XVII,565, 568, 628
 John XVII,623, 626, 679
 Samuel XVII,655, 670, 675
Snelling, James XIV,29
Snider, Mark XIV,343
Snow, Amos XV,629, 642-43;
  XVI, 26, 202, 223, 271,
  502, 606
 Benjamin XVI,909
 Daniel XV,732; XVI,21, 23;
  XVII,94
 Daniel Jr. XIV,644

Snow, Eli XV,24
 Ensign XIV,26
 Henry XIV,441, 527, 571,
  605; 45, 301; XV,459,
  606, 716; XVI,45, 301
 Hosea XV,7, 224
 James XVI,102
 Jesse XVI,536
 John XIV,96, 204; XV,48
 John Jr. XV,77, 79
 Joseph XV,207, 419, 529;
  XVI, 152
 Joshua XIV,548, 568, 659;
  XV, 610, 727, 734; XVI,10,
  43, 183, 209, 240, 277,
  521, 827
 Nehemiah XIV,280, 288;
  XV,150, 160; XVI,314;
  XVII,117, 251
 William XV,740
Snyder, John XVII,300
Soaper, Samuel XV,109
Sojir, Price XVII,299
Solomon, Isaac XIV,5
Somerville, James XVII,204
Somes, John XVI,297
 Timothy XIV,316, 365
Somers, Timothy XV,172
Soper, Joseph XIV,63, 186, 465;
  XV,268; XVI,926; XVII,3
 Samuel XIV,34, 91, 201
Souter, John XVII,528
Souther, James XVII,643
Southack, Cyprian XIV,119,
  150, 196; XV,753
 Ephraim XIV,309
Southick, Daniel XVI,933
Southmaid, John XV,381
Southmayd, John XVI,586
Soward, Richard XIV,237
Spafford, Asa XV,31, 144
 Amos XVI,82, 91, 221, 270,
  517, 794; XVII,291
 Bradford XVI,538
 Bradstreet XIV,297; XV,9
 Eldad XIV,436, 524; XVII,100
 Elijah XVI,138

Spafford, John XV,31, 368;
    XVII,104
    Moses XV,10, 27, 371
    Nathan XV,368
    Thomas XIV,476; XV,358;
        XVI,785
    Tyler XIV,597; XV,713
Spalding, Benjamin XVI,179
    Daniel XIV,463; XVII,78
    David XVI,935
    Dyer XV,138, 376
    Ebenezer XIV,247
    Ezra XV,138
    Henry XVII,92
    Jacob XIV,33; XV,744
    Joseph XV,374
    Oliver XV,426; XVI,310
    Rulaf XV,376
    Samuel XV,621, 663, 670;
        XVI, 95, 145, 619
    William XIV,42; XV,744
    William Jr. XV,744
    See also Spaulding
Sparhawk, Colonel XVII,1
    John XVII,333
    Thomas XIV,592, 595, 610,
        614, 634, 646, 655;
        XVI,866-67
Sparks, Deliverance XIV,8
    Joseph XIV,370, 377, 492,
        505, 515
    Thomas XV,724
Spaulding, Abel XV,38, 45, 373,
        378; XVI,465
    Abel Jr. XV 39
    Andrew XV,16
    Azel XIV, 274, 276, 289; XV,
        591
    Benjamin XVI, 157, 160, 178,
        536
    Charles XV, 39
    Daniel XVII, 66
    Dyer XV, 14
    Eben XV,21
    Edward XVI,140, 161, 235,
        268, 511, 729

Spaulding, Enoch XIV,392, 487,
        509, 513; XV,476
    Ezra XV,16
    Henry XV,100, 220, 360; XVI,
        238, 520, 839-41
    Jacob XV,88, 511
    John XVI,842
    Joseph XIV,105; XV,546;
        XVI, 285, 502, 607, 935
    Joseph F. XVII,257
    Lemuel XV,81, 83
    Levi XIV,38, 78, 87, 89, 155,
        201, 333; XV,220;
        XVI,426, 730
    Phinehas XVI,537
    Reuben XIV,464; XV,118,
        138, 554
    Samuel XIV,418; XV,683,
        689; XVI,87, 287, 508
    Stephen XVI,287
    Thomas XV,534
    William XV,81; XVI,321, 323,
        331, 334, 337, 339, 464
    See also Spalding
Spear, Allen XV,100, 104; XVI,
        840
    Elisha XIV,289, 292
    Joshua XIV,274, 277, 289;
        XVI, 312
    Major XVII,157-58, 201
    Robert XV,115, 174
    Samuel XIV,10, 412; XV,200,
        427, 733; XVI,47, 101,
        213, 266, 279, 303;
        XVII,418
    William XIV,34; XV,93, 356,
        534
    William Jr. XV,93
Speed, Eben XVI,766
    Ebenezer XVII,27
    Thomas XIV,119, 151, 196,
        563, 651; XV,729; XVI,28,
        189, 210, 527, 648
Speer, Allen XV,360
    Joshua XV,591
Speller, John XVII,426

Spence, James XVII,296
Spencer, Abednego XIV,235
  Amos XIV,234, 372, 384,
    496, 505, 516-17; XV,298;
    XVI,119
  Asa XIV,656; XV,459, 605,
    731; XVI,36, 39
  Daniel XV,473
  Ebenezer XIV,21, 228;
    XVI,256, 505
  Ebenezer Jr. XVI,256
  General XV,238
  Grace XVII,613
  Hobart XV,125
  Humphrey XVII,613
  J. B. XVI,287; XVII,438
  Isaac XVI,69, 80
  Jeremiah XV,26, 370, 654;
    XVI, 541
  John XIV,21, 408; XV,9, 34,
    108, 145, 571; XVI,119;
    XVII, 103, 249
  Joseph XIV,26; XV,10, 31
  Moses XIV,624; XV,618, 720;
    XVI,204, 233, 241, 272,
    504, 639
  Oliver XVII,159, 161, 188
  Reuben XV, 371; XVI,313,
    324, 329, 331, 340, 344-
    45, 465; XVII,249
  Robert XIV,251, 308; XV,61;
    XVII,98
  Thomas XVII,522
Spendergrass, Thomas XVI,102
Spenlow, Philip XIV,3
Sperling, Thomas XIV,191
Spicer, Jabez XV,39, 376
  Peter XIV,614; XV,434, 602,
    711
Spillard, Joseph XIV,76, 83, 198
Spiller, John XVI,262
  Joseph XVI,599
  Samuel XIV,359
Spinney, Caleb XIV,664; XV,431
  Daniel XIV,227, 257, 635;
    XV, 596

Spofford, Asa XVII,249
  David XIV,35; XVII,135
  Tyler XIV,105
Spooner, Daniel XVII,422
  James XV,145
  Jonathan XIV,5
Spottswood, Colonel XVII,196
Sprague, Abraham XVII,306
  Elkanah XV,39-40, 374, 591;
    XVII,67, 109
  James XIV,411
  John XV,9; XVI,605, 608
  Thomas XV,591
Spring, Jedediah XIV,25, 246
  John XIV,628; XV,456, 725;
    XVI, 207
  Seth XIV,67, 181, 246, 304,
    306, 465; XVI,281, 284,
    613
  Thomas XIV,167, 169, 246,
    274
Springer, Henry XIV,587, 656;
    XV, 732; XVI,36, 39, 195,
    212
  Joseph XIV,212, 215, 217,
    220
  Moses XVI,248, 269
  Samuel XIV,246
Springstreet, Christopher
    XIV,290
Sprouce, Thomas XVI,13
Sprous, Thomas XIV,581;
    XV,449, 600
Sprout, Michael XVII,98
Squire, Daniel XV,609, 723
  John XVII,118, 120
  Samuel XIV,346; XV,211,
    632, 636; XVII,61
Squires, Daniel XIV,589, 633
  Samuel XVI,35, 740
St. *See under Saint*
Stackpole, Abraham XIV,188
  Absalom XIV,126; XV,573;
    XVII, 11, 260
  Charles XIV,127, 188, 251;
    XVII,11

Stackpole, Douglass XVI,238,
    245, 274, 504, 624, 628
  Ebenezer XIV,119, 149, 196
  Henry XIV,127, 188, 251;
    XVII, 11
  James XIV,18
  Joshua XV,573; XVII,260,
    336
  Otis XVI,66, 77, 96
  Philip XIV,230; XV,573; XVII,
    260
  Samuel XIV,369, 374, 482,
    498; XV,628, 640;
    XVI,102, 622, 626
Stacy, Colonel XVII,240
  John XIV,259, 664; XVII,36
  Joseph XVII,139
  Samuel XIV,1, 158
  William XIV,664; XV,431
Stafford, John XIV,627; XV,442
  Nathaniel XIV,444, 543;
    XV,40, 374
  Stutely XV,16, 376
  Thomas XIV,394; XVII,89
Stalbird, Richard XVII,81, 83
Standley, David XV,348
  Dennis XV,705
  Jacob XV,698
Stanford, James XV,104, 427;
    XVI, 47, 55, 101, 303
  William XIV,11
Stanhope, Isaac XIV,91, 201
  Joseph XV,109
Staniels, Jedediah XV,267, 269-
    270, 273
Stanley, Benjamin XIV,51, 185
  David XV,349; XVI,700
  Dennis XV,590; XVI,289, 291
  Francis XVII,298
  J. XVII,760
  Jacoo XV,521; XVI,84, 95
  John XIV,6, 51, 185, 334;
    XV, 197, 216, 536
  Jonathan XVI,537
  Joseph XIV,36, 172, 175-77,
    315, 467, 548; XV, 20,
    182, 539

Stanley, Penticost XIV,428
  Samuel XV,98, 521, 539;
    XVI, 535-36
  William XIV,315
Stannard, William XV,30
Stanton, Benjamin XIV,4;
    XVII,754
  Charles XIV,560, 621;
    XV,722; XVI,205
  Elijah XVI,287, 511, 712
  John XIV,7, 234; XV,299
  Paul XIV,236
  Silas XVI,287, 519
  William XIV,235
  Zearle XVII,434
Stanwood, Daniel XVI,63, 73, 97
  Nehemiah XVI,63, 73, 97
  William XIV,325, 464;
    XVII, 139
Stanyan, Anthony XVII,528
  Jonathan XIV,261; XV,301,
    303-304, 306, 308
Staples, David XV,692
  Edward XIV,259; XVII,37
  Hezekiah XIV,259; XVII,36
  Isaac XVII,42
  Jacob XIV,264
  James XIV,664; XV,431
  John XIV,238, 250, 562, 636;
    XV, 445, 618, 627
  Simon XV,431
Starboard, John XIV,107, 122,
    187, 251, 369, 274, 482,
    498; XVI, 525
  Richard XV,593
  Simeon XIV,408; XV,299
  Stephen XIV,406; XV, 209
Starford, Joseph XV,740
Stark, Archibald XIV,59, 183;
    XV, 624, 726; XVI,8, 24,
    181-82, 208, 920;
    XVII,440
  Caleb XIV,59, 183, 465, 552,
    591; XV,710; XVI,2, 529;
    XVII,266, 418
  Ebenezer XVI,157
  George XV,95

Stark, John XIV,37, 40-46, 48,
    50, 52, 57, 153, 178, 481,
    552; XV, 139-41, 143,
    146, 149, 152, 158, 160,
    164, 167, 171, 174, 179,
    182, 185, 188, 191, 194,
    203, 206, 209, 216, 219,
    230-235, 276, 433, 592;
    XVI,2, 280, 307, 353, 389,
    417, 419, 422, 424, 443-
    44, 453, 482, 488, 732-33,
    832, 920, 923; XVII,3, 18,
    114, 143-44, 148, 218,
    232-33, 237, 240, 243,
    250, 266, 372, 418, 453,
    468
  Jonathan XIV,268, 270;
    XVI,314
  Moses XVI,315
  Phinehas XV,153; XVI,314
  Samuel XVI,733; XVII,461
  William XIV,268, 271;
    XVI,314; XVII,132
Starkey, Joseph XV,746; XVII,98
  Peter XV,205
Starr, Edward XVII,502
  Jonathan XV,52
Starret, William XIV,88, 200;
    XV,123
Starrett, William XVI,655-56,
    754
Start, George XVI,854
  John XIV,91, 201; XV,534
  William XIV,33; XV,353, 355
Stealing, John XVI,929
Stearns, Aaron XV,146;
    XVII,249
  Asa XV,711; XVI,198, 605;
    XVII, 468
  Benjamin XIV,336, 699;
    XV,214; XVI,143; XVII,62
  Daniel XIV,265, 614; XV,711;
    XVI,198, 605; XVII,468
  Dudley XV,483, 495; XVI,645
  Elias XV,25; XVII,104
  Ephraim XIV,265; XV,11, 369

Stearns, Isaac XIV, 33, 527,
    572, 596; XV,87, 210,
    611, 713, 744; XVI,269,
    518, 528, 822; XVII,214
  John XV,196, 303, 467, 472,
    479, 506, 629, 648;
    XVI,27, 102, 115, 643
  Jonathan XIV,423; XVI,98
  Joseph XV,632, 636; XVI,23,
    44, 690-91
  Joshua XIV,607
  Josiah XV,210
  Jotham XIV,608; XV,521,
    603, 714; XVI,84, 193;
    XVII,153
  Lieutenant XVII,423
  Peter XV,150, 160, 629, 654,
    662, 668, 676; XVI, 249,
    283, 643, 797
  Rev. Mr. XVII,13
  Samuel XIV,207; XV,7
  Samuel Jr. XVI,921
  Thomas XV,9,367,372;
    XVII,103
  Timothy XIV,34, 201;
    XVII,100
  Zachariah XV,518
  See also Sternes
Stebbins, Asahel XVI, 918
  Heman XV,33
  Lieutenant XIV,26
Stedman, David XVI,607
Steel, Benjamin XIV,244;
    XV,419
  Francis XVII,640
  James XIV,358
  John XIV,312, 420; XVI,898
  Joseph XV,201
  Josiah XV,340, 748
  Moses XIV,302, 312; XV,409
  Thomas Jr. XVI,898
  William XV,106
Steele, Benjamin XV,530, 686-
    87
  David XVI,286, 523, 793
  Josiah XV,321

Steele, Moses XIV,303
    Thomas XV,101
    William XIV,67, 181
Stelene, Carlisle XVII,489
Stephens, Abraham XVII,717
    Alexander XV,199
    Colonel XVII,196
    Daniel XV,279
    Jonathan XV,623, 641
    Josiah XVII,96
    Moses XIV,309
    Otho XV,623, 641
    Phinehas XIV,304
    William XIV,500, 512; XV,597
Stephenson, Joseph XV,295,
    468; XVII,610, 716
    Thomas XIV,13
Sterling, Archibald XIV,168-69,
    246, 275
    Hugh XIV,246; XVI,920
    Lord XVII,159, 161, 186-88,
    194, 197, 532
Sterne, Doctor XVI,530
    T. XVI,606
Sternes, Alexander XIV,147
    Asa XIV,578, 614
    Benjamin XIV,88, 200
    Daniel XIV,578
    Isaac XIV,88, 200, 267
    John XIV,247, 301
    Samuel XIV,103
    Timothy XIV,91
    William XIV,104
Sterrett, William XVII,160, 186,
    206
Stevens, Aaron XIV,125, 188,
    230; XVI,928; XVII,10
    Abel XV,38, 45, 373, 378;
    XVI, 150-51; XVII,108,
    416
    Abiel XIV,269-70, 289, 581-
    83, 653; XV, 448, 598,
    729; XVI, 30, 33, 59
    Alcock XVI,916
    Alexander XIV,196, 404
    Amos XIV,380, 489, 501,
    514, 602; XV,569

Stevens, Asa XIV,83, 198;
    XVI,670
    Bartholomew XIV,583, 604;
    XV, 716; XVI,201
    Benjamin XIV,226, 353;
    XV,115, 194; XVII,26
    Benjamin Jr. XV,116, 174
    Benjamin 3d XV,175; XVII,32
    Bimsley XVI,83, 94
    Caesar XV,322, 342
    Caleb XIV,247, 336; XV,214,
    518; XVII,62
    Calvin XVI,685
    Captain XV,602
    Cotton Mather XIV,239;
    XVII,23, 39
    Cutting XIV,316, 318
    Daniel XIV,135, 191, 225,
    296, 547; XV,280, 398,
    703; XVI, 539; XVII,92,
    253
    Daniel Jr. XVI,296; XVII,254
    David XV,557; XVI,795
    David Jr. XVII,258
    Ebenezer XVI,707, 732;
    XVII,32
    Edward XIV,9
    Elias XV,591; XVI,307
    Elihu XV,27-28, 371;
    XVI,608; XVII,279
    Ephraim XIV,91, 221, 468,
    577, 612; XV,93, 220,
    434, 711-12; XVI,198-99,
    735
    Francis XVII,134, 254
    Henry XIV,96, 204, 237, 265,
    336, 578, 598-99, 645,
    698; XV,145, 713; XVI,24,
    237, 245, 267, 519, 606,
    831; XVII,62, 224, 249,
    468
    Isaac XIV,165, 453, 532, 546;
    XVI,307; XVII,92, 114
    Isaac Jr. XIV,346
    Jacob XIV,459, 537; XV,116,
    399
    James XIV,25; XV,349, 396;

264

Stevens, James (Cont.) XVI, 534
  Jesse XV,129
  Job XIV,444, 542; XV,40
  John XIV,110, 133, 190, 226,
    240, 317, 320; XV,14,
    312, 468, 480, 493, 506,
    560, 699; XVI,214, 234,
    922; XVII,22, 30, 33, 111
  Jonathan XIV,16, 67, 91,
    180, 201, 237, 316, 319,
    438, 527, 611; XV,439,
    629, 718; XVI, 35, 44,
    202, 632; XVII,349
  Jonathan Jr. XVI,824
  Joseph XIV,231, 259, 346;
    XVI, 69, 638, 641, 914;
    XVII,22, 34, 37, 435
  Josiah XV,27, 35, 146, 148,
    158; XVI,605, 608
  Major XV,137
  Moses XIV,77, 83, 198, 313,
    340; XV,396; XVI,670;
    XVII, 32, 134, 254
  Nathan XIV,301, 391, 487,
    508, 512; XV,472, 490-91;
    XVI,247, 253, 501, 611
  Nathaniel XIV,56, 184;
    XV,116, 312; XVI,285;
    XVII,24, 692
  Nathaniel Jr. XVII,24
  Otho XV,589, 629; XVII,349
  Pelatiah XV,656, 666, 681;
    XVI, 816
  Peruda XVII,118, 120
  Peter XIV,7, 76, 83, 198, 319;
    XIV,469; XV,124, 494;
    XVI,224, 236, 242, 268,
    503, 617
  Peter R. XIV,211, 215, 217-
    20, 316, 567, 602;
    XV,607, 712; XVI,199,
    241, 268, 500, 577
  Phinehas XIV,145, 193, 305,
    466, 581-83, 653; XV,129,
    187, 448, 598, 729;
    XVI,31, 34, 59, 921; XVII,9
  Reuben XIV,341; XV,398

Stevens, Robert XVI,930
  Roger XIV,471; XV,371, 717;
    XVI,202, 218, 270, 515,
    770, 934
  Roswell XV,11, 27; XVII,105
  Samuel XIV,77, 83, 198, 233,
    358; XV,438; XVI,171, 177
  Samuel Jr. XV,707
  Simeon XV,584-86, 588;
    XVI,307
  Simon XIV,289, 292
  Solomon XIV,257, 259, 549;
    XV, 430
  Stephen XIV,233
  Theodore XIV,96, 204-5, 337;
    XVII,64
  Theophilus XIV,300; XV,565;
    XVII,25
  Thomas XIV,239, 267, 399;
    XV, 520; XVI,528
  Timothy XVI,314; XVII,81,
    83, 119
  William XIV,104, 126, 188,
    233, 402, 415; XV,422,
    730, 754; XVI,19, 922;
    XVII,11
  William Jr. XIV,484, 518;
    XVII, 86
Stevenson, James XVI,504
  Joseph XIV,322; XV,481,
    506; XVI,76, 236, 243,
    274, 624, 627-28, 776
  Philip XV,699; XVI,66, 77,
    93, 236, 243, 503, 624,
    628
  Robert XVI,270
  William XVI,274
Steward, Francis XV,427
  Henry XV,698
  John XV,221, 696, 698;
    XVI,141, 162, 929
  Jonas XVI,607
  Matthew XVI,286, 500
  Samuel XV,214
  Simpson XV,214
  William XV,520
Stewart, Allen XVI,91, 247, 498

265

Stewart, Charles XIV,227;
 XVI,930
 David XIV,110, 132-33, 190
 Francis XV,616; XVI,47, 55,
  303
 Henry XVI,86, 91, 107
 James XVI,929
 Joel XIV,95, 204; XV,79;
  XVII, 124
 John XIV,268, 271; XVI,214,
  234, 314
 Jonas XV,27
 Jonathan XIV,110, 132, 190
 Major XVII,155
 Matthew XVI,286
 Primus XVI,286
 Robert XIV,224; XV,562
 Samuel XIV,507, 516; XV,75;
  XVI,526
 Thomas XVI,792
 William XIV,244, 301, 337;
  XV, 75, 616; XVII,64, 297
 See also Stuart
Stickney, Amos XIV,244
 Benjamin XIV,25
 Daniel XV,478, 698; XVI,87,
  91, 99, 106, 264, 696;
  XVII,430-431
 David XVI,264, 696; XVII,430
 Duty XIV,51, 185
 Ezekiel XIV,167, 275, 429;
  XV, 406, 515
 James XIV,16, 19; XVI,252
 John XV,267, 269, 252
 Jonathan XV,750
 Joseph XIV,110, 133, 190;
  XV, 356; XVII,428
 Lemuel XIV,71, 179; XV,217,
  471, 502
 Levi XIV,642; XV,422, 457,
  730; XVI,18, 194, 211
 Paul XV,671, 683; XVII,428
 Reuben XV,658-59, 668, 679;
  XVI, 155, 252, 285, 501
 Richard XV,21, 220
 S. R. XIV,35
 Silas XV,533

Stickney, Simon XV,217
 Thomas XIV,210, 214, 217-
  20, 256, 260-61, 359, 429,
  432, 454-55, 478, 545-46,
  557, 565, 569, 588, 604;
  XV,127, 140, 161-62, 164,
  167, 171; XV,174, 179,
  182, 184-85, 188, 191,
  194, 232-35, 404-37, 491,
  607, 610, 631, 637-38,
  655, 663, 670, 688, 715;
  XVI,58, 104-5, 166, 201,
  263-64, 293-94, 400, 432,
  471-72, 609-10, 826, 910;
  XVII,50-51
 William XIV,429; XV,512;
  XVI, 909
Stileman, Elias XVII,512, 522-
  23, 527, 543, 547, 551,
  555, 561, 566-67, 618,
  620, 626, 639, 650-52
 Richard XVII,527, 649, 657
Stiles, Abner XVI,883
 Caleb XV,624, 632, 636;
  XVI,23, 44, 691
 Caleb Jr. XV,624, 632, 636;
  XVI,23, 44, 691
 Captain XIV,153
 David XVI,308-9
 Eli XIV,573; XV,613, 751;
  XVI, 509, 692-93
 Jeremiah XV,741; XVI,494
 John XIV,35; XV,95, 189
 Joseph XIV,695-96; XV,209,
  740
 Samuel XIV,89, 201
 Samuel Jr. XV,299
Still, David XVI,81
 James XVI,903
 John XV,11, 472, 501;
  XVI,270, 522, 903;
  XVII,104
 Reuben XVI,81
 Samuel XIV,3
 Thomas XVI,903
Stillings, Peter XIV,123, 168,
  187, 275, 353

Stillings, Samuel XIV,169
Stilson, William XIV,242, 313,
    315, 338, 465, 467, 548,
    695
Stimpson, Mr. XVII,710
Stinson, Aaron XIV,423
    Alexander XVI,920
    James XIV,75, 178; XV,739
    John XVI,630
    Robert XIV,71, 179; XV,586;
    XVI,920
    Samuel XIV,75, 178
Stish, Philip H. XV,295
Stockbridge, Abraham XV,
    544
    Isaac XIV,231, 448, 535;
    XVII, 27
    Israel XIV,229, 402, 414
    John XIV,9; XVI,313;
    XVII,642
    Moses XIV,9
Stockell, Robert XIV,240, 255,
    312, 617, 647
Stockels, Robert XV,444, 595
Stocker, Elijah XVI,159
    Michael XVI,237, 509
    Samuel XIV,314, 467, 548,
    567, 611; XV,608, 717;
    XVI,202
Stockings, Israel XVII,306
Stockton, Dr. Ebenezer
    XVII,441-442
Stockwell, David XV,43, 377;
    XVII,110
    Emmons, XVII,78
Stoddard, Benjamin XVI,48
    David XIV,84, 199
    Eleazer XIV,93, 202-3, 248;
    XV, 52
    Lemuel XV,223
    Thomas XV,50
Stoel, David XIV,325, 464
    Enoch XIV,436; XV,55
    William XV,11
Stokell, Robert XVI,804;
    XVII,29, 46

Stone, Abel XIV,36; XV,17, 43,
    197, 216; XVII,102
    Abijah XVI,138
    Andrew XIV,61, 182, 299,
    304, 306, 465, 586, 654;
    XV, 729; XVI,31, 34, 59,
    187, 210, 609, 914
    Benjamin XIV,225, 356, 405,
    476, 555, 656, 658; XV,
    425, 449, 458-60, 605-7,
    726; XVI, 7, 35, 37-38, 50,
    235, 237, 271, 286, 500,
    509, 530, 566, 568, 699,
    755; XVII,215, 221, 269
    C. B. XV,609
    Colonel XVII,160
    Daniel XV,47, 741
    David XIV,427
    Ebenezer XVI,311-12
    Eliphalet XV,102
    Enoch XIV,524
    Ephraim XIV,86, 199-200,
    263; XV,2, 654, 680, 686;
    XVI,166-167, 215, 286,
    523, 849, 879
    Ezekiel XIV,560; XV,131,
    183; XV,546, 623, 629,
    641, 719; XVI,102, 203,
    272, 514, 681, 771;
    XVII,257, 349
    Isaac XIV,84, 86, 264
    Jacob XIV,264; XV,48, 224
    James XIV,64, 181, 186;
    XV,608; XVII,4
    John XIV,64, 181, 186, 602;
    XV, 536, 712; XVI,159,
    237, 269, 505, 536; XVII,4
    Joseph XVI,16
    Josiah XIV,35, 91, 201, 334,
    394, 575, 639; XV, 39,
    534, 731; XVI, 26, 306,
    857-58; XVII,88
    Lieutenant XVII,223
    M. XVI,605
    Matthais XVI,608
    Nathaniel XIV,34, 421;

Stone, Nathaniel (Cont.) XV,356;
    XVI,763; XVII,525
  Salmon XIV,36; XV,97, 103,
    196, 216, 218
  Samuel XIV,578, 593;
    XV,716; XVI,137, 605;
    XVII,35, 468
  Silas XIV,577, 634; XV,724,
    750
  Thomas XIV,313
  Thomas Jr. XIV,302
  Uriah XIV,159, 161, 163; XV,
    277; XVI,326, 328, 332,
    341, 343, 345, 469;
    XVII,16, 92
  William XVI,609
Stoodley, Guppy XIV,239;
    XVII,23, 31
  John XIV,484, 500, 512;
    XV,326; XVII,86
  Thomas XV,324
Storer, Joseph XIV,454
  Samuel XV,416
  Thomas XIV,454
  William XVII,501
  Zachariah XIV,454
Storey, Joseph XIV,530, 546
  Thomas XIV,301, 467, 529,
    546, 548
  Zachariah XIV,530, 546
Storm, George XVI,932
Storms, Abraham XVII,307
Storrs, Aaron XV,39; XVI,528;
    XVII, 153
  Constant XV, 43
  Huckin XV, 374
  Nathaniel XV, 40; XVII, 369
Story, Charles XVII, 686-87,
    694; XVII,701, 703, 706,
    710
  Daniel XV,115, 176
  Thomas XV,182; XVI,588
  William XV,35; XVII,104
  See also Storey
Stouffer, Christian XVII,159
Stoughton, William XVII,524,
    532, 601

Stow, Abijah XVII,307
  Doctor XVI,583
  Jonah XVI,527
  Josiah XVI,928; XVII,86
  Thomas XVI,582
Stowe, David XV,593
  John XIV,640
  Jonah XV,29
  Jonathan XIV,265
  Josiah XV,584-85
Stratton, Daniel XIV,34
  Jabez XVI,598
  John XIV,223; XVII,490-91,
    500
  Nathaniel XIV,333
  Nehemiah XV,93, 220, 534;
    XVI, 235, 273, 514, 763
Straw, Benjamin XIV,388, 495,
    507, 516, 586, 647, 650;
    XV, 728; XVI,13, 519, 684
  Daniel XIV,230, 322, 446;
    XV, 294; XVII,28, 426
  Ezekiel XIV,24, 430; XV,548,
    698
  Gideon XV,482, 495
  Jacob XV,408
  John XIV,341, 566, 586, 653,
    657; XV,608, 729, 749;
    XVI, 31, 34, 39, 59, 187,
    210
  Jonathan XV,548; XVI,541,
    694, 914
  Jonathan Jr. XV,183
  Moses XV,699; XVI,237, 244,
    273, 505, 644
  Richard XIV,51, 185
  Samuel XIV,63, 181, 186,
    540; XVI,133, 163, 926;
    XVII,3
  Thomas XIV,61, 182, 249;
    XV,748
  William XIV,61, 182, 299;
    XV, 427; XVI,55, 101
Streeter, Amos XV,52
  Benjamin XV,224
  Ebenezer XV,57, 473, 503
  James XIV,36

Streeter, Zebulon XIV,355
Strickland, Daniel XIV,227, 257-
    258; XVII,30
Stringham, Peter XVII,306
Strong, Alexander XV,383
    Barnabas XIV,263
    Jesse XV,383; XVI,314
    Solomon XVII,118-19
Strongman, Richard XV,109
    William XIV,334
Stroud, John; XV,217; XVI,247,
    254
Strout, John XIV,101, 206-7
Stuard, Charles XIV,12
Stuart, Alexander XV,739
    Allen XVI,84, 251
    Charles XIV,257; XV,101,
        538; XVII,30
    David XIV,413
    Francis XVI,101
    Henry XV,696
    Joel XV,206
    John XIV,411; XV,73, 201
    Jonas XVI,313
    Jonathan XIV,424
    Josiah XIV,238
    Primus XVI,287
    Robert XVI,771
    Samuel XIV,388, 424, 494
    Simpson XV,73
    Thomas XV,552, 583
    W. XVII,296
    Wentworth XV,750
    William XV,654; XVII,102
    See also Stewart
Stubbs, Benjamin XVII,22, 34
    Isaac XV,748
    Sergeant XIV,2
Stuben, Baron XVII,413
Sturges, Samuel XIV,4
Sturtless, Asa XVI,99
Styles, Abner XIV,417
    Asahel XIV,358
    Samuel XIV,235
    Samuel Jr. XIV,409
Suckamug, John XIV,7

Sudrick, Job XVI,92
    Joseph XV,628, 640;
        XVI,199, 221, 268, 275,
        627
    Josiah XVI,622
    Michael XIV,372, 385, 496,
        506, 517; XV,295, 628,
        640; XVI, 197, 237, 245,
        272, 504, 622, 624, 627-
        28
Sufferances, Ephraim XVI,45,
    302
Sullivan, Daniel XIV,560, 563,
    621; XV,597, 722;
    XVI,103, 506, 649
    Dennis XIV,25, 228, 312, 338
    Ebenezer XV,749
    John XIV,31, 222, 228, 240-
        41, 522, 591; XV,489,
        496, 498; XVI,398, 434,
        450; XVII,127, 136, 154-
        210, 348, 376, 406, 447,
        454
    Valentine XIV,654
    Valentine O. XV,730
    William XVII,294
Sumerville, George XVII,302
Summers, James XVII,298
Sumner, Benjamin XVI,434, 488
    William XVI,95
    William A. XVI,81
Sutton, John XVI,264; XVII,431
    Michael XVI,236, 267, 502,
        594-595
    Stephen XIV,454, 530;
        XV,180
Swaddon, Philip XVII,501
Swain, Abraham XV,133, 171
    Benjamin XIV,232, 299, 387,
        450, 494, 535; XV, 256,
        258, 260, 262; XVI,65, 75,
        94, 106
    Benjamin Jr. XV,256, 258,
        260, 264
    Caleb XIV,2, 12; XVI,901
    Daniel XIV,22

Swain, Dudley XVI,131, 163; XVII,435
  Ebenezer XIV,312; XV,267, 269-270, 272, 474, 494; XVI,115
  Edward XIV,12
  Hezekiah XIV,580, 654; XV,448, 598, 729; XVI,31, 34, 59, 187, 210, 901
  Ichabod XIV,455, 530; XV,134, 171
  Jeremiah XIV,230, 413; XV,256, 258, 260, 262
  John XV,442; XVII,667
  Jonathan XVI,806-8
  Levi XV,167
  Nathan XV,284, 291
  Nathaniel XIV,34; XV,93, 355
  Phineas XV,267-68, 270, 272, 475, 494, 660-61, 668, 678; XVI,131, 163, 776
  Reuben XIV,133, 190, 413; XV, 523
  Roger XIV,235, 361; XV,249; XV,252, 254
  Theophilus XVI,128, 162
  William XIV,350
Swainson, Robert XIV,230; XV,286, 314-17, 336; XVII,29
Swallow, John XIV,346; XVII,61
  Silas XIV,439, 527, 545; XV,77, 347
Swan, Ca. XVI,305
  Ebenezer XIV,297; XV,23; XVI, 411, 864
  John XIV,325, 420, 464, 577, 634; XV,104, 357, 626, 724, 733, 739; XVI,47, 55, 101, 213, 303, 835
  John Jr. XV,104
  Joshua XIV,342, 347
  Robert XIV,333; XV,101
  Samuel XIV,14; XVII,730
  Timothy XIV,405; XV,390
  William XV,101; XVII,435

Swartzhousen, Christian XVII,295
Sway, Clement XIV,6
Swazey, Constable XVI,649
  Ebenezer XV,284, 287
  Abraham T. XIV,317, 319, 659; XV,607; XVI,42, 708
Sweat, Benjamin XIV,413; XVI, 873; XVII,433
  Daniel XV,629; XVI,641; XVII, 349
  Eliphalet XV,698
  Enoch XIV,329
  James XIV,239; XVII,23
  John XIV,113, 146, 195; XVI,873
  John P. XIV,317, 319
  John T. XIV,585
  Moses XIV,23, 405
  Peter XVII,32
  Samuel XIV,553, 610; XV,743; XVII,43, 266
  Stockman XIV,247; XVI,873
  Thomas XV,258, 260
  Thomas R. XVI,128
Sweet, Abraham XVI,9, 42, 183
  David XIV,239
  Giles XVII,536
  Samuel XVI,3
Sweetser, Nathaniel XV,200; XVI, 620
  Stephen XIV,647, 650; XV,595, 733; XVI,241, 516, 803-4
Swett, Abraham XIV,567; XVI,208
  Abraham T. XV,727
  Benjamin XIV,611; XV,320, 339, 406, 523, 718; XVI,202, 873
  Daniel XV,623, 641
  Eliphalet XV,513
  Elisha XV,195
  Enoch XVI,287, 516
  James XVII,31, 39
  John XIV,611; XV,284, 287, 718; XVI,202, 873;

270

Swett, John (Cont.) XVII,644
  Jonathan XV,578
  Joseph XIV,12; XVI,897;
    XVII, 619
  Moses XVII,659
  Moses G. XV,723
  Stephen XVII,641
  Thomas XV,256, 262;
    XVI,162
Swinerton, Benjamin XV,43
Swinton, Asa XIV,302
Switcher, Stephen XVI,12, 192,
  209, 232, 277
Sworn, John XV,427
Sylvester, H. H. XV,593
Symes, William XIV,442
Symms, William XVI,470
Symonds, Ephraim XV,742
  James XVI,519
  John XIV,333, 594, 646;
    XV,446; XVI,809; XVII,457
  Joseph XV,215
  Levi XIV,594; XV,446;
    XVII,457, 468
  Samuel XIV,185, 302, 304,
    467, 548
  Silas XIV,594; XV,446; XVII,
    457, 468
  Simeon XV,742
  William XIV,355
Syms, William XV,187
  T
Taber, Lemuel XV,106
  Philip XV,106
Tabor, Daniel XVII,144
  Pardon XVI,237, 523
Tacker, Jonathan XIV,406
Taggart, Archibald XIV,261; XV,
  127, 408, 546, 582;
  XVI,686; XVII,259
  James XIV,104, 106, 210,
  214; XIV,217, 219-20,
  463, 525, 553, 592;
  XV,427, 710, 733, 739;
  XVI,3, 47, 101, 213, 303;
  XVII,266, 378

Taggart, John XIV,332, 335,
  465, 572, 577, 589, 612,
  633; XV,104-5, 434, 539,
  611, 630, 646, 711, 723,
  739; XVI,206, 699, 812,
  839-40; XVII,291
  Joseph XIV,391, 487, 508,
  513, 568, 589, 633;
  XV,610, 723; XVI,206
  Robert XIV,50, 185; XV,465,
  467, 478, 504; XVII,248,
  289
  Thomas XVI,716
  William XIV,302, 390, 393,
  471, 486, 508, 512-13,
  554, 594, 632; XV,446,
  718; XVI,5, 202-203, 218,
  271, 518, 597, 619, 680,
  809, 935; XVII,259, 268
Taintor, Jedediah XV,360;
  XVI,738
  Michael XV,383
Talbot, Francis XVI,235, 242,
  271, 516, 803, 805
  William XVI,145
Tallant, James XV,359
  Joseph XIV,135, 191; XVII,7
Tambour, Joseph G. XVII,305
Tandy, Richard XIV,398
  William XIV,146, 196, 226
  William Jr. XIV,113
Tanner, Dr. XVII,388
  John XVII,511
  Joseph XVII,513
Tapley, Joseph XVII,23, 31, 39
Taplin, John XV,189, 429, 483,
  497
  Mansfield XIV,97, 204
Tappan, Samuel XIV,268, 272,
  290
Tarbell, Cornelius XVI,744-45
  Edmund XIV,100, 206-7,
  346; XV, 530
  John XIV,419; XV,530
  Nathaniel XIV,419; XV,81,
  211

Tarbell, Reuben XIV,85, 199;
  XV,48
  Samuel XIV,36; XV,97, 538,
    540; XVII,286
  Thomas XIV,100, 206-7;
    XV,209, 529-30
  Thomas Jr. XV,81
Tarbox, John XIV,411; XV,228;
  XVI,263; XVII,427
Tarleton, William XV,426, 584-
  85
Tarlington, Richard XVII,647
  Ruth XVII,621, 629
Tarlton, Elias XIV,18, 382, 490,
  501, 514, 519; XVI,317-19
  Elias Jr. XVI,318-19
  George XVI,317-19
  Isaac XVI,138
  Richard XVII,360
  William XIV,279, 287;
    XVI,307, 539, 927-29;
    XVII,251
Tarr, Benedict XIV,3, 14
Tash, Thomas XIV,22, 396-97,
  481; XVI,474, 898
Tasker, Daniel XV,311
  John XIV,13
  Jonathan XIV,235, 617;
    XV,444, 722; XVI,206,
    731-32
  Joseph XIV,235, 432
  Paul XV,195
  Samuel XVI,904
Tate, Benjamin XIV,230, 342,
  447, 540; XV,295, 468,
  480, 507; XVI,237, 244,
  272, 521, 836; XVII,29
  Joseph XV,295, 468, 480,
    507; XVI,119, 237, 244,
    272, 521, 836
  Mark XIV,473, 561, 621;
    XV,619, 722, 749
  Robert XVII,31, 39
Tatten, Isaac XV,371, 662, 669,
  681; XVI,712
  Isaac Jr. XV,662, 669, 681

Taylor,--- XV,699; XVII,746
  Abraham XIV,551; XV,221,
    320, 340; XVI,839
  Adam XV,196, 199
  Amos XIV,33; XV,744
  Anthony XV,124; XVII,528
  Benjamin XIV,56, 184, 234,
    242, 244, 404, 416, 600,
    667; XV, 73, 214, 284,
    287, 521, 615, 715;
    XVI,200; XVII,124, 742
  Benjamin Jr. XIV,244, 573
  Bradstreet XIV,563, 581,
    627; XV,449, 600, 721,
    748
  Captain XVII,265, 314
  Chase XIV,296; XV,162, 171,
    173, 232-33, 235;
    XVI,320-21, 323, 326,
    328, 331, 335, 338, 340,
    345, 397, 472
  Daniel XIV,33; XV,157, 688,
    744; XVI,64, 71, 93, 106
  David XIV,61, 182, 249, 328
  Dr. David XVI,436
  Edmund XIV,101, 206
  Edward XIV,463, 566, 653;
    XV, 459, 606, 609, 729;
    XVI,31, 34, 59, 187, 510;
    XVII,66
  Eldad XV,41
  Eleazer XV,96
  Elias XIV,264; XV,3
  Elijah XIV,85, 199, 264;
    XV,50
  Eliphalet XIV,409; XVI,712
  Elisha XVI,927
  Henry XIV,1
  Isaac XV,630, 643, 646, 664-
    65, 671, 676; XVI,22, 44,
    762, 855, 858-59
  Isaiah XV,538
  Jacob XIV,573, 590, 609,
    631; XV,456, 613, 711;
    XVI,51, 53, 198, 267;
    XVII,464

Taylor, James XV,85, 200, 463;
    XVII,51
  Jeremiah XVI,281
  Joel XV,125, 149, 160
  John XIV,118, 137 158, 192,
    287, 369, 375, 439, 482,
    498, 502, 511, 518, 547,
    580, 584, 600, 607-8, 624;
    XV,31, 134, 319, 339,
    394, 411, 422, 424, 428,
    437, 447, 476, 487, 489,
    498, 544, 567, 597-98,
    605, 630, 643, 646, 663,
    670, 684, 688, 715, 720,
    729; XVI,13, 19, 28, 121,
    159, 164, 194, 204, 211,
    220, 278, 508, 591, 679,
    751, 753, 840, 843;
    XVII,154, 156, 159-60,
    162, 181, 186-87, 191,
    203, 647, 651
  John Jr. XIV,651
  Jonathan XIV,103, 208;
    XV,125, 150, 160, 171,
    295, 520; XVI, 121, 164,
    255, 506, 534, 688
  Joseph XIV,12, 118, 139,
    158, 192, 255, 265;
    XV,371, 426, 522, 584-85,
    739, 749; XVI, 307, 312,
    902; XVII,218, 252, 644,
    667-68, 740
  Lieutenant-Governor
    XVII,723, 728
  Major XVII,298-99, 305
  Matthew XV,567; XVI,911
    Medad XIV,468, 607;
    XV,157
  Medad XV,603, 714; XVI,
    200, 225, 269; XVII,144,
    236
  Nathan XIV,143, 194, 589,
    633; XV,610, 700, 702-3,
    718, 723; XVI,46, 170,
    174, 206, 237, 275, 302,
    508, 685; XVII,8
  Nathaniel XIV,568

Taylor, Oliver XIV,566, 653;
    XV,459, 606, 609, 729;
    XVI,31, 34, 59, 187, 210
  Prince XVI,168
  Reuben XVII,297
  Richard XIV,11, 118, 139,
    158, 192, 255, 351, 531;
    XV,320, 339; XVII,740
  Samuel XV,201
  Silas XV,221, 537, 750;
    XVI,839
  Simeon XV,205, 329-30
  Simon XV,249-50, 255
  Thomas XIV,56, 184, 580,
    661; XV,393, 448, 468,
    480, 496, 599, 629, 648,
    727; XVI,10, 44, 67, 78,
    97, 547
  Timothy XVI,745
  William XIV,145, 193-94,
    212, 215, 218, 220;
    XV,327, 564, 596, 699;
    XVI,61, 63, 71, 92, 106,
    287, 519, 642; XVII,8
Tebbetts, Captain XIV,14
  Ebenezer XVII,261
  Ephraim XIV,187, 369, 482,
    498
  Henry XIV,3
  Jacob XIV,415
  John XIV,3, 15
  Jonathan XIV,245
  Joshua XIV,18
  Moses XIV,18
  Moses Jr. XIV,18
  Philip XIV,385, 506
  Samuel XIV,3, 14-15;
    XVII,656
  Samuel Jr. XIV,3
  William XIV,550
  See also Tibbetts
Tebbitts, Ebenezer XVI,817-19
Tedder, Stephen XVII,501
Temple, Archelaus XVI,287,
    362, 510, 702
  Ebenezer XVI,738
  Elijah XVI,46, 302, 311

Temple, Enos XVI,168, 878
  Isaac XIV,311, 465; XV,99;
    XVI, 442, 554, 839-40
  John XIV,35, 91, 201; XVI,
    298
  Mr. XVII,390
  Uriah XIV,355; XV,700, 702,
    704, 726; XVI,174, 208,
    522, 877, 879
  William XIV,264, 645;
    XV,473, 503, 633, 647,
    733; XVI, 23, 40, 190,
    311, 522, 886-87, 935
Templer, Samuel XIV,10
Templeton, James XVI,792
Tennant, Joshua XIV,650;
    XVI,13
Tenney, Benjamin XIV,35;
    XV,95; XVII,101
  Edmund XV,359
  Dr. John XVI,495
  Jonathan XVII,427
  Reuben XVII,144
  Samuel XV,413
  Dr. Samuel XVI,336, 351,
    360, 364, 373, 381, 395
  Silas XVI,150; XVII,109
  William XIV,33; XV, 102,
    216
  See also Tinney
Terhiger, Adam XVII,306
Termly, Ralph XVII,513
Terrill, Joshua XVI,28
  Richard XVI,906
Terry, Daniel XVI,41
  Ebenezer XV,9
Tessier, Joseph XVII,305
Tessie, Charles XVII,304
Tettier, Charle XVII,305
Tewksbury, Henry XIV,172,
    175-77, 301, 390, 393,
    486
  Isaac XVI,872
  Jacob XVI,871-72
  Josiah XV,560; XVI,615
  Thomas XV,321, 340

Thatcher, Benjamin XIV,644;
    XV,732; XVI,20, 23, 191,
    212
  Elisha XV,368
  Joseph XIV,356, 464; XV,62,
    741
  Peter XVI,153
  Peter Jr. XVI,307; XVII,114
Thayer, Allis XIV,421
  Benoni XV,383
  Caleb XIV,264
  David XVII,307
  Hezekiah XV,745
  Jonathan XV,204
  Joseph XV,471, 503
  Nehemiah XV,745; XVII,97
Thing, Bartholomew XVII,57
  Dudley XV,284, 291; XVII, 57
  Eliphalet XVII,57
  John XIV,12, 71, 179;
    XVII,27, 57
  Jonathan XIV,451, 532;
    XV,483, 657, 667, 679;
    XVII,693, 710
  Joseph XIV,12
  Levi XIV,398; XV,657, 667,
    678
  Nathaniel XV,284, 290, 748
  Peter XVII,57
  Samuel XVII,57
  Stephen XVII,57
  Winthrop XVI,255, 499, 582
  See also Thyng
Thissel, Josiah XV,329-30, 343
Thom, Barnard XVII,32, 425
  Benjamin XVI,889, 902
  Dr. Isaac XVI,453
  Jacob XVII,32
  James XVII,32
  Nathan XVII,32
  Thomas XV,517
  William XVI,547
Thomas, Anna XVI,322, 333,
    338, 474
  Benjamin XVII,644, 740
  Daniel XVI,153

Thomas, David XIV,85
  Edward XIV,283, 287;
    XV,435
  Elisha XIV,135, 191, 380,
    400, 489, 641; XV,169,
    256, 259-260, 263, 456,
    469, 565, 656, 666, 674;
    XVI,327, 329, 332, 342,
    345, 473, 772, 774; XVII,6
  Enoch XIV, 233, 581, 660;
    XV,449, 600, 727; XVI,10,
    43, 185, 209
  Israel XIV,85, 199
  Jacob XV,631, 650, 730, 735;
    XVI,18, 102, 194, 211,
    220, 278, 521, 827-28
  James XIV,108, 124, 187,
    566, 607-8; XV,311, 424,
    571, 590, 608; XVI,34, 59,
    119, 156; XVII,719
  John XIV,101, 206, 333;
    XV,21, 93, 356, 534;
    XVI,111, 166, 236, 270,
    515, 764
  John Jr. XV,324
  Jonathan XIV,23, 143, 194,
    231, 330; XVI,173, 238,
    270, 521; XVI,928; XVII,8,
    298
  Joseph XIV,210, 214, 127,
    219-220, 408, 570, 660;
    XV,311, 313, 317, 726;
    XVI,7, 333, 474; XVII,269
  Michael XVII,730
  Moses XIV,577; XVI,254
  Nathan XIV,427
  Nathaniel XIV,36, 421, 437,
    525; XV,348, 538
  Othniel XV,97; XVII,428
  Peter XIV,307; XV,267, 269-
    71, 629, 648, 725; XVI,581;
    XVII, 341
  Philip XIV,36, 38, 78, 98-99,
    155, 205, 248; XV,753
  Roland XIV,3
  Stephen XVI,637
Thomas, Stephen J. XIV,107,
    124, 187; XV,468-69, 480,
    493
  William XIV,23; XV,7; XVI,63,
    72, 91; XVII,694
Thompson--- XV,13
  Abraham XV,327; XVI,287,
    516, 805
  Alexander XVI,898
  Amos XIV,422
  Andrew XIV,89, 200
  Archibald XIV,260, 312;
    XVII,47
  Benjamin XIV,257, 304-5,
    357, 394, 484, 499, 512,
    518; XVI, 87, 99, 106,
    909; XVII,85
  Caesar XIV,566
  Captain XVII,375
  Charles XVI,109, 165, 306
  Daniel XIV,238
  David XIV,199-200; XV,256,
    258, 260, 263, 435;
    XVI,125; XVII, 425
  Ebenezer XIV,111, 168, 479,
    539, 550; XV, 13, 22, 34,
    36, 46, 63, 99, 142, 177,
    257, 299, 349, 363, 372,
    388, 395, 401, 403, 428,
    537, 655, 702; XVI,54,
    292, 364, 371, 375-376,
    380, 394, 533; XVII,15-16,
    54, 90, 111, 124, 126,
    217, 288, 323, 386, 445,
    455;
  Edward XVII,297
  Ensign XIV,26
  Ezra XIV,443, 542; XV,277;
    XVI, 314
  George XVI,85, 91, 106
  Henry XIV,471, 569, 576,
    586, 653; XV,609, 718;
    XVI,202, 219, 270, 509,
    512, 699, 726
  Isaac XV,98
  Jacob XIV,356

Thompson, James XIV,109, 124,
    171, 176-177, 187, 265,
    346, 583, 602, 604;
    XV,346, 436, 438, 712,
    716; XVI,199, 735, 910,
    930; XVII,89
  James S. XIV,346, 574, 579;
    XV, 453, 614
  Jesse XIV,264; XV,704, 726;
    XVI,176, 208
  Job XV,29, 368
  John XIV,14, 43, 99, 174,
    205, 223, 289, 291, 628;
    XV,28, 326, 458, 495,
    519, 721; XVI, 204, 256,
    272, 475, 510, 642, 715,
    735, 774; XVII,39, 360,
    427
  Jonathan XIV,12, 85, 199-
    200; XV,171, 476, 498
  Joseph XIV,234, 245-46;
    XV,299
  Joshua XIV,73, 178, 552,
    605; XV,710; XVI,3, 180,
    182, 197, 267; XVII,266,
    441-42
  Lieutenant XIV,579; XV,453
  Loren XV,434
  Loring XIV,614; XV,602, 711;
    XVI,198
  Matthew XIV,14, 231, 402,
    414
  Moses XV,700, 704; XVI,177,
    547
  Nathaniel XVI,621
  Paul XV,630, 637, 722;
    XVI,102, 889
  Peter XIV,333
  Prince XIV,566, 605; XV,607,
    716; XVI,201, 269
  Richard XIV,421
  Robert XIV,13; XVI,263, 725;
    XVII,426
  Roger XVII,98
  Samuel XIV,13, 66, 75, 124,
    178, 180, 187, 246, 347,
    411, 430, 571, 605;

Thompson, Samuel (Cont.)
    XV,200, 437, 624, 701,
    703, 710, 726; XVI,3, 46,
    171-72, 177, 182, 197,
    208, 240, 302, 504, 638,
    641, 922
  Seth XIV,329, 607-8; XV,424,
    714; XVI,158, 200
  Silas XIV,604; XV,58
  Solomon XIV,256, 260, 343;
    XV,326; XVI,907; XVII, 31,
    39, 46
  Thomas XIV,108, 124, 187;
    XVI, 413, 920, 925;
    XVII,141
  William XIV,145, 193, 271;
    XV, 20, 133; XVI,165, 236,
    238, 243, 245, 271, 508,
    512, 615, 750-51
Thomson, Isaiah XVII,293
  James XVII,35
  Jethro XVII,428
  John XVII,719
  Jonathan XVII,719
  Miles XVII,654, 656
  Robert XVII,719
Thorn, Barnard XV,691;
    XVI,124
  Barnet XIV,340; XV,658, 667,
    673
  James XIV,226, 404
  John XIV,25
  Nathan XV,560
  Robert XVI,932
  Stephen XVI,932
  William XVI,825
Thorndike, Joshua Jr. XV,537
Thorne, Barnet XVI,614
Thornton, Hugh XIV,573, 603;
    XV, 435, 616, 712
  Jesse XVI,138
  Joshua XIV,581, 659;
    XV,448, 590, 727; XVI,9,
    43, 183, 208
  Matthew XIV,120, 410, 457,
    478, 539, 557, 579; XV,
    140, 452-453, 630, 637-

Thornton, Matthew (Cont.) 38,
  655; XVI, 385, 433, 494;
  XVII, 13-15, 34
  Matthew Jr. XIV, 166, 168,
    170; XVII, 312
Thorp, Eliphalet XV, 754
Thrasher, William XVII, 22, 33
Thresher, Benjamin XV, 54
  Joseph XIV, 307; XV, 172
Thurber, Benjamin XIV, 298, 435
  Daniel XV, 55
  Hezekiah XV, 55, 745
  Isaiah XV, 669, 685; XVI, 810;
    XVII, 255
  Joseph XIV, 279, 287, 295,
    441; XVII, 254
  Samuel XV, 30
  Thomas XIV, 227, 257-58
Thurrill, Joshua XV, 729
Thurston, --- XVII, 236
  Abner XIV, 471, 563, 599;
    XV, 438, 717
  Ambros XIV, 308, 562, 580,
    620, 636; XV, 447, 598
  Caleb XIV, 400; XVII, 28
  Ezekiel XVI, 236, 242, 268,
    503, 617
  James XVI, 649, 651
  John XIV, 117, 353; XV, 300,
    302, 305, 309, 327;
    XVI, 111
  Jonathan XIV, 451, 532;
    XV, 284, 291
  Joseph XIV, 369, 377, 492,
    503, 515; XVII, 30
  Josiah XIV, 229, 401, 414
  Matthew XIV, 256
  Moses XIV, 298; XV, 30, 36,
    744
  Moses Jr. XV, 88
  Oliver XIV, 565, 630; XV, 725;
    XVI, 207, 275, 327, 329,
    331, 338, 340, 344-45,
    475, 581,
  Robert XIV, 642; XV, 597, 730;
    XVI, 18, 190, 211, 278,
    845-846, 900

Thurston, Samuel XIV, 455, 530
  Stephen XIV, 342; XVI, 111,
    844, 846
  Ward XIV, 165, 288
Thurton, Thomas XVII, 609, 618
Thwing, Nathaniel XIV, 119, 149,
  151
Thyng, Nathaniel XIV, 118
Tibballs, Henry XVI, 175
Tibbetts, Ebenezer XIV, 234
  Edmund XIV, 331; XV, 192
  Ephraim XIV, 108, 124, 375,
    502, 511, 518; XV, 179,
    485, 495
  Henry XIV, 455, 530; XV, 180,
    700, 703, 726; XVI, 46,
    171-172, 240, 302, 515,
    782
  Ichabod XIV, 114, 141, 192,
    236
  Jacob XIV, 224, 402
  Jedediah XV, 295
  Jeremiah XIV, 114, 322;
    XVI, 627
  John XIV, 230; XVI, 119, 287,
    521
  Jonathan XIV, 234
  Moses XIV, 115, 142, 193,
    250
  Philip XIV, 372, 497, 517
  Robert XIV, 363, 365, 455,
    530; XV, 194, 488, 498
  Simeon XIV, 549
  Stephen XIV, 230; XVI, 119
  William XV, 430
  See also Tebbetts
Tibbins, Henry XVII, 300
  Jonathan XVII, 57, 526
Tibbitts, Otho XVII, 693
Tibe, Michael XVII, 304
Ticknor, Elisha XV, 17, 38, 45,
  138; XVI, 543; XVII, 108
  Isaac XVII, 355-56, 358, 366,
    382
Tidder, James XIV, 34; XV, 21,
  356, 534
Tiffany, Benjamin XIV, 55, 184

Tilden, Charles XV,377; XVI,310
  Elisha XV,603
  Joel XV,156; XVI,543;
    XVII,143
  Joseph XV,375; XVI,543
  Joseph Jr. XV,40
  Stephen XV,603
Tilliard, Major XVII,155
Tillotson, Daniel XVI,924
Tilson, James XIV,356, 645;
    XVI, 24
Tilton,--- XV,699
  Caleb XIV,230, 350; XV,523;
    XVI,674-78
  Captain XIV,26
  Daniel XIV,312; XV,285, 291,
    320, 339, 464, 466, 477,
    505, 667, 678; XVI,587,
    644, 649; XVII,57, 692
  David XIV,11, 112, 146, 195,
    226; XV,400; XVI,614,
    616, 830
  Ebenezer XIV,118, 139, 158,
    192, 231; XV,128, 165,
    320, 339
  Elijah XIV,232
  Green XIV,388, 495, 508,
    516; XV,560
  Jacob XIV,145, 194; XVII,8
  Jeremiah XVI,65, 74, 76, 106
  Jethro XVI,906
  John XIV,112, 146, 230, 253,
    413; XV,256, 258, 260,
    263, 523
  Jonathan Jr. XVI,932
  Joseph XV,400; XVI,727-28
  Josiah XVII,24
  Levi XV,242, 245, 483, 495;
    XVI,131, 163
  Michael XIV,230
  Nathan XIV,230; XV,283, 290
  Peter XIV,230
  Philip XIV,107, 112, 120,
    146, 154, 194, 196; XV,
    559; XVI,706
  Reuben XIV,25
  Richard XVII,29

Tilton, Samuel XV,699; XVI,65,
    74, 93, 106; XVII,641
  Sherburne XIV,341; XV,400
  Timothy XIV,227, 387, 494;
    XVI, 526, 831; XVII,284
  William XIV,433; XV,513
  Tina, David XIV,550
  John XIV,550
Tinkham, Ebenezer XV,278
  Jeremiah XVII,95
Tinney, David XV,41, 375
  John XV,41
  Jonathan XVI,263
  Joseph XIV,34; XV,93, 355
  Reuben XV,157
  Silas XV,43, 375; XVII,67
  William XIV,419
Tirrell, Jonah XIV,358
Tisdale, Benoni XV,223
  Eliphalet XVII,307
Titcomb, Benjamin XIV,107,
    114, 140, 142, 154, 192-
    93, 250, 298, 553, 562,
    615, 620, 636; XV,447,
    456, 596, 598, 718; XVI,4,
    51, 180, 182, 203, 323,
    330, 338, 340, 624;
    XVII,247, 267-68, 365
  James XIV,28-29
  John XIV,115, 141, 193; XVI,
    128, 162, 628
Titus, Eleazer XVI,169
  Samuel XVI,924
  Sylvanus XV,23
Tiveto, John XVI,929
Tize, Jacob XVI,933
Tobey, Peter XVII,22, 34
  Richard XIV,13
  Samuel XIV,18
  Simon XIV,237; XVII,22, 33
Tobie, Richard XVI,833-34
Tobyne, Patrick XIV,369, 375,
    483, 498
Tocousen, Obadiah XIV,10
  Toby XIV,10
Todd, Andrew XV,201
  Colonel XVI,919

Todd, Daniel XV,169
John XIV,299,358, 458, 538;
XV, 95, 201, 364; XVII,
101
Joshua XVII,102
Nathaniel XIV,237, 240
Salmon XV,438
Samuel XIV,21, 369, 375,
483, 498, 502, 511, 518;
XVI,913
Solomon XIV,166, 170, 347,
579, 605; XV,453-54, 716;
XVI, 201, 331, 341, 484,
722; XVII,14
Thomas XVI,178-79
William XIV,240
Tokell, Robert S. XIV,260
Tolbart, William XV,75, 521
Tolbert, Philo XVI,558
Toleman, Benjamin XIV,93, 202-
3; XV,218, 542
Ebenezer XIV,93-94, 202,
213, 221
Thomas XV,159
William XIV,93, 202-3
Toles, James XVI,241
Tolford, Joshua XVI,420
Tolley, Thomas XIV,115, 141,
210, 215, 217, 220-21,
298
Toney, Daniel XVI,11
Toogood, Captain XV,608
Edward XVII,621, 655, 661,
667, 691-92, 757
Toombs, Andrew XIV,239;
XVII,23, 39
Toomey, John XVII,207
Toppan, Christopher XVI,390,
486
John XVI,642
Torr, Andrew XVI,621, 626, 628
Simon XIV,236, 476
Vincent XIV,124, 187, 623;
XV, 618, 720; XVI,204,
529
Torrey, Daniel XIV,312, 532,
565, 660; XV,727; XVI,41,

Torrey, Daniel (Cont.) 190, 209;
XVII,14, 28
Mr. XVII,381
Samuel XV,133; XVII,295
William XVII,142, 295
Tossey, John XVI,95
Joseph XV,746, 749
Towle, --- XV,699
Amos XIV,230
Anthony XIV,327-28; XV,749
Benjamin XVI,503, 617
Brackett XIV,410; XV,167,
464-467, 477, 749;
XVI,127, 162
Caleb XVII,643
Daniel XVII,25
Edward XVII,713
Eliphalet XV,321, 340, 523
Elisha XIV,253, 300; XV,562,
695, 699; XVI,807
Francis XV,749; XVII,642
Jabez XIV,118, 139, 158;
XV,411
James XIV,454, 529, 546
Jenness XV,696, 698, 754
Jeremiah XIV,327, 583, 600;
XV,437, 694, 749; XVI,
320, 323, 325, 328, 330,
337, 339, 343-344, 476,
530, 615, 684
John XIV,11; XV,191
Jonathan XIV,230; XV,319,
339, 487, 498
Joseph XIV,662; XV,730;
XVI,18; XVII,334, 644,
740
Joshua XIV,11, 230, 413;
XV,411
Josiah XIV,116, 129, 189,
230, 390, 486, 508, 412;
XV,523; XVII,25
Levi XV,327
Nathan XIV,118, 139, 158,
192, 224, 252, 255
Page XVI,287, 507
Philip XIV,1; XVI,672; XVII,
642

Towle, Reuben XVI,156, 252,
501, 600
Simeon XIV,230, 402, 415,
448, 534; XV,256, 259,
262, 527, 699; XVII,26
Simon XIV,253, 410; XV,168,
695
Solomon XIV,329; XV,351,
353; XVI,85, 92, 106
Thomas XIV,71, 179, 308
William XIV,24, 70, 179, 353,
584, 630; XV,168, 444,
724; XVI,207, 227, 240,
275, 518, 529, 807-8
William Jr. XIV,71
William 2d XIV,179
Zachariah XIV,118, 137, 158,
192, 255
Town, Edmund XVII,100
Elijah XIV,411
Francis XIV,421
Israel XVI,842
Nehemiah XIV,421; XVI,81
Richard XIV,416
Thomas XIV,416; XVI,884
Towne, Amos XV,349
Archelaus XIV,153, 246-47,
392; XV,488, 509, 513;
XV,632, 636; XVI,443-44,
557
Archelaus Jr. XIV,247, 302
Bartholomew XIV,247;
XV,520
Edmund XIV,437, 525;
XV,356
Ezra XIV,33, 38, 78, 89, 91,
155, 201; XV,103;
XVII,134
Ezra Jr. XIV,91, 201
Francis XIV,35, 436, 438,
460, 524; XVI,376
Gardner XIV,334
Jesse XIV,238
Nehemiah XIV,36
Thomas XIV,244
Towner, Comfort XV,10, 371
Ephraim XV,12, 30

Towns, Amos XV,539; XVI,158
Elijah XVI,263, 725; XVII,426
Gardner XV,536
Jacob XVII,98
Thomas XV,211
Townsend, David XIV,35, 333;
XV, 21; XVII,135
Ebenezer XIV,346, 527, 545,
573; XV,89, 210, 744
George XVII,761
John XIV,334
Josiah XVI,125
Oliver XVI,735; XVII,427
Thomas XVI,168
Townshend, David XV,534
Tozer, John XIV,333; XV,102,
216, 361, 751
Peter XIV,334, 576, 655; XV,
729; XVI,31, 34, 59, 187,
210
Richard XV,102, 109
Tozier, Peter XVII,468
Trafton, Benjamin XIV,237
Joshua XIV,238
Trask, James XVI,235, 522
Rufus XIV,103, 208
Traversie, Joseph XVII,133, 229,
237, 276-77, 290, 328
Travis, Robert XVI,10
Traynor, Michael XVII,300
Treadwell, James XIV,238
John XIV,283, 287
Nathaniel Jr. XVII,139
Samuel XIV,93-94, 202-3,
239; XV,739
Treat, Dr. Malachi XVI,350, 364,
374, 376, 423
Treble, John XIV,287
Tredick, Edward XIV,382, 490,
501, 514, 519
Tree, Richard XVII,670
Trefethen, George XIV,239, 256;
XVII,24, 31, 39, 85
John XIV,382, 388, 490, 495,
501, 514
William XIV,224, 248;
XVII,26

Tregowith, Nathaniel XIV,6
Trelanye, Mr. XVII,490
Treminick, James XVII,117
Trescott, Experience XV,603;
    XVII,67, 109, 236
  Jeremiah XVII,67
  Solomon XV,43
Trickey, Ephraim XIV,233, 322
  Francis XIV,330
  Isaac XVII,525
  John XIV,448, 463, 473, 535;
    XV,326, 590, 631, 638,
    730, 734; XVI,32, 34, 187,
    210, 220, 277, 320, 326,
    332, 341, 345, 479, 500,
    576-77; XVII, 29, 113
  Joseph XIV,402, 415; XV,325
  Samuel XIV,571, 618;
    XV,730; XVI,32, 34, 187,
    210, 220, 277, 513-14,
    778, 781
  Thomas XIV,119, 149, 196
  Zebulon XIV,12
Trief, Frederick XVII,306
Tripp, Gosperit XV,729; XVI,29
  Richard XV,300, 302, 304,
    308, 527
  Samuel XVII,139
Trisket, Experience XVI,47, 303
Trivet, Henry XIV,302; XV,75,
    213
Trott, John XVII,47
  Samuel XV,369, 643-44, 652
Trotter, Francis XVI,930
Troup, Robert XVII,233
Trout, Jacob XVI,930
Trowbridge, Edmund XV,751
  Edward XVI,679
  Luther XIV,92, 94, 213, 221
  Oliver XVI,152
Troy, Michael XIV,576
True, Aaron XIV,252, 350
  Abraham XIV,231, 353
  Benjamin XIV,585, 661;
    XV,267, 269, 271, 525;
    XVI,11, 65, 76, 97, 105-6;
    XVII,426

True, Benjamin Jr. XVI,262
  Daniel XVI,128, 162, 705;
    XVII, 433
  Edward XV,320, 340, 522;
    XVI, 127, 162, 705;
    XVII,433
  Ezra XV,249, 251-53
  Henry XIV,583, 600; XV,715
  Jacob XV,165
  Joseph XVI,130, 163, 260-
    61; XVII,432
  Reuben XV,400
  Samuel XIV,77, 224; XV,396,
    488, 499-500; XVII,32
  Thomas XIV,252
Truel, Daniel XIV,229
  David Jr. XVI,246, 252, 514
  Timothy XIV,537
Truell, David XV,754
Truelock, Hervey XVII,203
Trueman, Alexander XVII,204
Truesdel, Samuel XVI,109, 164,
    803
Truesdell, Aaron XVII,250
  Benjamin XIV,118-19, 150,
    196
  Ebenezer XVII,307
  Richard XVII,139
Trull, Israel XVI,921
Trumball, Jonathan XVI,391,
    436
  Nathaniel XV,549; XVI,131,
    163
  Samuel XIV,467, 548
  Simon XV,187
Trundy, John XVII,757
  Tobias XIV,224; XVII,26
  William XIV,382, 490
  William Jr. XIV,382, 490,
    501, 514, 519
Trussel, Moses XIV,43, 51, 186;
    XVI,320, 323, 325, 328,
    331, 341, 344, 481
  Reuben XIV,56, 184; XV,177-
    78; XVI,321, 331, 334
Tubbs, Abishai XV,12, 371
  Annanias XIV,264; XV,63,

Tubbs, Annanias (Cont.) 203;
  XVI,320, 326, 328, 332,
  341, 345, 486
  Benjamin XIV,3
  Ezra XIV,267
  Frederick XV,633, 643, 648,
  741; XVI,13, 44, 547, 661
Tuck, Benjamin XIV,118, 139,
  158, 192; XVI,286, 498,
  900
  Edward XIV,11
  James XIV,118, 139, 158,
  192; XIV,413
  Jeremiah XIV,230, 252, 413,
  642; XV,423, 455, 523;
  XVI,17
  Jesse XIV,232
  John XIV,76, 81, 198, 244;
  XVII,528, 693, 741
  Joseph XIV,244
  Samuel XV,284, 290, 292
  William XIV,89, 200
Tucker,--- XV,634
  Abijah XV,541
  Abraham XVI,287, 505
  Asahel XVII,67
  Benjamin XIV, 548; XVI,629,
  736-737
  Benoni XIV,315, 467
  Caleb XV,582
  Ebenezer XIV,112, 148, 196,
  404; XV,323, 341
  Elijah XV,430
  Ezra XIV,261
  Francis XVII,621, 629, 649,
  657, 672
  George XIV,550; XV,430, 693
  Hugh XIV,321
  Isaac XVI,138
  Jacob XIV,302, 467, 548; XV,
  127, 549; XVI,928
  John XIV,236, 260, 312, 451,
  532, 564, 630; XV,194,
  398, 725; XVI,287; XVII,
  22, 33, 46, 527, 648
  Jonathan XV,621, 645, 728,
  734; XVI,27, 102, 188,

Tucker, Jonathan (Cont.) 210,
  231, 277, 872, 874;
  XVII,438
  Joseph XIV,226, 340, 594;
  XV, 165, 446, 717;
  XVI,202, 247, 251, 285,
  499, 501, 510; XVII,32
  Josiah XV,658-59, 668, 679;
  XVI,247, 253, 297;
  XVII,438
  Jotham XVI,875
  Lemuel XIV,16; XV,633, 643;
  XVI,700
  Moses XIV,34, 93, 202-3; XV,
  102, 108, 355, 533, 535,
  541; XVI,736
  Nathaniel XIV,248, 380, 489,
  501, 514, 519; XV,608;
  XVII,26
  Nathan XV,698
  Richard XVII,527, 606, 669
  Samuel XV,647
  Sergeant XVII,157
  Stephen XV,618
  Stephen B. XIV,623
  Swallow XV,87; XVI,465
Tuckerman, John XVII,139
Tufton, Thomas XIV,91, 201
Tufts, Elijah XVII,435
  Eliphalet XV,312, 699;
  XVI,67, 78, 97
  Henry XIV,233
  John XVII,34
  Stephen XIV,476
Tulor, Moses XVI,147
Turkentine, Manly XVII,302
Turner, Ezra XIV,610; XV,718;
  XVI,202
  George XIV,255; XVII,28, 31-
  32, 38, 125
  Habakuk XVI,388
  Hugh XIV,571, 605
  James XIV,309, 576; XV,99,
  349, 427, 733; XVI,101,
  213, 266, 279; XVII,428
  John XIV,59, 183, 249, 411
  Joseph XV,99

Turner, Moses XIV,410; XV,754
  Solomon XV,99, 349
  William XV,98, 103, 536;
    XVI, 534; XVII,536
Turrel, Abel XV,362
Turrill, Joshua XIV,570, 651
Tuttle, Andrew XIV,372, 385,
    496, 505, 517, 519
  Benjamin XIV,236
  Benoni XIV,324, 464
  Daniel XIV,406; XV,312
  Ebenezer XIV,2
  George XV,311-13, 315, 317;
    XVI,710-12
  Gershom XIV,324, 464
  Isaac XIV,109, 123, 187
  Jacob XIV,314
  James XIV,371, 384, 496;
    XVI, 527
  John XIV,372, 385, 497, 506,
    517; XVI,66, 77, 96, 628;
    XVII,638, 648, 655-56,
    665, 670, 679, 710
  Nathan XIV,572, 597;
    XV,435, 611, 713;
    XVI,199, 558-60
  Nicholas XIV,109, 123, 187
  Oliver XV,27; XVI,606, 608
  Samuel XIV,235, 369, 374,
    482, 498, 502, 511, 518;
    XV,27; XVI,606, 608
  Stephen XIV,55, 184, 249,
    459, 537
  Stoten XVI,779, 781
  Thomas XIV,611; XV,718;
    XVI,874
  William XIV,314
Tuxbury, Thomas XV,340
Twead, Samuel XVII,86
Tweed, Samuel XIV,237, 484,
    512,518
Twilight, Ichabod XVI,285, 519
Twiman, John XV,427; XVI,47,
    55, 101, 303
Twiss, Asahel XVI,238, 273,
    509,692

Twitchel, Abijah XV,109
  Samuel XV,108, 536-37
Twitchell, Stephen XIV,420; XV,
    109
Twombly, Ebenezer XIV,407;
    XV,297
  John XIV,3, 236, 406, 447,
    540; XV,468, 480, 507;
    XVI,627
  Jonathan XVI,913
  Moses XV,242, 245, 747
  Nathaniel XV,249-53;
    XVI,776
  William XIV,233, 562, 636;
    XV, 312, 573, 624, 719;
    XVI,5, 203
  William Jr. XV,618
Tyce, William XV,587
Tyler, David XVII,134
  Ebenezer XV,384
  Isaac XVI,469
  Jeptha XIV,72, 179; XV,174,
    512
  Jeremiah XVI,286, 509
  John XIV,279, 656; XV,460,
    733; XVI,36, 39; XVII,221
  Jonathan XV,425
  Joshua XIV,424; XV,349
  Moses XV,267, 269, 273,
    513; XVI,810-11
Tyna, John XV,430

U

Udall, John XVI,313
  William XVI,313
Ugroufe, John XVII,501
Underhill, David XIV,457, 537;
    XV, 167
  John XV,167; XVI,168-69;
    XVII,501
  Jonathan XIV,410
  Nathaniel XVI,262; XVII,427
Underwood, Boston XIV,345
  James XIV,124, 187, 219,
    339; XVI,716
  Jeremiah XIV,34; XVI,158
  John XIV,227, 255, 260, 472,

Underwood, John (Cont.) 484,
    499, 512, 518; XVII,39,
    46, 85
  Thomas XIV,9; XV,75
Upham, Thomas XV,102, 361
Upsin, Elias XIV,10
Upton, Aaron XIV,417
  Eli XVI,159, 860
  Enos XIV,244
  William XV,220; XVI,159, 860
Uran, Daniel XV,187
Urann, James XIV,317, 319,
    454, 530, 546
  Jonathan XVI,236, 268, 500,
    935
Usher, Abijah XIV,336; XVII,63
  Eleazer XIV,247; XV,207
  John XVII,649, 652, 660-62,
    674, 694
  Robert XVI,159

V

Valarant, Michael XVII,299
Valette, Jaques XVII,305
Vance, James XIV,16; XVI,900,
    903
  John XIV,75, 178, 328, 348,
    583, 605; XV,427, 716,
    742; XVI,101, 201, 303;
    XVII,466
  William XV,754
Vanderburg, Cornelius XVI,286
  Cornelius P. XVI,522
  Henry XVI,932
  John XVI,932
Vandervort, Jacob XIV,289, 292
Vann, John XVI,47
Van North, Abraham XIV,577,
    634; XV,442, 724
Van Vliet, Dirk XVI,932
Vanzile, Egbert XVII,300
Varney, Benjamin XIV,3, 14
  Ebenezer XVII,710
  Ichabod XVII,435
  Joseph XIV,230; XVII,28
  Solomon XVI,893
Varnum, Benjamin XIV,246

Varnum, Ebenezer XIV,246;
    XV,607; XVI, 59, 210
  John XIV,43, 76, 81, 303;
    XVI, 102
  Joseph XVII,121
  Samuel XIV,25
Varrell, Edward XV,326
  John XIV,472; XV,325
  William XVI,61, 63, 72, 99,
    193
Varrick, Richard XIV,570
Varrill, Edward XIV,224, 248,
    448, 535; XVII,26
  John XIV,227; XVII,26
  Solomon XIV,248, 257;
    XVII,26, 30
  William XIV,381, 490
Vaughan, Captain XVII,710
  Colonel XIV,13, 15
  Daniel XVII,566
  Elliot XVII,761
  George XVII,710, 738, 761
  Jabez XIV,443, 542; XV,152-
    54, 158; XVI,924
  John XVII,205
  Joseph XVII,160, 184, 186
  Lieutenant XVI,314
  William XVII,527, 543, 555,
    563, 566, 568, 592, 594,
    599, 601, 612, 618, 631,
    650-52, 658, 661-64, 680,
    683, 761-62
Vaukleuk, Boltis XVI,932
Veal, Michael XIV,257, 383, 481
Veale, Michael XVII,30
Veasey, Daniel XIV,312
  Eliphalet XIV,191, 289, 307,
    402, 414; XV,724; XVII,6
  Jonathan Jr. XV,283
  Joshua XIV,181; XVII,6
  Samuel XIV,391, 488, 509,
    513
  Thomas XIV,191, 402, 415,
    488, 509, 513; XVII,6
Veazey, Eliphalet XIV,448, 535,
    635; XV,597; XVI,207,

Veazey, Eliphalet (Cont.) 274, 520, 845
  Henry XIV,94, 202
  John XV,6, 48
  Jonathan XV,290; XVII,27
  Simon XV,544
  Thomas XIV,392; XVI, 932
Veazie, Eliphalet XIV, 135, 289, 291
  Henry XIV, 202-3
  Joshua XIV,135
  Thomas XIV,135
Venner, Vane XVII,508
Verli, Michael XVII,304
Vernall, Mary XVII,646
Vernon, Ebenezer XV,729
  Robert XIV,10
  Samuel XV,588
Verry, John XV,145; XVII,249
  Thomas XIV,231
Vetch, Samuel XVII,707
Vicher, Ambrose XIV,662
Vicker, Ambrose XV,451, 453, 595; XVI,27, 724
Vickery, Benjamin XIV,336, 698; XVI,246, 252, 257, 513, 746; XVII,62, 64
  Elijah XIV,119, 151, 196, 353; XV,412; XVI,648
  John XIV,336; XV,207; XVII,63
  Joshua XV,256
  Merrifield XVI,597
Vicksham, Nicholas XIV,348, 560, 620
Victor, Felix XVII,309
Vincent,--- XVII,152, 229
  Anthony XIV,448, 535; XV,326; XVII,29
  Jonathan XIV,550; XV,430
  Joseph XV,15, 39, 376; XVII,89
  Leonard XVI,933
  Lewis XV,377
  Louis XVII,329
  Michael XVI,933
  Moses XV,377

Vincent, Thomas XIV,664; XV,431
  Timothy XV,376
  William XVII,29
Vinclair, Are XVII,304
Vinnette, Jean XVII,305
Vinson, Jonathan XIV,240
  Joseph XIV,394
Vintrom, Nicholas XV,443, 722
Virgin, Elisha XVI,105, 148
  Jeremiah XVI,263, 612; XVII,430
  Phinehas XV,405
Viron, Charles XIV,662; XV,450, 729
Vittum, William XIV,11, 269, 272, 290-91
Voitrin, Joseph XVII,299
Vorbeck, John XVI,83, 97
  Caleb XVI,928
Vosbeck, John XV,593
  Philip XV,590; XVII,81, 83
Vose, James XVI,574-75
  Thomas XVI,140, 161
  Thomas V. XV,557
  Uriah XVI,102
Vynes, Richard XVII,490

W
Wacomb, Caleb XVI,904
Wade, Edmund XVI,229
  Edward XIV,283, 287, 635; XV, 442, 456, 724; XVI,207, 241, 274; 508, 675-77
  Francis XIV,562, 636
  Jonathan XVII,756
Wadkins, Jared XVI,153
Wadleigh, Abraham XV,727; XVI,43
  Anne XVII,739
  Elijah XIV,571, 659; XV,727; XVI,41, 44, 209
  James XIV,452, 532; XV,285, 291, 482, 495
  John XIV,77, 83, 178, 341, 352, 587, 651; XV,329, 485, 500, 728; XVI,27,

285

Wadleigh, John (Cont.) 210,
    241, 277, 505, 526, 649
Jonathan XVII,710, 739
Joseph XV,284, 291, 523;
    XVI, 933
Joseph Jr. XVI,905
Mr. XVII,595
Nathaniel XIV,370, 493, 504,
    505; XV,243, 245; XVI,256
Robert XIV,12; XVII,526, 602,
    607
Simeon XV,482, 494
Thomas XIV,76, 83, 198, 532
Thomas Jr. XIV,342
Wadley, Abraham XIV,659;
    XVI,10
Benjamin XV,169
Elijah XVI,11, 190
Henry XVII,652
James XIV,312
John XIV,72, 83, 198, 563;
    XV, 343, 734; XVI,186,
    188, 221, 567, 670
Jonathan XIV,83, 198
Moses XIV,236
Nathaniel XIV,379; XV,247;
    XVI,500
Simon D. XVII,27
Thomas XIV,453; XVI,670
Wadsworth, Colonel XVII,350
Wainwright, Dr. Francis
    XVII,326, 730
See also Wanewright
Waistcoat, Richard XV,669, 685;
    XVI,810; XVII,255
Waisteat, Nathan XV,4
Wait, Jason XIV,264-66, 291,
    293, 553, 595, 599; XV,
    424, 435-436, 596, 602,
    710; XVII,224, 266, 444
John XIV,289, 648, 650;
    XV,595, 728; XVI,12, 192,
    209
Joseph XIV,262, 294;
    XVII,35, 72
Thomas XVII,118-19

Waite, Jason XVI,2, 51, 180,
    182, 188-89, 197, 267,
    300, 769
John XVII,315
Joseph XVI,333, 335, 448
Martha XVI,333-35, 339, 488
Nathan XVI,791
Stephen XVII,315
Thomas XVI,897
Waitstill, John XVII,502
Wakefield, Ebenezer XIV,103,
    207
Joseph XIV,103, 207
Peter XVI,259; XVII,437
Thomas XVI,555-56, 560,
    562
William XIV,103, 208
Wakeham, Caleb XIV,25
Edward XVII,717
Wakeland, James XVII,307
Wakely, John XIV,425
Walbridge, Isaac XV,15
Walcott, Roger XVII,104
Walden, Daniel XV,376
Nathaniel XVI,12, 192, 232
Nicholas XVII,656
Thomas XVI,13
Waldern, Richard XVII,501, 513,
    525, 537, 543, 555-56,
    559, 561, 565
William XVII,501, 616
Waldo, Dr. Albigence XVI,467-
    68, 480
Beulah XV,29
Calvin XV,12, 28
Daniel XV,29
Edward XIV,43, 297; XV,146,
    158; XVII, 103
Lieutenant XVI,545
Waldon, Jacob XIV,301, 467
Nathaniel XIV,648-49
Thomas XIV,344, 648, 650
William XIV,304-5
Waldron, David XIV,447, 540;
    XV,249, 251-52, 254
Ebenezer XIV,235, 312, 560,

Waldron, Ebenezer (Cont.) 620;
    XV,618, 722; XVI, 205,
    526
  George XIV,227, 243, 257,
    406, 476; XVI,60, 62, 70,
    99, 107
  Isaac XV,610; XVI,571, 915,
    921
  Jacob XIV,313, 315, 548; XV,
    549; XVI,868
  James XV,294; XVI,627
  John XIV,242, 244, 476; XVI,
    620, 623, 626, 628
  Nathaniel XV,595, 728; XVI,
    209, 277, 516, 803
  Richard XIV,235; XVII,548,
    551, 563, 568-69, 571-81,
    584, 592-93, 599, 601,
    604-5, 618, 631, 633,
    650-51, 661-64, 683, 685,
    723, 749
  Richard Jr. XVII,762
  Richard K. XIV,28
  Samuel XIV,245; XVII,29
  Thomas XIV,258; XV,595,
    728
  William XIV,227, 257, 466
Wales, Edward F. XVII,204
  James XVI,153
  Nathan XIV,285
  Nathaniel XIV,159-62, 262,
    287, 295, 546
  Nathaniel Jr. XVII,124
  Samuel XIV,247
Walford, Jeremiah XVII,606,
    609, 622, 644, 679
  Thomas XVII,512, 605-6, 609
  Thomas Jr. XVII,605
Walker, Abel XIV,297; XV,9, 31,
    37, 143, 145, 158, 707;
    XVI, 528, 531; XVII,103
  Alexander XIV,359
  Andrew XIV,6
  Asa XV,10, 368; XVI,137
  Benjamin XIV,358; XV,7; XVI,
    438

Walker, Bruce XIV,430; XV,267,
    269, 272, 515
  Charles T. XVII,760
  Daniel XVI,145
  Ezekiel XIV,166, 169, 246,
    274; XVI,284, 613
  George XVII,623, 693, 727,
    749-750
  Hannah XVI,666
  Isaac XIV,465-66; XV,31,
    368, 662, 669, 671, 680;
    XVI,234, 596; XVII,104,
    431
  Jabez XV,31
  James XV,40, 175, 386, 557,
    696, 698; XVI,611; XVII,
    258
  Jesse XV,21, 100, 356, 621,
    663, 669, 683, 689;
    XVI,235, 514, 664, 763,
    935; XVII,92
  John XIV,1-2, 34, 87, 115,
    141, 193, 201, 238, 322;
    XVII,692-693
  Jonathan XIV,165, 288, 607-
    8; XV,425, 714; XVII,81,
    83
  Joseph XIV,10; XVI,930
  Major XVII,395
  Nathaniel XIV,274, 276, 289;
    XV,11, 31, 145
  Robert XIV,359
  Samuel XIV,13, 28, 29, 247;
    XV, 21, 57, 97, 219, 539;
    XVI,60, 63, 65, 71, 76, 83,
    94, 97, 105, 107, 158,
    168, 235, 237, 244, 274-
    75, 514, 516, 553, 763,
    803, 805
  Seth XIV,239, 259; XV,9, 31-
    32, 143, 145, 158, 367;
    XVII,23, 37, 39, 148
  Silas XVI,666
  Supply XIV,166, 274
  Thomas XIV,465-66
  Timothy XIV,246; XVI,472,

Walker, Timothy (Cont.) 609,
   612, 893
   Timothy Jr. XIV,157-58, 175,
      246, 299, 316, 318, 320,
      365; XVI,610-11, 786;
      XVII,34, 445
   Tobias XVII,139
   William XIV,16, 38, 63, 78,
      95, 155, 181, 186, 203-4,
      299, 304-5, 438, 440, 465,
      527, 545, 566, 605;
      XV,79, 345, 607, 716;
      XVI,148, 201, 609, 909-
      10, 915, 926; XVII,3, 22,
      34
   Zaccheus XV,318, 744
Wall, Edward XVII,302
   James XIV,577, 593
   John XIV,258, 344
Wallace, Benjamin XVI,236,
      243, 274, 516, 803, 805
   Caesar XV,719; XVI,203,
      226, 271, 518, 771
   Ebenezer XIV,430
   Furnald XIV,338
   James XV,177-78, 368, 698;
      XVI,112, 717, 720;
      XVII,106, 324
   John XIV,69, 167, 170, 180,
      244, 468; XV,73, 175,
      201, 213, 479, 504, 711;
      XVI,267, 517, 898;
      XVII,14
   John Jr. XIV,69
   Johnes XVII,302
   Jonathan XIV,458, 537;
      XV,201
   Joseph XIV,103, 207; XV,272
   Levi XIV,501, 514
   Matthew XVI,793
   Robert XV,394, 429; XVI,359
   Samuel XIV,167, 170, 288;
      XVII, 14
   Spencer XIV,110, 133, 190;
      XVI, 648
   Thomas XIV,411; XV,200-1;
      XVI,717

Wallace, Thomas Jr. XV,597;
      XVI,717
Weymouth XIV,43, 69, 180; XVI,
      322, 330, 334, 337, 488
   William XIV,23, 330, 554,
      619, 641; XV,259-60, 264,
      567, 730; XVI,143, 211,
      262, 320, 325, 328, 332,
      341, 343-44, 489, 525,
      717-18
Walles, Caesar XIV,586
   John XV,465, 467
   Levi XIV,381, 490
   William XIV,381, 490; XV,422
Walley, John XVII,671
   Prince XV,630, 642-43; XVI,
      549
   Thomas XVI,55
Wallingford, Cato XIV,559; XVI,
      103, 208, 520, 836
   David XIV,33, 247, 407;
      XV,87, 89, 197, 209
   John XIV,14
   Jonathan XVI,119
   Samuel XIV,230, 243, 322,
      361, 446, 461; XVII,28
   Thomas XV,573
   Thomas Jr. XVI,905; XVII,
      260
Wallis, Caesar XIV,631; XVI,
      226, 771, 822
   Fernald XIV,312
   George XIV,353; XV,527;
      XVII, 511
   John XV,653; XVI,929
   Joseph XIV,416; XV,267, 269
   Nathaniel XIV,235
   Samuel XVI,821; XVII,25
   William XIV,332; XVI,5, 18,
      194, 775; XVII,267, 360,
      433, 693
   William Jr. XIV,228; XVII,
      693
Walls, Francis XV,724; XVI,230,
      275, 503, 624; XVII,378
   James XV,439
Walphy, Joseph XIV,448, 535

Walsh, Thomas XIV,69; XVII, 294
Walton, Abel XIV,579, 631; XV, 453; XVI,722
Abiel XIV,605; XV,454
Asa XV,428
Daniel XV,619
Davis XV,429
Elijah XIV,94, 202-3
Elisha XIV,94, 202-3; XV,52
George XIV,15, 227, 257, 345; XV,326; XVI,196; XVII,511, 755
John XV,395
Josiah XIV,34, 43, 91, 201; XV, 92, 219, 534
Moses XV,395
Nathaniel XV,7; XVII,357
Perez XVI,153
Reuben XIV,335; XVI,520, 840, 842
Rufus XIV,578, 596; XV,713; XVI,80, 199, 554
Samuel XIV,579, 604; XV,438, 453-54, 716; XVI,201, 721
Shadrach XIV,2-3; XVII,624, 629, 633, 638, 640, 643, 674, 702-3
Simeon XIV,432
Thomas XVI,554
Wampum, Gershom XIV,6
Wand, James XVII,307
Wanewright, Francis XV,726; XVI, 208
See also Wainwright
Wannerton, Thomas XVII,479-84, 487-88, 493-94, 522
Wanno, John XIV,7
Ward, Andrew XVII,435
Artemas XVII,121, 126
Benjamin XIV,398; XV,250-51, 255; XVI,236, 242, 270, 499, 582
Colonel XV,750
Daniel XIV,145, 193-94, 398; XVI,121, 164; XVII,9

Ward, Enoch XVI,801
Francis XVII,301
Henry XVII,124
Isaac XV,381
J. XIV,38-39
James XIV,635; XV,595, 724
John XIV,112, 148, 195, 350, 627; XV,457, 721; XVI,204, 226, 235, 272, 321, 326, 332, 341, 345, 490, 510-11, 703, 725
Melcher XIV,24, 351, 628; XV, 456, 721, 747; XVI,204, 226, 272, 508, 675-77; XVII,38
Michael XV,442
Nahum XVII,139
Nathaniel XV,412-13
Richard XIV,344; XV,595, 728
Samuel XIV,232, 353, 563, 623; XV,441, 725; XVI, 207, 231, 275, 514, 528, 766; XVII,26
Samuel Jr. XIV,213
Simeon XV,638
Simon XV,523, 631; XVI,127, 162, 867
Thomas XIV,11; XVII,642
Wardner, Jacob XV,11, 147; XVII, 249
Philip XIV,265
Wardwell, Jeremiah XV,747
Solomon XVI,693
Ware, Abiel XV,61
Jeremiah XIV,237
Richard XIV,650
Samuel XV,369; XVII,105
Warjwhott, Anthony XVII,293
Warmouth, Timothy XIV,312
Warner, Benjamin XV,573
Captain XV,650
Colonel XV,137, 424-25, 432
Daniel XIV,21, 85, 95, 199-200, 203, 205, 344; XV, 27, 61, 346, 509; XVII, 458

Warner, Elisha XIV,443, 543;
    XV,279, 281, 590; XVI,
    308; XVII, 73, 80, 82, 115
  Frederick XV,29
  Hugh XVI,92
  Job XIV,85, 199-200; XV,47;
    XVII,95
  John XV,7, 48, 93, 224; XVI,
    311; XVII,139
  Joseph XV,590; XVI,928
  Joshua XV,48
  Josiah XIV,477
  Levi XV,27
  Martin XV,52
  Seth XV,140; XVI,47;
    XVII,40, 153
  William XV,753
Warren, Aaron XV,156, 376;
    XVI, 178-79; XVII,143
  Andrew XIV,237
  Benjamin XIV,645; XVI,22,
    886; XVII,260
  Charles XVI,27
  Charles B. XIV,569; XV,610
  Cornelius XIV,105
  David XV,14, 138
  Francis XV,294-96, 317
  George XV,298
  Gilbert XIV,236
  Hugh XVI,80
  Isaac XVII,457
  J. XVI,350
  Joseph XIV,34
  Josiah XVI,527; XVII,463
  Moses XV,156, 376; XVI,178-
    79; XVII,143
  Pelatiah XIV,553, 615; XVI,4;
    XVII,268
  Phillips XVI,150
  Thomas XIV,143, 193-94,
    313, 561, 621; XV,595,
    719; XVII, 457
Washburn, Ebenezer XVII,105
Washer, Solomon XV,75, 520
  Stephen XIV,244; XV,73
Washington, George XIV,45,
    209, 221, 240-41, 270,

Washington, George (Cont.) 522,
    574; XVI,217, 249, 391,
    436, 438; XVII,51, 79,
    127, 156, 188, 200, 210,
    239, 281, 283, 290, 317,
    336, 348, 355, 363, 370,
    411, 444
Wason, James XVI,144; XVII,14
  John XIV,327; XV,753; XVI,
    156, 262; XVII,427
  Robert XIV,410
  Samuel XVI,697
  Thomas XIV,327, 418
Waterbury, Jacob XVI,195
Waterhouse, George XIV,228,
    242
  Richard XVII,527, 656, 667,
    669
  Samuel XIV,472; XVII,139
  Thomas XIV,151, 196, 650
Waterhouse, Timothy XVII,655
Waterman, Daniel XIV,422
  Silas XV,39, 374
  Zuriel XV,240-41
Waters, George XIV,227, 257;
    XVII,22, 33
  Hezekiah XV,17, 138
  John XIV,28, 160-61, 165,
    288; XVI,192
  Samuel XIV,227
  Samuel Jr. XIV,257
  Thomas XIV,28, 119-20, 647;
    XV, 595, 728, 734; XVI,12,
    209, 232, 241, 277, 516,
    803-4, 893
  William XVII,692
Watkins, Abner XV,165
  Elias XIV,105
  John XIV,423
  Michael XVII,306
Watson, Benjamin XVI,238, 245,
    273, 504, 624, 628
  Caleb XVI,169
  Daniel XIV,227, 234, 341,
    407, 624; XV,722;
    XVI,205, 526, 650, 817;
    XVII,424-25

Watson, David XIV,361, 564, 630; XV, 392, 725; XVI, 207, 230, 275, 514, 766-67
  Dudley XIV,400
  Ebenezer XIV,10
  Eleazer XIV,233; XV,545
  Elijah XIV,356
  George XVI,628
  Gloster XV,444, 723; XVI,206
  Isaac XIV,142, 193, 406, 618; XV,618, 699, 720; XVI,204, 621, 623, 627-28
  John XIV,20, 353; XV,465, 467, 469, 478, 481, 504, 506, 628, 640; XVI,237, 244, 255, 273, 519, 834, 862; XVII, 438, 492
  Jonathan XV,742; XVI,904
  Josiah XIV,231
  Mary XVI,623
  Nathan XIV,91; XV,475, 498; XVI,237, 244, 273, 510, 703, 706
  Nathaniel XIV,15, 21-22, 114, 141, 192, 298; XV,295; XVI, 627-28
  Otis XV,295; XVI,627
  Robert XVII,513
  Rufus XVI,287
  Samuel XV,191
  Stephen XV,325; XVI,67, 76, 98
  Thomas XVI,103, 202, 219, 270, 287, 509, 709; XVII,359
  Timothy XIV,239, 344, 448, 535
  William XIV,226; XV,249-51, 254, 274; XVI,623; XVII,261
  Winthrop XIV,114, 140, 193
Watts, David XV,29, 368
  Francis XVI,207
  Hugh XIV,75, 178, 458, 538; XV, 201
  Jesse XIV,54, 185

Watts, John XIV,569, 593; XV,29, 147, 201, 609, 717; XVI, 84, 92, 106, 929; XVII, 722-23, 728
  Jonathan XVI,138
  Moses XIV,458, 538
  Nathaniel XIV,16
  Timothy XV,13, 29
Waugh, James XV,552; XVII,259
  Robert XV,552; XVII,259
  William XV,552; XVII,259
Way, George XVII,500
  John XV,593; XVII,80, 82
  John Jr. XVI,308; XVII,115, 254
  Samuel XV,593; XVII,80, 82
Waymouth, Benjamin XVI,905
  James XIV,391, 487
  John XVI,897
  Joshua XIV,3, 15
  Samuel XIV,17
Waymouth, William XIV,2
Wealin, James XVI,100
Weare, Benjamin XV,249
  Daniel XIV,12, 110, 133, 190, 450, 534; XV,256, 258, 260, 263, 319, 339
  John XV,99, 616; XVI,930-31
  Jonathan XVI,564
  Joseph XV,153-54
  Meshech XIV,173, 368, 522, 531, 536; XV,2, 22, 45, 89, 91, 94, 114, 126, 130, 139, 193, 202, 208, 212, 215, 218, 222, 229, 289, 292, 296, 307, 318, 327, 404; XVI,389, 394, 588, 819; XVII,15, 40, 53, 56, 68, 80, 146, 211, 224, 338, 341-342, 346, 351, 354, 370, 374-376, 386, 394-95, 422, 444, 448, 450, 459
  Nathan XIV,253, 642; XV,423, 456, 624; XVI,8, 17, 26, 181-182, 208; XVII,440, 449

Weare, Nathaniel XIV,230;
   XV,383, 724; XVI,705-6,
   932; XVII,528, 594-95,
   601, 629, 633, 659, 669,
   683
   Peter XVII,715
   Richard XIV,109, 131, 190,
   555, 641-43, 648; XV,422-
   25, 448-449, 451, 455-58,
   460, 595, 597-600, 726;
   XVI,7; XVII, 269, 354
   Samuel XVI,162, 674-75
   See also Weir
Weatherbee, Jacob XVII,437
   See also Wetherbee
Webb, Azariah XV,278; XVI,538-
   39, 924
   Eliphalet XVI,257, 506
   George XVII,502
   John XVI,235, 242, 511, 725
   Joseph XVII,253
   William XIV,27
Webber, Captain XVII,420
   Christopher XIV,297; XV,11,
   23, 37, 146-48, 158;
   XVI,104, 135, 386, 864;
   XVII,103
   Colonel XVI,294
   Edward XV,633, 647, 732;
   XVI, 40, 190, 212, 228, 279,
   519, 820
   James XIV,8
   John XVI,285, 510, 706
   Richard XVII,527, 566, 753
   Thomas XVII,3
   William XV,534; XVI,51, 53
Webster, Abel XIV,423, 657; XV,
   732; XVI,37, 39
   Abel Jr. XV,459, 605
   Abraham XV,740
   Adonias XVII,528
   Amos XIV,279, 287, 295,
   556, 658; XV,459, 605,
   726; XVI,7; XVII,269
   Asa XV,586
   Benjamin XIV,273, 277, 289;
   XV, 754; XVII,30

Webster, Benedict XIV,428
   Caleb XIV,224
   Colonel XV,140, 655
   Cotton XIV,313
   Daniel XV,125; XVI,169-70,
   313; XVII,295
   David XIV,410; XV,124, 126,
   170, 382, 385, 453, 459-
   60, 584-85, 633, 647, 662,
   668, 708; XVI,58, 102,
   104, 166, 249, 294, 550;
   XVII,13
   Ebenezer XIV,261, 429, 588;
   XV, 127, 130, 162, 164,
   166, 232, 235, 237, 507,
   514, 516; XVI, 147, 149,
   294-95, 297; XVII, 642
   Eliphalet XVII,44
   Enoch XIV,246
   Enos XVI,823
   Gideon XVI,922
   Isaac XIV,226, 629
   Israel XIV,274, 276; XV,166;
   XVII,30, 644
   Jacob XIV,112, 146, 242,
   253, 340, 342; XV,560;
   XVI,650, 709; XVII,32,
   424
   James XV,328, 343; XVI,124;
   XVII,32
   John XIV,19, 246, 256, 295,
   412, 456-57, 478, 539,
   557, 582, 586; XV,113,
   388, 509, 550, 635, 638-
   39, 658-59, 667, 693-94;
   XVI,58, 104, 166, 262,
   300, 529, 589, 613, 807,
   913-15; XVII,296, 513,
   644
   John Jr. XVI,568
   John 2d XIV,273, 276, 288
   Jonathan XIV,471, 585, 611;
   XV,718; XVI,202, 509,
   530, 709
   Jonathan L. XV,421, 562;
   XVII,44
   Joseph XV,267, 269, 272;

Webster, Joseph (Cont.) XVI, 87,
90, 236, 275, 521, 827
Joseph S. XIV,65, 181, 186;
XVI,926; XVII,3
Moses XIV,76, 83, 198;
XV,169, 465, 467, 478,
505; XVI,65, 76, 97, 105,
107, 252, 501, 599-600
Moses Jr. XV,168
Nathan XIV,225, 405; XV,390
Nathaniel XIV,280, 288;
XV,194; XVII,251
Peter XIV,99, 205, 333;
XV,21, 217, 630, 643,
646; XVI,812, 849
Richard XIV,402, 415;
XV,256, 259-60, 263, 527;
XVI,822; XVII,26
Rev. Mr. XVII,15
Samuel XIV,35, 63, 181, 186,
327, 424; XV,95, 267,
269, 272, 588; XVI,551,
926; XVII, 3, 116, 135
Rev. Samuel XVII,134
Stephen XIV,181, 269, 271,
273, 276, 289-91, 569,
662; XV, 173, 609, 729;
XVI,30, 33, 187, 210, 277,
284, 529, 726-727, 796
Thomas XIV,119, 150, 196,
352, 559, 563; XV,719;
XVI,203, 272, 505, 527,
648-49, 651-652; XVII,644
Wedgewood, Captain XV,456
David XVII,740
James XIV,118, 137, 158,
191, 255, 555, 642;
XV,422-24, 733; XVI, 7,
350, 489, 531; XVII,235,
269
Wedgwood, John XIV,11;
XVI,128, 162; XVII,740
Jonathan XVII,528, 642
Josiah XVI,127, 162
Noah XIV,390, 486, 508,
512-13; XV,284, 288

Wedgwood, Samuel XIV,413;
XV,321, 333, 336-37, 339,
522
Weed, Benjamin XV,31, 143
David XIV,464; XVI,901
David Jr. XIV,325
Elisha XVI,832
Henry XVI,832
Jacob XIV,297
John XV,277; XVI,538, 924;
John XVII,133
Jonathan XIV,113, 148, 195
Weedon, General XVII,196
James XVI,931
Weeks, Abraham XIV,345;
XVI,214; XVII,42, 47
Amiel XIV,6
Benjamin XVI,876
Captain XIV,15
David XIV,160-61, 165;
XV,279, 281; XVI,542;
XVII,115
Elihu XIV,484, 500, 512
Elisha XIV,518; XVII,85
Jedediah XIV,253, 370, 379,
493, 504, 515; XVI,529
John XIV,401, 414-15;
XVI,103, 185, 213, 228,
239, 279, 506, 511, 649
Jonathan XIV,151, 197
Joseph XVI,902
Joshua XIV,118, 139, 145,
158, 192, 194, 255, 430,
448, 534; XVII,9
Josiah XIV,228, 448-49, 535;
XV,325; XVII,29
Leonard XIV,370, 377, 493,
503, 515; XVI,61-62, 72,
98, 107, 286, 514;
XVII,527, 656
Nathan XIV,229
Nicholas XIV,17
Pelatiah XIV,227, 257, 260;
XV, 431; XVII,46
Samuel XIV,227, 257, 485,
512; XVII, 87, 655, 705

Weeks, Samuel Jr. XIV,518
    Thomas XV,318
    Walter XIV,402, 414
    Ward Cotton XIV,134, 191;
        XV, 284, 287; XVII,6
    William XIV,229, 252, 255,
        638; XV,726; XVI,6, 281,
        668; XVII,269, 271, 291
Weir, James XIV,597; XV,745;
        XVI, 519, 809
    John XV,349
    Joseph XV,518
    Samuel XIV,613; XV,434;
        XVI,198
Welbourne, David XVII,94
Welch, --- XV,699
    Benjamin XIV,321, 624;
        XV,620, 720, 746;
        XVI,204, 231, 240, 272,
        511, 529, 710-12, 779
    Colonel XVI,937
    David XVI,234
    Ebenezer XIV,258
    Jacob XIV,233, 433; XVI,68,
        79, 92
    John XIV,235, 580, 624;
        XV,441, 447, 598, 720;
        XVI,204, 529, 779, 781;
        XVII,296
    John Jr. XIV,340
    Jonathan XIV,344
    Joseph XIV,396-97, 404;
        XV,388-393, 658, 667,
        673, 691; XVI, 64, 74, 94,
        107, 527, 794, 893
    Lewis XV,753
    Matthias XIV,570, 617;
        XV,627, 723, 746;
        XVI,206, 231, 274, 513,
        778, 818
    Michael XVII,306
    Moses XIV,238; XV,166, 514;
        XVI,125
    Paul XIV,406
    Robert XIV,3
    Thomas XIV,172, 177, 180,
        321, 570, 617; XVI,149,

Welch, Thomas (Cont.) 206, 231,
        241, 273, 287, 510, 513,
        529, 778
    William XIV,259; XVII,37,
        293
Weld, Aaron XVI,908
    Elias XVII,422
    Henry XV,630, 637; XVI,102,
        720, 774
    James XVII,88
    John XIV,394, 444; XV,16
Welland, Paul XIV,244; XVI,526,
        531
Wellen, Henry XVII,302
Wellman, Abraham XVI,287
    Isaac XV,15, 39; XVII,109
    Jacob XIV,43, 89, 201
    James XV,15, 44, 376;
        XVII,88
    James Jr. XIV,394
    John XV,110, 482, 646
    Reuben XIV,437, 525
    Samuel XV,360, 630, 643,
        646; XVI,751, 753
    Solomon XV,376; XVII,111
Wells, Abraham XIV,425
    Benjamin XIV,19; XV,124;
        XVII, 251
    Colonel XV,137
    Daniel XVI,307
    Ebenezer XIV,76, 81, 198;
        XV,267
    Edward XIV,14, 312, 432,
        636; XV,445, 618, 632,
        650, 725; XVI,13, 44, 102,
        237, 245, 272, 520, 832
    Eleazer XV,268-69, 272
    Ezekiel XIV,56, 184, 325,
        461; XV,15, 138, 155,
        698; XVII, 143
    Jacob XVI,684
    James XIV,354; XV,267-68,
        270-271; XVI,103, 207,
        227, 275, 518, 808
    John XIV,231, 397, 543, 570,
        641; XV,138, 422, 637,
        730; XVI,19, 64, 74, 98,

294

Wells, John (Cont.) 193, 777;
  XVII,25, 133
  Joseph XV,270
  Joshua XIV,69, 180; XV,373,
    378; XVII,111
  Josiah XIV,327, 583, 600;
    XV, 715
  Luke XVII,656
  Mr. XVII,375
  Nathaniel XIV,413; XV,487,
    499-500
  Obadiah XVI,922
  Paul XIV,279, 287, 656;
    XV,459, 605; XVI,36
  Peter XIV,469, 583, 586, 602;
    XV,460, 605, 712; XVI,
    199, 222, 268, 501, 600,
    682-84, 831
  Philip XIV,19
  Reuben XV,176; XVI,683-84
  Samuel XIV,72, 179, 469,
    583, 586, 602, 606;
    XV,712; XVI, 44, 198, 239,
    268, 519, 600, 683-84,
    784, 831
  Sargent XIV,340; XV,400
  Silas XIV,184, 424
  Stephen XIV,433; XVI,796
  Sylvanus XV,18, 138
  Thomas XIV,19, 327, 559,
    583, 621; XV,322, 341,
    722; XVI, 205, 240, 273,
    501, 600, 683-684;
    XVII,111
  Timothy XIV,112, 148, 195;
    XV, 323, 341
Wendall, Jacob XIV,336
Wendell, Jacob XVII,63
  John XVII,139
Wentworth, Amariah XVI,119
  Bart XIV,230
  Benjamin XIV,125, 188, 230;
    XV, 656, 666, 681;
    XVI,836; XVII, 754
  Benjamin 3d XVII,10
  Benning XIV,17, 20
  Caleb XIV,126, 188; XVII,11

Wentworth, Captain XIV,298
  Colonel XV,276; XVI,58, 104,
    261-62
  Daniel XIV,282, 286-87, 313,
    618; XV,444, 619, 723
  Drischo XIV,245
  Ebenezer XVI,818, 904
  Enoch XIV,309
  Evan XIV,230
  Ezekiel XIV,236; XVII,693,
    711
  George XVII,139, 354
  Gershom XIV,230; XV,295;
    XVII, 525
  Gershom Jr. XIV,230
  Henry XIV,233, 322, 365;
    XV,191
  Hunking XIV,379, 383, 389,
    393, 485, 493; XVII,35,
    139
  Isaac XIV,234, 407
  J. XVI,625
  James XIV,126, 188, 234,
    251, 407; XV,297, 750;
    XVII,11
  Jedediah XIV,127, 188, 230;
    XVII,12
  John XIV,29, 322, 365;
    XV,191; XVII,1, 29, 746-
    47, 754
  Jonathan XIV,107, 125, 127,
    154, 189, 251; XV,286,
    314-317, 581; XVI,108,
    363-64, 526, 836, 893,
    898; XVII,10, 214, 260
  Joshua XIV,338, 401, 404,
    414, 449; XV, 496, 583,
    595, 597, 628, 645, 665,
    693, 697-99; XVI,165-66,
    261-62, 430, 668, 843-44,
    926; XVII,139, 221, 245,
    274-75, 314-15, 350, 359,
    361-63, 371, 375, 421,
    448
  Lemuel XIV,43, 85, 199
  Mark XIV,245; XV,574, 628,
    640; XVI,102, 622, 627;

Wentworth, Mark (Cont.) XVII,
260
Mark H. XVII,322
Nathaniel XIV,125, 188;
XV,163,
Nathaniel XV,191; XVII,10
Nicholas XV,298
Paul XIV,473; XVI,119
Phinehas XIV,114, 140, 193,
298, 559, 623; XV,441,
720; XVI,204, 503, 531,
624; XVII, 452
Phinehas Jr. XVI,272
Richard XIV,230
Samuel XIV,245, 369, 374,
482, 498, 502, 511, 518;
XV,297; XVII,29, 527, 738
Spencer XIV,245; XVI,904
Thomas XIV,18
Tobias XIV,230, 322; XVII,29
William XVI,207, 229, 275,
836, 862; XVII, 368, 438,
528
Wescott, Nathan XVI,153
Wesson, Aaron XV,153-54;
XVII,81, 83, 118, 120
Daniel XVI,143, 259, 287,
498; XVII,437
Ephraim XIV,443, 542, 547;
XV, 153, 380; XVI,539;
XVII,73, 82
Ephraim Jr. XVII,80
James XIV,170; XV,379;
XVII,81, 83, 118, 120
Nathan XV,92, 733; XVI,51,
53, 213; XVII,457, 460
Peter XVII,81, 83
Roger XVI,143
West, Daniel XIV,571, 605
Edward XIV,85, 200, 308;
XVI, 105, 148, 285, 501,
935; XVII,511, 513, 753
Elizabeth XVII,672
Gilman XV,185, 515;
XVI,105, 147
John XIV,9; XV,371; XVI,64,
73

West, Nathan XV,15; XVII,109
Nathaniel XIV,268, 271, 290
Nehemiah XIV,135, 191, 341,
565, 660; XV,727; XVI,10,
43, 185, 209, 581; XVII,7
Noah XIV,430; XV,515
Thomas XIV,394; XV,14, 138;
XVII,88
Wilkes XV,169, 525
William XVII,308
Westbrook, Captain XIV,14-15
Westbrooke, John XVII,527, 619
Thomas XVII,691-92
Westcott, James XIV,428;
XV,204, 745
Westey, Robert XIV,213, 221
Weston, Ebenezer XVI,562
Nathan XIV,201
Southerick XIV,103, 266; XV,
751; XVI,525
Wetherbee, Abraham XIV,36
Daniel XV,81, 211
David XIV,199
Hezekiah XIV,99, 205;
XV,349, 631, 646;
XVI,763, 812
Jacob XVI,85, 100, 107, 259,
286, 512
Samuel XIV,297, 324, 326,
463
See also Weatherbee
Wetherall, David XIV, 85, 200;
XV, 47
Ephraim XV, 48, 680; XVI,
700-1
James XVI, 913
See also Witherell
Wethon, Arnold XVI,901
Weymouth, James XIV,508, 512
Timothy XIV,300; XV,243,
245, 247
William XIV,233
Whaley, James XVI,63, 73
Wheat, John XIV,8
Jonathan XIV,34, 333
Joseph XIV,281, 288, 441,
527, 545; XV,87, 511,

Wheat, Joseph (Cont.) 632, 636,
    732; XVI,40, 190, 212,
    228, 279, 509, 691-92
  Nathaniel XIV,33, 392, 488,
    509, 513
  Thomas XIV,33, 43; XV,744
  William XIV,246
Wheatley, Nathaniel XV, 38,
    375
  John XVII,149
  Luther XIV,607-8; XV,603,
    714; XVII,67
  Nathaniel XVII,109
  William XIV,286-87
Wheaton, Ezra XVII,22, 33
  James XIV,287
  John XIV,283; XV,156;
    XVI,930
  Joseph XV,482
  Lieutenant XVII,414
  Simeon XV,17
Wheeler, Aaron XV,84
  Abijah XIV,242; XV,328, 331,
    343; XVII,32
  Abner XIV,16, 52, 185, 342,
    349; XV,89, 210, 390
  Abraham XV,62; XVII,98
  Amos XV,93, 220
  Benjamin XIV,94, 202-3
  Charles XV,279, 281, 593;
    XVII, 89
  Daniel XIV,422
  David XV,541; XVI,737-38
  Ebenezer XIV,33, 419
  Ephraim XVI,933
  Ezekiel XV,590; XVII,69, 89
  George XV,590; XVI,314;
    XVII, 113, 117
  Glazier XV,593; XVII,89
  Isaiah XVI,519
  Jacob XVI,377
  James XIV,356; XV,51
  Jesse XIV,326, 464
  John XV,21; XVI,932
  Johnson XVI,308-9
  Jonas XIV,34; XV,100, 355,
    534; XVII,92

Wheeler, Jonathan XV,62, 227,
    741; XVII, 98
  Josiah XV,225; XVI,257
  Lebbeus XIV,33, 573, 590,
    609; XV,613, 714, 744;
    XVI,688
  Moses XV,31
  Nathan XVI,739-40
  Nathaniel XV,15
  Peter XIV,35; XV,220, 364
  Peter Jr. XV,96
  Plummer XIV,56, 184, 425
  Prime XIV,173, 176-77
  Reuben XIV,247, 572, 597;
    XV, 435, 611, 713;
    XVI,199
  Richard XV,100, 220
  Sampson XIV,405; XVII,32
  Samuel XV,220, 535
  Seth XIV,171, 173, 176-77;
    XV, 16; XVI,308-9;
    XVII,109
  Silas XIV,453, 532, 547; XV,
    329, 343, 425; XVII,32,
    81, 89
  Solomon XIV,341; XVI,709
  Thaddeus XIV,33
  Thomas XV,435, 437
  Timothy XV,82, 84
  Walter XV,472, 503; XVI,152
  Warren XV,390; XVII,32
  William XV,677; XVI,631;
    XVII, 208
  William Jr. XV,176, 621, 663,
    669, 689
  Zadoc XIV,436, 524; XV,227
Wheelock, Eleazer XVII,152-53
  Ithamar XIV,575, 593;
    XV,438
  James XIV,264; XV,377;
    XVI,153
  Joel XIV,34; XVII,100
  John XIV,660; XV,373, 378,
    426, 596, 711; XVI,306;
    XVII,150-153, 218, 229-
    33, 237, 239, 243, 248,
    311-12, 329

Wheelock, Jonathan XIV,577,
612; XV,101, 357, 538;
XVI,198
Lewis XVI,160
Phinehas XVI,531
Thomas XIV,468
Timothy XIV,34; XVII,100
Wheelwright, Daniel XIV,238
Joseph XIV,239
Whicher, Chase XIV,180
Whidden, James XV,321, 340;
XVII, 360
John XIV,300-1; XVII,513
John Jr. XIV,300-1
Jonathan XVII,622, 655, 692
Joseph XVI,303
Michael XIV,13
Samuel XIV,247, 300-1, 573;
XV, 616, 712; XVI,198;
XVII,513, 693
Thomas XVII,656, 667
William XVI,83, 90, 107
Whipple, Aaron XV,376
Daniel XIV,355, 645; XVI,22,
809
Israel XIV,355; XV,56;
XVI,810
Jabez XIV,645; XVI,24, 81,
95
James XV,631, 646; XVI,23,
44, 107, 812
Jeremiah XV,29
Job XIV,4
Joseph XVI,281; XVII,126
Moses XV,38, 45, 373, 378;
XVI, 531-32, 614;
XVII,111
Prince XV,282
Rufus XV,54, 446, 745;
XVI,809; XVII,96
Samuel XV,16, 138
Thomas XV,16, 138
William XIV,256, 401, 403,
414, 478, 556; XV, 139-
140, 276, 282, 286-93,
404, 433, 508, 514, 580,
582, 594, 655; XVI,397;

Whipple, William (Cont.) XVII,
15, 150, 213
Whiston, John XVI,308, 310
Whitam, Jeremiah XVI,47, 303
Whitcher, Andrew XIV,225, 382,
490
Benjamin XV,402
Chase XV,300-1, 304, 308
Daniel XIV,410
David XVI,308; XVII,115
Isaac XIV,225
Jacob XVII,425
James XVI,620
Jonathan XIV,231
Joseph XIV,231
Reuben XVII,254
Richard XV,754; XVII,32
Sargeant XIV,229, 402,
415
Stephen XV,728
Whitcomb,---XVI,101
Abijah XIV,94, 202-3
Asa XV,751
Benjamin XIV,281, 285, 287,
295; XV,131, 426, 700,
702-3, 718; XVI,46, 166-
67, 170-72, 174, 177-79,
203, 302, 782, 879; XVII,
150-51, 212, 317, 320,
348
Captain XV,424-25, 432
David XIV,437, 525; XV,62,
467, 479, 503
Elisha XIV,263; XV,46, 426;
XVI,412, 460, 812, 852,
927
Ephraim XIV,436; XVI,535
John XIV,437, 525; XV,63,
203, 669, 680; XVI,851,
927; XVII, 97, 255
Jonathan XIV,38, 78, 92, 94,
155, 202-3, 248, 671
Joseph XVII,97
Josiah XVI,83, 100, 107
Nathaniel XIV,85, 199-200;
XV, 701; XVI,46, 176, 302,
522, 877, 879

298

Whitcomb, Reuben XV,546;
  XVII,257
  Samuel XVI,159
  Silas XV,99
  Simon XIV,99, 156-57;
    XV,751
  Thomas XIV,264; XV,52;
    XVI,460
White, Abel XIV,264; XV,48
  Abraham XV,278
  Alexander XVII,294
  Andrew XV,483, 497, 622,
    634, 644, 729; XVI, 30,
    33, 187, 210, 219, 277,
    500, 753-55
  Aquila XIV,223
  Archelaus XV,329, 343
  Archibald XIV,91, 201;
    XV,106, 219, 369, 372
  Asa XIV,263
  Charles XIV,436, 524;
    XV,538, 739
  Constant XV,4, 55, 746
  Daniel XIV,91, 201
  David XV,538, 739; XVII,296
  Edward XVII,301
  Eleazer XIV,4
  Eli XV,591
  Ephraim XIV,348
  Ezekiel XIV,379
  Gideon XVI,254
  Henry XV,65
  Hugh XIV,263
  Isaac XVII,298
  James XIV,308, 485, 647,
    650; XV,221, 538, 595,
    728; XVI, 13, 906, 916;
    XVII,86, 498
  Joel XV,109
  John XIV,85, 199, 269-70,
    289, 295, 648; XV,21, 35,
    48, 101, 355, 593, 595,
    630, 643, 646, 681, 694;
    XVI,61, 64, 71, 94, 287,
    505, 520, 720, 724, 840-
    841, 917; XVII,96

White, John Jr. XV,664-65, 671;
    XVI, 793
  Joseph XV,47, 168, 588;
    XVII,25
  Joshua XIV,264
  Josiah XIV,110, 133, 190;
    XV, 256, 259, 264-65
  Jotham XV,31, 367, 372
  Major XVII,160
  Mr. XVII,385
  Moses XVII,300
  Nathan XIV,227, 472;
    XVII,25, 667
  Nathaniel XIV,160-61, 165;
    XVII, 331, 692
  Nicholas XV,588
  Noah XV,588
  Phillips XIV,479; XVII,77
  Pomp XIV,344; XV,325
  Samuel XIV,84, 327, 387,
    494, 507, 519; XV,106,
    474, 494, 537, 633, 643,
    648, 741, 754; XVI,13,
    547, 661; XVII,275
  Simpson XV,35
  Solomon XV,591
  Stephen XVI,159, 235, 270,
    506, 654-55
  Thomas XIV,7, 348
  Timothy XIV,323, 339
  William XIV,436, 525, 576,
    583, 600, 604-5, 612-13,
    631, 653, 656; XV, 357,
    434, 500, 504-5, 711, 715;
    XVI,198, 575, 599-600;
    XVII,135, 426
Whitehorn, George XVII,747-48
  John XIV,22; XVI,320, 322,
    325, 331, 335, 339, 343-
    44, 490
  Richard XVII,747-48
  Samuel XVI,256, 505
  Thomas XIV,226; XV,300-1,
    304, 308
Whitehouse, Charles XIV,245,
    372, 385, 517; XVI,623

299

Whitehouse, Daniel XIV,126,
    188, 230, 540
  Ebenezer XIV,473, 550;
    XVI,103, 208, 233, 241,
    241, 275, 520, 836
  Enoch XIV,473; XV,752
  John XIV,372, 385, 496, 505,
    517
  John Jr. XIV,372, 385, 497,
    506, 517
  Jonathan XIV,126, 188, 298;
    XVII,11
  Moses XVI,898
  Pumphrey XIV,2; XVI,913
  Solomon XV,175
Whitelock, John XIV,258
Whiting, Aaron XIV,85, 199-200
  Abel XV,453; XVI,510, 723,
    725
  Abiel XIV,600; XV,455
  Amos XVI,921
  Colonel XIV,26
  Cotton XVI,535
  James XIV,167, 170, 463;
    XVI, 921; XVII,14, 65
  John XIV,576
  Jonathan XIV,437
  Nathan XIV,54, 185, 458,
    538; XIV,539; XV,229
  Oliver XV,636; XVI,41, 44,
    880, 885
  Samuel XIV,634; XV,442,
    724; XVI,144, 814
  William XVII,672
Whitman, Abiel XV,473, 503
  Daniel XV,7
  Isaiah XVII,117
  Levi XV,621, 634, 645, 719;
    XVI,203, 271, 500, 574-75
Whitney, Aaron XVI,298
  Benjamin XIV,95, 204;
    XV,77, 79, 347
  Col. J. XV,753
  Elias XVI,535
  Ezra XVI,80, 90, 106
  Ithamar XV,7; XVII,95
  James XIV,427

Whitney, Joel XV,52
  John XIV,94, 202-3, 420; XV,
    109; XVI,138
  John Jr. XIV,94
  John 2d XIV,202-3
  Jonathan XIV,525
  Joseph XV,65
  Joshua XIV,430; XV,131,
    546; XVII,257
  Oliver XV,632
  Phinehas XIV,95, 204, 439,
    527, 545; XV,77
  Reuben XIV,525
  Richard XIV,303, 335;
    XV,419, 529; XVII,62
  Samuel XIV,576; XV,28
  Silas XVI,287, 515
  Thomas XVI,35
Whiton, Jeremiah XV,427
  Jonathan XIV, 3
Whittaker, Asa XVI,871
  Benjamin XIV,584
  Caleb XV,550
  Daniel XIV,446
  David XIV,361
  John XIV,438, 527
  Joseph XIV,397
  Laur XVII,495
  Moses XIV,77, 81, 198
  Thomas XIV,576; XV,487,
    499-500, 658-59, 667, 679
  William XVI,871
Whittam, Asa XVI,314
Whittemore, Aaron XIV,426; XV,
    188; XVI,787-89
  Amos XIV,425; XVI,728
  Asa XIV,310
  Benjamin XIV,459, 574; XV,
    615
  Ensign XVII,134
  Jacob XIV,438, 527, 545
  James XV,631, 637; XVI,102,
    609
  Joshua XIV,355
  Pelatiah XIV,89, 201, 554,
    622; XV,718; XVI,5, 51,
    182, 203, 248, 271, 761;

Whittemore, Pelatiah (Cont.)
XVII,268
Peter XVI,247, 253, 516
Samuel XIV,34; XVII,102
Zebadiah XV,93, 219
Whitten, Israel XIV,238
James XV,544
John XIV,263, 423, 657;
XV,15, 460, 605, 732,
735; XVI,36, 39, 212, 275,
278, 515, 686; XVII,143,
221, 705
Joseph XV,518
Mark XIV,69; XV,311, 545
Richard XIV,403
Samuel XIV,238, 603
Whittier, Benjamin XIV,299,
538, 585, 660; XV,562-63,
727; XVI,10, 43, 155, 157,
185, 209, 708, 807
Captain XV,694
Chase XIV,69
David XV,588
Jacob XVI,45, 301, 513, 737
James XV,525
John XVI,237, 244, 787
Joseph XV,285, 291, 528
Richard XIV,415; XV,283,
290
Whittle, John XV,519; XVI,144
Thomas XV,90, 207
William XVI,144, 246, 253,
511
Whittlesey, Josiah XV,593; XVII,
80, 82
Whittock, Thomas XV,711
Whitton, Simeon XIV,550
Simeon Jr. XIV,550
Whittridge, Josiah XIV,315
Whitum, David XV,465
Simeon XV,430
Wiatt, Francis XVII,495
Wibird, Richard XIV,13;
XVI,911; XVII,730, 746
Wickett, Henry XIV,7
Widden, Ichabod XIV,233

Wier, James XV,446, 745;
XVI,519, 809
John XIV,211, 216; XV,349
Joseph XV,518
Samuel XIV,576; XV,434,
711; XVI,198
Wiggin, Andrew XIV,72, 179,
232, 307, 331; XV,243,
245, 247; XVII,528, 673,
679
Asa XIV,321
Benjamin XIV,229, 369, 377,
492; XVII,30
Bradstreet XVI,111, 252,
520; XVII,693
Chase XIV,323, 361, 365
Cooker XV,597
David XIV,232, 248; XVII,26
Elijah XIV,370, 378, 493,
504, 515; XV,327
Gideon XIV,135, 191; XVII,6
James XV,192; XVI,65, 76,
99, 105, 107
Jesse XIV,322, 365; XVII,29
John XIV,233, 341, 408
Josiah XIV,321, 365
Major XVII,354
Mark XIV,229, 242, 367, 369,
377, 379, 492, 502, 510,
515, 521; XV, 318, 331-
33, 336-37, 543; XVI,319,
528, 842-44; XVII,30
Moses XV,325
Nathan XV,243, 245-46
Nicholas XIV,119, 150, 196
Noah XIV,229; XV,327;
XVII,27
Phinehas XIV,135, 191;
XV,327; XVII,6
Simon XIV,369, 377, 492;
XV, 544; XVI,109, 844;
XVII,27, 665
Theophilus XIV,232, 251,
400
Thomas XIV,135, 191; XVII,6,
486

Wiggin, Walter XIV,369, 377,
492, 503, 515
William XV,277; XVII,118-19
Winthrop XIV,108, 124, 187,
564, 630; XV,725;
XVI,207, 227, 275, 514,
764, 766-67
Wigglesworth, Colonel XV,457
Edward XVI,6, 325, 491-92
Dr. Samuel XIV,234, 339,
476; XVI, 637
Wight, John XV,216, 630;
XVI,102, 629
Wilbore, Nathan XIV,85, 199-
200
Wilbour, Elisha XV,48
Nathaniel XV,48
Philip XV,48
Wilcox, Asa XIV,357; XV,67, 226
Jesse XIV,298; XV,36, 370,
372, XVII,103
John XV,377
Obadiah XV,3, 67; XVII,96
Phinehas XV,30
Uriah XV,30, 37, 146-48, 158
William XVII,196-97
Wild, Joseph XVII,205
Wilder, Abel XV,373, 378; XVII,
108, 111
Ezra XVI,536
James XVI,291
John XVI,290
Jonas XV,705
Jonas Jr. XVI,289
Joseph XVI,535
Mark XIV,180
Moses Jr. XVI,290
Nathaniel XIV,645; XVI,23,
886
Peter XVI,81, 95, 107, 193
Silas XVI,254
Thomas XIV,325, 464
Wilhomet, Peter XIV,7
Wilkins, Andrew XIV,50, 186,
266, 477; XVI,259;
XVII,437
Archelaus XVI,884-85

Wilkins, Archibald XIV,244
Asa XIV,572, 639; XV,349,
612, 731; XVI,15, 25, 186,
211
Bray XIV,33, 247, 303, 312;
XV,552
Bray Jr. XIV,302
Daniel XIV,102-3, 266-67,
288, 292, 476-77;
XVI,236, 275, 498, 528,
531, 562;XVII, 463, 468
Eli XIV,102, 208; XV,74, 214;
XVI,560, 562
Elisha XIV,89
Elijah XIV,201
Isaac XVI,286, 500
Israel XIV,33
John XIV,34, 696
Jonathan XIV,103, 207, 247,
416; XV,73, 213, 520
Joseph XIV,425
Robert XV,624
Robert B. XIV,43, 89, 201,
439, 527-28, 572, 639;
XV,612, 727; XVI,8, 15,
19, 25, 182, 208;
XVII,441, 470
Samuel XVI,560
Sylvester XIV,267, 572, 596;
XV,611, 713; XVI,528
Thomas XVII,674
Uriah XVI,884
William XIV,584; XV,451-52;
XVI,588
William H. XIV,631; XV,711
Wilkinson, Benning XV,667;
XVI, 644
James XIV,18, 642; XV,422,
597, 730; XVI,18, 194,
211; XVII, 241
Thomas XVII,757
Willand, Nathaniel XVI,893;
XVII, 11
Paul XVI,623, 625
Willard, Caleb XIV,289, 292;
XVI, 921
David XV,368

Willard, Henry XIV,264
  Jeremiah XV,31, 368;
    XVI,311
  John XIV,264
  Jonathan XIV,326, 463, 473,
    553, 592; XV,446, 710;
    XVI,3, 51, 94, 180, 182,
    197, 267; XVII,65, 113,
    266, 445
  Josiah XVI,919-20, 922
  Langley XVI,81, 95, 298
  Lockhart XVI,435
  Nathaniel XIV,126
  Samuel XIV,444; XV,662,
    669, 671, 681; XVI,137,
    596
  Simon XVI,852, 888
  Wilder XIV,607-8; XV,602,
    714; XVI,200
  William XV,32
  Willoughby XV,144
Wille, Benjamin XIV,307, 362,
  569
  Ebenezer XIV,259, 323
  Ezekiel XIV,108, 124, 188
  John XIV,372; XVII,717
  John Jr. XVII,717
  Robert XIV,108, 124
  Samuel XIV,408; XVII,717,
    719
  Thomas XVII,719, 721
  William XIV,67, 244, 474;
    XVII, 716
  Zebulon XIV,307
Willen, Benjamin XV,441
Willet, Joshua XV,177-78, 742
Willey, Abel XV,124; XVI,586,
  861
  Allen XV,147; XVI,714
  Allen Jr. XV,35
  Andrew XV,249-51, 255;
    XVI,251,513
  Barnabas XV,25; XVII,104
  Benjamin XV,609, 619-20;
    XVI, 207, 227, 241, 275,
    500, 512, 572, 576

Willey, Charles XIV,226; XVI,68,
  76, 97, 776
  Darius XV,382
  Ebenezer XVII,42
  Ezekiel XIV,21, 188; XVI,710
  Jeremiah XIV,25
  John XIV,267, 385, 496, 505,
    517, 570; XV,656, 666,
    679, 740; XVI,66, 76, 95,
    570-72, 776, 780
  John Jr. XIV,330, 602;
    XV,300-301, 305, 308
  Jonathan XIV,225; XV,300,
    302; XVI,779
  Josiah XV,628, 640; XVI,102,
    622, 627
  Robert XV,242, 245, 247,
    468, 480, 496
  Samuel XIV,3, 13-14, 233;
    XV, 191
  Stephen XVII,22, 34
  Thomas XIV,1, 21, 235;
    XVI,904
  William XIV,212, 216, 470,
    570, 580-81, 602; XV,447,
    449, 598, 600, 628, 640,
    712; XVI, 102, 199, 222,
    268, 513, 659-660, 778-79
  William Jr. XVI,622
  Winthrop XIV,25, 259;
    XVI,519; XVII,37
  Zebulon XIV,119, 149, 196
Williams, Abraham XV,44;
  XVII,495
  Amos XIV,258; XVII,22, 33
  Asa XV,18; XVII,109
  Bartholomew XVII,295
  Benjamin XIV,34, 89, 201,
    340, 567, 585, 611, 657;
    XV,20, 197, 219, 533,
    535, 608, 717, 742;
    XVI,39, 64, 72, 92, 107,
    202, 708; XVII,32, 100
  Berry XVI,61
  Charles XV,297
  Daniel XV,40, 155; XVII,48

Williams, David XVII,144
    Ebenezer XIV,584, 631;
        XV,451-452, 711;
        XVI,557-60, 588
    George XVI,516, 803
    Henry XVII,607
    Isaac XIV,394; XV,386;
        XVII,88
    John XIV,108, 124, 187, 227,
        257-58, 411, 472, 549;
        XV, 323, 342, 358, 430,
        577; XVI, 248, 267, 285,
        511, 710, 716; XVII,74,
        716-17, 721
    Dr. John XVII,220
    Jonathan XIV,124, 187
    Joseph XIV,226, 340;
        XV,560, 570; XVI,638;
        XVII,32
    Lilburn XVII,208
    Martin XVII,621
    Moses XIV,225, 381, 490,
        501, 514; XV,499
    Moses B. XV,63
    O. H. XVI,217
    Dr. Obadiah XIV,46, 48; XVI,
        416, 482, 489
    Peleg XIV,553, 595; XV,446,
        710; XVI,3; XVII,266
    Peter XVI,285, 508
    Samuel XIV,6, 13, 103, 207,
        235, 322, 363, 394, 617;
        XV, 17, 109, 138, 618,
        723; XVI, 196, 206, 233,
        241, 273, 640; XVII,88,
        108, 717
    Smith XVI,296
    Thomas XVI,61, 64, 72, 92,
        107, 168, 257, 507, 793,
        878; XVII,429
Williamson, Caleb XVII,669
Willing, James XVII,22, 34, 37
Willis, Abiel XIV,445, 543;
    XV,40
    Edward XIV,562
    Elisha XIV,265; XV,741
    Jonathan XV,224; XVII,94

Willis, Reuben XVII,360
    Sylvanus XV,41, 138
    Thomas XIV,561
    William XV,256; XVII,307
Willoughby John XIV,563;
    XV,124, 126, 150, 381-82,
    385; XVI, 799; XVII,66
    John Jr. XV,160, 459
    Jonas XVI,297
    Joseph XIV,656
    Joshua XV,732
    Josiah XIV,586; XV,606;
        XVI,37, 39
Wills, Ebenezer XV,267
Wilmot, William XVII,207
Wilson,--- XV,699
    Aaron XIV,325, 464; XV,61
    Alexander XV,696, 698;
        XVI,86, 91, 107, 890;
        XVII,308
    Ambrose XVII,302
    Ammi XV,40
    Archelaus XIV,35; XVI,752
    Benjamin XV,3, 55; XVII,97,
        297
    Daniel XIV,356; XV,227, 741
    David XV,3, 24, 227, 394;
        XVII, 97
    Deliverance XVII,101
    Ebenezer XV,49; XVI,143
    Elihu XV,692; XVI,214, 234
    George XIV,336, 572, 597;
        XV, 215, 611, 713, 740;
        XVI,199, 235, 698, 839,
        890; XVII,63, 439
    Humphrey XVII,57, 526
    Isaac XIV,576; XV,155; XVII,
        109, 144
    James XIV,328, 333, 605,
        659; XV,16, 99, 103, 228,
        283, 288, 351, 353, 360,
        597, 698, 716; XVI,201,
        720, 753, 755, 840, 842,
        888, 918; XVII,109
    James Jr. XV,552; XVII,257
    Jeremiah XIV,94, 202-3
    Jesse XV,196, 228-29

Wilson, John XIV,72, 158, 246, 299, 658; XV,33, 39, 100, 525, 635, 639, 740; XVI, 39, 102, 284, 437, 513, 839-40, 890, 898

Jonas XV,355

Jonas Jr. XIV,34

Jonathan XIV,577, 593; XV,694, 716; XVI,65, 76, 96, 105, 107

Joseph XIV,36, 238, 468, 484; XIV,612; XV,218, 431, 442, 586, 632, 636, 692, 711; XVI,28, 198, 221, 224, 241, 267-68, 311, 498, 511, 557, 562, 729, 815; XVII,86

Joshua XIV,56, 184, 635; XV, 460, 605, 724; XVI,207, 229, 274, 515, 664, 682-83

Nathaniel XIV,296; XV,162, 194-195, 231

Richard XIV,240, 259; XVI,926; XVII,22, 33, 37

Richard Jr. XVII,22, 34, 42

Robert XIV,327, 411, 579, 605; XV,163, 167, 189, 351, 429, 453-54, 660, 694, 716, 748; XVI,201, 478, 527, 531, 600, 722; XVII,259, 293

Robert Jr. XV,169, 552

Samuel XIV,94, 202-3, 246, 627; XV,205, 457, 721; XVI,168, 205, 226, 272, 502, 529, 612, 703

Supply XIV,34, 90, 201, 420

Thomas XIV,75-76, 83, 178, 198, 283, 287, 411, 470, 578, 596; XV,169, 518, 526, 713; XVI, 199, 223, 268, 499, 553, 588, 599, 665-66

Titus XIV,577, 612; XV,434, 711

Warren XVI,121, 164

Wilson, William XIV,410; XV,17, 749

William Jr. XIV,410

Winch, Joseph XVI,236, 273, 517, 752

Samuel XV,218, 542; XVI,82, 95, 107

Winchester, David XIV,437, 525; XV,7

Jonathan XIV,437, 525

Lemuel XIV,102, 207

Wincol, Captain XIV,3

John XIV,1

Joseph XIV,344; XVI,62, 70, 94

Winfield, Matthew XVI,809

Winford, Ezekiel XVII,525

Wing, Israel XVI,287, 521

Wingate, Aaron XVI,68, 79, 96; XVII,435

Caesar XVI,238, 245, 523, 818, 820

Captain XVII,710

Daniel XIV,624; XV, 725; XVI,207, 817

Daniel Jr. XV,619

David XIV,234, 407; XVI,118

Edmund XIV,236

Enoch XIV,624; XV, 619, 725; XVI,207, 817

John XIV,13, 235; XV,575; XVI, 862; XVII,261, 525

Dr. John XVI,492

Jonathan XV,243, 245, 295, 469, 481, 507; XVI,627

Joseph XIV,407; XV,298, 325; XVI,119

Joshua XIV,209, 223, 231, 240, 339, 343, 346, 402, 414, 481; XV,570-76; XVII,27, 69, 261, 710, 740

Stephen XIV,363; XV,294, 699; XVI,128, 162, 627-28

William XVI,168-69

Winkell, Joseph XVII,22, 34

Winkley, John XIV,240

Winkley, Joseph XVI,60
  Mrs. XVII,639
  Samuel XVII,621, 646
  Samuel Jr. XV,299
Winn, Caleb XIV,99, 205;
    XV,349
  James XIV,43, 56, 184
  Joseph XIV,239; XV,69, 206
  Nehemiah XIV,97, 203-4
  Samuel XIV,238
Winship, Colonel XV,159
  Ebenezer XVII,233
Winslow, Edward XVII,307
  Elisha XIV,581, 641; XV,422,
    449, 600, 729; XVI,19,
    918
  Ephraim XIV,226, 340
  Jacob XV,321, 342
  John XVII,254
  Jonathan XV,249-51, 254
  Luther XIV,85, 199; XV,7, 50,
    223; XVI,153; XVII,97
  Samuel XIV,69, 180, 328,
    365, 515; XV,171; XVI,75
  Simon XIV,370, 378, 492,
    504; XV,482, 495, 656,
    666, 678; XVI,65, 98, 224,
    644, 703
  Zebulon XIV,327; XV,525
Winter, John XIV,263
Winthrop, John XV,591
  Mr. XVII,490
Winton, James XVI,178-79, 268,
    522, 877, 879
  William XIV,607-8; XV,603,
    714; XVII,153
Wisco, Lewis XIV,470, 578, 597;
    XV,446, 713; XVI,199,
    268, 519, 809
Wisdom, Henry XIV,624;
    XV,720; XVI,103, 516, 803
Wise, Abner XIV,469, 644;
    XV,711; XVI,221, 239, 267
  Daniel XIV,236
  Robert XIV,172, 177, 316,
    318; XVI,147
  Wyman XVI,913

Wiser, Benjamin XV,590
Witcher, Andrew XIV,501
Witham, Jedediah XIV,314
Withe, Zoe XVI,63, 72, 91, 720
  See also Withy
Witherell, Ephraim XV,7, 669;
    XVI,700-1; XVII,94, 255
  John XV,749
  See also Wetherell
Withers, Thomas XVII,522
Witherspoon, David XIV,327-28
Withington, Elisha XIV,419
  Matthew H. XIV,639; XV,731;
    XVI,16, 26, 278
  William XV,108, 542, 753
Withy, John XIV,597; XV,446;
    XVI, 519, 809
  Zoe XV,566, 698
  See also Withe
Witt, Artemas XV,704, 726; XVI,
    177, 878-79
  Benjamin XV,49
  Isaiah XV,11
  Moses XIV,325, 464; XV,24
  Zaccheus XV,360
Witten, Samuel XV,626
Wolcott, John XVI,286, 512, 935
  Roger XV,24
Wolstenholme, John XVII,494-
    95
Wood,--- XV,43
  Aaron XVI,275
  Benjamin XVI,554
  Caesar XVI,245, 273, 520,
    845
  Daniel XIV,418
  David XVI,578
  Dennis XIV,249
  Ebenezer XIV,184; XV,109
  Edward XIV,56, 184, 657;
    XV,732; XVI,36, 39, 195,
    212
  Dr. George XVI,354, 485
  Gideon XIV,587, 656;
    XV,732; XVI,37, 39, 195,
    212, 530
  Isaac XIV,36

Wood, James XIV,6, 421; XV, 192; XVII,434
John XV,740
Jonathan XIV,57, 94, 202-3, 355; XV,203
Joseph XIV,6; XV,10, 17, 156; XVI,920
Joseph Jr. XVII,143
Josiah XIV,359
Oliver XIV,97, 204
Paul XIV,95, 204, 573; XVI,635
Richard XVI,165; XVII,31
Samuel XIV,267, 439, 442, 544-545; XV, 30, 81, 147
Silas XVI,23
Stephen XVI,236, 273, 575
Thomas XIV,76, 135, 191, 587, 656; XV,732; XVI,36-37, 39, 195, 212, 530; XVII,7
Timothy XV,539
William XIV,33, 43; XV,209, 227, 718, 744; XVI,4, 322-23, 327, 329, 331, 334, 337, 339, 344-45, 494
Woodall, Timothy XIV,627; XV,443, 721
Woodbridge, Joseph XVII,731-32
Woodbury, Benjamin XV,390, 568
Captain XIV,249; XVII,244
Ebenezer XIV,225; XV,329, 343; XVII,32
Elisha XIV, 52-54, 153, 156, 184-85; XVI, 384, 452, 823
Hasadiah XV,483
Henry XV,390
Hezekiah XV,497
Israel XIV,628; XV,441, 721; XVI,204
Israel Jr. XIV,587
Jesse XVI,83
John XIV,398; XV,622, 663, 669, 683, 689

Woodbury, Jonathan XIV,53, 185; XVI,921
Joseph XVI,98
Josiah XIV,89, 425; XV,188
Levi XV,664, 670, 677; XVI,556; XVII,339
Luke XIV,52, 185, 554, 629; XV, 217-18; XVI,5, 180, 182, 203, 271, 374; XVII,268
Nathan XV,156; XVII,143
Nathaniel XIV,425; XV,188; XVI,909
Peter XIV,244
Samuel XIV,9; XV,349
William XIV,587, 628; XV,721; XVI,204
Zachariah XIV,452, 532
Woodcock, Elkanah XIV,264
Jonathan XIV,646; XV,446, 732; XVI,20, 23, 191, 212; XVII,98
Michael XV,538, 739; XVII,428
Woodcroft, David XVI,929
Woodhouse, David XIV,500, 512
Woodley, John XV,499
Woodman, Abner XV,390
Archelaus XIV,235, 242
Benjamin XIV,641; XV,595, 597
Daniel XIV,113, 148, 195, 309; XV,725; XVI,207, 625
David XIV,233; XV,243, 245-46; XVII,24
Edward Jr. XIV,233
Jeremiah XIV,389, 495; XVI,526
John XIV,234; XVII,620, 628, 635, 638, 641-45, 654, 665
Jonathan XIV,231, 300-1, 400; XVII,683, 719
Joseph XIV,453, 532; XVI, 507, 668
Joshua XIV,235, 476; XVI, 710-711; XVII,434, 461

Woodman, Levi XIV,382, 490, 501, 514
  Moses XIV,113, 148, 195
  Nathaniel XIV,240, 260; XVII, 22, 34, 47
  Samuel XIV,233, 351
  Thomas XIV,450, 534; XVI,69, 79, 92; XVII,384
Woods, Cornelius XVII,294
  Daniel XIV,573, 600; XV,615, 715; XVI,200
  David XIV,485; XVII,86
  Dennis XIV,61, 182
  Jonas XV,88-89, 210, 511
  Jonathan XV,77, 79, 347
  Joseph XV,144; XVII,249
  Nehemiah XV,89
  Paul XIV,600; XV,615, 715; XVI,200
  Richard XIV,239; XVII,23, 39
  Samuel XIV,527; XV,62; XVI,110, 165
  Stephen XVI,500
  William XV,62
Woodson, Major XVII,161, 185, 187
Woodward, Abel XIV,334; XV,541
  Abijah XVI,158
  Bezaleel XVI,388
  Captain XVII,72
  Daniel XV,144
  David XV,38-39, 45, 374; XVI, 528, 537; XVII,67
  Deliverance XIV,422; XV,18, 41
  Eleazer XV,17; XVII,67, 109
  Eliphalet XIV,135, 191; XVII,7
  Ezekiel XV,7
  Henry XV,15, 373; XVII,108
  Ithamar XIV,425
  Ithiel XV,19
  James XIV,547; XV,279, 281; XVI,539
  Jehial XV,138, 375

Woodward, Joel XVII,109
  Jonathan XVI,150
  Moses XV,577; XVI,929, 932; XVII,139, 419
  Nathaniel XIV,160-61, 165; XV, 19, 138
  Robert XV,629, 643, 733, 735; XVI,40, 190, 769, 847
  Samuel XVII,715-16, 722-23
  Theodorus XVII,118, 120
  Titus XV,15, 138, 157; XVII,144
  William XV,373; XVII,306
Woodworth, Elisha XVII,118, 120
  Joel XIV,269-70, 289; XV,384; XVI,538
  John XIV,443, 543; XV,277; XVII,48, 118-19
  Roswell XIV,280, 288; XV,153
  Samuel XIV,423
Wooldridge, Thomas XIV,308
Wooley, John XIV,355, 646; XV, 4, 54, 204, 732, 745; XVI,20, 22, 887
  Jonathan XIV,645; XVI,23, 323, 340, 492, 809
  Thomas XV,633, 643, 648; XVI, 23, 44, 603
Woolford, Thomas XVII,208
Woolister, George XV,530
Woolson, George XIV,101, 206-7
Woolvin, Thomas XIV,8
Wooster, Francis XIV,528
  James XIV,389
  Samuel XIV,392, 488, 509, 513
Worcester, Francis Jr. XV,125
  James XVI,12, 209, 232, 241, 277, 518, 803, 821
  Jesse XIV,346; XV,89, 511; XVI, 84, 90, 192
  Noah XIV,243; XV,209, 743; XVI, 584, 637, 688, 691
  Noah Jr. XIV,32; XV,87, 511

Worcester, Samuel T. XIV,42
Word, William XIV,255
Worden, Major XVII,181
Worker, Joseph XV,747
Works, Samuel XV,47; XVI,362,
   429, 462, 879; XVII,95
Wormall, Samuel XVII,57
Wormwood, Amos XIV,238
  Joseph XIV,22
  William XVII,717
Worsley, Robert XIV,101, 206,
   463; XV,226
Worster, James XIV,495, 545,
   647, 650; XV,596, 728,
   734
Worth, John XV,475, 498;
   XVI,285, 501, 874
  Timothy XIV, 340; XV,
   748
Worthen, E. XVI,703
  Enoch XV,522
  Ezekiel XIV,315, 350, 352,
   369, 377, 456, 492, 521,
   537; XV, 474, 476, 494,
   654, 672, 678, 686-87;
   XVI,527; XVII,21, 222
  Isaac XIV,549; XV, 474, 494;
   XVI,155
  Jacob XV,525; XVII,135
  Michael XIV,381, 490, 501,
   514; XV,321, 340
  Moses XV,460, 605; XVI,914
  Samuel XIV,174, 304-5, 465-
   66, 566, 653; XV,351,
   353, 381, 608, 729;
   XVI,31, 34, 59, 914
Worthlake, Benjamin XIV,6
Worthley, John XV,751
  Jonathan XIV,172, 174, 176-
   77; XV,550
  Nathan XV,698
  Samuel XVI,914
  Thomas XV,113, 550
  Timothy XIV,329
Wright, Aaron XIV, 223; XV,
   50
  Abel XV,18, 40

Wright, Atijah XIV,463; XV,124;
   XVI,496; XVII,66
  Amasa XIV,268, 274, 289
  Benjamin XIV,33, 206, 439,
   527, 545; XV,209;
   XVI,748; XVII,220
  Benjamin Jr. XIV,33
  Caleb XV,360; XVI,840
  Daniel XV,67, 741, 752
  David XIV,223, 607; XV,374,
   603, 714; XVI,200, 269;
   XVII, 67, 236
  Delino XV,43
  E. W. XIV,103
  Ebenezer XIV,263
  Edward XV,102, 109
  Francis XV,99; XVI,534
  Isaac XIV,103, 207; XVII,306
  James XIV,6
  Joel XIV,437, 525
  John XIV,620; XV,41, 44,
   596, 630, 646; XVI,528;
   XVII,296
  John Jr. XIV,418
  Jonathan XIV,85, 199, 264,
   419, 608; XV,603, 714;
   XVI,200; XVII,67
  Joseph XIV,34, 98, 205, 420,
   578, 598-99; XV,713; XVI,
   199, 606, 700; XVII,100,
   102, 224
  Lemuel XIV,347; XV,88
  Moses XIV,263; XV,12
  Nathaniel XV,14, 44, 138,
   373, 378
  Nehemiah XIV,97, 204-5, 418
  Oliver XIV,418; XV,24, 77,
   102-103, 108-9, 370, 630,
   643, 646; XVI,254, 517,
   736-38
  Paul XVI,840
  Phinehas XIV,607-8; XV,436,
   603, 714; XVII,104
  Samuel XIV,101, 206-7, 428,
   436, 438, 524; XV,15, 46,
   138, 196, 203, 205, 210,
   745; XVI,888

Wright, Silas XV,99, 103;
    XVI,442, 840
  Thomas XIV,15
  Uriah XIV,33; XV,89, 744
  William, XV, 63, 753
  Zebedee XV,207
Wyatt, Daniel XV,149, 160; XVI,
    585
  Francis XVII,495
  Josiah XVII,27
Wyer, John XIV,59
Wyman, Aaron XV,566
  Abel XVI,253
  Abiel XVI,246, 316
  Abijah XV,745
  Daniel XIV,418, 574, 626;
    XV, 615, 719; XVI,204
  Ezra XVI,259; XVII,437
  Isaac XIV,36-37, 39, 46, 48,
    80, 311, 324, 329, 335,
    421, 463, 467, 481, 548,
    669, 695; XV,542;
    XVI,662, 701
  James XIV,247
  Jasper XIV,9
  Jesse XIV,33, 438; XV,210;
    XVI, 263; XVII,427
  John XV,746; XVI,236, 521,
    860, 908
  Jonas XV,267, 269-70, 272;
    XVI, 86, 99, 107, 264;
    XVII,430
  Jonathan XVI,728
  Josiah XVI,63, 72, 90, 106,
    263; XVII,427
  Levi XV,229
  Seth XV,557, 621, 663, 669,
    677, 689; XVI,86, 92, 107,
    664; XVII,258
  Stephen XV,122, 228
  Thomas XIV,6, 16
  Timothy XV,553; XVII,259
        Y
Yarmon, John XV,21, 717
Yeaman, John XIV,575
Yeates, James XIV,227, 257-58

Yeaton, Adinton D. XIV,549
  Benjamin XIV,227, 257-58,
    550; XV,430
  Francis XIV,230; XVII,28
  Francis Jr. XIV,230
  George XIV,616; XV,440,
    595, 626; XVI,503, 624
  Hopeley XV,577; XVI,925;
    XVII,139
  John XVI,111, 261, 822;
    XVII, 432
  Jonathan XIV,322
  Moses XIV,17, 230, 243;
    XV,573, 574; XVII,28, 260
  Moses Jr. XV,573; XVII,28,
    260
  Paul XVI,119, 237, 244, 272,
    521, 836
  Philip XIV,3, 14, 236
  Richard XIV,388, 473, 495,
    507, 516
  Robert XVI,110, 166
  Samuel XIV,124, 187, 255,
    260, 408, 484, 499, 512,
    518; XVI, 118, 285, 522,
    638; XVII,31, 39, 46, 85
  William XIV,224, 239, 402,
    415; XVII,23, 31, 38
Yegoold, John XIV,661
Yeoman, John XV,438
York, Benjamin XV,655, 666,
    676, 698; XVI,67, 77, 96,
    623, 627-28
  Christopher XVI,608;
    XVII,249
  David XIV,233; XV,192
  Elijah XVII,24
  Eliphalet XIV,446, 540
  Ezekiel XVI,236, 243, 270,
    499, 582
  Gershom XV,27, 371;
    XVI,467
  John XIV,12, 25, 321, 365;
    XV, 191; XVI,66, 77, 96,
    316-17; XVII,513, 719
  Jonathan XIV,265

310

York, Joseph XIV,470, 570, 602;
    XV, 27, 294, 655, 666,
    677, 712; XVI,199, 225,
    268, 513, 527, 623, 627,
    778; XVII,105
  Josiah XVI,748
  Richard XIV,12
  Robert XVI,236, 242, 273,
    499, 582
  Samuel XIV,234; XV,667,
    677; XVI,103, 194, 213,
    220, 279, 513-14, 644-45,
    778
  William XV,27; XVI,313; XVII,
    252
Youer, John XIV,223
Young, --- XV,4
  Aaron XIV,226, 404; XV,322,
    331, 341
  Abner XIV,375, 385, 497,
    506, 517
  Abraham XV,754
  Andrew XVII,22, 33
  Benjamin XV,256-58, 260,
    264
  Caleb XV,589; XVI,83, 97,
    296, 307; XVII,114
  Captain XVII,129, 131-32,
    223, 232
  Christopher XV,144
  Clark XVI,257, 519
  Daniel XIV,12, 114, 141, 193,
    250, 273, 276, 289, 298,
    568, 605; XV,716;
    XVI,201, 525
  David XV,590, 746; XVI,308;
    XVII,115
  Ebenezer XIV,228, 446
  Edward XVI,80, 93
  Eleazer XIV,540
  Ephraim XVI,67, 77, 96, 628
  Ezra XIV,235
  George XVII,22, 34
  George J. XV,584
  Henry XVII,301
  Hezekiah XV,144
  Ichabod XV,65; XVII,95

Young, Isaac XIV,235, 409
  James XIV,571, 587, 628;
    XV, 267-68, 270-71, 608,
    725; XVI,207, 623;
    XVII,307
  Jeremiah XIV,28, 124, 187
  Jeremy XIV,108
  Jesse XIV,160-61, 163;
    XV,426, 589; XVI,928
  John XIV,25, 160-61, 163,
    369, 375, 483, 498, 502,
    511, 518; XV,197-98, 279,
    281, 426; XVI,526;
    XVII,289
  Dr. John XV,463; XVI,355,
    393, 440, 445
  Jonathan XIV,127, 188, 473;
    XV, 746
  Joseph XIV,540, 562, 637;
    XV, 445, 725, 741; XVI,
    207, 233, 241, 275, 295,
    526, 907; XVII, 29, 32
  Joseph Jr. XIV,447
  Joshua XIV,25, 160-61, 163,
    328; XV,152, 154, 528,
    585; XVI,307, 928; XVII,
    382
  Jotham XIV,65, 181, 186,
    304-5, 465; XV,129, 180;
    XVI,926; XVII,4
  Nathaniel XIV, 3, 14, 160-61,
    165; XV,754
  Richard XIV,165; XV,384
  Robert XIV,12; XVI,384
  Robin XVII,640
  Samuel XIV,160-61, 163,
    281-82, 284-85, 287, 292,
    295, 321; XV,426; XVI,
    307; XVII,73, 114-15
  Stephen XVI,128, 162, 628
  Thomas XV,192; XVI,913
  Timothy XVI,732
  Walter XVII,760
  Ward C. XV,390
  William XIV,114, 127, 188,
    647, 650; XVI,13; XVII,12,
    303

SUBJECT INDEX

A

Abington, MA XVI,55
Acworth, NH XIV,106, 298, 324-
  25, 470-71, 558, 578,
  592-93; XV, 37, 122, 438-
  39, 604, 630, 642, 669;
  XVI,80, 91, 93, 218, 320,
  328-32, 365, 383, 385,
  435-37, 546, 549, 934
Albany, NY XV,434-35, 437-38,
  440-42, 592
Alexandria, NH XIV,558;
  XV,151, 606, 633, 647,
  662, 668, 734; XVI,88,
  328-29, 331, 419-20, 499,
  550; XVII,3
Allenstown, NH XIV,42, 72, 519,
  557, 560, 570-71, 621;
  XVI, 86, 226, 498, 524,
  551; XVII, 3, 755
Almsbury (Warner), NH XIV,558;
  XVI,247, 253, 936
Alstead, NH XIV,43, 291,
  297,311, 325, 423, 553,
  558, 578, 592, 594-97;
  XV,37, 148, 369, 372,
  435, 501, 630, 642, 750,
  752; XVI,80, 84, 92, 218,
  298, 499, 524, 545, 551,
  934; XVII,249
Alton, NH XV,450, 599, 601,
  668, 690; XVI,282, 320,
  329, 331, 422, 554
  See also New Durham Gore,
  NH

Amesbury, MA XIV,112, 308;
  XV, 754
Amherst, NH XIV,39, 42, 43, 97,
  103, 242, 244, 247, 256,
  292, 311, 391-92, 416,
  418, 469-470, 553-54,
  557, 561, 572, 586, 589,
  595-97, 602-3, 606, 613,
  621, 632-33, 691, 701;
  XV, 68, 72, 74, 76, 123,
  140, 196-97, 435, 438,
  463, 521, 611-12, 622,
  632, 636, 654, 664, 670,
  689, 695, 739-40, 750-51;
  XVI, 83-84, 94-95, 98,
  104, 166, 218, 221-22,
  224-225, 233, 246-47,
  251-52, 259, 295, 297,
  320, 328, 330, 391, 393,
  417, 443, 498, 555, 935;
  XVII, 62-64, 339, 418,
  436-37
Andover, NH XIV,309; XV,162,
  231, 610, 612, 663, 670,
  688, 740; XV,754; XVI,88,
  92, 222, 224, 247, 251,
  297, 383, 499, 519, 562-
  63, 827; XVII,9, 50
  See also New Breton, NH
Andover, MA XVI, 55, 57, 492;
  XVII,40, 121
Andrews Hill XVII,493
Annapolis Royal XIV,4-10; XVII,
  707, 730
Antrim, NH XIV,632; XV,444,

Antrim, NH (Cont.) 583, 622,
634, 644, 689, 696;
XVI,47, 85, 91, 162, 246-
47, 251, 254, 303, 402,
498, 540, 564, 893, 935
See also Society Land, NH
Arlington, NH XVI,308-9
Arundel, ME XVII,38
Atkinson, NH XIV,76-77, 555,
557, 586-87, 658; XV,
343-44, 569, 606, 623,
641, 667, 691, 735, 743,
749; XVI,69, 79, 90, 94,
243, 245, 375, 498, 532,
565
Attleborough, MA XVI,55

B

Bakerstown, NH XVI,521
See also Salisbury, NH
Barnett, VT XVII,223
Barnstead, NH XIV,107, 296,
396, 557, 581-82, 603,
617, 619, 660; XV,163,
435, 449-50, 600-1, 628,
640, 668, 690; XVI,63-64,
67, 75, 90, 96, 98, 122,
233, 297, 499, 569, 626,
639
Barrington, NH XIV,18, 69, 107-
8, 114-15, 242, 307, 323,
384-386, 517, 554, 556,
617-19, 624; XV,444-45,
619-20, 628, 640, 654,
656, 666, 747; XVI, 69,
79-80, 227, 230, 244, 252,
256, 329-31, 363, 370,
372, 412, 499, 512, 524,
544, 569, 639; XVII,10,
434
Bath, NH XIV,159-60, 291, 468;
XV,425, 435-36; XVI,97,
307; XVI,321, 332, 403,
541, 573, 924; XVII,14,
121, 224
Battenkill XV,391
Battle of Brandywine XVII,154,
194, 196, 199, 300

Battle of Monmouth Court
House XVII,238-39, 246
Battle at Newtown, NY XVI,330,
356, 404, 475
Battle of Princeton XIV,481, 522
Battle of Saratoga XIV,652
Bedford, MA XV,239
Bedford, NH XIV,59, 210-12,
256, 258, 468, 470, 557,
573; XV, 111-12, 162,
345, 362-63, 435, 437,
616, 621, 634, 644, 689,
696, 740; XVI,85, 91, 100,
161, 219, 221, 247, 251,
253, 255, 295, 320, 328,
330-331, 383, 423, 499,
524, 544, 573, 600; XVII,
121, 256, 427
Bedford, RI XVI,231
Bemis Heights XIV,615; XV,276;
XVI, 330-32, 349, 374-75,
386, 387, 407, 412, 423,
447, 456, 476, 489;
XVII,147
Bennington Troops XIV,139-40
Bennington, NH, *See Society
Land, NH*
Bennington, VT XV,140, 154,
164, 174, 179, 185, 203,
216, 219, 230-33, 276,
428, 433, 435; XVI, 330-
32, 354, 361, 363, 379,
382-83, 386, 393, 396,
400, 419, 424-25, 432,
435, 440, 472, 486, 531,
536, 839, 860, 868;
XVII,147-48, 234
Benton (Coventry), NH XVII,342
Berwick, ME XIV,169, 291, 308,
369, 374-77, 381, 388,
414, 518, 553, 555, 615,
638; XV, 436-37, 661,
749; XVI,68, 223, 232,
491; XVII,12, 37
Beverly, MA XVI,935
Billerica, MA XVI,466; XVII,121
Boats, *See Ships*

Boothbay, ME XVII,328
Boscawen, NH XIV,42, 62, 211,
    316, 318, 469, 557, 567,
    585, 635; 607, 631, 638,
    663, 370, 688; XV,130,
    162, 187, 404-5, 435,
    700-3, 752, 754; XVI,46,
    88; XVI,94, 174-75, 220,
    224, 245, 251, 264, 296,
    302-303, 499, 524, 576,
    799, 935; XVII,50, 93, 430
Boston, MA XIV,282; XV,239,
    623; XVI,13, 55, 231, 266,
    350, 417, 430, 934-35;
    XVII, 349, 521, 529, 531,
    535-40, 561, 590, 603,
    651, 671, 724
Bound House XVII,509
Boundary, New Hampshire and
    Massachusetts XVII, 531,
    627, 632, 659, 677, 714-
    16, 742, 756
Bow, NH XIV,72, 169, 174, 309,
    316, 468-70, 558, 569,
    571, 606; XV,163, 437,
    610, 622, 631, 637, 663,
    670, 688-89, 754; XVI,66-
    67, 91, 222, 246, 247,
    253, 264, 499, 578, 660;
    XVII,431
Boxford, MA XIV,211; XVII,40
Bradford (New Bradford), NH
    XIV, 51; XVI,246
Bradford, MA XVII,40
Braintree, MA XVI,935
Brattleborough, VT XIV,326,
    645; XV,626; XVI,934
Brentwood, NH XIV,112-13,
    212, 307-8, 313, 379, 388,
    397-98, 469, 519, 556,
    562, 565, 616-617, 620,
    628, 630, 635-36, 660;
    XV, 292, 440, 442-43,
    445, 627, 629, 648, 667,
    734, 743, 746-48; XVI, 66-
    68, 75-76, 95, 98, 220,
    222, 224, 231, 233, 242-
Brentwood, NH (Cont.) 43, 245,
    255, 329, 331, 475-76,
    499, 542, 580, 933, 935;
    XVII, 7, 53, 435
Brimfield, MA XVI,934
Bristol, RI XV,669, 689
Brookline (Raby), NH XIV,42,
    59; XV,197, 614, 616,
    632, 636, 744-45; XVI,84,
    246, 253, 259, 331, 464,
    518, 584; XVII,121
Bunker Hill XIV,31-33, 38-40,
    45, 51, 120, 547, 680;
    XV,139, 739, 741, 743-45;
    XVI, 330-31, 351, 377,
    384, 388, 415-17, 431,
    443-44, 452, 464, 475;
    XVI,481-82, 488, 494,
    536, 544, 864, 893; XVII,
    4
Burnham's Garrison XVII,645
                C
Cambridge, MA XIV,33, 35, 46,
    216, 586; XV,282, 745-46,
    750, 753; XVI,351, 527,
    529-531, 534-45, 839,
    868; XVII, 214
Camp at Danbury XVI,41, 407,
    477, 849
Camp at Highlands XVI,162;
    XVII, 232
Camp at James River XVI,241
Camp at New Windsor XVI,306
Camp at Reading XVII,326
Camp at Soldiers Fortune
    XVI,893
Camp at Valley Forge XVII,210
Camp at White Plains XVI,411
Campton, NH XIV,339, 422-23,
    556, 558, 567, 587, 658;
    XV, 381, 459, 605, 609,
    633, 647, 662, 668, 708,
    709, 735; XVI,88, 90, 228,
    233, 247, 254, 288, 502,
    585, 680; XVII,14
Canaan, NH XIV,559, 608;
    XV,45, 378, 436, 604;

Canaan, NH (Cont.) XVI,503,
543, 587; XVII,108-9, 121,
143
Canada XIV,216
Candia, NH XIV,43, 76, 117,
242, 387-88, 469-70, 554,
557, 584, 628-30; XV,162,
402, 441, 452, 476, 495,
639, 658-660, 668, 693-
94, 734, 748, 754; XVI,66,
76, 97, 222, 229, 231,
233, 256, 262, 300, 500,
524, 544, 587, 808, 936,
938; XVII,426-27
Canterbury, NH XIV,107, 145,
210-211, 243, 318, 455,
557, 566, 606, 617-18,
660; XV,162, 387, 438,
513, 607, 663, 670, 688,
697, 700, 702-3, 735;
XVI,46, 62, 87, 90, 99,
174, 224-25, 232, 247,
253, 264, 296, 302, 320,
328, 332, 400, 458, 502,
524, 577, 591, 726, 899,
907; XVII,3, 4, 8-9, 21;
XVII,50, 430-31
Cape Ann XIV,307; XVI,701
Cape Cod XV,439
Cardigan (Orange), NH XV,604;
XVII,108, 110, 121, 143
Casco Bay, ME XIV,443,
Caughnawaga, Canada XVII,58-
59, 128, 152
Cavendish, VT XIV,701; XV,87,
106, 124, 701, 703;
XVI,175; XVII,72
Cedars, Canada XIV,290, 476;
XVI, 459-61, 525, 527-31,
868; XVII,48, 58-59, 211,
462, 465, 468
Chambly, Canada XVII,48, 152,
311
Charlestown, MA XIV,20, 39-40,
46, 156; XVI,404;
XVII,521-522, 603

Charlestown, NH XIV,43, 106,
213, 266, 292-93, 297,
325-26, 468, 471, 553,
558, 577-78, 586, 592-96,
610, 635; XV,37, 82-83,
90, 113, 115, 140, 142-43,
145, 231, 372, 435, 438-
39, 671, 703, 707, 741,
750; XVI,45, 80, 90-91,
177, 218, 221-25, 262,
264, 283, 301-2, 400, 502,
524, 595, 712-13, 768,
921, 934-35; XVII,106,
144, 148, 249, 358, 414,
422, 423, 429-30, 463,
503, 603, 725, 728, 730,
766, 783, 794, 796, 803,
818, 866, 873 (Fort
Number Four) 379, 420,
429, 454, 460, 463, 495,
497-98
Chateaugay, NY XVII,311
Chatham, NJ XVII,161-63, 166,
186-87
Chelmsford, MA XV,754;
XVII,121
Cheshire XVI,175
Chester, NH XIV,76, 83, 112,
256, 328, 387, 389, 422,
469-70, 553-54, 557, 559,
561, 572, 582-83, 601-2,
606, 621, 627, 628, 634-
35, 651; XV,162, 167,
388, 437, 442, 465, 513,
526, 612, 639, 643, 654,
658-660, 667-68, 691,
693-94, 734, 742-43, 749,
753-54; XVI, 65; XVI,76,
96-97, 166, 219, 222, 224,
226, 233, 242-244, 247,
252-53, 255, 262, 300,
320, 328, 330, 379, 476,
479, 501, 520, 524, 551,
599, 742, 808, 902, 915;
XVII, 3, 426, 428, 432,
755

Chester, NY XIV,610, 645
Chesterfield, NH XIV,43, 86,
    555, 598, 608, 645-46,
    655; XV,6, 53, 57, 59-60,
    196-97, 223, 225, 435-36,
    555, 633, 647-648, 651,
    669, 750; XVI, 81, 93,
    225, 320, 330, 459, 462,
    524, 531-32, 545, 601;
    XVII, 255
Chichester, NH XIV,43, 69, 211,
    354, 469, 558, 571, 606,
    630, 635, 641; XV, 303,
    438, 634, 661, 663, 668,
    674, 695; XVI, 66-67, 78,
    99, 255, 257, 299, 423,
    501, 604; XVII,50, 435
Chimney Point XIV,307-8, 310
Claremont, NH XIV,297, 324,
    553, 558, 578, 592-94,
    598, 614-615; XV,37, 142,
    145, 148, 372, 434, 438,
    629, 642, 654; XVI,80, 98,
    218, 221, 223, 232, 329,
    331, 335, 465, 468, 502,
    532, 541, 605, 607, 934;
    XVII,53, 99, 106, 249
Clarendon, VT XVI,488;
    XVII,120
Cloverick XV,441
Cocheco, NH XVII,622-23, 656,
    710
Cockermouth (Groton), NH
    XIV,210, 422, 553, 558,
    590, 608; XV, 436, 459,
    605, 633, 647, 708;
    XVI,88, 90, 296, 387, 503,
    668; XVII,14, 121
Cohos XV,277, 751
Concord (Penacook), NH XIV,36,
    62, 65, 67, 169, 174-75,
    242, 256, 299, 306, 371,
    379, 391, 416, 431, 468,
    555, 557, 566, 571, 585-
    86, 606, 655; XV, 127,
    130, 140, 162-63, 268,
    273, 404-5, 407, 434, 437,

Concord, NH (Cont.) 607-9, 631,
    637-38, 654, 663, 670,
    688, 752; XVI,86, 91-92,
    99, 105, 219, 222, 247,
    253, 263, 295-96, 299,
    332, 470; XVI,501, 524,
    546, 609, 613, 726, 820,
    915, 935; XVII,3, 21, 430,
    445, 452
Concord, MA XIV,33; XV,640;
    XVI, 525, 527, 537, 540,
    745
Continental Village XVII,421
Conway, NH XIV,168-69, 246,
    256, 291, 559, 566, 580;
    XV,427, 448, 598, 607,
    655; XVI, 45, 47, 104,
    219, 225, 242, 264, 281-
    84, 299, 302-3, 502, 612
Coos (Haverhill), NH XIV,211,
    282-83, 309; XVI,215,
    220, 228, 283, 288, 293,
    541, 543, 545, 869;
    XVII,65, 69, 77, 113
Corinth, VT, XVII,223
Cornish, NH XIV,106, 256, 324,
    422-23, 559, 596, 608,
    614; XV,1, 19, 38, 45,
    142, 157, 373, 378, 386,
    434, 436, 602, 651-52,
    654; XVI,223, 249, 431,
    466, 472, 502, 537, 935;
    XVII, 108-9, 120, 143-44,
    148-150, 376
Coventry (Benton), NH XVII,
    342
Coventry, CT XVI,935
Crooked Lane XVII,334
Crown Point XIV,19, 24-26, 291,
    308, 338, 364, 691, 700;
    XVI, 352, 492; XVII,59, 72,
    292
Croydon, NH XIV,471, 559, 594;
    XV,45, 378, 651, 750; XVI,
    328, 332, 503, 520, 532,
    613, 847, 935; XVII,108-
    10, 143

318

Cuckold's Town, NY XVII,162, 165, 168-73, 177, 182, 185, 187

D

Damariscotta, ME XVII,12
Danville (Hawke), NH XV,341-42, 450, 559, 561, 658, 667, 691, 742, 747-48; XVI,65, 75, 98, 243, 255, 508, 524, 614; XVII,424-25
Dartmouth (Jefferson), NH XVII, 144
Dartmouth College XVII,153
Deerfield, NH XIV,69, 72, 117, 210, 352-53, 387, 397-398, 469-70, 555-56, 570-71, 606, 628, 641, 651-52, 660; XV,268, 273-74, 292, 303, 313, 473, 506, 528, 623, 634, 649, 658-61, 668, 697, 735, 747-48, 754; XVI, 67-68, 78-79, 94-95, 98, 100, 220, 222, 224, 226, 231, 242, 244, 257, 320, 328, 330-31, 367, 395, 447, 449, 489-90, 503, 512, 524, 546, 548, 616, 634; XVII,349, 434
Deering, NH XIV,43, 557, 603, 632; XV,122, 444, 621, 638, 644, 689, 696, 744; XVI,86, 91, 161, 227, 246, 251-52, 329, 332, 405-6, 504, 619, 686, 935; XVII,438
Derry, NH XIV,211-12, 307, 470; XV, 438, 443, 751, 754; XVI, 719, 724-25, 902
Derry, Ireland XVII,332
Derryfield (Manchester), NH XIV, 36, 39, 211, 470, 552, 557, 572-73, 591, 602; XV,111, 434-35, 441, 612, 616, 622, 626, 644, 689, 696; XVI,85, 161, 247,

Derryfield, NH (Cont.) 253, 255, 503, 524, 667, 732, 823; XVII,121, 132, 246, 427, 453, 461
Dorchester, NH XIV,422
Dover, NH XIV,21-22, 107, 109, 114-15, 127, 142, 210, 242, 244, 256, 298, 366, 374-75, 384-85, 476, 517-18, 553-54, 556, 559-62, 615, 617-18, 620, 627-28, 640, 655, 666, 751-52; XVI,66-67, 69, 77, 93, 96, 221, 227, 229-31, 233, 242-45, 264, 357, 503, 524, 542, 620, 901; XVII, 4, 10-11, 36, 260, 424, 434-35, 510, 512, 524, 542, 547-48, 566, 605, 617, 623, 625, 648, 650, 655-56, 664-65, 676, 679, 685, 693, 710-11, 717, 720, 734, 737
Dover Combination XVII,501
Dover Neck XVII,656
Dracut, MA XVII,121
Dresden (Hanover), NH XV,603; XVII,321
Dublin, NH XIV,558, 575, 577, 597, 634, 702; XV,82, 197, 441-42, 537, 626, 630, 646, 664-65, 671, 741, 746, 750; XVI,82, 95, 246-47, 251, 255, 505, 524, 628; XVII,428-29
Dunbarton (Gorham), NH XIV,169, 175, 211-12, 254, 291, 359, 468, 557, 606; XV,439, 621, 622, 626, 637-38, 644-45, 689, 696, 740, 743, 751; XVI, 45, 67, 85, 90-91, 100, 161, 221, 246-47, 253, 301, 481, 484, 504, 524, 630; XVII, 19, 427
Dunstable, MA XVII,121
Dunstable (Nashua), NH XIV,43,

Dunstable, NH (Cont.) 97, 440, 468, 470, 545, 553, 555, 557, 596, 601, 606, 632, 638, 691; XV,77, 79, 197, 345-46, 437, 615, 632, 635, 636, 650, 664, 671, 695, 745, 754; XVI,84, 91, 223-24, 247, 251, 263, 259, 296, 330, 379, 504, 524, 547, 634, 687, 740; XVII,62-63, 121, 339, 436

Dunston, MA XIV,307

Durham, NH XIV,21-22, 31, 45, 107-9, 242, 307-9, 313, 339, 370, 374-77, 379, 390, 396, 518, 553-56, 559, 562, 591, 615-17, 623-25, 627, 635-38, 642, 647-48; XV,313, 421, 435, 440-43, 445, 469, 570, 618, 620, 628, 640, 654, 656, 666, 701, 703, 742, 749; XVI, 46, 64, 66, 74, 93, 166, 175, 177, 220, 227, 229-31, 233, 245, 302-3, 320, 328, 332, 463-64, 504, 524, 543, 625, 626, 637, 660; XVII,36, 38, 290, 434, 454, 466, 611, 621-623, 625, 635, 640-45, 657, 716-21, 733, 736

Duxbury School Farm (Milford), NH XIV,572; XV,297, 504, 748

E

East Kingston, NH XIV,475, 557, 585; XV,341-42, 420, 559, 623, 641, 667, 691; XVI,64, 69, 74, 243, 255-56, 510, 524, 641, 823, 901; XVII,44, 349, 425

East Town (Wakefield), NH XIV,309

Eaton, NH XVI,255

Effingham (Leavittstown), NH XV, 163, 449-50, 600-1;

Effingham, NH (Cont.) XVI,220, 257, 282, 505, 642, 862

Elizabeth Town, NJ XIV,308; XVII, 161-76, 186-87, 325

Enfield (Relhan), NH XIV,43, 173-174, 608; XV,378, 603; XVI, 335; XVII,121, 144

Epping, NH XIV,107, 116-17, 210-211, 242, 308-9, 330, 353, 369-71, 377-79, 381, 390-92, 399-400, 471, 513, 519, 554, 556, 564, 593, 599, 615-17, 630-31, 641, 647, 651, 661; XV,240, 265, 268, 410, 437, 440, 451, 484, 488, 495, 623, 626, 629, 648, 654, 657, 667, 701-3, 734; XVI, 45-46, 64, 67-68, 73, 98, 174, 218-19, 222-24, 227, 230, 242-45, 247, 251-52, 255-56, 265, 302, 489, 505, 643, 933-34; XVII,25, 349

Epsom, NH XIV,37, 42-43, 46, 69, 352, 354, 387, 468-69, 552, 555-56, 558, 570, 601-2, 604, 617, 651-52, 661; XV,162, 303, 434, 506, 626, 634, 649, 661, 663, 668, 695; XVI,64, 67, 73-74, 99, 221-22, 224, 231, 330, 368-69, 396, 416, 488, 505, 524, 646, 726; XVII,50, 434

Exeter, NH XIV,37, 69, 110-13, 116, 121, 242-43, 256, 307, 309, 311, 352-53, 370-71, 378-79, 381, 387, 389, 399-400, 435, 471, 553-56, 559, 561-63, 587, 599, 602, 615-616, 618, 620, 624-25, 627-629, 634-35, 637-38, 647, 651, 659; XV,240, 289, 434, 435, 438, 440-44, 453,

320

Exeter, NH (Cont.) 599, 626-27,
629, 648, 653, 657; XV,
667, 734-35, 743-744,
746, 748; XVI,57, 62-67,
71-72, 93-94, 97-99, 219,
221, 223-25, 227-33, 243-
45, 256, 316, 320, 328,
331, 335, 349, 391, 423,
505, 508, 524, 537, 647,
903, 932-34; XVII, 21, 53-
54, 56, 396, 404, 424-425,
510, 512, 525, 547, 602,
623-25, 640, 643, 650,
654, 664-65, 673, 676,
685, 693, 705, 710, 713

F

Fairlee, VT XIV,160, 291, 608;
XVII,119-20
Falmouth, ME XVII,315
Field's Garrison XVII,710
Fisheries, Coast XVII,337
Fishersfield (Newbury),NH XIV,
567; XV,608; XVI,224,
506, 936
Fishkill, NY XV,336, 435-37,
440, 754
Fitzwilliam, NH XIV,40, 94, 213,
553, 558, 575-76, 589,
632-634; XV,108, 463,
502, 532, 646, 664-65,
671, 746, 750, 753;
XVI,82, 95, 99, 324, 372,
433, 506, 541, 653;
XVII,428
Fort Ann, NY XIV,643; XVII,147
Fort in Bath XVI,541-42
Fort Carrillon XVII,58
Fort Dayton XVII,442
Fort Edward, NY XV,387, 440;
XVII, 147, 214
Fort George XIV,435, 466, 701;
XVI,364; XVII,147
Fort Herkimer XVII,442
Fort Hutchinson XVI,539
Fort in Piermont XVI,539
Fort in Piscataqua Harbor XVI,
540, 544

Fort Point XVII,459
Fort Rensalear XVII,442
Fort Sullivan XIV,240, 259, 480,
663; XV,430, 692;
XVI,214, 542-43; XVII,22-
23, 36, 42; XVII,74, 135
Fort Washington XIV,227, 252,
256, 258, 272, 549;
XV,429, 692; XVI,214,
234, 264, 378, 451, 531,
543, 619, 803, 926, 931;
XVII,20, 45, 74, 135, 383,
421, 451, 454
Fort Weare XVII,78-79
Fort William & Mary XIV,20, 27-
29, 31; XVI,317-19, 906,
912, 916; XVII,1, 55, 624,
628, 637, 641, 644, 667-
69, 674, 691, 694, 702,
757
Francestown, NH XIV,358, 557;
XV, 123, 197, 354, 622,
644, 654, 669, 689, 696,
753; XVI, 85, 95, 100,
161, 246, 251-52, 506,
521, 655, 935; XVII,19,
427
Franconia (Morristown), NH XVI,
83, 97; XVII,121
Freehold, NJ XVII,238
Fremont (Poplin), NH XIV,109;
XV, 451, 565, 629, 648,
667, 747; XVI,68, 79, 95,
97, 99, 221, 226-27, 244,
255, 257, 356, 517, 656,
802
Fryeburg, ME XIV,169, 392,
513; XV, 448, 598

G

German Flats XIV,283
Germantown, PA XVI,232;
XVII,170
Gilmanton, NH XIV,36, 116,
210, 212, 256, 296-97,
308, 364, 434, 469, 552,
557, 580, 582, 602-4, 619,
624, 627, 630, 636, 652,

Gilmanton, NH (Cont.) 660; XV,
162-63, 195, 437, 441,
447-48, 450, 598, 601,
627, 631, 650, 668, 690;
XVI,64, 65, 67, 74, 93, 98,
222, 226, 233, 242-43,
255, 257, 281-82, 297,
320, 328-29, 332, 409,
505, 524, 657, 726; XVII,
214-15
Gillensworth, CT XVI,934
Gilsum, NH XIV,325-26, 468,
558, 613, 645-46; XV,5,
46, 67, 196, 227, 434,
633, 648, 669; XV,741,
752; XVI,82, 92, 225, 507,
545-46, 661; XVII,255
Goddard's Creek XVII,605
Goffstown, NH XIV,57, 175, 210,
243, 358-59, 381, 470,
554-557, 562, 595, 597,
602, 606, 634-35, 658;
XV, 115, 117, 162, 435,
442, 543, 558, 614, 621,
644-45, 663, 669, 689,
696, 735, 740; XVI,69, 86,
91, 161, 219, 225, 229,
231, 232, 246-47, 253,
296, 357, 359, 435, 507,
663, 671; XVII,18, 121,
258, 427
Gosport (Rye), NH XIV,623
Grafton, MA XVI,934
Grafton, NH XIV,278, 291, 559,
608; XV,378, 604, 735;
XVII, 108, 110, 144, 385
Grantham (New Grantham), NH
XIV, 278, 559, 608; XV,
45, 378, 436, 602, 604;
XVI,151, 667; XVII,108,
414
Great Island (New Castle), NH
XIV,223
Greenland, NH XIV,21-22, 242,
369-70, 377, 379-82, 414,
449, 518, 554-56, 560,
592, 616, 621-22, 635,

Greenland, NH (Cont.) 638, 641,
659-60; XV, 303, 437,
442-43, 496, 597, 626,
628, 645, 665, 693, 735,
747; XVI,62-64, 72, 92-93,
98, 220, 228, 245, 257,
261-62, 507, 544, 667;
XVII,125, 360, 432-33,
705, 727
Greenwich XVI,243
Greenwich, RI XV,238
Groton (Cockermouth), NH
XIV,607; XV, 436, 459,
605, 633, 647, 708; XVI,
88, 90, 296, 387, 503,
668; XVII,14, 121
Groton, MA XVI,55
Guildhall, VT XV,435, 700; XVI,
782; XVII,78
Guilford, NH XIV,283
Guilford, VT XV,700-1, 704;
XVI, 174-76, 879
Gunthwaite (Lisbon), NH
XIV,160, 282, 470, 559,
567, 596, 608, XV,425,
435, 607; XVI,83, 97;
XVI,223-224, 306, 335;
XVII,330

H
Haddam, CT XVI,935
Halestown (Weare), NH XIV,211;
XV, 435-36, 734-35, 740;
XVI, 92, 95, 221, 231-32,
935
Half Moon, NY XV,221
Hampstead, NH XIV,43, 76-77,
83, 212, 283, 309, 380-81,
405, 470, 557, 586, 592,
602, 606, 627, 647; XV,
343, 396-97, 488, 559,
569, 623, 641, 658, 667,
691, 742-43, 752, 754;
XVI,63-65, 68, 94, 228,
247, 250, 253, 255, 482,
507, 601, 670, 934;
XVII,7, 121, 349
Hampton, NH XIV,107, 109,

Hampton, NH (Cont.) 139, 158,
242, 256, 555-56, 561,
602, 606, 620-21, 628-30,
635-36, 641-43; XV, 257,
411, 422, 433, 455-57,
489, 524, 656-57, 666,
695, 735; XVI, 62, 64, 71,
93, 99, 228-29, 232, 244,
255-56, 507, 546, 671,
845, 897-98, 934; XVII,
140, 424, 509, 512, 527,
547, 566, 602, 608, 623,
625, 627, 636, 638, 640-
44, 650, 654, 658, 664-67,
671, 675-676, 685-88,
693-94, 710, 727, 738,
740, 753
Hampton Falls, NH XIV,22, 109-
11, 555-56, 628-29, 635,
641, 643, 651; XV,292,
422, 443, 456, 489, 628,
640, 654, 656, 666, 695,
706, 734, 747; XVI, 65,
68, 75, 94-95, 220, 226,
228, 244, 255, 257, 506,
508, 524, 546, 674, 901,
933, 935; XVII,53, 80,
341, 374, 404, 433
Hancock, NH XVI,331, 335, 347,
402, 508, 678; XVII,429
Hanover, NH XIV,160, 422-23,
468, 553, 559, 592, 607-8;
XV,45, 157, 378, 435-36,
439, 603, 637; XVI,45, 47,
223, 225; XVI,229, 302-3,
320, 330, 388, 524, 537;
XVII,76, 108-9, 121, 144,
149, 226, 236, 290, 458
Hanover, NJ XVII,154, 163, 171,
176, 186
Harford, VT XIV,423; XV,439;
XVI, 218, 934; XVII,220
Hartford, CT XIV,404
Hartford, NY XIV,592-93
Harvard College XVII,590, 593
Haverhill, MA XV,244, 422; XVI,
402, 492, 935; XVII,40,

Haverhill, MA (Cont.) 121, 292,
756
Haverhill, NH XIV,159-60, 212,
291, 311, 546-47, 555,
587, 592, 596, 608, 643;
XV,142, 279, 281, 378-80,
424, 593, 637, 700-4; XVI,
45-46, 83, 97, 171, 174-
76, 179, 223, 249, 265,
295-96, 302-3, 307-308,
311, 508, 524, 527, 539,
679, 924; XVII,14, 16-17,
53, 69, 71-73, 81, 91,
120-21, 128, 132-33, 223-
24, 283, 382
See also Coos, NH
Hawke (Danville), NH XIV,380,
382, 388, 391, 557, 583,
596, 628; XV,341-42, 450,
559, 561, 658, 667, 691,
742, 747-748; XVI,65, 75,
98, 243, 255, 508, 524,
614; XVII,424, 425
Hemp XVII,743
Henniker, NH XIV,42-43, 65,
174, 291, 391, 558, 560,
568, 632, 660; XV,131,
162, 547, 608-9, 621, 623,
631, 638, 670, 688-689,
697, 742, 745, 751; XVI,
87-88, 95, 221, 246, 332,
432, 508, 680; XVII,4, 50,
62, 257, 349, 427, 431
Hertford, VT XV,602-3; XVII,241
Henzell's Island XVII,419, 466
Hill (New Chester), NH XV,126,
151, 381, 460, 605-6,
609-10, 622, 668; XVI,88,
97, 218, 515, 524, 681;
XVII,14
Hillsborough, NH XIV,42, 51,
210, 212, 390-91, 469,
513, 552-554, 558, 568,
572, 589, 604, 632-33;
XV,82, 84, 163, 408;
XV,427, 437, 444, 547,
582, 609-12, 621, 631,

Hillsborough, NH (Cont.) 638,
663, 670, 688, 751; XVI,
88, 95, 508, 684; XVII, 50,
259, 431, 438
Hinsdale, NH XIV,86, 558, 597;
XV, 6, 46, 50-51, 633,
648, 669, 753; XVI, 81,
93, 544, 86; XVII,255
Holderness (New Holderness),
NH XVI,423, 558, 587;
XV,126, 460, 605, 637,
662, 708, 735; XVI,244,
247, 254, 515, 546, 686;
XVII,215
Hollis, NH XIV,32, 39, 43-44,
243, 247, 292, 390-92,
468, 470, 552, 555, 557,
572-73, 590-591, 609,
640, 651; XV, 87, 89, 196-
97, 436, 511, 613-14, 624,
632, 636, 654, 664, 670-
671, 695, 743, 745, 750-
51; XVI, 84-85, 90, 220,
223-25, 228, 259, 297-98,
328-29, 331, 377, 431,
439, 494, 509, 524, 597,
687; XVII, 53, 121, 214,
339, 436-37, 457, 460
Hooksett, NH XV,513
Hopkinton,(New Hopkinton), NH
XV, 162-63, 182, 231,
404, 408-9, 439, 549, 606,
608, 631, 638, 654, 663,
670, 688; XVI, 87, 91,
100, 133, 220, 224, 246,
251, 264-65, 296, 320,
328, 331-32, 400, 481,
483, 509, 541, 694, 936;
XVII, 3, 50, 430, 443
Howland's Ferry, RI XV,239;
XVI, 332, 469
Hubbardton, VT XV,435;
XVII,221
Hudson (Nottingham West), NH
XIV, 89, 97; XV, 69, 196,
354, 437, 519, 614, 632,
635-36, 664, 670; XVI,84,

Hudson, NH (Cont.) 246, 253,
259, 296, 382, 515, 524,
545, 636, 696, 935;
XVII,60, 121, 339, 436
I
Indian Affairs XVII,77, 151,
211, 292, 311, 357, 465,
486, 490, 539, 543, 598,
640, 682, 688, 722, 724-
728, 732, 735, 746, 751
Indians, Bomazeen XVII,728
Caughnawaga XVII,242
John XVII,151
Micmac XVII,130, 227-28,
329
Mogg XVII,751
Norridgewock XVII,725
Peter XVII,153
Sabatis XVII,746
Satagan XVII,242-44
St. Francis XVII,128, 130,
227-228, 265, 282, 290,
328
Ipswich, MA XV,445; XVI,230,
546; XVII,509
Isle Aux Noix XIV,177, 290; XV,
311
Isles of Shoals XVII,487-88, 499,
521, 611, 665
J
Jackson's Creek XVII,710
Jaffrey, NH XIV,99, 213, 558,
575-576, 632, 699; XV,
103, 197, 427, 503, 630-
31, 646, 664-665, 671,
744, 751; XVI,82, 96, 100,
160, 254, 445, 509, 512,
534, 698, 741; XVII,121,
291, 428-29
Jaffrey's Point XVI,531
Jamaica Expedition XVII,
703
Jefferson (Dartmouth), NH XVII,
144
Jerry's Point XVI,526, 540, 542,
544
Jones's Garrison XVII,645

K

Keene, NH XIV,36-37, 39, 43, 94, 213, 311, 325-26, 429, 555, 558, 610, 632, 644-45; XV,2, 5, 46, 61, 64, 90, 111, 196-197, 428, 633, 643, 647-48, 652, 669, 735, 741, 752-53; XVI,81, 95, 225, 249, 254, 298, 320, 332, 434, 510, 532, 545, 597, 700; XVII, 62, 255

Kensington, NH XIV,107, 109-13, 121, 377, 389, 553, 556, 602, 615-16, 627-28; XV,240, 257-258, 265, 339, 442-44, 457, 476, 489, 524, 595, 656, 666-667, 695-96, 747; XVI, 65, 75, 94, 98, 223, 226-27, 231, 243, 244, 255, 321, 332, 490, 498, 510, 524, 542, 562, 702, 863-864, 901, 932-33; XVII,13, 433, 438

Kent, VT XVI,45, 301, 936

Kinderhook, NY XIV,283

Kingston, NH XIV,107, 112-13, 211-12, 242, 256, 309, 370, 380-81, 388, 553, 556-57, 562, 580, 585, 610, 616, 618, 623, 628, 636, 647-48, 659-661; XV,341-42, 344, 437, 440, 448, 559, 598, 623, 627, 641, 667, 691, 742-43, 746; XVI,62, 64-67, 73, 90, 98, 219, 224, 227, 230-31, 243-244, 247, 251, 253, 255-56, 509, 524, 706, 901-2, 935; XVII,7, 53, 349, 424, 688, 711, 756

Kingstreet, NY XV,337-38

Kittery, ME XIV,223, 236, 375, 387-88, 518-19; XV,282, 443; XVI,55, 221, 542,

Kittery, ME (Cont.) 544; XVII, 36-38, 43, 46-47, 280, 451, 539

L

Laconia, Province of XVII,475, 490, 500, 504, 552

Lancaster, NH XIV,559; XV,424-425, 702-3, 705; XVI,174, 289-91; XVII,78

Landaff, NH XIV,559, 585; XVII, 121

La Prairie, Canada XIV,177

Leavittstown (Effingham), NH XIV,111, 297, 364-65, 557; XIV, 581-82; XV,449-50, 600-1; XVI,220, 282

Lebanon, ME XVI,863; XVII,10-11

Lebanon, NH XIV,278, 294, 375, 385-86, 422-23, 517-18, 559, 607-8; XV,45, 157, 378, 436, 603; XVI,230, 543; XVII,72, 108-10, 121, 143, 149, 321, 369

Lee, NH XIV,108-9, 116, 242, 308, 374-75, 556, 617-18, 623-24, 651-52, 654; XV, 313, 441, 559, 619-20, 623, 627, 640, 656, 666; XVI,67, 93, 97, 227, 230, 233, 243-44, 511, 573, 710, 779; XVII,6, 349, 434, 435

Lempster, NH XIV,298, 324, 558, 578, 594, 610; XV, 35, 37, 372, 629, 741; XVI,218, 512, 543, 712; XVII,106

Lexington, MA XIV,32, 35; XVI, 351, 528, 544, 546

Lincoln, NH XVII,342

Lisbon (Gunthwaite), NH XIV, 160, 292; XV,425, 435, 606-7; XVI, 97, 223-24, 306, 335, 714, 924; XVII, 330

Litchfield, NH XIV,173-74, 339,

Litchfield, NH (Cont.) 435, 552-53, 557, 572, 574, 591, 602-4, 613, 365; XV,90, 187, 434-35, 543, 612, 614, 632, 635, 664, 670, 744-45, XVI,84, 95, 223, 246-47, 252, 259, 511, 524, 715, 890, 938; XVII, 339, 436, 437

Little Compton, RI XV,239

Little Harbor XVII,522, 542, 668-669

Londonderry, NH XIV,39, 42, 75-76, 168, 210, 242, 256, 309, 370-71, 279, 383, 391, 396, 457, 468, 470, 552, 554-55, 557, 559-62, 571, 591, 605-606, 616, 620-22, 624, 635-636, 647, 655; XV,163, 196-197, 394-95, 421, 427-29, 438, 450, 453-55, 465, 484, 567, 623, 630, 640, 654, 671, 677, 740, 742-45, 747, 750, 753-54; XVI, 47, 55, 63-65; XVI,72, 90-93, 100, 218, 222, 226, 228-29, 231-33, 242-43, 226, 251, 255-56, 263, 303, 321, 328-329, 331, 332, 351, 354, 407, 484, 510, 517, 524, 531, 600, 615, 716, 897, 901, 911, 916, 934-35; XVII,34, 40, 121, 219, 349, 426, 439, 444, 447, 465

Long Island, NY XIV,615

Long Meadow, MA XV,52

Losses at Bunker Hill XIV,79

Loudon, NH XIV,307, 558, 569, 585, 652, 662; XV,130, 132, 162, 179, 181, 292, 387, 513, 609, 663, 670, 688; XVI,87, 94, 100, 222, 255, 264, 297, 500, 503, 509, 512, 726, 935; XVII,8-9, 50, 430

Louisbourg, N.S. XVI,910

Ludlow, VT XVII,72

Lunenburg, MA XVI,466

Lunenburg, VT XV, 700; XVII, 71

Lyman, NH XIV,559; XV,425; XVI, 45, 301, 304

Lyme, NH XIV,159-60, 210, 292, 468, 558, 590, 608; XV, 277-278, 366, 383, 424-25, 436; XVI,99, 306, 314, 456, 543, 924; XVII,119-21

Lyndeborough, NH XIV,43, 89, 358, 359, 468-70, 553, 557, 601-2, 606, 612; XV,118-19, 138, 162, 188-89, 350, 352, 354, 437, 622, 644, 689, 696, 752; XVI,85-86, 99-100, 142, 161, 220, 224, 298, 328, 446, 511, 524, 540, 728, 935; XVII,121, 414, 426-27

Lynn, MA XIV,644

M

Madbury, NH XIV,108-9, 310, 374, 384-86, 517, 556, 562, 617, 623, 637; XV, 444, 620, 628, 641, 655, 666, 700, 703, 747; XVI, 68, 79, 96, 176, 233, 302, 304, 512, 524, 546, 730; XVII,435

Mails XVII,396, 635, 651

Malden, MA XV,435, 437; XVI, 232

Manchester (Derryfield), NH XIV, 59; XV,111, 434-35, 441, 612, 616, 622, 626, 644, 689, 696; XVI,85, 161, 247, 253, 255, 524, 732, 823; XVII,121, 132, 246, 453, 461, 755

Manchester, VT XIV,586; XV,140, 366

Mansfield, CT, XVI,934

Marblehead, MA XIV,308, 310;
XVI, 686
Marlborough, NH XIV,101, 117,
213, 555-58, 575-76, 586,
632, 638, 655, 702;
XV,103, 360-61, 393, 421,
502, 542, 604, 630, 646,
650, 664-65, 668, 671,
740, 746, 750-51; XVI,82,
92, 254, 373, 513, 524,
736; XVII,429
Marlow, NH XIV,298, 325, 469,
558, 575, 578, 596-98;
XV, 37, 369, 372, 501,
629, 642, 741; XVI,80,
92, 221, 545, 739;
XVII,106, 249
Mason, NH XIV,39, 43, 101,
557, 573-74; XV, 81, 83,
347, 531, 612-13, 632,
636, 664, 671, 695, 735;
XVI,85, 94, 100, 220, 259,
512, 524, 635, 739;
XVII,61, 121, 339, 436-37
Mason Hall XVII,534
Massabesic XIV,307; XV,747,
754
Maynesburg, NH, See Berlin,
NH
Medford, MA XIV,37, 44-46,
158, 160; XVI,923;
XVII,21, 457
Meredith (New Salem), NH
XIV,211, 296, 370, 378,
557, 580, 582, 635, 659;
XV, 133, 163, 389, 392,
440-41, 448, 450, 598,
601, 642-43, 668, 690,
697, 703, 735; XVI,65, 68-
69, 75, 94-95, 97-98, 219-
20, 227, 229, 233, 257,
281-82, 295, 512, 524,
741; XVII,7, 9
Merrimack, NH XIV,39, 97, 210-
11, 242, 338, 469, 557,
573, 603, 691; XV,85,
427, 434-35, 463, 614,

Merrimack, NH (Cont.) 616, 632,
635, 664, 671, 744, 751;
XVI,47, 83, 90; XVI,100,
145, 222, 225, 246-47,
251-52, 259, 265, 297,
303, 513, 524, 744, 934;
XVII,62-64, 121, 339, 414,
436-37
Methuen, MA XIV,169, 309,
616; XVII,40, 121
Middleton, NH XIV,109, 297,
364-366, 557, 560-61,
582, 620-621; XV,163,
443, 450, 599, 601, 668,
690; XVI,66, 77, 93, 96,
257, 282, 335, 512, 747,
817; XVII,10-11
Middleton, MA XIV,667
Mile Slip (Milford), NH XVI,504,
524, 748
Milford, (Duxbury School Farm),
NH XIV,103; XVI,748
Missisquoi Bay, VT XIV,295
Monadnock No, 5 (Marlborough)
NH XVI,524
Monmouth XVI,404
Monmouth Court House XVII,
238
Montreal, Canada XIV,282, 284,
290-91; XVII,59, 241, 277,
357
Mont Vernon, NH XIV,103
Moretown, VT XIV,159-60, 291,
608; XV,701, 703;
XVI,175, 812, 814;
XVII,364, 366
Morristown (Franconia), NH XIV,
283, 559, 596; XVI,83, 97;
XVII,121
Moultonborough, NH XV,162,
240, 392, 448-50, 599-
601, 632, 690, 701, 703,
734; XVI,46, 65, 75, 99-
100, 171-72, 175-176,
220-21, 228, 245, 282,
302, 512, 524, 726, 749;
XVII,9, 73

Mount Independence, VT
XIV,465, 693; XV,277,
701; XVI,934; XVII,126,
140

N

Nantasket, MA XIV,4

Narraganset XV,238

Nashua, NH *See Dunstable, NH*

Nelson (Packersfield), NH XIV,
576; XV,502, 630, 646,
664-665, 671, 740-41,
644-45; XVI,82, 100, 220,
254, 517, 546, 751, 935;
XVII,428-29

New Boston, NH XIV,43, 57,
210, 358-59, 391, 468-69,
471, 513, 557, 589, 603,
612, 633, 647; XV,163,
429, 434-35, 553, 622,
644-45, 670, 689, 696,
734, 740, 753-54; XVI, 47,
86, 91, 97, 100, 161, 218-
19, 221, 303, 320, 328,
331, 347, 360, 417, 419,
500, 524, 665, 753, 934-
35; XVII, 3-4, 19, 259,
426, 755

New Breton (Andover), NH
XVII,9, 50

New Britain (Andover), NH XIV,
316, 374, 558, 569, 572,
606; XV,610, 612, 740,
754; XVI, 222

Newbury, MA XIV,310; XVI,229,
935; XVII,40, 244, 509,
713

Newbury (Fishersfield), NH XIV,
211; XV,608; XVI,224,
506, 936

Newbury, VT XIV,160, 291, 608;
XV,425, 588; XVI,528,
538, 928-29; XVII,14, 69,
72, 240, 283, 469

Newburyport, MA XV,627;
XVII,40, 141

New Castle, NH XIV,21, 27, 31,
115, 142, 223, 247, 301,

New Castle (Cont.) 307, 374,
380-83, 387-88, 391, 479,
498, 519, 554, 556, 619,
623-24, 647-48; XV,440-
41, 596, 627, 734; XVI,
317-19, 515, 531, 542,
902; XVII,36, 74, 280,
334, 542, 603, 616, 621-
25, 632-33, 641, 643,
649-50, 657, 664-68, 676,
679, 681, 686, 693, 710-
11, 727, 735

New Cheshire, NH XIV,606

New Chester (Hill), NH XIV,291,
469-70, 558, 566, 569,
587; XVI,88, 97, 218, 515,
524, 681; XVII,14

New Durham, NH XIV,115, 296,
339, 366, 385, 517, 554,
557, 581; XIV,582, 617,
624, 635, 648; XV, 441,
444, 449-450, 469, 601,
668, 690; XVI, 66, 77, 96,
229, 257, 282, 329, 332,
473, 515, 755; XVII,10-12

New Durham Gore (Alton), NH
XIV, 297, 557, 582;
XVI,282, 320, 329, 331,
422, 554

New Garden XVI,66

New Glascow, MA, *See Blan-
ford, MA*

New Hampshire Grants, VT
XVI,175-176

New Hampshire Village XVI,191,
247

New Hampton, NH XV,241, 631,
650, 654, 668; XVI,69, 79,
92, 281-82, 320, 330, 454,
457, 523, 743, 758

New Haven, CT XIV,282-83

Newichewannock River
XVII,487-89, 503, 515,
523, 534

Newington (Bloody Point), NH
XIV, 108, 307, 374-75,
381, 518, 556, 562, 624,

328

Newington, NH (Cont.) 630, 635, 637, 641-42; XV, 440, 444, 582-83, 596-97, 628, 645, 654, 666, 693, 734-35; XVI,63, 68, 72, 93-94, 99, 220, 230-31, 233, 261, 514, 759; XVII,280, 433, 727, 737

New Ipswich, NH XIV,33, 39, 91, 173, 241, 335, 471, 553-54, 558, 575, 592-93, 622; XV,92-94, 103, 196-97, 219, 345, 355, 357, 438-39, 443, 502, 532, 535, 631, 646, 664-65, 671, 744-45, 751, 753; XVI, 83, 96, 218, 385, 428; 514, 524, 761, 934-35; XVII,100, 121, 134, 428

New Lebanon, NH XIV,283

New London, NH XIV,283, 567; XV, 608; XVI,523

New London, CT XVI,934

New Market, NH XIV,21, 37, 107-9, 136, 151, 211, 242, 307, 309, 352-53, 379, 388, 390, 400, 469, 513, 519, 554, 556, 563, 571, 615-18, 623-24, 627, 630, 635, 649, 651; XV,244; XV,289, 439-42, 570, 572, 596, 627, 629, 648, 667, 701, 703, 743, 747; XVI, 45-46, 67, 78, 93, 96-99, 175, 221, 227, 230-31, 233, 265, 302, 321, 332, 355, 373, 374, 514, 764; XVII,5, 6

New Marlborough, NH XV,437

New Plymouth XVI,232

Newport, NH XIV,298, 324-25, 471, 558, 578, 593; XV, 35, 37, 148, 372, 501, 629, 735; XVI, 98-99, 218, 515, 532, 768, 847, 934; XVII,53, 106, 249

Newport, RI XV,238; XVII,128

New Portsmouth XVII,755

New Salem (Meredith), NH XIV,77, 211, 660; XVI,97-98, 219-20, 257; XVII,7

New Salisbury, NH XV,734, 754

Newton, NH XIV,112, 380, 382, 475, 554, 557, 586, 627-29, 660; XV,341-42, 623, 627, 641, 658, 667, 691, 746, 748; XVI,67, 77-78, 226, 233, 257, 514, 524, 770; XVII,2, 349, 424-25

Newtown, NY XVI,330, 356, 404, 475

New Windsor, CT, XV,286, 289, 334, 336; XV,306

New York City XIV,282-83, 596

Nine Partners XIV,596

North Castle, NY XVI,728; XVII, 215, 246

Northfield, MA XV,359

Northfield, NH XIV,145; XVI, 296, 513, 772

Northampton, MA XV,392

North Hampton, NH XIV,139, 255, 379, 554, 556, 643; XV, 276, 334-36, 339, 422, 456-58, 524, 656, 666, 696, 735; XVI, 64, 67, 74, 98, 220, 228, 231, 256-57, 448, 489, 513-514, 540, 772, 845, 901; XVII,235, 432-33, 739

North Hill (North Hampton), NH XIV,562, 628, 636, 641-42; XVI,98, 220, 257

Northumberland, NH XIV,463, 559; XV,425, 638, 700, 703, 705-6; XVI,45, 166, 175-76, 290, 302, 515, 714, 782; XVII,77-78

Northwood, NH XIV,109, 330, 397, 469, 554, 556, 571, 618-19, 659-60; XV,250, 528, 572, 661, 668, 734; XVI,66, 68-69, 76, 95, 97, 222, 243-44, 251, 256,

Northwood, NH (Cont.) 332, 420,
480, 513, 660, 767-68,
775; XVII,434
Norwich, VT XIV,291, 422-23,
595, 608; XV,436-37, 603;
XVI,45, 265; XVII,236
Nottingham, NH XIV,36, 69,
117, 121, 210-12, 242,
308, 330, 352-53, 382,
397-98, 435, 468-71, 552,
554, 556, 566, 570-71,
580, 591, 602-3, 606,
615-17, 624, 627, 638,
641, 651; XV,268, 286,
421, 435, 437-41, 444,
447, 506, 598, 607, 627,
634, 638, 640, 649, 658-
59, 661, 668, 694-95, 703,
734, 744, 746; XVI, 64-66,
68-69, 75, 90, 92-100,
104, 174, 219-31, 242-43,
349, 407-9, 415, 421, 474,
490-91, 513, 537, 582,
639, 644, 768, 777, 900,
905, 935; XVII,434, 437
Nottingham West (Hudson), NH
XIV, 371, 379, 557, 574,
626; XVI, 84, 246, 253,
259, 296, 515, 524, 545,
636, 696, 935; XVII,60,
121, 339, 436, 439
Nova Scotia XIV,4, 388
Number 1 on Conn. R. See
Chesterfield, NH
Nutfield (Manchester), NH XVII,
755

O

Oblong, NY XVI,934
Onion River XVII,16
Orange (Cardigan), NH XV,378,
604; XVII,108, 110, 121,
143
Orford, NH XV, 154, 277, 383,
424, 705; XVI, 249, 385,
538, 783, 924; XVII,53,
119-21; XIV, 27, 159-60,
256, 267, 276, 278, 291,

Orford, NH (Cont.) 558, 608
Ossipee, NH XVI,783
Ossipee Gore, NH XVI,282, 747,
783
Otter Creek, VT XV,47, 65, 74,
82, 106; XVII,41
Oyster River, See Durham, NH

P

Packersfield (Nelson), NH XIV,
470, 558, 575-76, 593,
662; XVI,82, 100, 220,
254, 517, 546, 751, 935;
XVII,428-29
Panton, VT XVII,72
Paramus, NJ XVI,57
Parsonstown (Parsonsfield, ME)
XV,734; XVI,862
Pawlet, VT XIV,283
Pawtucket, RI XV,238
Peacham, VT XVI,215, 530-31;
XVII,366
Peekskill, NY XIV,547; XVII,131-
132, 237
Peirce's Island XVII,466
Pelham, NH XIV,42, 54, 210,
554, 557, 560, 625-26,
628, 635; XV,196, 345,
358-59, 441, 626, 637,
671; XVI,63, 72, 90, 223,
246, 253, 263, 383, 516,
525, 544, 719-20, 783,
884; XVII, 7, 110, 121,
427
Pemaquid, ME XVII,247, 491
Pembroke, NH XIV,42, 72, 174,
210-12, 242, 291, 339,
358-360, 426, 435, 552,
557, 571, 588, 592-93,
605-6; XV,162, 174, 177,
268, 273-74, 415, 437-38,
622, 631, 638, 645, 663,
669-70, 688-89, 696, 734,
747, 752; XVI, 55, 86, 88,
93, 97, 162, 228, 247,
253, 255, 264, 516, 524,
551, 779, 785; XVII,430-
31, 445

Penacook (Concord), NH
    XIV,470, 606; XVI,91-92,
    99, 915
Penobscot, ME XVI,331, 342-43;
    XVII,336, 341
Pepperell, MA XIV,33, 39;
    XVI,223
Perrystown (Sutton), NH
    XIV,211, 307, 316-17,
    558, 569, 592-593; XV,
    438, 609; XVI,223, 246,
    252, 518, 849, 936
Peterborough, NH XIV,42-43,
    106, 335, 468, 471, 553,
    558, 575, 577, 592-93,
    612-13; XV,103, 197, 427,
    434, 463, 540, 630, 637,
    646, 664-65, 671, 739,
    745, 750, 753-54; XVI, 47,
    54, 55, 82, 90-92, 218,
    221-23, 247, 254, 303,
    355, 389, 440, 445, 510,
    517, 520, 791, 934;
    XVII,121, 291, 378, 415,
    428
Peterborough Slip (Sharon), NH
    XV, 104-5, 664-65, 671,
    XVI, 82, 221, 518, 764,
    794, 835, 860; XVII,291
Petersham, MA XVI,935
Philadelphia, PA XIV,596
Pierce's Island XIV,228-29, 232
Pierce's Town XIV,309
Piermont, NH XIV,159, 291; XV,
    142, 277, 383-84, 425,
    436; XVI,47, 176, 297,
    303, 306, 517, 521, 538-
    39, 814, 924; XVII,14,
    120-21, 134
Pinkham's Creek XVII,727
Pirates XVII,730-32
Piscataqua, Grant of XVII,479,
    490-91
Piscataqua Harbor XIV,223,
    252, 256, 301, 481;
    XV,433, 692, 697, 736;
    XVI,215, 283, 399; XVII,

Piscataqua Harbor (Cont.) 35,
    38, 44, 55, 280, 446, 455,
    466, 488, 497, 499, 501
Piscataqua House XVII,487
Pittsfield, NH XVI,296-97, 320,
    330, 369-70, 856
Plainfield, NH XIV,278, 395,
    608, 662; XV,44-45, 602;
    XVI,935; XVII,90, 108-9,
    121, 144, 149, 236, 376
Plainfield, CT XVI,935
Plaistow, NH XIV,42, 44, 121,
    396, 471, 552, 557, 586-
    87, 591, 662; XV,343,
    388, 398-399, 488, 500,
    623, 629, 641, 667, 691,
    742, 749; XVI,67-68, 78,
    99, 100, 219, 232, 255,
    401-2, 502, 517, 532,
Plaistow, NH XVI,577, 794, 799;
    XVII,7, 40, 121, 349, 424
Ploughed Hill XIV,668-89
Plymouth, NH XIV,168, 211,
    256, 422-23, 440, 468,
    556, 558, 567, 571, 586-
    87, 590, 658; XV,124,
    126, 140, 142, 149, 163,
    381-82, 459-60, 605-7,
    633, 647, 654, 662, 668,
    708, 735; XVI,45, 88, 90,
    219, 224, 228, 232-33,
    243, 245, 249, 296, 301,
    320-21, 330, 332, 381,
    517, 524, 577, 600, 797;
    XVII,14, 17, 215
Pomfret, CT XVI,468
Pomfret, VT XIV,422-23
Poplin (Fremont), NH XIV,107,
    109, 113, 116-17, 387-89,
    398, 468, 470, 556, 565,
    606, 628, 651, 660;
    XVI,68, 79, 95, 97, 99,
    221, 226-27, 229, 244,
    255, 257, 517, 656
Port Royal XIV,3-4; XVII,707-8
Portsmouth, NH XIV,21, 27, 31,
    118, 151, 223, 242, 256,

Portsmouth, NH (Cont.) 301,
308-9, 339, 382-85, 387,
390-391, 468, 471-72,
517-19, 555-56, 560-62,
593, 596, 606, 616-17,
620-21, 623-24, 635, 637,
641, 647-49, 660; XV,282,
427, 431, 437, 439-440,
443-44, 595-97, 626-27,
692-93, 695, 699, 734-35,
742, 747, 749, 752-53;
XVI, 47, 62-64, 69-70, 94-
95, 98-99, 165, 196, 222,
228-33, 242-44, 260-62,
303, 317-20, 328-30, 332,
378, 394, 449-451, 479,
516, 524, 540, 542, 544,
803, 931; XVII,35-38, 46-
49, 55, 74, 138, 224, 280,
322-23, 335, 420, 432-33,
487, 504, 510, 512, 526,
542, 547, 566, 606-7, 612,
623, 625-26, 635, 643,
650-51, 654, 664-67, 676,
685, 693, 705, 726, 737
Post Office XVII,396, 403, *See
Also Mails*
Post Riders XVII,635, 651, 700
Powder Mill XVII,53-54
Pownal, VT XVI,303
Pownalborough, MA XIV,307
Princeton, Battle of XIV,481,
522
Prospect Hill, MA XIV,156, 668;
XV,750; XVI,403
Protectworth (Springfield), NH
XIV,559
Providence, RI XV,238, 243;
XVII, 12, 123-24
Public Houses XVII,649, 735
Public Loans, *See Loans*
Putnam's Point XIV,694
Putney, VT XIV,291, 597, 644;
XVI,701; XVII,255, 458

Q

Quebec, Canada XIV,553, 613;
XV, 739-41, 744-47; XVI,

Quebec, Canada (Cont.) 432,
525, 527; XVII, 241-44,
277, 311, 357, 421, 707-8
Quebec Expedition XIV,209, 474
Quomphegan XVII,711

R

Raby (Brookline), NH XIV,39,
392, 557, 574; XVI,84, 90,
246, 253, 259, 331, 464,
518, 584; XVII,121
Raymond, NH XIV,76, 116-17,
212, 307, 354, 370, 378,
387, 469, 519, 554, 557,
580, 538-85, 599, 619,
630, 659; XV,162, 439,
444-45, 447, 451, 598,
627, 639, 658-60, 668,
693-695, 734, 749; XVI,
68, 79, 97, 222-27, 232-
33, 243, 252, 262, 300,
365, 518, 524, 600, 806
Reading, CT XVII,215
Reading, MA XVI,686
Relhan (Enfield), NH XIV,559
Rhode Island XVI,330, 370, 391,
449
Richmond, NH XIV,43, 91, 438,
470, 558, 594, 597, 644-
45; XV, 5, 56, 196, 446,
633, 647-648, 669;
XVI,81, 93, 95; XVI,330,
410, 518, 546, 808;
XVII,255, 457
Rindge, NH XIV,37, 43, 99, 256,
422, 438, 552-54, 558-59,
561, 575-77, 621, 634;
XV,92, 103, 196-97, 216,
218, 348-349, 421, 441-
42, 502, 532, 540, 626,
630, 646, 650, 664-665,
671, 753; XVI, 83, 96,
176, 229, 254-55, 330,
376, 390, 445, 475, 518,
540, 812; XVII,100-2, 121,
137, 428
Rochester, NH XIV,18, 37, 114-
15, 121, 169, 242, 374,

332

Rochester, NH (Cont.) 384-85,
517-18, 554, 556, 559-60,
562, 624, 631, 637; XV,
286, 299, 437, 440, 445,
619-20, 628, 640, 656,
666, 740, 747, 750; XVI,
45, 68, 79, 90, 92, 223,
225-26, 230-31, 232, 242-
43, 245, 257, 301, 332,
335, 429, 523-24, 542,
756, 815, 898, 906, 912;
XVII,10-12, 37, 213-14,
261, 435
Rockingham, VT XIV,592; XVI,
218, 935-36; XVII,64
Roger's Creek XVII,727
Rolls Town, MA XIV,307, 309
Rowley, MA XVI,860
Royalston, MA XVI,411
Royalston, VT XVI,215, 530-31,
538, 540, 542, 840, 869;
XVII,72, 462
Rumney, NH XIV,210-11, 292,
309, 423, 441, 558, 560,
567, 586-587; XV,151,
460, 605-7, 633, 647, 662,
668, 708; XVI,88, 99, 220,
228, 232, 519, 799-800,
820; XVII,14, 215
Rupert, VT XVI,45, 265
Rutland, VT XV,92, 435;
XVI,228; XVII,234-35
Rye, NH XIV,116, 139, 242, 308,
380-82, 387, 414, 449,
519, 545, 556, 586, 623,
635, 641, 647-48, 651;
XV, 244, 257, 264-65,
441-42, 528, 596, 626,
693, 734, 750; XVI,63-64,
72, 98-99, 226, 228, 232,
244-45, 261, 329, 331,
350-351, 518, 524, 540,
542, 821, 845, 912; XVII,
220, 280, 432

S

Sagamore Creek XVII,609, 623
Saint. See also St.

Saint Croix XV,236-37
Saint George Channel XVI,429
Saint John, NS XVI,332
Saint John, PQ XVI,332, 458
Salem, MA XV, 754; XVI, 687;
XVII, 244, 509, 567
Salem, NH XIV,42, 54, 310, 554,
587, 628-29; XV,343-44,
390-391, 443, 623, 641,
667, 691, 743; XVI,63, 73,
233, 243, 320, 328, 330,
374-75, 519, 524, 544,
547, 822; XVII,7, 40, 349,
424
Salisbury, MA XIV,513; XVI,642;
XVII,509, 521, 730, 752
Salisbury, NH XIV,43, 62, 210,
316, 391, 469, 471, 548,
558, 568, 659; XV,130,
162-63, 516, 608, 610,
631, 638, 663, 670, 688,
706, 734, 754; XVI, 87,
90, 224, 243, 264, 294-
297, 521, 524, 564, 826;
XVII,9, 40, 50, 430
Salmon Falls XVII,711, 755
Sanbornton, NH XIV,145, 296,
313, 365-66, 374, 434,
557, 580, 582, 641, 659,
661-62; XV,162, 171, 173,
286, 448, 450, 599, 601,
631, 650, 663, 668, 690,
700-3, 735; XVI,46, 65,
74, 96, 174-76, 220, 225,
232, 243, 281, 296-97,
302, 320, 328, 331, 472-
73, 521, 547, 827; XVII,8-
9
Sandown, NH XIV,76-77, 112,
309, 387-88, 471, 519,
554, 557, 586-87, 606,
616-17, 647; XV, 341-42,
400-1, 436, 623, 641, 658,
667, 691, 743, 749; XVI,
46, 79, 100, 226, 245,
255-257, 499, 519, 524,
546, 563, 684, 829; XVII,

Sandown, NH (Cont.) 7, 349, 425

Sandwich, NH XIV,43, 297, 364, 557, 581-82, 641, 659; XV, 162, 449-50, 461, 600-1, 632, 650, 668, 690, 701, 703; XVI, 46, 65, 75, 94, 99-100, 176, 218, 225, 229, 242, 245, 281-283, 302, 320, 328, 330, 415, 520, 831, 934

Sandy Beach XVI,897

Sanford, ME XVI,55

Sapowet, RI XV,239

Saratoga, NY XV,140, 143, 226-27, 282, 293, 318, 345, 348-73, 421, 433, 755; XVI,57, 223, 330, 332, 379, 428, 448, 463, 494, 840, 935, 937; XVII,150, 442

Saratoga, Battle of XIV,652

Saville (Sunapee), NH XIV,298, 325, 435, 558, 578, 592, 606, 610; XV,439, 604; XVI,80, 93, 218, 520

Schenectady, NY XV,435, 438

Seabrook, NH XIV,111, 390-91, 513, 556, 628, 641-42, 662; XV,457, 489, 628, 639, 656, 666, 696, 734-35, 747; XVI, 65, 67, 78, 99, 220, 228, 232, 245, 255-56, 519, 833, 933-34; XVII,433, 443

Seal of the Province XVII,563

Seavey's Island XIV,233, 240

Sewall's Point XIV,676; XV,748

Sharon (Sliptown; Peterborough Slip), NH XV,104-5, 664-65, 671; XVI,82, 221, 518, 764, 794, 835, 860; XVII,291

Sheepscott, ME XIV,382

Ships, Sloops, Brigs, etc, XVII,. 520

Ship, Adventure XVII,340

Ship, Advice XVII,698

Ship, Ann & Mary XVII,646

Ship, Ardent XVII,324

Ship, Benjamin XVII,678

Ship, Bochacheco XVII,125

Ship, Dartmouth XVI,925

Ship, Dolphin XVII,701

Ship, Drake XVI,429-30

Ship, Druid XVI,413

Ship, Duke of York XVII,514, 519

Ship, Endeavor XVII,722

Ship, Experiment XVII,324

Ship, Falkland XVII, 673-74

Ships, Fire Rafts XVI,846

Ship, Fox XVII,1

Ship, George XVII,576-77, 615

Ship, Gift XVII,620

Ship, Guadaloupe XVII,370

Ship, Hampden XVI,215, 442; XVII,336, 353

Ship, Hannah XVII,340

Ship, Hazard XVII,340

Ship, Jupiter XVII,420

Ship, Lark XVII,567

Ship, Lion's Whelp XVII,493

Ship, McClary XVII,125, 270, 325

Ship, Newport XVII,670

Ship, Olive Branch XVII,420

Ship, Polly XVI, 926

Ship, Portsmouth XVII,324-25

Ship, Prince George XIV,472; XVII,19, 125-26

Ship, Prudent Sarah XVII,730

Ship, Raleigh XVI, 322, 325, 344, 413, 924-25; XVII, 141

Ship, Ranger XVI,332, 429-30; XVII, 145

Ship, Richard XVII,596

Ship, Royal Louis XVII,420

Ship, Salamander XVII, 608

Ship, St. John Baptist XVII, 698

Ship, Scarborough XVI,757

Ship, Seaflower XVII, 732

Ship, Spitfire XVI,326, 332, 344, 469, 470
Ship, Sullivan XVII,245
Ship, Susannah XVII,51
Ships, *See War Vessels*
Shirley, MA XVI,934
Shutesbury, VT XV,700, 703-4; XVI,175, 177
Skeensborough, VT XIV,692; XV, 441-42; XVII,147
Sliptown (Sharon), NH XIV,558, 575, 577; XV,671
Smallpox XVI,353, 364-65, 367, 395, 421, 423, 456
Socialborough, VT XVII,72
Society Land, NH XIV,174, 359, 557; XV,740; XVI,246, 252, 521, 524; XVII,19
Somersworth, NH XIV,107, 114, 127, 243, 308-9, 374-76, 473, 518, 554, 556, 559-62, 615, 618, 620-24, 636; XV,286, 296, 336, 440, 442-45, 574, 619-20, 656, 666, 749-50, 752; XVI,62, 66, 77, 96, 229, 233, 243-45, 321, 331, 442, 520-21, 524, 836, 863; XVII, 10-12, 260
Sorelle, Canada XIV,291; XVII, 278, 311
Southborough, MA XIV,308; XVI,934
South Hampton, NH XIV,110, 112, 212, 309, 380-81, 556, 617-618, 623, 627, 659; XV,427, 457, 489, 628, 657, 667, 696, 747; XVI,47, 66, 68, 77, 93, 98-100, 226, 231, 233, 245, 257, 303, 501 520, 836, 901; XVII,2, 20
Split Rock XVII,140
Springfield (Protectworth), NH XV,501, 604; XVI,218, 614, 934; XVII,249

Springfield, MA XVI,51, 53, 104-105, 262
Springfield, NJ XVII,161, 187
Springfield, VT XIV,692; XVI,935
Squamscot XVII,604, 673
Star Island (Gosport) XVII,611, 625, 665
Staten Island, NY XVII,154-209, 307
St. Francois, Canada XVII,132, 210, 241-42, 277
St. Johns, Canada XIV,176; XVII, 17, 76, 132-33, 151-52, 241-244, 277, 292, 311, 421
St. Johns, NS XVII,659
Stillwater, NY XIV,625, 638; XV, 164, 174, 179, 185, 191, 193, 203, 216, 219, 322, 324, 383, 438, 441; XV, 57, 330, 332, 374, 380, 395, 397, 404, 409, 420, 427, 429, 445, 937; XVII,465
Stoddard, NH XIV,468-69, 558, 575, 594; XV, 103, 502, 630-31, 646, 740, 746, 750; XVI,82, 92, 221, 331, 439, 441-42, 517, 520, 839
Strafford, NH XIV,291; XV,700; XVI,521; XVII,120
Stratford, NH XV,425, 705; XVI, 46, 166, 175-76, 292, 302, 782; XVII,78, 120
Stratham, NH XIV,136, 210, 223, 242, 291, 307, 339, 369-70, 375, 377-79, 403-4, 518, 555-556, 603, 606, 615, 635, 641-642, 647-49, 651-52; XV,332; XV,440, 543, 570, 597, 628, 645, 654, 665-66, 693, 734-35; XVI,62-64, 71, 92, 98-99, 220, 223, 228-29, 232-33, 245, 251-

Stratham, NH (Cont.) 52, 257,
261-62, 507, 520, 540,
668, 838, 842, 932-33;
XVII,6, 53, 432, 741
Sudbury, MA XVI,935
Sullivan, NH XIV,326
Sunapee (Saville; Wendell), NH
XV,439, 604; XVI,80, 93,
218, 520, 614, 847
Suncook, NH XIV,210-11, 618;
XV, 751
Sunsbury XVI,191, 404
Surry, NH XIV,43, 325-26, 558;
XV,46, 67, 197, 501, 633,
647, 669, 741; XVI,81, 92,
294, 298, 521, 545, 848;
XVII,255
Sutton (Perrystown), NH XV,
438, 609; XVI,223, 246,
252, 518, 849, 936; XVII,
3-4
Swanzey, NH XIV,36, 42-43, 94,
291, 311, 428, 438, 558,
594, 597, 645-46; XV,46,
196, 205, 293, 446-47,
633, 647, 650, 669, 701,
703, 735, 740, 746;
XVI,46, 81, 95, 174-75,
225, 254, 298, 302-3, 320,
328-29, 332, 388, 411,
469, 486-87, 493, 522-23,
850, 927; XVII, 99, 106,
255, 457
Swanzey, RI XV,239

T

Tamworth, NH XIV,211, 291,
297, 364-66, 557, 581-83;
XV,448-450, 598-99, 601,
631, 650; XVI,255, 282,
522, 853; XVII, 9, 73
Taunton, MA XV,239
Taunton, VT XV,435
Temple, NH XIV,35, 89, 101,
422, 468, 555, 558, 561,
575, 612, 621, 640; XV,
79 95-96, 196, 364, 502,
535, 613, 630, 646, 654,

Temple, NH (Cont.) 664-65, 671,
735, 740; XVI 752; XVI,82,
100, 220-21, 465, 498,
521, 524, 542, 562, 854;
XVII, 100-1, 134, 214,
291, 428, 470
Temple's Farm XIV,476
Tewksbury, MA XVII,121
Thetford, VT XIV,608; XV,425;
XVII,119-20
Thomlinson, VT XVI,492, 934
Thornton, NH XIV,423, 558; XV,
151, 460, 605-6, 638, 647,
708; XVI,247, 253, 860;
XVII, 13-14, 438
Ticonderoga, NY XIV,291, 343,
393, 435, 461, 481, 498,
591, 643, 692; XV,1, 6, 9,
14, 20, 22, 35, 38, 46, 50-
51, 54, 57, 61, 65, 68-69,
72, 74, 77, 79, 81-83, 85,
90, 92, 95, 97, 104, 106,
108, 111, 115, 118, 120,
122-24, 127, 131-33, 136,
139, 433, 435, 441; XVI,
331, 352, 364, 400, 404,
429, 491, 525-29, 531,
540, 840, 859, 934; XVII,
21, 72-73, 94, 100, 106,
108, 121, 126, 136, 140,
146, 216, 283
Tiverton, RI XV,239
Townsend, MA XV,434, 754
Trenton, NJ Battle at XIV,481,
522

U

Unity, NH XIV,113, 298, 325,
553, 558, 578, 593, 596,
610; XV, 37, 439, 627;
XVI, 80, 221, 257, 320,
330, 397, 399, 524, 545
Uxbridge, MA XVI,935

V

Valley Forge XV,434, 653;
XVI,57, 330, 365, 367,
404; XVII,291
Vermont Controversy XVII,342,

336

Vermont Controversy (Cont.)
406
Verplank's Point XVI,473

W

Wakefield (East Town), NH XIV,
243, 297, 366, 433, 557,
560-562, 581-82, 620-21,
627, 637, 651; XV, 193,
443, 449-450, 600-1, 631,
650, 668, 690; XVI, 62,
66, 68, 77, 96, 225, 230,
243-44, 257, 282, 510,
542, 861; XVII,11, 438
Waldoborough, ME XVI,45, 48,
301, 304
Walloomsuck, NY XVI,382, 432
Walpole, NH XIV,106, 256, 297-
98, 324-25, 442, 553, 555,
558, 578, 595-97, 610,
614, 644, 702; XV,1, 37,
85, 87, 146, 148, 196,
372, 435, 501, 629-630,
642, 644, 650, 700, 741,
744, 750; XVI,46, 80, 91,
175, 223, 226, 229, 233,
249, 298, 302, 331, 366,
382, 386, 522, 532, 864;
XVII,53, 106-107, 249,
445, 462
Warner (Almsbury), NH XIV,44,
51, 315, 568; XV,608,
610, 631, 638, 663, 670,
688; XVI,88, 90-91, 247,
253, 264, 329, 331, 335,
438, 867; XVII, 3, 4, 21,
50, 431, 438
War Vessels, Raleigh XIV,518
Scarborough XIV, 31
Warren, NH XVI,83, 409, 563;
XVII,120
Warren, RI XV,239
Warwick, MA XVII,255
Warwick, RI XV,238, 240, 245,
255, 261
Washington, NH XIV,558, 575-
76; XV,106-7, 115, 197,
372, 434, 502, 630, 646,

Washington, NH (Cont.) 664-65,
671; XVI,82, 92, 227, 254,
523, 869; XVII,255
Waterbury, CT XV,435
Watertown, MA XIV,45
Weare (Halestown), NH XIV,57,
169, 174-75, 212, 283,
329, 390-91, 468, 471,
513, 553, 557, 603, 610;
XV,113-14, 435-36, 439,
551, 621-22, 644-45, 689,
734-35, 740, 742; XVI,85,
91-92, 95, 161, 219, 221,
228, 231-32, 246-247,
252-54, 297-98, 532,
Weare (Halestown), NH XVI,
545, 870, 935; XVII,3, 19,
426, 438
Weathersfield, VT XIV,324
Wells, ME XVII,539
Wendell (Sunapee), NH XVI,
847
Wenham, MA XV,621
Wentworth, NH XIV,566-67,
573, 596, 608; XV,425,
607; XVI, 577, 876
Westford, MA XV,700, 704; XVI,
174, 934; XVII,121
Westminster, VT XIV,597, 644;
XV, 435; XVI,221, 935
Westmoreland, NH XIV,86, 291,
324, 558, 593, 610, 644-
45; XV,2, 6, 8, 47, 60,
196-97, 439, 443, 633,
648, 654, 664, 665, 668-
69, 671, 681, 700-4, 735,
751; XVI,46, 166, 174-
175, 225, 228, 302-3, 312,
320, 329, 331-32, 361-63,
393-94, 396, 399, 426-28,
522, 532, 547, 701, 876;
XVII,255
West Jersey XIV,291
West Point, NY XVI,58, 104-6,
109-65, 215, 249
West Town XIV,644
White Creek XIV,283, 586

White Plains, NY XIV,416, 431;
XVI,531, 768; XVII,247,
268
Williamsburg, VA XIV,638
Wilton, NH XIV,43, 101, 303,
390, 418, 440, 555, 557,
574, 597, 639-40, 667,
691, 699; XV,68, 74-76,
196, 419-20, 427, 531,
617, 632, 635-36, 664,
670, 735, 740; XVI, 45,
47, 85, 100, 220, 259,
297, 301, 303, 332, 354,
522, 524, 532, 540, 784,
880; XVII,62-63, 121, 339,
385, 436
Winchester, NH XIV,256, 291,
429, 558, 644-46; XV, 1,
46, 196, 203, 447, 503,
633, 647, 668, 746, 750;
XVI,81, 93, 95, 228, 298,
331, 403, 522-23, 852,
855, 927, 935; XVII,99,
255
Windham, NH XIV,42, 54, 254,
283, 468, 557, 560, 606,
620; XV, 443, 451, 453,
630, 637, 671, 740; XVI,
63-64, 73, 91, 95, 224,
247, 253, 263, 320, 328,
331, 452, 543, 719-20,
888; XVII,427, 439

Windsor, NH, *See Campbell's
Gore*
Windsor, VT XVI,934; XVII,72,
119-20
Winter Hill, MA XIV, 44, 222,
240, 242, 476, 668-89;
XV, 741, 745-46, 751; XVI,
465, 923, 927; XVII, 25-
26, 28, 33, 48
Wolfeborough, NH XIV,114-15,
296, 433, 557, 581-82,
660; XV; 449-50, 600-601,
619, 631, 650, 667, 690,
735; XVI,65, 76, 99, 221,
281-82, 524, 891; XVII,
439
Worcester, MA XV,436
Y
York, ME XIV,307; XV,435-36;
XVII,539
Yorktown, VA XIV,638

www.ingramcontent.com/pod-product-compliance
Lightning Source LLC
Chambersburg PA
CBHW071834270326
41929CB00013B/1997